P9-CAM-565

ECUADOR
& THE GALÁPAGOS ISLANDS

JULIAN SMITH & JEAN BROWN

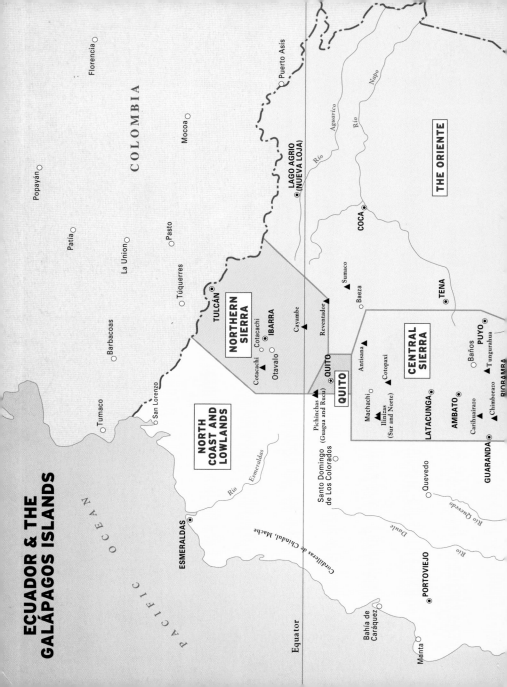

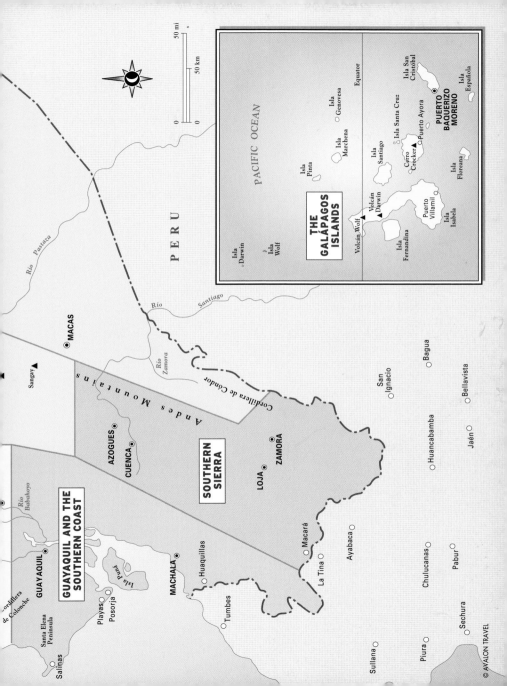

THE GALÁPAGOS ISLANDS

PACIFIC OCEAN

Equator

Isla Darwin

Isla Wolf

Isla Pinta

Isla Marchena

Isla Genovesa

Isla Santiago

Volcán Darwin

Volcán Wolf

Isla Fernandina

Isla Isabela

Puerto Villamil

Isla Santa Cruz

Cerro Crocker

Puerto Ayora

Isla Floreana

Isla San Cristóbal

PUERTO BAQUERIZO MORENO

Isla Española

GUAYAQUIL AND THE SOUTHERN COAST

SOUTHERN SIERRA

Andes Mountains

Cordillera de Condor

PERU

Río Pastaza

Río Santiago

Río Zamora

● MACAS

▲ Sangay

● AZOGUES

● CUENCA

LOJA

ZAMORA ●

Macará ○

La Tina ○

Ayabaca ○

San Ignacio ○

Bagua ○

Bellavista ○

Huancabamba ○

Jaén ○

Río Babahoyo

GUAYAQUIL ●

Isla Puná

Santa Elena Peninsula

Salinas

Playas ○

Posorja ○

Cordillera de Colonche

MACHALA ●

Huaquillas ○

Tumbes ○

Chulucanas ○

Pabur ○

Sechura ○

Piura ○

Sullana ○

50 mi

50 km

Contents

▶ **Discover Ecuador
& the Galápagos Islands 6**
Planning Your Trip 8
Explore Ecuador
& the Galápagos Islands. 11
• The Best of Ecuador 11
• Quito Festivals 12
• Galápagos Expedition. 13
• Galápagos Tour Operators 14
• Indigenous Past and Present . . 16
• Tigua Hide Paintings. 17
• Exploring the Natural World . . . 18
• Adrenaline Rush. 19
• Mountain Highs 20

▶ **Quito. 21**
Sights. 27
Entertainment and Events. 40
Shopping. 42
Sports and Recreation. 44
Accommodations 48
Food 52
Information and Services 56
Transportation. 62
Vicinity of Quito. 65

▶ **Northern Sierra 75**
Otavalo and Vicinity 78
Quito to Otavalo 92
Northwest of Otavalo. 97
Ibarra and Vicinity 102
Tulcán and the Colombian
  Border 113

▶ **Central Sierra 118**
Machachi and Vicinity 121
Machachi to Latacunga 123
Latacunga and Vicinity 128
Ambato and Vicinity. 135
Baños and Vicinity 141
West of Ambato. 152
Riobamba and Vicinity. 155

▶ **The Oriente. 168**
Quito to Baeza 172
Northern Oriente. 175
Lower Río Napo 183
South to Tena and Beyond 188
Southern Oriente 198

▶ **North Coast and Lowlands. . 206**
Western Lowlands. 209

North Coast 213
Central Coast 222

▶ **Guayaquil and the**
  Southern Coast **237**
  Santa Elena Peninsula 238
  Guayaquil and Vicinity 244
  Machala and Vicinity 262

▶ **Southern Sierra** **266**
  Cuenca and Vicinity 269
  Loja and Vicinity 288

▶ **The Galápagos Islands** **303**
  Visiting the Islands 306
  The Natural World. 320
  Santa Cruz and Nearby Islands . . 339
  San Cristóbal 348
  Santiago and Nearby Islands 353
  Western Islands 356
  Southern Islands 360
  Northern Islands 364

▶ **Background** **366**
  The Land 366
  The Natural World. 369

Environmental Issues. 376
History. 379
Government and Economy 390
The People 393
Culture. 397
Sports and Recreation 404

▶ **Essentials** **413**
  Getting There. 413
  Getting Around 416
  Visas and Officialdom 421
  Conduct and Customs 423
  Tips for Travelers 425
  Health and Safety 429
  Information and Services 436

▶ **Resources** **442**
  Glossary 442
  Spanish Phrasebook. 443
  Suggested Reading. 449
  Internet Resources 453

▶ **Index**. **455**

▶ **Map Index** **467**

Discover Ecuador
& the Galápagos Islands

I once made the mistake of leaving the Andes by bus one afternoon for a flight deep into the Amazon the next morning. I didn't have much choice – the road downhill was only open two nights a week.

Our bus pulled away from Baños's dripping green backdrop as the sun faded over the black church steeple. It started to rain, then pour. At the mouth of the first tunnel we waited three hours, with the roar of the Devil's Cauldron waterfall off in the darkness, until someone, somewhere, decided we could proceed.

The next thing I knew I was on a street corner in Puyo at 2 A.M., waiting for a connecting bus and holding my backpack over my head to keep from drowning. It arrived, we left, and I fell back asleep. Suddenly I was jostled awake to find our bus stopped and almost empty.

I followed my fellow travelers outside to find everyone lugging their bags over a swaying wooden bridge in the misty darkness. The main span was washed out in a flood, and another bus was waiting for us on the other side to continue on to Macas. Water dripped down the back of my neck as I wondered how much worse the journey could get.

Then, halfway across the bridge, the clouds parted and I halted in wonder. Stars like sand blazed down from above, turning the wide, lazy river into an ocean of light. On either side the dark forest echoed with alien cries, filling the air with the rich scent of earth and life. It was a moment almost too good to be true.

Despite its frustrations, Ecuador, in fact, sometimes seems too good to be true — a country the size of Colorado with twice as many birds as all of Europe, so volcanically lush that orchids grow like weeds and rows of fence posts take root and sprout leaves. In one handy package, Ecuador wraps up South America's big three attractions — the snowy Andes, the steamy Amazon, and hundreds of miles of Pacific beaches — together with the one attraction no other country on Earth has: the Galápagos Islands. And everything is within a day's travel of the capital.

So I'll leave my moment over the river as it is, along with the countless others I've accumulated over the years I've spent traveling in Ecuador: the smell of eucalyptus from the top of a bus in the thin air of the mountains, the ghostly roar of a howler monkey in the Amazon, a whale shark swimming past me in the Galápagos like a huge, spotted bus. Along with those go the memories of the stink of bus exhaust, the sting of sunburn, and the dull taste of potatoes, *again*. I'm leaving room for more in the decades to come.

And next time, I'm flying to the jungle.

Planning Your Trip

▶ WHERE TO GO

Quito

Ecuador's capital city is a welcoming, culture-rich metropolis with scenery that will take your breath away. Occupying a montane basin at nearly 3,000 meters, Quito boasts a perpetually agreeable climate and one of Latin America's richest concentrations of colonial churches, plazas, museums, and historic buildings.

Northern Sierra

High among Ecuador's Andean peaks you'll find stunning pastoral scenes, protected in part by several ecological preserves. Indigenous markets, like the famous one in Otavalo, offer crafts and household goods and food, and a full-blown animal market is an unforgettable sight.

Central Sierra

The Avenue of the Volcanoes boasts some of Ecuador's most inviting cities and outdoor pleasures. Numerous volcanic peaks are here for the climbing, including Cotopaxi and Chimborazo, or try camping by Laguna Quilotoa. Afterwards enjoy a soak in the hot springs of Baños, or spend a night at the award-winning Black Sheep Inn eco-lodge.

The Oriente

Rafting and jungle-hiking trips into this green expanse of Amazon rainforest can be easily arranged in the gateway towns of Baeza and Tena. Many tours stop by indigenous communities that continue to hold on to the ways of their ancestors. Other options include exploring caves and mining towns or staying at luxury jungle lodges farther afield.

North Coast and Lowlands

Along the Pacific coastline unspoiled beaches and resort towns attract budget travelers looking for surf, sun, and, occasionally, nightlife. Farther south, Machalilla National Park protects coastal forests and

Papallacta hot springs are a delight, especially on rainy days.

the gleaming high-rises and beaches of the Santa Elena Peninsula attract high-end tourists, while remnants of once-widespread mangrove estuaries are protected in the Manglares Churute Ecological Reserve nearby.

Southern Sierra

The colonial center of Cuenca rivals Quito in its profusion of churches, convents, and museums, yet it has the Old World feel prevalent throughout the southern region. The Ingapirca ruins look down the Cañar valley towards the coast, and south of Cuenca is the prize-winning eco-city of Loja. Even closer to the Peruvian border is Podocarpus National Park and the serene backpackers' getaway of Vilcabamba.

The Galápagos Islands

The unique ecosystem of this archipelago makes it one of the world's natural treasures. Here, a variety of wildlife including doe-eyed sea lions, birds with blue feet, and tortoises as big as armchairs roam free and fearless. The scuba diving is some of the best in the world. Visits are strictly monitored by the National Park Service to ensure the islands are minimally impacted.

Bicycles are much used in the lowlands, and repair shops are right on the street.

rich archaeological sites, as well as the "poor man's Galápagos" of Isla de la Plata. Birding in the western lowlands is excellent.

Guayaquil and the Southern Coast

The city center of Ecuador's biggest metropolis hosts a variety of shopping centers, museums, and nightlife options. West of the city,

► WHEN TO GO

Since it sits on the equator, Ecuador doesn't have hot and cold seasons like countries in temperate latitudes; here the only two seasons are *invierno* (winter), a hot, wet period, and *verano* (summer), which is dryer and cooler. Climatic cycles in different parts of the country don't coincide, so knowing which area(s) you plan to visit is the key in figuring out when to go.

Local tourist seasons occur near major holidays in late December and February–March. Many North American and European tourists come during the summer vacation months of June–August. I personally prefer in-between months like February and November.

Fans of local festivals might want to plan a trip to coincide with a few of the better ones, such as San Lorenzo's Santos Reyes and Santos Inocentes the first week in January or Cuenca's solemn Christmas processions. Many important indigenous festivals are clustered around the solstices and equinoxes in March, June, September, and December.

► BEFORE YOU GO

Passports, Tourist Cards, and Visas

Travelers to Ecuador will need a passport that is valid for at least six months beyond the date of entry. A tourist card (also called a T-3) is issued upon entry and must be returned upon leaving Ecuador. Stays of up to 90 days are permitted without a visa. Travelers must also be able to show "proof of economic means" (a credit card is usually good enough) and a return or onward travel ticket out of Ecuador.

Vaccinations

All visitors should make sure their routine immunizations are up to date. The CDC recommends that travelers be vaccinated against Hepatitis A and, in some cases Hepatitis B. Typhoid fever and rabies vaccinations are also recommended for those venturing into rural areas. Proof of yellow fever vaccinations is necessary when entering Ecuador from Peru or Columbia, but might be a good idea in any case.

Getting There and Around

Ecuador has two international airports: Mariscal Sucre International Airport in Quito and José Joaquin Olmedo International Airport in Guayaquil. You can get just about anywhere within Ecuador from either city in a few hours by plane or in a day by bus or car.

Ecuador's public transportation network is widespread but, at least on the ground, not always the quickest way to get around. If your time is limited, consider flying between larger cities instead of taking all-day (or all-night) buses, or renting a car. Renting a taxi and driver for the day is another economical and effective option.

What to Take

Pack light and leave room for souvenirs. In terms of clothing, pack appropriately for where you're heading: sandals and shorts for the beach; warm and waterproof layers for the Sierra; long sleeves and a hat for sun protection anywhere. For footwear, bring a comfortable pair of shoes or sneakers, and broken-in hiking boots if you plan to trek.

You can rent and buy camping equipment, mountaineering boots, and rubber boots (for the jungle) in Ecuador. And don't forget your camera—Ecuador is one of the most photogenic places you'll ever go.

From La Entrada, the road heads inland toward Alandaluz.

Explore Ecuador
& the Galápagos Islands

► THE BEST OF ECUADOR

You can manage to see a good chunk of the country and explore Ecuador's highlands in just two weeks. This itinerary features several of Ecuador's mainland highlights, from the capital city to the Amazon jungle.

If you have an extra week, consider adding a visit to Darwin's famous isles. Take a look at the *Galápagos Expedition* section (which follows) for helpful information on adding a tour of the islands to your trip and making the most of your time there.

Day 1
Fly to Quito and wander through Old Town. Have dinner in Teatrum overlooking the Plaza del Teatro. Spend the night in New Town. If you decide to add a trip to the Galápagos, book your trip now if you haven't already.

Day 2
Tour New Town, including the Casa de la Cultura and Avenida Amazonas. Book your Amazon trip and sleep where you did last night.

Day 3
Fly to Cuenca in the morning. Take a short trip to the Inca ruins at Ingapirca in the morning and then wander around the city center. End your day with the evening session at the nearby hot springs.

Day 4
More sightseeing around colonial Cuenca, or else a day tour to El Cajas National Park. Fly to Quito in the afternoon, or take an overnight bus to give yourself more time in Cuenca.

Moving quietly using only paddles is better for wildlife viewing.

Day 5
Head north from Quito to Otavalo, ideally in time for the Saturday market. Spend the night at a nearby hacienda such as Pinsaquí, where horseback riding is the main attraction.

Day 6
Spend another day around Otavalo, either on your own or on a guided tour. Head up to Ibarra in the evening.

Day 7
Take the bus to San Lorenzo, and visit the mangroves on the way to Esmeraldas. Head out to Playa Escondida for a mellow day at the beach.

Day 8
Beach time: nothing on the itinerary but relaxing.

QUITO FESTIVALS

Throughout Ecuador, historical, political, and religious holidays are festive occasions involving parades, fireworks, dancing, and special foods. The following are just some of Quito's biggest celebrations. As your tour of Ecuador is likely to include some time in the capital city, there's a good chance that you'll be just in time to celebrate.

- **January 6:** Día de los Inocentes – Street dances and bullfights lead up to major hangovers for many residents.

- **February or March:** Carnival – Pitched water-throwing battles last from Friday until Tuesday night.

- **March or April:** Good Friday – Thousands of residents fill the streets in solemn processions.

- **May 2:** Festival of Las Cruces – General merriment abounds in the neighborhoods of Cruz Verde on Bolívar and Imbabura in Old Town.

- **May 31:** Festival of La Cruz – This event is celebrated in the neighborhoods of Chaupicruz, Prensa, and Sumaco.

- **May 24:** Anniversary of the Battle of Pichincha – Military parades travel down Los Shyris.

- **August 10:** Independence of Quito – Military and school parades take place.

- **August:** Mes de los Artes (Arts Month) – Artistic performances occur throughout the city; the Casa de la Cultura can provide information on events.

- **September 23-24:** Fiesta de la Virgen de las Mercedes – Festivities center around the Iglesia La Merced, including a midnight Misa del Gallo (Rooster's Mass).

- **October 31:** Halloween – Costumed revelers march down Amazonas.

- **November 2-3:** Day of the Dead – Residents clean up graveyards and visit deceased friends and relatives.

- **December 1-6:** Founding of Quito – One of South America's largest fiestas. Events include the election of the Queen of Quito, bullfights, and parades, among many others. December 5 is the main day.

- **December 28:** Santos Inocentes (Holy Innocents) – Similar to April Fool's Day in the UK and US, innocent tricks are played on friends during this celebration.

- **December 31:** New Year's Eve – Life-sized or larger than life marionettes or sculptures depicting events from the past year are set up on Amazonas and street blocks.

homemade sweets and syrups made of guava or mora berries and raw sugar

Day 9

Head back up to Quito by bus. See the Mitad del Mundo and Pululahua crater in the afternoon, and spend the night back in the city.

Days 10-13

Jungle time: Visit the Amazon lodge of your choice by plane or boat, or take a bus to Tena and visit a nearby Quechua community. Take in some rafting on the upper Napo. Remember that getting to the jungle will be at least half a day on either end, so consider extending your stay by a day and forgoing Day 14's activities.

Day 14

If you're skipping the Galápagos tour, finish up your trip with a half day at the hot springs at Papallacta, perhaps combined with some hiking in the local lake district. Get back to Quito in time for a full night's sleep before your early morning flight.

► GALÁPAGOS EXPEDITION

The archipelago protects a unique ecosystem that is truly without parallel. Visitors have a rare opportunity to experience this amazing bubble of life firsthand, and for skilled divers, the scuba diving is some of the best in the world.

A tour of at least five days is recommended, and seven or eight days is even better, as it takes a half-day each way to get to and from the islands. Most travelers will visit the isles on packaged tours. Highlights of any tour should include the Charles Darwin Research Center in Puerto Ayora, Post Office Bay, Punta Suárez, and Punta Espinosa.

For more detailed information on planning your trip to the Galápagos, see *The Galápagos Islands* chapter (page 303). Here are a few tips to keep in mind when planning your trip.

Galápagos cruise boats anchored at Academy Bay in Santa Cruz

When to Go

The high tourist seasons occur December–January and June–August. If you are planning to travel to the islands during these months be sure to book your tour well in advance. Also note that many boats are dry-docked for repairs and maintenance during September and October.

During the dry season (June–November) the islands become brown and sere as dormant vegetation waits for the rains. Rains alternate with hot and sunny days during the wet season (January–April); the islands turn green, and sea turtles lay their eggs.

November and April may be the best overall months to visit—not too hot or cold and not too many tourists.

Planning Your Trip

Land or diving tours can be arranged in your home country or through a travel agency in Ecuador. Keep in mind that when booking a tour from abroad a deposit of at least $200 per person, via wire transfer or Western

GALÁPAGOS TOUR OPERATORS

Although dozens of tour operators throughout Ecuador offer trips to the Galápagos, only a handful earn consistently positive reviews. The following are your best bets for well-informed and responsible tour operators.

- **Andando Tours:** Mariana de Jesus E7-113 and Pradera, tel. 2/323-7186, fax 2/313-8309, info@andandotours.com, www.andandotours.com

- **Enchanted Expeditions:** De las Alondras N45-102 and De los Lirios, tel. 2/334-0525, fax 2/334-0123, headoffice@enchantedexpeditions.com, www.galapagosenchantedexpeditions.com

- **Galápagos Sub-Aqua:** tel. 4/230-5514 or 4/230-5507 in Guayaquil, tel. 5/252-6350 or 5/252-6633 in Puerto Ayora, www.galapagos-sub-aqua.com

- **Galasam Galápagos Tours:** Cordero and Amazonas, tel. 2/250-7080, www.galasam.com.ec; in Guayaquil: Ed. Gran Pasaje, tel. 4/230-6289, fax 4/230-1759; in the United States: 8306 Mills Dr., Ste. 460, Miami, FL 33183-4838, tel. 800/781-5089

- **Guide2Galápagos:** Amazonas N24-196 and Cordero, tel./fax: 2/250-8937, info@guide2galapagos.com, www.guide2galapagos.com

- **Lindblad Expeditions:** 96 Morton Street, 9th Fl., New York, NY 10014, tel. 212/765-7740 or 800/397-3348, www.expeditions.com

- **Metropolitan Touring:** Av. De Las Palmeras N45-74 and de las Orquideas, tel. 2/298-8200, ext. 2810, fax 2/246-4702, www.galapagosvoyage.com; in the United States through **Adventure Associates:** 13150 Coit Rd., Ste. 110, Dallas, TX 75240, tel. 800/527-2500, fax 972/783-1286, info@adventure-associates.com, www.adventure-associates.com

- **Oceanadventures:** Republica de El Salvador N36-84 and Naciones Unidos, tel. 2/246-6301, info@eclipse.com.ec, www.oceanadventures.com.ec

- **Quasar Nautica:** Brasil 293 y Granda Centeno, edif. IACA, piso 2, tel. 2/244-6996, fax 2/225-9305, info@quasarex.com, www.galapagosexpeditions.com; in the United States through **Tumbaco Inc.:** 7855 NW 12th Street, Ste. 221, Miami, FL 33126, tel. 305/599-9008 or 800/247-2925, fax 305/592-7060, infousa@quasarex.com

- **Safari Ecuador:** Foch E4-132 and Cordero, tel. 2/255-2505, fax 2/222-0426, admin@safari.com.ec, www.safari.com.ec

- **Scuba Iguana:** tel. 5/252-6497, info@scubaiguana.com, www.scubaiguana.com

climbing down the rocks to go fishing

deck at the Red Mangrove Inn in Puerto Ayora

Union (no credit cards by Internet or phone), is usually required.

Many travel agencies in Quito advertise tours, and shopping around is the way to go. Holding out for last-minute deals may save you anywhere from 5–50 percent, but be aware that it may leave you stranded as well.

Getting There

Transport to the islands is generally not included in the price of a tour. Flights to the Galápagos depart from Quito and Guayaquil daily. There are two airports in the Galápagos: one on Baltra, near the central island of Santa Cruz, and one on San Cristóbal. Make sure you're flying to the correct island to begin your tour.

If you are traveling to the islands without being booked on a tour, Puerto Ayora is the place to arrange a budget tour. However, note that getting from Baltra to Puerto Ayora is a journey in three stages involving two bus rides and a ferry ride.

Tour Boats and Guides

Tour boats are organized into five classes—economic, tourist, tourist superior, first, and luxury. Economic-class boats are the best option for those with a limited budget and/or time frame; tourist- and tourist superior-class boats are the most common in the islands; luxury tours and cruise ships offer services that match those in the finest hotels on the mainland. Prices vary widely, but all prices should include food, accommodation, transfers to and from your boat, trained guides, and all your shore visits.

There are also a few shore-based tours available for those who suffer from seasickness. However, precious time will be spent traveling to and from the islands every day, and some of the farther islands will be excluded from the itinerary.

A good guide is the most important factor in your visit. All Galápagos guides are trained and licensed by the National Park Service and qualify in one of three classes, in ascending order of quality. When booking a tour, ask about your guide's specific qualifications and what language(s) he or she speaks.

Diving

The underwater riches found here include manta rays, marine iguanas, and active volcano vents, just to name a few. At last count there were over 60 marine visitor sites throughout the archipelago, many on islands closed to visitors above the surface. The Wolf and Darwin Islands are sure to be highlights of any diving expedition.

However, note that diving here is not for beginners. Many dives are in open water, and the best marine life usually keeps to areas of strong currents—up to 3.5 knots in places. A wetsuit is essential, and in the cold season a wetsuit with hood, booties, and gloves becomes necessary. Many companies require a certain level of experience: an open water certification, a minimum number of dives, and sometimes a medical certificate.

Most large Galápagos tour agencies can book dive trips on live-aboard charters. See the *Galápagos Tour Operators* callout for more information on recommended agencies.

▶ INDIGENOUS PAST AND PRESENT

colorful dancers ready to celebrate during Corpus Christi

of the city's world-class museums, churches, convents, and cultural centers, including the Itchimbia Cultural Center, the preserved colonial home of María Augusta Urrutia, and the Centro Cultural Metropolitano in Old Town.

Days 3-5
The area near Otavalo, two hours north of Quito by bus, is rich with indigenous culture. Visit crafts villages such as Ilumán and Peguche. Bargain at the markets, like the famous one in Otavalo's Plaza de Ponchos, and sample a traditional plate of cuy (guinea pig) up near Ibarra. To complete the experience, stay in a centuries-old homestead such as the Hacienda Cusín near Laguna San Pablo.

Days 6-8
Head south past Quito to Latacunga, the starting point for the Latacunga Loop into the Andean hinterlands. Catch the bus in Latacunga (or drive yourself), spending a night at the Black Sheep Inn in Chugchilán and another at Llullu Llama in Isinlivi. Don't miss the hike from Laguna Quilotoa, where indigenous artists sell hide paintings on the breezy rim. Finish up at traditional Guantualo, whose Monday market is among the most authentic in the country. Take the afternoon bus to Latacunga and then head south to Cuenca overnight.

Ecuador is full of vibrant indigenous cultures and remnants of a history that spans thousands of years. Time your visit right and you can catch an outstanding local fiesta or two, such as Latacunga's Mama Negra (in early November) or San Lorenzo's Santos Reyes and Santos Inocentes (in early January). If your tastes run to all things historic and antique, you've come to the right place.

Days 1-2
Fly to Quito and whet your appetite at some

TIGUA HIDE PAINTINGS

The brightly colored paintings created by the artists of the Tigua valley are some of Ecuador's most distinctive (and portable) souvenirs. The paintings typically depict scenes of village life, such as *campesinos* tilling their fields as llamas look on and condors fly over a snow-covered volcano in the background.

This style of painting began as a way to decorate small drums used in traditional festivals. In the early 1970s, local artist Julio Toaquiza began to paint the Andean scenes on small canvases of sheep hide stretched over a wooden frame. Julio taught his family the skill and watched as the craft acquired a life of its own. Today more than 200 artists turn out the paintings in a handful of communities nestled in the Andes west of Latacunga. The Toaquiza family painters are still considered to be the best. Orlando Quindigalle in Pujilí is also renowned.

The original bright enamel paints have since been supplanted to an extent by more durable oils and acrylics. Many of the larger frames are works of art in themselves, covered with intricate patterns. The frame can often determine the overall quality of the work – when purchasing a painting, look for even, straight frames with taut hides.

Tigua paintings can be found all over Ecuador, but the best selection and prices are at the source. There's an artists' cooperative in the small community of **Tigua-Chimbacucho,** 52 kilometers west of Latacunga on the road to Quevedo, as well as a few artists in **Quilotoa** and **Pujilí** who sell their paintings at their residences.

In Quito, the **Tianguez** shop (Plaza de San Francisco, tel. 2/295-4326, 9:30 A.M.–6:30 P.M. daily, tianguez@andinanet.net, www.sinchisacha.org), run by the Fundación Sinchi Sacha, has a good selection. They are located below the Iglesia San Francisco. Also try **Artesanias Incario** (Juan León Mera N 2315 y Veintimilla, tel. 2/255-9834) for quality works.

Days 9-12

Four days in Cuenca should satisfy any lingering urges to explore history. Ecuador's third-largest city is near the top in terms of cultural offerings, from the ruins of an Inca palace to the outstanding blue-domed Catedral Nueva. At least a day or two should be spent beyond the city limits, taking in the well-preserved Inca ruins at Ingapirca and the indigenous villages of Gualaceo, Chordeleg, and Cañar. Spend the night in a restored colonial mansion, such as the Hotel Santa Lucía or the Mansion Alcazar.

Days 13-14

One option for the last two days of your trip is to head to the coast, where lively Guayaquil boasts culture of a slightly different sort. (Although with the anthropology museum of the Banco Central and the nearby Parque Historico, the city is no slouch in the ancient-history department, either.) Otherwise, keep going south from Cuenca through Loja to Vilcabamba, whose tranquil pace of life and way-out-in-the-country flavor are timeless. Either way, fly home from Quito or Guayaquil.

pre-colonial sacrificial stone

► EXPLORING THE NATURAL WORLD

It would take a year just to scratch the surface of Ecuador's incredible biological diversity, but in three weeks you can experience everything from spotting saki monkeys in the rainforest to snorkeling with miniature penguins around the Galápagos Islands.

Days 1-2

Start slow in Quito to give yourself time to adjust to the altitude and to the idea of a country with 1,500 species of birds. Visit the Botanical Gardens, the Vivarium, and the Quito Zoo in Guallabamba for a warm-up. Spend two nights in New Town, or else at the Hostería San Jorge in the Pichincha foothills, to get an early start on your birding. Book any tours to the Amazon or Galápagos now, if you haven't already.

Days 3-5

Head up to the Mindo-Nono area in the cloudforest for some world-class birdwatching astoundingly close to the capital. Comfortable lodges such as Tandayapa and Bellavista cater to birders, and reserves like Maquipucuna and Yanacocha are packed with life. Spend two nights up here and return to Quito the third.

Day 6

Book a day tour up into the foothills of the Antisana Ecological Reserve, where the South American condor—the largest flying bird in the world—still soars. Alternatively, visit Cotopaxi National Park for another chance to spot this magnificent creature.

Days 7-11

By now you should be prepared to take the next step to the Amazon, where the sheer abundance of life can, at times, be nearly overwhelming. A five-day tour to a lodge such as Sani Lodge will bring you in intimate contact with everything the Oriente has to offer—the whole vine-draped, gorgeous green mess of it. Birders will be in nirvana, and plant people will get the shakes.

Days 12-19

Then it gets even better. During a week in the Galápagos Islands you'll practically trip over animals you can't see anywhere else in the world. Giant tortoises, boobies, marine iguanas, and sea life galore: this is the kind of place that turns adults into kids and kids into naturalists. No natural-history tour is complete without a stop here. Deplane in Guayaquil.

Days 20-21

Spend your final days in Ecuador on the coast, either among the mangroves at Manglares Churute near Guayaquil, hiking the coastal dry forests of Machalilla, spotting whales off Puerto López, or ticking a few more birds off your life list in the coastal lowlands at a place like Tinalandia near Santa Domingo.

Local hotels and restaurants put out vegetable offcuts to feed the iguanas.

▶ ADRENALINE RUSH

Whether you get your adrenaline fix holding a paddle, an ice axe, or the handlebars of a mountain bike, satisfy your addiction with some high-energy fun in some of Ecuador's wildest spots. If you have a few more days at the end of this tour to cap things off by climbing a serious peak—say, Cotopaxi or Chimborazo—then you'll have to work in ascents of a few peaks over 4,000 meters along the way to acclimatize.

the freedom of downhill biking

Days 1-2

Fly to Quito and start with some slow sightseeing—hiking some of the steeper streets should get your heart pumping plenty. The San Francisco de Quito in the old city is close to everything. Spend one night in Quito and head to Baños the second night.

Days 3-5

Baños is the ideal spot to get the ball rolling on the eastern slope of the Andes. Choose from a multitude of hiking trails, a mountain-bike ride down the old road toward the Amazon, or swinging from a bridge over the Río Pastaza. At night, soak your aches away in the town's famous hot springs. Head to Riobamba the third day.

Days 6-7

From Riobamba, hike to the Collanes plain at the foot of El Altar for one of Ecuador's most impressive volcanic panoramas—the jagged peaks of Obispo, Monjes, and Tabernacle loom over Laguna Amarilla as glacier ice tumbles down the slopes. Camp up here for one night in the thatched *chozas*.

Day 8

Join Pro-Bici for an exciting ride from the refuge on Chimborazo back to Riobamba. You can also hike 5,000 meters to the upper climbers'

refuge. It's a spine-tingling ride down thousands of meters to the bottom of the volcano.

Day 9

Take the train from Riobamba or Alausí through Devil's Nose, an extraordinary feat of railway engineering that's all the more hair-raising when you're riding on the roof of the train. From Alausi, make your way south through the Andes to Achupallas by bus or truck.

Days 10-12

The Inca Trail to Ingapirca takes two nights, and arrives at Ecuador's foremost Inca buildings. From here, bus to Cuenca. The area around Cuenca is rich in alfresco entertainment. El Cajas National Park is worth at least one night in a tent. In between, sample some of the rich colonial character this historic city has to offer. Steer south to Loja for the third night.

Days 13-15

A trek through Podocarpus National Park can take you from the high Andes to the rainforest. Tour operators in Loja can arrange a multi-day stay in this little-known park, or you can arrange your own transportation and stay in the refuge near Loja or camp among the glacial lakes. Fly back to Quito the last night, or take an overnight bus.

MOUNTAIN HIGHS

A variety of high-altitude climbing options will keep mountaineers plenty busy in Ecuador. Beginning mountaineers will find the country an excellent training ground for higher, more difficult ascents elsewhere. There are certainly enough challenging climbs for seasoned veterans as well.

Several peaks, such as Pasochoa and Guagua Pichincha, are good starters for acclimatizing and getting into shape with minimum special equipment or training. Modest technical gear will do for the big three – Chimborazo, Cotopaxi, and Cayambe. And El Altar is considered to be the most difficult ascent in the country.

When planning your adventure, remember that many major peaks have roads leading close to or part way up their bases. The ascents themselves can be straightforward, but the conditions and routes vary drastically from year to year, even day to day. Never underestimate the mountains. Although climatic conditions will differ among regions, December-January are generally the best months to climb.

An experienced and responsible guide can make the difference between success and failure – and life and death. Always go with a licensed and qualified guide. For more information on guided hikes, contact **ASEGUIM,** the Ecuadorian Mountain Guide Association (tel. 2/223-4109, 3-6 P.M. Mon., Tues., and Thurs., www.aseguim.org). Also see each chapter's individual city listings for more information on local guides.

The following chart reveals the heights of many of Ecuador's loftiest peaks. These figures come from the most trustworthy source – the 1979 Instituto Geográfico Militar (IGM) surveys.

Mountain	Height (meters)	Volcanic Activity	Glacier/ Snow
Chimborazo	6,310	No	Glacier
Cotopaxi	5,897	Yes	Glacier
Cayambe	5,790	Yes	Glacier
Antisana	5,704	Yes	Glacier
El Altar	5,319	Yes	Glacier
Iliniza Sur	5,263	No	Glacier
Sangay	5,230	Yes	Glacier
Iliniza Norte	5,126	No	Rare
Carihuairazo	5,020	No	Glacier
Tungurahua	5,016	Yes	Glacier
Cotacachi	4,939	No	Rare
Sincholagua	4,893	No	Rare
Quilindaña	4,878	No	Rare
Guagua Pichincha	4,794	Yes	Rare
Corazón	4,788	No	Rare
Chiles	4,768	No	Rare
Rumiñahui	4,712	No	Rare
Rucu Pichincha	4,700	No	Rare
Sara Urcu	4,676	No	Rare
Imbabura	4,630	No	Rare
Atacazo	4,410	Yes	Rare
Fuya Fuya	4,262	No	No
Cerro Negro	4,260	No	No
Pasochoa	4,200	No	No

Days 16-18

Book a rafting trip on the Quijos River near Baeza and you'll enjoy the same white water (more or less) as the participants of the 2005 World Rafting Championships. The town itself, perched on the edge of the Amazon basin, is a great little place to spend a day or two hiking in the hills. From March to September, you can raft on the Rio Blanco near Santo Domingo.

tourist train waiting to descend Devil's Nose from Alausi

QUITO

Ecuador's capital is an intriguing mix of old and new: centuries-old colonial buildings huddle next to garish skyscrapers and fast-food outlets; professionals stride pass indigenous musicians and craft sellers; and electric trolleys glide silently by ancient buses belching clouds of exhaust. For all its contradictions, Quito is blessed with a wealth of historic architecture and museums, vibrant nightlife, a popular and convenient tourist sector, a near perfect climate, and one of the prettiest settings of any capital in the world.

After La Paz in Bolivia, Quito is the second-highest capital in Latin America (2,850 meters). The Pichincha volcanoes tower to the west, trapping fleecy clouds that would otherwise drift by and creating the spectacular peach and robin's egg blue sunsets captured in the *Paisaje de Quito* paintings by Oswaldo Guayasamín. Much of the population of Ecuador's second-largest city lives in *barrios* (neighborhoods) or shantytowns, either up the slopes of the mountains or spread north and south of the city center.

As the seat of Ecuador's government and its enclave of traditional values, Quito displays a deeply rooted conservative streak. On the other hand, a slew of schools, including the Central University, Catholic University, and the National Polytechnic School, along with modern businesses, inject a healthy dose of cosmopolitan attitude.

In 1978, Quito was the first city in the world to receive World Heritage Site status from UNESCO. After some slippage in the upkeep department, the municipal government got

HIGHLIGHTS

La Compañía: Of all of Quito's world-class colonial churches, none comes close to this one for sheer sacred splendor (page 32).

La Basílica: This vantage point offers tough-to-beat views of the city, plus armadillo gargoyles (page 35)!

Casa de la Cultura: This gleaming glass structure in Parque El Ejido houses museums chock full of colonial art, archaeology, musical instruments, and – best of all – gold (page 36).

Itchimbia Park and Cultural Center: Head up to the Itchimbia neighborhood overlooking Old Town to visit this impressive new center and have a chic sunset drink at Mosaico (page 36).

Capilla del Hombre: Oswaldo Guayasamín's Chapel of Man is a fitting coda for a life devoted to art and advocacy (page 39).

Mitad del Mundo: You can't visit Ecuador and skip the chance to stand with a foot in each hemisphere at the equator (page 67).

Mindo: The birding in the cloud forests is fantastic, and the town itself is charming (page 70).

LOOK FOR **(** TO FIND RECOMMENDED SIGHTS, ACTIVITIES, DINING, AND LODGING.

on the ball; since the new millennium began, it has been busily restoring the city's shine and civic pride. A new feeling of cleanliness and security pervades Old Town, with an increased police presence and horse-drawn carriages clopping past beautifully lit churches at night. Foundations are helping property owners in Old Town with loans and permits to restore historic buildings. The streets have been cleaned up, interior patios have been tastefully renovated, and street artists have replaced beggars and hawkers. Several large parking facilities and many new restaurants and museums have opened. Some traditions remain sacred, though—gorgeous old churches are starting to charge admission and prevent tourists from wandering in during mass.

HISTORY

According to a pre-Inca legend, the city of Quito was founded by Quitumbe, son of the god Quitu, in honor of his father. The valley that would eventually cradle Ecuador's capital was originally occupied by the Quitu tribe, which united with the Cara from the north to form the Shyris nation around A.D. 1300. In 1487, the Incas took over and turned the city into an important nexus of their northern empire, known as the Quitosuyo. Within a hundred years, the empire fell to infighting, leaving things wide open for the newly arrived Spanish to start almost from scratch.

The city of San Francisco de Quito was founded by Sebastian de Benalcázar on December 6, 1534, and named in honor

SANTA MARIANA DE JESÚS

Ecuador's first saint was so beautiful, they say, that she was forced to look at the world from beneath a dark veil her entire life. The one man who dared to look underneath was rewarded with the vision of a grinning skull. There were no more peeks.

A string of natural disasters and disease in the 17th century brought Quito to its knees. In 1645, at the age of 26, Mariana offered her life to God to spare the city's residents. Her blood was sprinkled in a garden, bringing forth a pure white lily, which has since been called the Lily of Quito.

CLIMATE

Quito reaps all the climatic benefits of its location in a mountain valley at 2,850 meters. The city's weather is often described as eternal spring, meaning balmy days of 8–21°C temperatures, warm direct sunlight cooled by light, steady breezes, and almost painfully picturesque clouds that usually gather for a short afternoon shower, all capped by a cool—but not cold—darkness. The saying goes that the city can experience all four seasons in a single day, and that isn't far off the mark.

Dry season in the capital lasts June–September, with July and August seeing the least precipitation. A shortened dry season runs December–January. More rain falls February–March and October–November, with at least half of April full of torrential downpours that take up most of the afternoon.

ORIENTATION

Quito extends about 47 kilometers north–south, and about eight kilometers across. Luckily for first-time visitors, the capital is

of fellow conquistador Francisco Pizarro. Benalcázar quickly set about appointing government officials, distributing land to his men, and constructing churches. Originally, Quito consisted only of the present-day section known as Old Town, bounded by the Plaza de San Blas to the north, the Pichinchas to the west, and the Machangara ravine to t he east. An art school founded in 1535 helped the city become a center of religious art during the colonial period, complete with its own style, the Quito School.

Since its founding, Quito has been an administrative—rather than a manufacturing—center. A population boom, aided by the discovery of oil, brought thousands of immigrants who spread their homes and businesses north into today's New Town, farther south of Old Town, and west up the slopes of Pichincha. By the mid-1980s, these makeshift *suburbios* housed as much as 15 percent of the city's population and had acquired most of the services that the older areas took for granted. Today, the city claims roughly 1.5 million residents. An earthquake in 1987 damaged numerous structures and left others in ruins, and the eruption of Guagua Pichincha in 1999 terrified many locals.

© JULIAN SMITH

carving on the door of La Compañia, Old Town

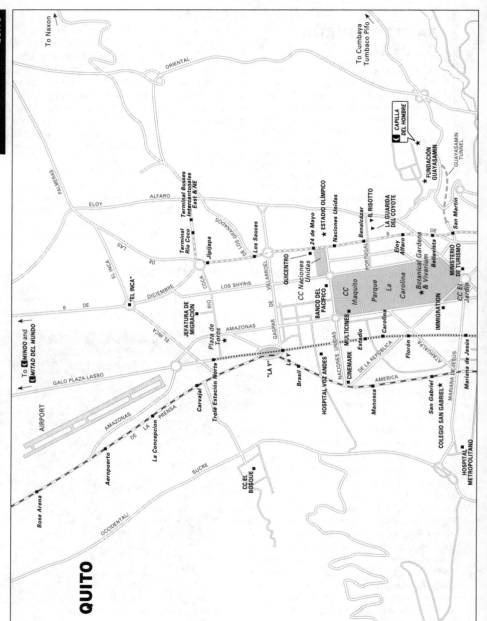

QUITO

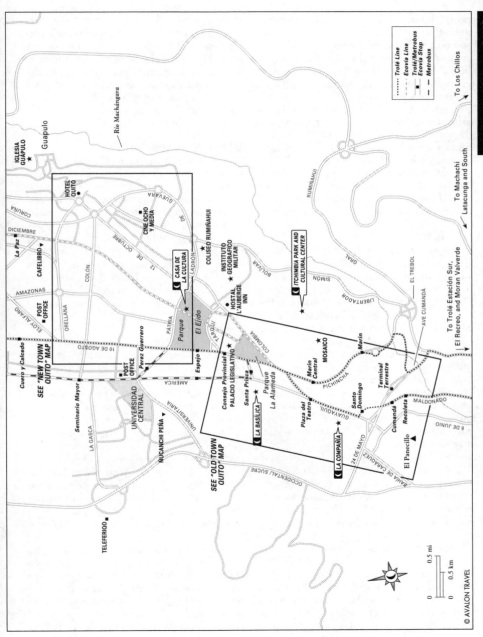

Trolé Line
Ecovía Line
Trolé/Metrobus
Ecovía Stop
Metrobus

To Los Chillos

To Machachi
Latacunga and South

To Trolé Estación Sur,
El Recreo, and Moran Valverde

IGLESIA
GUAPULO

Guapulo

Río Machángara

HOTEL
QUITO

CORUÑA

DICIEMBRE

La Paz

CAFELIBRO

AMAZONAS

POST
OFFICE

ELOY ALFARO

Cuero y Caledo

SEE "NEW TOWN
QUITO" MAP

POST
OFFICE

Seminario Mayor

LA GASCA

UNIVERSIDAD
CENTRAL

ÑUCANCHI PEÑA

TELEFÉRICO

CINE OCHO
Y MEDIA

12 DE OCTUBRE

COLÓN

ORELLANA

10 DE AGOSTO

AMÉRICA

Perez Guerrero

CASA DE
LA CULTURA

DE GUEVARA

LADRÓN

COLISEO RUMIÑAHUI

INSTITUTO
GEOGRÁFICO
MILITAR

Parque
El Ejido

PATRIA

Espejo

TARQUI

HOSTAL
L'AUBERGE
INN

COLOMBIA

Consejo Provincial
PALACIO LEGISLATIVO

Santa Prisca

Parque
La Alameda

LA BASÍLICA

Plaza del
Teatro

GUAYAQUIL

LA COMPAÑÍA

24 DE MAYO

BAHIA DE CARÁQUEZ

OCCIDENTAL SUCRE

SEE "OLD TOWN
QUITO" MAP

UNIVERSITARIA

ITCHIMBÍA PARK AND
CULTURAL CENTER

RUMIÑAHUI

GRAL

SIMON

BOLÍVAR

LIBERTADOR

EL TREBOL

AVE CUMANDÁ

MOSAICO

Marín
Central

PICHINCHA

Santo
Domingo

Cumandá

Recoleta

El Panecillo

MALDONADO

Marin

Terminal
Terrestre

5 DE JUNIO

N

0   0.5 mi

0   0.5 km

© AVALON TRAVEL

easily divided into zones: one for historical sights (Old Town); one for visitor services, restaurants, and accommodations (New Town); and then everything else. It's almost impossible to become disoriented—just look for the mountains to the west or, at night, for the lights on top of them.

A new system of street numbers was implemented in Quito in 2000, with letters prefixing the normal hyphenated numbers. The old numbers are often changed, so a business that was once at Foch 8–99 might be at Foch E4-132 now. Most addresses will also give the nearest cross street, so the full address would be Foch E4-132 y Cordero. As of 2008, this mostly applies to the north and central parts of the city.

Old Town

Quito's historical heart sits at the northern flank of El Panecillo (Little Bread Loaf) hill, whose statue of the Virgin is visible from most of the neighborhood. This area, also called Quito Colonial or the *centro histórico* (historical center), is roughly bordered by 24 de Mayo on the south and Parque La Alameda to the north. Most of the sights are situated within a few blocks of the central Plaza de la Independencia, the original core of the city.

Steep, narrow streets characterize this part of Quito, and cars barely fit in lanes designed for horse and foot traffic. Wrought-iron balconies hang over ground-level storefronts selling household wares, clothing, and an astounding number of shoes.

Most visitors come for the outstanding churches and museums, which were key in having Quito declared a World Heritage Site. Other visitors are content to wander the cobbled streets that evoke Ecuador's colonial past—despite the handbills and red graffiti from the latest political upheaval that occasionally mar the recent colorful paintwork.

New Town

The split wedge formed by the Parque La Alameda and El Ejido points away from the commercial hub of the capital. The Mariscal area is enclosed by Avenidas Patria, Orellana, 10 de Agosto, and 12 de Octubre. Tourists keep this part of Quito in business, supporting dozens of hotels and restaurants to suit every budget, along with enough souvenir shops, tour companies, and banks for two cities. Expensive apartments and some embassies fill many blocks, especially Gonzalez Suarez on the eastern edge of the valley, just before the drop-off to the Valley of the Volcanoes.

Other Neighborhoods

The section of Quito north of New Town sparkles with shiny high-rises that house a large part of the city's businesses, and it hosts much of the capital's industry. Modern shopping centers and chic restaurants cater to the middle and upper classes who live in this area or in the fast-growing Valle Los Chillos and Tumbaco valleys, both to the east. The steep old neighborhood of Guapulo spills down below Avenida 12 de Octubre and the lofty Hotel Quito. More residential neighborhoods occupy the lower slopes of Pichincha west and north of New Town.

SAFETY

With one of the highest concentrations of bodies in the country, Quito naturally has its share of crime. It's nothing to cancel your trip over, but it's definitely worth considering. By taking the standard precautions that you would in any major city and avoiding a few problem spots, you should have little to worry about.

The diciest area in the part of the city frequented by tourists is the Mariscal Sucre neighborhood of New Town, sometimes simply called "La Mariscal." Increased police presence, including dog patrols, has helped clean this area up since 2000, but it's still a good idea to take a taxi home at night. (Taxis are so inexpensive and plentiful that this applies to the entire city.)

Watch for pickpockets and bag slashers on the trolley, at the bus station, and in Old Town in general. Pay particular attention in crowded areas and when exiting tourist spots like churches. Keep all bags and cameras in front of you, and don't leave your wallet in your back pocket. Don't go into any parks after dark. If you suddenly find mustard on your clothes, beware of the kind, usually well-dressed person offering to help clean you up, because he is likely trying to clean you out.

El Panecillo, once off-limits to tourists even by taxi, has become safer since the local community started policing the streets—but taking a taxi to get there and back is still recommended. As of 2005, with the opening of the *teleférico* (aerial tram), Rucu Pichincha was no longer considered too dangerous to climb; then there were several assaults and muggings in late 2007. Security has been tightened up and there have been no more incidents, but it is always best to check locally about the current situation. Guagua Pichincha, on the other hand, is considered safe.

PLANNING YOUR TIME

Quito can be a little overwhelming in the sightseeing department. If you only have a couple of days here, spend one each in Old Town and New Town. Start with an overview at **El Panecillo, Itchimbia, Cima de la Libertad, Yaku,** or **La Basílica;** see the buildings around the Plaza Grande and the Plaza San Francisco; visit **La Compañía;** and wander the old streets a bit in between. The next day, hit the **Museo del Banco Central,** the **Guayasamín Museum,** and the **Capilla del Hombre,** and do some shopping and café-lounging in New Town. One more day would give you time to visit the equator at the **Mitad del Mundo,** or head uphill to **Pululahua** for a little bird-watching and crater-viewing.

You'll probably want to stay in New Town. Although more hotels and restaurants are opening in Old Town, they tend to be either cheap or upmarket, with little middle ground. Old Town is easily reached from New Town via the Trole, Ecovia, or Metrobus, three parallel bus routes with exclusive lanes (see map).

Sights

Quito's churches elicit more gasps than any of its other attractions. You'll certainly have enough opportunities to be impressed: The city is said to have at least 86 of them, most attached to monasteries or convents. Blank exterior walls symbolize the division between the outer and inner world, where nuns from wealthy and poor backgrounds worship side by side. Time away from prayer was often used to decorate the walls and ceilings with elaborate paintings, such as those in the refectory of El Carmen, that praised the glories of heaven while hinting at the treasures of the world outside.

Flash pictures are prohibited in most churches and historical museums to protect the fragile pigments of religious paintings and statues. Keep in mind that opening hours fluctuate almost daily; those provided here are a rough guide at best. Several churches are still under repairs following the earthquake of 1987, but all are open.

OLD TOWN

Quito's colonial section has been thoroughly cleaned up since the new millennium. Unlike just a few years ago, beggars and street vendors have been replaced with more police and horse-drawn carriages carting tourists around churches, which are beautifully lit at night. Traffic is prohibited 9 A.M.–4 P.M. on Sundays.

The municipality of Quito has put together an excellent **map/guide** to three historic walks through Old Town, written by Oscar Valenzuela-Morales and available at tourist offices. Even better are the **multilingual tours** given by municipal police from the tourist office (8 A.M.–5 P.M. daily, $10 pp includes some entry fees) in the Pasaje Arzobispal on the Plaza Grande.

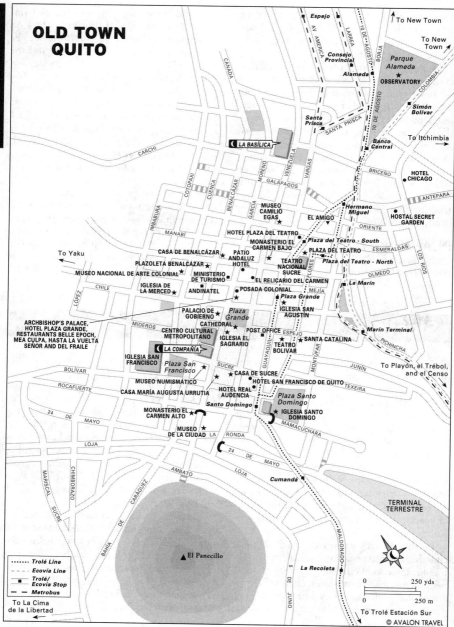

OLD TOWN QUITO

To New Town
To New Town
To Itchimbia
To Yaku
To Playón, el Trébol, and el Censo
To La Cima de la Libertad
To Trolé Estación Sur

Espejo
Consejo Provincial
Alameda
Parque Alameda
OBSERVATORY
Simón Bolívar
Santa Prisca
Banco Central
HOTEL CHICAGO
LA BASÍLICA
MUSEO CAMILIO EGAS
EL AMIGO
Hermano Miguel
HOSTAL SECRET GARDEN
HOTEL PLAZA DEL TEATRO
MONASTERIO EL CARMEN BAJO
Plaza del Teatro - South
PLAZA DEL TEATRO
CASA DE BENALCÁZAR
PATIO ANDALUZ HOTEL
TEATRO NACIONAL SUCRE
Plaza del Teatro - North
PLAZOLETA BENALCÁZAR
MINISTERIO DE TURISMO
EL RELICARIO DEL CARMEN
La Marín
MUSEO NACIONAL DE ARTE COLONIAL
IGLESIA DE LA MERCED
ANDINATEL
POSADA COLONIAL
Plaza Grande
PALACIO DE GOBIERNO
Plaza Grande
IGLESIA SAN AGUSTÍN
ARCHBISHOP'S PALACE, HOTEL PLAZA GRANDE, RESTAURANTS BELLE EPOCH, MEA CULPA, HASTA LA VUELTA SEÑOR AND DEL FRAILE
CATHEDRAL
CENTRO CULTURAL METROPOLITANO
POST OFFICE
Marín Terminal
IGLESIA EL SAGRARIO
LA COMPAÑÍA
TEATRO BOLÍVAR
SANTA CATALINA
IGLESIA SAN FRANCISCO
Plaza San Francisco
CASA DE SUCRE
MUSEO NUMISMÁTICO
HOTEL SAN FRANCISCO DE QUITO
CASA MARÍA AUGUSTA URRUTIA
HOTEL REAL AUDENCIA
Plaza Santo Domingo
Santo Domingo
IGLESIA SANTO DOMINGO
MONASTERIO EL CARMEN ALTO
MUSEO DE LA CIUDAD
Cumandá
TERMINAL TERRESTRE
El Panecillo
La Recoleta

Streets: Espejo, AV AMERICA, LARREA, BORJA, 10 DE AGOSTO, COLOMBIA, CANADA, SANTA PRISCA, CARCHI, MORENO, VENEZUELA, VARGAS, GALÁPAGOS, BRICEÑO, ANTEPARA, COTOPAXI, CUENCA, BENALCÁZAR, GARCÍA, IMBABURA, MANABÍ, ORIENTE, ESMERALDAS, LOS RÍOS, CHILE, FLORES, OLMEDO, LÓPEZ, MEJÍA, MIDEROS, ESPEJO, GUAYAQUIL, MONTUFAR, PICHINCHA, BOLÍVAR, SUCRE, TEXEIRA, JUNÍN, ROCAFUERTE, 24 DE MAYO, MAMACUCHARA, LOJA, LA RONDA, 24 DE MAYO, AMBATO, LOJA, MARISCAL SUCRE, CHIMBORAZO, CARAQUEZ, BAHÍA, DE JUNIO, 5 DE JUNIO, MALDONADO

Legend:
...... Trolé Line
--- Ecovía Line
■ Trolé/Ecovía Stop
— Metrobus

0 250 yds
0 250 m

© AVALON TRAVEL

© JEAN BROWN

panorama of Quito Colonial and El Panecillo

Plaza Grande and Vicinity

The heart of colonial Quito, officially called the Plaza de la Independencia, features a winged statue to independence atop a high pillar. In the park at its base, music, mime, and dance performances are watched by a legion of old men feeding the pigeons and enjoying the sun.

On the plaza's southwest side, the **Catedral** is actually the third to stand on this site (mass 6–9 A.M. daily). Other visits are available through the museum located on Venezuela (tel. 2/257-0371, 9:30 A.M.–4 P.M. Mon.–Sat., $1.50). José Antonio Sucre, the number-two man in South America's independence battles, is buried here. Behind the main altar is the smaller altar of Nuestra Señora de Los Dolores where, on August 6, 1875, president Gabriel García Moreno drew his last breath after being macheted outside the presidential palace. He is now buried here also, as is the country's first president, Juan José Flores.

Formerly the main chapel of the cathedral, the **Iglesia El Sagrario** (10 A.M.–4 P.M. Mon.–Fri., 10 A.M.–2 P.M. Sat.–Sun.) next door was begun in 1657 and completed half a century later. The walls and ceiling of the short nave are painted to simulate marble—even the bare stone is speckled black-and-white. Impressive paintings and stained-glass windows decorate the center cupola. Bernardo de Legarda, the most outstanding Quiteño sculptor of the 18th century, carved and gilded the baroque *mampara* (partition) inside the main doorway.

A long, arched atrium to the northwest lines the front of the **Palacio de Gobierno** (8 A.M.–5 P.M. Mon.–Fri., when the government is not in session). The ironwork on the balconies over the plaza, originally from the Palais des Tuileries in Paris, was purchased just after the French Revolution. At the entrance to the main courtyard off the walkway stand two long-suffering guards in full uniform. Considering how often they're photographed with grinning tourists, it's probably for the best that guns aren't a part of the ceremonial outfit.

The **Palacio Arzobispal** (Archbishop's Palace) on the northeast side leads to a three-story indoor courtyard housing a number of small shops and snug eateries. Cobbled courtyards, thick whitewashed walls, and wooden balconies make it worth a peek. The plaza's colonial spell is broken only by the modern **City Hall** to the southeast. The church of **La Concepción** (10 A.M.–4 P.M. Mon.–Fri., 10 A.M.–2 P.M. Sat.–Sun.) stands at the corner of Chile and Garcia Moreno. The attached convent is Quito's oldest, dating to 1577, and is closed to visitors.

At the corner of Benalcázar and Espejo, the **Centro Cultural Metropolitano** (tel. 2/295-0272, 9 A.M.–4:30 P.M. daily) houses the collection of the relocated **Museo Alberto Mena Caamaño** (tel. 2/295-0272, ext. 135, 9 A.M.–4:30 P.M. daily, $1.50), including colonial and contemporary art and a set of wax figures depicting the death throes of patriots killed in 1810 by royalist troops. True to its name, the new cultural center includes lecture rooms, the municipal library, and gallery space for temporary art exhibits.

Plaza del Teatro and Vicinity

This small plaza at Guayaquil and Manabí is surrounded by restored colonial buildings, including the **Teatro Nacional Sucre,** one of Quito's finest theaters. The gorgeous building, erected in 1878, reopened in 2004 after extensive renovations, complete with a wonderful restaurant called Theatrum on the second floor above the lobby. The theater hosts frequent plays and concerts, including opera, jazz, ballet, and international traveling groups. Tucked in the far corner is the renovated **Teatro Variedades.** Its previous life as a porn cinema has ended, and it has been reborn as an elegant dinner theater. Next door is the delightful and popular **Café Teatro.**

Enter the **Monasterio El Carmen Bajo** (Venezuela between Olmedo and Manabí, 8 A.M.–noon daily, free) through huge wooden doors dating to the 18th century. Whitewashed stone pillars support a two-story courtyard inside, surrounded by nun's quarters and schoolrooms.

Teatro Bolívar

Scorched by a fire in 1999, only two years after an extensive restoration, this opulent theater is being restored yet again as of 2008. The 2,200-seat building was built in 1933 by a pair of American theater architects, and it incorporates elements of art deco and Moorish styles. The theater is on the 100 Most Endangered Sites of World Monuments

Plaza de la Independencia and the presidential palace

© JEAN BROWN

Watch and is currently open during restoration. Your ticket price will help fund the ongoing work, or you can give more—you could even buy a seat for a year and get discounted entry to events.

Iglesia San Agustín and Vicinity

In the church (Chile and Guayaquil, 7 A.M.–noon and 1–6 P.M. daily) no surface is left unpainted, including with the likenesses of saints, which line the arches against a pastel background. A black Christ occupies a side altar. The adjoining **Convento y Museo de San Agustín** (Chile and Flores, tel. 2/295-5525, 9 A.M.–12:30 P.M. and 2:30–5 P.M. Mon.–Fri., 9 A.M.–1 P.M. Sat., $1) features loads of colonial artwork on the walls and surrounds a palm-filled cloister. Ecuador's declaration of independence was signed in the *Sala capitular* on August 10, 1809. (Don't miss the incredible carved benches and altar.) Many of the heroes who battled for independence are buried in the crypt.

QUITO

Plaza San Francisco and Vicinity

This gently sloping, cobbled expanse can easily keep you occupied all afternoon. Head up the set of circular stairs to the **Iglesia San Francisco** (8 A.M.–noon and 3–6 P.M. daily), the largest and oldest colonial edifice in the city. It was begun on the site of an Inca royal house within weeks of the city's founding in 1534. The first wheat grown in Ecuador sprouted in one of its courtyards, and Atahualpa's children learned their three *R*s in its school.

Two white spires flank a glowering stone facade, which sets the perfect mood for the interior. Inside, it's easy to imagine yourself in the 16th century, amid the musty odor drifting up from the creaking wooden floorboards. Bare lightbulbs are almost swallowed by the dusty gloom, with little help from the small, high windows. Its decorators seemed to gild first and ask questions later—thick encrustations cover almost every square inch. Seeing the carved roof alone is worth a visit. Notice how many of the design motifs come from the indigenous cultures, including the smiling/frowning faces of sun gods, repeated several times, and harvest symbols of flowers and fruit.

To the right of the main entrance, the **Museo Fray Pedro Gocial** (tel. 2/295-2911, 9 A.M.–6 P.M. Mon.–Sat., 9 A.M.–noon Sun., $2 pp) houses one of the finest collections of colonial art in Quito, dating from the 16th–19th centuries. Guides are included in English, Spanish, and French. On the other side, the **Capilla de Catuña** (8 A.M.–noon and 3–6 P.M. daily) also has colonial art on display. As the story goes, this chapel was constructed by an indigenous man named Catuña who promised to have it completed in a certain length of time. When it became obvious that he wasn't going to come close to his deadline, he offered his soul to the devil in exchange for help getting the job done. Then Catuña finished and had a sudden change of heart, begging the Virgin Mary to save him from his hasty agreement. Sure enough, a foundation stone was discovered missing during the inauguration, negating his deal with the devil. The Tianguez café and gift shop downstairs (9:30 A.M.–6:30 P.M. daily, open later Wed.–Sat.) is a great place to spend some time and souvenir dollars.

© JEAN BROWN

The immense Plaza San Francisco has the same proportions as the previous building on the site, an Inca compound.

Plaza Santo Domingo and Vicinity

A statue of Sucre pointing to his victory site on the slopes of Pichincha decorates this plaza at the southern corner of Old Town. Crowds often surround performance artists in front of the **Iglesia Santo Domingo** (7 A.M.–noon and 3–6 P.M. daily), which was begun in 1581 and finished in 1650. Four clock faces and an off-center tower decorate the stone facade. Despite the stained glass behind the altar, the decorative elements inside somehow don't seem to work together, although the baroque filigree of the Chapel of the Rosary to one side is stunning. The attached **Museo Fray Pedro Bedon** (tel. 2/228-2695, 1–5 P.M. daily, $1) has obligatory guides and takes you through the reserved chapels, too.

Nearby is one of the best-preserved colonial streets in Old Town. Also called Calle Juan de Díos Morales, **La Ronda** was nicknamed for the evening serenades (*rondas*) that once floated through its winding path. The narrow lane is lined with painted balconies, shops, and a hotel. It's reached most easily via Guayaquil, sloping down from the Plaza Santo Domingo.

Plaza Santo Domingo and church

© JEAN BROWN

The extensive renovations and an artsy atmosphere have turned this into a destination for Quiteños and tourists; it is well guarded and totally pedestrian. Take an evening stroll and look into the bars or cafés—you may find one with live entertainment.

🄲 La Compañía

This church, said to be the most beautiful in the Americas, is definitely among the most ornate. Seven tons of gold supposedly ended up on the ceiling, walls, and altars of "Quito's Sistine Chapel," which was built by the wealthy Jesuit order between 1605 and 1765. The church (10 A.M.–5 P.M. Mon.–Fri., 10 A.M.–4 P.M. Sat., noon–4 P.M. Sun., $2) was still being restored from the damage caused by the 1987 earthquake when a raging fire set work back a couple of years. It is now open to the public in all its glory.

Even the outside is overwhelming, crammed with full-size statues, busts, sculpted hearts, and a garden's worth of leaves carved in stone. The interior has eight side chapels, one of which houses the guitar and possessions of Santa Mariana de Jesús—her remains are under the main altar (see sidebar). Some of the more expensive relics, including a painting of the Virgin framed with gold and precious stones, are locked away in a bank vault between festivals. One of the more eye-catching objects in La Compañía is a painting depicting hell, where sinners—each labeled with one of the deadly sins—are receiving imaginative, excruciatingly appropriate punishments.

Across Sucre from La Compañía is the **Museo Numismático** (tel. 2/258-9284, 9 A.M.–1 P.M. and 2–5 P.M. Mon.–Fri., 10 A.M.–1 P.M. and 2–4 P.M. Sat.–Sun., $1), which traces the history of Ecuador's various currencies, from shell currency to the adoption of the U.S. dollar. An inflation chart will make you glad you're not one of the country's financial ministers. Also housed here is the national music library, where there are often free concerts in the evenings. On the opposite side of García Moreno from the museum is the **Casa de María Augusta Urrutia** (García Moreno 760 between Sucre

© JEAN BROWN

recent restoration of La Ronda

and Bolívar, tel. 2/258-0107, 10 A.M.–6 P.M. Tues.–Sat., 9:30 A.M.–5:30 P.M. Sun., $2), a wonderfully preserved 19th-century mansion. Doña María passed away in 1987, and her house is a virtual window onto the past, with three inner patios and luxurious accoutrements from all over the globe, as well as a virtual gallery of Victor Mideros's paintings.

Heading east on Sucre brings you to the **Casa de Sucre** (Venezuela 513 and Sucre), once home to Bolívar's southern counterpart. The building has been preserved in its original, early 1800s state; and the collection, naturally, is heavy on the militaristic side.

Monasterio El Carmen Alto

This monastery, at Rocafuerte and García Moreno, was the home of Santa Mariana de Jesús from 1618 to 1645. Abandoned children were once passed through a small window in the patio to be raised by the nuns; adjacent, there is a small store that allows visitors to purchase cookies, chocolate, honey, creams, and herbs (9–11 A.M. and 3–5 P.M. Mon.–Fri.). The church is only open for 7 A.M. mass. The **Arco de la Reina** (Queen's Arch) over Garcia Moreno marks the original southern entrance to Quito's center and once sheltered

worshippers from the rain. Across Rocafuerte, peanuts and other nibbles are roasted fresh every day.

The **Museo de la Ciudad** (García Moreno and Rocafuerte, tel. 2/228-3882, 9:30 A.M.–5:30 P.M. daily, $2) traces the history of the city from pre-Hispanic times to the beginning of the 20th century. It's set in the old Hospital San Juan de Dios,·founded by the order of King Philip in 1565. The collection, which is very well presented, includes Inca burials, photographs, clothing, and religious and scientific artifacts, as well as a large painting depicting Francisco de Orellana's descent of the Amazon. Tours in English, French, Italian, and German can be arranged for an extra charge.

Iglesia de la Merced

The entrance to one of Quito's newest churches, completed in 1742, is on Chile, just up from the corner with Cuenca. The 47-meter tower is the highest in the city and houses the largest bell in town. Enter the high-vaulted nave, decorated with white stucco on a pink background from the Plaza. The church (6:30 A.M.–noon and 12:30–6 P.M. daily) is dedicated to Our Lady of Mercy, whose statue inside is said to have saved the city from an eruption of Pichincha in

QUITO

© JEAN BROWN

Monasterio El Carmen Alto and the Arco de la Reina

1575. To the left of the altar is the entrance to the **Monasterio de la Merced,** housing Quito's oldest clock, built in London in 1817; a new clock face was recently installed. Here again are many paintings by Victor Mideros depicting the catastrophes of 1575.

Across Mejía is the **Museo Nacional de Arte Colonial,** home to Quito's finest collection of colonial art. Works by renowned artists Miguel de Santiago, Caspicara, and Bernardo de Legarda make up part of the collection, which, as of 2008, was still closed for major renovations.

Casa de Benalcázar

The Colonial Patio (Olmedo 962 and Benalcázar, tel. 2/228-8102, 9 A.M.–noon and 2–4 P.M. Mon.–Fri.) was built the year of Quito's refounding. Wednesdays at 6:30 P.M., Pan-Hispanic films are shown; call for details.

La Cima de la Libertad

In the foothills of Pichincha stands this military museum and monument to Sucre's decisive victory over the royalist forces at the Battle of Pichincha on May 24, 1822. At the **Templo de la Patria,** an expansive mosaic of the

independence struggle by Eduardo Kingman competes with the view of the city and snow-capped volcanoes on clear days. The **Museo de las Fuerzas Armadas** (tel. 2/228-8733, 8:30 A.M.–4:30 P.M. Mon.–Fri., 10 A.M.–4 P.M. Sat.–Sun., $0.50) displays historical military tools and weapons. A taxi here should cost about $5, and there is a bus route that returns visitors to the city.

Yaku

Families traveling with children will be happy for them to be entertained at this lovely overview of the city. The museum, dedicated to many aspects of water, is on the hill in El Placer (take a taxi up and walk down). The bubble room is fun for all ages, and traveling photo and art exhibitions on water themes are interesting.

El Panecillo

A 30-meter statue of the Virgin of Quito punctuates this hill at the southern end of Old Town. You can climb up inside the base (9 A.M.–5 P.M. Mon.–Sat., 9 A.M.–6 P.M. Sun., $1) to an observation platform for a sweeping

© JEAN BROWN

sculpture of the Virgin overlooking Quito from El Panecillo

view of the city and its impressive environs. Take a taxi here, as the neighborhood on the way up is still somewhat dangerous. The surrounding plaza is secured until 7 P.M., and a taxi ride up and back costs about $5. There is a restaurant with great views and acceptable food overlooking the city to the north.

La Basílica

A fine alternative view of the city can be found to the north up Venezuela, eight blocks from the Plaza Grande. Even though construction began in 1892, the basilica (9 A.M.–5 P.M. daily, $2) is still unfinished. Tours start with the stained glass and powerful gilt statues in the nave, then move on to the 115-meter Condor Tower, with views easily comparable to those from El Panecillo. Notice that the "gargoyles" are actually a menagerie of local animals, including armadillos. You can buy a pass to the upper floors and have a coffee with a view at the café. If you're feeling bold, climb the bell tower. (Although it's not part of the tour, you may be able to step up to the altar to see the Virgin of Quito atop El Panecillo, framed in a heart-shaped glass window.)

PRISON VISITS

If you're looking for something different to do in Quito and feel like spreading some cheer, consider visiting a fellow countryperson being held in one of the city's two prisons. Foreigners are incarcerated in all of them, mostly on drug charges, and they greatly appreciate the chance to speak their own language and meet new people. It's an easy way to brighten someone's day and a safe way to get a glimpse into the dark side of traveling abroad. Inmates appreciate small gifts like toiletries, snacks, and books, but leave your valuables at home. Bring a photocopied ID to leave with the guards. The South American Explorers keep a list of foreigners currently being held.

To reach the **Carcel de las Mujeres** (women's prison, tel. 2/241-4593), head east three blocks from the El Inca roundabout and take a left onto Las Toronjas, then continue for another 1.5 blocks to the prison on your right. Visiting hours are 10 A.M.-3 P.M. Wednesday, 10 A.M.-noon and 1-4 P.M. Saturday and Sunday. (No entries or exits noon-1 P.M.) Prisoners may receive calls (tel. 2/241-4619) 9 A.M.-6 P.M. Wednesday–Sunday.

The **Penal García Moreno** (Rocafuerte and Chimborazo, tel. 2/228-1298) holds men. It's 10 blocks uphill along Calle Rocafuerte from Plaza Santo Domingo in Old Town. Visiting hours are 9 A.M.-5 P.M. Wednesday, Saturday, and Sunday, with last entry at 3 P.M. and no entries or exits noon-1 P.M.

Santa Catalina

This church has been closed and cloistered since its construction on the ruins of the Inca Palace of the Virgins. The newly opened **Convent Museo Santa Catalina** (Espejo and Flores, tel. 2/228-7213, 8:30 A.M.–5:30 P.M. Mon.–Sat., $1.50) displays religious art and artifacts in situ.

BETWEEN OLD TOWN AND NEW TOWN

Parque La Alameda

Ornamental lakes and a monument to Bolívar hold down opposite ends of this triangular park. In the center stands the oldest **astronomical observatory** in South America, inaugurated in 1864 by then president García Moreno. The beautiful old building also houses a museum (tel. 2/257-0765, 9 A.M.–noon and 2:30–5:30 P.M. daily, $1) filled with books, photos, and antique astronomical tools, including a gorgeous brass telescope that still works. Visitors can sometimes view the stars on clear nights; call ahead for a schedule and information on occasional astronomy lectures. It is currently closed for renovations, but should be open in 2009. Many of the large trees found here were planted in 1887, when the park began as a botanical garden.

Palacio Legislativo

Drop by Gran Colombia and Montalvo when this arm of Ecuador's government is out to lunch (really), and you can peek through the fence to see Guayasamín's infamous mural titled *Imagen de la Patria*. The huge work, depicting and protesting injustice in Latin America, caused a stir during its unveiling at a formal ceremony of ambassadors and dignitaries. An evil-looking face with a helmet labeled CIA caused the U.S. ambassador to storm out of the room. Copies of the mural are available in the Guayasamín Museum.

Following a fire in 2003, the legislators met in the Banco Central building on 10 de Agosto and Briceño. While the new constitution is being written in Montecristi, both buildings are closed.

◖ Casa de la Cultura

An unmistakable curve of mirrored glass surrounds the best collection of museums in one spot in the city (tel. 2/222-1007, 9 A.M.–5 P.M. Tues.–Fri., 10 A.M.–4 P.M. Sat–Sun., $2). The Casa de la Cultura Museum was remodeled in 2005. It includes sections called the **Museo Colonial y de Arte,** the **Museo de**

Instrumentos Musicales (musical instruments), the **Museo de Arte Moderno** (modern art), and the **Museo de Traje Indígena** (indigenous clothing).

There is a separate entrance to **Museo del Banco Central** (tel. 2/222-3258, 9 A.M.–5 P.M. Tues.–Fri., 10 A.M.–4 P.M. Sat–Sun., $2), which is a world unto itself, with 1,500 pieces of pre-Inca pottery and other relics labeled in English and Spanish. A vault downstairs protects a dazzling collection of gold pieces, and various *salas* (salons) display colonial and contemporary art and furniture.

The **Agora,** a huge concert arena in the center of the building, hosts concerts. (Admission depends on the event.) There's also a *cine* showing art and cultural films most evenings.

The old building on 6 de Diciembre, facing the park, houses occasional exhibits and a bookshop that sells its own publications. Next door is the **Teatro Prometeo,** which is open for evening performances.

Parque El Ejido

Avenidas Patria, 6 de Diciembre, 10 de Agosto, and Tarquí form the wedge filled by Quito's most popular central park. It's all that remains of the common grazing lands that stretched for more than 10 kilometers to the north. Heated games of Ecuavolley fill the northwest corner of the park most evenings and weekends, and a children's playground takes up the northeast corner. You can also often see people playing an Ecuadorian version of a French game of *boules*. On weekends, the area near the arch at Amazonas and Patria becomes an outdoor arts and crafts market; paintings line the sidewalk along Patria, and Otavaleños and other artists sell textiles, antiques, and jewelry.

◖ Itchimbia Park and Cultural Center

The old Santa Clara market building—imported from Hamburg in 1899 and brought to the highlands, by mule, in sections—has been rebuilt in all its glass-and-metal glory on top of a hill east of Old Town. The structure is now a cultural center (tel. 2/295-0272, ext.

137, 10 A.M.–6 P.M. daily, $1) hosting occasional traveling exhibitions. It's surrounded by a park that is being reforested and laced with footpaths. It's all beautifully lit at night, and it's no slouch in the view department by day. Just below on Samaniego is Mosaico, along with several new happening spots for drinks and elite elbow-rubbing that justify their prices every evening at sunset.

NEW TOWN

If you're going to bump into anyone you know in Quito, it'll be along **Avenida Amazonas,** New Town's wide commercial artery. Banks, shops, offices, travel agencies, and restaurants cluster like grapes on a vine, and the sidewalk cafés are the place to be seen with a cold beer and a pizza. Andean bands play occasionally in the Plaza de los Presidentes at Washington and Amazonas.

The exponentially expanding development around the **Plaza del Quindé,** at the intersection of Foch and Reina Victoria, has resulted in such a concentration of restaurants and night

© JEAN BROWN

Plaza del Quindé, the newest gathering place in the Mariscal

spots that it defies making recommendations. Visit any Thursday, Friday, or Saturday and mill with the crowds. On other days, it is a little quieter, but there's a 24/7 coffee shop that's never empty.

Museo Jacinto Jijón y Caamaño

The family of a prominent Ecuadorian archaeologist donated his private collection of colonial art and archaeological pieces to the Universidad Católica after his death. Now it's on display in this museum (tel. 2/299-1700, ext. 1242, 8 A.M.–4 P.M. Mon.–Fri., $0.60), located within the university compound on the third floor of the main library building. Enter off 12 de Octubre near Carrión—ask the guard to point you in the right direction. Nearby in the Central Cultural block is the extensive **Weilbauer** collection (tel. 2/299-1700, ext. 1681, 8 A.M.–1 P.M. and 2 P.M.–5 P.M. Mon.–Fri., free).

Museo Amazonico

The small **Abya Yala** complex (12 de Octubre 1430 and Wilson, tel. 2/396-2800) contains a bookstore with the city's best selection of works on the indigenous cultures of Ecuador. Shops downstairs sell snacks, crafts, and natural medicines, while the second floor is taken up by the excellent museum (8:30 A.M.–12:30 P.M. and 2–5 P.M. Mon.–Fri., $2). The guided tours available in Spanish will take you past stuffed jungle animals, stunning Cofán feather headdresses, and real Shuar *tzantzas* (shrunken heads). The pottery depicting Lowland Kichwa gods, each with its accompanying myth, is particularly interesting, as are photos of oil exploration and its environmental impact.

Mindalae Ethnic Museum

Run by the Sinchi Sacha Foundation, which promotes indigenous cultures, fair trade, and responsible tourism, the Mindalae Museum (Reina Victoria and La Niña, tel. 2/223-0609, 9:30 A.M.–6 P.M. daily except Sun., $3) has five floors with comprehensive collections of ethnic clothing, artifacts, and ceramics from all regions, plus a shop and a restaurant.

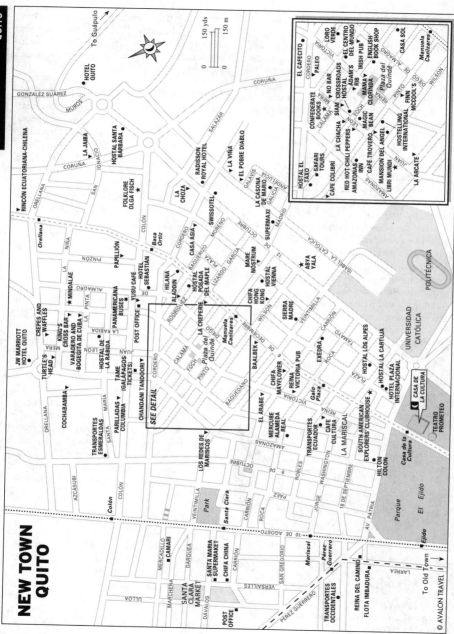

NEW TOWN QUITO

© AVALON TRAVEL

NORTH OF NEW TOWN
Parque La Carolina

Quito's largest park stretches from the intersection of Orellana and Eloy Alfaro almost one kilometer east to Naciones Unidas. It's popular with early-morning joggers, and the *laguna* has two-person paddleboats for rent for $3/30 min. Three large **shopping malls** anchor its corners: El Jardín, at Avenida de La República and Amazonas; Iñaquito, at Amazonas and Naciones Unidas; and Quicentro, at Naciones Unidas and Avenida de Los Shyris.

Natural history is the focus of the dusty **Museo de las Ciencias Naturales** (Rumipamba 341 and Los Shyris, tel. 2/244-9824, 8:30 A.M.–4:30 P.M. Mon.–Fri., $2), at the east end of the park. Here, the Casa de la Cultura administers displays on zoology, botany, and geology, including an anaconda skeleton. Fans of creepy-crawlies can get their fill at the **Vivarium** (Amazonas 3008 and Rumipamba, tel. 2/227-1820, 9:30 A.M.–5:30 P.M. Tues.–Sun., $2.50), with more than 100 live reptiles and amphibians. The collection includes poisonous and constrictor snakes from the Oriente. If you're more into flora than fauna, visit the Jardín Botanico (between Ciencias Naturales and Shyris, 9 A.M.–5 P.M. daily), which features plants from all over Ecuador, including lots of orchids.

Museo Fundación Guayasamín

Ecuador's most famous artist once lived in this palatial place, overlooking New Town in the Bellavista suburb. It's now a museum (Bosmediano 543, tel. 2/244-6455, 10 A.M.–5 P.M. Mon.–Fri., $3) run by the Fundación Guayasamín. Pre-Columbian figurines and pottery fill the first building, while Guayasamín's paintings and an impressive collection of colonial art wait further on. Guayasamín's large-scale paintings are alternately tender and tortured, but affecting either way. The balcony outside has a cafeteria. In the gift shop, ask to see the many unique pieces of jewelry designed by the master himself. To get there, take a bus bound for Bellavista (marked Batan–Colmena) or hail a taxi.

◖ Capilla del Hombre

Completed three years after his death in 1999 by the Guayasamin foundation, Oswaldo Guayasamín's masterwork is a must-see for visitors to Quito. The Chapel of Mankind (Calvachi and Chavez, tel. 2/244-8492, www.capilladelhombre.com, 10 A.M.–5 P.M. Tues.–Sun., $3) is dedicated to the struggles endured by the indigenous peoples of the Americas, both before and after the arrival of the Spanish. Vistors receive a discount on entrance fees if they visit both the chapel and Guayasamin museum in the same day.

Huge paintings fill the open, two-story building, which is centered on a circular space beneath an unfinished dome mural portraying the millions of workers who died in the silver mines of Potosí, Bolivia. Other works cover topics both heartening and wrenching, from the innocent faces of children to the gigantic *Bull and Condor*, symbolizing the struggle between Spanish and Andean identities. In the center of the ground floor burns an eternal flame. Guided tours are offered in English and Spanish.

Entertainment and Events

BARS AND DANCE CLUBS

Probably the most popular nighttime destinations for teenage and young Quiteños, dance clubs and discos go in and out of popularity faster than the phases of the moon. Many places with music have a small cover charge, a drink minimum, happy hour 5–8 P.M. or thereabouts, and a dress code (relaxed slightly for gringos). Unaccompanied males may have trouble getting in. So many new popular places, discos, bars and restaurants, have sprung up around the **Plaza del Quindé** (Foch and Reina Victoria) and on nearby Calama, there is often gridlocked traffic from 10 P.M. to midnight, and taxis wait around until the wee hours, as at least one café is open 24/7.

Papillon (Yanez Pinzon and Colón) is very popular with locals—and probably the loudest place you can find. On weekends, it may get so crowded that you have no choice but to hang your coat on a rafter and dance to the Latin music on a table—or the bar.

With its college feel, **No Bar** (Calama and Juan León Mera) is popular with locals and gringos. Somewhere among the gyrating bodies is a pool table. Some classier discos, such as **El Cerebro** (Shyris and 6 de Diciembre) have stricter standards of dress and bigger cover charges, but at least here, the cover includes a free drink.

Jazz and the occasional singer or poetry reader fill **Café Libro** (Almagro and Pradera) to bursting. Well-stocked bookshelves and photos of writers decorate this literary place, which is open until midnight Monday–Saturday. **El Pobre Diablo** (Isabel la Católica E12-06 and Galavis) is still one of the best places for live music in Quito on Wednesday nights, and other nights when advertised. It's quite stylish, frequented by a sophisticated and attractive crowd—an art-and-wine kind of place. A Swiss chap runs **Ghoz** (La Niña 425 and Reina Victoria). Darts, pool, foosball, and pinball fill the large upstairs of this

smoky cave. On the first floor, there's a wide selection of quality beers, board games, and a kitchen that whips up a good set meal—Swiss food, of course—for $4–7.

Step into the pastel rainbow inside the chic **Boca del Lobo** (Calama 284 and Reina Victoria), and you'll feel like you're in Los Angeles: martinis, panini, and bumping tunes. In the neighborhood of Guápulo is **Ananké** (Camino de Orellana 781), a funky little spot with great views from both floors by day, and DJs and chill-out rooms upstairs by night. The decor is somewhat surreal: Barbies, balloons, and an orange fridge.

Reservations are recommended at **Varadero and La Bodeguita de Cuba** (Reina Victoria 1721 and La Pinta), where Cuban rhythms will set your toes tapping and your hips swiveling. Live music starts at 8 P.M. Thursday–Saturday. **Seseribó** (Veintimilla and 12 de Octubre) has been offering *pura salsa* for more than a decade. It occasionally has live music, too. Other popular *salsatecas* include **Mayo 68** (Lizardo García 662 and Juan León Mera) and **Cali Salsateca** (1699 Colón).

To brush up on your gyrating, spend a few hours (or days, if you're like me) at one of the **dancing schools** listed in the *Sports and Recreation* of this chapter.

Gay bars are harder to find—city residents are your best source of information. The best-known are **Matroiska** (Pinto and Juan León Mera), **Blackout** (Baquedano and Reina Victoria), and **Pride Lounge** (Almagro and Pinto).

PEÑAS

Live folk music happens after 9 P.M. Wednesday–Saturday at **Ñucanchi Peña** (Universitario 496 and Armero). Things get going around the same time on Thursdays and Fridays at **Noches de Quito** (Juan León Mera and Carrión), which also runs a hostel upstairs, I doubt you'll get much sleep there, but if it's too late to go home, it could be a godsend.

PUBS

Quito's sizable population of British, German, and North American immigrants supports a handful of authentic taprooms. The **Reina Victoria Pub** (Reina Victoria 530 and Roca, tel. 2/222-6369), located in a 100-year-old house, is one of the best known. Chosen as one of the 22 best gathering places in the world by *Newsweek,* it's been open since 1973. Relax with a Guinness in front of the fireplace, or down a Newcastle between games of darts or pool. A small restaurant serves sandwiches and light fare. **Finn McCool's** (Pinto 251 and Reina Victoria, tel. 2/256-4953) is actually run by Irish expats and attracts a multinational crowd for pool, foosball, and pub food.

King's Cross Bar (Reina Victoria and La Niña) features a good selection of ales, and **The Turtle's Head** (La Niña 626 and Juan León Mera) is a Scottish-owned pub that proudly promotes its wide selection of draught microbrewed beers. They have pool, darts, and food. The **Irish Pub** (Lizardo Garcia 559 and Reina Victoria) offers $1 beers on Monday from 5 P.M.

CINEMA

The *El Comercio* newspaper has a daily cinema schedule. Multicines (in the C.C. Iñaquito at Naciones Unidas and Amazonas, tel. 2/226-5061 or 2/226-5062; and at the C.C. El Recreo on Maldonado in south Quito) and Cinemark (Naciones Unidas and America, tel. 2/226-0301) get mainstream releases a few months after they appear in the United States. Ticket prices run $3–4.

For a more artistic lineup, look to **Ocho y Medio** (Valladolid N24-353 and Vizcaya, tel. 2/290-4720), an alternative theater in La Floresta neighborhood. Pick up its monthly program at many hotels and restaurants.

THEATERS AND CONCERTS

El Comercio also runs information on theater performances and music concerts. When possible, advance tickets are a good idea. The **Teatro Politecnico** (Ladrón de Guevara and Queseras) hosts the National Symphony; tickets are a steal at $1. The colorful, indigenous-themed **Jacchigua Ecuadorian Folklore Ballet** performs at the Casa de la Cultura on Wednesdays at 7:30 P.M. Tickets are available at the theater or in advance from several travel agencies for $15.

The **Teatro Malayerba** (Sodiro 345 and 6 de Diciembre, tel. 2/223-5463), next to the Iglesia El Belén, is one of the better places to see a play in the city. Smaller performance houses include the **Patio de Comedias** (18 de Septiembre 457 and Amazonas, tel. 2/256-1902). Rock concerts, including some by international stars, pass through the **Coliseo Rumiñahui** and **Estadio Olímpico**—if someone big is coming to town, you'll know it.

CITY TOURS

The **tourist information office** on the Plaza Grande in Old Town (tel. 2/258-6591, 8:30 A.M.–5 P.M. daily) offers four daily tours of Quito's municipal highlights ($12 pp), as well as two nightly tours. Admission to places such as churches is included.

What better way to enjoy a newly spruced-up Old Town than in a **horse-drawn carriage?** These depart from the Plaza Grande next to the Government Palace 6 P.M.–midnight daily ($4 pp or $12 per carriage).

CABLE CAR

In early 2005, the *teleférigo* (tel. 2/225-0825, www.teleferiqo.com) climbing up the slopes of Pichincha was completed. It departs from above the Avenida Occidental, where a tourist center with restaurants, café, and carnival rides were built. The cable car climbs to 4,050 meters, affording fabulous views over the city and the Andes—on clear days, sunset is a lovely time to be up top.

QUITO

Shopping

Even if all you see of Ecuador is Quito, don't worry about souvenirs: There are plenty to buy. As far as something typical of the city, consider one of Oswaldo Guayasamín's prints of a Pichincha sunset, available at the Fundación Guayasamín, or a bouquet of roses at the airport.

CRAFTS AND GALLERIES

Once again, New Town is the place to spend your money—almost every block in the Mariscal district has some sort of crafts shop or sidewalk vendor's stand. Take your time, shop around, and compare quality. There are also a few standouts in Old Town.

Hungarian-born Olga Fisch came to Ecuador to escape the ugliness brewing in Europe in 1939. After opening her first shop in 1943, she became a world-renowned expert on South American crafts and folklore; during her lifetime, she was sought by the Smithsonian and collectors worldwide for her advice. **Folklore Olga Fisch** (Colón E10-53 and Caamaño, tel./fax 2/254-1315, www.olgafisch .com, 9 A.M.–7 P.M. Mon.–Sat.) was her house until her death. The first floor is filled with gorgeous, pricey ceramics and textiles from all over the continent. Out back, in what was once a storeroom, is a lovely restaurant called El Galpon. There are outlets of Fisch's shop in the Hilton Colón (tel. 2/252-6667), Swissôtel (tel. 2/256-9003), and the new Patio Andaluz in Old Town.

If you only have time for one crafts store in Quito, make it **Tianguez** (tel. 2/223-0609, 9 A.M.–6 P.M. daily), which is run by the Sinchi Sacha Foundation (a nonprofit set up to help support the people of the Oriente) underneath the Iglesia San Francisco. The store, which also has a small outdoor café on the Plaza San Francisco, features an excellent selection of quality handicrafts from around the country for surprisingly low prices. Profits from the masks, ceramics, Tigua hide paintings, jewelry, and weavings go to fund their programs to benefit indigenous communities.

La Bodega (Juan Leon Mera and Carrion) stocks high-quality artisan works, from adorable ceramic Galápagos creatures to jewelry. **Artesa** has several outlets selling excellent ceramics, some of which are updated versions of pre-Columbian designs. One store (tel. 2/246-4484) is on the ground floor of the Quicentro shopping mall. For suede and leather, try **Aramis** (Amazonas N24-32 and Pinto, tel. 2/222-8546), where they can make clothes or handbags to order.

Mindalae (Reina Victoria 17–80 and La Niña, tel. 2/223-0609) is also operated by the nonprofit Sinchi Sacha Foundation. It houses a shop selling indigenous crafts and a small restaurant. The **Camari Cooperative** (Marchena and 10 de Agosto) provides a place for indigenous and fair-trade groups from throughout Ecuador to sell their crafts. The store features a wide selection with good prices and quality. **Excedra** (Carrión 243 and Tamayo, tel. 2/222-4001) serves as a combination art gallery, folklore and antique outlet, and tea room. It's an offbeat little place with a nice selection of crafts. Beautiful, high-quality wool textiles for less money than you'd think are the specialty at **Hilana** (6 de Diciembre 1921 and Baquerizo Moreno, tel. 2/250-1693).

Professional browsers could spend a whole day on Juan León Mera and Veintimilla, where half a dozen highbrow crafts/antique stores and art galleries cluster within two blocks of Libri Mundi. Try **Galeria Latina,** or **Artesanias Incario** across the street for Tigua hide paintings, and other quality works; or stop by the weekend arts-and-crafts market in the park by Avenida Patria.

BOOKS

Libri Mundi (Juan León Mera and Wilson N23-83, tel. 2/223-4791, www.librimundi .com) is probably the best bookstore in Ecuador. Along with a wide range of titles in Spanish, it sells new and a few used foreign books (English, German, and French) at a markup. Flyers posted outside the door are a handy way to find out about artistic and literary goings-on around Quito. Libri Mundi also has branches in the Plaza del Quindé, Centro Comercial Quicentro and in Cumbayá. For used paperbacks, head for the large used library of **Confederate Books** (Calama 410 and Juan León Mera, tel. 2/2527-890) or **The English Bookshop** (Calama and Reina Victoria). **South American Explorers** (see the *Tourist Information* section of this chapter) has the best selection of guidebooks in Quito, a borrowing library, and a book exchange. An extensive library, **Damas Norteamericanas y Britanicas** (12 Octubre 26–138 and Orellana Ed. Lincoln, tel. 2/222-8190, damasnyb@ yahoo.com, 10 A.M.–noon Wed.–Sat.) is run by Alfonso, who knows his book selections well.

MAGAZINES AND NEWSPAPERS

Foreign magazines fill the shelves at **Libro Express** (Amazonas 816 and Veintimilla). Street vendors all along Amazonas also stock a few foreign publications. Bookshops in expensive hotels sell foreign magazines and newspapers, but be sure they don't try to mark up the latter over the printed price.

SPORTING EQUIPMENT

If you're looking for a mask and snorkel (or even a wetsuit) for your Galápagos trip, you'll find them—along with a whole store full of modern sporting equipment—at **KAO Sport** (Almagro and Colón, Ed. Ecuatoriana, tel. 2/255-0005 or 2/252-2266). Other KAO branches are located in many of the city's *centros comerciales.*

OTHER ITEMS

Hugo Chiliquinga (Huachi N67-34 and Legarda, tel. 2/259-8822) is considered by many to be the best guitar maker in Ecuador. He both makes and sells guitars, but he may have a waiting list, since he has an international reputation. **Marcel G. Creaciones** (Roca 766 between Amazonas and 9 de Octubre, tel. 2/265-3555, fax 2/255-2672) carries a good selection of Panama hats. For exclusive jewelry designs, stop by the **Museo Fundación Guayasamín** or **Ag** (Juan León Mera 614 and Carrión, tel. 2/255-0276, fax 2/250-2301). Many small leather-working shops in New Town can custom-make clothes, boots, bags, and other accessories for surprisingly reasonable prices. Try **Zapytal** (Pinto 538 and Amazonas, tel. 2/252-8757).

MARKETS

Vendors have been moved off the streets, making driving and walking around the old city much easier, if a little less colorful. For streetside shopping in Old Town, go to Ipiales (clothing and shoes), Calle Cuenca between Mejía and Olmedo (crafts and bazaar items), San Roque (food and furniture), and Plaza Arenas ("recycled" stolen goods, clothes, and hardware). Watch your wallet or purse carefully, and don't fall· for the mustard-on-the-clothes trick.

On weekends, the north end of Parque El Ejido becomes an outdoor art gallery with a selection of paintings, sculpture, and jewelry. **La Mariscal** artisan market in New Town occupies half of the block south of Jorge Washington between Reina Victoria and Juan León Mera. Just about every indigenous craft in Ecuador makes an appearance daily.

Local produce is the main draw to New Town's **Mercado Santa Clara,** along Ulloa and Versalles just south of Colón (main Wednesday, also Sunday). Every Friday, a fruit and vegetable market fills Galaviz between Toledo and Isabel La Católica, where children sell baskets of spices and wealthy shoppers hire elderly basket carriers to tote the day's purchases.

Boutiques, supermarkets, and movie theaters find a home in Quito's many *centros comerciales* (malls), some of which would be right at home in downtown Beverly Hills. Major ones include **El Bosque** (Al Parque and Alonso de Torres), **El Jardín** (República and Amazonas), **Iñaquito** (Amazonas and Naciones Unidas), **Multicentro** (6 de Diciembre and La Niña), **C.C.Nu** (Naciones Unidas and Amazonas), and **Quicentro** (6 de Diciembre and Naciones Unidas); and, in the south **El Recreo** trolley terminus.

Sports and Recreation

CLIMBING AND MOUNTAINEERING
Climbing Companies

A few of the many tour companies in Quito specialize in climbing—they have the experience and professionalism to get you back down in one piece, should anything go wrong. Founder and head guide Ramiro Cunalata brings almost two decades' worth of experience climbing in South America and Europe to the **Ecuadorian Alpine Institute** (Ramirez Davalos 136 and Amazonas, Of. 102, tel. 2/256-565, fax 2/256-8949, eai@ecuadorexplorer.com, www.volcanoclimbing.com). The climbs and treks are well-organized, professionally run, and span all experience levels—they even got me to the top of Cotopaxi in 2000.

The **Compañía de Guías** (Jorge Washington 425 and 6 de Diciembre, tel. 2/255-6210, tel./fax 2/250-4773, guisamontania@accessinter.net, www.companiadeguias.com) is a guide cooperative whose members speak English, German, French, and Italian. **Safari Tours** (Foch E4-132 y Cordero, tel. 2/255-2505, fax

---

TOUR COMPANIES

It seems that absolutely everyone now offers tours around Ecuador, which is all the more reason to heed positive reviews. Ideally, a tour should give you extra knowledge that you can't find in a guidebook. Guides should get you to interesting places efficiently, introduce you to fascinating people, and take the worry out of where you're going to eat or sleep next. Activities like climbing, rafting, bird-watching, and horseback-riding require specialized equipment and experience, as well as the most up-to-date knowledge of local routes and conditions. Of the dozens of general tour operators working out of Quito, a few stand out for their quality, professionalism, and value.

One of the largest tour operators in the country, **Metropolitan Touring** was the first to organize high-quality Galápagos trips in the 1960s. Since then, the company has branched out to include just about every kind of tour in Ecuador, including hacienda stays, city and market tours, train trips, and mountain-climbing. It has branch offices throughout the country, including a main one in Quito (De los Palmeras N45-74 y Las Orquideas, tel. 2/298-8200, www.metropolitan-touring.com). Information and bookings are available in the United States through Adventure Associates (13150 Coit Rd., Ste. 110, Dallas, TX 75240, tel. 800/527-2500, fax 972/783-1286, info@adventure-associates.com, www.adventure-associates.com).

Nuevo Mundo Travel and Tours (18 de Septiembre E4-161 and Juan León Mera, tel. 2/250-9431, nmundo@interactive.net.ec, www.nuevomundotravel.com) was started in 1979 by a founder and former president of the Ecuadorian Ecotourism Association. Its tours and facilities, therefore, are among the most environmentally conscious in Ecuador – the company doesn't even advertise some of them to minimize impact on the destinations. Along with the usual Galápagos and Oriente tours, several unique options include shamanism programs and one-month Spanish courses combined with environmental studies.

Safari Tours (E4-132 and Cordero, tel./fax 2/222-0426, tel. 2/255-2505, fax 2/222-3381, admin@safari.com.ec, www.safari.com.ec) is one of the most frequently recommended operators in the country. Owner Jean Brown knows Ecuador intimately and can take you in the company's trusty four-wheel drive vehicles to just about anywhere to climb, hike, bird-watch, camp, or mountain-bike. Safari has a complete Galápagos database and can book last-minute spaces or make reservations online.

Quasarnautica (Jose Jussieu N41-28 y Alonso de Torres, sector El Bosque, tel. 2/225-

2/222-3381, tel./fax 2/222-0426, admin@ safari.com.ec, www.safari.com.ec), with highly recommended climbing trips to any peak in the country. At **Sierra Nevada** (Pinto 637 and Cordero, tel. 2/255-3658 or 2/222-4717, fax 2/255-4936, snevada@accessinter .net, www.hotelsierranevada.com), bilingual owner Freddy Ramirez occasionally serves as a guide. Rafting, climbing, the Galápagos, and Amazon trips are all on the list. Positive reports have also come in about **Agama Expeditions** (Venezuela 1163 and Manabí, tel. 2/251-8191, fax 2/251-8196), which offers guided climbs of Cotopaxi's south face, and **Moggely Climbing** (Amazonas and Calama,

tel. 2/255-4984, moggely@hotmail.com, www.moggely.com).

Climbing and Camping Equipment

Quito has by far the best selection of outdoor gear merchants in the country. Everything from plastic climbing boots and harnesses to tents, sleeping bags, and stoves is readily available, although not always of the highest quality or state of repair. Needless to say, check all zippers, laces, and fuel valves before you head off into the wild. Large-size footgear (U.S. size 12 and up) may be hard to locate. Plenty of gear is available for sale as well, either imported (at a high markup) or made in Ecuador. **Tatoo**

7878, www.quasarex.com) also operates land tours under the name Amerindia Tours. The company operates and books up-market trips around the country. Contact Quasar in the U.S. through Tumbaco (7855 N.W. 12th St., Ste. 221, Miami, Fl 33126, tel. 305/599-9008 or 800/247-2925, fax 305/592-7060, info@ quasarnauticausa.com).

Tropic Ecological Adventures (info@trop iceco.com, www.tropiceco.com) is run by Andy Drumm, a fellow of the Royal Geographic Society and the president of the Amazon Commission of the Ecuadorian Ecotourism Association. These trips have won awards for socially responsible tourism and are especially strong in the Oriente, where they introduce travelers to the Huaorani, Cofán, and Achuar.

Green Planet (Juan León Mera 2384 and Wilson, tel. 2/252-0570, fax 2/252-1426, greenpla@interactive.net.ec) operates out of a little shop under a tree, across from Libri Mundi. Trips to Cuyabeno and Yasuní are both recommended for the guides and the food. Many one-day tours are available to places like Otavalo and Cotopaxi.

Enchanted Expeditions (De Las Alondras N45-102 y Los Lirios, tel. 2/334-0525, fax 2/334-0123, headoffice@enchantedexpedi tions.com, www.enchantedexpeditions.com) covers the entire country, with a focus on the

Galápagos – the boats *Cachalote* and *Beluga* receive frequent praise. **Ecuador Adventure** (Pasaje Cordova N23-26 and Wilson, tel. 2/222-3720, fax 2/254-4073, info@ecuado radventure.ec, www.ecuadoradventure.ec) has a long list of adventure outings, including mountain-biking, rafting, horseback-riding, Amazon tours, and ocean kayaking.

Sangay Touring (Amazonas 1188 and Cordero, tel. 2/250-8937, fax 2/256-0426, info@ guide2galapagos.com, www.sangay.com) is a British-and-Ecuadorian-run agency that has been offering tours around the country since 1992. Sangay recently split off a sister company, Guide2Galapagos (www.guide2galapa gos.com) to handle island bookings.

After the eruption of Tungurahua, **Rain Forestur** (Amazonas N4-20 y Robles, tel./ fax 2/223-9822, rainfor@interactive.net.ec) moved from Baños to Quito. Its Cuyabeno trips have been applauded, but there's also a full slate of other options, including skiing on Carihuairazo.

Dracaena (Pinto E4-353 and Amazonas, tel./ fax 2/254-6590, dracaena@andinanet.net, www.amazondracaena.com) is best known for its Cuyabeno trips of four and five days. Also recommended in Quito is **Surtrek** (Amazonas N23-87 and Wilson, tel. 2/223-1534, fax 2/250-0540, info@surtrek.org, www.surtrek.org).

(Juan León Mera and Baquedano) has export-quality gear for sale.

Tracking down gas for camp stoves can get your adventure started prematurely. White gas, also known as Coleman fuel or *gaz blanco,* can be hard to locate. It is an ingredient used in the processing of coca leaves into cocaine and therefore a controlled substance, so only small quantities are available. Try one of the various hardware stores *(ferreterías)* in town: **Ace Hardware** has an outlet in the C.C. Iñaquito (Naciones Unidas and Amazonas, tel. 2/225-2041); and **Kywi** hardware can be found at Luis Cordero 1641 and 10 de Agosto (tel. 2/250-1713) or in the Centro Commercial Olímpico (6 de Diciembre and Portete, tel. 2/243-4631). Hardware stores may have propane/butane canisters *(gaz para camping)* or methylated spirits *(alcohol industrial)*—bring your own bottle to fill.

For climbing gear for sale or rent, try **Altamontaña** (Jorge Washington 425 and 6 de Diciembre, tel. 2/255-8380) or **Antisana Sport** (tel./fax 2/246-7433) in the El Bosque Shopping Center, also good for large-sized hiking boots. Other places to buy camping gear include **Camping Cotopaxi** (Colón 942 and Reina Victoria, tel. 2/252-1626), **The Explorer** (Reina Victoria 928 and Pinto, tel. 2/255-0911), and **Los Alpes** (Reina Victoria 2345 and Baquedano, tel./fax 2/223-2326). **Equipos Cotopaxi** (6 de Diciembre N20-36 and Jorge Washington, tel. 2/225-0038) makes its own sleeping bags, backpacks, and tents for less than you'd pay for imported items. The various **Marathon Sports** outlets in the Centros Comerciales El Bosque, El Jardín, Iñaquito, San Rafael, and Quicentro stock light-use sportswear at decent prices.

OTHER ACTIVITIES
Biking

Colored wire sculptures of mountain bikes mark the office of the **Biking Dutchman** (Foch 714 and Juan León Mera, tel. 2/254-2806, www.bikingdutchman.com), which runs well-reviewed day trips to Cotopaxi, Papallacta, and the Tandayapa-Mindo area for $49 pp, which includes bikes and safety gear, lunch, and van transport up the steeper sections. The 30-kilometer descent down Cotopaxi is guaranteed to raise your blood pressure. Two-day trips ($132 pp) to Cotopaxi/Quilotoa and the upper Amazon include meals and overnight accommodations. For true pedaling fanatics, 5- and 12-day trips are also offered.

The **Aries Bike Company** (Pinto and Amazonas, tel./fax 2/222-3220, ariesbikecompany@latinmail.com, www.ariesbikecompany.com) also offers biking and hiking tours from 1–14 days all over Ecuador. The guides speak English, Dutch, and Spanish.

Once a fortnight on Sundays, a long north–south section of road through Quito is shut down to cars and open only to cyclists, skateboarders, skaters, and walkers.

Rafting and Kayaking

Yacu Amu Rafting (Foch 746 and Juan León Mera, tel. 2/290-4054 or 2/254-6240, fax 2/290-4055, info@yacuamu.com, www.yacuamu.com) is the leader in white-water trips out of Quito. The year-round day trips down the Toachi and Blanco Rivers offer more rapids per hour than anywhere else in Ecuador ($79 pp Toachi, $89 pp Quijos, $59 pp Tena)—plus cold beers at the end of every trip. The Toachi/Blanco trip can be stretched to two days for $219 pp, and two-day trips down the Quijos ($239 pp) and five-day trips on the Upano are offered August–February ($749 pp). Customized itineraries are possible, as are kayak rentals and kayak courses.

Horseback Riding

Sally Vergette runs **Ride Andes** (tel. 9/973-8221, rideandes@rideandes.com, www.rideandes.com), offering top-quality riding tours through the highlands. From the foothills of Imbabura to cattle round-ups near Cotopaxi, the trips use local horse wranglers, support vehicles, and healthy, happy animals. Guests stay in some of the country's plushest haciendas along the way. The options range from $90 pp for two people on a one-day tour to an eight-day hacienda-to-hacienda trip starting at $2,156 pp. You must have some riding experience—six hours in the saddle will leave you walking funny if you're not used to it—but you'll be amazed at how fitting it is to experience this scenery from atop a horse. Astrid Müller of the **Green Horse Ranch** (tel. 9/971-5933, ranch@accessinter.net, www.horseranch.de) offers riding trips starting in Pululahua Crater from $75 pp for one day, $180 pp for two days, and up to $1,380 pp for nine days. These are for people of all experience levels, and the prices include food, accommodations, and transportation to and from Quito. Multilingual guides accompany all trips.

Spectator Sports

Soccer *(fútbol)* games fill the Estadio Atahualpa (6 de Diciembre and Naciones Unidas) when the national team plays. Take the Ecovia to the Naciones Unidas stop to get there. The Casa Blanca, which is the Liga stadium, rocks with roars and groans on weekend afternoons. Buy tickets ahead of time at Casa Blanca at the "Y" junction and take the Metrovia to the Ofelia terminal. **Bullfights** are held year-round on publicized dates at the Plaza de Toros (Amazonas and Juan de Azcaray), just south of the airport. (Take the trolley north to La Y). The festival of the founding of Quito during the first week of December is an especially popular time for bullfights. Smaller evening bullfights are sometimes held at the remodeled Plaza Belmonte near San Blas.

Art and Dance Lessons

The **Academia Superior de Arte** (Jorge Washington 268 and Plaza, tel. 2/256-4646)

offers drawing and painting courses next to the Hotel Amaranta. Courses in tai chi and other martial arts are taught at Carrion and 10 de Agosto.

Sign up for Latin and Caribbean dance classes—including salsa, merengue, cumbia, and vallenato—at the **Ritmo Tropical Dance Academy** (Amazonas N24-155 and Calama, tel. 2/255-7094, ritmotropical5@hotmail.com). The **Tropical Dancing School** (Foch E4-256 and Amazonas, tel. 2/222-0427) also offers Latin dance lessons, as does **Son Latino** (Reina Victoria N24-211 and Lizardo García, tel. 2/223-4340). Prices at all of these schools are approximately $6 pp per hour for one-to-one or couple lessons.

Public Pools and Gyms

The Concentración Deportiva de Pichincha maintains the indoor, heated **El Batán** pool at Cochapata and Manual Abascal (tel. 2/246-0660). Swim caps are required, and lockers and keys are provided. Other heated indoor pools can be found at **Jipijapa** (Río Coca and Isla Fernandina, tel. 2/226-5752) and **Miraflores** (10 de Agosto and Nicaragua). All of these facilities cost $3.50 pp per day and have daily public swimming hours. **Oasis** (Ulloa 3315 and República, tel. 2/245-9473 or 2/245-9478) offers a sauna, steam room, hot tub, and pool for $9 pp (women get in for half price on Monday and Friday). It also has a cafeteria, locker room, and massage therapy onsite. Bring your own towel.

Nonguests can pay $18 to use the gym, spa, and pool at the Hotel Quito, or else head to **Fitcenter** (Alpallana 505 and Whymper, tel. 2/250-8851, $10 pp), a clean gym with weight machines and aerobics and spinning classes.

Accommodations

Like any good capital, Quito offers the entire spectrum of accommodations, from by-the-hour rats' nests to luxury hotels rivaling any in the world. Most are found in New Town, with an increasing number scattered about Old Town, where you should be careful in some of the uphill districts. A few crop up outside both areas.

Reservations are a good idea for busy times, such as holidays, especially Christmas and Easter. Book by phone or fax whenever possible. A tax of up to 22 percent will be added to bills in the more expensive hotels, and a separate charge may be tacked on for paying by credit card.

UNDER $10

With so many budget travelers passing through on a regular basis, Quito has sprouted a bumper crop of budget hotels. Most are concentrated in New Town, and many are excellent values. At last check, all those listed here passed the bug/brothel/bathroom test—no cockroaches, no rooms by the hour, and no crud in the showers—but things change, so take a glance for yourself before signing the register. All have hot water, and most offer luggage storage.

New Town

Remember that beach house you and 14 of your closest friends rented the summer before college? It's been relocated to Quito in the form of **El Centro del Mundo** (Lizardo García 569 and Reina Victoria, tel. 2/222-9050, centrodelmundo@hotmail.com). This archetypal backpackers' crash pad has dorm rooms with foot lockers for your stuff for $8 pp, and private rooms for $12. Breakfast and Internet access are included in the prices. The small rooftop patio features cooking facilities, and the cable TV is always on in the cushion-strewn common room.

You'll find the headquarters of the Ecuadorian Hostal Association in the clean and modern **Hostelling International** (Pinto E6-12 and Reina Victoria, tel. 2/254-3995). Cramped dorm rooms with shared baths are $8–12 pp (more expensive ones have private baths), including continental breakfast in the restaurant downstairs. IYH cardholders get a $1 discount. ISIC cards are issued in the hostel office.

The **Crossroads Café and Hostal** (Foch 678 and Juan Leon Mera, tel. 2/223-4735, crossrds@uio.satnet.net) occupies a restored colonial house that seems to go on forever. Dorm rooms in the yellow building are $7 pp, and private rooms are $33 d, with plenty of hot water in the bathrooms and a VCR and cable TV downstairs. There's a café on the first floor that serves all meals, plus kitchen facilities. (Be warned that the intersection of Foch and Juan León Mera can get loud at night.)

A few blocks uphill from New Town is a neighborhood called La Floresta. Not to be confused with La Casona in Old Town, **La Casona de Mario** (Andalucia 213 and Galicia, tel./fax 2/223-0129 or 2/254-4036, lacasona@punto.net.ec) is a comfortable house run by a friendly Argentine who offers a garden, kitchen, patio, and laundry facilities. Rooms run $9 pp.

The modern and friendly **Hostal Vienna** (Tamayo 879 and Foch, tel. 2/223-5418) costs $10 pp with private bath and TV.

Old Town

Right before the southbound Plaza del Teatro *trole* stop, the **Hotel Plaza del Teatro** (Guayaquil 1373 and Esmeraldas, tel. 2/295-9462 or 2/295-4293) is as nice inside as it looks from the street. A popular restaurant and bar fill the first floor, and private parking is available for guests. Rooms cost $10 pp with TV and private bath.

Another good pick in Old Town is the attractive and popular **Secret Garden** (Antepara E4-60 and Los Rios, tel. 2/295-6704, hola@secretgardenquito.com, www.secretgardenquito.com) with bunk rooms ($9 pp) and rooms with private baths ($22 per room—as they say, "three in a bed—that's fine with us!"). The rooftop terrace is a great place to watch the sun go down. The family-run **Chicago** (Los Rios and Briceño, tel. 2/281-1695) is popular and clean ($8 pp), with private bathrooms.

$10-25

All hotels in this category offer rooms with private bathrooms, unless otherwise noted.

New Town

I wonder how many of the hungry hundreds who dine at **The Magic Bean** (Foch 681 and Juan León Mera, tel. 2/256-6181, magic@ ecuadorexplorer.com, www.ecuadorexplorer .com/magic) know that there are four comfortable (if dim) rooms upstairs for $10 pp with shared bath and $30 d with private bath, with continental breakfast. More colorful is **El Cafécito** (Cordero 1124 and Reina Victoria, tel. 2/223-4862, quito@cafécito.net, www.cafécito .net), a quiet place attached to one of Quito's best café/restaurants. Shared rooms in the cozy, artistic hostel upstairs are $6 pp, and the owners speak English. The small and inviting **Hostal Posada del Maple** (Juan Rodriguez E8-49 and 6 de Diciembre, tel. 2/290-7367, admin@ posadadelmaple.com, www.posadadelmaple .com) is another one of those funky old homes that seems to go on forever in a maze of staircases, balconies, and plant-filled courtyards. Private quarters are $17 s, $29 d, including a full breakfast and use of the TV room. Right in the heart of New Town, the **Loro Verde** (Rodriguez 241 and Almagro, tel./fax 2/222-6173) offers a safe and friendly haven for $12 pp, including breakfast. There are many other options on Rodriguez, Garcia, and Calama.

Old Town

The Swiss-owned **Hostal L'Auberge** (Gran Colombia 1138 and Yaguachi, tel./fax 2/256-9886) is an inviting spot just northeast of Old Town that features a kitchen, garden, pool table, sauna, and fireplace. Dorm rooms are $8 pp, and private rooms are $9 pp with shared bath and $10 pp with private bath. Yet

another former colonial home now houses the **Hotel San Francisco de Quito** (Sucre 217 and Guayaquil, tel. 2/228-7758, tel./fax 2/295-1241, jorgeparedes@hotmail.com). A fountain and ferns fill the courtyard, and rooms with TV and private bath are a deal at $24 s, $38 d. The long-running **Vienna International** (Chile and Flores, tel. 2/295-9611) still offers good service with rooms around an interior patio ($17 pp).

$25-50
New Town

A small rise in price brings you into the realm of charming old guesthouses, with all the amenities, plus a healthy dose of character.

Warm colors and wood floors welcome visitors to the ◖ **Casa Sol** (Calama 127 and 6 de Diciembre, tel. 2/223-0798, info@ lacasasol.com, www.lacasasol.com), a cheery spot with a tiny courtyard owned by *indígenas* from Peguche, near Otavalo. Rooms are $37 s, $56 d, including breakfast. They have a TV room and a book exchange in front of a fireplace. The highly accommodating staff of the **Hotel Plaza Internacional** (Leonidas Plaza 150 and 18 de Septiembre, tel. 2/252-4530, tel./fax 2/250-5075, hplaza@uio.satnet .net, $28 s, $38 d) speak English, French, and Portuguese. Look for the attractive building behind the French embassy.

Opened in 1999, the bright yellow **Hotel La Cartuja** (Plaza 170 and 18 de Septiembre, tel. 2/252-3577, fax 2/266-2391, info@hotelacartuja .com, www.lacartuja.com) occupies a converted neocolonial mansion that once held the British Embassy. Twelve rooms ($46 s, $57 d, including continental breakfast) are arranged around a quiet courtyard. English, French, and Italian are spoken.

Another restored colonial building houses the **Hostal Santa Barbara** (12 de Octubre N26-15 and Coruña, tel. 2/222-5121, tel./ fax 2/256-4382, santabarbara@porta.net, $46 s, $59 d), just downhill from the Hotel Quito. Each of the 16 rooms has cable TV, and some have balconies. The Italian owner offers some of the best Italian food in the city in the hotel's restaurant.

Old Town

Tucked upstairs facing, La Concepción Church, is the renovated **Posada Colonial** (Garcia Moreno and Chile, tel. 2/228-1095), where comfortable rooms are $25 s, $35 d.

Enjoy a sunset cocktail on the top-floor bar of **Hotel Real Audencia** (Bolivar 220 and Guayaquil, tel. 2/295-2711 or 2/295-0590, realaudi@hoy.net). Rooms are spacious (ask for a quiet one at the back) and spotless, if a little overpriced, at $28 s, $45 d.

$50-75
New Town

Setting high standards for midprice hotels throughout Ecuador is the 【 **Mansion del Angel** (Wilson E5-29 and Juan Leon Mera, tel. 2/255-7721, $65 s, $105 d), a discreet little place with 10 beautifully appointed rooms, antiques, and attentive service, plus luxurious private bathrooms and a buffet breakfast included. You need to book well in advance.

Thick fur rugs in front of the fireplace and one of the more beautiful dogs in the city add to the old-world feel of **Hostal Los Alpes** (Tamayo 233 and Jorge Washington, tel./fax 2/256-1128, alpes@accesinter.net). Rooms, including breakfast, cost $64 s, $72 d.

The bright and clean **Hostal de La Rábida** (La Rábida 227 and Santa Maria, tel./fax 2/222-2169, larabida@uio.satnet.net, www.hostalrabida.com) bills itself accurately as "a small and stylish corner in Quito." Rooms ($61 s, $77 d) have cable TV and down comforters. There's a fireplace in the living room and a garden out back, the home of resident rabbit Brownie.

$75-100
New Town

A nine-story building is home to the **Hotel Sebastian** (Almagro 822 and Cordero, tel. 2/222-2300, fax 2/222-2500, hotelsebastian@hotelsebastian.com, www.hotelsebastian.com), which could be considered Quito's first "eco-hotel." Only organically grown vegetables free of pesticides are served in its restaurant, and the building boasts one of the best water-purification systems in the country. Forty-nine rooms and seven suites start at $73 s, $85 d.

Café Cultura (Robles 513 and Reina Victoria, tel./fax 2/222-4271, info@cafécultura.com, www.cafécultura.com) is set in a beautifully restored colonial mansion, formerly the French cultural center. The hotel is full of dark wood and paintings, and it manages to be cheery and classy at the same time. The owners speak English, French, and German. There's a gourmet café downstairs, a small private garden out back, a library full of guidebooks, three stone fireplaces, and a grand staircase in the center of it all. Rates are $89 s, $110 d, with a few suites for $130 and up.

Old Town

Once a family home, **El Relicario del Carmen** (Venezuela and Olmedo, tel. 2/228-9120, hotelrelicarm@andinanet.net) has been meticulously renovated and made into a comfortable retreat for travelers wishing to stay in the colonial part of the city. Rooms are $91 s, $118 d and include breakfast.

$100-200
New Town

The venerable **Hotel Quito** (González Suárez N27-142 and 12 de Octubre, tel. 2/254-4600, fax 2/256-7284, hotelquito@orotels.com) gazes over the city and the valley to the east on the eastern shoulder of New Town. New owners have made few changes other than the price, but the view will always be one of the best in Quito, especially at sunrise from the glass-walled restaurant. Rates are $122 s, $134 d, and there's a pool for guests.

Smack in the middle of Amazonas sits the luxury oasis of **Hotel Mercure Alameda Real** (Roca 653 and Amazonas, tel. 2/256-2345, fax 2/256-5759, apartec@uio.satnet.net). The 22 rooms run $145 s, $162 d, and 130 suites featuring a kitchenette, minibar, and cable TV start at $181. There's a comfortable, stylish lounge and reading room on the ground floor and a great pastry window on the sidewalk on Amazonas.

Rates at the **Radisson Royal Quito Hotel** (Cordero 444 and 12 de Octubre, tel. 2/223-3333, fax 2/223-5777) start at $152, and suites are $165 each. Guests can expect the same service and amenities as at any luxury hotel back home, including a business center, conference facilities, and a spa. For refueling, there's a bar, a café, and a restaurant.

A complete makeover in 1997 transformed the Hotel Colón into the **Hilton Colón** (Amazonas 110 and Patria, tel. 2/256-0666, fax 2/256-3903, reserv@hiltoncolon.com, fax 2/256-3903, reserv@hiltoncolon.com, www.hiltoncolon .com). Towering over the Parque El Ejido, it's probably the most popular spot for tourists who have unlimited budgets. Facilities include an excellent gym, a 10-meter pool, reading room, casino, shops. Its 415 rooms and suites start at $181. Reservations can be made in the United States by calling 800/HILTONS.

Old Town

Patio Andaluz (Garcia Moreno and Olmedo, tel. 2/228-0830, cialcontel@cialco.com) was a massive project, restoring an old colonial home with two interior patios, spacious rooms, and split-level suites are air-conditioned and comfortable. There is an excellent restaurant in the first-floor patio, with carved stone pillars; and even the staff are clothed to fit the ambience. Single or double rooms are $183.

MORE THAN $200
New Town

Uphill from the Hilton Colón to the east, the **(C Swissôtel** (12 de Octubre 1820 and Cordero, tel. 2/256-7600, fax 2/256-8079, ask-us.quito@swissotel.com, http://quito.swissotel .com) has 277 wheelchair-accessible rooms and a private health club, along with Japanese and Italian restaurants, a casino, and a gourmet deli. It's quite a sleek, comfortable place—if you're looking for the equivalent of a four-star hotel back home, head here. Rooms are $311, with suites starting at $420.

The newest and perhaps largest luxury hotel in Quito is the **JW Marriott Hotel Quito** (Orellana 1172 and Amazonas, tel. 2/297-2000, fax 2/297-2050). This glass palace contains 257 rooms ($242 each) and 16 suites ($350) with all the bells and whistles, along with a business center, business facilities, an outdoor heated pool, a health club, and a Mediterranean restaurant.

Old Town

Quito's first hotel was the Majestic, which overlooked Independence Plaza from a lovely baroque building. Today, fully reconditioned and reborn as the luxury **Plaza Grande** (Garcia Moreno and Chile, tel. 2/251-0777, toll-free 888/790-5264, info@plazagrandequito.com), it has 15 suites, three restaurants, ballroom, champagne and brandy bars, and all the luxury you require—the marble bathroom floors even have built-in heating. The cheapest suite will run you a cool $450, but the ground-floor café offers a bottomless pot of coffee and traditional dishes.

LONGER STAYS

Most **hotels** will arrange a discount for stays of a few weeks or more. For example, the **Residencial Casa Oriente** (Yaguachi 824 and Llona, tel. 2/254-6157) offers apartments with kitchens for $80 per month ($60 per month with shared kitchen), with a minimum stay of two weeks. Spanish lessons are available, and English, French, and German are spoken. You can also try the **Casa de Frederico** (Benalcázar 1235 and Oriente, tel. 2/228-9661, quitoantiguo@yahoo .com), where five three-room apartments with kitchen facilities go for $200 per week, including meals and four hours of Spanish lessons per day ($10 per day with meals).

On a more personal note, a **family stay** is a great way to practice your Spanish and get to know Ecuadorian culture from the inside. Plus, it's often just as affordable as a budget hotel, as long as you're willing to make a longer commitment. Options change like the weather, so check at the South American Explorers' Quito Clubhouse for the latest list, or arrange it through your language school. The clubhouse is also a reliable source for information on **apartments** for rent, as are the classified ads in the local papers.

Food

Every major world cuisine is represented in Quito's culinary spectrum, with a healthy serving of cafés and fast-food joints tossed in for good measure. Many restaurants outside New Town close by 9 or 10 P.M. There's no pattern as to which are open or not on weekends and Mondays; if you can't call ahead, have an alternate plan ready.

OLD TOWN

Part of colonial Quito's recent renaissance is an upsurge in high-end eateries. Some of the best restaurants in the city are now south of Parque El Ejido. At the top of the list is **Theatrum** (tel. 2/228-9669), on the second floor of the Teatro Sucre. This ultrastylish place overlooking the Plaza del Teatro is half wine bar and half red-walled restaurant. The service is gracious, and the fusion cuisine is excellent and artfully prepared. A six-course set menu is $33–38 pp for dinner (à la carte dishes are also available), and there's an extensive wine list. **Mea Culpa,** which overlooks the Plaza Grande, has a dress code, so leave your trainers at home if you want to try out the special fare. Next door, in the hotel Plaza Grande, is French restaurant **La Belle Époque.**

Beneath the Itchimbia Cultural Center is **Mosaico** (Samaniego N8-95 and Antepara, tel. 2/254-2871, dinner Mon.–Tues., lunch and dinner Wed.–Sun.), one of Quito's hottest new cafés. The emphasis here is on drinks, especially at sunset, when the views of Old Town are unbeatable from the mosaic-inlaid tables on the terrace. Arrive early to secure a table, because this stylish spot fills up quickly with Quito's elite. The limited menu lists Greek dishes, sandwiches, and desserts ($5–9), including the only real New York cheesecake in Ecuador. A taxi is $1.50 from Old Town. There are several other new places on this short street.

The old **Círculo Militar** (8 A.M.–6 P.M.) on Venezuela and Mejía has been extensively renovated and now has a café on the ground floor. The upper floors are open to the public for visits, too. Facing Plaza San Francisco on Bolívar is the spacious new **Café San Francisco** (tel. 9/903-4164, from 11 A.M. Wed.–Sun.), with views over the plaza.

With live music Thursday–Saturday and 360° views over the colonial city, the **Vista Hermoso** (Mejía 453 y Garcia Moreno) offers pizzas, snacks, and cocktails under the stars. The elevator is operated by a uniformed attendant, and the terrace has gas heating for cool nights.

The **Panaficador Superior** (Garcia Moreno N1-56 and Bolívar) is a coffee shop that bakes excellent pastries daily. Three quiet cafés are located in Pasaje Amador—just the place to escape the bustle of Garcia Moreno, together with the locals. The old city doesn't have many spaces for sidewalk cafés, but Espejo facing the Teatro Bolívar has several, plus an excellent frutería.

For budget Ecuadorian dishes, you could do much worse than **Angelo's** (Mejía 265 and Guayaquil) or **El Amigo** (Guayaquil between Esmeraldas and Oriente), both of which have been recommended for typical meals and coffee. The **Chifa Asia,** on Flores and Olmedo, offers some variety from the usual budget Old Town eateries.

NEW TOWN
Asian

Hundreds of inexpensive *chifas* fill the city, but some are better than others. The classy **Casa China** (Cordero 613 and Tamayo) offers the best value for your money, with **Chifa China** (Carrión and Versailles) and **Chifa Hong Kong** (Wilson between Tamayo and Plaza) close behind. **Happy Panda** (Isabel la Católica and Cordero) offers Hunan cooking for a little variety on the Chinese scene. **Chifa Mayflower** (Carrión 442 and 6 de Diciembre, tel. 2/254-0510) is one of seven in a small Quito chain, which includes branches in the El Bosque, El Jardín, Quicentro, and El Recreo malls. They all share the same fast-food plastic feel, bright but pleasant, with combinations around $4–7, including drinks and free rice. Home delivery is also an option (tel. 800/629-356, www.mayflower.com.ec).

Siam offers a delectably peanut-laden pad Thai for $4.25 on a candlelit balcony over the gringoland at Calama and Juan León Mera. It has a large drink list and also offers sushi on Mondays ($4–9). **Tanoshii,** at the Swissôtel, is also excellent for sushi. **Yu Su Café,** facing the Panamericana bus terminal on Colon, is small and spotless and offers the best sushi prices in town. **Uncle Ho's,** on Calama and Almagro, has a nice selection of Thai and other Asian dishes.

Bakeries and Sweets

With a great selection of French and wholemeal breads, as well as pastries, **El Cyrano** (Portugal 860 and Los Shyris) is constantly lauded as the best bakery in town. **Corfu** next door is described as "ice cream heaven." Three bakeries closer to the center of action are **El Túnel** (6 de Diciembre and Jorge Washington), **Sal & Pimienta** (outside the Hotel Colón), and **Pan del Río** (on Cordero just east of Amazonas). Grab a $0.50 croissant and an espresso *para llevar* (to go) at the street side window of **Spicy** (Amazonas N21-168), at the foot of the Hotel Mercure Alameda Real.

The daughter of Rosalía Suárez (see the sidebar *Helados de Paila* in the *Northern Sierra* chapter) runs **Helados Rosalía Suárez** at Los Shyris and Holanda, facing the bleachers in Parque La Carolina. Along with the authentic, hand-stirred *helados de paila,* this small place steams some of the best *humitas* in Quito.

Breakfast

Crepes and Waffles (Orellana and Rábida) is one of the few places in Quito open on Sunday nights. Ignore the gaze of the fat-figured Botero posters as you choose from a gigantic menu that includes crêpes (sweet and savory), pita pizzas, salads, and waffles for $4–8. Service is efficient, and there's even a nonsmoking section. You can find real bagels at **Mr. Bagel** (Portugal 948 and 6 de Diciembre, tel. 2/224-0978).

Breakfast is especially recommended at the **Café Colibrí** (Pinto 619 and Cordero), where $3.50–6 gets you enough sustenance to keep going all day. It also has German food for around $5 per plate and serves German beers in the outdoor patio garden. The weekday morning buffets at the **Hotel Colón** and the **Swissôtel** are sumptuous ($15–17); it's hard to imagine, but they're even larger and better on Sundays.

Burgers and Steaks

Burgers, grilled plates, and BBQ in the $4–7 range are the specialties at **Adam's Rib** (Calama and Reina Victoria) and **The Texas Ranch** (around the corner at Juan León Mera 1140 and Calama). Three branches of the popular **Parilladas Columbia** (Colón 1262 and Amazonas, Tarquí 785 and 10 de Agosto, and 6 de Diciembre 4531 and Pasaje El Jardín) serve good-quality steaks for $6–9. The restaurant **Los Troncos,** facing Carolina Park (Los Shyris and Portugal), serves huge steaks with a selection of sauces, as does **La Casa de la Abuela** (Reina Victoria and La Pinta), which has maintained a great reputation for more than 30 years. A fireplace and a penthouse view complement the cuts at **Terraza del Tartaro** (Veintimilla 1106 and Amazonas, tel. 2/252-7987).

Cafés and Coffee Shops

El Cafécito (Cordero 1124 and Reina Victoria, tel. 2/223-4862) serves a tasty, inexpensive *menú del día* for $6 in a pastel, candlelit dining room that livens up after dark. Candles and crayons for coloring your placemat make things even cozier than the fireplace would on its own.

Another comfy place for a quality cuppa is the **Café Trovero** (Juan León Mera and Pinto, 2/256-4157), with a caffeinated happy hour (half-price drinks) 5–6 P.M.

For a quick pick-me-up, stop by the sidewalk window at **The Magic Bean** (Foch 681 and Juan León Mera, tel. 2/256-6181); and for a late-night fix, stop by the 24-hour **Coffee Tree** in the Plaza del Quindé (Foch and Reina Victoria or Plaza de los Presidentes, Washington and Amazonas). The **Café Conquistador** (Ríofrío and Larrea, between Old Town and New Town) serves great coffee and *humitas,* a Latin American snack staple.

Cuban

The cuisine of this Caribbean island has become quite popular in Ecuador, although its cultural ebullience and beguiling music don't hurt either. The popular **Varadero Sandwiches Cubanos** (Reina Victoria and La Pinta) has a selection of—you guessed it—Cuban sandwiches for $5. Things heat up at night, with live music by the bar. **La Bodeguita de Cuba** (Reina Victoria 1721 and La Pinta) is popular for its Cuban *bocaditos* (appetizers) for $4, as well as the live Cuban music on Thursday nights.

Ecuadorian

Restaurants that serve "local" fare conspicuously can be a strange thing. Dressed-up versions of everyday plates share the bill with traditional recipes that might otherwise be forgotten. **La Choza** (12 de Octubre 1821 and Cordero, tel. 2/223-4839) is a popular midprice place. Appetizers such as *tortillas de maíz* run $2–4, with main dishes like the tasty *locro de papas* going for $4 and up. Tour groups often empty their buses here. For larger, less expensive portions, steer toward

Mama Clorinda (Reina Victoria 1144 and Calama, tel. 2/254-4362), where you can get *llapingachos* and a quarter of a chicken for $6. The **Rincon Ecuatoriano-Chileno** has been around forever, and faithful clients fill it for weekend lunches (6 de Diciembre and Belo Horizonte). On weekdays, though, you don't have to queue for a table.

French

Gallic cuisine tends to be served in the most upscale of Quito's foreign restaurants, those favored by natty executives and wealthy tourists. **Rincon de Francia** (Roca 779 and 9 de Octubre) is among the best restaurants in the city. Make reservations and dress sharp. A French bakery occupies the ground floor of **Chantilly** (Roca 736 and Amazonas).

The small fondue bar at **Île de France** (Reina Victoria 1747 and La Niña, tel. 2/255-3292) is more intimate. **La Creperie** (Garcia 465 and Almagro, tel. 8/222-6274) is one of the longest-running restaurants in the city, and it's often packed on Friday nights for live music. Crêpes, of course, are the mainstay, but the cheese fondue ($18 for two people) is hard to beat.

Italian

As the city has spread north, several classy restaurants have followed the business-lunch crowd up Eloy Alfaro. One of the best is the **Il Risotto** (Eloy Alfaro and Portugal, tel. 2/222-0400), with a great view of the city from the main dining room northeast of the Mariscal. Good service and generous portions make the prices ($5–10 per plate) more bearable, as does the heavenly tiramisu. Many local gourmands will name **La Viña** (Isabel La Católica and Cordero) as Quito's best restaurant. Delicious pastas and other Italian plates are around $9–15.

Le Arcate (Baquedano 358 and Juan León Mera) has pastas and a bewildering array of wood-oven pizzas (the "Russian" has vodka as an ingredient) for $6–9. At **La Bella Italia**

(Cordero and Pinto corner), almost everyone orders pizza for good reason: They're baked in a wood oven. The pastas are also excellent, for around $4–8. **La Briciola** (Toledo 1255 and Cordero) has delicious dishes starting at $6 (try the ravioli classico), a good wine list, and a fire to ease the chill of a cold Quito evening. It's near the Radisson Royal and the Swissôtel. **La Chacha** (corner of Juan Leon Mera and Foch, weekdays only) does a roaring trade in budget pizzas and pastas.

Mexican

On Portugal, close to Eloy Alfaro, **La Guarida del Coyote** is solid and inexpensive, with tasty south-of-another-border dishes ($5–7) and a pleasant atmosphere. A plate of fajitas at **Red Hot Chili Peppers** (no relation to the band—Foch and Juan León Mera, tel. 2/255-7575) will easily fill two people to bursting. It's a tiny place with a big TV and graffiti covering the walls, and it just may well serve the most authentic Mexican food in town. Dishes are $5–9.

Middle Eastern

One delectable specialty of Ecuador's Arab establishments—up there with hummus and grilled kebabs—is the shawarma (a serving of grilled meat in a warm pita with yogurt sauce and vegetables). **El Arabe** (Reina Victoria 627 and Carrión) also serves a good version either inside or to-go—order from the sidewalk. Another newer branch on Coruña and Whimper is more expensive and comfortable; guests lounge on floor cushions in front of a fireplace, in a room decorated like a Bedouin tent. The **Baalbek** on 6 Diciembre and Wilson is often packed for lunches. In the evenings, it opens by reservation only.

The patio at **Aladdin** (Almagro and Baquerizo Moreno) is always packed at night. The water pipes and 16 kinds of flavored tobacco probably have something to do with it, along with the $1 falafel and shawarma.

Pizza

A plethora of options exist for ordering pizza to go. **Ch' Farina** (Carrión and Juan León Mera, tel. 2/244-4444 or 2/255-4961) is the local champ, followed by **Roy's Pizza** (tel. 2/245-9594) and **El Hornero** (tel. 2/254-2518).

Seafood

Two restaurants stand out immediately in the *pescado* category. **Mare Nostrum** (Tamayo 172 and Foch, tel. 2/252-8686) claims to have "70 ways of serving fish," and the ones I've tried have been outstanding. Boat models, suits of armor, low lights, and dark wood beams set the stage for delicious cream soups and *encocados* served in half a coconut shell. Dishes start at $5, but go much higher. Try El Arroz del Capitán, combining rice and fresh seafood with soy, cilantro, and onions. The same owners run **Los Redes de Mariscos** (Amazonas 845 and Veintimilla), which has an extensive wine list. **La Jaiba** (Coruña and San Ignacio, tel. 2/254-3887) has a pleasant atmosphere and plates for $5–9—try the shrimp in whiskey.

Spanish

La Casa Vasca (18 Septiembre and Paez) specializes in large servings of seafood for $7–18 per plate. **La Paella Valenciana** (Republica and Almagro) specializes in you-know-what and has other traditional dishes ranging $6–20.

On the budget end, the **Mesón Español** (Carrión 974 and Páez) offers a filling *almuerzo* in a pleasant setting across from the restaurant El Toro Partido. Dishes start around $4. Sit upstairs or on the patio at the **Puerto Español,** next door at 9 de Octubre and Carrión; breakfast and lunch are bargains at $3 each.

Vegetarian

After all that meat, it's good to know that Quito also has a healthy range of vegetarian options. Veggies at the cheery **El Maple** (Foch 476 and Almagro, tel. 2/223-1503) are washed in purified water. The Indian-run

Chandani Tandoori (Juan León Mera and Colón, tel. 2/222-1053) does vegetarian curries, as well as chicken dishes. The *menú del día* is about $3.

Although there are animals on the menu, **The Magic Bean** (Foch 681 and Juan León Mera, tel. 2/256-6181) is still a vegetarian restaurant at heart. Salads, pizzas, and Colombian coffee—served inside or on the covered patio—have made this place one of the more popular gringo stopovers in New Town. At $5–7 per dish, the food is dependably good and comes in generous portions. There's also a long list of natural juices. Other mostly vegetarian restaurants include **El Cafécito** (Cordero 1124 and Reina Victoria, tel. 2/223-4862) and **Mr. Bagel** (Portugal 948 and 6 de Diciembre, tel. 2/224-0978).

Other International

For a tangy Swiss fondue, try **Paleo** (Cordero E5-48 and Juan León Mera), which also serves great raclette. The tiny **Cochabamba** (Gangotena and Orellana) bakes delicious traditional or chicken Salteñas weekdays.

Doña Arepa is a tiny nook in the Centro Commercial El Obelisco (Amazonas and Colón) that does Venezuelan food—all meals—for about $3.

MARKETS AND SUPERMARKETS

Gleaming aisles and air-conditioning make the larger Ecuadorian supermarkets almost indistinguishable from their North American and European equivalents. **Supermaxi** is the biggest, with a branch at La Niña and Yanes Pinzón, one block off 6 de Diciembre, as well as in the Centros Comerciales El Bosque, Iñaquito, Multicentro, America, El Jardín, and El Recreo, among others. **Mi Comisariato** is in the Centro Commercial Quicentro, as well as at Rodrigo de Chávez and Galte, García Moreno and Mejía, and Nuñez de Vela and Ignacio San Maria. They're all open 9 A.M.–7 or 8 P.M. on weekdays and close earlier on weekends. The **Santa Maria** stores are a little cheaper and open 8 A.M.–8 P.M. There's one by Santa Clara Market, and another near the Ofelia bus terminal.

A more economical food alternative is the **Santa Clara Market** (7 A.M.–3 P.M. Mon.–Fri., mornings only Sat.–Sun.), at Ramirez Dávalos between Carrión and Antonio de Marchena, two blocks from 10 de Agosto. This place has countless small food stands and meals to go, along with a few inexpensive markets.

Information and Services

TOURIST INFORMATION

The main office of the **Ministerio de Turismo** (Eloy Alfaro N32-300 and Tobar, piso 3, tel. 2/250-7555, 8:30 A.M.–12:30 P.M. and 1:30–5 P.M. daily), near the Parque La Carolina, is one of the most helpful in the country and can assist with hotel reservations. It has maps, and some staff speak English. The **Corporation Metropolitana de Turismo** (Reina Victoria and Cordero, tel. 2/255-1566, 9 A.M.–5 P.M. Mon.–Fri.) has a glass kiosk in a little park in New Town. It also has branches at the airport (tel. 2/330-0164), in Old Town (García

Moreno N12-01 and Mejía, tel. 2/257-2566 or 2/228-3480), and at the Museo Nacional del Banco Central (tel.2/222-1116).

Officers of the **Oficina Información Turística** (tel. 2/258-6591, 8:30 A.M.–5 P.M. daily) are clad in blue and found around the Plaza Grande in Old Town—either on the street, at the kiosk in the plaza, or in the office in the Pasaje Arzobispal. Some speak English.

The name may imply a smoky room full of wealthy expats in tweeds trading tales about running from the natives, but the **South**

QUITO

American Explorers association (SAE, Jorge Washington 311 and Plaza, tel./fax 2/222-5228, quitoclub@saexplorers.org, www.saexplorers.org, 9:30 A.M.–5 P.M. Mon.–Fri., open until 8 P.M. Thurs., 9:30 A.M.–noon Sat.) is actually a houseful of bright-eyed, underpaid, and overworked vagabonds who know the country inside and out.

Although nonmembers are welcome to stop by the Quito clubhouse for a brief visit, the SAE puts most of its energy toward dues-paying members, making the annual fee ($60 pp, $90 per couple) a solid investment for those who plan to stay in Ecuador more than a month or travel through many countries in South America.

With branches in Ithaca, New York, Lima and Cuzco, Peru, and Buenos Aires, Argentina, the club stocks a wealth of information readily accessible to members by mail, email, fax, or in person. Members can also store equipment, peruse the library, enjoy a cup of tea on the couch while listening to some mellow music, and ask the staff for advice on anything from bread recipes to river rafting. An SAE membership card entitles you to discounts at many hotels, tour agencies, and Spanish schools in Quito and around the country. Well-organized files of trip reports written by members give the latest scoop on destinations throughout the continent. The SAE has greatly expanded its volunteering database, making it the best place in the country to find information on volunteer positions.

Classes and movies in French are only a few of the offerings of the **Alliance Française** (Eloy Alfaro N32-468 and 6 de Diciembre, tel. 2/224-6589, 2:30–6:30 P.M. Tues., 8:30 A.M.–12:30 P.M. Wed.–Fri., 8:30 A.M.–12:30 P.M. Sat.).

VISAS
Tourist visa extensions beyond the standard 90 days are the main reason most travelers end up at the **Jefatura Provincial de Migración** (Isla Seymour 1152 and Río Coca, tel. 2/224-7510, 8 A.M.–12:30 P.M. and 3–5 P.M. Mon.–Fri., 8 A.M.–noon and 3–6 P.M. Sat.). Go early and be ready to wait.

MAPS
The hike up Paz y Miño is worth it for the commanding view of the city from the **Instituto Geográfico Militar** (IGM, tel. 2/250-2091, 8 A.M.–4 P.M. Mon.–Fri.). While you wait for the staff to process your map order (bring a book), consider a show at the **planetarium.** The IGM often closes early on Fridays, and visitors must surrender their passports at the gate to enter.

POST
Quito's main **post office** is in New Town (Eloy Alfaro 354 and 9 de Octubre, tel. 2/256-1218, 8 A.M.–6 P.M. Mon.–Fri., 8 A.M.–noon Sat.). The Express Mail Service (EMS) is at this office (tel. 2/256-1962). There's also a branch one block east of the Plaza de la Independencia in Old Town (Espejo between Guayaquil and Venezuela, tel. 2/228-2175, 8 A.M.–6 P.M. Mon.–Fri.).

There's a **FedEx** branch (Amazonas 517 and Santa María, tel. 2/227-9180), and **DHL** has several offices throughout the city, including on Eloy Alfaro and Av. de Los Juncos (tel. 2/397-5000), Colón 1333 and Foch (tel. 2/255-6118), and at the Hilton Colón and the airport.

TELECOMMUNICATIONS
Telephone
There has been a communications revolution all over the country: On almost any street corner, even in the smallest towns, there are *cabinas* offering telephone service. The national companies **Andinatel** and **Pacifictel** no longer have a monopoly—together with Porta, Movistar, and Alegro, they both run competing offices. Movistar and Porta also have pay phones everywhere, and each type requires its own brand of prepaid card.

Internet Access
The "Gringolandia" area of the Mariscal

QUITO EMERGENCY TELEPHONE NUMBERS

- Police   101
- Fire Department   102
- Red Cross   131
- Emergency   911

Sucre neighborhood is rife with Internet cafés. Expect to pay $1 or less per hour and to have access at most cafés 8 A.M.–9 P.M. daily, possibly later on weekends. Although connection rates and computer quality vary widely, most cafés have fax service, scanners, printers, and Internet phone programs, allowing foreign visitors to call home for a fraction of the cost of a normal connection. The term "café" may be misleading, however, because many offer only water and snacks.

Listing Internet cafés in Quito is an inherently futile gesture, because they open and close faster than a fifth-grader's mouth at recess, but several are more convenient and offer better quality. In New Town, the block of Calama between Juan León Mera and Reina Victoria has a handful, and there are a few in the basement of the Ecuatoriana building at Almagro and Colón. **Papaya.net** (Calama and Juan León Mera) is an old standby, with food service, a popular bar, and Internet telephones. Also try **La Sala,** on Calama and Reina Victoria, which has Internet telephones, all the standard services, a waiting area and a small café.

MONEY
Banks and ATMs
ATMs for most international systems (Plus, Cirrus, Visa, and MasterCard) can be found at major banks along Amazonas and around

the shopping centers. These tend to have limits on how much you can withdraw per day (usually $500), so if you need to, say, pay cash for a Galápagos trip, you'll have to go to the Banco del Pacífico head office on Naciones Unidos and Los Shyris for cash advances.

Exchange Houses
Since the introduction of the dollar, exchanging other currencies has become more difficult. Try to bring U.S. dollars travelers' checks, as rates are poor for Canadian dollars, U.K. pounds, and even the euro. Exchanging those currencies outside of Quito, Guayaquil, and Cuenca is difficult, if not impossible. **Vaz Cambio** (Amazonas and Roca, tel. 2/252-9567), facing the Hotel Mercure, is one of the most convenient *casas de cambio* in Quito.

Credit Card Branches
There's a **Visa** office (Bosmediano E11-09 and 6 de Diciembre, 9 A.M.–4:30 P.M. Mon.–Fri., 9 A.M.–1 P.M. Sat.). **American Express** (tel. 2/256-0488, 8:30 A.M.–5 P.M. Mon.–Fri.) has an office on the fifth floor of the Ed. Rocafuerte at Amazonas 339 and Jorge Washington. Card members can buy travelers' checks using personal checks against their accounts for a 1 percent fee. Quito also houses the **MasterCard** head office (Amazonas and Pereira, tel. 2/298-1300, 8:30 A.M.–5 P.M. Mon.–Fri., 9:30 A.M.–1:30 P.M. Sat.).

Money Transfers
Western Union has many locations around the city—check www.westernunion.com for a list of offices worldwide (8 A.M.–6 P.M. Mon.–Fri., 9 A.M.–5 P.M. Sat.–Sun.) The company charges $52 for a same-day transfer of $1,000, plus local taxes. It'll cost you $25 to transfer any amount to and from the Americas ($35 to/from Europe) at the **Banco del Pacífico** at Amazonas and Jorge Washington. (You are expected to cover the cost of contacting

EMBASSIES AND CONSULATES IN QUITO

- **Argentina:** Amazonas 477 between Robles and Roca, Ed. Banco de los Andes, piso 5, tel. 2/256-2292, 9 A.M.-1 P.M. Mon.-Fri.

- **Bolivia:** Eloy Alfaro 2432 and Ayarza, tel. 2/224-4830, 8 A.M.-4 P.M. Mon.-Fri.

- **Brazil:** Amazonas 1429 and Colón, Ed. España, piso 10, tel. 2/256-3086, 9 A.M.-3 P.M. Mon.-Fri.

- **Canada:** 6 de Diciembre 2816 and Paul Rivet, tel. 2/223-2114, 9 A.M.-noon and 2:30-5:30 P.M. Mon.-Fri., appointments required, Australians also welcome.

- **Chile:** Sáenz 3617 and Amazonas, piso 4, tel. 2/224-9403, 8 A.M.-5 P.M. Mon.-Fri.

- **Colombia (Consulate):** Atahualpa 955 and República, piso 3, tel. 2/245-8012, 8:30 A.M.-1 P.M. Mon.-Fri.

- **Colombia (Embassy):** Colón 1133 and Amazonas, Ed. Arist, piso 7, tel. 2/222-8926, 9 A.M.-1 P.M. and 2-4 P.M. Mon.-Fri.

- **Costa Rica:** Rumipamba 692 and República, tel. 2/225-4945, 8 A.M.-1:30 P.M. Mon.-Fri.

- **Cuba:** Mercurio 365 and El Vengador, tel. 2/244-3904, 9 A.M.-1 P.M. Mon.-Fri.

- **Denmark:** República de El Salvador 733 and Portugal, Ed. Gabriela 3, piso 3, tel. 2/243-7163, 9:30 A.M.-1:30 P.M. and 3-5 P.M. Mon.-Fri.

- **France (Consulate):** 18 de Septembre 115 y Leonidas Plaza, tel. 2/294-3840, 8:30 A.M.-1 P.M. and 3-5:30 P.M. Mon.-Fri.

- **France (Embassy):** Plaza 107 and Patria, tel. 2/294-3800, 8:30 A.M.-1 P.M. and 3-5:30 P.M. Mon.-Fri.

- **Germany:** Naciones Unidas and República de El Salvador, Ed. Citiplaza, piso 14, tel. 2/297-0820, 8:30-11:30 A.M. Mon.-Fri.

- **Guatemala:** República de El Salvador 733 and Portugal, Ed. Gabriela 3, piso 3, tel. 2/245-9700, 9 A.M.-1 P.M. Mon.-Fri.

- **Israel:** 12 de Octubre and Salazar, Ed. Plaza 2000, piso 9, tel. 2/223-7474, 10 A.M.-1 P.M. Mon.-Fri.

- **Italy:** La Isla 111 and Albornoz, tel. 2/256-1077, 8:30 A.M.-12:30 P.M. Mon.-Fri.

- **Japan:** Amazonas N39-123 y Jose Arizaga, Ed. Amazonas Plaza, piso 11, tel. 2/227-8700, 9:00 A.M.-noon and 2-5 P.M. Mon.-Fri.

- **Mexico:** 6 de Diciembre 4843 and Naciones Unidas, tel. 2/292-3770, 9 A.M.-1 P.M. Mon.-Fri.

- **Netherlands:** 12 de Octubre 1942 and Cordero, tel. 2/222-9229, 8:30 A.M.-1 P.M., 2-5 P.M. Mon.-Fri. by appointment

- **Paraguay:** 12 de Octubre and Salazar, Ed. Torre Sol Verde, piso 8, tel. 2/223-1990, 8:30 A.M.-2:30 P.M. Mon.-Fri.

- **Peru:** República de El Salvador 495 and Irlanda, tel. 2/246-8389, 9 A.M.-1 P M. and 3-5 P.M. Mon.-Fri.

- **Spain:** (Consulate): La Pinta 455 and Amazonas, tel. 2/322-6296, 8:30 A.M.-noon Mon.-Fri.

- **United Kingdom:** Naciones Unidas and República de El Salvador, Ed. Citiplaza, piso 14, tel. 2/297-0800, 8:30 A.M.-12:30 P.M. and 1:30-5 P.M. Mon.-Thurs., 8:30 A.M.-1:30 P.M. Fri.

- **United States:** Avigiras y Guayacanes, tel. 2/398-5000, 8 A.M.-12:30 P.M. and 1:30-5 P.M. Tues.-Fri.

- **Venezuela:** Amazonas N30-240 y Eloy Alfaro, Ed. Cedatos, piso 8, tel. 2/255-7209, 9 A.M.-12:30 P.M. and 2 P.M.-4 P.M. Mon.-Fri.

your home bank.) If that much cash makes you itch, you can change it into American Express travelers' checks at the main branch of the Banco del Pacífico at República 433 and Almagro. This transaction costs $10 to change up to $1,000, and 1 percent of the total from there on up.

HEALTH
General Concerns
Unless you're from somewhere like La Paz or Nepal, you'll feel Quito's **altitude** within the first few hours after arriving. Take it easy the first few days, drink lots of water, and get plenty of sleep. Save the jogging and the *cuba libres* for next week, if possible. Other than the altitude, the only health risks particular to the capital are the unforgiving **sun** and the **smog** from all the traffic. Busy streets seem to trap and hold the noxious gases, so smart pedestrians avoid them whenever possible.

Hospitals and Clinics
The American-run **Hospital Voz Andes** (Villalengua 267 and 10 de Agosto, tel. 2/226-2142) receives the most business from Quito's foreign community. It's described as fast, competent, and inexpensive, with an emergency room and outpatient services. To get there, take the *trole* north along 10 de Agosto to just past Naciones Unidas. The **Hospital Metropolitano** (Mariana de Jesús and Occidental, tel. 2/226-1520) is also recommended, although it's more expensive.

The 24-hour **Clínica Pichincha** (Veintimilla E3-30 and Páez, tel. 2/299-8777) has a laboratory that can perform analyses for intestinal parasites. Blood and stool tests are also performed at the **Laboratorio Leon** (see Renato Leon under doctors). Yellow-fever shots are dispensed at the **Centro de Salud No. 1** (Rocafuerte 1545, tel. 2/315-1711) near the Plaza Santo Domingo. Women's health problems should be referred to the 24-hour **Clínica de la Mujer** (Amazonas N39- 216 and Gaspar de Villarroel, tel. 2/245-8000).

Private Doctors
Dr. John Rosenberg (Foch 476 and Almagro, tel. 2/252-1104, jrd@pi.pro.ec) is a highly recommended general practitioner who speaks English and German. He is the doctor for the U.S. Embassy and performs house calls. He has office hours weekdays after 3:30 P.M. and can administer hepatitis vaccines. **Eduardo Larrea** (Centro Medico Metropolitano, piso 3, Of. 311, tel. 2/226-7652 or 9/919-4665) also speaks English.

Carlos Ribadeneira (Mariana de Jesús and A street, tel. 9/448-9115) is a gynecologist who speaks English.

Renato Leon (Ascazubi and 10 Agosto, tel. 2/223-8342 or 2/255-2080) is a tropical- and infectious-disease specialist who speaks English and does parasite lab tests more quickly and cheaply than the hospitals. Check with various embassies for doctors who speak languages besides Spanish and English.

Roberto Mena (Coruña and Isabel la Católica, tel. 2/256-9149) comes very highly recommended for quality dental work. He speaks English and German.

SPANISH LESSONS
Ecuador is quickly becoming one of the best places to learn Spanish in Latin America. Not only do Ecuadorians speak slowly and clearly in comparison to their quick-talking, slang-tossing neighbors, but competition among dozens of schools keeps prices low and quality up—and it's a great place to travel.

Almost 60 Spanish schools in Quito offer intensive Spanish instruction. With such intense competition, it's worth your while to shop around for one that fits your needs perfectly. Tuition usually includes four–seven hours of instruction per day, either in groups or one-on-one (some veterans say that four hours is plenty). Costs range $6–9 per hour. An initial registration fee may be required, and discounts are often possible for long-term commitments. Make sure to get a receipt when you pay, and check to see if any extras are not included in the hourly rate. SAE members often receive discounts of 5–15 percent.

Many schools draw business by offering extras, such as email and fax service, sports facilities, and extracurricular activities. Some will even house you (for a fee) or arrange for a home stay with a local family (typically $10–25 for full board, $9–12 for lodging only). Don't sign any long-term arrangements until you're sure of both the school and the family.

The following schools have received many positive reviews:

Amazonas (Jorge Washington 718 and Amazonas, Ed. Rocafuerte, piso 3, tel./fax 2/250-4654, info@eduamazonas.com, www.eduamazonas.com)

Beraca (Amazonas 11–14 and Pinto, piso 2, tel. 2/290-6642, office@beraca.net, www.beraca.com)

Bipo and Toni's (Carrión E8-183 and Plaza, tel. 2/255-6614, bipo@pi.pro.ec, www.bipo.net)

Cristóbal Colón Spanish School (Colón 2088 and Versalles, tel./fax 2/250-6508, info@colonspanishschool.com, www.colonspanishschool.com)

Instituto Superior de Español (Darquea Terán 1650 and 10 de Agosto, tel. 2/222-3242, fax 2221-628, superior@ecnet.ec, www.instituto-superior.net)

La Lengua (Colón 1001 and Juan León Mera, Ed. Ave Maria, piso 8, tel./fax 2/250-1271, info@la-lengua.com, www.la-lengua.com)

Simón Bolívar (Foch E9-20 and 6 Diciembre, tel. 2/223-4708, info@ecuadorschools.com, www.simon-bolivar.com)

Recommended private teachers include **Ana-Maria Muñoz** (Buga N12-44 and Haití, tel. 2/258-1346, anashome@hotmail.com, http://come.to/anashome) and **Mariana Gonzalez Parra** (tel. 2/234-9355 or 2/250-1271, spanishteachermariana@yahoo.com), who teaches in the Chillos Valley.

OTHER SERVICES
Laundry
Wash-and-dry places are common in New Town: Three are on Pinto near Reina Victoria and the youth hostel, and there are two more on Foch. A few may even let you use the machines yourself. Laundry services are available in many hotels, and the receptionists in more expensive ones can point you toward a dry cleaner *(lavaseca)*.

Photography
You can buy slide film at **Fuji** (Amazonas and Carrión) and develop it at **Ecuacolor** (Orellana and Coruña). **Fotografos y Aficionados** (6 de Diciembre 1944 and Cordero) is a good all-around custom photo lab, and **Di Foto** (Amazonas 893 and Wilson) will develop panoramic shots with excellent quality. If your camera isn't working, take it to Gustavo V. Gomes, a competent repairman at **Cemaf** (Asunción 130 and 10 de Agosto, Ed. Molina, Of. 1, tel. 2/223-0855, beeper 2/222-7777). Most Internet cafés will download your photos onto a CD for a small charge.

Transportation

GETTING THERE AND AWAY

Air

The **Mariscal Sucre International Airport** (tel. 2/294-4900) is north of New Town, beyond the intersection of 10 de Agosto, Amazonas, and De la Prensa. Buses marked "Aeropuerto" head down 9 de Octubre, 12 de Octubre, and Juan Leon Mera. You can also take the trolley along 10 de Agosto and then transfer onto the Rumiñahui connecting bus *(alimentador)* from the Estación Norte, or onto the Metrobus on America, which stops at the airport.

Upon arriving in Quito, hop a bus heading south (left) to reach both New and Old Town. A taxi ride from the airport to Old Town or New Town during the day should cost about $5–7 (subtract $1 if you walk out onto De la Prensa and find one yourself, and add $1–2 after dark).

Services at the airport include tourist information, a post office, late-night money exchange, duty-free shops, Andinatel, and a few restaurants and cafeterias.

TAME (Amazonas and Colon, tel. 2/396-6300) has flights from Quito to Baltra in the Galápagos ($350–407 round-trip), Coca ($61), Cuenca ($63), Esmeraldas ($59), Guayaquil ($63), Lago Agrio ($61), Loja ($83), Macas ($66), Machala ($93), Manta ($68), and Tulcán ($50). **Icaro** (Palora 124 and Amazonas, tel. 2/245-0928) has daily flights to Coca ($61 one-way), Cuenca ($68), Manta ($68), and uayaquil ($69). **Aerogal** (Amazonas 7797 and Juan Holgún, tel. 2/225-7202) goes to Guayaquil and the Galápagos for $1 more than TAME; the airline also have daily flights to Cuenca ($69). The newest line is **VIP** (Foch and 6 de Diciembre, which have smaller planes to Coca ($60), Lago Agrio ($60), and seasonally to Salinas.

National Buses

At press time, two new bus terminals were scheduled to open in December 2008, replacing the existing central terminal at Cumandá.

The new interprovincial bus terminal at Quitumbe, in south Quito, will serve all long distance routes traveling west, east, and south. It will also service routes to Esmeraldas via Santo Domingo.

Those traveling long distances north and northwest bound will use the new Terminal Norte, at the intersection of Eloy Alfaro and the Panamericana Norte. Note that this new terminal should not be confused with the existing intercantonal (inter-county/short distance) terminus at La Ofelia.

By December 2008 the rapid transit routes, Trole, Ecovia, and Metrobus, are also scheduled to extend their services to include transport through the city center, passing by the airport. City planners also hope to extend the hours of operation for rapid transit. Currently the Trole runs until midnight on weekdays and 10 p.m. on weekends; a "skeleton" service running 24 hours a day at selected stops is being proposed.

La Marín (a long, curving section along Pichincha) is the departure point for buses heading to destinations into the Chillos Valley, especially to the south. Ask here about buses to places such as Sangolquí, Alóag, and Machachi.

Rio Coca is currently the northern end of the Ecovia route and the interchange for buses to the Tumbaco valley, El Quinche, and the eastern villages.

A few private companies have their own small departure terminals. **Panamericana Internacional** (Colón and Reina Victoria, tel. 2/255-1839) travels to Guayaquil ($8–9, eight hours), Machala and Huaquillas ($12–14, 13 hours), Tulcán ($5, 4.5 hours), Loja ($16, 16 hours), Cuenca ($12, 14 hours), Manta ($8, eight hours), Portoviejo ($9, nine hours), and Esmeraldas ($6, six hours). **Flota Imbabura** (Larrea 1211 and Portoviejo, tel. 2/223-6940) heads to Cuenca ($12), Guayaquil ($8), and Manta ($8). **Ecuatoriana** (Jorge Washington and Juan León Mera, tel. 2/222-5315) sends

INTERNATIONAL AIRLINES IN QUITO

- **Air France/KLM:** 12 de Octubre N24-562 and Cordero, Ed. World Trade Center, Of. 401, tel. 2/252-4201, shared offices

- **American Airlines:** Amazonas 4545 and Pereira, tel. 2/226-0900

- **Avianca:** Coruña 1311 and Bello Horizonte, Loc. 3, tel. 800/003-434

- **Continental:** 12 de Octubre and Cordero, Ed. World Trade Center, Of. 1108, tel. 800/222-333

- **Copa:** República de El Salvador 361 and Moscu, tel. 2/227-3082

- **Cubana de Aviacón:** Felix Oralabal 599 and Marco Jofre, tel. 2/243-2714

- **Delta:** Los Shyris y Suecia, Edificio Renazzo Plaza, Loc 3, tel. 2/333-1691 or 800/101060

- **EL AL:** Juan León Mera 453 and Roca, Of. 302, tel. 2/256-4109

- **Iberia:** Eloy Alfaro 939 and Amazonas, Ed. Finandes, tel. 2/256-6009

- **Icelandair:** Diego de Almagro 1822 and Alpallana, tel. 2/256-1820

- **Japan Airlines:** Juan León Mera 453 and Roca, Of. 302, tel. 2/252-5354

- **Lan:** Orellana 557 y Coruña, Edificio Coruña, piso 3, tel. 2/299-2300 or 800/101-075, Lan Chile, Ecuador, and Peru together

- **Lufthansa:** Amazonas N47-205 and Río Palora, Edif. Harmonia, tel. 2/226-7705

- **Mexicana de Aviación:** Naciones Unidas and Amazonas, Ed. Banco La Previsora, Of. 410, tel. 2/246-6493

- **Taca:** República de El Salvador N34-67 and Portugal, tel. 2/292-3170 or 800-TACA-EC (800/822-232)

- **TAME:** Amazonas 13-54 and Colón, tel. 2/250-9375 or 2/292-2187 (airport)

- **United Airlines:** Amazonas 724 and Ventimilla, Edif. Gonzales, piso 3, tel. 2/290-2158

- **Varig:** Portugal 794 and República de El Salvador, Ed. Porto Lisboa, tel. 2/225-0126

plush buses to Guayaquil ($8). **Reina del Camino** serves Manabí from Pedernales to Puerto López, including Manta and Portoviejo, from its terminal at 18 Septiembre and Larrea.

The new northern terminal at Ofelia, which is only for county buses, is where **Coop Pichincha** serves Guayllabamba and El Quinche, **San Jose de Minas** serves the northwest (Nanegal, Minas, Chontal, Cielo Verde), **Flor de Valle** goes to Cayambe, Pacto, and Mindo, **Transportes Otavalo** doesn't go to Otavalo—only Minas and Pacto, and **Malchingui** and **Cangahua** travel to various locations. The installation is so new that no phone lines have been installed yet. Ofelia is the end of the Metrovia route, and dozens of connections spread out into the northern parishes from here. It is clean, organized, and well signposted. The Mitad del Mundo buses come through here—use your existing bus ticket and pay just a little extra for the transfer.

Rental Cars

Renting a car may be a good way to get out of the city, but take into account the convenience and cheapness of buses and the many vagaries of driving in Ecuador (see *Getting Around* in the *Essentials* chapter). It's definitely not the way to see the city.

Small cars start at $50 per day. Several major car-rental companies operate in Quito:

Avis: At the airport, tel. 2/330-0667

Bombuscaro: At the airport, tel. 2/330-3304, www.bombuscarorenta car.com

Budget: Colón 1140 and Amazonas, tel. 2/223-7026

Hertz: At the airport, tel. 2/225-4257

Localiza: tel. 800/562-254, www.localiza .com.ec

Safari Tours (E4-132 and Cordero, tel. 2/255-2505, fax 2/222-3381, tel./fax 2/222-0426, admin@safari.com.ec, www.safari.com. ec) has some four-wheel-drive vehicles and drivers available to head into the mountains, and it can arrange larger cars and buses for groups. **Moggely Climbing** (Amazonas and Calama, tel./fax 2/255-4984, moggely@hotmail.com, www.moggely.com) and the **Ecuadorian Alpine Institute** (Ramirez Davalos 136 and Amazonas, of. 102, tel. 2/256-5465, fax 2/256-8949, eai@ecuadorexplorer.com, www .volcanoclimbing.com) has four-wheel-drive vehicles as well.

Hernan Bonilla (Amazonas and Wilson, tel. 2/256-5028) can carry up to six people in his Chevy Blazer for $120 per day. **Manuel Hidalgo Transporte** (tel. 2/254-1872 or 2/255-2991) has a 14-passenger van for trips, and **Hugo Abata** (tel. 2/259-6530) has been recommended as a driver with 12- and 16-passenger vehicles.

Trains

Quito's **train station** is at Sincholagua and Maldonado, a few kilometers south of Old Town. The trolley is the easiest way to reach it: heading south, get off at the "Jefferson Pérez" stop and walk uphill along Maldonado, or exit at Cardinal de la Torre, then pass over the hill and down Maldonado. The Chimbacalle stop on the northbound trolley is right at the station. Until the train line leaving southern Quito is repaired, you will be bussed from there to Tambillo, where the adventure begins.

The only service still running is to Boliche Recreational Area adjacent to Cotopaxi National Park at 8 A.M. on Saturdays (also Sundays in high season) for $10 pp each way—it's a gorgeous ride through the Avenue of the Volcanoes when the weather's clear. Passengers have about two hours to gaze and wander at the western edge of the park before heading back to Quito. You could also walk out to the Pan-American Highway and change to a bus to Riobamba, then take the famous train ride through the Devil's Nose below Alausí.

GETTING AROUND
Local Buses

The easiest way to get around Quito is by bus. Rather than try to decipher the city's web of local bus routes, travel between major intersections. Find an intersection near you and one near where you want to go, locate a bus connecting the two, and walk a few blocks at either end. Most major avenues, especially Amazonas and 10 de Agosto, have buses passing every few minutes in either direction.

Any of 10 de Agosto's major crossroads, including Patria, Orellana, and Naciones Unidas, are likely places to find a bus heading south to Old Town or north as far as the turning to Mitad del Mundo. "La Y," at the meeting of 10 de Agosto with América and De la Prensa, along with El Inca (technically Parque Huayna Capac) at 6 de Diciembre and El Inca, are both major bus intersections.

Taxis

Digital meters are required by law. When—not if—the driver tells you it is "out of order" *("no funciona"),* offer to find another cab or report him using the four-digit number on the door or windshield. Such statements have a strange tendency to fix malfunctioning meters instantly. Meters start at $0.35, with a $1 minimum charge, and run except when the cab is stopped. Rides within Old and New Town shouldn't be more than $2 during the day. Prices increase at night, but shouldn't more than double.

Freelance yellow cabs prowl the streets, and various small taxi stands exist all over the city, especially in front of expensive hotels.

QUITO

These have a set price list for destinations and are usually more expensive than a metered ride.

Radio taxis can be called on a moment's notice, or arranged the day before, to pick you up. Try the **Central de Radio Taxi** (tel. 2/250-0600 or 2/252-1112) or **Taxi Amigo** (tel. 2/222-2222 or 2/222-2220). Both are reliable and available at any hour. **Taxis Lagos de Ibarra** (Asunción 381 and Versalles, tel. 2/256-5992) sends five-person taxis to Ibarra for $8 pp, or to Otavalo for $7.50. **Sudamericana Taxis** (tel. 2/275-2567) sends cabs to Santo Domingo—or stops en route, such as La Hesperia or Tinalandia—for $15 pp.

Trolley Systems

From a commuter's point of view, Quito's new electric trolley system seems almost too good to be true: It's clean, quiet, and fast. **El Trole** runs north–south between several endpoint stations: One (Estación Norte) is north of New Town, near La Y; and the others are south of Old Town at El Recreo or the extension to Moran Valverde (Estación Sur). The main *trole* thoroughfare, 10 de Agosto, reserves a pair of center lanes for the whirring plastic carriages, detouring down Guayaquil and Maldonado in Old Town, then continuing on Maldonado south of El Panecillo.

Passengers pay $0.25 each upon entering the station and simply board the next car, which will pass in 5–10 minutes. No hassle, few lines, and everyone's happy but frequently overcrowded—just watch your bags and wallets in the stations and in the cars. Trolleys run 5:30 A.M.–11:30 P.M. Monday–Friday, 6 A.M.–10 P.M. Saturday and Sunday. Plans to connect a new southern bus terminal at Quitumbe are moving ahead, but already at least one year behind schedule. The terminal may open in 2009.

The **Ecovia** is similar, just without the overhead wires. It also runs north–south, from its northern Río Coca terminal along 6 de Diciembre to La Marín near Old Town (6 A.M.–10 P.M. Mon.–Fri., 6 A.M.–9:30 P.M. Sat.–Sun.). Most turn around at La Marín, where there are interchanges with many country bus routes to the south and the valley; and an extension continues past the exit of the Cumandá terminal to Avenida Napo.

The third line, called the **Metrobus** (5:30 A.M.–10:30 P.M. Mon.–Fri., 6 A.M.–10 P.M. Sat.–Sun.), runs from the Marin up Santa Prisca and along Avenida América, La Prensa, and north to the new Ofelia terminal, where there are connections to the Mitad del Mundo, Calderón, Mindo, and most counties north and west of the province.

Vicinity of Quito

CALDERÓN

Just outside Quito's northern suburbs, the Pana passes this tiny town—actually closer to Quito's Mariscal Sucre Airport than El Panecillo—where artisans craft figures out of a varnished dough called *masapan*. This technique, unique to Ecuador until Playdough came along, originated with the annual making of bread babies for Day of the Dead celebrations in November. Artisans in Calderón developed more elaborate and lasting figures, adding salt and carpenter's glue, and the villagers gradually created new

techniques. With the introduction of aniline dyes, the masa became colored.

Today, Calderón is filled with artisan shops and private houses that turn out the figurines by the hundreds. Tiny indigenous dolls called *cholas* stand in formation on tables and shelves next to brightly painted parrots, llamas, fish, and flowers. Each flour-paste figure is molded by hand or rolled and cut with a pasta maker and pastry cutter. They are then dried, painted, and varnished. The figures make unusual, inexpensive gifts and are popular

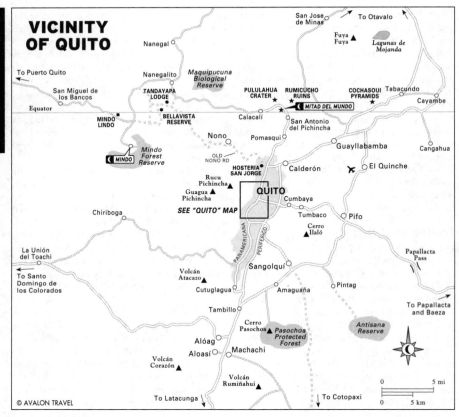

VICINITY OF QUITO

San Jose de Minas
To Otavalo
Fuya Fuya ▲
Lagunas de Mojanda
Nanegal ○

To Puerto Quito ←
Nanegalito ○
Maquipucuna Biological Reserve
PULULAHUA CRATER ★
RUMICUCHO RUINS ★
COCHASOUI PYRAMIDS ★
Tabacundo ○

San Miguel de los Bancos ○
TANDAYAPA LODGE
◖ MITAD DEL MUNDO
Cayambe ○

Equator ●
MINDO LINDO ■
BELLAVISTA RESERVE ●
Calacalí ○
San Antonio del Pichincha ●

◖ MINDO
Mindo Forest Reserve
Nono ○
Pomasqui ○
Guayllabamba ○
Cangahua ○

OLD NONO RD
HOSTERIA SAN JORGE ●
Calderón ○
El Quinche ○

Rucu Pichincha ▲
QUITO
Chiriboga ○
Guagua ▲ Pichincha
SEE "QUITO" MAP
Cumbaya ○

Tumbaco ○
Pifo ○

PANAMERICANA
PERIFERICO
Cerro Ilaló ▲

La Unión del Toachi ○
Sangolquí ○
Papallacta Pass

To Santo Domingo de los Colorados ←
Volcán Atacazo ▲
Amaguaña ○
Pintag ○

Cutuglagua ○
To Papallacta and Baeza →

Tambillo ○
Antisana Reserve

Cerro Pasochoa ▲ Pasochoa Protected Forest
Alóag ○
Aloasí ○
Machachi ○

Volcán Corazón ▲
Volcán Rumiñahui ▲

© AVALON TRAVEL
To Latacunga ↓
To Cotopaxi ↓

0   5 mi
0   5 km

as Christmas ornaments. Models of crèches, Santa Claus figures, and decorated trees are sold everywhere. Shops line the main street, and buses for Calderón leave regularly from the Ofelia terminal. In Quito, there are feeder buses on Ulloa near the Santa Clara Market.

GUAYLLABAMBA AND VICINITY

Winding its way down into a dry gorge, the Pana crosses the Guayllabamba River and ascends on the other side to the town of the same name. Head toward the main part of Guayllabamba, half a kilometer from the highway, and you'll notice piles of odd-looking fruit for sale. These are *chirimoyas,* which, along with small, dark avocados on the next table, grow well in the lush valley. They may look like relics from the Pleistocene epoch, but *chirimoyas* (also known as custard apples or sweetsops) are actually quite tasty, once you get past the scaly-looking skin.

Guayllabamba is home to the **Quito Zoo** (tel. 2/236-8898 or 2/236-8900, 8:30 A.M.–5 P.M. Tues–Fri., 9:30 A.M.–5 P.M. Sat.–Sun., $3.50), which opened in 1997 and is now considered one of the best and most spacious zoos in Latin America. The largest collection of native fauna in the country occupies the 12-hectare spread, including several animals rescued from the illegal fur trade. The focus is on mammals such as jaguars, spectacled bears, wolves, monkeys, and pumas. Macaws, parrots, eagles, Andean condors, and toucans represent native birds, and a Galápagos tortoise rounds things out. The zoo is three kilometers from the center of town—take a taxi or follow the signs. Tours are available.

El Quinche

Six kilometers away, through the dry, eroded landscape south of Guayllabamba, is the village of El Quinche. The town's ornate church and sanctuary dedicated to the Virgin of Quinche draw crowds of pilgrims from Quito in search of the Virgin's blessing year-round, and especially at processions honoring the Virgin held on November 21. The shrine is thought to grant special protection to truck and taxi drivers. From here, you can follow the road south to Pifo, then west into Quito's valley suburbs and up into the city. Quito's new airport is being constructed close to the town, but don't expect to fly in there for a few more years.

🅲 MITAD DEL MUNDO

"The Middle of the World" lies beyond the village of **Pomasqui,** past dry hills scarred by gravel quarries, at the gate of the village of **San Antonio del Pichincha.** Just before San Antonio, a long, paved pedestrian avenue slopes up to the left to the base of a massive monument resting *almost* smack on the equator.

A huge globe tops the square pedestal, which is bisected by a bright red line marking the planet's waistline. Here's your chance to shake hands or kiss from two different hemispheres, or pose with one foot on either side of the equator. An elevator inside the monument will take you to the top for a view of the encircling hills. You descend on foot through an excellent **ethnographic museum** (tel. 2/239-5637, 9 A.M.–6 P.M. Mon.–Thurs., 9 A.M.–7 P.M. Fri.–Sat., $1) filled with clothing, artwork, and reams of information on Ecuador's indigenous

cultures. Free tours are available in English and Spanish.

In the Disney-style "tourist village" next to the monument are numerous gift shops and traditional restaurants, a bullfighting ring, and a scale to find out if you really weigh less when you're this far from the center of the earth (since it bulges at the middle). Tourist agencies offer package tours to Pululahua and Rumicucho. **Calimatours** (tel. 2/239-4796 or 2/239-4797) has tours leaving daily for $6 pp, minimum four people.

Along the avenue, which is lined with busts of members of La Condamine's expedition, is a mediocre **planetarium** and a surprisingly neat model of colonial Quito in the **Fundación Quito colonial** (tel. 2/239-4319, 9:30 A.M.–5 P.M. daily, $1). The three-square-meter model took almost seven years to build at a scale of three blocks to one meter, with labeled streets. Make sure to stay for "sunrise" and "sunset," which arrive complete with tiny

Mitad del Mundo equator monument, north of Quito

© JULIAN SMITH

lights and sound effects. Models of Cuenca, Guayaquil, and various old ships are also part of the display.

The **Heroes del Cenepa** monument near the entrance is dedicated to the soldiers killed in border fighting with Peru in 1995, and the **French Museum** southeast of the monument traces the story of the ill-fated equator expedition (see the sidebar *Measuring the Earth* in the *Northern Sierra* chapter). Admission is free with a ticket to the ethnographic museum. You might have your bubble burst at the **Solar Culture Museum** south of the monument—its organizers claim that the real equator line actually goes through the barely visible ruins on Cataquilla Hill to the southeast. The computerized presentation on the archaeoastronomy of Ecuador's prehistoric sites is quite interesting.

North of the complex—exit and head left along the outside of the wall—is the excellent **Museo de Sitio Inti-Ñan** (tel. 2/239-5122, 9:30 A.M.–6 P.M. daily, $3). Its name means "Museum of the Path of the Sun" in Kichwa, and the family that owns and operates it has done a nice job with the collection, which includes displays on local plants, indigenous cultures, and even a live Galápagos tortoise. You'll hear yet another claim of the *exact* equator line, which they say goes right through the museum (and will pull out a fixed GPS to prove it).

To get here, take the Metrobus on Avenida America to the Ofelia terminal and catch the connecting Mitad del Mundo bus.

Pululahua Crater and Geobotanical Reserve

Where a volcano once burbled thousands of years ago, a steep-sided crater now yawns wide enough to support numerous farms on its flat, fertile bottom. This 3,200-hectare reserve, five kilometers north of Mitad del Mundo, was officially created in 1978 to protect the rich subtropical ecosystem within what is said to be the largest inhab-ited crater in South America—and possibly the world.

Regular buses and taxis take the road from the base of Mitad del Mundo's pedestrian avenue toward the village of Calacalí. Along the way, a dirt lane leaves the road to the right (after the gas station) and climbs to the lip of the crater at Moraspungo. You can also hike to Pululahua up a road that starts at the Sangria Restaurant between San Antonio de Pichincha and Calacalí and passes the Ventanilla viewpoint; this becomes a path that continues down into the crater.

El Crater (tel./fax 2/243-9254) is a restaurant and hotel that perches on the edge of the crater near the viewpoint. The panoramic view from the large windows easily outdoes the restaurant's small art gallery. Plates are $5–9, and it's open daily for lunch and dinner. There's also a smaller café that sells drinks and snacks.

A few hours' hike will bring you to the bottom of the crater and left up the Calacalí road to the **hikers' refuge,** where you can spend the night; the stay is included with your admission to the reserve ($5 pp). Bring all your own food, because there aren't any restaurants down there, and a sleeping bag. Hike over the rims to rejoin the paved road to Calacalí (10–15 km, three–four hours), where you can catch a bus back to the Mitad del Mundo. It's also possible to circle the crater rim on foot. **Horseback tours** of the crater are available through Astrid Müller's **Green Horse Ranch** (tel. 9/971-5933, ranch@accessinter.net, www.horseranch.de) in Quito.

Rumicucho Ruins

Often tacked onto the end of tours of the area, these modest pre-Inca ruins (7:30 A.M.–5 P.M. daily, $0.50 pp) consist of a series of rough stone walls and terraces on a small hilltop with a commanding view of the dry, windswept surroundings. To get there, take 13 de Junio (the main drag) northeast out of San Antonio de Pichincha, then turn right at the

Rumicucho sign. Guided tours in Spanish may be available.

THE PICHINCHAS

Quito's volcanic headboard is actually a pair of sibling peaks. Both are named Pichincha, which is thought to come from indigenous words meaning "the weeper of good water." **Rucu** ("Elder") is actually shorter (4,700 meters) and nearer to the city, whereas **Guagua** ("Baby") stands 4,794 meters high and has always been the worse behaved of the two.

Guagua sat quiet from 1660, the year it last erupted (and was first climbed by Friar Juan Romero), until October 1999, when it belched a mushroom cloud of ash that blotted out the sun over Quito for a day and covered the capital in ash. Although things seem to have calmed down, this activity prompted the Ecuadorian Geophysical Institute to close civilian access for several months. Although things seem to have calmed down, you should still check with the South American Explorers for the latest update.

Climbing Rucu isn't too difficult—no special equipment is needed—but robberies and attacks along the route around the turn of the millennium made climbing too dangerous. The situation improved with the opening of the *telefériqo* cable car and attendant development in 2006, but incidents were reported again in 2007. Increased security since 2008 seems to have cured the problem, but inquire locally if the route from Cruz Loma is safe enough to attempt.

Private transportation—preferably four-wheel-drive—is almost essential to reach Guagua, the farther peak. The real starting point is the pueblo of **Lloa,** almost due west of El Panecillo but reached by a roundabout route to the south of Quito. A tortuous dirt road leaves the main plaza and heads up the valley between the Pichinchas, ending in a shelter maintained by the Civil Defense. Park here, pay the entry fee of $1 (this goes toward the guardian's salary), and don't leave anything of value in the car. Sleeping space for 10 people costs $5 pp per night, including running water and cooking facilities.

Another hour will bring you from the shelter to the summit. The west-facing crater is pocked by smoking fumaroles, active domes, and collapsed craters. A rocky protrusion called the Cresta del Gallo (Rooster's Crest) separates the old, inactive side to the south from the newer, active area to the north. If you're considering descending the 700 meters to the bottom, think again—it has been declared off-limits since the latest eruption. And besides, 7 of the 10 highest peaks in the country are visible from the rim already.

HOSTERÍA SAN JORGE

Four kilometers up the road from Cotocollao to Nono—as close to Quito's airport as New Town—is a 230-acre mountain reserve (km 4 via Antigua a Nono, tel. 2/224-7549 or 2/249-4002, info@hostsanjorge.com .ec, www.hostsanjorge.com.ec) run by the friendly and enthusiastic George Cruz. The traditional country house, once owned by former Ecuadorian president Eloy Alfaro, offers wonderful views of the Quito valley from 3,000 meters in the Pichincha foothills. Gardens, a lake, and a spring-fed swimming pool and hot tub surround the guestrooms ($67 s, $73 d), warmed by fireplaces on chilly evenings. Three meals are $41 pp per day. It's a good place to acclimatize, and the owners offer a wealth of activities, from birding in the backyard to treks on pre-Inca trails to the coast. The Mindo and Nono areas are within mountain-biking distance. You can get there by taxi or call them for a pickup ($10–13 pp).

MAQUIPUCUNA BIOLOGICAL RESERVE

More than 4,500 rugged hectares purchased by the Nature Conservancy in 1988 protect one of the last remaining chunks of cloud forest in northwestern Ecuador. Most of this privately owned and managed reserve is undisturbed primary forest, ranging from a low-altitude

(1,200 meters) subtropical zone to cloud forest at the base of 2,800-meter Cerro Montecristi. It's less than three hours from Quito and surrounded by another 14,000 hectares of protected forest.

Temperatures vary 14–24°C, allowing thousands of plant species to thrive in a wide range of climates. More than 330 species of birds include the cock-of-the-rock and the empress brilliant. The reserve is also the first place where spectacled bears have been reintroduced into the wild. Wander farther afield, and chances are you'll stumble across a burial mound or a *culunco*—a half trail, half tunnel between the Andes and the Oriente—left by the pre-Inca Yumbos tribe.

Accommodations and guided tours center around the open-air Thomas Davis Ecotourism Center at 1,200 meters. Separate research stations keep visiting scientists busy between field trips, and nearby rivers and waterfalls are perfect for a quick dip. Admission is $5 pp, and you can secure a private bedroom with shared hot showers and three meals a day for $73 pp per night. Guides are $10 per group. Try to give the reserve notice before you arrive, even if you're visiting only for the day. For more information, contact the Fundación Maquipucuna in Quito (Baquerizo Moreno 238, tel. 2/250-7200, fax 2/250-7201, root@maqui.ecuanex.net.ec, www.arches.uga .edu/~maqui).

The road past Mitad del Mundo, Pululahua, and Calacalí eventually passes **Nanegalito** to reach **Nanegal,** the nearest village to Maquipucuna. Transportes Minas at La Ofelia send buses to Nanegal and beyond daily at noon, 1:30 P.M., 3 P.M., and 4:40 P.M.

From Nanegal, you'll have to hire a truck or taxi to take you to Marianitas, which is four kilometers from the reserve entrance. You can also get off the bus at a big green house with yellow trim known as La Delicia (bus drivers know where it is) and walk two kilometers to Marianitas, then another four kilometers to the reserve.

MINDO

This small, tranquil village has been receiving more and more visitors as its reputation as a birding hotspot has spread. Set in a quiet, lovely valley dotted with flowers and surrounded by forested mountains, Mindo is smack in the middle of one of the best birding areas in South America. Part of the Chocó Bioregion, Mindo and its environs count hundreds of species of birds, from flycatchers and hummingbirds galore to woodcreepers, manakins, and cotingas. Nineteen endemic bird species share the Tandayapa Valley with pumas, spectacled bears, ocelots, and 80 species of orchids.

Almost 21,000 hectares of forest, from tropical jungle to *páramo,* fall within the **Mindo-Nambillo Protected Forest,** which wraps around the town to the east and south. Drained by the ríos Mindo, Nambillo, and Cinto, the area is run by the **Amigos de la Naturaleza** (tel. 2/390-0423, amigosmindo@ hotmail.com), a local conservation group that has an office two blocks from Mindo's plaza. The forest is home to more than 400 species of birds, including toucans, barbets, and golden-headed quetzals. Local guides can lead you to Andean cock-of-the-rock leks, where brilliant crimson-colored males compete for females.

Mindo is still a low-key place, but word has gotten out—at last count, the town had more than 60 hotels. Because it's so close to Quito, it is a frequent weekend getaway. The surrounding forest has started to be affected by an influx of settlers and tourists. Most worrisome was an oil pipeline from Quito to Esmeraldas, which the Ecuadorian government put right through the middle of the area. With the help of foreign tourism operators and business owners, locals fought to stop it—to no avail—and the scar through the forest is only slowly fading.

Recreation and Tours

A German-Ecuadorian couple owns a section of land uphill from Mindo called **Mindo Lindo** (tel. 9/244-3820), which offers easier access to the cloud forest than other properties in town.

They charge $2 pp to use the trails and charge $25 pp for accommodation. A few freelance **birding guides** operate out of Mindo and can lead visitors on day trips out of Quito. Vinicio Pérez is highly recommended; ask for him in town. He charges around $50 for a morning's guiding. **Andean Birding** (Salazar Gómez E-1482 and Eloy Alfaro, tel./fax 2/224-4426, info@andeanbirding.com, www.andeanbirding.com) also operates out of Quito.

Local guides are recommended for **hiking** and charge about $25 per day to take you to nearby waterfalls, such as La Cascada de Nambillo (entrance $5 pp), at the end of the Vía Mindo Gardens. Ask at the Centro de Información or at one of the hotels in town for details on hiking and **tubing** on nearby rivers. The **Mariposas de Mindo** butterfly garden ($3 pp) is two kilometers away via Mindo Gardens.

Accommodations

The cheapest place to stay in Mindo is the **Casa de Cecilia** (tel. 2/276-5453), just off the main plaza. Rooms open to the forest are $5 pp, and there's a restaurant downstairs. The **Hostal Arco Iris** (tel. 2/390-0405) on the plaza offers clean rooms for $8 pp. Next to the soccer field and sports complex one block from the main plaza, the **Hostal Rubby** (tel. 9/340-6321) offers shared rooms with balconies and mosquito nets for $8 pp. It's a backpacker kind of place, with hammocks and a café/bar downstairs. Another rustic place adjoining the soccer field is the **Hostal Armonia** (tel. 2/390-0431), which is packed full of orchids and has private rooms with hot water for $14 pp. It runs river tubing and other outdoor tours for $6 pp.

The Amigos de la Naturaleza organization offers lodgings in the **Centro de Educación Ambiental** (Environmental Education Center), about four kilometers from town via Mindo Gardens. Cabins without electricity are $10 private or $5–6 shared, and camping is $4 pp. Basic food is served at the restaurant (plates around $4). Follow the vía Mindo

Gardens to the hotel **Mindo Gardens Lodge** (tel. 2/225-2490, $50 d), with comfy cabins on 350 hectares and a restaurant right on the Río Mindo. The cabins have private bathrooms with hot water, and breakfast is included in the price.

Near the Mindo Gardens Lodge, **El Monte Sustainable Lodge** (tel. 2/390-0402) is run by American Tom Quesenberry and his Ecuadorian wife, Mariela Tenorio. They offer three wood cabins at the edge of the Río Mindo with hot water, private baths, and thatched roofs. The cabins are $67 pp per night, including all meals and birding guides for the hiking trails nearby. You have to cross the river on a small cable car to reach the hotel, but once you do, you can take your pick of whitewater tubing, nature walks, and a snooze in a hammock.

Food

Mindo's eating options outside of the various hotels are improving. A few inexpensive restaurants and cafés along the main street in town include the **Café Mindo,** the **Restaurant de la Señora Niquito,** and the **Restaurant Francisco,** which all serve inexpensive set meals.

Information

There's a **Centro de Información** (7 A.M.–6 P.M. daily) on Quito near the plaza. Ask for a list of members of the local naturalists' guide association.

Transportation

The old cobbled road to Mindo passing through Nono on its way northwest from Quito has been overtaken by a new paved road running west from the Mitad del Mundo. It joins the old road just north of Mindo and continues west to Puerto Quito. An eight-kilometer road connects Mindo to the main road. Direct buses from Quito with the Cooperative Flor del Valle leave at 8:20 A.M. and 4 P.M. Monday–Saturday; at 7:40 A.M. and 9:20 A.M. Saturday; and at

7:40 A.M., 8:20 A.M., 9:20 A.M., 1:45 P.M., and 5 P.M. Sunday. Daily buses leave Mindo for Quito between 6:30 A.M. and 2 P.M. Trucks and buses to other destinations can leave you at the main road at the top of the hill, where you can catch a passing bus to Quito.

Yanacocha

The old Nono–Mindo road, rough as it is, offers great birding along almost its entire length. One particularly good spot is this 964-hectare reserve of elfin Polylepis forest in the Pichincha foothills. Take a turnoff to the left (south) 18 kilometers from Quito and drive up to the gate. Explain to the caretaker, if he's there, that you're there to watch birds *("para observar las aves")*, and he will collect a $5 pp entry fee, which helps the Fundación Jocotoco (www.fjocotoco.org) protect special bird areas around Ecuador. Twenty-two species of hummingbirds have been spotted in the vicinity, including the very rare black-breasted puffleg, which has been observed only in the tiny reserve.

Tandayapa Lodge

Iain Campbell, a geology expert turned birding guide, runs this luxury birder lodge along the old Nono–Mindo road. He bills Tandayapa (Reina Victoria 1684 and La Pinta, Ed. Santiago 1, Dep. 501, tel./fax 2/244-7520, tandayapa@tandayapa.com, www.tandayapa.com) as "the only lodge in the world designed by birders, owned by birders, and run for birders by birders." You can tell it's the real thing: 4 A.M. breakfasts are no problem, and they've already planted 30,000 trees in the immediate area to help combat deforestation.

Rates ($109 s, $185 d) include all meals, and the 12 guestrooms all have private baths with hot water. They're in a single building with a fireplace, bar, and a balcony overlooking the cloud forest, making it easy to start your day with a few new sightings. They've seen 18 species of hummingbirds from the balcony feeders alone, and a total of 320 species of birds on their trails. Many species are "staked out," meaning the guides know where they are on a regular basis. Packages including guides and transportation are available. One-day birding packages from Quito are $95 pp (two-person minimum), including transportation, lunch, and two guided walks.

To reach Tandayapa, either head up the old Nono–Mindo road (now called the *Ecoruta Paseo del Quindé*) or take the new road and get off the bus at the turnoff, at km 52. It's seven kilometers to the lodge from there (11 kilometers from Nanegalito).

Bellavista Cloud Forest Reserve

British ecologist and teacher Richard Parsons began with 100 hectares of prime cloud forest near the town of Tandayapa, where he built a four-story, thatched-roof lodge looking out over the moss-covered treetops. The ground floor of the geodesic dome—one of most distinctive accommodations in Ecuador—encloses the living and dining rooms, while guest rooms upstairs have private baths, hot water, and balconies with hummingbird feeders. Interested ornithologists and friends have helped increase the size of the reserve to 500 hectares, and three comfortable houses plus a research station for students and scientists have all been added. Birders can search through the premontane cloud forest (1,400–2,600 meters) for the tanager finch, giant antpitta, and white-faced nunbird that frequent nearby streams.

Private rooms in the dome buildings are $101 s, $173 d, with all meals ($65 s, 100 d without), and accommodations in the shared quarters upstairs are $57 pp with meals ($29 pp without). For more privacy, choose one of the three newer houses for the same prices. Campsites are available for $7 per night, and hostel-style lodging in the research station is $12 pp per night. Day trips from Quito, including guides, transport, and two meals, run $99 s, $158 d, and two- and three-day packages are also possible. Arrange visits through the reserve's office in Quito (Jorge Washington E7-23 and 6 de Diciembre, tel./fax 2/223-2313, info@bellavistacloudforest.com, www.bellavistacloudforest.com).

Transportation can be arranged from Quito, or you can take a public bus to Nanegalito from the terminal at la Ofelia. (Any bus to Pacto, Puerto Quito, San Miguel de los Bancos, or Mindo passes Nanegalito.) Ask in Nanegalito about renting a pickup truck to take you the last 15 kilometers to the reserve. If you're driving yourself, head for the Mitad del Mundo and Calacalí on the new road to Esmeraldas, and turn left at km 52, just across a bridge (look for the Bellavista sign). Follow this road six kilometers to the village of Tandayapa, then uphill another six kilometers to the reserve. You can also continue on the road to Esmeraldas through the town of Nanegalito to km 62, then turn left and follow signs along the ridge for 12 kilometers to Bellavista. The third access is at km 77, just one kilometer from the Mindo entrance; then drive the 12 kilometers of unpaved road to the reserve.

SANGOLQUÍ

Corn is king in this town southeast of Quito. A 10-meter statue of a cob, called "El Choclo,"

greets visitors in a traffic circle at the entrance. In late June, festivities mark the end of the harvest. During the fourth and final day, bullfights become arenas for raging displays of machismo, as alcohol-numbed locals goaded by "friends" try to get as close to the bull as possible without getting killed—unsurprisingly, someone usually gets injured. The central plaza area has been beautifully restored, and the town hosts an excellent indigenous market on Sundays and a smaller one on Thursdays. To get there, take a Sangolqui bus from the local terminal at Marin Bajo.

PASOCHOA PROTECTED FOREST

This long, sloping valley preserves the original lush, wooded state of the area surrounding Quito. Fundación Natura administers the reserve, which ranges 2,700–4,200 meters. Primary and secondary forest topped by *páramo* supports a wide diversity of birds, from the sword-billed hummingbird—whose upturned bill is longer than its body—to a

© JEAN BROWN

Pasochoa summits

family of condors living atop Cerro Pasochoa (4,200 meters).

Loop paths of varying lengths and difficulty lead higher and higher into the hills, ranging two–eight hours in length. It's also possible to climb to the lip of Cerro Pasochoa's blasted volcanic crater in five–six hours. Campsites and a few dorm rooms with showers and cooking facilities are available near the bottom, along with a small souvenir store. Free guided tours are sometimes available. The reserve is open daily; admission for foreigners is $10 pp.

To get here from Quito, take a bus from the south end of the Plaza La Marín (Playon) below the Old Town to the village of Amaguaña ($0.60, 30–40 minutes). Hire a pickup ($5–8) from the plaza of Amaguaña to the turnoff for the reserve, which is marked by a green sign facing south one kilometer toward Machachi on the Pana. From there, a dirt road leads seven kilometers up a rough, cobbled road to the reserve. Drivers may agree to come back for you, or you could catch a ride down with the reserve personnel in the evening. Take a phone card, and you can call from the cell phone at the entrance for a taxi to collect you.

GUÁPULO

Take the precipitous Camino de Orellana down the hill behind the Hotel Quito—or else the footpath from the park and playground—to reach this hillside neighborhood. Narrow, cobbled streets are lined with shops, cafés, and homes, including lavish walled-in residences favored by ambassadors. At the center is the 17th-century plaza fronting the beautiful **Iglesia de Guápulo,** which was built between 1644 and 1693 on the site of an even older convent. The sparkling church can be seen from far above and houses a collection of colonial art, including crucifixes and a pulpit carved by Juan Bautista Menacho in the early 18th century.

NORTHERN SIERRA

Ecuador's northern highlands, stretching from Quito to the Colombian border, enclose everything that makes the Sierra special: incredible scenery, picturesque towns with bustling indigenous markets, unspoiled national parks, and ice-capped volcanoes. It's no surprise, then, that the northern Sierra is one of the country's most popular regions for tourists. What may surprise you is how easily you can leave the beaten path and find yourself in rural areas and nature reserves you'd swear no traveler had ever seen before.

Otavalo's textile market, one of the most spectacular in South America, is the biggest draw in the region. Many of the smaller villages around Otavalo specialize in particular crafts; the city and its environs demand at least a few days of exploring. Farther north, the quiet colonial "White City" of Ibarra is larger but calmer. Unless you have some urgent unresolved business with the border police, there's no excuse not to stop by the famous topiary cemetery in Tulcán near the Colombian border.

Parks and nature reserves offer hiking, camping, and mountaineering to rival any in Ecuador. The Cotacachi-Cayapas and Cayambe-Coca Ecological Reserves spill from the highlands into the coastal lowlands and the Oriente, respectively. Many smaller private reserves, such as Intag and Cerro Golondrinas, are tucked into the corners of the larger ones. After a long hike to a remote *laguna,* soak your aches away in one of the many hot springs that bubble up from the hillsides.

The inter-Andean plateau is lined by towering mountain ranges on its way northeast to

© JEAN BROWN

HIGHLIGHTS

Textile Market: Otavalo's Saturday market is justifiably famous, with acres of multi-hued textiles and crafts of every description (page 78).

Hacienda Cusín: One of Ecuador's oldest and most elegant haciendas is a sumptuous step back in time (page 87).

Laguna Cuicocha: Take a boat through the Dream Canal on the icy waters of this lake high in the Andes at the foot of Volcán Cotacachi (page 99).

El Angel Ecological Reserve: One of Ecuador's most pristine *páramo* reserves is home to odd plants in a high, misty setting (page 112).

Tulcán's Municipal Cemetery: With its extraordinary topiary works, this graveyard has been called "so beautiful, it invites one to die" (page 113).

LOOK FOR ◖ TO FIND RECOMMENDED SIGHTS, ACTIVITIES, DINING, AND LODGING.

Colombia. Dry river valleys and cold alpine lakes punctuate the land between the peaks. Near the border, highland valleys climb into damp, moody *páramo* straight out of a Scottish historical epic. Earthquakes occasionally rattle the region, explaining mountaineer Edward Whymper's description of the local topography as "not very unlike that of a biscuit which has been smashed by a blow of the fist."

PLANNING YOUR TIME

The northern Sierra is the most compact Andean region covered in this book. It's possible to see the highlights in four–five days—or, if you're really pressed for time, hit Otavalo in a long day trip from Quito. Otavalo's environs and Ibarra are each worth a few days, and Tulcán merits a quick stop on the way into or out of Ecuador overland. If you want to go backpacking or visit a remote private reserve, give yourself at least a week.

Otavalo and Ibarra each make good home bases for exploring. **Otavalo's Saturday textiles market** is a must and within day-trip distance of both the **Hacienda Cusín,** a premier historic hotel, and the twin domes in **Laguna Cuicocha** part of the gigantic Cotacachi-Cayapas Ecological Reserve. Farther north (and father afield) is the chilly, otherworldly expanse of **El Angel Ecological Reserve.** At the Colombian border, **Tulcán's municipal cemetery** is the prettiest place in the country to be buried.

NORTHERN SIERRA

Otavalo and Vicinity

Despite its modest size, Otavalo is probably the best-known city in Ecuador outside of Quito. Every Saturday, thousands gather in the Plaza de Ponchos to buy, sell, haggle, or simply watch the granddaddy of all Andean markets. Otavalan textiles and indigenous music are carried around the world by this distinctive indigenous group (see the sidebar *The Indígenas of Otavalo*), making the city a must-see for most travelers to Ecuador. Add in the beautiful surrounding countryside, dotted with crafts villages and Otavalo's proximity to Quito, and you have one bustling—yet somehow still authentic—market town.

Nestled in the lovely Valle del Amanecer (Valley of the Sunrise) at 2,530 meters, Otavalo (pop. 31,000) is said to be the second-oldest town in Imbabura Province. It was a market town before the Incas arrived, surviving as a trading center for produce and animals

brought up from the lowlands. Since then, textiles have become the product of choice, earning the Otavalo *indígenas* global fame and a quality of life worlds apart from most other indigenous groups in South America. It's easy to see that there's money here, with shiny new four-wheel-drive vehicles blasting contemporary music in the streets. But as the drivers flip their long braids and adjust their woven blouses, you'll notice that both the town and its inhabitants seem to have kept in solid touch with their heritage.

Sadly, the high number of tourists has led to occasional robberies and assaults. Never leave your hotel room unlocked, and be careful of bag slashers and pickpockets in the crowded markets. Also, try to explore the area's trails and more remote locations in groups, because lone hikers have sometimes been robbed. On the whole, however, the streets of Otavalo are safe at night.

SIGHTS
(Textile Market

The reason most tourists come to town (and the reason you probably can't find a hotel room on Friday night) is the Saturday textile market. Vendors from town and surrounding villages set up shop well before dawn. Coffee steam mingles with clouds of breath as vendors chat, gobble a quick breakfast, and set up scaffolding to display their wares. By 8 A.M., the animal market is under way, and soon the Plaza de Ponchos is packed with a brightly colored, murmuring throng of vendors and tourists haggling over every imaginable type of textile and craft. The market has become so successful that it is now open every day of the week. The Saturday market is still the biggie, though, and it's worth experiencing even if you don't intend to buy anything. Just getting up early and watching the place slowly come to life as the sun rises over Volcán Imbabura is a wonderful experience.

If it can be made out of wool, cotton, or

© JULIAN SMITH

Otavalo Street

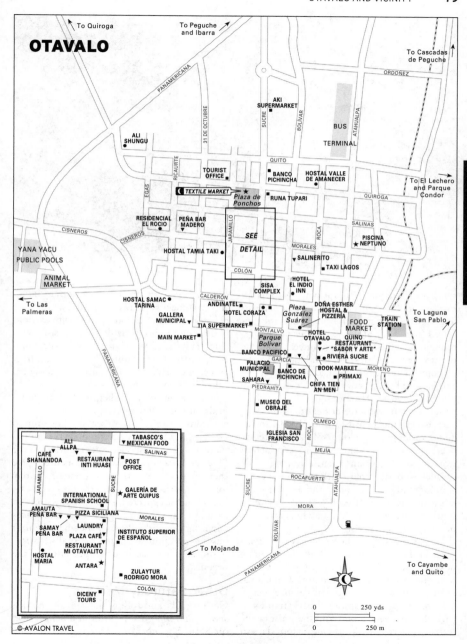

OTAVALO

NORTHERN SIERRA

© AVALON TRAVEL

animal market

© JULIAN SMITH

synthetic yarn, you'll find it here. Wall hangings are popular, woven with abstract patterns or designs of intermeshed birds and lizards (inspired by a book of M. C. Escher's drawings brought by a Peace Corps volunteer years ago, the story goes). Thick wool and alpaca sweaters come in interesting color combinations, and carpets and blankets of the same materials are often covered in llama designs. Piles of hats made of felt or wool teeter next to mounds of surprisingly inexpensive wool mittens, socks, and handbags and cloud-soft alpaca teddy bears. The best (and most expensive) ponchos, worn by the Otavalans themselves, are made of thick wool dyed blue with indigo imported from abroad, with a collar and gray or plaid fabric on the inside. Ponchos are also made of synthetic materials like orlon, which is less expensive but more garish.

Long cloth strips called *fajas,* used by *indígenas* in the Sierra to tie back their hair, hang next to their wider cousins called *chumbis.* Many of these belts are woven in La Compañía, on the other side of Lago San Pablo. A single belt woven on the traditional backstrap loom (stretched between a post and the waist of the seated weaver) can take as long as four days to complete. Jewelry similar to that worn by indigenous women is spread out on tables: necklaces of black or red beads, interspersed with earrings of turquoise and lapis lazuli. Other treasures include raw fleece, yarn, and dyes, textiles from Peru and Bolivia, painted balsa-wood birds, and piles of assorted junk hiding the occasional valuable antique.

For the Saturday market, it's best to spend Friday night in town; arrive early or make reservations ahead of time to secure a hotel room. Get up early Saturday morning for the animal market and the best selection and prices in the Plaza de Ponchos, because vendors often give their first customer the best price of the day for good luck—or they say they do, anyway. Bargaining is expected, even in many stores in town, and proficient hagglers can talk prices down significantly. Prices peak when the tour buses from Quito are in town, usually 9 A.M.–noon, so arrive early or linger late for the best deals.

Other Saturday Markets

Get up early and follow the squeals, honks, snorts, and moos to the **animal market,** held on Saturday mornings starting at sunrise.

Enough farm animals to film a Disney movie are for sale, from cows to guinea pigs, although the conditions would probably make old Walt shudder. To get there, head west on Morales or Calderon and cross the bridge, passing the stadium. The market is straight ahead across the Pana. The **produce market** overflows with food, housewares, and clothes in and around the Plaza 24 de Mayo all day.

Museums and Galleries

The **Museo del Obraje** (Sucre 6–08 and Olmedo, tel. 6/292-0261, 8 A.M.–12:30 P.M. and 3–5 P.M. Mon.–Sat., $2) showcases the textiles that have made the area famous. It also offers courses in weaving and other handicrafts.

In the center of town, the **SISA** complex (Calderón 409 between Bolívar and Sucre, tel. 6/292-0154) packs a handicrafts shop, bookstore, art gallery, bar, and restaurant into two floors. The name is an acronym for "Sala de Imágen, Sonido y Arte" (Image, Sound, and Art Space), and it also means "flower" in Kichwa. Live music is performed on weekend nights.

ENTERTAINMENT AND EVENTS
Fiestas

Inti Raymi, the Inca festival of the northern solstice, has been absorbed into the Catholic **Festival of San Juan** held in late June. Boats of every description dot the Lago de San Pablo, and people cheer local favorites (of both species) in bullfights. In the San Juan barrio northwest of Otavalo, a ritual rock-throwing called *tinku* frequently results in serious injuries.

Yamor, the festival everyone looks forward to, takes place close to the equinox, traditionally beginning during the first weeks of September. In Otavalo, the Inca festival of Colla-Raymi, a harvest celebration of the earth's fertility, was combined with the festival of San Luis Obispo, the patron saint of the harvest. Today, Yamor has become a two-week blowout of the largest order. Parades, marching bands, bullfights, outrageous costumes, and dances are all fueled by a special *chichi de*

jora made of seven different grains and drunk only during the festivities. Be warned—all that alcohol can occasionally bring out revelers' less pleasant sides.

In the *entrada de ramos* (entrance of the branches), food and animals—from bread and fruit to live guinea pigs—are displayed, re-creating a ritual presentation of food to the landowner dating to colonial times. A highlight is the appearance of the *coraza,* often a patron of the festivities. The only participant on horseback, the *coraza* wears an elaborate costume with a three-cornered hat and silver chains covering his face.

Nightlife

Good Andean music is easy to find in Otavalo's *peñas* (nightclubs). Ask around to find out when and where to go, since live bands aren't always on the ticket. If you're lucky, you might find the music interspersed with poetry readings, dramatic monologues, and indigenous dance performances. Grab a high-octane pitcher of *canelazo* (hot cinnamon tea with *aguardiente*), sit back, and enjoy.

Your best bets are the **Amauta Peña Bar** (Morales between Jaramillo and Sucre), the **Peña Bar Madero** two blocks west (Morales between 31st Octubre and Ricaurte).

Public Pools

After a long, hot ramble through the countryside, take a dip in the **Yana Yacu** public pools (8 A.M.–5 P.M. daily, $0.50 pp), west of town across the Pana. Changing rooms are available.

SHOPPING

If you can't spend your money here, you can't spend it anywhere. In addition to the markets, stores throughout town carry huge selections of woven goods. **Antara,** a store on Sucre near Colón, sells handmade Andean musical instruments. For more work by local artists, try the **Galería de Arte Quipus** (Sucre and Morales), which specializes in oils and watercolors. You can buy, sell, or trade books at **The Book Market** (Roca and Garcia Moreno at hostal

Riviera Sucre), which has a good selection of works in several languages.

RECREATION AND TOURS

Tour companies have sprouted up all over town to accommodate visitors who want to watch the actual production of crafts and textiles and see how the artisans live. Competition keeps prices low, and seeing the work and skill that goes into the crafts is fascinating. Most agencies have a spectrum of options available, including hiking, driving, biking, and horseback trips of varying lengths and itineraries. All agencies offer tours in English.

Kitty-corner from each other at Colón and Sucre are two recommended tour operators. **Diceny Tours** (tel./fax 6/292-1217) bills itself as the "original" and stresses the fact that it's owned by Zulay, who is *indígena*. The staff runs excellent all-day tours to weaving villages, Cotacachi, and Lago Cuicocha for

MEASURING THE EARTH

By 1735, most people agreed that the earth was round. But another question remained: *how* round was it? Some scientists posited that the rotation of the earth caused it to bulge outward slightly in the middle, but others found that idea ridiculous. With explorers setting out daily to the far corners of the globe, it became more and more important to determine how much, if any, the earth bulged in the middle, since navigational charts off by a few degrees could send ships hundreds of miles in the wrong direction.

To answer the long-standing debate, the French Academy of Sciences organized two expeditions to determine the true shape of the earth. One team headed north to Lapland, as close to the Arctic as possible. The other left for Ecuador on the equator. Each team was tasked with measuring one degree of latitude (about 110 kilometers) in its respective region. If the degree at the equator proved longer than the degree near the Arctic, then the earth bulged. If not, it didn't.

The Ecuadorian expedition was the first organized scientific expedition to South America. At the time, Ecuador was part of the Spanish territory of Upper Peru. It was chosen because of its accessibility – much easier than alternative locations along the equator: the Amazon basin, Africa, and Southeast Asia. The Ecuadorian expedition was led by academy members Louis Godin, Pierre Bouguer, and Charles-Marie de La Condamine. With them came seven other Frenchmen, including a doctor/botanist, Godin's cousin, a surgeon, a naval engineer, and a draftsman.

Tensions hampered the expedition from the start, as Bouguer and La Condamine quickly learned they did not get along. Bouguer was stern, stoic, and accused of being paranoid of competitors, whereas La Condamine, a protégé of Voltaire's, was easygoing. This personal rivalry sparked numerous quarrels, as the extroverted, enthusiastic La Condamine effectively became the leader of the expedition.

The group arrived in Cartagena, Colombia, in 1735. There they were joined by two Spaniards, both naval captains under secret orders from the king of Spain to report back on the French expedition and conditions in the Spanish territories. In March 1736, the party sailed into Ecuador's Pacific Port of Manta and soon traveled by way of Guayaquil to Quito. Quiteños received the earth measurers with delight, and dances and receptions filled the days following their arrival. As the festivities continued, Pedro Vicente Maldonado Palomino, an Ecuadorian map maker and mathematician, was chosen to join the historic expedition.

Eventually, the group got down to business. For the sake of accuracy, it was decided that the measurements would be made in the flat plains near Yaruquí, 19 kilometers northeast of Quito. As the work progressed, troubles mounted. The French and Spanish, unused to the altitude and the cold of the Sierra, began

$16 pp, and does trekking and horseback-riding tours as well.

Opposite Diceny is **Zulaytour Rodrigo Mora** (tel. 6/292-2791), on the second floor above a telephone/fax/money-exchange business. Tours are offered in French and German.

On the Plaza de Ponchos, **Runa Tupari** (tel. 6/292-5985) provides the most authentic indigenous experience in town. The company can set up home stays in small nearby communities, where you can live with and learn from traditional families, who actually see some financial benefit from the arrangement. They work with 15 families in five small communities and charge $25 pp, including meals and transport. Runa Tupari also sells products from various local community projects.

You can do tours of the area yourself almost as easily by hiking or renting a mountain bike or taxi. The rolling countryside around Otavalo is spider-webbed with country

to fall ill. Soon the group suffered its first casualty: the nephew of the academy's treasurer, one of the youngest team members.

As the mourning scientists wandered the plains with their strange instruments, local residents grew suspicious. Rumors began circulating that they had come to dig up and steal buried treasure, maybe even Inca gold. The situation became so tense that La Condamine and a fellow member of the expedition were forced to travel to Lima to obtain the viceroy's support. They finally returned in July 1737 with official papers supporting their story. The measurements continued, and by 1739, the goal of determining the true shape of the earth was in sight. Then disastrous news arrived from the academy: The Lapland expedition had succeeded. The earth was flattened at the poles. The verdict was already in.

As La Condamine tried to keep the expedition from disintegrating, more bad luck seemed to strike from every side. The party surgeon, Juan Seniergues, became involved in a dispute over a Cuencan woman and was beaten and stabbed to death at a bullfight in the Plaza de San Sebastian by an angry mob sympathetic to his local rival, the woman's former fiancé. The rest of the group sought refuge in a monastery. In the confusion, the team botanist, Joseph de Jussieu, lost his entire collection of plants – representing five years' work, this loss eventually cost him his mind as well. The team draftsman was killed in a fall from a church steeple near Riobamba. La Condamine had to fend off accusations from the Spanish crown that he had insulted Spain by omitting the names of the two Spanish officers from commemorative plaques he had already erected at Oyambaro.

Finally, in March 1743, the remaining scientists made the last measurements, confirming the Lapland expedition's findings and bringing the expedition to an end. Even though they had come in second, the group's efforts did lay the foundation for the entire modern metric system. Some members decided to stay on in Ecuador – two had already married local women – while others traveled to different South American countries. Most went back to Europe. La Condamine, accompanied by Maldonado, rode a raft down the Amazon for four months to the Atlantic Ocean. From there, the pair sailed to Paris, where they brought the first samples of rubber seen in Europe and were welcomed as heroes. Maldonado died of measles in 1748, while La Condamine enjoyed the high life in Paris until his death in 1774.

In 1936, on the 200th anniversary of the expedition's arrival in Ecuador, the Ecuadorian government built a stone pyramid on the equator at San Antonio de Pichincha in honor of the explorers and their work. This pyramid was eventually replaced by the 100-foot monument that stands today. Busts along the path leading to the monument commemorate the 10 Frenchmen, two Spaniards, and one Ecuadorian who risked their lives – and sanity – for science.

lanes, and you could easily spend days wandering aimlessly from one village to the next. If you're in the mood for a moderate climb, head east on Morales, up past the large cross, to the **Mirador El Lechero** for a great view of Otavalo and the Laguna de San Pablo. **Parque Condor** is a short continuation of the Lechero hike, and for many, it's a unique chance to see condors, hawks, eagles, owls, and other raptors in close quarters. Open since 2005, the park (9:30 A.M.–5 P.M. Tues.–Sun., $3 pp, www.parquecondor.org) started with European support. The birds are well cared for, and they fly freely for half an hour each morning at 11:30 and each afternoon at 4:30. A taxi from Otavalo to the park is $4 one-way.

ACCOMMODATIONS

Otavalo has no shortage of hotels, especially in the budget category, but rooms may still be scarce on busy nights. At some hotels, water is heated only during certain hours.

Under $10

The **Hostal Valle del Amanecer** (Roca and Quiroga, tel. 6/292-0990, fax 6/292-1159) has a *Gilligan's Island* theme in its cobbled, plant-packed courtyard and outdoor fireplace. Rates run $9 pp with shared bath, $10 pp private. The hostel has a restaurant and offers motorcycles and bicycles for rent ($40 and $6 per day, respectively).

One of the best budget deals is at the immaculate **Hostal Maria** (Jaramillo and Colón, tel. 6/292-0672). For only $5 pp, you can have a private room with 24-hour hot water and TV. At the friendly **Hostal Tamia Taki** (Jaramillo 5–69 and Morales, tel./fax 6/292-0684), rates are $4 pp with shared bath, $5 pp with private bath (try to get a room on one of the upper floors, because the ground floor can be a bit noisy). The attached Café Paris gets kudos from readers. The **Residencial El Rocio** (Morales between Ricaurte and Egas, tel. 6/292-0584, $6 pp) is clean and friendly, with attractive cabins across the Pana ($10 pp) for those who want quiet and a parking space.

$10-25

I've never gone wrong with the colorful **Riviera Sucre** (Moreno 380 and Roca, tel./fax 6/292-0241), with its open courtyard and large, cozy rooms for $12 (shared) and $16 pp (private bathrooms). The managers are friendly, the showers are hot, and breakfast at the downstairs cafeteria is a good way to start the day.

The venerable **Hotel Otavalo** (Roca 504 and Juan Montalvo, tel. 6/292-0416, hotavalo@im.pro.ec, www.hotelotavalo.com.ec) offers the best midprice value at $22 s, $36 d, including breakfast. It has 30 large, simple rooms. Rooms at the **Hotel Coraza** (Calderón and Sucre, tel./fax. 6/292-1225) are especially comfortable, equipped with TVs, and go for $15 s, $30 d.

Over $25

The **Hotel El Indio Inn** (Bolívar 904, tel. 6/292-2922 or 6/292-0325, $23 s, $47 d) has in-room TVs, private parking, and a restaurant. The carefully renovated colonial **Doña Esther** (Montalvo 444 and Bolívar, tel. 6/292-0739 info@otavalohotel.com) has a lovely central patio and excellent wood oven for pizzas, the specialty of restaurant Il de Roma. Simple, spotless rooms are $22 s, $32 d.

Otavalo's most distinctive hotel is the ◖ **Ali Shungu** (Quito and Quiroga, tel. 6/292-0750, alishungu@uio.telconet.net), at the northwest corner of town. The hospitable American owners, Frank Keifer and Margaret Goodhart, employ a bevy of local women in traditional clothing who do everything from ordering you a taxi to stoking the fire in the sitting room on chilly nights. Each wall of the hotel is lined with colorful masks, dolls, and weavings, and leafy plants fill all the corners. Out back is a patio overlooking the flower garden and gift shop. The restaurant offers vegetarian and meat entrées for around $5, along with hefty sandwiches. Live Andean music entertains guests and diners on Friday nights. Rooms are $43 s, $55 d, and two apartment suites are available for two-night minimum stays ($95 d, $108 t).

There are also many excellent lodging options outside of town in this price range. For more information, try www.codeso.com/TurismoEcuador/HotelsImbabura.html.

FOOD
Near the Plaza de Ponchos
On the south side of the Plaza de Ponchos, **Café Shenandoa** has been serving home-made fruit pies and sandwiches ($2–4) for about 30 years. Next door, **Ali Allpa** offers meat and vegetarian options for $3–4. **Tabasco's Mexican Food,** with a good view of the plaza from its second-story patio, serves Mexican dishes, pizza, and pasta for $3–5.

Elsewhere in Town
Low tables, straw mats, and candles hint at the falafel, hummus, and shawarmas to come at **Sahara,** on Piedrahita behind the Palacio Municipio. A limited range of dishes go for $3–4, plenty of drinks are available, and water pipes are $2.

The **Quino Restaurant "Sabor y Arte"** is an intimate little place with art on the walls and a yellow plastic ceiling that gives it an underwater, otherworldly glow. The seafood, for about $3.50, is recommended. The best of the many *chifas* is the **Chifa Tien an Men,** which is popular with locals for its generous portions (around $2.50).

With all these tourists around, it's no surprise that pizza is one of the most popular dishes in town. The ever popular **Pizza Siciliana** (Morales and Sucre) also serves other kinds of Italian food, starting at $5 for a small pizza. It has music most nights. Try the Trucha Otavalito (trout in a seafood sauce) for $4 in the sunny open patio of **Restaurant Mi Otavalito** (Sucre and Morales).

If you're shopping for food to make your own meal, try **Salinerito,** a gourmet deli with organic fruits and vegetables, bread, honey, cheeses, and sandwiches, on Bolívar near Colón. The best *panadería* in Otavalo is on Jaramillo under the Hostal Maria.

INFORMATION AND SERVICES
There's a **tourist office** on Quiroga and Jaramillo (tel. 6/292-7230, 8:30 A.M.–1 P.M. and 2–6 P.M. Mon.–Fri., 9:30 A.M.–1 P.M. Sat.–Sun.), at the corner of the Poncho Plaza. Two good general-information websites about Otavalo are www.otavalo.com and www.otavalo-net.com.

The **Banco Pichincha** (Bolívar and García Moreno; Sucre and Quiroga) has ATMs. **Banco del Pacifico,** on the Central Plaza (Sucre and Garcia Moreno) will change travelers' checks. You can also try **VAZ money exchange** on Sucre and Colón, which handles many foreign currencies, travelers' checks, and Western Union money transfers. Some tour agencies change cash and travelers' checks as well. Many Otavaleño traders accept payment with travelers' checks. The **post office** is on the corner of Sucre and Salinas (8 A.M.–7 P.M. Mon.–Fri., 8 A.M.–1 P.M. Sat.).

Most hotels do laundry, or you can try **Lavanderia,** beside the pizzeria (Morales and Sucre). Internet cafés, as usual, have sprung up all over town. Two of the best are on Sucre, south of the Plaza de Ponchos: **C@ffé.net** and **Native c@ffé.net,** both of which charge around $1 per hour and offer food and Internet phone calls.

Spanish Lessons
The **Instituto Superior de Español** (Sucre 11–10 and Morales, tel. 6/292-2414, fax 6/292-2415, institut@superior.ecuanex.net.ec) is repeatedly recommended as having the best Spanish classes in Otavalo. One-on-one instruction ($5.75 per hour) is offered for speakers of English, German, and French, and the school can arrange home stays ($14 per day) and tours for students. Another option is the **Mundo Andino Spanish School** (Salinas 404 and Bolívar, tel./fax 6/292-1864, espanol@interactive.net.ec, www.geocities.com/mundo_andino), which offers four–seven hours of classes per day ($5 per hour) and home stays ($13 per day) with local families.

NORTHERN SIERRA

TRANSPORTATION

Otavalo's **bus terminal** is on the northeast corner of town at Atahualpa and Ordoñez. Here, you can catch buses to Quito ($2.50, 2–3 hours) and Ibarra ($0.50, 30 minutes), as well as to nearby villages such as Ilumán, Carabuela, Peguche, and Agato. You can also catch any bus heading north along the Pana and ask the driver to let you off at the appropriate intersection, then walk from there. Coming back is even easier—just flag down any bus heading south.

Taxis, which congregate at the plazas and parks, charge about $8 per hour around town and $10 per hour for more out-of-the-way locations like the Lagunas de Mojanda. Try **Taxi 31 de Octubre** (tel. 6/292-0485). **Mountain bikes** are another possibility for extended excursions. The best ones for rent are at **Primaxi** (Atahualpa and Moreno) and **Indy Aventura**

(on Salinas across from the Plaza de Ponchos). Both charge $8 per day.

LAGUNA DE SAN PABLO

The lake at the foot of Volcán Imbabura, circled by pastoral hamlets, is a beautiful sight. Legend has it that a giant living in the lake reached out and grabbed Imbabura long ago, giving it its characteristic indentations; look for the heart-shaped dark patch on the southern end.

A road surrounds the lake, perfect for a day's bike ride or drive. The bus from Otavalo marked "Araque" follows this road (catch it in front of the market on Atahualpa). The festivals of Corazas (August 19) and Los Pendoneros (October 15) are celebrated in the tiny shoreline villages, which specialize in such crafts as fireworks and woven reed mats. The walk south from Otavalo to the lake takes about an hour.

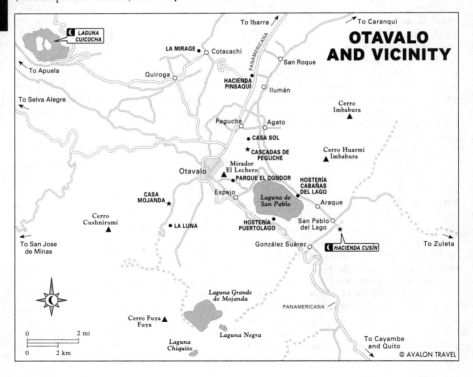

NORTHERN SIERRA

© JEAN BROWN

riding near Hacienda Cusín and Laguna de San Pablo, with Imbabura in view

◖ Hacienda Cusín

Outside the town of San Pablo del Lago is one of the most famous and luxurious country inns in South America. Built in 1602, the Hacienda Cusín (tel. 6/291-8013, fax 6/291-8003, hacienda@cusin.com.ec, www.haciendacusin.com, $98 s, $146 d) is one of the oldest in the country, named after a young local warrior who fought bravely against the Inca. Situated in a wide, scenic valley just south of Imbabura at 2,400 meters, the hacienda is a relaxing, old-world type of place where llamas and sheep graze in the shadows of avocado trees. Old stone walls topped with moss encircle two acres of gardens, which bloom continuously in the mild climate. Hummingbirds can't seem to believe their luck in the forests of bougainvillea, belladonna, orchids, and foxglove.

Twenty-five rooms are spread over seven guesthouses, all with private bathrooms and garden views. Some have bathtubs and fireplaces. Fifteen garden cottages echo the white walls and terra-cotta tile roof of the main building. This ancient edifice, decorated with colonial antiques and tapestries, houses the game room, conference room, and library graced by French windows. The outstanding restaurant seats 40 under a beamed ceiling. Food is served on carved wooden plates in front of a log fire. Horses are available to rent, and many kilometers of trails wind into the hills and fields. Rates include breakfast.

More Accommodations and Food

A billboard along the Pana points down a dirt road to the **Hostería Puertolago** (tel. 6/292-0900 or 6/292-0920, fax 6/292-0901, efernand@uio.satnet.net), on the southern shore of the lake. Meticulously mowed grounds surround a main building housing a nautical-motif bar, a restaurant, and an atrium with a wide window over the lake. Posh rooms with TV and fireplace are $73 s, $91 d. Rowboats and kayaks are available by the hour or the day, as are motorboats and paddleboats. Lake tours are $5 pp, day or night.

The comfortable **Hostería Cabañas del Lago** (tel. 6/291-8001, cablago@access.net.ec), around on the eastern lakeshore, caters to family groups and has two restaurants specializing in trout. Foot-powered paddleboats and motorboats are available for rent. Two-person cabanas with fireplaces and private baths run $73, including breakfast and tax.

LAGUNAS DE MOJANDA

Half an hour from Otavalo by car lie three moody, beautiful lagoons in the shadow of jagged mountains. The Lagunas Grande (also known as Caricocha), Negra (Huarmicocha), and Chiquita (Yanacocha) are clustered 18 kilometers up a steep, cobbled road through the *páramo*, 1,200 meters below Otavalo. Clouds play across the dark surfaces of the lakes and wrap themselves around Fuya Fuya (4,263 meters) to the west.

A taxi from Otavalo costs $8–10, depending on how far up the road you're going.

Casa Mojanda

For the price, it doesn't get much better than this: an ecologically and socially minded hotel with some of the best views from any rooms in Ecuador. A Brooklyn-Ecuadorian couple opened Casa Mojanda (tel. 9/973-1737 or 9/972-0890, mojanda@uio.telconet.net, www.casamojanda.com) in 1995. Five kilometers south of Otavalo at 9,800 feet, on the road to the Lagunas de Mojanda, the hotel clings to the edge of a valley facing Cotacachi and the Cerro Cushnirumi, one of the few undisturbed tracts of Andean cloud forest in Ecuador. All the buildings were constructed using the *tapial* (rammed-earth) process in a tasteful, simple style, with white-washed walls, wood, terraces, and hammocks.

The airy main building houses the dining and living rooms, and a separate library building is outside; a small amphitheater faces the valley. The owners provide plenty to keep their guests busy: hiking trails, mountain bikes, an outdoor hot tub with a great view, gentle riding horses, videos, and a two-seater kayak, for starters. They also oversee the nonprofit Mojanda Foundation, working for the environmental protection and social welfare of surrounding communities. Donations and requests for more information can be directed to the hotel.

Eight guest cottages cost $150 d, including breakfast and dinner, and housing in the two 10-person hostels is $60 pp for groups of four or more.

La Luna

Just up the road to the *laguna* from the Casa Mojanda is this budget *hostería* (tel. 9/315-6082), with private rooms ($13.50 pp), dorm rooms ($6 pp), and campsites ($3). The main building has a small restaurant and bar, and you can rent videos, take a four-wheel-drive tour, or just enjoy the setting and resident dogs. To get here, take the first left past the Casa Mojanda and head downhill a few hundred yards, then over the bridge. The hosts can pick you up in Otavalo for free until 6 P.M.

PEGUCHE

One of the most financially successful indigenous villages near Otavalo, Peguche (pop. around 4,000) is rapidly growing. It's home to a few *tiendas* (shops) and restaurants (more every year), as well as artisans who turn out all kinds of textiles and musical instruments. Ñanda Mañachi (tel. 6/269-0076), just a couple of blocks north of the plaza, is an interesting place to visit—they give demonstrations of making and playing many varieties of panpipes. Through open windows drift the clack of mechanical looms and music from newly made *flautas* (reed flutes) and *rondadores* (Andean panpipes).

Various homes and workshops around town specialize in rugs, blankets, tapestries, and scarves. If you're looking for fine tapestries, stop by the home/workshop of either **Jose Ruiz Perugachi** or **José Cotacachi** (ask around for directions).

Cascadas de Peguche

This small park's waterfall is perfect for cooling your feet after a day's hike. From Otavalo, the 45-minute walk begins by following the railroad tracks north out of town. Follow the road when it leaves the tracks up to the right, and look for the sign at the park entrance. A dirt road leads straight from the Pana through Peguche, passing under two white arches and the remains of an old *obraje* (colonial weaving workshop) to the sign and park entrance.

Small stands sometimes sell food at the entrance. The wooded valley has relatively clean

THE *INDÍGENAS* OF OTAVALO

Otavaleños are a special case among indigenous groups. Their unusual financial success and cultural stability have allowed them to travel and educate their children abroad, while still keeping a firm hold on their traditions at home.

Although many of Otavalo's residents are white or mestizo, more than 40,000 full-blooded Otavalo *indígenas* live in town and the surrounding villages. Their typical dress and unmistakable carriage makes Otavaleños easily recognizable. "They walk, sit, and stand with exquisite grace," wrote Ludwig Bemelmans in the early 20th century. "The men have historic, decided faces, and the women look like the patronesses at a very elegant ball." Women traditionally wear elaborately embroidered white blouses over double-layered wool skirts, white underneath and black or dark blue on top. Shawls ward off the sun, keep them warm at night, or carry their babies. Necklaces of gold metal or red beads (once coral, now usually colored glass or plastic) are worn around the neck, and their long, black hair is tied back in a single braid and wrapped in a woven *faja*.

Men also wear their long, black hair braided in a *shimba,* often to the waist. (Their hair is such an important symbol of ethnic identity that *indígenas* of any tribe aren't required to cut it off when they enter the army). Blue wool ponchos are worn in all types of weather over white calf-length pants and rope sandals. A straight-brimmed felt fedora tops it off.

The history of the Otavaleños famous weavings starts before the arrival of the Incas, when the backstrap loom had already been in use for centuries. The Incas, appreciating the fine work, collected the weavings as tribute. Specially chosen women dedicated their lives to weaving fine textiles, some of which were burned in ritual offerings to the sun. Upon their arrival, the Spanish forced the Otavaleños to labor in workshops called *obrajes*. Despite the terrible conditions, the Otavalo *indígenas* became familiar with new weaving technology and learned how to produce textiles in mass quantities.

In the early 20th century, Otavalo's weavers caught the world's attention with a popular and inexpensive imitation of fine woven cloths from Asia called *cashmir*. The 1964 Law of Agrarian Reform turned weaving into a true cottage industry, as locals were now able to weave in their own homes. Today, the clack and rattle of electric looms turning out rolls of fabric can be heard in the smallest towns. Most private homes have at least an antique, treadle-operated sewing machine or two, along with a free-standing manual loom. Many weavers, though, still go through the entire wool process by hand cutting, washing, carding, dying, and weaving wool over a period of days. Some backstrap looms are still in use; weaving a blanket on one can take over a week. Men traditionally operate the looms, either full time or after finishing the day's work in the field, while women perform the embroidery. Families start training children as young as three to weave.

Most important, Otavaleño weavers have been able to hold onto their roots while keeping their business feet firmly in the present. Otavalo's *indígenas* own most of the businesses in town, as well as many stores throughout Ecuador and in other countries in South America. They travel extensively abroad to sell their products or simply travel in the Americas, Europe, and Asia. The election of Otavalo's first indigenous mayor in 2000 shows how strong the native presence is in the Valley of Sunrise – organized indigenous strikes can bring the entire region to a standstill – and gives hope to other more downtrodden groups.

This success and visibility attracts both admiration and envy. Spend some time here, and you'll see that Otavaleños have learned to straddle the fine line between making a profit and selling out their culture, and they seem to have come out ahead for their efforts.

picnic areas in eucalyptus-scented clearings. A clear path leads under tall trees toward the falls, but the footing at the base can be tricky, especially when crossing the damp logs. Some robberies have been reported at the falls, so don't go alone or at night. Part of the $0.50 entrance fee is supposed to go toward paying guards, but they aren't always around.

Accommodations

Peguche offers a few options for those who want to stay outside of—but still near—Otavalo. Just up the hill from the entrance to the Cascada de Peguche is one of the loveliest new developments in northern Ecuador. Marcos Lema, a well-traveled, bilingual Otavaleño looking to promote a revaluation of his culture, took six years to fashion a colorful and comfortable hillside retreat called **La Casa Sol** (tel. 6/269-0500 or 2/223-0798 for the office in Quito, fax 2/222-3383, www .lacasasol.com). It opened in 2006. Prices of $37 s, $56 d include breakfast and dinner. The 10 bedrooms and two suites were built using traditional materials and methods. Balconies and terraces offer enticing views over Peguche and the Otavalo Valley, and the locally grown ingredients used for cooking, the friendly staff from the community, and the hotel's involvement in educational projects all make this a very special place.

Peguche Tío Hostería (tel./fax 6/269-0179, huillart@uio.satnet.net) calls to mind a big wooden spaceport. Inside are a dance floor, restaurant, and music, video, and book libraries specializing in local culture. The 12 rooms outside near the gardens all have hot water, fireplaces, and private bathrooms ($10 pp). Take note, though: the hotel is frequently closed, so make reservations in advance.

Straddling the railroad tracks farther into town is the **Hostal Aya Huma** (tel. 6/269-0333, fax 6/269-0164, ayahuma@ayahuma .com, www.ayahuma.com). This beautiful place opened in 1995, and it's as comfortable as they come: fireplaces, hammocks, a book exchange, Spanish classes, a vegetarian restaurant, live Andean music on Saturday nights, and a garden to die for. Hot water runs 24 hours a day, and fax and laundry services are available in the main building. Entrées in the restaurant (serving all meals) are around $5. Follow the signs through town, or ask directions. Rates run $17 s, $24 d with private bath.

AGATO

About four kilometers northeast of Otavalo is another weaving village, a few kilometers east of the Pana up the base of Imbabura, above Peguche. Artisans here are known for their traditional-style weaving and fine embroidery, and there's no better place to see them in progress than at the

La Casa Sol overlooks the dawning valley.

©JEAN BROWN

ILUMÁN'S NATIVE HEALERS

Along with its crafts, Ilumán is known for its *curanderos* (native healers), who can be hired to cure or curse. Residents have passed down knowledge of natural remedies and spiritual cures here for centuries, treating everything from back problems to cancer. In 1988, there were 85 registered faith healers in Ilumán (eight of them women), but according to locals, only a small percentage were genuine. Dozens of locals come to Ilumán daily to be cured or to hire black magic, and even a few foreigners seek the wisdom of the healers every year.

Curing rituals are a blend of ancient wisdom, folklore, and modern faith. Invocations in Quechua to Mama Cotacachi and Taita Imbabura, the old gods of the volcanoes, are sent up alongside prayers in Spanish to the Christian God and Jesus. *Curanderos* spit water or blow cigarette smoke on the patient, or rub the patient with special stones. A candle is passed over the patient's body, then lit to learn about the patient by studying the flickering flame. Cures can take the form of prayers or medicinal herbs like eucalyptus, poppies, and lemon, either rubbed on the patient's body or drunk as a tea.

Less public are the *brujos*, practitioners of the black arts. Traditionally working only at night, these wizards will cast malignant spells for jilted lovers or failing businessmen – for the right price, of course. Rumor has it that their powers extend even to murder.

workshop of master weaver **Miguel Andrango** and family (tel. 6/269-0282). You can watch the artists weaving wool on backstrap looms, while others create intricate embroidery on the finished cloth. Miguel has woven fine ponchos and blankets for 60 years and continues to teach younger weavers, who will carry on the traditions. Many of their high-quality textiles are for sale. Practically anyone in town can give you directions to the workshop, and many area tours stop by there as well. Look for a sign to the right of the Pana, just past Peguche, or ask in Peguche for the road toward Agato. There are local buses from Otavalo train station to Agato.

ILUMÁN

A little farther up the Pana from Peguche, across from the entrance to Pinsaquí, lies this small town noted for its felt hats and weavings. Follow the cobbled road uphill straight toward Imbabura, and turn right when it levels out to reach the center of town and the plaza. South of the plaza on Bolívar is a sign for Carlos Conteron's **Artesanías Inti Chumbi** workshop (tel. 6/294-6387). The couple at this workshop present backstrap-loom weaving demonstrations and sell textiles and beautiful indigenous dolls. Throughout Ilumán are workshops specializing in the colorful felt fedoras worn by the area's *indígenas*. Signs for the native healers carry the word **Yachaq.** Buses from Otavalo go straight to the town center.

HACIENDA PINSAQUÍ

An equestrian theme pervades this hacienda just north of Otavalo, on land that has been in the family of owner Pedro Freile for centuries. Pinsaquí began in 1790 as a textile workshop that supported as many as 1,000 workers at one

entrance to the lovely Hacienda Pinsaquí

© JEAN BROWN

time. Simón Bolívar was a repeat guest on his way between Ecuador and Colombia during the struggles for independence.

Horse racing and hunting trophies grace the bar area, next to pictures of fine horses. At night, the bar's fireplace roars. The 30 rooms and suites feature thick walls, canopied beds, fireplaces, and tiled floors, and some suites contain hot tubs. Across the railing from the main hall and its fountain is a 120-seat restaurant and lounge with "walk-in" fireplaces. These fireplaces are large enough to pull a bench into, similar to some older Elizabethan houses in England. Day tours on horseback will venture up the lower slopes of Imbabura. For rates and information on longer trips, contact Ride Andes in Quito.

Quito to Otavalo

LAS TOLAS DE COCHASQUÍ

Fifteen pre-Inca pyramids, built by the Caranqui in A.D. 700, gaze out from below Mojandas. By A.D. 1200, the eight-hectare site had reached its peak, with an estimated local population of 70,000. It was abandoned by the time the Spanish wrested control from the Inca, around 1533, and was rediscovered only in 1932. Three decades passed before excavations began into the earth-covered hills. Shamans still come here to absorb the site's "special energy," and festivals are held at the solstices (June 22 and December 22) and equinoxes (March 21 and September 23).

The ruins are no Chichén Itzá, but the setting itself is worth the trip. The view from 3,000 meters is spectacular—on a clear day, you might spot Cotopaxi, the Ilinizas, Antisana, and even El Panecillo in downtown Quito. The purpose of the site is still unclear, but an astronomical-observatory theory is supported by a solar calendar atop pyramid 14: Two circular platforms represent the sun and moon, and the shadows thrown by upright stones are thought to have marked the best times to plant and harvest.

One mound, found by a German excavation team in 1932, contained 400 skulls, probably

food stall in the Otavalo area

© JEAN BROWN

from ceremonial sacrifices. The relatively soft volcanic blocks of up to 200 kilograms, brought from five kilometers to the north, have been protected from the elements by the gradual accumulation of earth and grass.

Even if you're not an archaeology buff, Cochasquí (9:30 A.M.–3:30 P.M. Tues.–Sun., $3) is great for a picnic lunch in the sun. Visitors must be accompanied by a guide. Free tours leave hourly, and the guided tours (mandatory) are definitely worth a tip. An outdoor scale model of the site makes it easier to visualize, and two small museums display artifacts found nearby, as well as traditional buildings with medicinal gardens. Campsites are available uphill of the ruins, and hiking up and over to the Lagunas de Mojanda makes a gorgeous six-hour trip.

Getting There

Take a bus that travels from Quito to Otavalo by way of Tabacundo (verify this ahead of time), and have the driver drop you off at the new tollbooths beyond Guayllabamba. From the cement sign for the ruins (Pirámides de Cochasquí) it's eight kilometers up a cobbled road to the site. If you plan on walking, bring water—it can be a hot two hours uphill. Time it right, and you might be able to hitch a ride with the site's employees either up to the site in the morning or down to the Pana for a bus back to Quito in the afternoon.

Guided tours from Quito also include other local places of interest.

CAYAMBE

Nestled in a wide, shining valley, the quiet burg of Cayambe (pop. 17,000) is surrounded by the heavily cultivated pastures of old haciendas. This rich agricultural region is known for cheese, and many of the surrounding acres have been planted with ornamental flowers (see the sidebar *Flower Exports: To Russia, with Love* in the *Central Sierra* chapter). Market day is Sunday, and the traditional market plaza is several blocks up the hill from the church. Over it all looms Volcán Cayambe, whose snow-covered dome is blinding in the sunlight and

THE LANGUAGE OF THE INCAS

More people speak Quechua today than in the 16th century, when the last Inca died. Also known as *runasimi*, "the language of the people," Quechua is pronounced similarly to Spanish, with the addition of glottal stops popped in the back of the throat and indicated by apostrophes (as in *hayk'aq*, meaning "when"). The consonant "q" is exaggerated until it sounds almost like the "g" in "guitar," and "th" is aspirated toward the sound of "t" alone. The accent is always on the next-to-last syllable.

- *Ama sua, ama llulla, ama quella* – Don't steal, don't lie, don't be lazy (traditional Inca greeting)
- *Quampas hinallantaq* – To you likewise (traditional response)
- *Napaykullayki* – Greetings
- *Alli tuta manta* – Good morning
- *Alli p'unshaw* – Good afternoon
- *Alli tuta* – Good evening
- *Allichu* – Please
- *Imamanta* – What's up?/What's happening?
- *Yupay chany* – Thanks for everything
- *Alli shamuska* – You're welcome
- *Tayta/Mama* – Sir/Madam
- *Wayki* – Brother, friend (said to another man of the same age)
- *Allinllachu kanki?* – How are you?
- *Allimi* – Fine
- *Ima shuta kanki?* – What is your name?
- *Ñuca [Bill] shutimi kani* – My name is Bill
- *Maymanta shamunki?* – Where are you from?
- *Ñuca [Chicago]-mi-manta kani* – I am from Chicago
- *Allilla* – Good-bye
- *Kavakama* – See you later

NORTHERN SIERRA

seems to glow even at night. The city is a good jumping-off point for climbing Cayambe or Sararucu to the east, or for visiting the ruins at Cochasquí to the west.

The **Fiesta de San Pedro y Pablo** (Festival of Saints Peter and Paul) on June 28 and 29 is one of the most elaborate in Ecuador, because San Pedro is the patron saint of the district. During the festival, the streets are filled with indigenous groups representing their communities. There may be more roosters suspended from poles than you'd ever expect to see. This is for the *entrega de gallo* (delivery of the rooster), a reminder of a colonial tradition in which hacienda workers gave the *patrón* (owner) a ceremonial gift of a rooster every year.

Accommodations

The flashy **Hotel La Gran Colombia** (tel. 6/236-1238, $14 d) opened in 1996 on Avenida Natalia Jarrín, about half a kilometer south of the city center. Guests enjoy TV, private bathrooms, and a children's playground out back. The hotel's restaurant is popular with locals. Half a kilometer further out is the **Hostería Mitad del Mundo** (Ave. Natalia Jarrín 208, tel. 6/236-1607 or 9/984-6734, $12 s, 14 d). Along with the usual bar and restaurant, it boasts a covered pool, sauna, and steam room. The clean rooms have private baths, hot water, and TVs.

Ten kilometers south of Cayambe sits the **Hacienda Guachala** (tel. 2/236-3042, tel./fax 2/236-2426, info@guachala.com, www.guachala.com, $40 s, $54 d), a 400-year-old estate straddling the equator. The hacienda dates from 1580, when the land was bought by a Spanish colonist whose grandson eventually acquired the title for 300 ounces of silver. La Condamine's globe measurers lodged here in 1743; and two centuries later, the hacienda was inherited by Neptali Bonifaz Ascazubi, who was elected president of Ecuador but then disqualified for being of Peruvian nationality. It was opened as a hotel in 1993.

Old saddles line the entrance hallway, giving off the smell of old leather. All the buildings were built with terra-cotta tile roofs in the rammed-earth style except the church, built with brick in 1938. An underground spring feeds the sun-heated pool, which Is surrounded by vibrant flowers. Browse through hundreds of pictures from the early 20th century in the photographic museum. The 30 rooms are simple and comfortable, and horses and bicycles ($10 per hour) are available for exploring the countryside, which extends as far as a set of Inca ruins on a windy hilltop.

Getting There

The Pana passes almost directly through Cayambe, briefly becoming Avenida Natalia Jarrín before heading north to Otavalo and Ibarra. Cayambe buses leave from the new terminal in Quito at La Ofelia (see Quito's new bus routes), as do buses to Mindo and most northern, eastern, and western routes within the province of Pichincha. Just at Cayambe, the road forks, heading to the right toward Olmedo, Zuleta, and eventually Ibarra. The main branch to the left peaks at the Cajas police checkpoint before descending toward Lago San Pablo and Otavalo.

CAYAMBE-COCA ECOLOGICAL RESERVE

The second-largest Andean reserve in Ecuador spills from the snowy heights of Cayambe down the eastern face of the Cordillera Oriental. The reserve's 404,685 hectares stretch across four provinces and range in altitude 800–5,790 meters. Three major peaks and more than 80 lakes dot the incredibly varied landscape, which includes everything from alpine tundra to tropical forest. Most visitors come to climb Cayambe, but that leaves tons of natural areas to explore on foot—including a great multiday hike from the Andes down into the eastern jungle. Be sure to bring a machete and sharpening stone for the trip—and know how to use them—as the northern trails are little used. However, the southern, or Oyacachi, route is continually improved and today presents few obstacles.

Artifacts found in Cayambe-Coca evidence a prehistoric migration from the Amazon to the Andes. Today, about 600 Cofán *indígenas* live in a handful of communities near the northeastern corner of the reserver. Descendants of the Caranqui tribe inhabit the more southern, tropical part as high as Oyacachi, where their ancestors fled after a massacre at the hands of the Inca at Lago Yahuarcocha.

Volcán Cayambe

The top of Ecuador's third-highest peak (5,790 meters) is a unique and beautiful spot: It's not only the highest point in the world on the equator, but, according to some, also the farthest point from the center of the earth due to the equatorial bulge. It's also the only place in the world where temperature and latitude reach zero simultaneously.

The name for this wide, white mountain means "water of life" in Kichwa. Cayambe has the reputation of being a dangerous climb, especially since three famous Ecuadorian climbers were killed by an avalanche in 1974 on the mountain's slopes. Edward Whymper and the Carrels were the first to summit the volcano's northeast peak in 1880, but their route wasn't repeated until 1974, by Quito's San Gabriel Climbing Club.

Cayambe is recommended only for advanced climbers. The main obstacle is the ever changing network of crevasses. Climbers also face unusually high winds, strong snowstorms, and the occasional avalanche. The Bergé-Oleas-Ruales refuge (4,600 meters) offers the services of a permanent guardian, cooking stove, and hot showers for $16.50 pp per night. It's owned by the San Gabriel Climbing Club and is administered by Alta Montaña in Quito (tel. 2/225-4798). Snacks, water, soda, and beer are for sale.

The IGM 1:50,000 *Cayambe* and *Nevado Cayambe* maps cover the mountain.

Cerro Saraurcu

One of the few nonvolcanic peaks in Ecuador, Cayambe's smaller sister (4,676 meters) isn't climbed nearly as often as Cayambe. The "Corn Mountain" (from the Kichwa *sara,* meaning "corn") is also known, more ominously, as Devil Mountain in both Kichwa (Supaiurcu) and Spanish (Cerro del Diablo). Even so, it's pretty and a straightforward climb, aside from the awful approach through kilometers of boggy *pantano,* the evil cousin of the high-altitude *páramo.*

The IGM 1:50,000 *Cangahua* and *Cerro Saraurcu* maps cover the area.

Oyacachi Trail

One of the country's best hikes crosses the entire southern part of the reserve from Cayambe, by way of Cangahua and Oyacachi, to El Chaco in the Oriente. The partly cobbled trail dates back to pre-Inca times. This gorgeous trail is strenuous, with rough terrain. Due to weather, it's only easily passable November–March.

Trucks and buses leave hourly from Cayambe for Cangahua, the starting point for a full day's hike to Oyacachi. For those who just want to enjoy the semideveloped hot springs, buses leave Cayambe for Oyacachi at 8 A.M. on Saturdays and Sundays, returning at 3 P.M. There are now several small hostels in town for $10 pp.

In Oyacachi, you can camp near the hot springs across the river. Horses are available for rent as far as Cedro Grande (1–2 days) for about $10 per day, and guides can be hired for $20 per day plus food. After that, you'll probably have to pack all your supplies for yourself, because the going gets rougher and the rivers widen. Forests nearby hide red-crested cotingas, grey-breasted mountain toucans, and the shining sunbeam hummingbird.

The trail east to El Chaco follows the left side of the Río Oyacachi. You'll have to cross a few rivers along the way. Often, the "bridge" is simply a cable—locals use loops of barbed wire to slide across, but a climbing harness and pulley will also work. Wading is possible in places. You'll have to ford the Ríos Cariaco, Chaupi, and Santa María during the descent to El Chaco (horses can go only as far as the Río Cedro). From the El Chaco end, the road continues to extend toward the Santa Maria,

NORTHERN SIERRA

which is much appreciated by kayakers who enjoy paddling the lower Oyacachi river.

The IGM 1:50,000 *Oyacachi/Santa Rosa de Quijos* map covers most of the hike.

Getting There

You can enter the reserve from a few different directions. From the west, the route that climbs the Volcán Cayambe, via Juan Montalvo and the Piemonte guard post, is the most direct. Alternatively, a recently paved road leads from the town of Cayambe through Olmedo and east to the Guaybambilla guard post and the Laguna San Marcos. Here, at 3,400 meters, you'll find an interpretation center, paths, and campsites. You can also follow the road from Chota in the north through Pimampiro and Nueva America to hike to the Lago Puruanta. This beautiful lake, high in the *páramo,* is one of the unspoiled jewels of the Ecuadorian Andes.

From the east, the La Virgen guard post is a few kilometers before Papallacta by the road from Quito to Baeza. From here, the Laguna Sucos is a 45-minute hike. Beside the Papallacta springs is the newest entry leading up to the guard post in the *páramo,* on the new road that crosses the reserve to Oyacachi. Between Baeza and Lago Agrio, the El Chaco and Aguarico guard posts provide access to the more difficult and less explored eastern section of the reserve. The Volcán Reventador and the San Rafael Falls (see the *Oriente* chapter) are both found along this stretch of road.

The entrance fee to the reserve is $5 pp for foreigners.

HACIENDA ZULETA

This venerable estate (hacienda@zuleta .com, www.zuleta.com) was owned by former Ecuadorian presidents Leonidas Plaza and Galo Plaza Lasso, the latter from the 1940s until 1987. Family members still take an interest in all operations, and they may actually conduct some of the guided visits. The original farmhouse, nine kilometers north of Olmedo on the road from Cayambe, dates to 1691. It was later augmented with workshops and a chapel when the Spanish crown deeded the entire region to the Jesuits.

Zuleta is best known for the signature embroidery turned out in its handicraft shops. Inspired by crafts in Italy and Spain, Galo Plaza Lasso's wife set up the original workshop to put the local women's embroidery talents to work. The Peace Corps helped get things going in the 1960s, and today the hacienda and its environs are famous for the "Zuleteño" style, in which intricate, colorful designs are sewn onto white cloth shirts, napkins, and wall hangings. The hacienda's Galo Plaza Lasso Foundation oversees a condor rehabilitation project, as well as the women's community embroidery project.

Andean peaks loom beyond the grass fields, eucalyptus, and native forests that fill the 1,800-hectare spread. Tree-lined lanes and an enormous cobbled central plaza set the stage for home-cooked meals of organic vegetables, fresh trout, and dairy products straight from the farm. Guided tours on horseback, mountain bike, and foot can take you to indigenous villages on steep mountainsides, where endangered spectacled bears are returning. You can also check out some of the 140-plus mounds and pyramids left by the pre-Inca Caranqui tribe.

One-day to two-week horseback-riding programs are available. The Hacienda's own breed of horses (Zuleteños) are strong and well adapted to the altitude. More than 100 horses—both workhorses and fine riding animals—graze these lands. Zuleta is a working farm that employs more than 100 workers from the community, along with 20 who are learning English and specializing in tourism.

A minimum stay of two nights is recommended, and the price of $250 pp includes all meals, snacks, refreshments, farm visits, and taxes. There are discounts for longer stays and families. Reservations are necessary for the 15 comfortable guestrooms. German, French, English, and Spanish are all spoken.

Northwest of Otavalo

COTACACHI

Across the Río Ambi gorge from the Pana, Cotocachi (pop. 7,500) is said to have been created during an earthquake when Volcanes Imbabura and Cotacachi made love. The town is a smaller, quieter version of Otavalo, with leather goods instead of wool. Shops along the main streets are filled with the bags, saddles, jackets, boots, vests, and purses for which the city is known—so many that you can smell the cowhide from a block away. Just about anything that can be made out of suede or leather is available here or can be crafted to order. Quality is generally high, although it does fluctuate, and prices are reasonable (some bargaining is possible on larger purchases). The main market day is Saturday.

Thousands of people pack the streets for the **Fiesta de San Juan** (June 24), during which local men dance and drink at night in the main plaza until their wives drag them home. On the last day, though, it's the ladies' turn to carouse while their husbands watch over them.

Sights

The **Museo de las Culturas** (tel. 6/291-5945, 9 A.M.–12 P.M. and 2–5 P.M. Mon.–Fri., 2–5 P.M. Sat., 10 A.M.–2 P.M. Sun., $1) is a small but well-done museum one block off the main square on García Moreno. Set in a lovely colonial building, it houses displays on local music, festivals, arts, and more, with descriptions in English. Guided tours are available. The area around Abdón Calderón Plaza has several other restored colonial buildings worth a look.

The **crafts market,** in the Parque San Francisco at 10 de Agosto and Rocafuerte, two blocks south of Bolívar, is tiny during the week but blooms to a respectable size on Saturday and Sunday.

Accommodations and Food

For the budget-minded, the friendly folks at the **Tierra Mia** (Bolívar 12–26 and 10 de Agosto, tel. 6/291-5327) offer the best deal in the area. The hotel and its restaurant are on the second floor (enter on Bolívar), and there's private parking below. Breakfast is available, and you can use the kitchen when you want. Rooms (some with balconies) are $7 pp with private bath. Around the corner on Bolívar is the **Inti Huasi** restaurant, which specializes in trout and serves a tasty, economical *menú del día* for $2.50. It's not uncommon to find the town's mayor dining with guests at the **Leñador** (Sucre 1012 and Montalvo, tel. 6/291-5083), which caters to all tastes with huge servings of traditional fare.

Next to the museum sits the **Hostería El Mesón de las Flores** (tel. 6/291-6009, fax 6/291-5828, $72 s or d). Inside the spacious colonial building, you'll find a bright, three-story courtyard with sky-blue balustrades. Flowers spill over the edges, and old musical

© JEAN BROWN

Plaza del Sol monument at the entrance to Cotacachi

peacocks on the manicured lawns of La Mirage

© JEAN BROWN

instruments grace the walls. Notice the murals in the Imbabura coffee shop, and don't miss the cozy Pisabo bar, with its leather chairs and fireplace. All rooms have private baths and phones, and some have TVs. Breakfast is included.

Just outside of Cotacachi on 10 de Agosto is **La Mirage Garden Hotel and Spa** (tel. 6/291-5237 or 6/291-5561, fax 6/291-5065, mirage1@mirage.com.ec, www.mirage.com.ec), a 21-year-old luxury hotel designed in the style of an old hacienda. La Mirage was accepted into the prestigious Relais & Chateaux International Association in 1997, making it the only member in Ecuador and only one of seven in South America.

Five hectares of spectacular gardens, brimming with bougainvillea and exotic flowers and pollinated by eight species of hummingbirds, are all maintained by a bevy of full-time gardeners. Oriental rugs and tiled floors decorate the whitewashed buildings. As you wander the grounds, you'll come across a gym, a gift shop, a small private chapel used occasionally for weddings and baptisms, and a comfortable bar with roaring fire and large sofas. Each of the 23 palatial rooms features a high canopied bed, an antique writing desk, a fireplace, and cable TV. Outstanding hiking, biking, horseback riding, and birding are available in the surrounding countryside beneath Volcán Cotacachi. The spa has hot tubs, a steam room, a solar-heated indoor pool, staff trained in massage, aromatherapy, facials, reflexology, and a traditional shaman is available from a local community.

La Mirage's restaurant is universally excellent, and the wine selection (displayed on a converted church confessional) includes varieties from Chile, Argentina, France, and the hotel's own Perafan vineyard, the highest vineyard in the world. *Quiteños* and diplomats converge here every week to stay the night or simply enjoy a gourmet meal while watching the tame peacocks wander across the grounds.

Rooms start at $427 and sumptuous suites run up to $976, including one used by Queen Sofia of Spain. Breakfast, dinner, and taxes are all part of the package. Hotel staff all speak some English and will meet guests at the airport or at their hotel in Quito. Weekend lunches are popular, so call ahead. In the United States, make reservations through the Latin American Reservation Center (tel. 800/327-3573, fax 863/439-2659, larc1@att .net, www.larc1.com).

Transportation

Frequent buses run to Otavalo and Ibarra from the bus station at Sucre and 10 de Agosto, returning just as often. Trucks to Laguna Cuicocha cost $5, and you can arrange to have them pick you up later.

COTACACHI-CAYAPAS ECOLOGICAL RESERVE

This huge reserve northwest of Cotacachi stretches from the chill Andean *páramo* over the western edge of the Andes and well into the tropical western lowlands. In 1979, its 206,000 hectares were defined as reaching north from the Laguna Cuicocha to the old Ibarra–San Lorenzo rail line and west over the Cordillera de Toisán to the headwaters of rivers flowing into the Pacific.

Cotacachi-Cayapas is defined by water. The Ríos Bravo Grande, Agua Clara, San Miguel, and Santiago all drain the reserve's lower regions, and waterfalls like the Salto del Bravo and the Cascada de San Miguel await a few hours upstream by boat from the San Miguel guard post. The Andean part of the reserve is dotted with trout-stocked lakes, including the Lagos Yanacocha, Sucapillo, and Burrococha at the feet of Yana Urcu de Piñan (4,535 meters).

Harboring a range of rich habitats, the reserve is a naturalist's dream. It includes the southern part of the Chocó biological zone, which encompasses the region between the Andes and the coast from southwest Colombia to northwest Ecuador. With its abundance of rainfall (the reserve's rainforest can get up to five meters of precipitation a year), the Chocó is one of the most biologically diverse zones on earth. All four species of monkey that live in western Andean tropical forests swing through the trees here, including black howlers, and *nutria* (river otter) tracks often turn up on the banks of the muddy rivers. One of Ecuador's three species of tapir hides in the underbrush,

along with the occasional jaguar and ocelot. The rare Andean spectacled bear inhabits the Cordillera de Toisán and the Andean forests on the flanks of Cotacachi.

Access

From Cotacachi, a road leads west through the town of Quiroga to a park entrance gate near Laguna Cuicocha. A guard post near Lita, halfway along the route between Ibarra and San Lorenzo, offers entrance into the reserve's lower-altitude cloud forests. Boats are available from Borbón, near San Lorenzo, to travel up-river to the San Miguel guard post, where the Río San Miguel joins the Río Cayapas. From here, you can rent motorized canoes to enter the reserve's lowest regions. The entrance fee is $5 pp for foreigners.

◖ Laguna Cuicocha

This distinctive lake is one of the most visited in Ecuador, thanks to its beauty and easy access. At the foot of Volcán Cotacachi, 3,070 meters up in the Andean *páramo,* this icy crater lake is full of azure water, and silvery grebes make their homes in water so clear that you can see the caldera's steep sides plunge almost straight down into the depths.

No outlet for the lake's water has ever been found. The two islands that huddle in the center, Teodoro Wolf and Yerovi, are separated by a narrow channel known as the Canal del Ensueño (Dream Canal).

The park entrance is manned (8 A.M.–5 P.M. daily), and a **visitors center** (9 A.M.–4 P.M. daily.) overlooks the water, with exhibits on the ecology, geology, and human history of the lake. Just down the hill, the **Muelle Restaurant** on the lakeshore offers a large selection of entrées for around $3. Boat rides are available from the restaurant's dock for $1 pp.

A few hundred meters almost straight up-hill behind the Muelle is the **Restaurant El Mirador** (tel. 6/264-8039), with better views and food for $2–5, including a *plato típico* for $2.50 and a *cuy* (guinea pig) special for $6. From behind the restaurant, you might glimpse Volcanes Cayambe, Imbabura, and Fuya Fuya off in the hazy distance. Ernesto the owner is a recommended guide for climbing and back-country exploration in the area, and he rents basic rooms next to the restaurant for $7 pp with hot water. He also has some new rooms over the restaurant, with great views, for $10 pp.

From here, a lovely trail winds around the lake, with views of Cotacachi and the islands. The hike takes 4–6 hours, so bring water, sun-screen, and sturdy boots. Tour groups often come to El Mirador, and it's a good place to meet people to hike around the lake with or share a truck back to Cotacachi. Driving from Cotacachi, take a left at the park entrance gate and follow the road uphill.

Buses run regularly from Otavalo to Cotacachi and Quiroga. From Cotacachi, take a left at the last traffic light in town on 31 de Octubre, and follow the road west through the town of Quiroga to the park entrance gate near the Laguna Cuicocha. From Quiroga, you can also hire a private truck from the main plaza for about $5, or tackle the two-hour uphill hike on foot. The scenery on the way to the lake is spectacular.

Volcán Cotacachi

According to local folklore, Mama Cotacachi (a.k.a. "Mother Ti-Ti") wears a cap of snow after a visit by her lover, Taita Imbabura, dur-ing the night. The 4,939-meter climb, first done in 1880 by Edward Whymper and the Carrels, is fairly straightforward and nontech-nical, and the lower part is worth hiking even if you don't intend to reach the summit. The top can be tricky (some climbing experience and a helmet are a good idea, because of the loose rock), so climb with a partner or be sure you know what you're doing.

Yana Urcu de Piñan

This mountain is climbed much less often than Cotacachi, because the approach can take up to three days. It rises from the *páramo* in a less-visited region of the reserve near the Gualaví guard post north of the Volcán Cotacachi. One route leaves south from the Juncal bridge, where the Pana passes over the Río Chota north

of Ibarra. It can also be approached from the south near the Hacienda El Hospital. Reserve personnel at the entrance may be able to help you plan a route. The ascent itself, up the southeast ridge, is relatively simple and should take five–six hours. The hike northwest from Irunguichu (four kilometers west of Urcuquí) to the **Piñan Lakes** at the base of the moun-tain is a beautiful way to spend three or more days. For more information on hiking in this area, see the *West of Ibarra* section.

LOS CEDROS BIOLOGICAL RESERVE

The largest privately owned reserve in Ecuador is tucked against the southwestern corner of Cotacachi-Cayapas, whose southern flank and watershed it helps protect from human intru-sion. The Centro de Investigaciónes de los Bosques Tropicales (Tropical Forest Research Center) runs this remote reserve 70 kilometers from Otavalo. Founded in 1991 and named for the cedar trees once found in abundance here, Los Cedros is a small chunk of what a good third of Ecuador used to be like: humid rainforest and cloud forest covering rough mountains and deep valleys like a damp green blanket, woven by tumbling, crystalline rivers. Three river systems tie together three moun-tain ridges within the reserve, drenched by up to 3.5 meters of rain per year.

Preliminary studies have found more than 160 species of birds in the reserve, including the Andean cock-of-the-rock and the spectac-ular golden-headed quetzal. Troops of brown-headed spider monkeys, endemic to the region, share the branches with white-throated capu-chins and howler monkeys. Botanists will appreciate the 200 known species of orchids found amid ferns and palms galore. At night, huge, silent moths of every color and pattern crowd light bulbs like rush-hour commuters at subway turnstiles.

The reserve is set up primarily for research-ers and volunteers. A 100-meter canopy walk-way and lodge are available, the food has been described as "jungle gourmet," and the water comes fresh from mountain streams. The driest months, and thus the best for visits, are July and September. Research opportunities are wide open, including nature tourism and various programs on environmental and health education being developed with local communities. Contact the center (tel. 8/460-0274, jose@reservaloscedros.org) for more information. Rates are $40 per day, including all meals, and volunteers are expected to contribute $350 per month.

Reaching Los Cedros is half the adventure. Buses run from Quito to El Chontal (four hours). It's a six-hour hike from there to the reserve. Mules can be arranged for riding or hauling baggage.

INTAG CLOUD FOREST RESERVE

The Cotacachi-Cayapas reserve bends around the town of Apuela, leaving a large oxbow of land outside the border. Luckily, the Intag Cloud Forest Reserve is there to take up the slack. This 505-hectare private reserve is owned and operated by Carlos Zorilla and his wife, Sandy, and, like Los Cedros, has been opened to the public to help defray operating costs. Similarly, Intag's mission is not only to preserve the area's ecosystem, but also to bring local communities directly into the conservation picture through educational programs and projects. The reserve ranges in altitude 1,850–2,800 meters—70 percent of the acreage is primary or secondary cloud forest. Some parts receive up to 2.5 meters of precipitation during the October–May rainy season.

The bird-watching, naturally, is outstanding, offering occasional glimpses of the plate-billed mountain toucan or the white-rimmed brushfinch, as well as more than 20 species of hummingbirds. When he's available, Carlos serves as an interpretive guide. Hiking trails ranging one–five hours in length lead into primary and secondary forests; for the more casual visitor, there's a waterfall less than 10 minutes from the cabins.

Facilities at Intag include a main building with an attached dining area and library nearby. Simple but comfortable guest cabins feature sun-heated showers and solar lights. Much of the organic, vegetarian food is grown nearby in a part of the reserve dedicated to sustainable agriculture, and the coffee is roasted on the farm. The atmosphere is strictly informal, and guests are encouraged to pitch in with dish washing, milking the cows, and feeding the chickens.

To help fight the destruction of the surrounding forests, the Zorillas founded the **Organization for the Defense and Conservation of the Ecology of Intag** (DECOIN) in 1995. Through the group (tel./fax 6/264-8593, decoin@hoy.net, www.decoin.org), they've successfully organized resistance to government-funded mining projects that would have destroyed even more of the cloud forest, and they have organized a local organic coffee growers' association, as well as a province-wide environmental congress. If you'd like more information on their work or would like to make a donation, contact the group.

Staying at the reserve costs $45 pp per day. Because the number of visitors is strictly controlled, reservations are a must. The minimum group size is eight people and a two-night minimum stay is required. No walk-ins, please—remember, this is also their home.

APUELA

This isolated village, at 2,000 meters on the western edge of the Cordillera Occidental, serves as a good starting point for even more remote destinations northwest of Otavalo. The bus ride here, through the cloud forests of the western Andes, is spectacular in itself. The road to Apuela leaves to the left of the Cotacachi-Cayapas entrance gate near Laguna Cuicocha, heading up and over into the Río Intag valley. Accommodations are available in town at the inexpensive **Residencial Don Luis** (tel. 6/264-8555, $5 pp), a few blocks from the main plaza. **La Forastera** restaurant is recommended for inexpensive, tasty local dishes.

The area around Apuela just begs to be explored by foot. The clean, quiet hot springs of the **Piscinas Nangulví** operate six new triple rooms (tel. 6/264-8291, $20 pp) about seven kilometers from the town center. Accommodations are also available near the baths at the pretty **Cabañas Río Grande** (tel. 6/264-8296, $20 pp) for a cabin with private bath. Flowers surround each cabin's porch, and the restaurant is good and inexpensive. Reservations are recommended, especially on weekends. Buses from Otavalo may take you all the way to the baths—ask first—or you can catch one from Apuela bound for García Moreno.

If you'd prefer to walk, take the main road out of Apuela to the crossroads after the second bridge. Head left to the *piscinas* (one hour) or right to the **Gualimán** archaeological site (two hours). At Gualimán, you'll find pre-Inca burial mounds, a run-down pyramid, and a small museum, with breathtaking views all around. The elderly Pereira couple who take care of the site can feed and house you for $6 pp per day, if you call ahead (tel. 6/264-8588 to leave a message).

Four buses leave from Otavalo to Intag daily, passing through Apuela (three hours). Buy your ticket at least one hour before departure.

Ibarra and Vicinity

The sign at the entrance to Ibarra (pop. 153,000) calls it "The city you always come back to," and a few hours in town will show you why. The wide, clean streets are lined with the whitewashed colonial buildings, most no more than two stories tall, that give Ibarra the nickname La Ciudad Blanca (the White City). Ibarra enjoys a slow, dignified pace of life more suited to a small town than a provincial capital.

Wander the outer residential streets by day, dodging horse-drawn carts and peeking into garden courtyards of old houses, and it seems as if you have the whole city to yourself. At night, the Parque Pedro Moncayo is alive with families chatting and children playing in front of the cathedral and municipal government building. Even the climate here, at 2,225 meters, is pleasant and mild.

Ibarra was founded in 1606 under the name Villa de San Miguel de Ibarra. It served early on as the administrative center for the textile *obrajes* of the Otavalo region. In August 1868, an earthquake tore through the quiet streets, laying the city to ruin and many of its 6,000 inhabitants to rest. Passing through a decade later, Edward Whymper found most of the city, save the fragile but resilient homes of the *indígenas,* still in rubble. Today, Ibarra is home to a mixture of highland *indígenas,* especially Otavaleños, and black Ecuadorians (called "negros" or "morenos" locally) from the western lowlands and Río Chota valley. There's a lot to see in the area, making Ibarra a good home base for a week of hiking, climbing, or just daydreaming. The streets in the city center are safe to walk at night, but take care farther downtown.

© JEAN BROWN

church and plaza in Ibarra

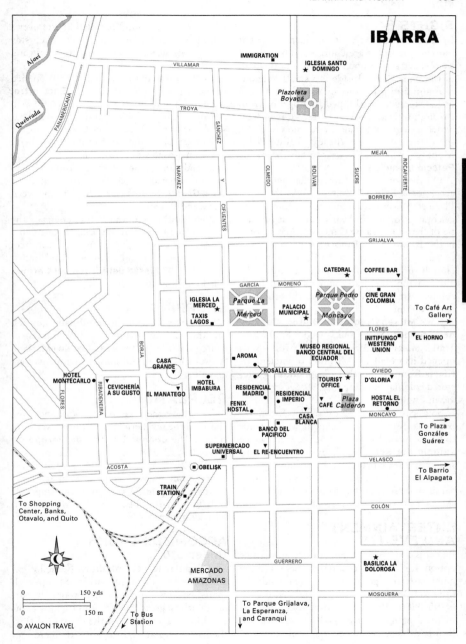

IBARRA

Ajaví

Quebrada

PANAMERICANA

VILLAMAR

IMMIGRATION

IGLESIA SANTO
★ DOMINGO

TROYA

Plazoleta
Boyacá

SANCHEZ

NARVAEZ

Y

CIFUENTES

OLMEDO

BOLIVAR

SUCRE

MEJÍA

ROCAFUERTE

BORRERO

GRIJALVA

CATEDRAL
★

COFFEE BAR

GARCÍA   MORENO

Parque Pedro

IGLESIA LA
MERCED ★

Parque La
Merced

PALACIO
MUNICIPAL
★

Moncayo

CINE GRAN
COLOMBIA

To Café Art
Gallery

TAXIS
LAGOS ■

FLORES

BORJA

CASA
GRANDE
▼

AROMA

Rosalía Suárez

MUSEO REGIONAL
BANCO CENTRAL DEL
ECUADOR

INITIPUNGO
WESTERN
UNION

EL HORNO

OVIEDO

HOTEL
MONTECARLO ●

RIBADENEIRA

CEVICHERÍA
A SU GUSTO

EL MANATEGO

HOTEL
IMBABURA

RESIDENCIAL
MADRID

RESIDENCIAL
IMPERIO ●

TOURIST
OFFICE ★

CAFÉ

D'GLORIA ▼

HOSTAL EL
RETORNO

To Plaza
Gonzáles
Suárez

FLORES

FENIX
HOSTAL ●

Plaza
Calderón

CASA
BLANCA

MONCAYO

ACOSTA

BANCO DEL
PACIFICO

SUPERMERCADO
UNIVERSAL   EL RE-ENCUENTRO

VELASCO

● OBELISK

To Barrio
El Alpagata

COLÓN

TRAIN
STATION

To Shopping
Center, Banks,
Otavalo, and Quito

GUERRERO

BASILICA LA
DOLOROSA
★

0   150 yds

MERCADO
AMAZONAS

0   150 m

MOSQUERA

To Bus
Station

To Parque Grijalava,
La Esperanza,
and Caranqui

© AVALON TRAVEL

SIGHTS

In such a placid city, it's not surprising that most of the sights are churches. The **Iglesia La Merced** stands on the west side of the park of the same name. Inside is a small religious museum and a famous image of the Virgin of La Merced, worshipped by pilgrims from throughout the province. The **cathedral,** which underwent a major restoration in 2000, shares the north side of the leafy Parque Pedro Moncayo, while to the west stands the stately **Palacio Municipal.**

On the north end of town, the drab, modern **Iglesia Santo Domingo** backs the small Plazoleta Boyacá, decorated with a monument celebrating Simón Bolívar's victory at the battle of Ibarra in nearby Caranqui. Across town is the **Basílica La Dolorosa,** at the corner of Sucre and Mosquera. Built in 1928, this church suffered a collapsed dome during the 1987 earthquake, but was reopened in 1992. A huge, ornate wooden altar fills the otherwise plain interior.

The **Museo Regional Banco Central del Ecuador** (Sucre and Oviedo, 8:30 A.M.– 1:30 P.M. and 2:30–4:30 P.M. Mon.–Sat.) opened its excellent collection of ancient artifacts from the northern highlands in a restored colonial building in 1999. Descriptions are in English.

Southeast of Ibarra on the road to Esperanza is the colorful village of Caranqui, which claims to be the birthplace of Atahualpa. Here, at the **Templo del Sol,** a small underground museum fills the plaza (9 A.M.–1 P.M. and 2–5 P.M. Tues.–Sun. $0.50), and a nearby archaeological site located three blocks behind the church shows Inca artifacts and structures.

ENTERTAINMENT AND EVENTS

Ibarra is a sleepy city, but it does have a few options for after-hours entertainment. On the quiet eastern edge of town is a real find: the **Café Art Gallery** (Salinas 543 and Oviedo, tel. 6/295-0806, from 5 P.M. Mon.–Sat.), opened by local painter Olmedo Moncayo in 1996. Browse exhibits of contemporary paintings and sculpture by local and national artists over a cappuccino or burrito, and maybe even stay for a music recital, poetry reading, or theater performance on a weekend evening.

El Re-encuentro (Olmedo 9–59) opened in the space once occupied by **El Encuentro,** formerly described as the "best little bar in northern Ecuador," with saddles instead of bar stools. It is now located on Gonzales in the Urbanization Municipal. **Baraka** (Rocafuerte between Rosales and Mosquera) has a pool table and dancing on weekends. You'll have to stop by in person to see what's showing at the **Cine Grand Columbia,** on Moreno between Sucre and Rocafuerte.

Neighboring Laguna Yahuarcocha is the focus of the **Fiesta de los Lagos,** celebrated the last weekend of September with car races around the water and an agricultural/industrial fair. The **Fiesta del Virgen del Carmen** is held on July 16.

SHOPPING

Musicians will love the handmade guitars, mandolins, and *requintos* (small guitars) of Marco Carrillo at **Guitarras Carillo** (Mariano Acosta 13–32 and Galindo). Instruments start at $100.

RECREATION

Do you have the urge to see Ibarra and a big chunk of the northern Sierra from above? If so, ring up the **Condor Escuela de Parapente** (Oviedo 913 and Sanchez y Cifuente, tel. 6/295-3297 or 6/295-1293, flyecuador@ yahoo.com, www.flyecuador.com.ec) for a tandem paragliding ride from the slopes of Imbabura ($40). The school also rents and sells equipment.

ACCOMMODATIONS
Under $10

The popular **Hotel Imbabura** (Oviedo 933 and Narváez, tel. 6/295-0155, $6 pp with shared bath) is a good bet, with roomy if spartan quarters, great showers, and friendly owners. Little caged birds in the courtyard fluff themselves up at night against the cold and sing in the morning as you eat breakfast. A few blocks away, the **Residencial Madrid** (Olmedo 857 and Oviedo, tel. 6/295-1760) is clean and friendly at $6 pp for rooms with private bath, hot water, and TV, as is the **Residencial Imperio** (Olmedo 8–62, tel. 6/295-2929) across the street. The Imperio also features a disco and costs $8 pp with private bath, TV, and hot water in the morning and evening.

You can enjoy the view from the terrace of the pleasant **Hostal El Retorno** (Pedro Moncayo 4–32 and Sucre, tel. 6/295-7722) for $8 pp with TV and private bath. It's at the mouth of the alley between Sucre and Rocafuerte. The pink and yellow **Fenix Hostal** (Pedro Moncayo 7–44, tel. 6/295-3993), is a good deal with a covered parking garage, cable TV, and restaurant for $8 pp.

Over $10

Probably the nicest place in Ibarra for the money is the **Hotel Montecarlo** (Rivadeneira 5–61 and Oviedo, tel. 6/295-8266, fax 6/295-8182, $18 s, $32 d). The small pool, hot tub, sauna, and steam room are open to the public (7:30–9 P.M. Wed.–Fri., 10 A.M.–9 P.M. Sat., 10 A.M.–10 P.M. Sun., $3.50 pp). Rooms include cable TV and phone. A few hundred meters down the Pana is the **Hotel Ajavi** (Mariano Acosta 16–38, tel. 6/295-5221, fax 6/295-5640, $59 s, $76 d). Rate includes breakfast, and midweek 25 percent discounts are available. Luxurious amenities include a pool, a sauna, a gym, and private parking.

Several high-quality hotels can be found among the estates and flower farms just south of Ibarra along the Pana. The magnificent **◖ Hostería Chorlaví** (tel. 6/293-2222 or 6/295-5777, fax 6/293-2224, ventas@haciendachorlavi.com, $45 s, $50 d) sits four kilometers south along the Pana. It's been owned by the Tobar family for 150 years, since the days when the *hostería* commanded farmlands stretching to the slopes of Imbabura, and was opened to tourists in 1972. The name supposedly translates as "nest of love lulled by the waters of the yellow river," but with a pool, sauna, tennis and squash courts, cockfighting

ring, and a soccer field to keep you busy, you might not have time left for anything else. On weekends, services are held in the tiny church, and folkloric music and dance performances are offered on Saturday and Sunday afternoons. Antique art and furniture adorn the 52 rooms, some of which sport fireplaces. An excellent restaurant serves organic vegetables grown in the gardens smack in the middle of the grounds. Evening cocktails are served next door at the **Taberna Los Monjes** (Monks Tavern, 6 P.M.–midnight Thurs.–Sat.).

Down the same cobbled road west of the Pana is the **Rancho Carolina** (tel. 6/293-2444, ranchoc@andinanet.net, $23 s, $34 d). They seem to be going for the Hacienda Minimalist style here, with dark wood railings contrasting with the thick, whitewashed walls. The dining room surrounds a pretty covered courtyard with a fountain. All food—including the rabbits—is grown on the premises. Seventeen rooms decorated with plants and antiques surround the pool and whirlpool.

Finally, six kilometers south of Ibarra near the village of Bellavista is the **Hostería Natabuela** (tel. 6/293-2032, tel./fax 6/293-2482, $30 s, $37 d), more a classy hotel than an antique hacienda. Neatly trimmed hedges and flowers line the brick paths between the 19 rooms, pool, sauna, steam room, and gym. Take time to venture down country lanes (ask directions to the Paso de los Incas, a nearby fragment of Inca highway), but leave time to enjoy the folkloric music on Sunday afternoons. Rooms come with TV, phone, private bath, and fireplace.

FOOD

Ibarra definitely has a sweet tooth. Besides its *helados de paila,* Ibarra is known for its *arrope de mora* (a blackberry syrup) and *nogadas* (nougat candies). Numerous shops selling these and other sweets crowd the southeast corner of Parque La Merced. Several *chifas* and small restaurants line Olmedo south of the park, enough so you can dine at a different one every night for a week.

HELADOS DE PAILA

Ibarra's most delicious product is its famous *helados de paila*. A type of sherbet (*helado* means iced), these treats are made by hand in a *paila*, which looks like a big copper wok. Ice, sugar, and fruit – the only ingredients – are mixed by hand with a large wooden paddle. Salt sprinkled on the ice under the *paila* keeps the mixture from freezing solid. The result is a delectable treat, as close to pure frozen fruit as you can get.

The process of making *helados de paila*, begun by Rosalía Suárez in her kitchen in 1896, has been carried on virtually unchanged by her descendants since her death at age 105. The *heladería* (ice cream shop) on the south side of Olmedo at Oviedo is run by Rosalía's daughter, and one run by her grandson is across the street. Now *helados de paila* are sold everywhere, but only Rosalía's are the real thing. A branch of Rosalía's Helados serves Quiteños on Los Shyris, across from Carolina Park.

For starters, the **Rico Donut Pastry Shop** has great fresh doughnuts and cakes. **El Horno** (Rocafuerte 6–38 and Flores) makes a good pizza. At the **Cevichería A Su Gusto,** or any of the other cevicherías on Oviedo and Rivadeneira, they'll whip up a shrimp, clam, or oyster ceviche to your taste for $4 a bowl. The **Casa Blanca Restaurant** (Bolívar and Moncayo) serves a good *menú del día* ($3) in the open courtyard of an old colonial house. It's a good choice for breakfast, too. **D'Gloria** on Oviedo and Sucre is popular with Ibarreños for lunch and dinner. **El Mantego,** on the corner of Oviedo and Narvaez, does a roaring trade in lunches during the week. **Caribou Bar and Grill,** a favorite with Ibarrens, is on Guerrero 5–37 and Sucre.

To buy your own food, head to the covered **Mercado Amazonas,** near the railway station, or the **Supermercado Universal,** within a few blocks. The new shopping center on the road south to Otavalo has large supermarkets, coffee shops, restaurants, and much more. You can find *cuyes* at the Amazonas market, but for the best in the area, you'll have to go five kilometers west to the town of San José de Chaltura, where a whole little squeaker costs $8, cooked to order.

INFORMATION AND SERVICES

There's a helpful **municipal tourist office** (tel. 6/295-5051, 9 A.M.–noon and 3–6 P.M. Mon.–Fri., 9 A.M.–noon Sat.) in the Plaza Calderón.

A **post office** is way to the east on Salinas, one block from the Iglesia San Francisco and the Plaza González Suárez. Keep trudging north for the **immigration office,** on Villamar next to the Iglesia Santo Domingo. Internet cafés abound.

A set of public showers called the **Baños Amazonas** on Sucre is open 6 A.M.–6 P.M. daily ($0.40 pp), but for a real treat, try the facilities of the Hotel Montecarlo, which are open to the public.

The **Banco del Pacífico,** on Olmedo and Moncayo, changes travelers' checks. You can have money wired to you via **Western Union.**

Blanca Vaca Rosero (tel. 6/264-1408) has been repeatedly recommended for excellent Spanish lessons ($5 per hour). She can be contacted through the Hotel Imbabura.

TRANSPORTATION

A taxi is one of the best ways to see the area and costs about $5 per hour or $25 per day. **Taxis Lagos de Ibarra** (Flores 9–24 and Cifuentes, tel. 6/295-5150) can be hired for local tours and run shared services all the way to Otavalo and Quito. A ride to the capital will cost you $8 and takes a fraction as long as the bus.

Midway between Quito and the border, Ibarra is a travel hub of the northern Sierra. All buses now leave from the new bus terminal south of the *mercado.* **Cooperativa**

Trans Espejo runs buses to El Angel at 30 minutes past every hour ($1, one hour); and **Cooperativa Cotacachi** sends buses to Cotacachi every 15 minutes from morning to night ($0.30, 30 minutes). **Transportes Valle de Chota** runs one daily bus via Julio Andrade and La Bonita directly to Lago Agrio ($7, six–seven hours). **Aerotaxi Andina** drives to Quito four times per hour ($3, two–four hours), as well as Esmeraldas, Guayaquil, and Santo Domingo. Other companies go to Tulcán ($2.50, three hours) and San Lorenzo ($3–4, four hours), and CITA operates a direct route to Ambato that bypasses Quito—the quick way to get south. Buses to San Antonio de Ibarra leave regularly from the obelisk for the 15-minute journey.

SOUTH OF IBARRA
San Antonio de Ibarra

On an early-morning walk through this town, known for its wood carvers, you'll hear wooden mallets striking chisels, smell fresh cedar shavings, and glimpse bands of sunlight slanting through clouds of sawdust. The back streets and main plaza are lined with workshops, which are often just the artists' empty living rooms, where they hew, plane, and sand blocks of cedar and *naranjillo* wood.

Pieces range from artistic (copies of Michelangelo's *David* and the *Venus de Milo*) to religious (saints, crucifixes, angels) to frivolous (cute animals and busty nudes). The abstract works are often the most attractive. Some of the sculptures of people, especially saints destined for religious processions, have ingeniously articulated limbs. Many pieces are painted or varnished; carved furniture, frames, and utensils round out the selection. Prices range from $1 into the hundred of dollars.

The main plaza has the largest stores, including one with interesting abstract stone sculptures. The gallery of **Luis Potosí** (tel. 6/293-2056) is the most famous, with a selection of beautiful and expensive carvings.

Buses to San Antonio de Ibarra leave from the obelisk in Ibarra ($0.25, 15 minutes). If your bus lets you out on the Pana, follow the street uphill to the east to the town's main plaza.

La Esperanza and Imbabura

Many Ibarrans relocated to this pretty town (officially called La Esperanza de Ibarra), nine kilometers south of Ibarra, after the 1868 quake. In the hopes of avoiding future catastrophes, La Esperanza's new residents dedicated their town to Santa Marianita, the patron saint of earthquakes. At 2,505 meters, La Esperanza sits at the foot of **Volcán Imbabura** (4,609 meters), making it a good departure point for climbs of the volcano or its smaller sibling, **Cubilche** (3,802 meters). "Taita" (Father) Imbabura is still a very real figure to the local *indígenas,* who ask his blessing for an abundant harvest from the crops planted on his flanks (when it's raining on the valley, it's said to be Imbabura relieving himself). No one is sure when the first ascent was made, but local *indígenas* used to climb the mountain to collect ice to sell in Ibarra.

The climb up Cubilche takes about four hours from La Esperanza, and you can descend

The Caranqui Museum is on the way to La Esperanza.

NORTHERN SIERRA

the other side to Lago San Pablo in another three hours or retrace your steps. Watch the deep, matted grass in the valley between Cubilche and Imbabura on the way down; it can be a hassle to wade through. Climbing Imbabura is a bit more of an undertaking, but it's still possible to reach the summit and get back in one long day with no special equipment. Plan on leaving at or before dawn and taking a solid 8–10 hours round-trip from La Esperanza. The IGM 1:50,000 *San Pablo del Lago* map covers the mountain, although it's not crucial for the climb.

A **day hike** around the base of Imbabura is another option, best done clockwise starting from La Esperanza. Along the way, you'll pass cows grazing and children waving from fields of grass, all in the mountain's shadow, until Lago San Pablo comes into view around the corner. To fully enjoy it, plan on a full day with an early start.

Señora Aida Buitrón has run the rustic, tranquil **Casa Aida** (tel. 6/266-0221) for more than three decades. She'll reminisce about visits from Bob Dylan and Joan Baez in the '70s, when the famous musicians used to search for magic mushrooms in the fields after rains. Hot bread and *huevos criollos* start the day, and tasty vegetarian meals are $2.50. The guesthouse is on the main (really, only) road in town and costs $5 per bed, with hot showers, a garden, and plenty of pets.

Cooperativa La Esperanza buses run from the Parque Germán Grijalva in Ibarra, on Mosquera five blocks south of the obelisk on Sánchez y Cifuentes ($0.50, 30 minutes). Taxis to La Esperanza cost $5.

LAGUNA YAHUARCOCHA

Northeast of Ibarra, Yahuarcocha takes its name (Blood Lake) from the legend that its waters turned red when the Incas slaughtered thousands of local chieftains in the 15th century for daring to side with the Spanish invaders. Despite its gruesome moniker, Yahuarcocha is quite pretty, surrounded by mountains and lined by *tortora* reeds, which are woven into *esteras* (mats) and Titicaca-style canoes. The

wide road encircling the lake is used for annual car races and by local teens learning to drive (usually not simultaneously). On weekends, it's lined with vendors selling lake trout, and at a few places near the entrance from the Pana, you can rent rowboats for $2 an hour. Birders should keep an eye out for many waterbirds near the shore.

To get here, head north from Ibarra along the Pana to the large sign announcing the lake turnoff to the right. Alternatively, you can turn right slightly earlier onto a dirt road that leads up to a hilltop with a beautiful view of Ibarra and the lake. Pass the small disco and bar, and descend the other side to the lakeside pueblo of **San Miguel de Yahuarcocha**, known locally for its *curanderos* (faith healers) and *brujos* (witches). Buses run to Yahuarcocha every few minutes from the market in Ibarra at Guerrero and Sanchez y Cifuentes.

Accommodations and Food

Overlooking Yahuarcocha is the **Hotel El Conquistador** (tel. 6/295-3985, fax 6/264-0780), with a large restaurant and an expensive discotheque. Rooms with TV and private bath are cheap at $20 s, $40 d. Next door is the newer, slightly nicer **Hotel Imperio Del Sol** (tel. 6/295-9794 or 6/295-9795, fax 6/295-9796, $43 s or d), which includes breakfast with similar rooms and facilities. You'll pass the **Hostería El Prado** (tel./fax 6/295-9570 or 6/264-3460, $37 s, $55 d) on the Pana just before arriving at the entrance to the lake. It's a pleasant country hotel with an indoor pool, sauna, steam room, mini-zoo, and restaurant. Ten huge rooms have phones, color TVs, and private baths, and laundry service is available. Rates include an American breakfast.

WEST OF IBARRA
Piñan Lakes Hike

Ibarra is a good starting point for the southeastern portion of the Cotacachi-Cayapas Reserve. Transportes Urcuquí buses from the terminal in Ibarra head west every half hour via **Urcuquí** (one basic hotel) to **Irunguicho** ("Irubincho" on the 1:250,000 *Ibarra* map), four kilometers away. Irunguicho is the departure point for the lovely loop hike to the numerous **Lagunas de Piñan** at the base of Yana Urcu de Piñan. (The Laguna Doñoso, farther to the west near the hamlet of Piñan, actually has a more official claim to the title of Laguna Piñan; but for clarity, I'll refer to it as Doñoso and the lakes around Yana Urcu as the Lagunas de Piñan.)

A clear, steep path leaves from Irunguicho to the north-northwest. At Cerro Churuloma, one hour away, you'll find campsites and the last available water until the lakes. Heading west, you'll pass Cerro Hugo (4,010 meters), with beautiful views of Cayambe, Cotopaxi, and Cotacachi, followed by Cerro Albuqui (4,062 meters). Five to six hours from Irunguicho lies Lago Yanacocha, the first of this cluster of tiny *páramo* jewels.

Lago Yanacocha is just east of Yana Urcu and mirrored by Lago Sucapillo to the west. To the south is the larger Lago Burrococha, with a good campsite to the south. To reach it from Yanacocha, climb the ridge to the south, then head west-southwest past some small ponds until you hit a trail heading west. Many other small lakes and ponds dot the landscape. It's possible to continue from here another 12 kilometers west to the larger and more remote **Laguna Doñoso.**

The hike out winds south, then east, joining with a dirt road. The last two hours of the six-hour walk are on a cobbled road, leading to **Otavalillo** and the Hacienda El Hospital. From there, it's one more hour uphill to Irunguicho, three kilometers north, where you can catch a ride back to Urcuquí or Ibarra. The IGM 1:50,000 *Imantag* map is sufficient, but the 1:25,000 *Cerro Yana Urcu* provides more detail. Take a compass regardless.

Chachimbiro Hot Springs

These mineral-water pools, 42 kilometers northwest of Ibarra, are run by a local foundation dedicated to encouraging sustainable development and environmental education in

© JEAN BROWN

Hosteria Pantavi is a lovely country hotel.

the area. Surrounded by trails and organic gardens, the pools range from cool to scalding and are used by locals to treat a range of illnesses. There's also a steam bath and sauna.

A daily bus leaves from the terminal at 7 A.M. and takes two hours to reach the pools. You can also hire a taxi for $10 each way from Ibarra (one hour), but be warned that the road deteriorates seriously for the final third of the ride, so your driver must (and, granted, probably will) have nerves of steel. Taxi drivers will often wait to take you home. Entrance is $1 pp, and you can spend the night in a cabin ($8–18 pp). The place is often packed on weekends, when the open restaurant at the springs is open. Lodging, three meals a day, and full use of the facilities (including horses) is $25 pp. A few hundred meters down the hill from Tumbabiro and 7 kilometers from Chachimbiro is the attractive **Hosteria Pantavi** (tel. 6/293-4185, www.hoteriapantavi.com, $36 s, $47 d), built on the foundations of the old San Clemente hacienda. There are attractive rooms, mature gardens, and a swimming pool, with plans for a sauna and vapor rooms, and the restaurant and bar are filled with artwork. Prices include breakfast.

IBARRA TO THE COAST

The once famous train ride to San Lorenzo, in the mangroves near the Colombian frontier, has been out of service for years owing to landslides and a much faster road to the northern beaches. However, the first part of the route to "Primer Paso" now functions on a daily basis (tel. 6/295-0390). The single carriage has limited seating and leaves at 8 A.M., so get there early to get a ticket especially weekends.

Traveling from Ibarra to the beach is considered a four–five hour journey, and many buses ply this spectacular route daily. New destinations are opening in the forests on the way. The Siete Cascadas near Lita lives up to its name, offering accommodations ($10 pp) or simply a lunch stop with time to hike and explore the set waterfalls set in luxurious vegetation.

Guallupe

Also known as La Carolina or Limonal, Gallupe is on the new road to the coast from the Chota valley. Many buses stop here for lunch, and there are several small food stands and a couple of pleasant hostels with pools. Consider renting a bike in Ibarra and taking it on the bus or train to Salinas, then riding downhill to Guallupe for an overnight stay, return by bus the next day. There is also access from here to the Hacienda Primavera Wilderness Ecolodge in the cloud forests. The price of $83 pp includes full board, horse rides, pool, and comfortable accommodations.

Bospas Fruit Forest Farm

Belgian Piet Sabbe manages a tropical farm (tel. 6/264-8692, bospasforest@gardener.com, www.ecuativer.com/bospas) near Limonal in the Mira Valley, 1.5 hours northwest of Ibarra on the road to San Lorenzo. The farm is an ongoing experiment in sustainable organic farming, and its staff constantly experiments with crop diversification, agroforestry, and permaculture techniques. Traditional crops such as beans, yucca, and corn are grown among fruit trees that provide shade, timber, water conservation, and soil anchoring, aided by vetiver grass planted in contour lines on the slopes.

Three private rooms in a stone guesthouse surrounded by forest gardens are available for travelers for $10 d per night, complete with private bath and porches with hammocks. Dorm rooms ($6 pp) and campsites ($3 pp) are also available. Piet's wife, Olda Gabriela, is an excellent cook and serves three meals a day. Hiking and horseback rides in the surrounding mountains can be arranged, and a four-day tour of the northern highlands' many distinct ecological regions can be arranged for $32–71 per day per person, depending on the size of the group.

Guests are encouraged to learn about tropical farming techniques, and the farm accepts interns and volunteers interested in learning about sustainable farming practices. Volunteers are asked to contribute $190 per month for room and board or $15 per day for shorter stays (minimum five days).

Cerro Golondrinas

Northwest of Ibarra, this small cloud-forest reserve protects a wide range of habitats, from *páramo* at 4,000 meters to premontane forest below 1,500 meters. Birders stand a good chance of adding to their life lists here: 210 species of birds have been recorded near Cerro Golondrinas peak (3,120 meters), along with condors in the mountains and toucans and parrots at lower elevations. Sloths, monkeys, and coatimundis hide in the lower forests, and foxes and deer inhabit the *páramo*.

You can enter the reserve from the bottom via the village of Guallupe, which is near La Carolina on the road to San Lorenzo, or from the top by way of the town of El Angel. One of the best ways to see the reserve is to go on the four-day trek organized by the **Fundación Golondrinas.** This moderately strenuous journey takes you by foot and horse from the *páramo* in El Angel down to the cloud forest and Guallupe ($250 pp, $220 pp for groups of five–eight).

It's possible to do the trek on your own. Independent travelers can stay in the foundation's **El Tolondro** hostel in Guallupe (tel. 6/264-8679), which costs $18 pp per night, including all meals. To get there, ask to be let off the Ibarra–San Lorenzo bus in Guallupe (48 kilometers from Ibarra), then walk 10 minutes uphill, following the signs. During the trek, you can also stay at the foundation's **El Corazón Cloudforest Lodge,** at 2,200 meters in the heart of the reserve. It takes four hours to get there (local guides and horses can be arranged at the foundation's office in Guallupe), and it's a bit spartan, with only four bunk beds, an outhouse, and a fire for cooking—but for $5 pp per night ($15 with all meals), the incredible views from the ridge top are a steal.

Also along the trek route, the inhabitants of the village of **Moran** on the edge of the *páramo* (access from El Angel) run the **Cabana de Moran** for $10 pp with all meals, plus the $2 pp entrance fee. For reservations, contact Fernando Calderón, the driver of the local milk truck. If you're pressed for time, the foundation also offers two-day visits to the lower reaches of the reserve from Guallupe for $120 pp.

In addition to managing the reserve, the foundation is deeply involved in local conservation and education issues. It draws inspiration from its founder, Maria Eliza Manteca Oñate, who won a Rolex Award for Enterprise in 2000 for her efforts in promoting sustainable farming techniques in the Andes. The foundation's main goal is to protect the forest from lumber interests and encroachment by settlers. They administer conservation, environmental education, and agroforestry programs in local communities, along with demonstration farms. The foundation accepts visiting scientists, as well as short- and long-term **volunteers.** The latter need some experience in horticulture or permaculture techniques and should have a solid grasp of Spanish. Contributions of $240 pp per month are requested for stays of at least one month, in exchange for room and board. You can contact the foundation at manteca@uio .satnet.net or www.fundaciongolondrinas.org.

IBARRA TO TULCÁN

North of Ibarra, the Pana follows the Río Chota upstream and soon splits in the village of Mascarilla, giving you a choice of routes to reach Tulcán. The older, rougher route heads north through Mira and up into the wilds of El Angel. The newer, southern route is far more trafficked (including countless cargo trucks) and passes through Chota, Bolívar, and San Gabriel. Once you leave the hot, dry Río Chota valley, both routes wind through cloud forest–covered mountains sparkling with lakes, waterfalls, and rivers.

Mascarilla

The friendly inhabitants of this small village, just a short walk from the Pana, will be happy to show you their handicrafts projects, which include making beautiful, expressive pottery masks and bowls, as well as paper recycling. They have a small store opposite the tiny, clean hostel. Accommodations run $6–10 pp ($10 per day includes breakfast and dinner).

El Angel

By the time your bus finally chugs all the way up to El Angel (pop. 6,000), the town's motto—"Paradise Closer to the Sky"—doesn't seem so far from the truth. It definitely feels like you're up on top of something here at 3,000 meters. The clouds are closer and the air a bit thinner. There's even a street called Río Frío (Cold River). Most travelers come here to visit the Reserva El Angel to the north, even higher in the bright, cold *páramo*.

The rough topiary works in the **Parque Libertad** were begun by José Franco, the father of Tulcán's famous topiary cemetery. A small collection of pottery is displayed in the **Museo Arqueológico Municipal** in the municipal building.

The **Hostería El Angel** (tel. 6/297-7584 or 2/222-1489, rsommer@uio.satnet.net), right at the turnoff, is easily the nicest lodging in town. Eight rooms are surrounded by flowers, and facilities include a living room with fireplace, a cafeteria, laundry service, and—bless them—hot water. Private rooms go for $25 s, $37 d with private bath, and shared rooms are $15 pp (all prices include breakfast). The owners offer tours of the *páramo* by foot, mountain bike, horse, or car.

The best of the handful of restaurants in town is the **Asadero Los Faroles,** on the Parque Libertad, which serves a full meal of chicken, french fries, and soda for less than $3. For cheap meals and grocery shopping, the **Mercado Central** is on Salinas 9–74, next to the Ministerio del Ambiente (INEFAN) office. The Monday market fills the surrounding streets.

For information on the El Angel reserve, stop by the office (Salinas 9–32, tel. 6/297-7597), inside the small courtyard and on the second floor.

Cooperative Trans Espejo (tel. 6/297-7216) has an office on the Parque Libertad. Buses run to and from Quito ($4, four hours), Ibarra ($2, two hours), and Tulcán ($2, two hours). If you miss the last bus of the day, hitch a ride or hire a taxi to take you to the Pana at Bolívar, where it's easy to flag down a bus passing in either direction.

El Angel Ecological Reserve

High above the town of the same name is Ecuador's premier *páramo* reserve. Created in 1992, El Angel reserve ranges 3,650–4,770 meters across some of the most pristine high-altitude country in Ecuador. Throughout the reserve's 15,700 hectares, you'll see the spiky heads of the giant *frailejón* plant for which El Angel is famous. Locals use it for various curative purposes, including relief of rheumatism—crush a piece of leaf to release the medicinal turpentine smell. Sharing the plant's fuzzy green leaves, but without the tall stem, is the *orejas de conejo* (rabbit ears). Andean and torrent ducks swim in the streams flowing between lakes stocked with rainbow trout. Hawks and the occasional condor soar on the thermals over the heads of grazing deer.

It is possible (and highly recommended) to camp out here, but be prepared for serious weather. Temperatures in El Angel can drop below freezing, and 1.5 meters of rain per year is not uncommon. Wherever in the reserve you go, take care with the fragile vegetation—a misplaced footprint can last for months. The best season to visit is during the relatively dry season of May–October, when high winds and intense daylight sun alternate with clouds, drizzle, and nightly chill. The November–April wet season is marked by mud and more precipitation, including snow. Admission is $10 pp.

From the town of El Angel, hire a taxi or jeep or hike north through La Libertad into the reserve. This dirt road leads to the crystalline Laguna Crespo, near the Cerro El Pelado (4,149 meters). To the west are the Colorado guard post, the Cerro Negro (3,674 meters), and the Laguna Negra.

An alternative entrance route is along the old road to Tulcán, past the guard post at La Esperanza. Look for a parking area 16 kilometers from El Angel. A 45-minute trail leads from here to the striking Lagunas Voladero and Potrerillos. The road from Tufiño to Maldonado traverses the northern part of the reserve, skirting Volcán Chiles and the Lagunas Verdes.

For more information on the reserve and how to get there, visit the office in El Angel. **Gerardo Miguel Quelal** has been recommended as a guide, and **Fernando Calderón** as a jeep driver.

Bolívar

Several years ago, visiting scientists uncovered a trove of Mammoth bones just a kilometer out of town. The collection has been cleaned and now awaits the completion of a new museum in which to be housed. Meanwhile—next to the museum's future location—a 3-D mural with freestanding sculptures forming a small plaza at the northern entrance to the village has been executed in gory color and detail.

Gruta La Paz

One of the most famous icons of Ecuador's northern Sierra sits in a natural cave just north of Bolívar. The Gruta La Paz (Peace Grotto), also called Rumichaca, contains a chapel dedicated to the Virgen de Nuestra Señora de la Paz and is dwarfed by a huge, natural stone overhang. Stalactites and stalagmites lend the site a gothic atmosphere that is amplified by the fluttering bats and dark waters of the Río Apaquí. In addition to the subterranean chapel, attractions include a set of thermal baths (open Wed.–Sun.) just outside the cave. There's also an inexpensive guesthouse for pilgrims, who fill the cave on weekends and holidays, especially during Christmas, Holy Week, and the **Fiesta del Virgen de la Paz** on July 8. At other times, you can have the bat-filled cavern almost completely to yourself. Private buses can be hired from Bolívar or San Gabriel, and trucks carrying groups leave from San Gabriel and Tulcán on weekends.

Tulcán and the Colombian Border

Tulcán, the highest provincial capital in the country (3,000 meters), seems like an old shopping mall someone stuck up on a chilly shelf and forgot about. A wintry cold descends at night and lingers well into the morning, making it feel a lot further than 125 kilometers from the springtime mildness of Ibarra. Tulcán (pop. 47,000) isn't the prettiest place, but the amazing topiary gardens in the municipal cemetery can easily occupy an afternoon. Throughout the city, no hedge is left unshaped both in parks and on military bases. For visitors with more time, the high *páramo* road west through Tufiño and Maldonado is unique in Ecuador.

Approximately six kilometers from Colombia, Tulcán bustles as only a border town can. You can buy anything here, from shoes and leather jackets to toasters and chainsaws. It's also shifty, as only a border town can be—without something to buy or sell, you might feel somewhat out of place, and you should take care walking around at night. Since the introduction of the dollar, more Ecuadorians have started crossing over into Colombia for shopping deals than vice versa.

SIGHTS
◖ Tulcán's Municipal Cemetery

Local resident José Franco started the famous topiary works in Tulcán's municipal cemetery decades ago. Today, Franco is buried amid the splendor of his creations in the Escultura en Verde del Campo Santo (Sculpture in Green of the Holy Field), under an epitaph that calls his creation "a cemetery so beautiful, it invites one to die." Monumental cypresses have been trained and trimmed into figures out of Roman, Greek, Inca, and Aztec mythology, interspersed with arches, passageways, and intriguing geometric shapes. The cemetery has become such a tourist attraction that vendors sell film and ice cream outside the gates. Needless to say, exercise discretion if a burial procession is in progress.

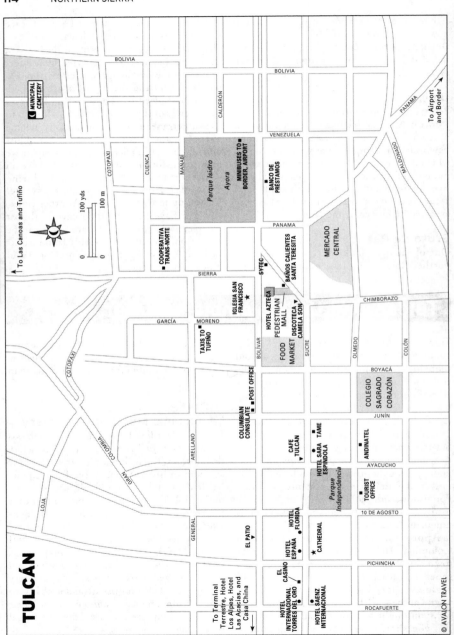

TULCÁN

MUNICIPAL CEMETERY

BOLIVIA

BOLIVIA

CALDERÓN

VENEZUELA

↑ To Las Canoas and Tufiño

To Terminal
Terrestre, Hotel
Los Alpes, Hotel
Las Acacias, and
Casa China
↓

COTOPAXI

CUENCA

MANABÍ

Parque Isidro
Ayora

MINIBUSES TO
BORDER, AIRPORT

BANCO DE
PRÉSTAMOS

To Airport
and Border →

PANAMA

MALDONADO

PANAMA

MERCADO
CENTRAL

0   100 yds
0   100 m

COOPERATIVA
TRANS-NORTE

SIERRA

IGLESIA SAN
FRANCISCO ★

SYTEC

BAÑOS CALIENTES
SANTA TERESITA

CHIMBORAZO

GARCÍA

MORENO

HOTEL AZTECA
PEDESTRIAN
MALL
DISCOTECA
CAMELA SON

OLMEDO

COLÓN

TAXIS TO
TUFIÑO

FOOD
MARKET

BOLÍVAR

SUCRE

BOYACÁ

COLEGIO
SAGRADO
CORAZÓN

COTOPAXI

POST OFFICE

COLUMBIAN
CONSULATE

JUNÍN

ARELLANO

CAFÉ
TULCÁN

HOTEL SARA
ESPÍNDOLA

TAME

ANDINATEL

AYACUCHO

GRAN COLOMBIA

Parque
Independencia

TOURIST
OFFICE

10 DE AGOSTO

LOJA

GENERAL

EL PATIO

HOTEL
FLORIDA

HOTEL
ESPAÑA

CATHEDRAL ★

PICHINCHA

EL
CASINO

HOTEL
INTERNACIONAL
TORRES DEL ORO

HOTEL SÁENZ
INTERNACIONAL

ROCAFUERTE

© AVALON TRAVEL

ENTERTAINMENT AND EVENTS

There are dance clubs all over town—one of the more popular is the **Discoteca Camela Son,** behind the Hotel Azteca. **El Casino** on Sucre and Pichincha is open every day until 3 A.M. The **Fiesta Municipal** warms things up every year on April 11, as does the **Fiesta del Provincilización del Carchi** on November 19.

SHOPPING

Tulcán is like one big shopping mall: It seems like every other door opens into a clothing store. The main **food market** spreads along Boyacá between Bolívar and Sucre, and there's another between Sucre and Olmedo, two blocks west of Rocafuerte. The *mercado central* has the usual clothing and food stalls.

ACCOMMODATIONS

None of Tulcán's hotels are particularly notable. Double-check if and when hot water is available. Down the Pasaje San Francisco, between Bolívar and Atahualpa, the **Hotel Azteca** (tel. 6/298-0481) provides some of the best of Tulcán's lower-end accommodations. The 52 rooms are $7 pp with cable TV, and there's a disco downstairs (light sleepers beware). The **Hotel Saenz Internacional** (tel. 6/298-1916, fax 6/298-3925) is a good deal at $8 pp (suites are available for $16) with private bath and cable TV. The hotel also has a bar, disco, and restaurant. Across Sucre is the **Hotel Internacional Torres del Oro** (tel. 6/298-0296), with a restaurant and guarded parking. Rates are $12 pp with private bath and cable TV.

Near the Parque Independencia are the **Hotel Florida** (tel. 6/298-3849) and the **Hotel España** (tel. 6/298-3860), both with decent private rooms and 24-hour hot water for $5 pp. Near the *terminal terrestre,* the **Hotel Los Alpes** (tel. 6/298-2235) and the **Hotel Las Acacias** (tel. 6/298-8830) both have rooms with private bath and TV for $5–7 pp. **Sara Espindola** (just below the central plaza on Sucre and Ayacucho, tel. 6/298-2464, $40 s, $50 d) is the best in town. It has a good restaurant, and its spa facilities are open to nonresidents for $5 pp.

FOOD

Tulcán's food picks are even thinner than its hotel selection. Several restaurants specializing in Colombian food are scattered throughout town, including **El Patio,** on Bolívar between Pichincha and 10 de Agosto, with a tiled courtyard decorated with old photos and antiques. Set meals cost around $2. The **Casa China,** two blocks past the terminal, serves up tasty *chaulafan* for $2.50. The **Cafe Tulcán,** across from the Hotel Sara Espindola, is perfect for reading the paper over coffee or ice cream and offers a set lunch menu $1.50.

INFORMATION AND SERVICES

The **tourist information office** is on Olmedo on the Parque Independencia. The **post office** sits across the street from the food market on Bolívar. Sidewalk money changers along Ayacucho are happy to transform your dollars into pesos. Rates are better in Tulcán proper than at the border or in Colombia. The **Banco Pichincha** (Sucre and 10 de Agosto) and the **Banco de Préstamos** (on Parque Ayora) change travelers' checks.

TRANSPORTATION
Buses

The *terminal terrestre* (bus terminal) is at the annoyingly far southern end of Tulcán—a $0.50 taxi ride, $0.20 bus ride, or 30-minute walk from the main plaza. It's surrounded by small restaurants. Being the only northern border town, Tulcán has buses leaving for just about every major city in the country, including Quito ($5, five–six hours), Ibarra ($2.50, two–three hours), and even an *ejecutivo* to Huaquillas ($20, 18 hours). A new service on Transportes Putumayo connects Tulcán directly with Lago Agrio and Coca along the new frontier road through La Bonita, Puerto Libre, and Lumbaquí. One bus a day runs to either destination ($7, seven hours to Lago Agrio, nine to Coca).

NORTHERN SIERRA

In town, **Cooperativa Trans-Norte** buses depart hourly to Tufiño ($1, one hour) in the morning and, when full, in the afternoon. Trans-Norte also sends buses to Chical ($4, four hours) at noon daily, plus 1 P.M. Monday–Thursday and Sunday and 11 A.M. on Thursday. *Colectivo* taxis on García Moreno and Avellano run to Tufiño when four people fill the seats; for a little extra, they will continue to Agua Hediondas. *Colectivos* also run to the border and the airport from the Parque Isidro Ayora, when full ($0.75).

Air

The **TAME** office(tel. 6/298-0675) next to the Hotel Sara Espindola sells tickets to Quito (Mon., Wed., Fri., Sun.; $50 one-way) and connections for Guayaquil (Mon., Wed., Fri.; $116 one-way) and Calí, Colombia ($78 one-way). The airport is two kilometers north on the road to the border; a taxi costs $1 each way.

COLOMBIAN BORDER

Seven kilometers north of Tulcán, a bridge over the Río Carchi marks the border with Colombia. It's open around the clock and crawls with moneychangers, but if you need your passport stamped coming in or out, cross between 6 A.M. and 10 P.M. Keep your eyes open if you decide to change money on either side of the border; official Ecuadorian changers should have photo IDs. There's an ATM on the Colombian side, but it does not have U.S. dollars.

Exit formalities from Ecuador are relatively more straightforward, if less orderly, than in Colombia. Direct any questions to the **Ecuadorian immigration office** (tel. 6/298-0704, open 24 hours) or the **Ministerio de Turismo** office (tel. 6/298-3892, 8:30 A.M.–1 P.M. and 1:30–5 P.M. Mon.–Fri.), both located in the CENAF buildings at the bridge.

Taxis from Tulcán to the border cost $4 one-way, and microbuses leave from the Parque Isidro Ayora, when full, for $0.75. On the Colombian side, it's 13 kilometers to Ipiales, and *colectivos* make the trip regularly for 600 pesos. Buses run from Ipiales to Pasto, 90 kilometers farther (500 pesos, two hours).

WEST OF TULCÁN

The road west from Tulcán follows the Río San Juan (called the Mayasquer in Colombia), which serves as the international border, much of the way to the ocean. This unspoiled area has been described as even more beautiful than the El Angel Reserve, because it's even more remote. Condors circle over kilometers of untouched *páramo* and cloud forest all the way to El Chical, and the road becomes impassable soon after.

Tufiño

Thermal baths bubbling up from the smoldering core of Volcán Chiles are the main attraction in this town, 18 kilometers from Tulcán. There aren't any places to stay in Tufiño, but you can get a meal in the market or at one of several small shops. A restaurant/disco is open on weekends. Bring your passport to cross the border to the pools.

The **Balnearios Aguas Termales** are actually in Colombia, but crossing for the day should be no problem. The three-kilometer walk there isn't difficult, but asking for directions can't hurt. Cross the border and look for the large green sign, where you head left. Admission to the warm pools is free, but the nicer hot pools are in private complexes and cost $1 pp.

To get to the **Aguas Hediondas** ("stinking waters") pools—the hottest and most scenic—head west from Tufiño on a dirt road for three kilometers, then turn to the right at the large sign and go another eight kilometers into a beautiful, remote valley. Several buses a day connect Tulcán with Tufiño, but only the noon one travels up this dirt road to the turnoff. A direct bus to the pools leaves on Sunday at 8 A.M. A truck to the pools costs $8, and the driver will wait for you. Camping here is possible—bring a tent and a warm sleeping bag.

Past Tufiño, the road enters the El Angel Reserve and climbs the lower reaches of Volcán Chiles, approaching on the right. The higher the road winds, the more windswept and impressive the *páramo* becomes. You'll pass at least five waterfalls on the way to the town of **Maldonado,** some within a short walk of the road.

Volcán Chiles

Climb this summit (4,768 meters), and you can stand with one foot each in Colombia and Ecuador, because Chiles' peak pokes right through the border. The scenery is unusual, even for Ecuador: rough, strange, and studded with alien-looking *frailejón* plants. The weather is the main concern in this otherwise straightforward ascent: Dress for rain and snow, and be prepared to be clouded in most mornings. Guides can occasionally be found in Tufiño.

The trailhead is about 20 kilometers and 30 minutes past Tufiño. A private truck to the trailhead from Tufiño costs $3, or you can hop off a bus on its way to Maldonado or El Chical. The climb from the road to the peak and back takes about six hours. The IGM 1:50,000 map *Tufiño and Volcán Chiles* is helpful, but it may be hard to buy, because of border tensions.

CENTRAL SIERRA

Quito and Cuenca are the bookends enclosing the Avenue of the Volcanoes, a perpetually impressive stretch of real estate that makes up the bulk of Ecuador's mountainous spine. Strung along the Pan-American Highway like beads on a string, large colonial cities rest beneath soaring peaks. Each city is tucked into its own river basin, and farmland fills in most of the level space in between. The more remote and spectacular areas, fully stocked with volcanoes, lakes, and rivers, have been set aside as parks or reserves.

Whether you're seeing how far that dirt road goes past the next village or hiking a well-worn trail around the base of a volcano, you can't beat the scenery, air, and just plain open space that permeate this part of the Sierra. The Avenue of the Volcanoes,

Alexander von Humboldt's 19th-century nickname for this part of Ecuador, stuck for good reason. The territory ranges from broad, confident Chimborazo to wrinkled Rumiñahui, lurking in the shadow of Cotopaxi. Rivers tumble and join to drain the Andean snows into either the Amazon or the Gulf of Guayaquil, and glacier lakes sparkle in the farther reaches.

Home to roughly half of Ecuador's population, the Central Sierra is farmed on almost every available acre. Large plantations hearken back to the days when forced labor supported farms stretching beyond the horizon. Small communities in the mountains plant crops at elevations as high as 4,000 meters, supplementing their income through shepherding and crafts.

© JEAN BROWN

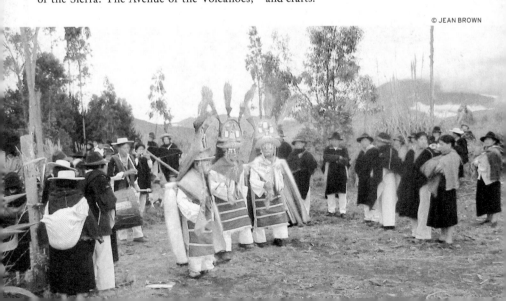

HIGHLIGHTS

◖ **Cotopaxi National Park:** Home to Ecuador's flagship peak, wild horses, and llamas, this park is only 90 minutes south of Quito (page 123).

◖ **Laguna Quilotoa:** Neon waters in a stunning setting make this lake, midway around the Latacunga Loop, well worth the extra mileage (page 134).

◖ **Hiking in Baños:** Of all its attractions – waterfalls, restaurants, and outdoor activities galore – the outstanding hiking earns Baños a spot on most travelers' list of favorites (page 146).

◖ **Chimborazo Fauna Reserve:** Encircled by roads connecting Riobamba, Guaranda, and Ambato, Chimborazo's summit is well over 6,000 meters, and it's flanks are home to the reintroduced herds of vicuna (page 152).

◖ **Nariz del Diablo Train Ride:** Riding on top of this train has been suspended, but the journey through the Devil's Nose below Alausí wil give you a new appreciation for the problems faced by railroad engineers in the Andes (page 166).

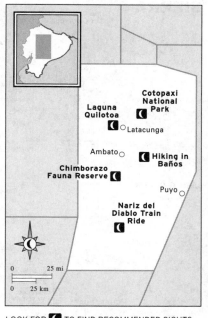

LOOK FOR ◖ TO FIND RECOMMENDED SIGHTS, ACTIVITIES, DINING, AND LODGING.

The Central Sierra has always been the most dyed-in-the-wool indigenous region of Ecuador. During their reign, the Incas established outposts all along the road to Quito to keep the local populations in line. Today, 75 percent of Chimborazo Province residents consider themselves of native descent. Dozens of different groups inhabit the highlands, often each in its own town. Clothes and customs are the most distinguishing characteristics, from the white-and-black garments of the Salasaca to the white-fringed red ponchos of the Quisapinchas.

PLANNING YOUR TIME

For travelers on a tight time budget, a quick day trip to Cotopaxi is all they see of the Central Sierra, except a glimpse for the scenery flying in and out of Quito. Baños, the most popular destination in the region, is well worth two–three days, and the **Latacunga Loop** to the **Laguna Quilotoa** merits another two–four. A full week would give you time to do this part of the country reasonable justice, but climbers, backpackers, and lollygaggers will want even more.

The best cities to base your travels around are Baños, Riobamba, and Ambato (in that order). **Cotopaxi National Park** sees the most traffic in the Ecuadorian Andes, while it's likely that no one has seen some parts of sprawling Sangay National Park in centuries. If climbing 5,000-meter mountains isn't your thing, give a thought to the trek to the **Collanes plain** at the foot of El Altar.

More sedate diversions also beckon. Several

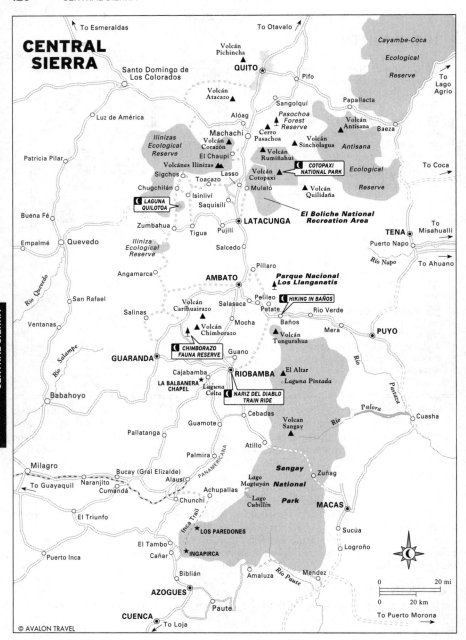

CENTRAL SIERRA

CENTRAL SIERRA

To Esmeraldas
To Otavalo
Volcán Pichincha ▲
QUITO ⊙
Santo Domingo de Los Colorados
Pifo
Cayambe-Coca Ecological Reserve
To Lago Agrio
Volcán Atacazo ▲
Sangolquí
Papallacta
To Coca
Luz de América
Alóag
Pasochoa Forest Reserve
Volcán Antisana ▲
Baeza
Patricia Pilar
Machachi
Cerro Pasocha
Volcán Sincholagua ▲
Antisana Ecological Reserve
Ilinizas Ecological Reserve
Volcán Corazón ▲
El Chaupi
Volcán Rumiñahui ▲
Volcánes Ilinizas ▲▲
Sigchos
Lasso
Toacazo
Volcán Cotopaxi ▲
COTOPAXI NATIONAL PARK
Chugchilán
Isinliví
Mulaló
Volcán Quilidaña ▲
Buena Fé
LAGUNA QUILOTOA
Saquisilí
El Boliche National Recreation Area
Zumbahua
Tigua
Pujilí
LATACUNGA
To Misahualli
Empalmé
Quevedo
Iliniza Ecological Reserve
Salcedo
Puerto Napo
TENA ⊙
Río Napo
To Ahuano
Angamarca
Píllaro
AMBATO ⊙
Parque Nacional Los Llanganatis
San Rafael
Pelileo
HIKING IN BAÑOS
Volcán Carihuairazo ▲
Salasaca
Patate
Río Verde
Salinas
Mocha
Baños
Mera
PUYO
Ventanas
Volcán Chimborazo ▲
Volcán Tungurahua ▲
CHIMBORAZO FAUNA RESERVE
Guano
Guano
GUARANDA ⊙
Cajabamba
RIOBAMBA
El Altar ▲
Laguna Pintada
Babahoyo
LA BALBANERA CHAPEL
Laguna Colta
NARIZ DEL DIABLO TRAIN RIDE
Guamote
Cebadas
Volcan Sangay ▲
Cuasha
Pallatanga
Atillo
Palmira
Milagro
Bucay (Grál Elizalde)
Sangay
Zuñag
To Guayaquil
Naranjito
Alausí
Lago Magtayán
National
Cumandá
Achupallas
Chunchi
Lago Cubillín
Park
MACAS
El Triunfo
Sucúa
LOS PAREDONES ★
Logroño
Puerto Inca
El Tambo
INGAPIRCA ★
Cañar
Biblián
Amaluza
Mendez
AZOGUES ⊙
Río Paute
To Puerto Morona
Paute
CUENCA
To Loja

0   20 mi
0   20 km

© AVALON TRAVEL

fine old haciendas offer luxury accommodations with a colonial flavor, such as the famous **La Ciénega** near Cotopaxi Park. Indigenous markets range from the authentic bustle of Saquisilí and Zumbahua to anything-goes spreads in Ambato and Riobamba. A stop in the resort town of **Baños** is compulsory for most travelers.

In a class of its own is the train ride through the famous **Nariz del Diablo** (Devil's Nose), a set of hair-raising switchbacks west of Alausí—especially if you ride on the roof!

Machachi and Vicinity

After the ugly urban sprawl immediately south of Quito, this quiet, pretty little city is an oasis. The small valley it occupies is surrounded by peaks in almost every direction: Face north toward the Volcán Atacazo and rotate to the right to see Pasochoa to the northeast, Sincholagua to the east, Rumiñahui to the south, the Ilinizas to the southwest, and Corazón to the west. Machachi is a good base for climbing any of these.

Machachi's central plaza is surrounded by an ornate painted church, the Teatro Municipal, and a handful of mediocre restaurants. A few scattered leather shops sell clothes and shoes, and the main market day is Sunday.

SIGHTS

Machachi's main tourist attraction is the **Güitig factory,** four kilometers out of town to the east. Mineral-water pools take on a slightly different meaning here—this is the same stuff, more or less, that comes in those plastic bottles you see all over Ecuador. The three crystal-clear pools (two cold, one lukewarm) just past the bottling plant are set among gorgeous flower gardens, picnic areas, and sports facilities. Tours of the plant itself are available on weekdays (ask the guards at the entrance). Taxis to the plant cost $0.80 one-way, or you can just walk east on Pareja out of town, following it as it turns into Ricardo Salvador about halfway to the factory (7 A.M.–4 P.M. Mon.–Fri., $0.20).

ACCOMMODATIONS

One good place to spend the night is the **Hospedaje Chiguac** (three blocks east of the church plaza, tel. 2/231-0396). Rooms with private bath and hot water have views of Rumiñahui out the windows, almost close enough to touch. The $12 pp rate includes breakfast, and other meals are also available.

A more pleasant option is in the nearby village of Aloasí, at the foot of Corazón Volcano. **La Estación de Machachi** (tel. 3/230-9246, $34 s, $39 d) has a friendly atmosphere and wood stoves to ward off the high-altitude chill. Get there via a $2 taxi ride from Machachi or a local bus from the church.

TRANSPORTATION

Any bus running south along the Pana can drop you off at one of the two entrances to Machachi, leaving you with a two-kilometer walk into town. Buses from Quito run from the *terminal terrestre,* and more often from the *trole's* southern station at El Recreo ($0.75, one hour). Buses back to Quito leave from two blocks west of the plaza (if you want to go to the *terminal terrestre,* ask if your bus is going all the way there). Taxis can be hired to take you up the rough roads to the bases of nearby mountains; a one-way trip to Cotopaxi runs about $30.

ILINIZA ECOLOGICAL RESERVE

Set aside none too soon in 1996, this 149,000-hectare reserve encloses its twin namesake peaks, as well as Cerro Corazón, Laguna Quilotoa, and a significant chunk of cloud forest. Most visitors enter the reserve near Machachi to climb. The entrance fee, charged only for those climbing the Ilinizas, is $5 pp.

CENTRAL SIERRA

FLOWER EXPORTS: TO RUSSIA, WITH LOVE

You've probably noticed the long, plastic-sided greenhouses that line the landscape throughout the Sierra. In the last few decades, the ornamental flowers grown in these greenhouses have become the Sierra's most economically important export. In 2007, the total export of flowers exceeded $400 million, $300 million of which was roses. The other leading flowers are Gypsophilia (baby's breath) and Hypericum. Cut flowers are Ecuador's fourth-largest export trailing only petroleum, bananas, and shrimp. More than 5,800 hectares are now covered by greenhouses and flower farms 3,000 of which are roses.

All this success results from Ecuador's climate, which is ideal for flower growing. Twelve dependable hours of daily sunlight year-round, rich volcanic soil, and a particular combination of altitude and humidity produce what some florists call the highest-quality roses in the world. Around 80 varieties are currently grown for export.

Many old haciendas have been converted into flower farms to take advantage of the rise in demand. The greenhouses are run with scientific precision, regulated by computer-monitored humidity readings. Ecuadorian floriculturists can now buy plants in-country that they once had to import.

The next time you happen to buy roses in Moscow, take a second look: A third of Ecuador's 500 flower farms grow plants exclusively for the Russian market, shipping $57.8 million worth of flowers in 2007. Even though some Russian flowers are cheaper, imported blossoms are in great demand. The majority of Ecuador's production is flown out to Miami on its way to the European and U.S. markets. KLM and Iberia also top off their luggage areas with flowers. This could explain why your plane home to Madrid or Amsterdam might be particularly fragrant – many Ecuadorian flowers are shipped across the Atlantic on passenger flights.

Roses have become one of Ecuador's major exports.

For information on the Laguna Quilotoa and the western part of the reserve near Chugchilán and Zumbahua, see the *Latacunga Loop* section.

Climbing Volcán Corazón

A short distance west of Machachi across the Pana sits this extinct volcano, first climbed in 1738 by Charles-Marie de la Condamine while on a break from measuring the planet. At 4,788 meters, Corazón is a challenging day climb, consisting mostly of easy uphill hiking through grassy fields, with some moderate but exposed rock scrambling for the last 500 meters. With a four-wheel-drive vehicle, you can get to within two hours of the top, but you'll need permission to go through the private land en route. Count on about five to six hours of hiking from the Pana. A taxi from Machachi can drop you off partway up the road (usually near the tree farm) for about $8, cutting the ascent time by one to two hours.

Climbing the Ilinizas

The sister peaks are remnants of what used to be one volcano, and they're like night and day for climbers. **Iliniza Sur** (5,265 meters), the higher and more difficult of the two, is the sixth-highest peak in Ecuador. Besides El Altar, Iliniza Sur was the only mountain in Ecuador that Edward Whymper couldn't climb, although he tried twice. The trusty

Carrel brothers, though, made the 1880 expedition a success by reaching the summit on their own. The first Ecuadorian climber reached the top in 1950. Even though glacial retreat is well under way on Iliniza Sur, it's still a challenging endeavor and a good introduction to Ecuador's more difficult peaks above 5,000 meters. Check in Quito for the latest route information.

Iliniza Norte, Ecuador's eighth-highest peak (5,126 meters), was one of the few in the country to be first climbed by Ecuadorians—in this case, by Nicolás Martínez and Alexandro Villavicencio, accompanied by the Austrian climber Franz Hiti, in 1912. In the dry season, technical equipment and experience are not necessary, making Iliniza Norte accessible part of the year to hardy hikers undaunted by some minor rock climbing.

The approach to both leads from the Pana to a hut on the saddle separating the two peaks. Ten kilometers south of Machachi, look for a wooden sign saying "Ilinizas" just before Jambelí Creek. The turnoff is 50 meters north of the bridge and leads seven kilometers

southwest across the train tracks to the village of El Chaupi. Buses run to El Chaupi from Machachi as well.

Three kilometers beyond the village, you'll find the **Hacienda San José del Chaupi** (tel. 9/971-3986), a working farm that provides a good starting point for climbing any of the peaks in the area. Rooms with hot water, kitchen, and fireplace cost $10 pp, with continental breakfast included. Horses are available for rent for $5 per hour and $25 for an entire day.

Next stop is the **Nuevos Horizontes hut,** at 4,600 meters, only about 500 meters below either peak. One of the oldest mountaineering huts in Ecuador, it can accommodate about 24 people and features bunk beds, stoves, and cooking and eating utensils. One of the 13 beds will cost you $10 pp per night, and water is available from a nearby stream.

It's a good idea to check at **Hostal Llovizna** $12 pp just past the church in Chaupi. Vladimir Gallo (tel. 9/969-9068), who runs the hut, owns this *hostal* and can arrange horses to carry luggage. La Ensillada, the saddle between the peaks, is above the hut.

Machachi to Latacunga

▣ COTOPAXI NATIONAL PARK

Ecuador's premier Andean park is within a few hours of Quito and covers the intersection of Pichincha, Cotopaxi, and Napo provinces. In all of Ecuador, Cotopaxi is second only to the Galápagos in number of visitors annually. Inside the 33,400 stunning hectares, you'll find the park's namesake volcano, one of the most beautiful in the Americas, along with two other peaks higher than 4,700 meters. Wild horses gallop between the mountains, and llamas graze grassy *páramo* dotted with wildflowers.

Flora and Fauna
Wet montane forests fill Cotopaxi's lowest altitudes. There's not much of this zone left, but

riding near Hacienda La Alegría

what does remain ranges from 3,600 to about 3,800 meters. Sub-Andean *páramo* covers everything between 4,000 and 4,500 meters, which is where you'll find most of the park's animals: puma, dwarf deer, *páramo* rabbits, and the endemic marsupial mouse. Even casual birders will probably spot carunculated caracaras, shrike- and ground-tyrants, great thrushes, rufous-naped brush finches, Andean gulls, noble snipe, and brown-backed chattyrants (related to flycatchers). Speckled teals and yellow-billed pintail flock around the park's lakes, while Andean lapwings claim the shoreline. Above it all soars the occasional Andean condor.

Shrubby blueberries and lupines bloom next to Indian paintbrush and members of the daisy family, while the occasional terrestrial bromeliad is probably pollinated by hummingbirds. You might spot the *urcu rosa*, a small blue mountain rose, hidden among the tough *ugsha* grass. Above 4,500 meters to the snowline at 4,700 meters, plunging temperatures keep the mossy tussocks of the Andean tundra relatively empty.

Access

A badly rutted road runs southeast from Machachi to enter the park from the north, but to reach the main entrances to Cotopaxi, head farther down the Pana. There are two turnoffs: The first, 16 kilometers south of Machachi, is also the entrance to El Boliche National Recreation Area. It passes the CLIRSEN satellite tracking station (with a new museum) before forking three ways. Take the right-hand fork and follow the train tracks for 500 meters. From here, it's six kilometers downhill through a forest to a campsite with fireplaces and simple cabins. One kilometer farther along is the Raúl Daule campsite, with water available from a nearby river.

The second entrance turnoff is nine kilometers farther south down the Pana and is marked by a cement billboard. This is the best of all the entrances and sees the most traffic, making it easier to hitch a ride into the park, especially on weekends (although it does wash out occasionally in the rainy season). It joins with the other Pana access road at the park boundary, where you pay the entrance fee ($10 pp) at the gate, which is open daily.

The road through the park curves in a semicircle north around Volcán Cotopaxi. As it heads northeast, it passes the administrative center at Campamiento Mariscal Sucre, 10 kilometers from the gate. Here, a small museum has exhibits on the geology, history, flora, and fauna of the park. Shortly beyond the museum, you'll reach the Llanura de Limpiopungo, a wide plain at 3,800 meters between Cotopaxi and Rumiñahui. The birding along the shore of the **Laguna Limpiopungo** is excellent.

On a small hill 15 kilometers beyond the lake are the oval ruins of **El Salitre,** formerly an Inca *pucara* (fortress). Competition for this scenic assignment was probably fierce, but the spectacular views of Cotopaxi, Rumiñahui, Sincholagua, and Pasochoa weren't enough to make up for Cotopaxi's constant eruptions—El Salitre was all but abandoned after the arrival of the Spanish.

A trail leads around the lake to the northwest for access to Rumiñahui. Shortly beyond that trail, another jeep track heads south nine kilometers to the Cotopaxi refuge. After joining the road from Machachi, the park road eventually crosses the eastern park boundary, passing north of Cerro Chuguilasín Chico. Ten kilometers outside the boundary, the gated road meets the Río Tambo and a hacienda of the same name near the base of Quilindaña. The IGM 1:50,000 *Cotopaxi, Mulaló, Machachi* and *Sincholagua* maps cover the park.

Climbing Volcán Cotopaxi

Tack another 2,000 meters onto the perfect conical point of Japan's Mount Fuji and stick it in the middle of the Andes, and you'll have a good picture of Volcán Cotopaxi (5,897 meters). There's some debate as to whether this famous mountain is the highest active volcano in the world, but it's definitely in the top three.

It's hard to believe this beautiful peak, whose name means "neck of the moon" in Kichwa, is also one of Ecuador's most historically destructive volcanoes. The first recorded eruption

© JULIAN SMITH

climbing Cotopaxi

experienced climber who is fully up to date on the changing glacier conditions.

Although Cotopaxi can be climbed year-round—it sees more clear days than almost any other peak in the Ecuadorian Andes—the best months are December and January. August and September are also good but windy. February–April can be clear and dry as well, whereas August–December are usually windy and cloudy. Acclimatization is essential.

The road to the refuge heads south from the main park road for nine kilometers to the parking area at 4,600 meters. A half-hour hike up a steep, sandy trail brings you to the José Ribas refuge, which was built in 1971 by the San Gabriel Climbing Club, stands at 4,800 meters, and is administered by Alta Montaña in Quito (tel. 2/225-4798). The two-story shelter is fully equipped with 70 bunk beds, cooking facilities, running water, snacks and water for sale, and lockable storage space for gear. A night's stay is $20 pp. (Keep an eye out here: a surprise avalanche on Easter Sunday in 1996 buried dozens of day trippers in the uphill courtyard, killing 11.)

The open crater peak, anywhere from 6–10 hours' climb from the refuge, contains smoking fumaroles reeking of sulfur. Leave the refuge between midnight and 2 A.M., and plan on three–six hours for the descent.

A hike completely around Cotopaxi's 20-kilometer base is another ambitious undertaking. Follow the park road clockwise to the eastern border, then follow the Río Tambo upstream to the southwest after crossing the park boundary. From there head west, passing north of Quilindaña to eventually reach the Pana. The full circuit can take up to one week.

disrupted a battle between the Spanish and the Inca in 1534, and eruptions in 1742 and 1768 flattened Latacunga, killing hundreds of people. A deceptively quiet century followed before the volcano began to belch again in 1853. The latter half of the 19th century saw many eruptions, including one in 1877 that sent a *lahar* (landslide of earth and melted ice) all the way to the Pacific, leveling Latacunga again for good measure. The 20th century was relatively quiet, with only about two dozen minor murmurings.

A German and Colombian climbing team first set foot on Cotopaxi's glacier-covered peak in 1872, followed 10 years later by Edward Whymper, who opened the northern route still in use today. The climb is not difficult, as the many climbers who scale the ice-covered slopes regularly will attest. Crevasses are usually large and obvious, making the climb mostly an uphill slog. It's not for the inexperienced, however—technical equipment is necessary (ice axes, crampons, ropes, and marker wands), along with the services of a guide or

Climbing Volcán Rumiñahui

This homely mass, 13 kilometers northwest of Cotopaxi, was named after Atahualpa's stoic general (who in turn takes his name from the Kichwa word *rumi,* meaning stone, plus *ñawi,* for eye). The straightforward climb is a mixture of uphill hike and scramble, but because the quality of rock can be poor, a rope and climbing protection are recommended for the

CENTRAL SIERRA

more exposed stretches. Rumiñahui has three peaks: the northern and highest peak (4,712 meters), a southern peak (erroneously labeled Rumiñahui Central on the IGM map), and a central peak.

The east side of Rumiñahui is reached through Cotopaxi Park along tracks that skirt Laguna Limpiopungo to the north or south. A path toward the central peak is clearly visible along a well-defined ridge. From the lake to the base is about a two-hour hike, and camping along the way is possible. The south peak involves some moderate technical rock climbing (class 5.5). The IGM 1:50,000 *Machachi* and *Sincholagua* maps cover this area.

EL BOLICHE NATIONAL RECREATION AREA

Ecuador's smallest nationally protected area (1,077 hectares) hugs the southwestern side of Cotopaxi Park. Boliche is perfect for visitors who are more interested in weekend family picnics and mild hikes than mountaineering, offering cabins, camping spots, sports fields, and self-guided trails. The habitat here at 3,500 meters is similar to Cotopaxi's *páramo*

and Andean forest, but with less of the original flora and fauna. Half the area is covered with pine trees planted through reforestation programs in the 1960s and 1970s. Visitors may catch sight of deer, rabbits, and the occasional wolf. Llamas and guarizos (offspring of llamas and alpacas) have been released in the park and are reproducing well. The entrance to El Boliche is the same as the northern turnoff for Cotopaxi off the Pana—16 kilometers past Machachi and the CLIRSEN tracking station with its newly opened museum, and across the train tracks. Admission to the area is $10 pp and is combined with the entry to Cotopaxi.

ACCOMMODATIONS NEAR COTOPAXI
Hacienda San Agustín de Callo

This ancient hacienda (tel./fax 3/271-9160, info@incahacienda.com, www.incahacienda .com) owes as much of its history to the Inca as to the Spanish. It was originally built as an Augustinian convent on the site of a ruined Inca outpost. The chapel and dining room both incorporate massive Inca stonework, and Inca remains have been unearthed during

CENTRAL SIERRA

© JEAN BROWN

llamas at Hacienda San Agustín de Callo

restorations. The nearby Cerro de Callo is a perfectly round hill thought to be an Inca burial mound.

Lodging, including breakfast and dinner, starts at $268 s, $335 d, and lunch is $30. The hacienda sits along the road that parallels the Pana north of Mulaló. Take the southern turnoff to Cotopaxi park and turn right (south) toward Mulaló instead of continuing straight into the park. You'll pass the Hacienda Los Nevados before reaching the San Agustín turnoff to the west, opposite an arrow painted on a white rock.

Hacienda La Ciénega

Your first glimpse of the **🅲 Hacienda La Ciénega,** at the end of a long dirt lane lined with towering eucalyptus trees, is also the most impressive. One of Ecuador's oldest haciendas, La Ciénega (3/271-9052, $55 s, $77 d, hcienega@uio.satnet.net) now operates as a hotel and restaurant. The setting is straight out of the 17th century, when the estate belonged to the Marquis of Maenza and stretched from Quito to Ambato. La Condamine, von Humboldt, Juan José Flores, and Velasco Ibarra all found shelter here over the centuries.

The main building has been aptly described as a "living museum," with meter-thick whitewashed walls, wrought-iron banisters, and bare stone steps worn down by centuries of traffic. The square building surrounds a flower-filled courtyard with a fountain, where a set of ornately carved wooden doors open into the small private chapel. Horses graze near flower-filled greenhouses to the rear of the courtyard.

Of the 28 rooms, those in the original main building are more authentic (i.e., smaller and without fireplaces). More rooms have been added in the old servants' areas. Room eight, the only one on the third floor, is the honeymoon suite, with excellent views of the estate. Breakfast is included, and lunch and dinner are $15–18 pp.

A sign on the west side of the Pana one kilometer south of Lasso points down a paved lane, where the hacienda gate opens on the left after one kilometer.

Hostería San Mateo

Located in Lasso about 10 minutes by car south of the main park entrance, this *hostería* (tel.3/271-9015, fax 3/271-9471, san_mateo@yahoo.com, www.hosteriasanmateo.com) has five beautiful rooms with private bath and cabins for up to four people decorated in Ecuadorian country style. The proper service at the restaurant, where the outstanding *menú del día* is $9.50, and the general air of classiness about the *hostería* make it good value for $67 s, $73 d.

There's a swimming pool and bar for those who don't take advantage of the horseback riding and hiking. Owner Francisco Baca's family has a four-century history in Ecuador, and he maintains interests in cattle and dairy ranching, as well as organic vegetable farming.

Tierra del Volcán (Volcano Land)

The northern entrance road to Cotopaxi park passes this relatively new lodge shortly before it hits the park boundary. The three Ecuadorian owners offer tours on foot, mountain bike, and horseback near the nearby hills. Straw mats on the roof and walls and fireplaces in the dining room and living rooms give the *hacienda* a comfortable air. Enjoy homemade food from the farm or a board game in the game room/bar above the dining room. Horse-riding day tours from Quito are $99 pp with at least two people and include transport and a hacienda lunch.

The views of Sincholagua and Cotopaxi from the large patio, complete with beehive bread oven (a type of outdoor oven), are spectacular. Rates for rooms and breakfast are $85–120 for two people, depending on how long you stay. You can also get just a bed and breakfast for $24 pp, with lunch or dinner an additional $14 each. For more information, contact the office in Quito (San Ignacio N27-127 and Gonzáles Suárez, tel. 2/323-7372, info@volcanoland.com, www.volcanoland.com).

Hacienda Yanahurco

Opened in 1995, this retreat is east of the volcano, and access is normally from the northern entrance road to Cotopaxi park. The hacienda (tel. 2/244-5248, www.haciendayanahurco.com) offers outdoor activities on the lands of an old family hacienda: guided hiking, fishing, bird-watching, and especially horseback-riding excursions over 26,000 private hectares. Seven rooms in the ranch-style buildings have fireplaces and private baths. The fishing here is particularly good; brook, rainbow, and brown trout fill the streams. The annual roundup of wild horses is a very special three-day weekend event that should be reserved well in advance.

All-inclusive packages, including activities, food, and accommodations in the expansive main hacienda, are $205 pp per day (transport from Quito is $160 round-trip for up to three passengers). There are cheaper options to visit including a camping area. The private, locked entrance road is reached by turning east from the main park entrance road at the Laguna Limpiopungo.

Hacienda La Alegria

Gabriel Espinosa and his friendly family run the comfortable 【 Hacienda La Alegria (tel.2/246-2319 or 9/980-2526, info@alegriafarm.com, www.haciendalaalegria.com) on the old railroad line in the shadow of Volcán Corazón. Horse riding is the focus here—horses and guides are both excellent, and they run day and overnight trips into the hills in every direction. You might find yourself clattering down a cobbled country lane beneath a row of eucalyptus trees or stopping at a store while trotting through Machachi or Alóag to ask directions from the saddle.

Old equestrian photos and equipment decorate the beautiful old building, which can accommodate 24 guests in newer extensions. Meals include produce from the hacienda's organic farm.

Rates range from $67 pp for bed and breakfast to $120 pp for full board, including rides and hacienda visits. Transport from Quito can be arranged.

Hato Verde

Immense pumice walls greet visitors to this lovely hacienda, with nine warm cozy bedrooms and a homey family atmosphere. The house has retained much of the 120-year-old building's character, and it was carefully renovated and decorated before opening as a guesthouse in 2004. At night, the fires are lit and shutters closed; in the mornings, they are opened to display great views of Cotopaxi volcano and the farmlands. Fresh milk and cheese produced on the farm are a feature of the country breakfasts included in the price ($79s, $89 d). Hato Verde (tel. 3/271-9348 or 3/271-9902, www.haciendahatoverde.com) is just a few hundred meters from the Pan-American Highway south of Cotopaxi.

La Quinta Colorada

A $3 taxi ride from the old train station in Lasso brings you to this pleasantly restored country farmhouse, where accommodations with dinner and breakfast cost $22 pp. Rooms have fireplaces and private bathrooms. Pedro and Elvia prepare traditional foods, often grown in the front garden.

Latacunga and Vicinity

Before returning to his capital of Cuzco, Tupac Inca Yupanqui left his regional chiefs to oversee his newly conquered northern domains with the words *"Llagtata-cunuai"* ("I leave this land in your care"). From this edict comes the name Latacunga, claimed today by a midsize colonial city (pop. 52,000). Less than 30 kilometers from Cotopaxi, Latacunga has been repeatedly destroyed by Cotopaxi over the years, but something keeps drawing its inhabitants back to the banks of the Río Cutuchi.

The first volcanic stones were laid for Latacunga in the late 1500s. Early on, the city prospered from textile sweatshops and the

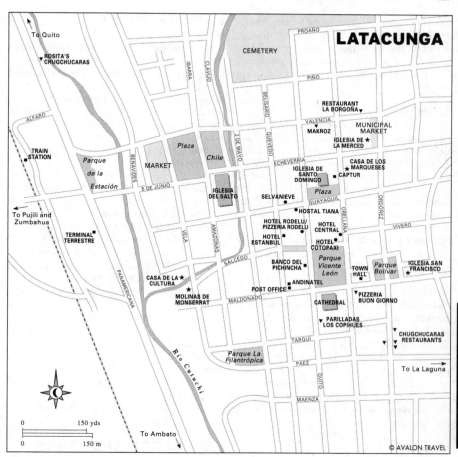

spoils of a nearby Inca gold mine. Cotopaxi always loomed to the northeast, and it made good on its silent threat on December 21, 1742, in an eruption that obliterated most of the city. Survivors described birds falling from the sky, asphyxiated by sulfur fumes. The city was rebuilt, only to be partially destroyed again in 1768. Stubborn residents dug themselves out and repaired the city yet again. More than a century of peace followed—until 1877, when a third massive eruption brought Latacunga III to an end.

The inevitable emigrations between erupti-ons left the city as a sort of time capsule, halting further growth while preserving what Cotopaxi hadn't yet ruined. Today, its modest but pretty colonial heart—across the Río Cutuchi from the ugly stretch of the town along the Pana— is a network of bumpy streets cobbled with volcanic blocks and lined by narrow sidewalks. Courtyards open off just about every block, and the only structures taller than two stories are churches and municipal buildings.

Latacunga is a travel crossroads between the Sierra and the coast, and it makes a good base for climbing and hiking in the area. Its residents are friendly and proud of their hometown—don't be surprised if children come up to you on the street and ask you how you like their city. Mountain-guiding services and a preponderance of beauty salons complete the picture.

SIGHTS

The central **Parque Vicente León** features a few topiary works in a garden setting that's locked tight at night. South of the park sits the plain white **cathedral,** a solemn building with ornate carved wooden doors and a small, picturesque gallery behind. To the east, the **town hall** also borders the west side of **Parque Bolívar,** while across Ordóñez is the **Iglesia de San Francisco.** A few blocks southwest, **Parque La Filantrópica** is guarded by the grand old **Hospital General,** a historic landmark to the south.

Markets

Plaza Chile near the bridges hosts Latacunga's **market,** which spills down almost to the river on Tuesdays and Sundays. Huge, colorful bundles of yarn and felt hats (for small heads) predominate, while the cilantro-scented fruit section features impressive pumpkins, melons, and watermelons. To the east, the less spectacular daily **municipal market** borders the **Iglesia de la Merced** between Valencia and Echeverría.

Museums

Built on the site of an old Jesuit flour mill along the river, the **Molinas de Monserrat** (8 A.M.–noon and 2–6 P.M. Tues.–Fri., 8 A.M.–3 P.M. Sat., $0.50) contains part of the old mill rush, as well as an impressive ethnographic collection of ceramics, paintings, dolls in indigenous festival costumes, and colonial artifacts. A bridge over a rushing stream in the gardens leads to the **Casade la Cultura** next door.

The lovely flower-filled courtyard of the hodgepodge **Casa de los Marqueses** (8 A.M.–noon and 2–6 P.M. Mon.–Fri., free) is more interesting than the rusty tools, stamps, paintings, and antique furniture that fill it.

ENTERTAINMENT AND EVENTS

Latacunga's **Fiesta de la Santissima Virgen de la Merced** (September 22–24), known familiarly as the **Mama Negra,** is one of the more colorful and outstanding events in Ecuador. It centers around a small black icon of the Virgin, which was carved by an indigenous artisan in the 17th century. The festival was first dedicated in 1744 (in vain, as it turned out) to Latacunga's patron saint to protect against Cotopaxi.

During the Mama Negra festivities, the streets are filled with a colorful cast of characters. Verse tellers—more or less public jesters—tell poems and recite bawdy *loas* (limericks) filled with nuggets of ironic truth. Whip-wielding *camosonas* share the stage with *huacos,* dressed in dazzling masks and white costumes decorated with an intriguing assortment of trinkets, buttons, religious images, and scraps of glass and plastic. *Huacos* wander the street in pairs brandishing painted sticks and animal skulls, looking for patients (or victims) on whom to work their ceremonial healing powers. The Angel de la Estrella (Angel of the Star), played by a young boy in plaster wings, asks the Virgin on behalf of the entire city for her protection against future natural disasters.

Latacunga's **Independence Celebration** is held on November 11.

RECREATION AND TOURS

Latacunga's location between volcanoes, while occasionally dangerous, does make it a good climbing and excursion base. **Rinallacta Tours** (Guayaquil 5–32 and Quito tel. 3/280-0357, www.rinallactatours.com) and **Expeditiones Tovar** (Guayaquil and Quito, tel. 3/281-1333) sends tours to Zumbahua and Quilotoa. Both offer guided mountain climbs, hikes in the Andes, jungle tours, and trips to indigenous markets.

ACCOMMODATIONS

Although Latacunga has a few decent hotels, those in search of luxury should head to one

SAQUISILÍ'S THURSDAY-MORNING MARKET

Cotopaxi gleams in the early morning sun as vendors labor to set up one of the most authentic and economically important markets in the country. This market isn't oriented toward tourists: the atmosphere in Saquisilí is strictly business, and almost everything for sale serves a utilitarian purpose, from crates full of chickens to homemade shotguns.

Buses from Latacunga drop shoppers in the Plaza Condordia, where racks of tools and mountains of neon-colored yarn line the square. Grab a 20-cent *pan dulce* (Andean-style cornbread) and head in just about any direction. The entire city has become one big market. Although most of the major buying and selling takes place in one of eight plazas, new municipal ordinances have moved many vendors off the connecting streets. Each has its own particular offering – some of which earn a double take. In one area, you can find car radios dangling from wires; head down and over a block for the fried pig heads. While chickens are confined to the food market, along with the roosters, rabbits, and guinea pigs, pullets (young hens) are sold in a different area altogether. Tinny loudspeakers trumpet miracle herbal cures for everything from diarrhea to gonorrhea, as ragged old men shuffle by with crates of goods secured on their backs by rough lines around the shoulders.

Past the food market, with its haggling crowds and pots stewing over smoking coal fires, you'll eventually reach the large metal roof shading the textile market. Otavalan weavers display sweaters and tapestries, and garish wooden festival masks from Cotopaxi Province in the form of dogs, monkeys, and clowns glare off racks. To one side sits a row of elderly tailors, each pumping the treadle of an antique Singer sewing machine. Many tables are covered with intricate, colorful paintings from the Tigua Valley to the southeast.

Follow the pig squeals about one kilometer out of town to the animal market, where creatures of every description are bought, sold, and bartered. This market is also divided into sections: placid, dreadlocked llamas cluster with cloud-fleeced alpacas near the entrance, while cows, sheep, and horses congregate toward the back.

Some women resemble strange parodies of New York City dog walkers, with dozens of piglets on strings milling around their ankles. Occasionally, someone screams, but no one turns to look – it's just a huge hog being loaded into the back of a truck by a group of sweating, swearing farmers. Aside from a few tourists with cameras, this scene in the blowing dust and harsh equatorial sun seems plucked out of time.

Accommodations in Saquisilí are available at the **San Carlos Hotel** (tel. 3/227-1057) for $5 pp with private bath and hot water – or, more comfortably, at **Gilocarmelo** (tel.3/272-1634, www.hosteriagilocarmelo.com), a five-minute walk east of the main northern bus parking area.

© JEAN BROWN

Llamas wait patiently for the loads they will carry home from market.

of the **haciendas** a short drive north or south on the Pana.

Under $10

Latacunga's best hotels are within a block or two of Parque Vicente León. The quiet **Hotel Estanbul** (Quevedo 6–44 between Salcado and Guayaquil, tel. 3/280-0354) is a perennial budget traveler's favorite, run for 50 years by a gaggle of feisty proprietresses. Good views of the mountains await from the rooftop balcony, and luggage storage and parking facilities are available. Rooms have desks and—hey!—garbage cans. Rooms go for $10 pp with shared bath ($12 pp private). Newly opened, the **Tiana** (Guayaquil 5–32 and Quito, tel. 3/281-0147, www .hostaltiana.com) surrounds a lovely colonial patio, efficiently run by a Dutch/Cañari couple. There are private rooms and dorm rooms, hot showers, and breakfast for $8–14 pp.

$10-25

The best rooms in the musty **Hotel Cotopaxi** (tel. 3/280-1310, $12 s 16 d) overlook the plaza and have private baths. The **Hotel Rodelu** (Quito 1631 and Salcedo, tel. 3/280-0956, fax 3/281-2341, rodelu@uio.telconet.net, www .rodelu.com.ec, $18 s, $30 d) has rooms with private bath, TV, and in-room telephones. The facilities are clean, and the first-floor restaurant is one of the best in town.

The **Hotel Makroz** (Valencia and Quito, tel. 3/280-0907, hotelmakroz@latinmail.com, $20 s, $30 d) is the newest and probably the best lodging available. All rooms have private baths, hot showers, and comfortable beds, and there's an interior patio and space for parking.

FOOD

Local specialties include *chugchucara*—a singular fried dish that includes chunks of pork, crispy skins, potatoes, plantains, and fresh and toasted corn—and *allullas* (ah-YU-zhahs), doughy cookies made with cheese and pork fat.

The pleasant **Restaurant Española** (2 de Mayo and Guayaquil) does not cater to vegetarians, but offers excellent meat dishes. Near the municipal market, **La Borgoña** is good for cheap traditional dishes. Watching a soap opera may take precedence over taking your order for the staff at the **Pizzeria Rodelu,** but the pies, which are topped with enough cheese to induce a heart attack and start at about $4.50, are worth waiting for. Pizzas at **Pizzerias Buon Giorno** on the plaza are similarly priced, and a heaping helping of lasagna is $4.50. There's also a wide range of huge salads.

SERVICES

On Parque Vicente León, the **Banco Pichincha** handles some foreign currency. The **post office** is on Quevedo and Maldonado.

CAPTUR (Sanchez de Orellana and Guayaquil, tel. 3/281-4968, 9 A.M.–6 P.M. Mon.–Fri., 9 A.M.–1 P.M. Sat.) is the local tourist office. Maps, brochures, and a little information in Spanish are available.

TRANSPORTATION

Latacunga's new **bus terminal** on the Pana, one block south of the footbridge, is open for business, though buses use a bypass and can be caught at the south end of the block. Various companies go to Quito ($2, two hours), Ambato ($1, one hour), and Saquisilí ($0.50, 20 minutes). Transportes Cotopaxi heads to Quevedo ($5, five hours) via Zumbahua. Transportes Primavera buses go to **Salcedo** ($0.50, 20 minutes), and Transportes Pujilí will take you to Pujilí ($0.25, 15 minutes).

Taxis are available for day trips to Zumbahua and/or Quilotoa and Cotopaxi Park ($40–50).

LATACUNGA LOOP

The loop road west of Latacunga offers independent travelers one of the easiest ways to get into the remote reaches of Ecuador's Sierra. Along the way are dusty market towns and a striking lake in a volcanic caldera, while in every direction roll the windswept earthen waves of the high Andes.

Plan on taking at least three–four days to do the entire loop at a reasonable pace, and more like a week to really explore the region, even with your own transportation. Less than half of the 200 kilometers are paved, leaving the outer section between Sigchos and Quilotoa merely a rough dirt track.

Transportation

Along the Latacunga Loop, getting there is half the fun and most of the effort. The rough road is not for the faint of heart or axle—buses getting stuck in the mud or stopped by landslides are the norm, rather than the exception, in the rainy season—but if you're willing to hop aboard (or better yet, on top) and focus on the scenery rather than the comfort or lack thereof, this can be one of the most enjoyable parts of your trip.

Two regular buses make the loop on any given day, one in either direction. One, called "La Iliniza," heads counterclockwise around the loop from Latacunga to Chugchilán, leaving from the bus terminal at 11:30 A.M. on its way through Saquisilí and Sigchos. Another bus, also called "La Iliniza," leaves daily at noon from the bus terminal, heading clockwise around the loop via Zumbahua. (The "Vivero" bus leaves for Isinliví at 1 P.M.). On Thursdays, all buses leave half a block from the crafts market in Saquisilí. Both "Iliniza" buses spend the night in the plaza at Chugchilán, bidding farewell around 3:30 A.M. the next morning as they head in opposite directions back to Latacunga. In either direction, it's $3 pp and four hours to reach Chugchilán from Latacunga. The ride on top of either of these buses is one of the most fun and scenic in the country. (Be ready for any kind of weather, low branches and power lines, and plenty of dust.)

Regular buses leave Latacunga every half hour for Zumbahua ($1:50, two hours) on their way to La Mana and Quevedo, heading back just as often until 9 P.M. daily. The El Salado bus that leaves around 1:30 P.M. will turn off the paved road at Huairapungo (windy pass) and thread its way around the hilltops before descending to Malinguapamba, where friendly indigenous hosts can accommodate two to six people in their guesthouse for $10 per day. The price includes simple meals and a genuine cultural experience.

Renting a private truck can make the farther reaches of the loop easier to navigate. Pickups to Quilotoa ($25–35) and Chugchilán (about $40) can be hired in Zumbahua (expect to pay more for them to wait for you). On Saturday mornings, many vehicles are making the trip already, but by the afternoon they're all off taking people home to villages in the hills. Many of the winding backroads are recommended for scenic (if long) walks or bike rides, especially the ones fanning out from the crater—paths spider-web off in all directions.

The owners of the Black Sheep Inn (see *Chugchilán*) can arrange private transportation from Quito for $100 (up to four people) to $125 (five or more).

Isinliví

The **Llullu Llama Hostal** (tel. 3/281-4790, info@llullullama.com, www.llullullama.com) opened its door in this tiny town in 2000. It's set in a renovated old country house with five private rooms ($9 pp), four loft rooms ($7 pp), and a dormitory ($6 pp). The name means "new flame" or "baby llama" in Kichwa and Spanish. Breakfast and dinner are available, as are box lunches on request. You can rent horses with local guides, clear hiking maps and instructions are available.

There are many excellent hiking and mountain-biking routes in the area, including trails to Quilotoa (seven hours by foot), Chugchilán (four hours), and the colorful Monday market in Guantualó (one hour) Malinguapamba community (2–3 hours). The owner is trying to promote permaculture techniques in the local community, and the view from the composting toilet is excellent. An Italian-run cooperative in the village does superb woodworking.

Sigchos

Unfiltered sunlight warms this high, bright town, which is stuck abruptly in a lovely terrace as if it fell out of the sky. A Sunday market and a few basic *residenciales* await visitors who decide to stay for more than a few minutes as their buses pass on to Chugchilán or Latacunga.

Chugchilán

A poor, remote mountain village north of the Laguna Quilotoa is home to about 25 families and the award-winning **(Black Sheep Inn** (tel. 3/281-4587, info@blacksheepinn.com, www.blacksheepinn.com), run by Michelle Kirby and Andy Hammerman from the United States. Over the years, they've turned the place into a model of ecological sustainability and self-sufficiency. Composting toilets (illustrated instructions provided), organic gardens, a greenhouse, and a full recycling program are already in place, and a sauna is also up and running. In the main lodge, guests can play a board game, snuggle up near the wood stove, or check their email. The steam room and a new hot tub with great views are a short climb from the main lodge. Llamas, ducks, dogs, chickens, and—sure enough—a few black sheep wander the grounds, which spill down the hillside above the town proper.

Six beds are $25 pp, six private rooms with two or three beds are $90 d, and the double cabins with private bathrooms are $50 pp. Prices include hot showers, tea and coffee, breakfast (or a box lunch), and a vegetarian dinner, where bright orange nasturtium flowers may add their peppery flavor to a garden-fresh spinach salad. Snacks and other drinks are extra.

The inn is a great base for exploring the area; photocopied maps are available to point the way to Laguna Quilotoa, the local cheese factory, and pre-Inca ruins on the edge of the cloud forest. Horseback tours are $10 for four hours, and they organize four-wheel-drive and mountain-biking tours as well.

In Chugchilán, the **Hostal Mama Hilda** (tel. 3/281-4814) offers comfortable, basic accommodations for $11 pp, including a vegetarian breakfast and dinner. Mama Hilda herself is a dear, and she can arrange horseback riding in the area. The nearby **Hostal Cloud Forest** (tel. 3/281-4808, $5–7 pp) has the most popular restaurant in Chugchilán, and you can buy provisions at stalls in the **Sunday market** or at a few small shops in town. There's an **Andinatel** office on the plaza, where phone calls can be made Tuesday–Sunday. It's the only public line in town, so residents listen for the speaker announcements to see who incoming calls are for.

It's possible to hike from Chugchilán to Laguna Quilotoa or back in a long day. Time your trip to catch a bus back, or spend the night at the lake. Most days, a truck takes hikers up to the lake in the morning, price depends upon the number of passengers. The six-to-seven-hour hike starts uphill from the main square. Descend to the Río Toachi cross and climb a switchback trail up and out of the steep canyon. Pass through the tiny community of Guayama (why-AM-ah), where you can buy a soda or fresh roll for your final push up the edge of the crater. Follow the signposts to join the road between Chugchilán and Zumbahua. In the opposite direction, the route is more downhill (see *Laguna Quilotoa*). The hike west to Isinlivi or Guantualó (traditional Monday market) starts on the road about three kilometers north of Chugchilan. Take the path opposite the road to the cheese factory or the turning at Chinaló to reach Itualó, and cross the bridge over the Toachi River.

(Laguna Quilotoa

Bright turquoise water—the color is caused by dissolved minerals—makes this deep crater lake a startling mirage-like sight amid the breezy surrounding hills. Now part of the Iliniza Ecological Reserve (see *Machachi and Vicinity*), the *reserve* charges a $1 pp entrance fee. Accommodations can be found along the turnoff from the main road, where a few Tigua artists run humble shelters with fireplaces, wool blankets, and not much else. Humberto Latacunga's **Cabanas Quilotoa** (tel. 3/281-4625) has rooms with fireplaces for $8 pp. It includes a small *tienda* (shop) and a dirt-floor restaurant, where Humberto's beautiful paintings and carved wooden masks are for sale. Next door is the bare-bones **Hostal Quilotoa** ($3 pp).

The precipitous hike around the rim takes four–five hours, and the steep plunge down to the lake itself can be done in three hours round-trip. Horses are available for rent at the rim for the ascent. (The water is said to contain too many minerals to be purifiable.) A walk of five hours takes you back to Chugchilán. You can buy sodas and snacks at a small *tienda* in the village of Guayama. The route descends into the precipitous Río Toachi gorge at Sihui, then makes the final uphill push to Chugchilán. Maps are available at the Black Sheep Inn in Chugchilán and at the Cabanas Quilotoa. Buses run from Chugchilán to the laguna before dawn, passing as high as 3,914 meters along the way.

Zumbahua

This high up, it can feel as much like the Himalayas as the Andes. The rocky knobs along the road from Latacunga have become spires, and the wind carries a distinctive hint of grit and loneliness particular to high mountain towns. Zumbahua itself is a bleak, dusty place surrounded by steep hillsides and inhabited by foul-tempered dogs, children asking for handouts, and, oddly enough, opuntia cacti.

Zumbahua's **Saturday market** brings the place to life from 6 A.M. onward. A sea of felt fedoras and bright shawls swirls around piles of onions and potatoes. Llamas led by a rope through a hole in the ear don't seem to notice the tinny sales patter blaring out of loudspeakers in Spanish and Kichwa.

A few basic hotels cluster around the main plaza. The **Hostal Quilotoa** and **Hostal Richard** are the best, for $5 pp with shared bath and hot water. The **Hotel Oro Verde** has also been recommended for budget lodgings. It can be hard to find a room on Friday night, so try to arrive early to give yourself a chance to catch a bus back if no accommodations are available. Tigua painters at Chimbacucho have a gallery next to the new community *hostal,* **Samana Huasi** (tel. 3/282-4868, $6), on the main road towards Pujilí. Tucked into the valley a few kilometers to the east is the family-run **Posada de Tigua** (tel. 9/161-2391), a working farm with cozy rooms and home-cooked meals—the price is $20 per day, including meals.

Pujilí

West of Latacunga, the road winds up into the hills, where patches of evergreen dot a landscape that becomes more and more barren. Soon you're into that moody Andean landscape that is so hard to capture on film: cloud shadows racing over undulating fields as the wind sends waves through an ocean of grass. *Indígenas* in ponchos provide the occasional flash of color, as shepherds follow ragged white and brown sheep, shaggy burros, and placid llamas.

In Pujilí itself, the markets on Sunday (main) and Wednesday draw *indígenas* from even tinier settlements. Gustavo Quindigalle sells excellent Tigua-style paintings from his house in the *ciudadela* Vicente León (ask locally for directions). The festivals of Carnival and Corpus Christi parades are especially colorful.

Ambato and Vicinity

Only slightly ahead of Riobamba in size, the capital of Tungurahua Province (pop. 155,000) serves as the commercial hub for the section of the Sierra between Quito and Cuenca. In his book *The Inca Smiled,* Richard Poole tells of a rivalry between the neighboring provincial capitals: "To an Ambateño the inhabitant of Riobamba is a *chagra,* a yokel…whereas for the Ríobambeño, the inhabitant of Ambato is something of a city slicker."

Although lacking character, Ambato does have a few things to offer. The city's markets are among the most important in the Sierra. A reassuring number of bookstores are scattered throughout town, while *indígenas* in red ponchos and colorful felt hats—white

CENTRAL SIERRA

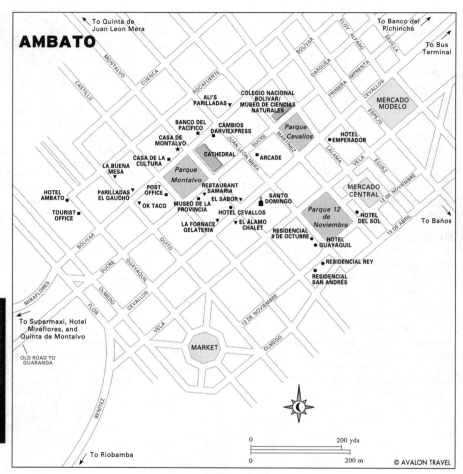

bowlers and green and brown fedoras—conduct their business. The setting, although geologically volatile, is pretty, with steep hillsides to the southeast sandwiching the city against the river to the northwest. For a pleasant afternoon stroll, head west along Bolívar as it turns into Miraflores and follows the banks of the river. Out here, you'll find a few of the city's better hotels, along with the country houses of famous local sons Juan Montalvo and Juan León Mera, and the new Supermaxi store.

HISTORY

Ambato's interesting past has left it a rather dull city. The immediate area was inhabited for millennia before the Inca arrived. The Cara conquered the original inhabitants, the Cashapamba, before being overrun themselves by the Inca. The invaders from Cuzco soon established a way station here along the Inca highway to Quito. The city of Ambato was founded in 1535 on the bank of the Río Ambato by Sebastián de Benalcázar, founder of Quito.

Then the fun started. In a pattern that had become common in the Sierra, the inhabitants of Ambato found themselves shaken, stirred, and occasionally buried by the restless earth. The fledgling city was first destroyed by an earthquake in 1698, leading the surviving residents to rebuild a few kilometers south of the razed site. The most recent quake to cause severe damage occurred in 1949. As a result, Ambato has seen most of its colonial character reduced to rubble, leaving it a relatively faceless city compared to many in Ecuador. Much of what hasn't been rebuilt within the last four decades is run down.

Ambato managed to become an intellectual gathering place in the 19th century, drawing writers and intellectuals from Quito and Guayaquil. The writers Juan Montalvo and Juan León Mera owned country homes outside Ambato in the 1800s, both of which are now within the city and preserved as museums. The city also hosted political essayist Juan Benigo Vela (1843–1920), as well as Pedro Fermín Cevallos and Luis Martinez—all well-known intellectuals in their time, who today are immortalized in countless Ecuadorian street names.

For some reason, Ambato has two street-numbering systems in operation. The ones used here are found on the white signs, not the blue ones.

SIGHTS

The **Parque Montalvo,** graced by a statue of Juan Montalvo, is backed by Ambato's drab modern **cathedral,** which was rebuilt after the most recent earthquake and contains some well-executed wood carvings of the stations of the cross. On the corner of Montalvo and Bolívar is the **Casa de Montalvo** (tel. 3/282-4248, 9 A.M.–noon and 2–6 P.M. Mon.–Fri., 10 A.M.–1 P.M. Sat., $1), where author Juan was born and laid to rest. Tours of the house and

lavish mausoleum are available. The Montalvo Experience is completed by a visit to the writer's summer home, known as the **Quinta de Montalvo** (8 A.M.–6 P.M. Tues.–Sat., free) in the suburb of Ficoa, west on Miraflores and across the river onto Avenida Los Guacamayos.

The home of the other Juan is also along the Río Ambato. Juan León Mera sought solace at the **Quinta de Mera** (9:30 A.M.–5 P.M. Wed.–Sun., $1) between penning his country's national anthem and *Cumandá,* a novel depicting indigenous life in 19th-century Ecuador. The old mansion rests amid well-maintained gardens in the suburb of Atocha, north of the city center. To get there, take a taxi or walk north on Montalvo to a bridge over the river. From here, you can take a bus labeled Atocha or walk, taking a right on Capulíes. The walk should take about one hour.

For some reason, almost every stuffed monkey in every museum in Ecuador is posed with its claws out and its teeth bared. The **Museo de Ciencias Naturales** (8:30 A.M.–12:30 P.M. and 2:30–6:30 P.M. Mon.–Fri., $0.50), in the Colegio Nacional Bolívar on Parque Cevallos,

© JEAN BROWN

entrance gate to Parque Montalvo in Ambato

is no exception. Menacing herbivores notwith-standing, the museum's collection is quite good. Highlights include some beautiful birds, especially the condors, and a display of historical photographs taken around the turn of the 19th century by famous Ecuadorian mountaineer Nicolás Martínez. In the back, you'll find incredibly ornate Píllaro festival costumes down the hall from a menagerie of barnyard freaks. Open daily (9 A.M.–1 P.M. and 2–6 P.M.), the **Museo de la Provincia,** inside the lovely renovation of the *Casa del Portal,* is the latest addition to Parque Montalvo. Admission is free, and traveling exhibits share space with permanent displays.

ENTERTAINMENT AND EVENTS

The new **Mall de los Andes** (Atahualpa and Victor Hugo) contains the recently opened Cinemark, with three theaters. It's a gathering place in the evenings.

Festivals

The end of February brings two large fiestas to town. Ambato's **Carnival** is famous for what it lacks: the traditional water throwing, which was officially outlawed by the city government. The concurrent **Fiesta de las Frutas y las Flores** (Fruit and Flower Festival) is one of Ecuador's most lavish annual affairs. Activities range from the usual bullfights, parades, and midnight dancing in the streets to a book fair and painting and theater exhibitions. Hotels are often full during this time, so book ahead if you plan to spend the night.

SHOPPING

Although there might not be much to see in Ambato, there's certainly no lack of things to buy. In addition to the city's huge markets, Ambato is the leather center of the Central Sierra. Almost every block has its own upscale boutique selling suede and leather clothes, luggage, shoes, and accessories. You can also have clothes custom-made by several private *sastres* (tailors). Almost everything is high quality, so expect to pay accordingly. For the best deals,

take the rural bus to Quisapincha from Ficoa, near the Supermaxi ($0.50).

Markets

Ambato is famous for having some of the largest markets in the country. The **Mercado Central,** east of Parque 12 de Noviembre, has hosted a main market on Mondays and smaller ones on Wednesdays and Fridays since 1861. (Markets are held daily, but those three days are the largest.) The flowers are one of the main attractions, grown in farms throughout the central Sierra and sold in gaudy, fragrant bunches along a whole row of stalls. There's also the **Mercado Modelo,** a few blocks northeast of the Mercado Central. More than half a dozen smaller markets throughout the city specialize in everything from vegetables and fruit to shoes, animals, and tourist goods. For supermarket goods, try the new Mall de los Andes, south on the road to Huachi.

ACCOMMODATIONS
Under $10

Most of Ambato's budget accommodations are clustered around Parque 12 de Noviembre. The **Residencial 9 de Octubre** (tel. 3/282-0018, $4 pp) and the **Residencial San Andres** (tel. 3/282-1604, $5 pp) both have rooms with shared baths and hot water. The **Hotel Guayaquil** (tel. 3/282-3886, $6 pp) is a small step up; rooms have private bath and TV.

$10 and Up

The most swank accommodations in Ambato are at the **Hotel Ambato** (Guayaquil and Rocafuerte, tel. 3/242-1793, info@hotelambato.com, $43 s, $56 d). Overlooking the Río Ambato, the hotel has all the amenities: gift shop, casino, laundry facilities, Internet, and room service. Their Restaurante Ficoa is one of the best in the city. Rates include private bath, phone, radio, cable TV, and breakfast ($43 s, $61 d). The **Hotel Cevallos** (Cevallos and Montalvo, tel. 3/242-2009, $16 s, $29 d) is also recommended. The classy new **Hotel Casino Emperador** (Cevallos and Lalama, tel. 3/242-4460, $51 s, $73 d) has a casino, pool, spa, and one of the most popular nightspots. Prices include breakfast.

FOOD

For traditional Ecuadorian food, the Swiss-run **Alamo Chalet** (Cevallos 6–12 and Montalvo) is the local choice, with *comída típica* and spaghetti on the menu. Dishes are around $3.50, and the restaurant boasts a pleasant setting with art-covered walls. **Parilladas El Gaucho** (Bolívar and Quito) is also recommended, with traditional food for around $4.50 a plate.

Wood-oven pizzas at **La Fornace** average $4–6, with service so good you might momentarily forget you're in Ecuador. The folks at **OK Taco** (Quito and Guayaquil) will sing the praises of their eponymous entrée, but they also offer a few other Mexican favorites for $3–5.

If you're after a snack, try **El Sabor,** serving sandwiches, frozen yogurt, and fresh-baked breads and cakes. The renovated **Casa del Portal** (Sucre facing Parque Montalvo) is home to the new **Museo de la Provincia** and two new gathering places, the elegant **Samaria** restaurant (tel. 3/282-0538) in an interior patio and **El Portal** (tel. 3/242-4507) offering coffee, snacks, and cocktails in very cozy surroundings.

INFORMATION AND SERVICES

Ambato's **tourist information office** (Guayaquil and Rocafuerte, tel. 3/282-1800, 8:30 A.M.–noon and 2–5 P.M. Mon.–Fri.) is beside the Hotel Ambato.

Darviexpress (Bolívar 17–07) exchanges travelers' checks and a good selection of foreign currencies with surprising efficiency and a very low commission. The **Banco del Pacífico,** on Montalvo and Bolívar, handles travelers' checks as well. The **post office** holds down the southwest side of Parque Montalvo.

TRANSPORTATION

Ambato's **bus station,** two kilometers north of town, can be reached by taxi ($1) or local bus from Parque Cevallos. Quito is three hours north by bus ($3), and Latacunga is one hour ($1). Riobamba is one hour south ($1), and Baños is 45 minutes southeast ($0.80). Buses heading to Riobamba and other southern cities flash by around the new bypass, avoiding the city completely. To catch one, take the local bus to "Montalvo" from Parque 12 de Noviembre, or take a taxi to the "Mercado Mayorista." Frequent departures also leave for Guaranda ($2, two hours) from the terminal, and buses for **Píllaro** leave regularly from the corner of Colón and Nacional, north of the city center ($0.50, 40 minutes). Local taxis use meters.

PÍLLARO

A little less than 20 kilometers northeast of Ambato, San Antonio de Píllaro sits at 2,800 meters amid rich farmland planted with grains, papayas, and oranges. The bus ride there is lovely (once you get past the quarry and garbage dump), traveling through a deep, snaking valley. Píllaro's main claim to fame is access to the Llanganatis, an area cloaked in mystery and clouds. Much of Atahualpa's gold treasure is said to be hidden in this area,

The Rio Verde is one of the many crystal rivers flowing out of the Llanganatis Reserve.

© JEAN BROWN

and Píllaro is one of the starting points for many expeditions that have searched in vain (or been kept very quiet)—see the sidebar **The Inca's Ransom.**

This sleepy town comes to life during its outstanding fiestas. Examples of traditional, ornate **Corpus Christi costumes** worn in Píllaro during the June festival are on display in Ambato's Museo de Ciencias Naturales. At New Year and until January 6, the Diabladas parade the streets dressed exotically in red with exuberant devil masks. Parades and dances for the **Celebration of Apostle Santiago the Elder** (St. James) beginning on July 25 and lasting into August, bullfights are the culmination, a Pamplona-style bull run thunders through Píllaro's narrow streets.

Budget lodging is available at the **Novo Hostal** (Rocafuerte and Sucre, tel. 3/287-4936). You can get a bed with private bathroom for $7 pp. Tucked away on Guzman and Montalvo is the **Hotel Chelo's** (tel. 3/287-3404), where an immaculate room with hot showers and cable TV will cost $10 pp. Trekkers or treasure hunters might want to begin their trip with an overnight at **El Porvenir** (tel. 3/286-0458) also known as the Puerta de los Llanganatis, where rustic cabins with great views and lots of clean air cost $6 pp. The cabins are near the community of Santa Rosa, eight kilometers beyond Pillaro.

SALASACA

Fourteen kilometers southeast of Ambato, Salasaca is home to an indigenous group of the same name, one of the most distinctive in the Ecuadorian highlands. The ancestors of the Salasaca *indígenas* were relocated to Ecuador from Bolivia by the Inca under a policy intended to minimize local uprisings among conquered tribes by sticking them in unfamiliar surroundings.

Happily, the Salasaca prospered in their new home. Today, they're known by their distinctive dress, most of all the long black ponchos (the color supposedly represents perpetual mourning for the Inca Atahualpa). Men wear *calzónes* (wide white pants), and both sexes wear white hats of bleached and felted wool.

Most of the local *indígenas* make their living working the land, spending their spare time weaving the famous Salasaca *tapices* (narrow tapestries). Unique in Ecuador, these cloth decorations usually feature fine weaving and intricate designs of animals, birds, and plants. Weaving is the domain of men, and boys first sit at the looms as early as age 10.

Shopping and Services

You can buy Salasaca weavings in the Plaza Central daily, but choices are particularly good on weekends. Weaver **Alonso Pilla** welcomes visitors to his home/workshop, where he weaves *fajas,* the traditional Andean belts. His house sits about 50 meters across from the Gasoline station, where a dirt road meets the main road—look for the sign. Alonso is very friendly and offers customized tours to surrounding villages for $5 per hour. He and his family run the cozy little *hostal Runa Huasi* (tel. 9/984-0125) beside his mother's house—call for the latest rates.

For food, the **Samarina Restaurant/Peña** one block north of the market is the only game in town, offering cheap basic meals.

Festivals

During the festival of **Corpus Christi** in June, residents dress up in elaborate masks and costumes and dance accompanied by marching bands. **San Vinicio** on June 15 is also significant, and during the **Day of the Dead** festivities November 2–3, Salasaca hosts the **Tzawar Mishki** festival of Andean music and dance.

PATATE

This quiet town filled with evacuees when Tungurahua volcano woke up in 1999. Several hotels offered "volcano watches" from a safe distance, and there was a short-lived tourist boom. It is now on the main evacuation route from Baños to the highlands, and people stop in the plaza to sample the traditional *arepas* (the recipe is said to be pre-Inca) with glasses of *enmaserado,* a local cane spirit macerated with grape juice.

The high road to Baños passes the historic haciendas **Leito** ($67 pp gets you breakfast, a spacious room, and great views of the volcano, tel. 3/285-9329, www.haciendaleito.com) and **Manteles** ($79 s, $89 d, includes breakfast, reservations required, tel. 2/223-3484, www.haciendamanteles.com), before dropping through cloud forests to the "Ojos del Volcan" and crossing the Pastaza over the new San Francisco bridge.

Baños and Vicinity

Ecuador's premier resort town (pop. 10,500) counts natural hot springs and one of the most beautiful settings in the country as key elements of its almost irresistible draw. Add an important religious shrine, extensive nightlife and eating options, and dozens of choices for outdoor adventure, and you have a recreation destination popular with both Ecuadorian and foreign tourists. Between the hikes and the spas, the travel agencies and the zoo, you may well find yourself spending weeks where you meant to spend days—that is, if the town all isn't buried by *lahars* first.

Perched on a shelf at 1,815 meters between the base of the Tungurahua volcano and the Río Pastaza gorge, Baños enjoys a mild subtropical climate year-round. Water flows on every side: The Cascada Cabellera de la Virgen (Virgin's Hair Waterfall), visible from anywhere in town, tumbles down the steep hillside, and Bascún Creek to the west joins the brown Pastaza to rush downhill into the Oriente. Hot springs bubble up from the depths of Tungurahua to the south, which is often wreathed in clouds. Flowers dot the dripping green backdrop and burst over house walls in eruptions of purple, red, orange, and yellow.

Ecuadorian tourists are drawn not just to the town's beauty, but also to the Church of Our Lady of the Holy Water, one of the more

CENTRAL SIERRA

© JEAN BROWN

sugar cane stand in Baños

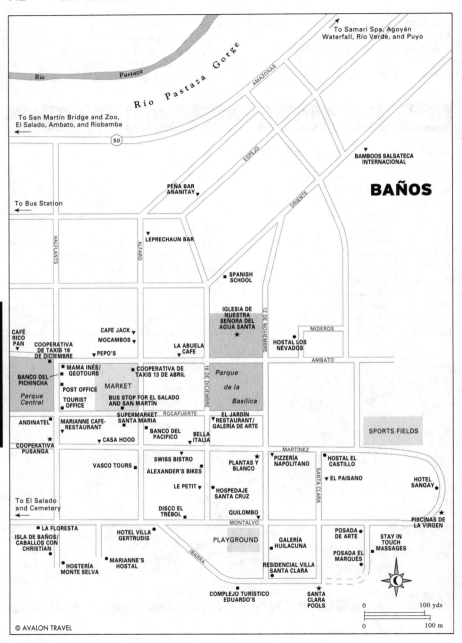

To Samari Spa, Agoyán
Waterfall, Río Verde, and Puyo

Río Pastaza Gorge

Río Pastaza

AMAZONAS

Río Pastaza Gorge

To San Martín Bridge and Zoo,
El Salado, Ambato, and Riobamba

50

ESPEJO

BAMBOOS SALSATECA
INTERNACIONAL

ORIENTE

BAÑOS

PEÑA BAR
ANANITAY

To Bus Station

HALIFANTS

ALFARO

LEPRECHAUN BAR

SPANISH
SCHOOL

IGLESIA DE
NUESTRA
SEÑORA DEL
AGUA SANTA
★

12 DE NOVIEMBRE

MIDEROS

CAFÉ
RICO
PAN

CAFE JACK
MOCAMBOS

COOPERATIVA
DE TAXIS 16
DE DICIEMBRE

PEPO'S

LA ABUELA
CAFE

HOSTAL LOS
NEVADOS

AMBATO

BANCO DEL
PICHINCHA

MAMA INÉS/
GEOTOURS

POST OFFICE

TOURIST
OFFICE

MARKET

COOPERATIVA DE
TAXIS 13 DE ABRIL

BUS STOP FOR EL SALADO
AND SAN MARTÍN

16 DE DICIEMBRE

*Parque
de la
Basílica*

*Parque
Central*

ANDINATEL

MARIANNE CAFE-
RESTAURANT

CASA HOOD

SUPERMARKET
SANTA MARIA

ROCAFUERTE

BANCO DEL
PACIFICO

BELLA
ITALIA

EL JARDÍN
RESTAURANT/
GALERÍA DE ARTE

SPORTS FIELDS

COOPERATIVA
PUSANGA

VASCO TOURS

SWISS BISTRO

ALEXANDER'S BIKES

LE PETIT

PLANTAS Y
BLANCO

HOSPEDAJE
SANTA CRUZ

MARTÍNEZ

PIZZERÍA
NAPOLITANO

SANTA CLARA

HOSTAL EL
CASTILLO

EL PAISANO

HOTEL
SANGAY

PISCINAS DE
LA VIRGEN

To El Salado
and Cemetery

DISCO EL
TRÉBOL

QUILOMBO

MONTALVO

LA FLORESTA

ISLA DE BAÑOS/
CABALLOS CON
CHRISTIAN

HOTEL VILLA
GERTRUDIS

PLAYGROUND

IBARRA

GALERÍA
HUILACUNA

POSADA
DE ARTE

POSADA EL
MARQUÉS

STAY IN
TOUCH
MASSAGES

HOSTERÍA
MONTE SELVA

MARIANNE'S
HOSTAL

RESIDENCIAL VILLA
SANTA CLARA

COMPLEJO TURÍSTICO
EDUARDO'S

SANTA
CLARA
POOLS

0   100 yds

0   100 m

© AVALON TRAVEL

important pilgrimage sites in the Central Sierra. Foreign travelers, on the other hand, come by the busload to relax in the hot pools, enjoy fresh fruit–topped pancakes for breakfast, and hike and ride horses through the hills above town.

Although this influx hasn't yet destroyed Baños's undeniable charm, the active volcano towering overhead is another matter. A limited eruption in September 1999 prompted the government to order the evacuation of the city. Residents protested but were forcibly removed by the army. Four months later, about half the city's inhabitants returned, finding Baños still in one piece but many of their homes and businesses emptied by burglars.

The orange alert, which presumed a major eruption within weeks, was held until August 2000, by which time many businesses had closed or relocated. More recent activity at the beginning of 2008 again had authorities talking of evacuation, but the locals are not moving. Baños has regained much of its former glory, most of its inhabitants have returned, and once again it's hard to walk a block without being offered a bike or horse for rent. And on the up side, the lava and ash spewed out to the west by the erupting volcano have added an entirely new tourist attraction to the town's already long list.

SIGHTS
Iglesia de Nuestra Señora del Agua Santa

The Church of Our Lady of the Holy Water is unmistakable in the center of town. The black rock walls of the Dominican church are accented with red trim and twin white-topped towers. Vendors pack the streets outside selling candles and rosaries, and the trays of flickering candles and ornate red-and-gilt altar inside evoke a baroque atmosphere.

Paintings around the perimeter of the nave record instances dating to the 17th century when the Virgin began saving the faithful from Tungurahua's eruptions, car wrecks, and numerous plunges into the Pastaza. In each case, the legend goes, victims were saved after entreating the Virgin for protection.

The statue of the Virgin sits near a spring of holy water to the left of the main body of the church. Upstairs, a museum (7 A.M.–4 P.M. daily, $0.50) houses religious relics and stuffed animals, along with piles of discarded canes and crutches—testimonials to the Virgin's healing powers.

Volcán Tungurahua

A narrow appendage of Sangay National Park reaches north to enclose Tungurahua, only 10 kilometers south of Baños. The young volcano has one of the more lengthy rap sheets in the Ecuadorian Andes—a look at the paintings in Baños's church would lead you to believe that during the 18th and 19th centuries, the volcano erupted every day and twice on Sundays. Especially destructive eruptions came in 1711 and 1877, and the two Germans who first climbed the peak in 1873 must have been crushed to hear that subsequent eruptions changed the mountain's appearance so drastically that, in effect, a new unclimbed summit was created.

Tungurahua II was first climbed in 1900 by Ecuadorian mountaineer Nicolás Martínez. The eruptive sequence that began in October 1999 forced the evacuation of Baños, blocking roads with slides of mud and ice. As of 2005, the crater had expanded to more than 400 meters in diameter—five times wider than it was when it began to erupt.

Tungurahua used to be considered the easiest snow climb in Ecuador—one of the few in the country where you started out amid tropical vegetation and finished in snow and ice. Until the risk of eruption alert lessens, however, climbing is highly discouraged.

The volcano still puts on a good show from afar. Incandescent blocks and plumes of steam and ash accompany explosions, tremors, and landslides. Climb any of the trails the facing hills to see the volcano (see *Hiking*), which is especially impressive at night. (Just make sure you bring a flashlight and can make your way back

THE INCA'S RANSOM

Placed in the town of Píllaro, ask for the farm of Moya, and sleep (the first night) a good distance above it; and ask there for the mountain of Guapa . . .

Thus opens the guide to Atahualpa's ransom, one of the richest and most plausible treasure legends in South America.

The story begins in 1537, with Atahualpa in the hands of the Spanish. Pizarro has just declared that the Inca will be killed unless he buys freedom with a room full of gold and silver. Llama trains from all over the Inca empire start creaking toward Cajabamba, laden with riches. When the news arrives that Atahualpa has been strangled, his general, Rumiñahui, quickly hides the ransom, estimated at 15,000 kilograms of gold and silver, including an 82-kilogram throne of solid gold. Every ingot is spirited away almost overnight on the shoulders of porters who are later ordered by nobles to take their own lives. Soon no one is left who could lead the Spanish to the treasure, despite a frantic campaign of interrogation, torture, and killing. As they are burned alive, Inca nobles taunt the invaders, saying that treasure will never be found.

Over the years, accounts of the treasure's size, location, and very existence have drifted like clouds over the Andes. In the mid-18th century, a poor farmer named Sanchez Orinjana came across a cache of gold earrings, noseplugs, and ingots in the Quinara Valley near Vilcabamba. Orinjana promptly took his treasure to Quito and bought himself the title of Marquis of Solana, and the modern quest for Atahualpa's gold began in earnest.

The Llanganati Mountains soon emerged as the most probable location of the lost riches. Part of the Eastern Cordillera, the range stretches from the Río Patate Valley north almost to Volcán Quilindaña, with the highest point at Cerro Hermoso (4,571 meters). Rumiñahui could hardly have found a more inhospitable, forbidding spot in the entire Inca empire. It's a wild, untouched place where trout fill the streams and the hillsides choke with dripping greenery. Gold nuggets, fishhooks, and nails found among the sheer hills and icy rivers kept the legend alive. (The IGM 1:50,000 *San José de Poalo, Sucre,* and *Mulatos* maps cover most of the area – at least the part that has been mapped – and January–March is the least miserable time to visit.)

The first organized expedition set out for the Quinara Valley under orders from the king of Spain, headed by the magistrates of Latacunga and Ambato. Three days later, the group emerged from the forest, treasure-free and minus a friar who disappeared mysteriously one night. Despite the expedition's apparent failure, the story continues to circulate that the group actually did find the treasure and stole it away to Europe – a rumor substantiated by the 1803 departure of the ship *El Pensamiento* from the port of Lambayeque in northern Peru, laden with $1 billion in gold, silver, and jewels later deposited in the Royal Bank of Scotland.

Then, in a plot twist that would make Hollywood proud, a map and a treasure guide turned up. It seems that a poor Spanish soldier under Pizarro named Valverde married an indigenous girl in Latacunga. He must have made quite an impression on the in-laws, because his wife's father – the chief of Píllaro, the closest town to the Llanganatis – told

in the dark.) Several companies run trips up to the antennas at **Ojos del Volcan** (Eyes of the Volcano), and in the daytime, you can return down to Baños on a bicycle or rent a dune buggie for the round trip. The view from Runtún is excellent. A new cable car was completed at the junction of the old road to Riobamba. It gives great views of the volcano at night, and connects to one of the emergency escape routes, so it is possible to walk back to Baños on the north side of the Río Pastaza via Lligua.

Check with the SAE or locally for the latest volcano update. The best source is the Ecuadorian Geophysical Institute, which maintains a frequently updated website at www.igepn.edu.ec.

him about the ransom and where to find it. Whether or not Valverde profited isn't certain, but on his deathbed in Spain, he dictated his famous *Derrotero* ("Path") for the king of Spain.

The original *Derrotero de Valverde* remains in the Archivo General de los Indies in Seville, but numerous copies are circulating. The British botanist Richard Spruce came across a copy in the Latacunga city archives in the mid-19th century. He also uncovered a map drawn by Anastasio Guzman, a Spanish botanist and farmer who had lived in Píllaro. Building on the knowledge of many trips into the Llanganatis, Guzman's 1800 map roughly corresponded with Valverde's guide. Seven years later, Guzman walked off a cliff in his sleep. The account of the treasure, along with a copy of the *Derrotero*, appeared as the final chapter in Spruce's *Notes of a Botanist on the Amazon and Andes*, published in 1908.

The route is simple and detailed, yet maddeningly vague in crucial passages. One penciled squiggle directs seekers around a mountain, after leading them through "quaking-bogs," "great black lakes," tunnels, ravines, and streams running with gold grains. The lake where the treasure supposedly lies, described as man-made, is said to lie between three peaks that form a triangle.

Atahualpa's riches have inspired countless treasure hunters – usually foreigners – and authors to spend years unraveling the mystery. Commander George Miller Dyott, famous for his quest for Colonel Fawcett in Brazil's Matto Grosso, was among the first explorers to mount a serious expedition. The first half of the 20th century saw three books that detailed the legend: *Llanganati*, by Luciano Andreade Marin (1937, reprinted in Spanish in 1970); *Fever Famine and Gold*, by Erskine Loch (1938); and *Buried Gold and Anacondas*, by Rolf Blomberg (1954). German adventurer Eugene Brunner spent decades in the 20th century compiling information and maps and venturing into the Llanganatis, and he died convinced that he had pinpointed the treasure lake. Peter Lourie tells Brunner's tale in his own book of treasure fever, *Sweat of the Sun, Tears of the Moon*.

The sheer impossibility of the terrain and its horrendous weather have kept the story a legend. During one trip, Brunner said he saw the sun three times in 127 days, and had only five days in which the weather was good enough to travel. Marin writes off the Llanganatis as "a region which without doubt should be marked on the maps, as few others in the world, with the words FOREVER UNINHABITABLE." Some say the mountains are cursed, sending compasses spinning and clouding the mind of anyone foolish enough to venture in. There's even a legend that a lost indigenous tribe inhabits the deepest valleys. Airplane pilots consider the Llanganatis similar to the Bermuda Triangle: probably an old wives' tale, but best to avoid all the same, just in case. Planes crash regularly in the mountains – at least reportedly, because wreckage and bodies are seldom recovered.

But the legend continues to draw seekers, and the *Derrotero* lures them into the hills. After describing a final ambiguous landmark, it ends:

> . . . *and in this manner thou canst by no means miss the way.*

ENTERTAINMENT AND EVENTS
Nightlife

The **Mocambo,** popular with gringos for its food and atmosphere, is on Alfaro and Ambato. Upstairs are darts, pool, and music videos. Graffiti art marks the outside of the **Full Jack Café,** on Alfaro between Ambato and Oriente, while the **Bamboos Salsateca Internacional** has moved farther out of town to Oriente and Suárez, with much more dance space.

The **Peña Bar Amanitay** (16 de Diciembre and Espejo) has folkloric music from 9:30 P.M. on weekends, the **Trebol** on Montalvo and

16 de Diciembre is currently the most popular disco. The **Leprechaun Bar** (Alfaro and Oriente) is open late and continues to draw evening revelers.

Festivals

Baños's **Canonization Festival** is celebrated December 15–16 with bands and processions, and the festival of **Nuestra Señoradel Agua Santa** brings in crowds of pilgrims in October.

SHOPPING

Baños's most plentiful souvenirs—along with the usual postcards, T-shirts, and hats—are woven straw bags, baskets, hand-stretched toffee, and heart-shaped cakes of *guayaba* (a sweet guava paste). Browse through the handful of antique stores, and you might come across something interesting, from kitschy paintings of Ché Guevara to old tools and pre-Columbian-style artifacts.

Albert Guzñay Saenz of **El Cade** has been carving tagua nuts for almost four decades, and he offers one of the best selections of carvings in Ecuador. The nearby area of Maldonado, between Espejo and Oriente, is full of crafts shops and taffy pullers, as is Calle Ambato.

The **Galería de Arte Huillacuna** (12 de Noviembre and Montalvo, tel. 3/274-0909, 8 A.M.–7:30 P.M. daily) displays sculptures, paintings, and drawings by local artists and offers accommodations upstairs.

On the way out of town on Oriente, look carefully to the left one block before the junction with the main road: You should find the family that makes *maracas*. For more than 20 years, they have been painting various designs on these typical instruments and exporting them all over the Caribbean and Central America. For a small fee, you can get a personalized set with your name artfully carved on them.

RECREATION AND TOURS
Thermal Baths

The thermal springs from which Baños takes its name are touted for the curative properties of their dissolved minerals. Because many locals use the springs as actual baths, it's probably not a good idea to submerge your head. Don't worry, though—the brown color is from the minerals, and most baths are cleaned and the water changed at least a few times per week.

Piscinas de la Virgen (4:30 A.M.–5 P.M. and 6–10 P.M. daily, $1–2 pp), the most popular baths in town, are also the hottest (50°C) and the prettiest, located at the foot of the Virgin's Hair waterfall. Cold, chlorinated pools are also available, or stand under the cold spouts if you dare. Facilities for washing clothes are around the side. Frequented by locals and children, the tepid **Santa Clara Pools** (9 A.M.–6 P.M. daily, $1 pp) feature water slides, a sauna, and a steam room. The **Complejo Turístico Eduardo's,** on Ibarra across from Santa Clara, is the newest set of baths. For access to the pools alone, you'll pay $0.50, but $2 lets you use the sauna, steam room, hot tub, and gymnasium.

El Salado Hot Springs (4:30 A.M.–5 P.M. daily, $1.50 pp), with both hot and cold pools, sits on the far (east) side of the Bascún Creek canyon, 1.5 kilometers out of town. Look for a paved road just across the bridge, east of Baños on the way to Ambato and Riobamba. Buses from the center of town run to the springs every half hour throughout the day, or else it's a 40-minute walk or 10-minute drive, passing the Chalets Bascún along the way. Another route down the opposite side of the canyon begins where Martínez leaves town to the west.

◖ Hiking in Baños

The steep hillside west of town can be scaled by two routes. Head south on Mera and go to the right past the cemetery to reach the **Virgen Mirador,** an overlook at the eastern edge of the hillside with a statue of the Virgin. The walk up takes about half an hour, and the views of Tungurahua around the corner are great. The path continues above the statue all the way to the top of the hillside and Runtún, or a downhill branch can be taken back down to Mera (to ascend this way, head left initially from Mera).

The hillside flattens out eventually at the small village of **Runtún** at 2,600 meters, named for the Kichwa word for fortress. Needless to say, the views of Baños and Tungurahua are worth the climb, which takes a whole day up and back. East of Runtún is the aptly named **Bellavista,** with its huge cross lit up lime-green after dark, seeming to float in the night sky above Baños. Another route leads uphill from the end of Maldonado in Baños directly toward Bellavista, with a side branch to Runtún. Runtún and Bellavista, along with the village of **Puntzan,** can be reached by car, as well as via a back route from the village of **Ulba,** a few kilometers east of Baños along the road to Puyo.

More good hikes follow the Pastaza: Cross the main road and the new mirador road bridge at **Puente San Francisco.** A network of trails crisscrosses the hillside facing Baños. The village of **Illuchi,** about a two-hour hike from the river, is a good turning-around point, with views of Baños, Tungurahua, and the river.

The **Puente San Martín** crosses the Pastaza just to the west of town. To reach it, cross the bridge out of Baños, pass the turnoff to El Salado, and turn right near a religious shrine and police checkpoint. Near the bridge is the **Cascada Inés María,** a small waterfall, and the **San Martín Zoo,** opened in 1994 as a refuge for sick and injured animals from the Amazon. The collection of birds and mammals was evacuated to Quito during Tungurahua's activity, but most have been returned. Across the Puente San Martín is the village of **Lligua,** a three-to-four-hour hike to where the Río Lligua enters the Río Pastaza. Farther up is the crest of Chontilla Hill (2,700 meters), followed by a radio antenna on the hilltop. A loop up this hillside is a good option for a day hike, crossing at one bridge and re-crossing at the other.

Mountain Biking

Baños couldn't be in a better setting to explore by wheel power. Most guided trips are four hours, with some time spent driving to or from your destination. One of the more popular bike excursions is down the old road to Puyo, along the gorge of the Río Pastaza. This spectacular ride is all downhill, leaving it up

to you to pedal back up or catch a bus. This dirt road can be very muddy during the rainy season, but at least it keeps you away from the traffic for much of the journey—some parts are on the new paved road. You can usually arrange with your rental company to leave your bike at one of several places en route and take a bus back.

Five kilometers from town is the Agoyán Hydro station, a kilometer beyond the Agoyán Waterfall, followed by an unlit tunnel. Another seven kilometers past the tunnel, the Río Verde spills into the Pastaza from the north near a small village of the same name, forming the **Cascadas San Miguel.**

Horseback Riding

Horses are another popular way to get into the hills. Expect to pay about $16 for a three-hour ride, and be wary of operators willing to be bargained down to less than $10. Baños's most acclaimed horse trips are with **Caballos con Christían,** at the Isla de Baños hotel. Christían Albers offers 10 years of experience and robust horses.

Keep in mind that reports of ill or mistreated horses have been on the rise in the last few years, to the point that an association was being organized to fix fair prices and ensure proper veterinary treatment of the animals. Look for healthy, well-treated animals, and try out the saddle for fit before you head out on your ride. Don't accept blankets instead of saddles.

Rafting and Kayaking

Río Loco (Maldonado and Martínez) offers rafting trips, including transportation, a guide, and lunch. Rates are $60 pp for a whole day of shooting rapids and $30 pp for half days (10 percent SAE discount). Experienced rafters and kayakers with their own equipment should consider the Río Patate between Patate and Baños (also known as the "crazy river"). The Río Pastaza is farther downstream, closer to Puyo (the stretch below Shell is recommended), and the Río Topo empties into the Río Pastaza in the direction of Puyo.

CENTRAL SIERRA

Tours

So many tour agencies operate in Baños that it's tough to keep the trustworthy separate from the fly-by-night rip-off artists. The following agencies have been repeatedly recommended, but it's a good idea to check with the South American Explorers' clubhouse in Quito for a current list. Almost all agencies offer hiking, rafting, kayak, canyoning, pendulum, and mountain-biking tours, climbing trips, and rainforest expeditions. Many agencies that offer climbing trips buy, rent, and sell new and used mountaineering equipment. Rates for overnight trips should be $40–50 pp per day, all-inclusive.

Geotours (Ambato and Halflants, tel./fax 3/274-1344, geotoursbanios@yahoo.es) runs biking, horseback riding, rafting, and trekking tours. It also handles reservations for Río Loco rafting trips. **Cordova Tours** (Maldonado and Espejo, tel. 3/227-4093, ojosvolcan@hotmail.com) does general tours and rents four-wheel-drive vehicles.

A few agencies specialize in tours of the Amazon. **Sebastian Moya Expediciones** (16 de Diciembre and Martínez, tel. 9/923-0986, wulopez@hotmail.com) is owned by the Shuar guide Sebastián Moya and run under the auspices of the Yawa Jee Shuar Indigenous Foundation, a private nonprofit dedicated to sustainable, low-impact tourism to benefit Shuar communities. Along with highly recommended jungle tours, **Tsantsa** offers work and study opportunities at research stations in the Oriente. It has an information center on Parque Central. **Expediciones Amazonicas** (Oriente between Alfaro and Halflants, tel. 3/274-0506) has gotten positive reports.

Most feedback on **Rainforestur** (Ambato and Maldonado, tel./fax 3/274-0743) has been positive. Guides speak English, French, and German, and offer tours of the surrounding area and Cuyabeno (four–five days, $45 pp per day, including all meals). **Vasco Tours** (Alfaro and Martínez, tel. 3/274-0017, www.vascotoursbanios.com) is run by Flor Vasco and Juan Medina in Quito. People returning from Vasco jungle trips rave about the guides' knowledge, professionalism, and relationship with the Huaorani tribes the tours visit.

Relaxing

At the end of a long, active day, many tired travelers take advantage of several massage and therapy spots. Frequently recommended are the husband-and-wife team Geoffrey and Edith at **Stay in Touch** on Santa Clara (tel. 3/274-0973). A one-hour full-body massage costs $25.

ACCOMMODATIONS

Baños has more than 120 hotels, and competition keeps prices down. Most will negotiate their rates midweek and double them on national holidays (and/or demand a minimum three-night stay), when it's not uncommon to see people sleeping in the street after all the hotel beds are booked.

Under $10

The **Hostal Plantas y Blanco** (Martínez and 12 de Noviembre, tel. 3/274-0044) is well known among visitors for its rooftop terrace, guest services, and value. The hotel's fresh-fruit double pancakes are one of the best breakfasts in town, served early in a dining room overlooking the city. Board games, music, and honor-system beer and sodas are available to guests until the patio closes at night. A special therapeutic steam bath is open to anyone in the morning, and movies on the VCR, luggage storage, and laundry service are available downstairs. Rooms are comfortable, cleaned daily, and have wonderful hot showers—all this for only $8.50–10 pp. A friendly Salasacan named José, but better known as "Zaracay," sells his wares through the hostel.

Plantas y Blanco's owner has opened the **Hospedaje Santa Cruz** (16 de Diciembre and Martinez, tel. 3/274-0648, $7.50 pp), with two ground-floor patios with fireplaces, games, magazines, and a self-service bar. Off Montalvo near the waterfall is the **Posada El Marqués** (tel. 3/274-0053), a homey, family-run place with newly upgraded rooms for 38 people in the large main house. Rooms are spacious, clean, and quiet, with private bath and hot water for $15 pp. Laundry service and *queña* flute lessons are available.

Within one block of the church is the friendly **Hostal Los Nevados** (Ambato and 12 de Noviembre, tel. 3/274-0673 or 3/274-0827, $6 pp). Clean rooms feature private bath and hot water. The **Hostal El Castillo** (Martínez and Santa Clara, tel. 3/274-0285) is painted black with white lines around the rocks. The hostel exchanges travelers' checks, rents bikes and horses, runs a small book exchange, and offers Internet service in the cafeteria. For $6 pp, you get a private bath and hot water. At the southern end of 12 de Noviembre, the **Residencial Villa Santa Clara** (tel. 3/274-0349) has rooms in the main house with shared bath for $10 pp and private cabins in the back with their own bathrooms for $11 pp.

$10-25

The **Isla de Baños** (Montalvo 131, tel./fax 3/274-0609, $14–20 pp in double rooms) is run by Christían Albers of Caballos con Christían. The glass-walled atrium on the first floor looks out onto a well-tended flower garden—the perfect place for one of the hotel's famous breakfasts. A book exchange, breakfast, security boxes, and baggage storage are all included. Opening soon, from the same people who run the excellent restaurant **Marianne,** a hostel of the same name hidden down a quiet lane off Montalvo between Halflants and Alfaro. All the $15 pp rooms have balconies.

$25-50

Probably the prettiest hotel within Baños proper, the **◖ Hostería Monte Selva** (tel. 3/274-0566, fax 3/285-4685, $38 s, $63 d) consists of a collection of cabanas at the foot of the hillside at the south end of Halflants. Papasan chairs and a bamboo bar remind you that above all else, this is a place to relax. The beautiful pool, sauna, and steam room are open to the public for $10 pp ($5 for children).

Family cabins are $15 pp, and all prices include breakfast and use of the extensive facilities.

Head west down Montalvo to reach the **Hotel Villa Gertrudis** (Montalvo 20–75, tel. 3/274-0441, fax 3/274-0442, $15 s, $29 d), a villa-style old home surrounded by beautiful gardens. Rates include breakfast. The Olympic-size covered pool across the street was previously part of the hotel; now it functions with a therapy center and is open to the public daily 7 A.M.–1 P.M. and 2–6 P.M. for $3 pp.

The big peach-colored building at the base of the waterfall is the **Hotel Sangay** (tel. 3/274-0490, fax 3/274-0056). Guests can choose between rooms in the main hotel, cabanas out back, and executive suites beyond that. Guests can work up a sweat with tennis or squash before crossing the street to the baths. The hotel's restaurant is highly recommended. Rooms are $25 s, 35 d, and cabins are $35 s, $45 d. Prices include breakfast and use of the facilities.

Over $50

On the crest of the hill overlooking Baños sits **◖ Luna Runtún** (tel. 3/274-0882, fax 3/274-0376, carmen@lunaruntun.com, www.lunaruntun.com, $155 s, $207 d), an "adventure spa" that offers luxurious lodgings. The hacienda feel is enhanced by flower gardens, fountains, and tiled roofs. Eucalyptus beams, handmade bricks, and hand-cut windows adorn the plush rooms. Enjoy massage, reiki, and beauty treatments in the garden spa, which uses plants from the garden and ashes and volcanic stones from the volcano. The Swiss/Ecuadorian owners speak Spanish, English, French, Swedish, and German, and they offer Spanish courses and tours of the area. A taxi to the hotel from Baños costs about $8, and a private shuttle is available.

Samari Spa (tel. 3/274-1855, fax 3/274-1859, www.samarispa.com, $99 s, $139 d) is on the road to the jungle just one kilometer out of town, so it's quiet and relaxing. The opulent facilities include 37 rooms, plus suites, a covered pool, a sauna, steam-hydro massage, and therapy and massage rooms. The original building of volcanic rock has been tastefully restored and sits in beautifully landscaped gardens. The acclaimed restaurant offers all meals and caters to conventions or small groups.

FOOD

The main options for eating in Baños—and there are plenty of options—are healthy and international. It seems like just about every country in Europe has a representative restaurant in town, while countless others offer pizza, salads, and other meat-free fare. Most restaurants close by 10 P.M.

International Cuisine

Le Petit Restaurant (16 de Diciembre and Montalvo, tel. 3/274-0936) is part of Le Petit Alberge hotel, serving excellent (albeit pricey) French food. The fondues are especially good. For dishes from the south of France, try the **◖ Marianne Cafe-Restaurant** (on Halflants between Martínez and Rocafuerte), a neat little place serving lunch and dinner. This is one of the best restaurants in town, with main dishes for $4–7.

Pasta in all its variations can be found at the popular Italian restaurant **Mama Inés**, on Ambato by Parque Central. Pizzas or spaghetti dishes are around $3–5 at **La Bella Italia** (tel. 8/256-8610) on Martinez and Alfaro. Just across the street, the new **Swiss Bistro** offers fondue, raclette, and many other European specialties.

Other Options

The building housing **El Paisano** (Santa Clara 288 and Martínez) doesn't look very inviting, but the vegetarian fare is inexpensive and excellent, making good use of fresh ingredients. Take a look at the paintings.

Pizzeria Napolitano, across the street from Plantas y Blanco, cooks up 11 different kinds of pizza, along with meat and seafood dishes. For creative surroundings and cooking, try **Quilombo** (Montalvo and 16 de Diciembre), a small place that offers meat dishes with zest. **La Caldera,** on Ambato and

16 de Diciembre, offers a good selection of traditional Ecuadorian fare.

Ambato between Halflants and Alfaro hosts an overwhelming array of bars and cafés. The tiny **Pepo's Cafe** serves breakfast and sandwiches, and **La Abuela Cafe** offers pasta, salads, soups, and vegetarian dishes in a cozy atmosphere with *buenas vibraciónes* (good vibrations). One block west, the **Cafe Rico Pan** is popular for its breakfasts, pizza, and homemade breads.

For more vegetarian options, **El Jardín Restaurant/Galería de Arte** (Rocafuerte and 16 de Diciembre) has a good selection. Breakfast is inexpensive, and the outdoor garden/patio is perfect for afternoon cakes and coffee. The **Casa Hood** (Martinez and Halflants), long a Baños mainstay for travelers because of its healthy food, has funky art and comic books to keep you busy until your tasty food arrives, accompanied by fresh juice, pastry, or herbal tea. Prices are around $2.50–5 for main dishes. It has a bookstore, a large message board, and videos at night. **Cafe Hood,** overlooking the plaza on Montufar and Rocafuerte, offers a *menu del día* lunch for $1.50, as well as excellent home-baked cakes and coffee.

INFORMATION AND SERVICES

Head to the **Departamento de Turismo del Municipio** (Halflants and Rocafuerte, tel. 3/2740-483, 8 A.M.–5:30 P.M. daily) for the scoop on Baños's long list of places to stay, places to eat, and things to do.

The **Banco del Pacífico** (Rocafuerte and Alfaro) has an ATM and changes travelers' checks.

Spanish Lessons

Outside of Quito and Cuenca, Baños is probably the most popular place in Ecuador to stay and study Spanish. Most schools offer individual and group instruction. At the northeast end of town, the **Raíces Spanish School** (tel./fax 3/274-0090) occupies the yellow house of J. Silva Romo at 16 de Diciembre and Suarez. It features flexible schedules with instruction for $6 per hour, as well as laundry and fax services.

José María Pepe Eras runs the **16 de Diciembre Spanish School** (tel. 3/274-0232 or 3/274-0453), marked by a big sign reading "Spanish School." He has been teaching for 15 years and employs four other teachers. Dr. Martha Vaca Flores is the director of the **International Spanish School for Foreigners** (Espejo and 16 de Diciembre, tel. 3/274-2612, martaiss@hotmail.com), where instruction is $6 per hour.

The **Baños Spanish Center** charges $6 per hour (Oriente and Cañar, tel./fax 3/274-0632, baniosspanishcenter@hotmail.com) and is run by Elizabeth Barrionuevo, who speaks Spanish, English, and German. She has been recommended as an excellent teacher, and she offers dancing and cooking lessons in addition to language instruction.

TRANSPORTATION

The central **bus station** is bordered by Reyes and Maldonado, along the main road at the north end of Baños. Buses run to most cities in the Sierra, as well as to the Oriente: Quito ($4, four hours), Ambato ($1, one hour), Riobamba ($1.50, 1.5 hours), and Puyo ($2, two hours). (The road from Baños to Riobamba is basically gone, with washed-out canyons up to 10 meters deep.) Local buses to **El Salado** and **San Martín** leave regularly from the bus stop at Alfaro and Martinez, beside the Santa Maria supermarket.

Taxis can be found at the **Cooperativa de Taxis** (Ambato and Halflants) and the **Cooperativa de Taxis 13 de Abril** (Rocafuerte and Alfaro). You can also find lots of taxis at the bus station.

EAST OF BAÑOS

The road to Puyo is now fully paved—vehicles use a series of tunnels, while bikers and hikers can enjoy the canyon views from the old road along the cliff face. This is the famous Valley of the Waterfalls, which has developed into an adventure tourist's playground, with pendulum swings, gondola cable crossings, canyoning, hikes, rafting, and many other fun activities.

About 14 kilometers from Baños is the Machay Bridge, where a spectacular pendulum swing between the adjacent bridges over the river is $10. Two cable cars cross the river ($1 pp) near the Manta de Novio waterfall, 16 kilometers from Baños. The people who operate the cable crossing will keep an eye on your bicycle for a small fee.

In Río Verde, 18 kilometers from Baños, there are several small restaurants and places to leave bikes while hiking. You'll see a sign indicating a path down to the river and a suspension bridge. From the middle of the bridge is the best view of **El Pailón del Diablo** (Devil's Cauldron), a waterfall tumbling between vertical walls into a deep depression. (Look for the devilish faces in the rocks above the waterfall—there are supposed to be six.) The villages of Río Verde and Río Negro both offer overnight facilities for tourists. **Miramelindo** (tel. 3/288-4194, www.miramelindo.banios.com, $15 pp) is beside the river between the Río Verde tunnels: look to the left and spot the colorful roof tiles, just like in the famous paintings by Gonzalo Endara Crow. There are comfortable rooms overlooking a garden full or orchids and birds, with a huge pressure bubble-filled hot tub overlooking the river. It's a lovely spot to relax, and your insurance company shouldn't invalidate your coverage because you stayed to close to an active volcano. If Miramelindo is full, a couple of kilometers further down is **Pequeno Paraiso** (tel. 9/981-9776, $12 pp), where comfy cabins sit on grounds full of fruit trees, and a Bellevue looks over the canyon. **El Encanto Natural** (tel. 6/288-4028), at Las Estancias between Río Verde and Río Negro, is another option. Río Negro has one simple hostel in the village and a couple of places across the river at the edge of the forest. Puyo is another 40 kilometers downhill, past Mera and Shell.

West of Ambato

One of the most spectacular detours in the country leaves Ambato to the west and moves up and over the flank of Volcán Chimborazo, down to Guaranda, and onward to Babahoyo and the coastal lowlands. The road was once one of the main thoroughfares between Quito and Guayaquil. Today, traffic crosses the Cordillera Occidental elsewhere, but the 100-kilometer route—the highest paved road in Ecuador—has retained all its beauty.

Cultivated fields cover every square meter of countryside along the initial stretch west of Ambato. Soon you'll be climbing into the misty, moorish *páramo,* where chunks of the rich, dark-brown hillside have crumbled onto the road as it cuts between pine forests. Suddenly, less than 10 kilometers away, squats ancient, massive Volcán Chimborazo, the highest mountain in Ecuador. Volcán Carihuairazo sulks deferentially to one side.

Hardly any vegetation reaches this high up, and wind across the bleak base of the mountains whips grit into the air. Somewhere in this rocky, sandy moonscape, the road peaks at higher than 4,000 meters. Soon you begin the descent into the Tolkien Valley, where Guaranda awaits—Chimborazo lingers in the distance, its snowy cap shining brilliantly in the sun.

The journey takes about two hours by bus. Because the road from Guaranda to Riobamba is almost as thrilling, the ride out and back is a highly recommended detour if you're heading north or south on the Pana, even if Guaranda isn't on your list. Just sit back, trust your driver, and enjoy the views.

◖ CHIMBORAZO FAUNA RESERVE

The provinces of Cotopaxi, Tungurahua, and Bolívar intersect within this 58,560-hectare reserve that encloses Chimborazo and Carihuairazo. The four Holdridge life zones within the reserve are all basically *páramo* by another name, ranging from the low, dry mountain steppe to the more humid mountain

and sub-Andean forests. Much of the original vegetation has been cut down. A camelidae reintroduction program oversees the breeding and care of llama, vicuña, and alpaca herds with the direct participation of local indigenous communities.

The reserve can be entered either near Pogyos on the road between Ambato and Guaranda (look for the sign reading "Yacupartina"), or from Mocha on the Pana, south of Ambato. Admission is $10 pp. The IGM 1:50,000 *Quero* and *Chimborazo* maps cover the area.

Climbing Volcán Chimborazo

Ecuador's highest peak (6,310 meters) caps the southern tip of the Cordillera Occidental, a final upward thrust before the mountain chain fades off to the south. Chimborazo, whose name comes from the Kichwa for "snowy place to be crossed," actually consists of two peaks with five separate summits between them. The climb is challenging and not that straightforward.

Chimborazo used to be considered the highest mountain in the world, a fact that perhaps eased the sting when both La Condamine and Humboldt failed to achieve the summit (the latter repeatedly). Whymper and the Carrels, in what was probably the sweetest moment in their travels in Ecuador, were the first to stand atop Chimborazo in 1880, having ascended via what is known today as the Whymper Route. Although Mount Everest has since been deemed higher, Chimborazo has one thing over Everest: even if it is shorter when measured from sea level, its peak is actually farther from the center of the earth than Everest's, because of the earth's equatorial bulge.

While the route isn't technically difficult, it still demands knowledge, experience, and—above—all acclimatization. (Keep in mind Whymper's writings on his ascent: "We arrived upon the summit of Chimborazo standing upright like men, instead of groveling, as we had been doing for the previous five hours.") The upper slopes are prone to avalanches—a bad one in 1993 killed 10 climbers. The melting of the mountain's glaciers has led to recent changes in the route. Although Chimborazo can be climbed year-round, the best months have been December and January. April brings heavy snowfall; by June, you can expect high winds, a clear sky, and good snow.

On the road from Ambato to Guaranda, look for a solitary abandoned white house on the left where the road reaches its highest point, a little west of Pogyos. A paved road leads southeast, forking southwest of Chimborazo after 10 kilometers. Straight ahead to go to Riobamba, or turn left to reach the Whymper hut: It's at 5,000 meters at the foot of Thielmann Glacier, 10 kilometers uphill. Accommodations in this refuge, which is operated by the Alta Montaña agency in Riobamba (tel. 3/294-2215), include cooking facilities and mattresses. Taxis from Riobamba, Ambato, or Guaranda may go as high as the lower hut.

From here, your choices include the old, deteriorating, and possibly dangerous Castillo Route and the relatively new Glacier Route. Allow at least 8–10 hours for the ascent from the Whymper Hut and half as long for the descent. Alternative access in 2007 and 2008 has been on the northeast glacier, using the camp at the Yacupartina community building or horses from Urbina. This route is much safer but longer, taking three or four days.

Climbing Volcán Carihuairazo

Sharing the Abraspungo Valley with its big brother Chimborazo, Carihuairazo (ka-ree-why-RAH-zo) takes its name from the Kichwa for "strong, freezing wind." Both the Maxima (5,020 meters) and Mocha (height disputed) peaks are covered with snow and ice, making technique and experience necessary for the ascent. Both summits are part of a large caldera almost two kilometers in diameter, open to the north. Whymper and the Carrels first climbed the Mocha peak in 1880, while Maxima remained unconquered until a Colombian,

German, and French expedition reached the summit in 1951.

The Mocha peak is accessed most easily from the town of Mocha, midway between Ambato and Riobamba on the Pana. A dirt road leads northwest from Mocha and is partially accessible by four-wheel-drive vehicle (trails also lead west from Mochapata and 12 de Octubre, two smaller villages a few kilometers south of Mocha). The trail passes a ruined hut at 4,300 meters, near Cerro Piedra Negra peak (4,500 meters). To ascend the Maxima peak, head east from Pogyos to Yacupartina, where you can camp in the community house, or hike further and use a spot near the Laguna Negra.

The town of Mocha can also be used as a starting point for the beautiful, challenging **hike between Chimborazo and Carihuairazo.** The four-to-five-day trip heads west, skirting the southeastern flank of Carihuairazo and passing between the volcano's two main peaks and two smaller side hills (Cerro Piedra Negra to the south and Loma Piedra Negra to the southeast). It ends near Pogyos, on the Ambato–Guaranda Road.

SALINAS

If few travelers experience the road to Guaranda, even fewer make it another 20 kilometers up to Salinas, an isolated little town at the foot of interesting cliff formations. Developed with help from the Swiss, Salinas's food cooperatives are considered one of the most successful development projects in the Americas. They turn out several quality products, including some of Ecuador's best European-style cheese, sausages, chocolates, coffee, cookies, bread, and mushrooms. An artisan store sells crafts made of wood, tagua, ceramic, and porcelain, and the **Quesera de la Cooperative Salinas** (Salinas Cooperative Cheese Factory) offers tours. You can arrange guides, bikes, and horse tours through the **tourism office** on the main plaza. Look at the map on the main plaza for information on walking routes in the area. Cheese, other food staples, and handicrafts are for sale in a **shop** on the second floor of the west side of the plaza.

There are mineral-water springs 15 minutes from town, and old salt mines are a two-hour walk past the stadium (inquire locally for directions). Snug accommodations are available in the nearby **Hotel Refugio** (tel. 3/239-0022). Rooms with breakfast are $6–14 pp, and you can also eat at the friendly community kitchen on the main plaza, which is open to all. Carnival brings the **Fiesta de la Lana** (Wool Festival), celebrated with food and music. Three daily **buses** leave from Guaranda, or you can rent a pickup or catch a bus to *Quatro Esquinas* (Four Corners), the intersection with the road to Salinas, and hitch the 20 kilometers from there to Salinas.

GUARANDA AND VICINITY

Guaranda's nickname, "the Rome of Ecuador," seems to make about as much sense as "the Quito of Italy," but a glance at the city's setting explains it. The capital of Bolívar Province is built on, around, and between a set of rolling hills—seven, to be exact, just like ancient Rome. Guaranda's setting is made even more superb by the snowy bulk of Volcán Chimborazo over the hills to the northeast. Cobbled streets climb through this bright, breezy town (so breezy, in fact, that power outages from blown-down lines are not uncommon).

Like Latacunga, Guaranda (pop. 21,000) is a provincial capital with a small-town feel; it has kept its hilly charm intact. After an evening *paseo* around Parque Bolívar, you'll hear your footsteps echo down the steep side streets, while elsewhere children play soccer and roller-skate in the narrow, sloping Plaza Rojo along Calle Enriquez. No longer part of the main land route between Quito and Guayaquil, the road still offers one of the more spectacular drives from the Sierra, and many buses travel this way daily.

Sights

The city's castle-like **cathedral** sits on the edge of Parque Bolívar, solidly built of large stone blocks. Overlooking the town is **El Indio Guarango,** a five-meter statue of a heavily muscled warrior. The views from the small plaza surrounding the statue are worth the hike, and a museum with local archaeology is below. Follow the same road to the La Colina complex and keep going a kilometer past it—or hire a taxi.

Entertainment and Events

Carnival in Guaranda is rated as one of the most festive and traditional in the highlands—expect plenty of drunken street dancing, water balloons, and sprayed foam. If you can't wait until then to party, try **Los Balcones de la Pila**, at García Moreno and Pichincha, and the **Cafetacuba,** downstairs from the Corte Superior de la Justicia on Parque Central.

Shopping

There are a few small **supermarkets** around the city, or try one of the city's two **markets,** held on Saturday and Wednesday in the Plaza 15 de Mayo and the concrete Mercado 10 de Noviembre. A few cobblers around the city can custom-make you a pair of cowboy boots or walking shoes for surprisingly little.

Accommodations

Guaranda's poshest digs are above the city at the 19-room **Complejo Turístico La Colina** (117 Guayaquil, tel./fax 3/298-0666 or 3/298-1954, $35 s, $60 d, includes breakfast). It has a bar and restaurant, along with a pool and sauna open to the public (8 A.M.–6:30 P.M., $3 pp). Tours can be arranged to nearby villages and sights. To reach the hotel, head east on Moreno and take a left uphill on Guayaquil.

Next to the municipal building in the city center is the **Hotel Cochabamba** (García Moreno and 7 de Mayo, tel. 3/298-1958, fax 3/298-2125, $15 s, $24 d). The hotel's restaurant is probably the best in town, with entrées for $2–3 and a set lunch for $2. The owners also organize local tours.

My favorite part of the pleasant **Hotel Bolívar** (Olmedo and Pichincha, tel. 3/298-0547, $13 s, $24 d) is the 10-meter cactus in the plant-filled inner courtyard. The hotel is two blocks down from the plaza on the northwest corner, and the rooms have rugs, TVs,

© JEAN BROWN

avocados and other chopped ingredients waiting to be added to a rich potato soup

and hot water. Pastel wall stripes reminiscent of the 1960s decorate the **Hotel Santa Fe** (10 de Agosto and 9 de Abril, tel. 3/298-1526, $7 s, $14 d), which has rooms with private baths and electric showers. There's also a restaurant.

Food

Guaranda is seriously lacking in the food department—no Roman feasts here. Along with the restaurant at the Hotel Cochabamba, the best possibility for a decent meal in the city is the **Restaurant El Rincón del Sabor** (Convention1884 and Olmedo). Otherwise, try a pizza at the **Pizzeria Buon Giorno** (Sucre and Garcia Moreno, tel. 3/298-3603); they start at $4.

Services and Transportation

Guaranda's **bus station** is a 20-minute walk east from the city center on Moreno. At the **Flota Bolívar** ticket window (Enriquez and Azuay), you can book passage to Ambato, Guayaquil, Quito, Santo Domingo, and Babahoyo.

Toward Riobamba

The narrow road east from Guaranda is as exciting for its knuckle-biting danger as its scenery. Clinging desperately to the side of green velvet hills, the dirt road is barely wide enough for one lane of traffic. Don't look down around the curves, or you might see the bus tires skirting the edge of a sheer 100-meter drop-off. The surrounding hills are so steep that houses are built on shelves dug out of the hillsides, and field workers can till the ground in front of them standing up straight. Above a tiny trickle of river, the reforested slopes sport tiny, evenly planted saplings. Workers enveloped in clouds of sawdust saw larger pine trees along the road.

CENTRAL SIERRA

Riobamba and Vicinity

There were moments in Riobamba...usually in the early morning and evening, when I felt myself so transfixed by the gentleness of the light, the softness of the breeze and the scented stirrings of the eucalyptus, that I had no desire to move from where I was ever again.

– Richard Poole, *The Inca Smiled*

The history of the capital of Chimborazo province begins in prehistoric times. Puruhá *indígenas* were the first to settle here at the south end of the Avenue of the Volcanoes, among the low, rolling hills within sight of Chimborazo, Tungurahua, and El Altar. Next came the Inca, followed in 1534 by the Spanish, who founded their first capital near the present-day city of Cajabamba. An earthquake in 1797 destroyed most of Riobamba, prompting the surviving

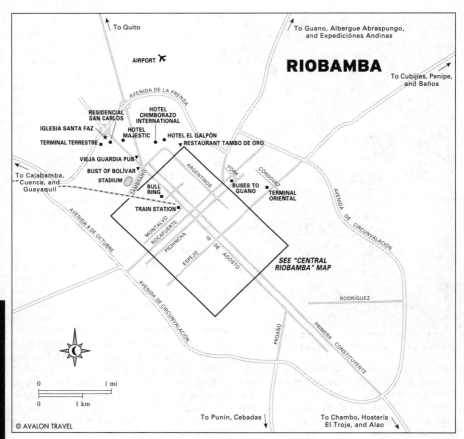

residents to rebuild in the city's present location. Ecuador's first constitution was written and signed here, an event commemorated in the name of the city's main thoroughfare, Primera Constituyente.

Riobamba's nickname, "Sultan of the Andes," suits the city perfectly. It has an elderly, settled feel, as if nothing has changed in a long while, and that's just fine. Cobbled streets and well-maintained antique cars add to the air of comfortable complacency. Colonial buildings in every imaginable pastel shade line the city's short blocks. Turquoise, peach, lime, and lavender facades frame elderly women selling ducklings out of cardboard boxes on street corners. It's no surprise that a long lunch hour (noon–3 P.M.) is the norm.

As a trading center for the south-central Sierra, Riobamba (pop. 123,000) sees more indigenous traffic than most cities its size. Cattle being led down the street are a common sight, and even the city's name reflects its mixed heritage—a combination of the Spanish word for river and the Kichwa word for valley. Riobamba is also known for the chill winds that blow through its streets, sent down from the slopes of Chimborazo and El Altar.

Riobamba is a good place to plan a climb of

one of the nearby peaks or break up a long land journey north or south. You can take a day trip to Chimborazo or shop for crafts in one of the nearby villages.

SIGHTS
Museums and Galleries
One of South America's foremost religious art museums is housed in the former **Convento de la Concepción** (Argentinos and Larrea, 9 A.M.–noon and 3–6 P.M. Tues.–Sat., $4) in the church of the same name. This 16th-century convent was donated to the city when the convent life began to fall out of vogue among young women. Today, the former nuns' cells hold priceless works of colonial religious art. Paintings, sculptures, and crucifixes abound. Don't miss the incredibly inlaid *barguesos* (chests of drawers) or the museum's priceless monstrance—a gold-and-jewel-encrusted vessel in which the consecrated host was displayed to the faithful during mass. The monstrance was stolen in 2007, but the section containing the host was recovered, along with a few other parts, and returned to the nuns in mid-2008. A reconstructed nun's room, complete with wire scourges, gives an idea of spartan convent life during the colonial period. Free guided tours are available, with a tip expected and deserved.

Parks, Churches, and Monuments
Named after the date on which Riobamba was founded, the **Parque 21 de Abril** occupies a small hill called La Loma de Quito at Argentinos and León. It offers a great view of the city and mist-shrouded volcanoes on the horizon, along with a mural depicting the history of Ecuador, with special emphasis on Riobamba. Climbers, take note: one of the park's outer walls offers good bouldering practice. On the north side of the park sits the small **Iglesia San Antonio de Padua,** with an impressive wood altar. Crypt visits (bring a date!) are held 3–6 P.M. on Saturday and Sunday.

The **basilica** next to the **Parque La Libertad** is famous for being the only round church in the country. Riobambeños are

particularly proud of this one, because local talent was responsible for most of its design and construction during the late 19th century. A few blocks west, the pleasant colonial **Parque Maldonado** encloses a monument to Pedro Maldonado under the gaze of the city's **cathedral.** Two blocks north sprout the spires of the **Convento San Alfonso,** resembling an old gray Victorian house.

Markets
Most of the goods sold in Riobamba's many markets are of the household, tool, or food variety, but a few offer tourist items as well. Of particular note are the baskets and mats woven by nearby *indígenas* out of reeds from the Laguna Colta. Saturday is the main market day, with Thursday close behind. Crafts and indigenous clothing are sold in **Parque de la Concepción** at Orozco and Larrea, south of the convent. The produce market in **Plaza Simón Bolívar** also carries pottery and baskets. Also significant are the **Mercado Borja** (across Espejo from the Iglesia La Merced), the **Mercado La Condamine** (five blocks south of the train station), and the **Mercado San Francisco** (between 10 de Agosto, Primera Constituyente, Velasco, and Benalcázar).

ENTERTAINMENT AND EVENTS
Lectures and video showings are sometimes held at the **Casa de la Cultura** (Rocafuerte and 10 de Agosto, Tues.–Sun.), and at the **Colegio Nacional Maldonado** on Parque Sucre. The latter is home to the tiny **National Science Museum** (8 A.M.–noon Mon.–Fri., $0.20), which is even better than the one in Ambato.

Festivals
The **Founding of Riobamba,** celebrated April 19–21, coincides with an **agricultural, livestock, and crafts fair** to produce the city's largest annual festival. Other occasions to tie one on and dance all night include the **Independence of Riobamba** on November 11.

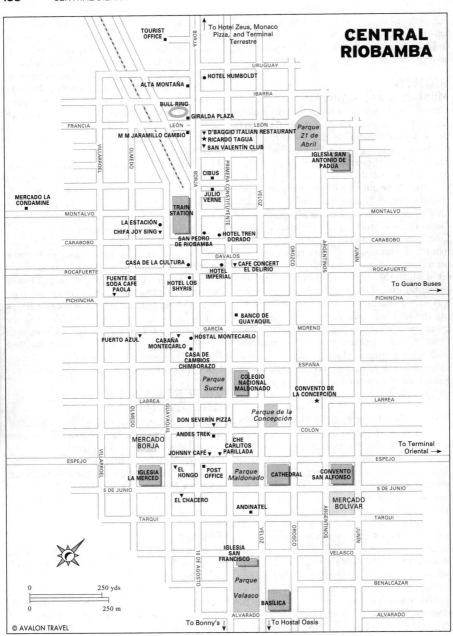

CENTRAL
RIOBAMBA

To Hotel Zeus, Monaco
Pizza, and Terminal
Terrestre

TOURIST
OFFICE

BORJA

URUGUAY

HOTEL HUMBOLDT

ALTA MONTAÑA

IBARRA

BULL RING

GIRALDA PLAZA

FRANCIA

LEÓN

LEÓN

M M JARAMILLO CAMBIO

D'BAGGIO ITALIAN RESTAURANT
RICARDO TAGUA
SAN VALENTÍN CLUB

Parque
21 de
Abril

VILLARROEL

OLMEDO

BORJA

PRIMERA CONSTITUYENTE

VELOZ

IGLESIA SAN
ANTONIO DE
PADUA

CIBUS

JULIO
VERNE

MERCADO LA
CONDAMINE

MONTALVO

TRAIN
STATION

MONTALVO

LA ESTACIÓN
CHIFA JOY SING

SAN PEDRO
DE RIOBAMBA

HOTEL TREN
DORADO

OROZCO

ARGENTINOS

JUNÍN

CARABOBO

CARABOBO

CASA DE LA CULTURA

DAVALOS

CAFE CONCERT
EL DELIRIO

ROCAFUERTE

HOTEL
IMPERIAL

ROCAFUERTE

To Guano Buses

FUENTE DE
SODA CAFE
PAOLA

HOTEL LOS
SHYRIS

PICHINCHA

PICHINCHA

BANCO DE
GUAYAQUIL

GARCÍA

MORENO

PUERTO AZUL

CABAÑA
MONTECARLO

HOSTAL MONTECARLO

CASA DE
CAMBIOS
CHIMBORAZO

ESPAÑA

Parque
Sucre

COLEGIO
NACIONAL
MALDONADO

CONVENTO DE
LA CONCEPCIÓN

OLMEDO

GUAYAQUIL

LARREA

DON SEVERÍN PIZZA

Parque de la
Concepción

LARREA

ANDES TREK

COLÓN

MERCADO
BORJA

CHE
CARLITOS
PARILLADA

To Terminal
Oriental

JOHNNY CAFÉ

VILLARROEL

ESPEJO

IGLESIA
LA MERCED

EL
HONGO

POST
OFFICE

Parque
Maldonado

CATHEDRAL

CONVENTO
SAN ALFONSO

ESPEJO

5 DE JUNIO

EL CHACERO

5 DE JUNIO

ANDINATEL

MERCADO
BOLÍVAR

TARQUI

ARGENTINOS

JUNÍN

TARQUI

10 DE AGOSTO

IGLESIA
SAN
FRANCISCO

VELOZ

OROSCO

VELASCO

Parque
Velasco

BASÍLICA

BENALCÁZAR

0   250 yds

0   250 m

ALVARADO

ALVARADO

To Bonny's

To Hostal Oasis

© AVALON TRAVEL

Nightlife

The bar **El Tentadero** (Borja and Leon) is a local hotspot. The **Vieja Guardia** pub, popular for drinking and dancing, sits at Flor and Zambrano near the bust of Bolívar.

SHOPPING

Several shops on Borja sell tagua nut carvings. **Ricardo Tagua** (Borja and León) is one of the best, as is **The Tagua Shop,** which shares the office of Alta Montaña (Daniel León Borja 35–17 and Ibarra). You can watch the carvings being made at the latter, which stocks other crafts as well. **Giralda Plaza** is a small *centro commercial* with cafés, shops, and a supermarket on Borja and Leon.

RECREATION AND TOURS

Within range of a sizable handful of Ecuador's most popular peaks, Riobamba hosts several high-quality mountain-guide services. All of the organizations and individuals listed are fully licensed. **Alta Montaña** (Daniel León Borja 35–17 and Ibarra, tel./fax 3/294-2215, aventurag@ch.pro.ec) is the most well known and trusted. It offers trips for just about any destination and activity you can imagine, from climbing and hiking the Inca Trail to birdwatching and horseback-riding. Alta Montaña's guides really have their act together. A four-person trip up Chimborazo costs $160 pp, all-inclusive. They also operate and take reservations for **La Estación** *hostal* at the Urbina railway station (tel. 9/969-4867).

Marcelo Puruncajas directs **Andes Trek** (Colón 22–25 and 10 de Agosto, tel./fax 3/294-0964). He has climbed since 1958 and speaks English. Chimborazo for four costs $160 pp. The shop rents equipment, runs mountain-biking trips and Amazon tours, and has four-wheel-drive service available.

Marco Cruz operates **Expediciones Andinas** (tel. 3/296-4915, marcocruz@laserinter.net), three kilometers toward Guano and across the street from the Albergue Abraspungu. Climbing is its specialty, but llama treks and mountain-biking tours are also on the bill. A four-day, four-person trip

Coconuts travel well and are a preferred, safe refreshment in many a market.

© JEAN BROWN

up Chimborazo costs $400 pp, including use of the high-quality equipment, which is also available for rent.

The **Julio Verne** travel agency (Pasaje El Espectador 22–35 and Borja, tel. 3/296-3436, julver@interactive.net.ec) relocated here from Baños after the eruption of Tungurahua. It receives regular recommendations for its climbing, trekking, and jungle trips, and the staff speaks German, Dutch, English, and a little French. Climbing Cotopaxi or Chimborazo is $180 for two people, with one guide for every pair of climbers.

Galo Brito of **Pro Bici** (Primera Constituyente 23–51 and Larrea, tel. 3/294-2468 or 3/294-1880, probici@probici.com, www.probici.com) guides mountain-biking excursions personalized for each group's ability, from extreme descents of Chimborazo to quiet village tours. Galo, who offers high-quality Cannondale aluminum-frame bikes and a support vehicle, speaks English and a smattering of French and German. Day trips are about $80 for one person, $45 pp for two.

ACCOMMODATIONS
Under $10

Many of the budget hotels clustered around the train station redefine the word *basic,* offering little more than a mattress and a door that closes. The **Hotel Imperial** (Rocafuerte 22–15 and 10 de Agosto, tel. 3/296-0429) has laundry, luggage storage, and mail service for $6 pp with private bath. The friendly owner runs tours to Chimborazo and Tungurahua and has a small book exchange.

The friendly and clean **Hotel Los Shyris** (10 de Agosto and Rocafuerte, tel. 3/296-0323) is another good deal for $10 pp, with private bath and hot water. With its quiet garden, the **Hostal Oasis** (Veloz 15–32 and Almagro, tel. 3/296-1210, $10 pp) is calm and a good value.

$10-25

Facing the station on Guayaquil, the newer, popular **La Estación** (tel. 3/295-5226) charges $12 pp, including breakfast, and offers help in getting train tickets. The **Hotel Tren Dorado** (Carabobo 22–35 and 10 de Agosto, tel. 3/296-4890, $11 pp) has a restaurant, TV and VCR room, and rooftop balcony. Nicely decorated rooms with private bath and hot water are an excellent value. The staff will make you an early breakfast before you catch the train, and they also run tours of the area.

Four blocks west of the train station, the friendly **Hotel Humboldt** (Borja 35–48 and Uruguay, tel. 3/296-1788 or 3/294-0814, $18 s, $26 d), has a bar, restaurant, private parking, and a lounge with a TV and VCR. Rooms include TV and phone.

$25-50

Two of Riobamba's fancier hotels command a view of the city from a hill on the elbow of Zambrano and Argentinos, in the suburb of La Giralda. Both show their age a bit, but they're still good deals. Up the steps at the end of Argentinos is the unmistakable pink edifice of the **Hotel Chimborazo International** (Argentinos and Nogales, tel. 3/296-3474 or 3/296-3475, fax 3/296-3473, $38 pp). Each of the 36 rooms features color TV, phone, and private bath, and guests can enjoy the pool, sauna, and whirlpool on the first floor. The **Hotel El Galpon** (tel. 3/296-0981 or 3/296-0982, fax 3/296-0983, $19 s, $29 d) has a disco, indoor pool, private parking, and an upscale restaurant.

The **Hotel Zeus** (tel. 3/296-8036) on Borja has spectacular views, an elegant restaurant, and a spa center. Comfortable rooms with bathtubs are $24 s, $36 d. The small **Hostal Montecarlo** (10 de Agosto 25–41, tel. 3/296-0557, $15 s, $30 d) is brimming with character. It has a covered courtyard and marble floors. The 17 small rooms all have TV and private bath.

Over $50

Begun in 1555, the Hacienda Chuquipoggio of Don Hernando de la Parra oversaw 151,700 hectares of land at its peak, spread across four provinces. Simón Bolívar himself once graced Chuquipoggio—conveniently located between Quito and Cuenca—with his liberating presence. The hacienda's main buildings were recently converted after five years of restoration into the **(Hostería Andaluza** (tel. 3/294-9370, handaluz@ch.pro.ec, $60 s, $72 d), a fine country hotel 16 kilometers north of Riobamba along the Pana.

The hotel boasts 55 rooms, including four suites, and a pair of restaurants in the former stable area that are capable of holding 150 people. Iron stoves steam beneath deer- and bull-head trophies inside, near old horse saddles gleaming in the firelight. A gym, sauna, steam room, game room, and playground are elsewhere on the grounds. Tiled roofs and fountains lead back to the workshops, where the *hostería's* famous Andaluza hams are slowly cured in sea salt, as they have been for centuries. Rooms include private bath and satellite TV.

Set in the Las Abras suburb three kilometers north of Riobamba, on the way to Guano, the **Albergue Abraspungu** (tel. 3/294-0820 or 3/294-0821, fax 3/294-0819, abraspungo@ andinanet.net, www.hosteria-abraspungu.com,

$55 s, $75 d) began its career as a pre- and post-climbing lodge before metamorphosing into a country inn in 1994. Everything here rings of mountaineering, from the hotel's name (after the valley between Chimborazo and Carihuairazo) to the black-and-white photos of climbers and mountains on every wall, taken by Marco Cruz of Expediciones Andinas, across the lane. Four-wheel-drive vehicles fill the parking lot, and antique climbing gear hangs from the walls. Each of the 42 rooms is named after a different Ecuadorian mountain, and they're all connected by whitewashed hallways trimmed with rough wood beams and decorated with indigenous hats, masks, and old farming tools. Breakfast costs $5; lunch and dinner are $12 each.

FOOD

At night, an entire colony of food kiosks lines Carabobo near the train station, making it a popular place among locals for dinner. Most Riobamba restaurants close by 10 P.M.

Simón Bolívar once owned the building where you'll find the **(Cafe Concert El Delirio** (Primera Constituyente and Rocafuerte, tel. 3/296-6441), a snug, classy restaurant surrounding a small courtyard garden. The ambience inside is pure old-world Spain, with movie posters, paintings, and a fireplace to ward off the chill. Dishes run $7–8. Another upscale pick is the **Cabaña Montecarlo** (García Moreno 21–40), offering decent Ecuadorian fare and pasta in a chalet atmosphere for less than $5. A welcome addition to the local dining scene is **El Chacero** (5 de Junio 21–46 and 10 de Agosto, tel. 3/296-9292), with a good variety of Italian dishes in a cozy atmosphere for $4–7.

Monaco Pizzería (Borja and Duchicela) has vegetarian pizzas and lasagna. **Cibus** (Borja and Lavalle) is the new in place to be well fed and entertained; it's popular for dinner or just coffee and a snack. The **Chifa Joy Sing** by the train station has been serving standard Chinese fare for about 20 years. A little further out of town, not far from the bus station, is **Il Encontro,** with Italian and other international specialties served by a chef with medals pinned to his uniform. Comfortable dining, good choices, and immense portions can be found at **Bonny,** on Primera Constituyente and Darquea.

On Pichincha and Olmedo, the **Fuente de Soda Cafe Paola** serves breakfast and fruit salads and is a quiet place for a snack and a cup of coffee in the evening. For another good breakfast option, head to **Johnny Cafe** (Espejo and Primera Constituyente), a funky little place decorated with old photos of Riobamba, just off Parque Maldonado on Espejo. The **San Valentine Club** almost feels like a '60s soda fountain, except they serve pizzas, Mexican food, and—well, why not?—Mexican pizzas. Small pies are less than $4 and a vegetarian burrito is $3. It's only open in the evenings. For lunchtime fish dishes, try **Punto Azul** (Moreno and Olmedo).

My favorite eatery in all of Riobamba is still **(El Hongo,** a mushroom-shaped snack stand that adds a touch of Smurfs to the solemn street corner of Espejo and Guayaquil.

INFORMATION

The **tourist information office** (tel. 3/294-1213) is behind the Centro de Arte y Cultura at Borja and Pasaje Municipal. Staff can recommend mountain guides and equipment sources in the city. There is now a tourist information office at the revamped train station (9 A.M.–5 P.M. daily). The **Ministerio del Ambiente** (tel. 3/296-3779, 8 A.M.–1 P.M. and 2–5 P.M. Mon.–Fri.) has a small, green-roofed office to the left of the larger Ministerio de Agricultura y Ganadera building on 9 de Octubre. This is the headquarters for Sangay National Park, and therefore the place to go for any information on the park or climbing Volcán Sangay or El Altar. The guard posts at Candelaria and Alao can be contacted from here by radio to check on trail conditions.

SERVICES

The **post office** is one block north, under the fish-scale clock dome. Internet cafés are scattered around the train station.

CENTRAL SIERRA

Money

MM Jaramillo Arteaga (Borja and Leon) and **Chimborazo** (beside the Hostal Montecarlo) exchange travelers' checks efficiently and at good rates, and they handle a reasonable selection of other currencies. Find an ATM at the **Banco de Guayaquil** (Primera Constituyente and Garcia Moreno).

TRANSPORTATION
Bus and Taxi

Riobamba's main terminal terrestre is on the west end of town, about one kilometer from the train station at La Prensa and Borja. Buses come and go between here and Quito ($4, 3.5 hours), Ambato ($1, one hour), and Cuenca ($6, six hours). To reach Baños ($2, 90 minutes) and cities in the Oriente, like Tena ($6, seven hours), you'll have to get to the Terminal Oriente, 12 blocks north of Primera Constituyente along Espejo. Buses to Guano leave from Pichincha and York, nine blocks north of Primera Constituyente.

A **private taxi** to the refuge on Chimborazo costs about $40 and can hold up to five people.

Train

The status of the train heading toward the coast from Riobamba is constantly changing, so it's a good idea to check with the South American Explorers or the train office in Riobamba for the latest update. As of 2004, the train was running from Riobamba to just below the Nariz del Diablo (Devil's Nose), the spectacular set of switchbacks below Alausí, then returning uphill to Riobamba the same day. Trains leave Wednesday, Friday, and Sunday at 7 A.M. for $15 pp one-way and return in the late afternoon.

NEAR RIOBAMBA

A few kilometers south, at the intersection with the road to Bucay and Guayaquil, is **La Balbanera Chapel,** the oldest church in Ecuador. When the Spanish first arrived in Ecuador in 1534, one of the first things they built was this church on the shore of the reedy

Laguna Colta. Since then, it has undergone a complete renovation—by man and earthquake—but stepping inside the meter-thick stone walls still comes close to taking you back centuries (except for the steel grill in front of the altar).

Eight kilometers north of Riobamba, artisans in the craft village of **Guano** turn out distinctive wool rugs and wall hangings and leather shoes. Abstract and pre-Colombian motifs predominate in the weavings, which are much thicker and more durable than the usual thin tapestries. Carlos Orozco's store and home workshop sells quality textiles, along with a craft shop on the main plaza. Ancient ruins stand watch on a nearby hillside. Saturday is market day. From Guano, it's a 20-minute walk to the tepid **Los Elenes thermal baths,** which at least have great views of the volcanoes to the east. Camping is permitted, and there's a small cafeteria.

SANGAY NATIONAL PARK

The largest park in Ecuador's Central Sierra connects Chimborazo, Tungurahua, and Morona-Santiago Provinces. The park contains three of Ecuador's best climbs—to the tops of Volcanes Tungurahua, El Altar, and Sangay. At the time of its creation in 1979, the park protected 270,000 hectares of such biological richness that UNESCO declared it a World Heritage Site four years later. In 1992, the Ecuadorian government more than doubled the size of the park to 517,725 hectares.

One year after that, Sangay was placed on UNESCO's World Heritage in Danger list primarily because of problems caused by the construction of a road bisecting the park from Guamote to Macas. No environmental impact studies were ever ordered to predict the impact of this road on Sangay's delicate ecosystems. Most of the park's backcountry, though, is still pristine and hard to reach.

Flora and Fauna

The park's 4,400-meter altitude range encloses 10 different life zones, from lowland

Roofs thatched with *páramo* grass keep highland housing warm.

rainforest to alpine tundra, and not surprisingly is home to a staggering diversity of flora and fauna. Most of the larger animals are concentrated in the park's lower, southern side, including anteaters, jaguars, monkeys, and most of Sangay's estimated 500 species of birds. The higher regions protect one of the last sizable refuges of the Andean tapir near Volcán Sangay. The highly endangered pudú deer can also be found in Sangay Park, but you'll have to look carefully—the nocturnal deer is one of the world's smallest, weighing in at 10 kilograms and standing 40 centimeters at the shoulder. The pudú's stubby horns have earned it the nickname "Mephistopheles" from scientists.

Indigenous Cultures

Two indigenous groups currently live in Sangay Park: the Canelos (lowland) Kichwa to the north, and the Shuar near Macas. Artifacts in the valley of the Río Chiguaza (a tributary of the Pastaza) date back as far back as 500 B.C., and a ceremonial center uncovered 30 kilometers north of Macas is considered perhaps the most important archaeological site in the Ecuadorian Amazon. The Río Upano area around Macas was the home of the Río Upano culture during the Formative Period (4000–500 B.C.).

Access

The main gateways to Sangay from the west are through Alao, southeast of Riobamba, via Chambo, Guayllabamba, Pungala, Licto, or Atillo, and further southeast via Cebadas. Hiring a private truck or taxi is the most certain way to make the journey to Alao. Trucks also leave from Parque Libertad heading to Alao on Monday, Wednesday, Saturday, and Sunday at 1 P.M. Buses run from Riobamba at least as far as Licto. For the return, a milk truck leaves Alao for Riobamba early every morning.

There aren't any restaurants or hotels in Alao, but you might be able to sleep in the park office if it's open. If not, break out the tent. Admission to the park is $10 pp. The trail continues into the park between El Altar and the Volcán Sangay to the abandoned settlements of La Esperanza and Huamboya along the Río Palora, with a southern spur to the base of the Volcán Sangay. Near the end of the route is a site called El Placer, 20 kilometers from Alao, where a small refuge has been built near a set of hot springs.

Daily buses (Transportes Riobamba from the Oriente terminal) take the new road to Macas, which is mostly paved to Atillo. You can stay here at Saskines in a cabana for $5 pp. Meals and guides are available, and the lakes are just

© JEAN BROWN

a kilometer along the road. From Guamote, a road connects before Cebadas (pick up good cheese at the *queseras*) to the Atillo road. Further south past Palmira is another road to the guard post near the Lagunas Ozogoche. There is an excellent hiking trail between Atillo and Ozogoche Lakes. Climbers can reach El Altar from Penipe between Riobamba and Baños via a track located southeast past the Candelaria guard post.

Local Guides

The **Asociación de Guías Indígenas de Guarguallá** (AGIG) is a confederation of indigenous mountain guides from Guarguallá, a valley south of Alao. Guides offer four-day horseback excursions to the foot of Sangay, as well as climbing and hiking trips. All profits from their activities go directly to help the marginalized communities of Chimborazo Province. None of the guides speak English, so having someone in your group who speaks Spanish will help. You can contact them in Riobamba through the office of the Movimiento Indígena de Chimborazo (1430 Casa Indígena, Guayaquil and Juan de Velasco, tel. 3/294-1728), or through the Hotel Canadá (Borja and La Prensa, tel. 3/294-6676).

Climbing Volcán Sangay

Summiting Ecuador's most active volcano adds rockfall, tremors, and enough sulfur to turn your ice-axe yellow to the normal mountaineering dangers of avalanches, crevasses, and plain old falling. Towering above the jungle on the edge of the Cordillera Oriental, smoky Sangay (5,230 meters) is a mountain few ever see, let alone scale. But if its name (from the Kichwa *samkay,* meaning "frighten") and reputation don't scare you off—and if the cosmic dice governing volcanic eruptions roll in your favor—you just might be able to say you've completed one of the most difficult and dangerous climbs in South America.

Sangay's recorded history of activity dates back to 1628, and the mountain hasn't let up since: a French expedition in 1849 counted more than 250 explosions in one hour. The first successful ascent was made in 1929, followed by the first national ascent in 1962. But Sangay didn't go quietly: an eruption killed two members of a British expedition in 1976 (a story recounted in Richard Snailham's book *Sangay Survived*). More recently, Sangay shot out a column of ash 25 miles high in January 2004.

The mountain's continual activity makes any detailed route description obsolete, because the contours of the peak are continually being reformed. You should definitely hire a guide and pack animals for the long, difficult hike to the base of the mountain. Members of the guide co-op in Alao will be up to date on the mountain's activity and the safest current routes. Vinicio Cazin is a recommended guide, and visitors can ask for him upon arrival.

Take rubber boots and wear a helmet, because the hike to the base can be muddy, and lava-rock bombs are harder than your head. Protect your gear in plastic bags. Ice axes and crampons are helpful for the smooth, compacted snow near the top. Finally, leave for the peak attempt early in the morning and ascend and descend quickly to minimize your time on the slopes. Most guides won't even make the ascent themselves, instead choosing to point out the way and wait for you at the bottom. The best months to make the climb are October–February, the driest time in the area. July and August are sodden, making the hike to the base more of a two-day slog. Several IGM maps will make your life easier: 1:50,000 *Sangay* and *Laguna Tinguichaca,* and the 1:25,000 *N IV-F3c Río Culbreillas* and *NV-B1.*

Approaching El Altar

The jagged remains of El Altar's crater bear witness to what must have been an incredible cataclysm, as one of the highest mountains in the world blew apart in an ancient explosion, leaving a C-shaped crater larger than three kilometers in diameter open to the west. Also known as Capac Urcu (Grand Mountain), El Altar is merely a shell of its former self, but it's still the fifth-highest mountain in Ecuador and probably the most technical climb.

Nine separate summits echo El Altar's religious name. Counterclockwise from south to north, they are: Obispo, "the bishop," El Altar's highest (5,315 meters); Monjas Grande (5,160 meters) and Chico (5,080 meters), "the big and little nuns"; Tabernáculo, "the tabernacle," actually three peaks, of which Sur (5,100 meters) is the highest; Los Frailes, "the friars," a quartet topped by Grande (5,180 meters); and finally, Canónigo (5,260 meters), "the canon." None of these peaks were climbed before 1963, when an Italian team led by Marino Tremonti first stood atop El Obispo. All have been climbed since then, but many new routes remain open.

Even with one of the longest approaches in the country—or perhaps because of it—El Altar is thought by many to be Ecuador's finest climb. It's not something you can toss off in a weekend, so you have no choice but to enjoy the valley, lakes, and views along the way. Climbers should check with outfitters in Quito or Riobamba on the condition of the track to the base and find out if the guard post near Candelaria is open. A recommended equipment list includes snow picks, ice screws, runners, two ropes, helmets, and a small rack of rock protection. Hikers can enjoy the trek to the base, one of the most impressive mountain spectacles in Ecuador, with jagged snowy peaks cupping a volcanic lake. The IGM 1:25,000 *Cerros Negros* and *Laguna Pintada* maps cover the area.

Two routes to El Altar leave from the road between Riobamba and Baños. A trail to the stunning **Collanes Plain** at the foot of El Altar begins in Penipe, just across the Río Pastaza 22 kilometers northeast of Riobamba, reachable by any bus to Penipe. From Penipe, make your way southeast to Candelaria. Buses leave from the market plaza on Sunday; otherwise, rent a pickup or hike the 12 kilometers. Cargo trucks leave the Terminal Oriente in Riobamba for Candelaria on Wednesdays, Fridays, and Saturdays. A small telephone office in the Candelaria's center can call a truck from Penipe for the return trip, if there isn't one waiting already ($8 one-way). A milk truck also runs back downhill a few times per week.

Two kilometers past the center of Candelaria (don't blink) is the left-hand turnoff for the ranger station, where you register and pay the park entrance fee. About one kilometer up the track is the Capac Huasi *hostal* at the Hacienda El Releche (tel. 3/284-7160 in Candelaria, 3/296-4133 or 3/296-0848 in Riobamba). Surprisingly comfortable accommodations with shared hot-water showers, kitchen facilities, and a great fireplace for drying sodden clothes are $12 pp, and horses can be rented (a good idea for the trek to the base).

The first part of the track beyond the hacienda is a confusing maze of cow paths, so try to get directions at the ranger station if it's open. After four–five hours of moderate uphill hiking, the Collanes Plain and El Altar itself come into view. The owner of the Releche *hostal* has built a set of inexpensive bunkhouses at the near end of the plain ($12 pp). Each has bunks and kitchen facilities, and booking in advance is recommended.

During rainy periods, the plain becomes a sodden bog, but in clear weather the view competes for best in the country. Those muted rumblings aren't planes crossing overhead, but rather ice sliding into the *laguna* from steep glaciers inside the crater. You'll have to climb the 350-meter rocky ridge east of the plain to reach the crater; stay to the left, as the right-hand route is dangerous. The crater shelters the gray-green Laguna Amarilla in the shadow of El Altar's pious peaks.

The mountain is usually climbed from the outer face (the crumbly inner face wasn't scaled until 1984). To ascend Obispo or any of its southern neighbors, you'll want to first head south to the Campamiento Italiano (Italian campsite), a set of tent platforms between the Lagunas Azul and Mandur just south of Obispo. It's a six-hour walk from the Collanes plain and four hours by horse from the Vaquería. For the northern peaks (clockwise from Canónigo), a trail leaves northeast from the Collanes plain.

GUAMOTE

Market day is Thursday, and this small town seems to sleep in a quiet mountain basin during the rest of the week, with only the morning trains on Wednesdays, Fridays, and Sundays to disturb the peaceful and deserted streets. On Thursdays, you must maneuver with care along any of the colorfully filled streets connecting various plazas. They're full of everything you might want if you live in these parts, and very little, apart from a few handicrafts, if you don't. This is one of the thriving unspoiled markets of the Sierra. To see the market at its best, you need to spend the night and get up early. There are a couple of older, cheap hostels close to the train station, and the lovely, well-run **Inti Sisa** (tel. 3/291-6529) just up the hill. This small hostel with a few private rooms and a spacious dormitory, uses its profits to support educational programs in town and the area. For $10 pp (make a reservation), you get a bed, breakfast, and the chance to help with local projects.

ALAUSÍ

Market day is Sunday, and indigenous people come down from the nearby *páramo* wearing their best and most colorful clothing. Less than 100 kilometers south of Riobamba, this train town rests on a ledge overlooking the Andes's steep western plunge. A few kilometers below, the Quito–Guayaquil train line tackles the Nariz del Diablo (Devil's Nose), one of the more impressive feats of rail engineering in the Americas. Most tourists come the night before to take the ride. There's nothing else special about Alausí, but you could do much worse than this pretty, quiet town for a night's stopover before taking transport up to Achupallas and hiking the Inca Trail to Ingapirca. San Pedro is the patron of Alausí, and a huge statue of him presides over the center of town, visible from all sides. The town's festival is celebrated on June 29 with bullfights and colorful parades.

Nariz del Diablo Train Ride

Alausí's **train station,** the goal of most visitors, sits behind the small plaza at the north end of 5 de Junio. The train through the famous Nariz del Diablo (Devil's Nose) now runs only on Wednesdays, Fridays, and Sundays—and be happy for that. It starts in Riobamba at 7 A.M., stops off in Alausí near 11 A.M. for about half an hour, then descends through the famous switchbacks that are so tight, the entire train has to back up momentarily to fit through. Sit on the right-hand side of the roof if you can. In 2007, two Japanese tourists were decapitated by a telephone line on another section of the railway when they stood up. The furor that the accident caused shocked the train authorities to their very core. Roof riding is now discouraged. Just below the switchbacks, the train stops near Sibambe, turns around, and climbs back through the entire route. The whole trip from Riobamba to Sibambe and back up costs $15 pp and takes all day, but you can buy a ticket in Alausí through the Nariz itself and back up for less. Be at the window at 10 A.M. at the latest to make sure of a seat. Buses wait in Alausí in the early afternoon to pick up passengers when the train stops on the way back up, then take them to Riobamba, Quito, or Cuenca.

Accommodations and Food

Almost everything is along the main street, 5 de Junio, which ends at the train station. Buses stop in front of the **Hotel Pan-Americano** (tel. 3/293-0278), with a restaurant downstairs and decent rooms with private bath and hot water for $8 pp. The narrow, plant-filled **Hotel Tequendama** (tel. 3/293-0123) makes a good rest stop for budget travelers, with shared-bath rooms for $4 pp and breakfast for $1.50. One block from 5 de Junio, the **Hotel Europa** (García Moreno 159 and Chile, tel. 3/293-0200) offers rooms for $8 with shared bath and $12 with private baths (probably the nicest in town). Your best bet for food in Alausí is one of the various hotel restaurants; try the Hotel Gampala on 5 de Junio.

Information and Services

You can exchange travelers' checks at the **Banco de Guayaquil** (5 de Junio and Ricaurte), on the ground floor of the Municipal Building near the train station. The **post office** (García Moreno and 9 de Octubre) is one block uphill from 5 de Junio, past the Hotel Pan-Americano. A covered **market** spreads along García Moreno between Pedro Loza and Chile, uphill from 5 de Junio.

Buses head to Ambato ($3, three hours), Cuenca ($5, five hours), Guayaquil ($5, five hours), Quito ($6, 5.5 hours), and Riobamba ($2, two hours) from the corner of 9 de Octubre and 5 de Julio. More buses pass on the highway up the hill (taxi, $1), picking up passengers at the gas station on the Pan-American highroad.

Occasional trucks bound for Achupallas (market on Saturday) leave from the hotel Tequendama on 5 de Junio. There is more transport available 30 minutes south at the road junction at **La Moya,** just after the river crossing.

THE ORIENTE

"El Oriente," muses Henri Michaux in *Ecuador: A Travel Journal,* "an Ecuadorian says this word as if it were Paris: both dangerous, hard to reach, and presumably awe-inspiring." Though Ecuador's eastern half isn't as dangerous as it once was—the Shuar *indígenas* no longer perform their famous head-shrinking ritual, at least not on humans—it remains the wildest part of the country, with thousands of square kilometers accessible only by motorized canoe or airplane. And it still has the ability, in its fiery sunsets, endless coiling rivers, and sheer explosion of life, to leave you speechless with wonder that a place like this still exists on earth—especially since you can visit it so easily and inexpensively.

The Oriente ("the East") comprises everything east of the Ecuadorian Andes, which by most definitions approaches half the country, but only 5 percent of Ecuador's people live there. Although the Pacific traces the coast and the mountains comprise the Sierra, the Oriente finds its heart in the rivers that tie it to the Amazon basin and, eventually, the Atlantic Ocean. The inexorable waters can undercut a huge clay bank or snip a bend overnight, stranding an oxbow kilometers long. The muddy Río Napo, more than one kilometer wide in spots, drains the Ríos Coca and Aguarico and heads off into Peru. Colombia's Amazon lies across the Río Putumayo to the north. Farther south, the Río Pastaza flows from Sangay National Park.

The Quijos region west of Coca was well known to the Incas, who ventured downhill to meet lowland tribes in peace and battle. It was

© JULIAN SMITH

HIGHLIGHTS

◖ Papallacta Hot Springs: Start your visit to the Oriente with a soak at these hot springs on the road from Quito – perhaps after a hike through the nearby lakes (page 174).

◖ Napo Wildlife Center: One of the newest lodges in the Ecuadorian Amazon is run by an indigenous community down the Río Napo that is happy to show you the wonders of their unspoiled home (page 185).

◖ Yachana Lodge: A visit to this lodge, down the Napo River from Tena, is a fascinating educational experience – go on a rainforest hike, then enjoy a cup of coffee made from beans you picked yourself and roasted over an open fire (page 188).

◖ Tena: A white-water and jungle-tour hotspot, Tena is easier to reach than most other cities in the Oriente and a pleasant place to spend a few days exploring (page 190).

◖ Kapawi Ecolodge: Reachable only by float plane, Kapawi is Ecuador's most remote – and luxurious – Amazon experience (page 204).

LOOK FOR ◖ TO FIND RECOMMENDED SIGHTS, ACTIVITIES, DINING, AND LODGING.

also the first area east of the Andes to be penetrated by the Spanish (see the sidebar *Francisco de Orellana*). The anniversary of the European discovery of the Amazon River (February 12) is still celebrated with markets and fairs in jungle cities. Within a few centuries after European contact, most of the region's tens of thousands of inhabitants had fallen victim to smallpox and cholera. But the remaining cultures, though splintered and scattered, were safe—for the moment.

The discovery of oil in the 1960s brought this once stagnant backwater into the national consciousness. In the north, the oil pipeline serves as a constant reminder of the vast reserves that make Ecuador the third-largest oil exporter in Latin America, while simultaneously wielding the power to obliterate entire cultures and ecosystems within decades.

Throughout the region, Kichwa words on maps show the influence of the Lowland Kichwa, who inhabit the foothills and forests in western Napo and northern Pastaza Provinces. Also in the north are pockets of Siona/Secoya and Cofán. The Huaorani have a huge reserve in central Napo Province and spill over into Yasuní National Park. To the south, the Shuar and Achuar saw their ancestral lands divided and torn by the decades-long border dispute with Peru, which ended in 1998.

PLANNING YOUR TIME

The northern Oriente, most of which is within a (long) day's bus trip of Quito, sees the most

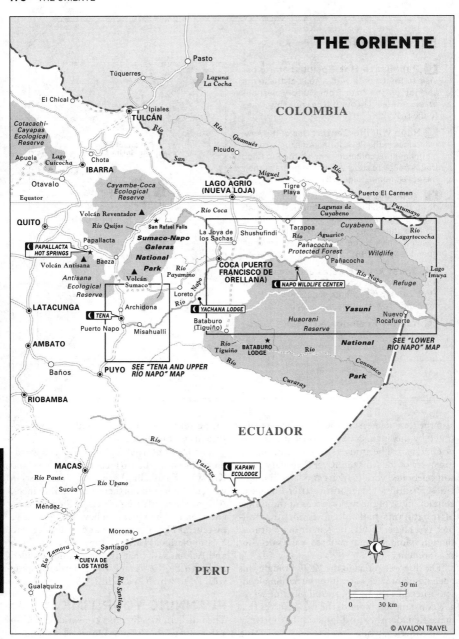

THE ORIENTE

Pasto

Túquerres

Laguna La Cocha

El Chical

Ipiales

TULCÁN

Río

Río

Guamués

COLOMBIA

Cotacachi-Cayapas Ecological Reserve

Picudo

Apuela

Lago Cuicocha

Chota

San

IBARRA

Miguel

LAGO AGRIO (NUEVA LOJA)

Río

Tigre Playa

Puerto El Carmen

Otavalo

Cayambe-Coca Ecological Reserve

Putumayo

Equator

Río Coca

Lagunas de Cuyabeno

Volcán Reventador ▲

QUITO ⊕

Río Quijos

★ San Rafael Falls

La Joya de los Sachas

Shushufindi

Tarapoa

Cuyabeno

Río Lagartococha

🕯 **PAPALLACTA HOT SPRINGS**

Papallacta

Sumaco-Napo Galeras

Río

Aguarico

Wildlife

Volcán Antisana ▲

Baeza

National

Pañacocha Protected Forest

Pañacocha

Antisana Ecological Reserve

Volcán Sumaco ▲

Park

Río Payamino

COCA (PUERTO FRANCISCO DE ORELLANA)

Río Napo

Lago Imuya

Refuge

Loreto

🕯 **NAPO WILDLIFE CENTER** ★

LATACUNGA ⊚

Archidona

Río Napo

🕯 **YACHANA LODGE** ★

Yasuní

Nuevo Rocafuerte

🕯 **TENA**

Puerto Napo

Misahualli

Bataburo (Tiguiño)

Huaorani Reserve

AMBATO ⊚

Río Tiguiño

★ **BATABURO LODGE**

Río

National

SEE "LOWER RÍO NAPO" MAP

Baños

PUYO ⊚

SEE "TENA AND UPPER RÍO NAPO" MAP

Río

Cononaco

Park

Curaray

RIOBAMBA ⊚

Río

ECUADOR

MACAS ⊚

Pastaza

🌙 **KAPAWI ECOLODGE**

Río Paute

Río Upano

★

Sucúa

Méndez

Morona

Santiago

Río Zamora

★ **CUEVA DE LOS TAYOS**

PERU

Gualaquiza

Río Santiago

0 ____ 30 mi

0 ____ 30 km

© AVALON TRAVEL

traffic. Bidding the Andes a final farewell after the **Papallacta Hot Springs,** the road east from Quito hits Baeza, where white-water rafting on the Quijos River is justifiably soaring in popularity. Oil's influence predominates here, creating unpleasant jungle cities such as Lago Agrio and Coca, as well as the roads that have opened the region to non-indigenous settlers and tourists.

On the upper reaches of the Río Napo, the area around **Tena** and Misahualli is popular with travelers who come for the white water or to visit Kichwa villages with indigenous tour operators. There isn't much primary forest or wildlife left around here, but there are still places worth visiting, primarily the educationally and culturally minded **Yachana Lodge.** On the other hand, lodges along the lower Napo, such as the **Napo Wildlife Center,** offer access to some of the most unspoiled rainforests in Ecuador.

The southern Oriente offers a glimpse of how the entire Amazon basin used to be. Here you'll find what is probably Ecuador's premier rainforest destination: the **Kapawi Ecolodge,** practically at the Peruvian border.

If you're not interested in the rainforest and its inhabitants—human or otherwise—then the Oriente is probably not for you. The bus rides are long, the weather is hot and sticky, and the stinging insects can be ruthless. But if the rainforest appeals to you, you'll be hard-pressed to find a country in the world with easier access to pristine Amazon rainforests still inhabited by traditional indigenous tribes.

The best ways to get here are by local bus and plane—many tours and lodges fly visitors from Quito to the nearest town and plop them

INDIGENOUS ORGANIZATIONS

- **Abya Yala Fund for Indigenous Self-Development in South & Meso America** (P.O. Box 28386, Oakland, CA 94604, tel. 510/763-6553, fax 510/763-6588, abyayala@earthlink.net, http://ayf.nativeweb .org): This organization seeks to support indigenous peoples in economic, social, cultural, and spiritual ways, including with the publication of a journal on Indian rights.

- **Confederation of Indigenous Nationalities of Ecuador (CONAIE)** (Granados 2553 y 6 de Diciembre, Quito, tel. 2/245-2335, conaie@ecuanex.net.ec, http://conaie.nativeweb.org): Formed in 1986, the largest indigenous organization in Ecuador serves as a political mouthpiece for its members, focusing on ecology, land rights, education, and indigenous culture.

- **Confederation of Indigenous Nationalities of the Ecuadorian Amazon (CONFENIAE)** (6 de Diciembre 159 and Pazmino, of. 408, Quito, tel. 2/290-1125, confeniae@applicom

.com, www.unii.net/confeniae): The Shuar, Achuar, Huaorani, Siona-Secoya, Cofán, Zaparo, and Lowland Quechua groups banded together in 1980 to defend and legalize their historical territories in the Ecuadorian Amazon. Their umbrella organization seeks to promote the social, political, and economic development of indigenous communities.

- **Indigenous and Peasant Federation of Imbabura (FICI)** (M. Jaramillo 608 and Morales, Otavalo, tel./fax 6/292-0976, inrujta-ccfici@andinanet.net, http://fici.nativeweb.org): A political group of Quechua *indígenas* in Imbabura Province.

- **Scientific Institute of Indigenous Cultures (ICCI)** (Calle Gaspar de Carvajal N26-27 and Luis Mosquera Narváez, Quito, tel. 2/320-3696, icci@ecuanex.net .ec, http://icci.nativeweb.org): This private, nonprofit institution works toward the organization and preservation of different indigenous groups.

in a boat from there. Most tours run four–eight days; unless you're planning on going from town to town or visiting more than one lodge, a week is plenty of time to get the feel of the place. Even four-day tours are adequate for some, especially since you'll often be roused at dawn to spot animals before they go to sleep for the day. As a result of the frequency of flights

to and from the jungle towns, most trips begin and end on Mondays or Fridays. Departures on other days are normally arranged with groups of four or more.

The in-and-out nature of Amazon tourism makes the idea of a home base somewhat moot, but Baeza, Tena, and Macas are all pleasant enough towns in which to spend a day or two.

Quito to Baeza

Of the handful of roads that connect the Oriente to the rest of Ecuador, the one to Baeza is used the most. It was built in the early 1970s to provide access to the oil towns of Lago Agrio and Coca, as well as the all-important oil pipeline. Countless oil tankers, supply trucks, and buses follow the pipeline as it snakes up out of the jungle. The winding road is narrow but paved, and in good condition for most of the way to Lago Agrio.

The gradual, relentless climb out of Quito up the Eastern Cordillera slows buses to a crawl, but this pace gives you more time to enjoy the rugged scenery as the air grows cold and the landscape looms rocky and barren. Just as most vehicles are ready to gasp and die, Papallacta Pass opens a window onto the entire Amazon basin. An entrance to the Cayambe-Coca Ecological Reserve is across from a statue of the Virgin, with trails leading off into the *páramo*. If the weather's clear, look for a stupendous view of the Volcán Antisana to the south. From here it's all downhill, with the roadside vegetation turning almost instantly to cloud forest fed by the Amazon mists from below.

Despite the heavy traffic, the excellent **birding** makes the road to Baeza from Quito worth a jaunt for birders who don't have the time or inclination to plunge all the way into the jungle. Pull off on a side road and you might glimpse buff-winged starfrontlets, viridian metaltails, buff-breasted mountain tanagers, or one of a few types of quetzals native to the area.

ANTISANA ECOLOGICAL RESERVE

Since 1993, this reserve has protected a large chunk of the Ecuadorian Andes between the provinces of Pichincha and Napo. An altitude range of more than 4,500 meters, all the way to the top of the Volcán Antisana (5,704 meters), encloses two distinct ecosystems. Temperatures in the lower, humid cloud forest (1,200–3,800 meters) can reach 25°C, while nights in the high *páramo* (3,800–4,700 meters) often drop well below freezing.

The reserve's upper reaches are home to more than 50 bird species. One of the most significant condor populations in the country (about 10 of an estimated 70) soar through the high, thin air. Other rare species, such as the carunculated caracara and black-faced ibis, stick closer to the ground. Tapirs, spectacled bears, pumas, and dwarf pudú deer hide in the lower forests. Such species richness partly comes from proximity to the Cayambe-Coca Ecological Reserve and Sumaco-Napo Galeras National Park: animals can migrate between Antisana's 325,000 acres and the other reserves relatively easily, and conservation efforts often carry over area boundaries.

The Antisana Reserve protects one of the most important watersheds in the country, providing 75 percent of the capital's potable water. The glaciers of Antisana Volcano feed the Río Quijos to the west and trout-filled Laguna Micacocha in the direction of Sincholagua. Hunting, overgrazing, and encroachment by settlers fill out the usual list of threats, which also includes timber extraction in the eastern reaches. Further damage has been done by EMAPQ (the Quito Water Authority) in constructing an access road and dam across the Micacocha to provide water to the capital. The condor population has suffered particularly badly.

Visiting the Reserve

There is no visitors center at the reserve, so head to the Ministry of the Environment offices in Quito for information. Before leaving for Antisana, contact Jose Delgado, the owner of the Hacienda Pimantura (tel. 2/246-2013), for permission to use the access road from Pintag that crosses his farm (a situation of dubious legality, but that's how it is). He charges $10 pp, which also grants admission to the reserve itself.

Climbing Volcán Antisana

Ecuador's fourth-highest peak looms southeast of Quito in a remote, cloudy area seldom visible even from afar. Four peaks surround an ice-filled crater that was active into the 18th century. Edward Whymper and the Carrels first climbed the highest peak in 1880, leaving the other three (all within a hair of 5,500 meters) for later adventurers. Its remote location, bad weather, and lack of huts make Antisana a difficult climb.

The route begins six–seven kilometers east of Sangolquí on the road to Pifo, passing through the villages of Pintag (five kilometers) and the Hacienda Pimantura of Sr. Delgado (12–13 kilometers) as it heads southeast toward the mountain. The IGM 1:100,000 *Pintag* map covers the area.

PAPALLACTA
Lake District

Shortly after the road to Baeza crests the Eastern Cordillera, about 60 kilometers from Quito, it approaches the Papallacta lake district on the northern (left) side. This gorgeous stretch of country, filling the southern tip of the Cayambe-Coca Ecological Reserve, offers plenty of hiking possibilities among moody

walkway on a jungle lake

© JEAN BROWN

glacial lakes and crumbling hills that evoke the craggy countryside of Scotland. It's only a few hours from Quito, and any bus heading toward Tena or Lago Agrio can drop you off along the way. Be ready for wet, boggy conditions during the rainy season. The IGM 1:50,000 *Papallacta, Laguna de Mica,* and *Sincholagua* maps cover the area.

At the crest of Papallacta Pass (4,064 meters), a statue of the Virgin on the south side of the road marks the start of a great day hike among the lakes. Head up the dirt road opposite the Virgin toward the antenna-topped hill to the north, stop at the new guard-post house to pay your entry fee and head up to the "360 hill," which has a sweeping 360 degree view of the surrounding *páramo.* From here, hike downhill to the northeast toward the southern end of Laguna Parcacha, then southeast from there toward the park guard station south of Laguna Loreto. A dirt road heads south to the Papallacta hot springs, where you can soak your aching bones and catch a bus back to Quito (leaving every hour in the afternoons until evening) in time for bed.

THE ORIENTE

The rest of the Lake District spreads north from Papallacta, with multiday hikes connecting bordering towns like Pifo and Oyacachi. Laguna Papallacta, the largest in the area, lies to the south of hot springs on the Río Papallacta. An old lava flow has stuck a tongue into its eastern side.

C Papallacta Hot Springs

A sign on the left-hand side of the road to Baeza, a few kilometers past the Laguna Papallacta, points you up a dirt track to the finest set of developed hot springs in Ecuador. Nestled in a steep Andean valley at 3,225 meters, the springs attract crowds of Quiteños on weekends. It's hard to beat the combination of steaming water and dripping cloud forest, especially after a hike among the lakes.

It's 1.5 kilometers up to the Termas de Papallacta. Along the way, you'll pass the **Hostería Pampa de Papallacta** (tel. 6/232-0624), with bunk beds in simple rooms for $15 pp with private bath. Shortly beyond that, there's a fish hatchery on the left, built with the help of the Japanese government, and three restaurants serving the trout (trucha) that have been introduced into many of Ecuador's mountain streams.

At the top of the road, you'll reach the **Termas de Papallacta** (tel. 2/256-8989 or 2/250-4787, termasuio@termaspapallacta .com, www.termaspapallacta.com). There is a public section open 6 A.M.–9 P.M. daily for $7 pp, as well as spa pools with water jets and bubble jets open 8 A.M.–7 P.M. daily for $17 pp. The spa center also offers massages, sauna and other treatments. Ranging from kiddie-wader to swimming-pool size, and from river-cold to boiled-lobster (36–42°C) in temperature, the pools are pleasantly landscaped and surrounded by facilities, including changing rooms, bag storage, towel and locker rental, a pricey café/restaurant, and a small store. Horse trips leave the ticket window on weekends.

If you just can't tear yourself away, reserve one of the 36 rooms or 12 cabins at the **Hotel Termas de Papallacta,** right next to the baths. Family cabins are $165–220 for up to six people, and rooms with private baths are $120 for one–three people, including access to the hotel's private baths. The hotel has an office in Quito at Foch E7-38 and Reina Victoria, on the fourth floor. It also operates a 250-hectare ranch on the Papallacta River for birding and hiking excursions into the cloud forest.

The Fundación Terra operates an information center on the hill to the right of the baths called the **Exploratorio** ($2), which introduces visitors to the ecology of the section of the Papallacta River canyon between the baths and the border of the Cayambe-Coca Reserve. Three short walking trails have been developed: you can traverse the one-kilometer trail on your own, but the two- and four-kilometer trails require a guide.

Cheaper options for accommodations and food are available at the **Hostal Antisana** (tel. 6/232-0626, $17 s, $30 d), located near the termas, and the budget **Hotel Coturpa** (tel. 6/232-0640, $12 s, $15 d) in town. The Coturpa's pools are not nearly as nice as the termas uphill, but cost only $3 pp (7 A.M.–5 P.M. Mon.–Fri., 6 A.M.–6 P.M. Sat.–Sun.).

BAEZA

After the ride down from Papallacta, this pretty little mountain town is a good place to break up the long bus journey to the Oriente from Quito. It was founded in the 16th century as a mission settlement on the eastern slope of the Andes—since then, it hasn't progressed much beyond wide-spot-in-the-road status. Horses carry riders down the main street past well-kept wooden houses lined with potted plants, and frogs chirp in the roadside grass at night. The beginnings of the Amazon spread out to the east.

The road from Quito splits just west of town. The left fork follows the oil pipeline and the Río Quijos northeast toward Lago Agrio, then south to Coca. The right fork heads through the middle of Baeza to Tena. A gas station and bar-restaurant Don Gonzales at the crossroads are usually the last stops for buses bound from the jungle to Quito. The old section of Baeza comes first, consisting of a few streets sloping

THE ORIENTE

up steeply toward the church. A newer section of town sits a bit farther along across the Río Machángara.

Thanks to local government efforts, the Quijos Valley in which Baeza, Borja, and El Chaco sit are poised to take advantage of the newly paved road from Quito and the proximity of Papallacta Hot Springs to become a prime nature and adventure tourism destination.

Recreation

A few great hiking trails take full advantage of Baeza's lofty views. To follow the **Camino de la Antena** (Antenna Trail), head up through the old part of town to the right of the church. You'll pass a cemetery on your way to a fork in the trail just across the Río Machángara. The right-hand fork continues along the river for quite a ways, whereas the left fork climbs up to a set of antennas overlooking the area. A farther branch continues along the mountaintop over town, with great views of the entire Quijos Valley on clear days. Expect to take three–four hours to reach the antennas, more if the trail is muddy from recent rain. Whichever path you pick, the **birding** in the pastures and cloud forest is bound to be great: dusky pihas, grass-green tanagers, Andean guans, and black-billed mountain toucans may all make an appearance. The **Granary Trail** connects the old and new villages, beginning by the road below Bar-Restaurant Gina (sign). It goes to the south past a small waterfall and through the forested hillside to the south end of the new village. It tends to be a little muddy at times, so good boots are advisable; and the bird-watching is good, so allow at least an hour.

Accommodations and Food

Some of the better choices in the new town are **Bambu's** (tel. 6/232-0219, $8 pp), with a pool and sauna, or **Gina's** (tel. 6/232-0471, $8 pp), above the restaurant of the same name in the old part of town.

The **Hotel Samay** (tel. 6/232-0170, $6 pp) in the new section is clean, friendly, and simple. Hot showers are available on the first floor. The most promising of Baeza's scant selection of eateries is in the old section of town, where **Bar-Restaurant Gina** serves great trout dishes for $3–4. There are even a couple of vegetarian options.

Information and Services

A tiny **police** station sits in the old section of town, along with a small military base.

Transportation

Any bus between Quito and cities in the northern Oriente passes through Baeza, making it easy to hop on or off in town. Buses to and from Coca and Lago Agrio pass by "La Y" (pronounced "La Yay"), the highway intersection just west of town, whereas those to Tena and spots south head right through town. Buses to Quito ($3, three hours) stop below the market in new Baeza.

Northern Oriente

The road northeast from Baeza descends into the wide, flat valley of the Río Quijos, where the jungle becomes more and more dense as the altitude drops. It's a beautiful and surprisingly unspoiled landscape for most of the way. Trees take over completely as the road leaves the slate-green Quijos to join the Río Aguarico flowing west.

As far as travelers are concerned, the towns in this part of the Ecuadorian Amazon are mostly jumping-off points for jungle tours or white-water rafting. Lago Agrio and Coca are best avoided, except in transit; but travel information is provided here, in case you get stuck for the night. It's possible to arrange trips out of Tena and Misahualli, even at the last minute, but be aware that there is little primary forest left nearby. Remote Amazon lodges are your best bet for wildlife and unspoiled nature.

Sitting on top of a bus, gritty and windy as

it may be, is a good way to see a slice of frontier life. People play volleyball and soccer in fields backed by towering, vine-laden trees, and lines of bright, freshly washed clothes stretch from house to tree to house.

SAN RAFAEL FALLS

The highest waterfall in Ecuador roars over a rock shelf in the Río Quijos, 66 kilometers and 1.5 hours from Baeza. A small bus stop on the right marks the turnoff, flanked by a small sign reading "Entrada Al Campamiento San Rafael y La Cascada." One hundred meters up the hill is the **Hotel San Rafael** (tel. 6/2281-8221, $10 s, $12 d). Follow the dirt road downhill over the small Río Reventador and past a guard post (deserted as often as not), where foreigners are supposed to pay $10.

The two-kilometer trail to the falls starts between two of the yellow bunkhouses. Painted green arrows mark the way at first. Continue down the hill beyond the campsite, ignoring a blocked-off branch to the right after 500 meters. The trail is clear, but it can get muddy as it crosses streams and winds though a series of wooden gates. Bromeliads and cecropia trees decorate the forest alongside giant ferns with fronds as big as horses. Birders, keep your eyes peeled: Guiana cock-of-the-rocks are frequently seen here. After about 45 minutes, you'll arrive at a small clearing overlooking the falls as they fill a leafy gorge with mist. Be careful near the edge: The small cross is in memory of a Canadian photographer who fell to his death. The best view of the brown torrent is from a little farther down. The path continues to the base of the falls, a three-hour round-trip of steep and slippery scrambling.

VOLCÁN REVENTADOR

True to its name (which means "exploder" in Spanish), Reventador is one of the most active volcanoes in Ecuador. It protrudes from the cloud forest on the eastern edge of Cayambe-Coca Ecological Reserve, well east of the main Avenue of the Volcanoes. Lava rocks on the way up are warm to the touch, reminding nervous climbers of the ancient explosion that chopped down one of the highest mountains in the country (judging from the size of its caldera) to a mere 3,562 meters. The peak shows just how big this mountain used to be. The entire south rim of the old three-kilometer crater is missing, opening a view of a new, smaller volcanic cone in the middle, surrounded by sulfur-encrusted rocks. Reventador's recorded activity began in 1541. It erupted in 2002 with less than 12 hours' notice, and continued to rumble into 2004. Most recently, in July 2008, it began another cycle of activity.

Since its first ascent by a scientific expedition in 1931, Reventador hasn't been climbed often because of its muddy approach and constant, if low-level, activity. Because the three-to-five-day trek to the top crosses everything from pastures to lava-covered wasteland, hiring a guide is a good idea. The approach is sodden and the peak is often clouded over, so climbers should bring machetes, rubber boots, waterproof tents and rope, compasses, and maps. The IGM 1:50,000 *Volcán El Reventador* map covers the area.

© JULIAN SMITH

San Rafael Falls

The trail begins shortly past the entrance to San Rafael Falls. There's a refuge at 2,300 meters, about four–five hours from the road, with eight bunk beds and a fire pit. It takes seven–eight hours to reach the summit from the refuge, and another five or so to descend. It's possible to make it to the summit and back to the refuge in one long day, but be warned that finding your way over lava in the dark is difficult, and water may not be available past the refuge, depending on the season.

CASCALES

This quiet little agricultural village, just 40 minutes from Lago Agrio, offers a pleasant alternative to overnights in the noisy oil town. If you choose to travel by day to see the spectacular scenery, you can make stops at Papallacta and San Rafael and overnight at **Paraiso Dorado** ($7 pp, tel. 9/471-5191), or overnight here at the end of a jungle trip before continuing to Quito. Several short jungle walks are offered by Paraiso Dorado's owners.

LAGO AGRIO

The capital of Sucumbíos Province, Lago Agrio (pop. 35,000) was carved from the jungle in 1972 as a field headquarters for Texaco's explorations in the Oriente. Although it's officially named Nueva Loja, the city is better known by the Spanish translation of Sour Lake, Texas, where Texaco got its start at the turn of the 20th century.

"Lago" is an oil town, pure and simple—a scruffy frontier outpost that's hot, remote, and best bypassed. Its lawless feel has grown with the recent influx of drug trafficking and guerrilla activity from Colombia, only 25 kilometers north. The most exciting thing to do in Lago is probably to take the TAME flight into the city, which scrapes the rooftops on its initial buzz of the center before landing.

Accommodations

Most hotels in town don't bother with hot water, but in this heat, you won't miss it. The well-run **Hotel Oro Negro** (Quito 164, tel. 6/283-0174, $4 pp) has basic but clean budget rooms with fan and shared bath. Across the street at the popular **Hotel D'Mario** (tel. 6/283-0172), rooms with TV, air-conditioning, and private bath are $15 pp; add hot water, telephone, and a refrigerator for $3 pp. The poshest places in town are the **Hotel El Cofán** (12 de Febrero between Quito and Añasco, tel. 6/283-2409) and **La Cascada** (Quito and Amazonas, tel. 6/283-2229). The latter has a pool and spa. Both are $25 s and $37–39 d, and all rooms come with private bath, cable TV, minibar, and air-conditioning.

Food

Several restaurants along Quito spill out onto the sidewalk and cater to tourists. **Restaurant D'Mario** does a decent pizza for $4.50 and is often packed with gringos after hours. It also has good ice cream. For typical fare, the **Restaurant La Chola Cuencana** on Añasco has a large selection—make your choice from the paintings of dishes on the wall (dishes average $3), or ask for the English menu. The small restaurant in the **Hotel Cofán** has air-conditioning and good choices, but it's a little more expensive than other places in town. The **Panadería/Cafetería Jackeline** (Amazonas and Quito) serves juice, fruit salad, and ice cream, while the **Heladería Milwaukee,** just south of the plaza, offers a range of fast food and, of course, ice cream.

Transportation

There is a *terminal terrestre* north of town, but almost everyone goes directly to the bus company offices instead. **Transportes Baños** has the most daily departures to Quito ($7–8, eight hours) and a 7 P.M. overnight bus to Guayaquil ($15, 14 hours). **Transportes Loja** goes to Loja ($20, 24 hours), Cuenca ($18, 18 hours), Ambato ($9, 10 hours), and Machala ($18, 19 hours). **Transportes Putumayo,** at the southwest corner of the market, drives to Quito and Coca ($2.50, three hours), as well as Tarapoa ($2). *Rancheros* to Coca and Shushufindi ($2, three hours) leave often from Amazonas. The **Valle de Chota** company has a daily bus from the bus terminal to Ibarra via the frontier road through La Bonita.

TAME (9 de Octubre and Orellana, tel. 6/283-0113) flies to Quito every day of the week except Sunday for $64 pp one-way. Book a few days in advance if you can. VIPSA also has daily flights in its 40-passenger plane. Local buses run to the airport, or you can go to the TAME office and try to find fellow passengers to share a cab.

CUYABENO WILDLIFE REFUGE

Most of the eastern half of Sucumbíos Province falls within this gigantic reserve created in 1979, including some parts that are so unspoiled, researchers have dubbed it the "Pleistocene Refuge." Persistent oil activity and settlement in the western part of the reserve throughout the 1980s prompted the government to more than double the reserve's size, in an effort to compensate indigenous peoples and protect even more of the Río Cuyabeno's watershed from colonization. President Rafael Correa has suggested a novel way of protecting this area, having calculated how much income the reserves could contribute to Ecuador's economy. He would like Ecuador to be paid by international organizations to "keep the oil in the ground."

Today, Cuyabeno covers four million hectares, including most of the Río Aguarico, all the way to the Peruvian border. More difficult access promises to keep much of the park pristine for the foreseeable future (a day-long motorboat ride is the only way to reach the new eastern section). Most important, Cuyabeno serves as an example of how a combination of profitable ecotourism and politically active indigenous populations can keep "progress" in check. After a visit to the reserve in 1993, then president Sixto Duran pledged to keep the park free from development.

The Río Aguarico is Cuyabeno's main outlet, emptying into the Río Lagartococha, which forms the Peruvian border as it flows south into the Napo. Pink freshwater dolphins and endangered giant river otters inhabit the Lagartococha's upper reaches. Fourteen major lagoons are interspersed with countless seasonal

SPEAKING COFÁN

Meenga'kay – How are you?
Hayo – Yes
May'en – No
Chietzafpopoem – Thank you
Chieegaychu – Goodbye
Vatoova – Caiman
Cornsipeendo – Harpy eagle
Taysy – Jaguar
Na'en – River
Coovy – Tapir
Tsa'coer – Water

marshes and lagoons. In the west, terra firma forests stay dry most of the year, whereas seasonally flooded areas of low-water marshes border permanently flooded forests to the east. More than three meters of rain in a year are not unusual.

More than 200 species of trees per hectare have been recorded here, including many species of palm, guavas, and native trees like the *zapote silvestre* (forest apple), *uva de arbol* (tree grape), and *cerezo de tierra* (ground cherry). Birders won't be disappointed, because Cuyabeno contains at least a third of all the bird species in the entire Amazon basin. Raucous blue-and-yellow macaws fly overhead, and the ringed kingfisher, the largest of five species in the reserve, is often startled from its riverside perch by passing canoes. Mammal species include the fisher bat, which snatches fish from lakes and rivers, and saki monkeys with long, furry tails.

The Siona-Secoya tribe inhabits the upper reaches of the Río Aguarico near the Río Cuyabeno. Groups of Lowland Kichwa are occasionally encountered downstream, along with a small enclave of Cofán at Zábalo. Two Shuar communities have recently moved into the far eastern part of the reserve.

A $20 fee is charged to enter the reserve.

Visiting Cuyabeno

The only real way to experience the reserve is by going on a tour or staying at a permanent

floating dock with airplane disco and bar behind Hotel La Misión

lodge. Access is via the road southeast from Lago Agrio, where groups board motorboats at Dureno or Chiritza to be whisked downriver. The **Dracaena** and **Green Planet** tour agencies in Quito offer weekly trips via Lago Agrio to camps inside Cuyabeno for $200 pp (four days) to $230 pp (five days), plus the reserve entrance fee ($20 pp). These usually visit primary rainforest, the Laguna Grande (keep an eye out for river dolphins), and local Siona communities.

Set near the refuge's Laguna Grande, the luxury **Cuyabeno Lodge** offers comfortable bungalows built with natural materials and private baths. Some of Ecuador's finest naturalist guides lead hikes and canoe trips into the forest in conjunction with Siona natives. Four- and five-day expeditions cost $295 and $355 pp, respectively, not including transport from Quito and the reserve entrance fee. For reservations, contact Neotropic Turis (Pinto E4-338 and Amazonas, Quito, tel. 2/252-1212, fax 2/255-4902, info@neotropicturis.com, www.neotropicturis.com).

COCA

If the Oriente is Ecuador's Wild West, Coca is its Dodge City. Since the streets were paved, some of the frontier feeling has been lost—but

here on the banks of the Río Napo, many taxis are pickup trucks, and helicopters and puddle-jumper planes roar overhead. Oil workers and colonists keep the dozens of bars and pool halls in business, while residents watch Peruvian TV shows in front of slowly spinning fans.

Officially named Puerto Francisco de Orellana, Coca (pop. 25,000) was declared the capital of the newly made province of Orellana, which split off from Napo in 1998. It's the closest sizable city to undisturbed rainforest in Ecuador—Yasuní National Park is just downstream—but still better left to the locals. Book your jungle tours in Quito or Baños.

Recreation and Tours

Coca serves as the gateway to Ecuador's upper Amazon, offering relatively easy access to the rainforest down the lower Napo River. If you arrive without a tour already booked, there are plenty of dubious operators in town. Because most destinations are far down the Río Napo, tours of less than three days—and those that don't leave the Río Napo itself—are seldom worth the effort. You need at least four days to visit Yasuní National Park or the Huaorani Reserve (make sure your guide has written permission to visit this tribe—only a few do).

THE ORIENTE

FRANCISCO DE ORELLANA

One of the most remarkable journeys in the history of the Americas almost ended before it began. In 1539, Francisco de Orellana, the former governor of Guayaquil and a relative of the Pizarros, was assisting Gonzalo Pizarro in leading a few hundred Spanish soldiers, thousands of natives tribesmen, and an ark's worth of dogs, horses, and food animals in an exploration of the upper Amazon. Half of the party, including 2,000 *indígenas*, perished during the grueling journey over the Eastern Cordillera without ever seeing the jungle. The rest survived by eating their horses, then their saddles.

When the group finally stumbled across the Río Napo, Pizarro ordered Orellana to build a boat to carry the weakest members and explore downriver in search of food. Two months' labor produced a large raft, which was pushed from the muddy shore on January 1, 1542. Within minutes, the strong brown current had swept the raft and its crew of 57 Spaniards and several hundred natives out of sight. Foremost on every Spanish mind was the legendary golden city of El Dorado, along with a fabled land of spices peopled by the Canelos, the "People of Cinnamon."

The first part of the river, through what would become Ecuador, passed quietly. Native villages received the explorers with peaceful offers of food, and the Spanish planted crude crosses to claim the land for the king. Within a month, the party had reached the Napo's confluence with the Río Aguarico.

A strange encounter followed when the group stopped in a native village to build a larger boat. Gaspar de Carvajal, a Dominican friar who served as the journey's chronicler, wrote how one day four tall, light-skinned men dressed in gold stepped out of the trees. This account began a long series of rumors about a wealthy tribe of "white Indians." The rumors persisted throughout the New World for centuries, despite a complete lack of concrete evidence.

Aboard the new raft, Orellana's group began to fight for their lives as they entered a region of increasingly hostile natives. By June 3, the exhausted survivors were amazed to reach the great joining of waters (today near Manaus in Brazil), where the coffee-black Río Negro (named by Orellana) joins the lighter Río Marañon, and the two flow side by side for kilometers without mixing.

An attack shortly after the meeting of the rivers sparked another legend. The Spanish soldiers described being set upon by a native group that included tall, light-skinned women armed with bows and arrows. The defenders dubbed the fierce females "Amazones," after the mythical women warriors of Greek legend. Just as the story stuck in the world's collective imagination for centuries, the name stuck to the river as well.

On August 26, the waters suddenly spread to the horizon, and a tang of salt drifted in on the breeze. The straggling band had finally reached the Atlantic Ocean, becoming the first

Jungle trips from Coca start at around $35 pp per day. Julio Jarrin of **Expediciones Jarrin** (tel. 6/288-0860, tel./fax 2/252-5096, opposite the hotel Oasis, exjarrin@impsat.net .ec) has been leading tour groups to visit the Huaorani for many years. He runs the company with his family and employs some female and English-speaking guides on trips of 4–10 days. He also visits Yasuní and a lodge in Pañacocha.

Evenings come to life along the pedestrian section of the Malecón facing the public wharf,

as cafés, bars, and food kiosks fill with locals and visitors.

Accommodations

Only a few of the many budget hotels are passable, and most of them don't have hot water. The **Hotel Florida** (tel. 6/288-0177), on the road to the airport, costs $10 pp for a basic room with private bath. In the center of town, the **Hotel El Auca** (Napo between Rocafuerte and Moreno, tel. 6/280-0127 or 6/288-0600) is a popular meeting place for tour groups.

Europeans, and most likely the first human beings, to travel the entire length of the world's longest river – a trip that was not repeated for more than a century.

After skirting the coast north of the Margarita Islands off what would become Venezuela, Orellana rested and dispersed his group before leaving in May 1543 for Spain. King Charles I was delighted with Orellana's tale, making him governor of the territories he had discovered and authorizing (though not financing) him to lead a follow-up colonization expedition. In 1545, Orellana left Spain with a ragtag force, paid for out of his own pocket and consisting of 300 men on four small ships. By the time the expedition reached the mouth of the Amazon six months later, one boat had been lost and half the men had died or deserted. Some of the crew managed to reach Venezuela, but Francisco de Orellana died of fever in November 1546, somewhere in the lower delta of the river that made him famous.

ORELLANA'S JOURNEY 1542-1543

© AVALON TRAVEL

Wooden cabins fill an inner courtyard filled with hammocks, flowers, and jungle birds. Cabins are $28 s, $45 d with private bath, fan, TV, and hot water. The hotel features a restaurant with a patio overlooking the street, plus newer, more expensive rooms with air-conditioning in the main building.

Oil-company managers and other bigwigs stay at the new **Grand Hotel del Coca** (tel. 6/288-2666 or 6/288-2311, $60 s, $75 d), on a quiet side street past the Hotel la Misión. Rooms with private bath, hot water, TV, and air-conditioning cost $23 s, $33 d at **Hotel La Misión** (tel. 6/288-0544, fax 6/288-0263, www.hotelmision.com), near the docks. A restaurant, pool with "toboggan," and airplane disco sit next to the balcony, overlooking the muddy Río Napo. Nearly tame toucans, parrots, and the occasional monkey perch next to the pool. **Hotel Oasis** (tel. 6/288-0206, $9 s, $12 d) sits beside the Mision and serves as the operations center for Yarina Lodge. Several other companies also use the hotel's docking facilities.

THE ORIENTE

loading up an Amazon bus, Coca

© JULIAN SMITH

Food

Coca's best restaurants are in its hotels, including **La Misión** and **El Auca.** At the latter, a large and varied menu includes *camarones al ajillo* (shrimp in garlic sauce) and *chuleta Hawaiana* (Hawaiian pork chops), as well as a few vegetarian options. Entrées range $4–6.

The **Chifa Dragon Dorado** (Bolívar and Napo) gets points for food (plates average $3), service, cable TV, and air-conditioning. A full, heart-stopping *parillada* costs $10 at the **Parilladas Argentina,** on the wood-covered second floor along Cuenca.

Transportation

Coca's *terminal terrestre* is eight blocks north of the river, off Napo Street (most directions in Coca are given in relation to this street or the river). However, the major long-distance bus companies have private terminals closer to the center, all on Napo. The road that connects Coca to the road between Baeza and Tena, heading through Loreto and south of Sumaco-Napo Galeras National Park, is the shortest route to Quito. *Rancheros* to Lago Agrio ($2.50, three hours) line up just north of the bridge and leave frequently.

Three companies share the route to Tena ($6, six hours), sending buses roughly every hour 5 A.M.–10 P.M. **Transportes Baños** sends the most comfortable buses to Tena twice a day from its office in town. It also offers six buses a day to Quito ($8, 10 hours) in the morning and evening, along with service to Ambato ($10, 10 hours) and Guayaquil ($20, 22 hours). **Transportes Loja** goes to Quito, Machala ($19, 20 hours), and Loja ($25, 27 hours). **Transportes Esmeraldas** goes to Quito ($8, 10 hours) with connections to—you've guessed it—Esmeraldas.

TAME (tel. 6/288-1078), **VIPSA** (tel. 6/288-1747), and **Icaro** (tel. 6/288-3384), fly to Quito every day of the week for about $61 pp. **Boats** down the Río Napo leave at 8 A.M. on Monday and Thursday, heading as far as Nuevo Rocafuerte (where the **Municipal** hotel $5 pp) on the Peruvian border for $30 pp (10 hours), with a possible stop at Pañacocha.

Lower Río Napo

Ecuador's largest river is a great brown highway flowing into the lowland wilderness that stretches all the way to Brazil. Even though the main channel has lost most of its original wildness, watery back roads and side streams reach into virgin rainforest where the 20th century has yet to make an appearance.

As towns become fewer and smaller, several lodges take advantage of the wide river's easy access, from wooden shacks to luxury bungalows. Booking in advance is the only remotely convenient way to tour the area, including Yasuní National Park, which, like all of Ecuador's jungle reserves, should only be visited in the company of a qualified guide.

YARINA BIOLOGICAL RESERVE

Opened in 1998 on 470 hectares of primary forest, Yarina Lodge is still run professionally by the original owners. Despite the reserve's location just one hour downriver from Coca, the wildlife viewing here is quite good—caimans are particularly common. Top-notch native guides take visitors to visit local homes, pan for gold, and climb the 40-meter-tall observation tower. During night floats on the nearby lagoon, luminous insects resting on aquatic plants give you the feeling you're paddling through the sky. A night in one of the 20 double huts, meals (including tasty vegetarian options), guided trips, and a translator costs $67 pp per day (10 percent SAE discount, 5 percent students and large groups). For reservations, contact the Yuturi Travel Agency (Amazonas N24-236 and Colón, tel. 2/250-4037 or 2/250-3225, info@yarinalodge.com, www.yarinalodge.com).

LIMONCOCHA AND VICINITY

The **Limoncocha Biological Reserve** was created in 1985 to protect some 28,000 hectares of rainforest surrounding the lake of the same name and a five-kilometer stretch of the Río Napo. Once considered one of the premier birding spots in the country, Limoncocha boasted more than 400 species sighted within 12 square kilometers of the lake. Seventeen species of hummingbirds, hoatzins, the rare agami heron and pale-eyed blackbird were all common along the shore.

The area has seen its share of turmoil. For decades, oil companies have blasted and drilled almost directly on the shores of the lake. In 1991, six years after the creation of the reserve, Metropolitan Touring decided that the local habitats were impacted too much by oil drilling and discontinued their operation in the jungle. In 1982, the Ecuadorian government ordered the Summer Institute of Linguistics (SIL), the largest missionary/linguistic organization in the world, out of its Ecuadorian headquarters in Limoncocha. Because the SIL provided many services that the small town otherwise lacked, the group's abrupt departure left Limoncocha's fate in jeopardy.

Things have recovered somewhat since local communities lobbied the oil companies to build a road bypassing the village and alter their blasting methods. Bird populations have begun to rebound, and now the lake echoes with screeches and caws more often than with the roar of dynamite.

© JEAN BROWN

Yarina Lodge

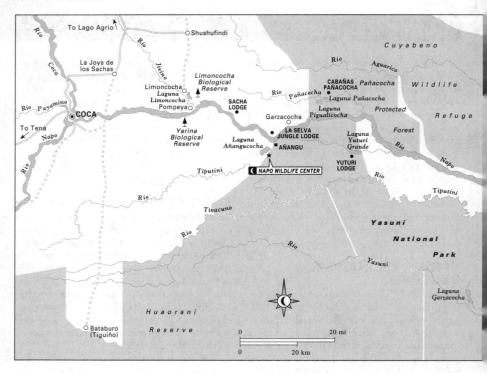

Besides its birds, the oxbow lake is known for an important ceramics find nearby. Pieces from the Napo Phase (circa A.D. 1190–1480) reflect a great aesthetic jump in indigenous pottery. Archaeologists have deduced from the works' decoration that the ancient inhabitants practiced secondary burial, a practice in which bodies were buried, then exhumed after a few months and reinterred in large ceramic containers sculpted especially for the ritual.

The three cabins called **Cabañas Limoncocha** were graciously left to the local indigenous community by Metropolitan Touring. Today, they are among the least expensive accommodations on the river. For prices and reservations, contact the Asociación Indígena de Limoncocha (AIL), c/o CONFENIAE (6 de Diciembre 159 and Pazmino, Of. 408, tel. 2/254-3973, fax 2/222-0325, confeniae@ applicom.com, www.unii.net/confeniae/ english). Entrance to the reserve is $5 pp.

Also on the lake is the Kichwa village of **Limoncocha,** where locals have formed an ecotourism cooperative that provides Kichwa lessons, guided tours, and accommodations to visitors. It's possible to stay in town and explore the area for about $40 pp per day, including lodging in cabanas, food, and guides. Two small shops sell supplies, and canoes can be rented. To get here from Coca, take one of the frequent buses or *rancheros* to Shushufindi ($2, two hours), then catch another bus to Limoncocha. One leaves in the early morning, another near noon, and a third late in the afternoon ($1.25, 90 minutes). The Hotel El Auca in Coca is a good source of information about Limoncocha, because one of its guides is from the area.

LOWER RÍO NAPO

Zábalo

Río Lagartococha

Zancudo

Laguna Zancudococha   Laguna Imuya

E C U A D O R

Tiputini

Río Cocaya

Nuevo Rocafuerte

Laguna Jatuncocha

P E R U

© AVALON TRAVEL

A short ride downriver is the Capuchin mission and archaeological museum at **Pompeya,** on a small island near the north bank of the Napo. Keep going to the **Isla de los Monos** (Monkey Island), where a few different species of primates roam wild—with a good guide, sightings are nearly guaranteed. These two sights are often combined with a visit to Limoncocha and can easily be visited independently from the town.

SACHA LODGE

This Swiss-owned lodge offers first-class accommodations and service only 2.5 hours downstream from Coca. The lodge owns 2,000 of the more than 7,000 hectares of mostly primary rainforest that surround the small complex on the shore of Laguna El Pilche. Ten cabins with private baths and gas-heated

hot water are connected by thatched walkways to the dining hall, where gourmet meals are the norm.

A 43-meter viewing tower built around a kapok tree affords guests the occasional view of Volcán Sumaco to the west, along with at least some of the 200 bird species that have been spotted from the tower. Birders will love the 270-meter canopy walkway and the salt lick just downriver near Añangu, where squawking flocks of parrots, parakeets, and macaws squabble over the mineral-rich soil exposed by the river.

All nature-viewing excursions from the lodge are accompanied by two guides (one local and one English-speaking biologist) for every four–seven people. A five-day visit costs $870 pp, not including airfare from Quito (10 percent SAE discount), and a four-day trip is $690 pp, leaving on Monday or Friday. For reservations, contact the lodge in Quito (tel. 2/250-9115, sales@sachalodge.com, www .sachalodge.com).

◖ NAPO WILDLIFE CENTER

One of the newest Amazon lodges in the country (opened in 2003), the Napo Wildlife Center is also one of the best. The lodge sits on Añangu Lake inside Yasuní National Park. It is run by local Kichwa Indians, who ensure

mealy Amazon parrots, yellow-crowned parrots, dusky-headed parakeets, and blue-headed parrots at clay lick on the Napo River

© JULIAN SMITH

THE ORIENTE

walking jungle tour near Napo Wildlife Center

that visitors have an outstanding wildlife and cultural experience while causing as little impact as possible. After a two-hour motor canoe ride down the Napo from Coca, guests switch over to dugout canoes and are paddled two more hours upstream to the lake. Ten comfortable, thatched-roof bungalows each have private baths and mosquito nets, and a five-story observation tower overlooks the dining room and lounge.

Excursions include climbing the 36-meter canopy observation tower, visiting local indigenous communities, hiking through the forest, and spending time at two of the most easily accessible clay licks in the country, where dozens of parrots and parakeets converge at once (the best months for this are December and January). More than 560 species of birds have been recorded nearby. Packages include four- and five-night visits that run $650–795 pp, including airfare from Quito.

LA SELVA JUNGLE LODGE

Ever since it won the main ecotourism award from the World Congress on Ecotourism and the Environment in 1992, La Selva Jungle Lodge has been Ecuador's most famous jungle lodge. It's also the (relative) granddaddy,

having offered a combination of luxury accommodations and outstanding experience since 1985. Many people come to Ecuador just to stay at La Selva.

The main lodge and 16 cabins overlook the Laguna Garzacocha. The menu features a combination of French, North American, and Ecuadorian cuisine, along with a dash of the rainforest, including local river fish and a special Amazon pizza. Residents of two local indigenous communities are employed at the lodge, whose list of services includes the Slothful Laundry, where clothes are "washed and often dried" but "never ironed."

Guests can go birding with native experts, climb the 30-meter canopy tower, or venture out by night to spot black caimans in the lake shadows. Those who stay close to the lodge can visit the **butterfly farm** in the nearby village of Garzacocha. Here, in the first professional operation of its type in South America, 30,000–35,000 pupae from 24 species are reared from eggs to be exported abroad. If you meet an intent-looking person along a trail peering into the canopy or measuring a root diameter, chances are he or she is from the **Neotropical Field Biology Institute,** a field station begun here in 1992.

© JULIAN SMITH

Large canoes with canopies are used for longer journeys on the jungle rivers.

Four- and five-day packages cost $697 and $832 pp, respectively, not including airfare to and from Coca. Guests arriving from other countries can be met at the airport and escorted to the lodge. Make reservations in Quito at the lodge's office (San Salvador E7-85 and Carrión, tel. 2/255-0995, info@laselvajunglelodge.com, www.laselvajunglelodge.com).

SANI LODGE

This fairly new lodge is located in 37,000 hectares of Kichwa-owned communal lands, and the staff at Sani are proud of their preservation work within the community. The aim is to become a model of ecological, community-based tourist development, while training the local people and maintaining international standards of service. Comments so far have been positive, and the impressive list of wildlife is enticing to nature lovers. Programs are four days ($510 pp) or five ($680 pp), and clients are met at Coca airport for transfers by river to the lodge, located three hours downstream.

YUTURI LODGE

One of the upper Napo's more remote lodges sits on a hill overlooking the Río Yuturi, five hours from Coca. More than one million hectares of flooded primary forest encompass countless lagoons, streams, and marshes fed by the blackwater river. All of it is leased from the Kichwa community of Samona, whose Spanish-speaking residents serve as native guides working with bilingual guides many from Quito. Twenty cabins built in the traditional style—except for electricity and private baths—are comfortable, and the meals are excellent, even for vegetarians.

With more than 500 species of birds in the surrounding forest, including orange-cheeked parrots, black-crowned tityras, collared puffbirds, and paradise tanagers, bird watchers can almost be guaranteed to add to their life lists during a visit. For reservations, contact the Yuturi Travel Agency (Amazonas N24-236 and Colón, tel. 2/250-4037 or 2/250-3225).

RIVER BOAT TRIPS

When Metropolitan Touring stopped its operations in the jungle, it looked like the end of an era for this type of trip. Although not an *African Queen*–style adventure, these comfortable floating hotels move on the jungle highway of the Río Napo and choose the most interesting sights for their day visits. They cater to clients who like to be on the move in well

THE ORIENTE

appointed, air-conditioned accommodations. Kempery tours (tel. 2/250-5599, www.kempery.com) had a boat custom built and operates four day trips for $520 pp and 5 day trips for $630 pp on the **Jungle Discovery,** which leaves from Coca on Mondays and Fridays. They are trying to promote longer trips to Pantoja and Iquitos in Peru during the high seasons.

The **Manatee** (tel. 2/244-8985, www.manateeamazonexplorer.com), taking its name from the aquatic mammal also known as the sea cow, offers similar trips on a custom-built boat along the Río Napo. Four days cost $511 pp and five days cost $635 pp.

The Misión hotel in Coca operates the **Flotel La Misión** (tel. 2/256-7148, www.hotelmision.com) aboard the reconditioned Metropolitan Touring craft. Trips are four or five days long, and they aim for middle-budget travelers at $100 per day.

◖ YACHANA LODGE

FUNEDESIN, a foundation that fosters long-term community development in the Ecuadorian Amazon, operates this complex, located three hours, by motor, upstream from Coca. It's aimed at educating visitors while providing a source of funds for local community development—and it must be working; it won *Condé Nast Traveler's* Ecotourism Award in 2004 and the National Geographic Award in 2008. Perched near the village of Mondaña, the lodge oversees 280 hectares of land stretching for 30 kilometers in either direction, including primary and secondary forest and agricultural land.

Yachana bills itself as "a place for learning," giving guests the opportunity to do things like become a beekeeper for a day (bee suit included). Canoe excursions and 15 kilometers of trails allow you to enjoy the rainforest on your own or under the direction of local guides, before returning to the rustic but comfortable accommodations for the night. Yachana isn't a place to see animals in the virgin forest, but if you'd like to meet local people and know that part of your fee goes toward supporting the local health care center, then Yachana is for you.

Packages, including transport upstream from Coca, are $480 pp for four days and $640 for five days (students and SAE members receive discounts). Regular canoe service runs to Yachana on Tuesday and Friday. Make reservations in Quito (Solano E12-62 and Oriental, tel./fax 2/252-3777, info@yachana.com, www.yachana.com).

South to Tena and Beyond

Ecuador's central Amazon sees more traffic closer to the base of the Andes. Most of the forests near the gateway towns of Tena and Misahualli have been disturbed, but whitewater rafting and cultural visits are still a great way to get to know the area. Down the Napo River, things get wild quickly. This part of the river isn't as remote as the lower section, but the farther you venture from the waterway, the more undisturbed you'll find the ecosystem.

BAEZA TO TENA
Cabañas San Isidro

Señora Carmen Bustamente and her family have welcomed visitors to their cattle farm in the Cosanga Valley since the 1970s. The Cabañas (sanisidro@ecuadorexplorer.com, www.cabanasanisidro.com) are very eco-minded: a quarter of the income earned from tourism goes toward buying more land for conservation. Eleven cabins with private baths and hot showers surround a main farmhouse enclosing the dining area, bar, and sitting room. An observation tower overlooks the surrounding cloud forest, where numerous trails lead off to archaeological sites, streams, and waterfalls. A biology station has been opened nearby.

San Isidro sits a few kilometers on the road above Cosanga. Rooms are $97 pp, including all meals but not naturalist guides. Reservations are essential.

Sumaco-Napo Galeras National Park

Volcán Sumaco juts from the rainforest east of Baeza, anchoring one of Ecuador's newest national parks. Created in 1994, Sumaco-Napo Galeras covers more than 200,000 hectares of lowland and high-altitude rainforest, where countless tributaries of the Ríos Napo and Coca begin. A small island section of the park encloses the Cordillera Galeras, south of the road between Narupa and Coca.

Cloud forests on the slopes of the volcano are special, completely isolated from other cloud forests by the intervening lowland rainforest farther down. Many unique species have evolved as a result, including 28 species of bats and 13 types of rodents. Pumas, jaguars, and tigrillos leave their prints in the mud, and river otters occasionally doze on riverbanks. Up to four meters of rain per year is the norm, and temperatures can range 10–25°C. The dry season runs November–February. The entrance fee is $5 pp, and three basic refuges within the park cost $3 pp. They are poorly maintained but dry.

East of the Cordillera Galeras, the Olalla Torres family runs a small lodge on their farm. It's a great base for climbing Sumaco or just getting away—*far* away—from it all. The turnoff for Cotapino, the closest village to the farm, is about 50 kilometers out on the road to Coca, near the town of Venticuatro (24) de Mayo, west of San José de Dahuano and Avila. A rolling dirt trail leads south to the farm. Arrangements to visit can be made in Venticuatro de Mayo, or just show up (prices are negotiable).

The few people who venture into Sumaco-Napo Galeras are usually intent on scaling the park's namesake volcano. The 3,900-meter **Volcán Sumaco** was first climbed in 1865. It's a long, difficult approach requiring five–six days of hiking and hacking before the final steep ascent.

Sumaco is called "potentially active" because, although there aren't any recent records

bird-watchers terrace at Wildsumaco Lodge

© JEAN BROWN

of eruptions, its conical shape indicates activity within the last few centuries. Odds are low that it will erupt when you're on it, but smart money says it isn't dead yet. October–December offer the driest conditions and clearest views from the summit. Look for the IGM 1:50,000 *Volcán Sumaco* map to check out the ascent.

Take the road east from Narupa to Coca to begin the ascent. Ask for guides in the Kichwa settlement of Wawa Sumaco, the guard post and visitor's center is just a few hundred meters from the main road, up the entry to Pacto Sumaco. Guides cost around $10–15 pp per day, and a small monetary contribution to the community ($25) is expected as well.

Wildsumaco Lodge

Nearly seven kilometers from Wawa Sumaco, this newly opened lodge (www.wildsumaco .com, $125 pp) offers superb bird-watching, great views over the forest, and extensive, well made forest trails. There are 10 comfortable double cabins and a dining area with a fireplace for cold evenings, plus a spotters' deck at canopy level. Here, birders can locate such special finds as the yellow-throated spadebill, grey-tailed piha, military macaw, coppery-chested jacamar, napo sabrewing, chestnut-crowned gnateater, and more than 370 other species.

THE ORIENTE

The price includes all meals, transport from Narupa or Coca, and a local guide; specialized bird guides are available.

Jumandy Caves and Tourist Complex

Four kilometers north of Archidona, on the Baeza to Tena road, sits an eight-hectare ecological park (9 A.M.–5 P.M. daily, $5 pp) centered around the largest of many caves in the region. A slow river flows out of a large, dark opening in the hillside, filling a pool equipped with water slides and surrounded by playgrounds and sports fields. There's also a restaurant and a bar.

The main cave is named after a warrior chief who fought against the Spanish. It was rediscovered in the late 1960s by a priest chasing an ocelot that disappeared into the cave's hidden mouth. The beginning section is heavily trafficked, illuminated, and riddled with graffiti, but the entire complex extends for kilometers underground. Three hundred meters in, you have to swim across a small lake, and that's just the beginning. Guides are available for aspiring spelunkers. The complex also has a hotel with private rooms with hot water for $5 pp.

◖ TENA

The steady descent from Baeza, across rattling metal bridges over muddy streams, eventually leads to Tena (pop. 17,000), the capital of Napo Province. Ecuador's self-proclaimed "cinnamon capital," located at the confluence of the Ríos Tena and Pano, began in the 16th century as a missionary and trading outpost—about as far into the forest as the Spanish were willing to settle.

Tena is not at all what you might expect from a midsize jungle town—it's peaceful, orderly, and clean, in a beautiful setting surrounded by forested hills, with the edge of the Andes just visible to the west. It's also more geared toward tourists than many of its counterparts, making it a better choice for longer stays. Many inexpensive hotels, tourist agencies, and restaurants serving vegetarian food cater to backpackers who use the

town as the starting point for trips into the rainforest.

Tena's location—a perfect storm of steep topography, dazzling jungle scenery, and tons of flowing water—have slowly made it one of Ecuador's white-water hotspots. It's a great place to learn to kayak or raft, with warm water and many rivers nearby.

Sights

To kill a free day in town, you could do worse than **Parque Amazonico La Isla** (8:30 A.M.–6 P.M. daily, $1 pp), a well done jungle-style park occupying the wedge-shaped piece of land between the two rivers. Gravel paths wander through 22 forested hectares, past spacious cages with native animals and reptiles. (Warning: Don't get to close to the monkey who lives near the animal cages—he likes to steal cameras.) Highlights include the canopy view from the mirador, and an ornamental and medicinal plant garden. Precocious kids wait at the covered bridge to act as guides.

Entertainment and Events

The **Gallera Bar** at the Hotel Puma Rosa is a good spot to shoot some pool or play table tennis. It also has one of the city's largest and most popular discotheques upstairs. On the other end of the scale, the **Boli Bar** on Orellana near the river is tiny, but it has a good music selection (note that in such close quarters, darts may not be such a good idea). Other bars line the river between and around the two bridges. Tena celebrates its **founding** on November 15.

Shopping

You'll find Tena's best selection of souvenirs, particularly woven bags and jewelry, at **Eco Artesania** on the main plaza.

Recreation and Tours

Ríos Ecuador (tel. 6/288-6727, info@ Ríosecuador.com, www.Ríosecuador.com) is run by Quito's Yacu Amu Rafting on Garcia Moreno, next to Chuquitos restaurant. It offers rafting and kayaking on the Napo and Anzu

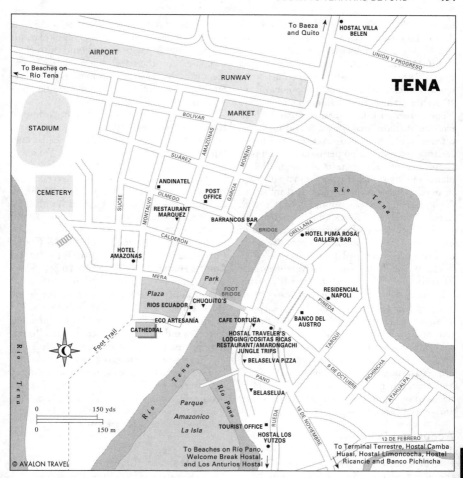

To Baeza and Quito

HOSTAL VILLA BELEN

UNION Y PROGRESO

AIRPORT

To Beaches on Río Tena

RUNWAY

TENA

MARKET

BOLIVAR

AMAZONAS

STADIUM

SUÁREZ

MORENO

ANDINATEL

POST OFFICE

GARCIA

OLMEDO

Río Tena

CEMETERY

SUCRE

RESTAURANT MARQUEZ

MONTALVO

BARRANCOS BAR

BRIDGE

ORELLANA

HOTEL PUMA ROSA/ GALLERA BAR

CALDERON

HOTEL AMAZONAS

MERA

Park

FOOT BRIDGE

RESIDENCIAL NAPOLI

PINEDA

Plaza

RIOS ECUADOR

CHUQUITO'S

ECO ARTESANÍA

CAFE TORTUGA

BANCO DEL AUSTRO

CATHEDRAL

Foot Trail

HOSTAL TRAVELER'S LODGING/COSITAS RICAS RESTAURANT/AMARONGACHI JUNGLE TRIPS

TARQUI

Río Tena

BELASELVA PIZZA

9 DE OCTUBRE

PICHINCHA

PANO

Río Pano

BELASELUA

15 DE NOVIEMBRE

ATAHUALPA

0   150 yds

Parque

Amazonico

RUEDA

0   150 m

La Isla

TOURIST OFFICE

12 DE FEBRERO

HOSTAL LOS YUTZOS

To Beaches on Río Pano, Welcome Break Hostal, and Los Anturios Hostal

To Terminal Terrestre, Hostal Camba Huasi, Hostal Limoncocha, Hostel Ricancie and Banco Pichincha

© AVALON TRAVEL

($59 pp), and on the Misahualli ($79). The trips are safe, professional, and fun.

Operating out of the Hostal Traveller's Lodging, **Amarongachi Jungle Trips** (tel./fax 6/288-6372, pattyco64@hotmail.com) offers well-reviewed tours within a relatively short distance of town. A four-day trip visiting low-land Kichwa communities and viewing wildlife from the Cabañas Shangri-La atop a 150-meter riverside cliff costs $160 pp.

The **Cerda family**—Olmedo, Oswaldo, Fausto, and Blanca—are all frequently described as excellent private guides for the upper Río Napo. Tours of two–eight days focus on indigenous cultures and the native flora and fauna, and they can be based out of cabins or tents for $35–45 pp per day. The family also offers rafting and motorized canoe tours. Some English and German are spoken.

Another branch of the Cerda family runs **Sapo Rumi Jungle Adventure** (tel. 6/288-7896, fax 6/288-6608, ecerdafamily@hotmail .com). The company, located on 15 de Noviembre near the bridge, has gotten good reviews for four-day "difficult" trips, starting at $45 pp per day; and three-day "easy" trips, from $30 pp per day. None of the guides speaks English.

RICANCIE (Jumandi and Radio Oriental, tel. 6/288-8479, ricancie@hotmail.com, www.ricancie.nativeweb.org) is a network of 10 Kichwa communities along the upper Río Napo that offer hiking, canoeing, and explanations of traditional lifestyles and medicine during well-run two-to-seven-day programs starting around $30 pp per day. You can pick the minds of local experts about medicinal plants and forest life, visit with a shaman, learn to make pottery or play traditional music, or participate in a *minga* (communal work event). Some of the guides speak a little English, but you'll get more out of the experience if you or someone in your group knows some Spanish, or if you ask for a translator.

On weekends, it seems as if everyone under 21 (and quite a few over) in Tena is wearing a bathing suit and carrying an inner tube. They're headed for one of the riverbank **beaches** near town, which can be reached on foot and packed into a truck. The "playa del sol" (sun beach) and "isla del amor" (island of love) are west of town on the Río Tena—keep going past the end of the airport runway. There are a few more beaches south of the main plaza (reached by a foot trail from Misión Josefina) and on the Parque Amazonico La Isla.

Accommodations

The friendly Rivadeneyra family runs the **Hostal Villa Belen** (tel./fax 6/288-6228), at the north edge of town, with a small, open cafeteria under a thatched roof. The 18 rooms all have fans, private baths, cable TV, and hot water for $10, and breakfast is $3. The clean, modern **Hostal Traveller's Lodging** (tel. 6/288-6372) offers good beds, luggage storage, and a strongbox. Private rooms with cable TV, hot water, and private bath start at $8 s, $17 d, and more luxurious rooms on the top floor cost twice that. Cositas Ricas Restaurant and Amarongachi Jungle Trips operate out of the same building, near the eastern end of the footbridge.

The **Hotel Amazonas** (tel. 6/288-6439), at the northwestern corner of the main plaza, is a tightly run ship with second- and third-floor balconies over the street. Three-dollar rooms are a mixed bag, with thin mattresses and no fans, but the quiet location and friendly owners make it worth considering.

A popular newer option is **A Welcome Break** (tel. 6/288-6301), where clean rooms are $8 pp with private bath. It is located on a quiet street near the more expensive Yutzos.

On the hill, catching the breeze and enjoying the quiet, is the spotless, German-run **Hostal Limoncocha** (tel. 6/288-7583, $8.50 s, $15 d). Rooms have private bath and fans, and a small terrace is available for sitting and watching the sunset.

Down 15 de Noviembre on Via del Chofer (turn right past the bus terminal) is the **Hostal Camba Huasi** (tel. 6/288-7429, $6 pp), where decent rooms with private bath but no fans are often full of tour groups. Rooms at the newer **Hotel Puma Rosa** (tel. 6/288-6320, $13 s, $24 d), on Orellana north of the bridge, are centered around a plant-filled courtyard. Rooms have private baths, hot water, and cable TV.

The closest thing to luxury accommodations in town can be found at the **Hostal Los Yutzos** (tel. 6/288-6717 or 6/287-0091, yutzos@uchutecan.com), on Rueda along the Río Pano. Rooms with private baths, cable TV, hot water, fans, and refrigerators are $31 s, $41 d.

Food

Chuquitos, a local favorite below the plaza, has a great riverside location. The portions are immense, and few items on the huge menu—which ranges from seafood to Chinese—will set you back more than $4, except the frog legs (around $7).

The **Cositas Ricas Restaurant,** in the Hostal Traveller's Lodging, serves generous breakfasts, vegetarian plates, muesli, and yogurt, and—like the hotel—is always packed with gringos. Most meals, including pizza, vegetarian spaghetti, and fried chicken are about $4 (breakfast is $2). Up the spiral staircase, you'll find a more elegant dining option, with air-conditioning and river views and an extensive international menu.

Information and Services

The staff at Tena's **tourist office** (tel. 6/288-8046 or 6/288-6536, 8:30 A.M.–12:30 P.M. and 2–5:30 P.M. Mon.–Fri.), on Rueda near Hostal Los Yutzos and the market, are friendly and helpful. They offer a free map and city brochure, and they take their job of overseeing tour companies seriously (stop by with any complaints).

Travelers can change money at the **Banco del Austro,** on 15 de Noviembre between the bridges. The local **police station** is next to Villa Belen, which is near the airport, and the **post office** is on Olmedo near Amazonas.

Transportation

The *terminal terrestre* sits about one kilometer south of the footbridge on 15 de Noviembre. Local buses labeled "Terminal" run down 15 de Noviembre. The ride to Quito takes six hours ($6) and is longer and more expensive by way of Ambato. Other buses run to Baeza ($3, three hours), Puyo ($3, three hours), Baños ($4, four hours), and Coca ($6, six hours). Buses to Misahualli ($1, one hour) pass the bus stop on 15 de Noviembre in front of the terminal more or less hourly. Buses to Archidona and the Jumandy Caves leave often from the corner of Bolívar and Amazonas. (Buses to Coca and Quito via Baeza also pass here.)

MISAHUALLI

Seven kilometers south of Tena is Puerto Napo, once the main port on the upper Río Napo. Two roads lead east from here along the river—one on the south side across the bridge, and one on the north to the town of Misahualli.

Set on a rocky spit where the Río Misahualli empties into the lazy Río Napo, Misahualli is still only a speck of a town with a few cheap hotels, restaurants, tour agencies, and stores stocked with jungle supplies. In a living lesson of the danger of feeding wildlife, the monkeys who frequent the main plaza and the beach one block away have developed a kleptomaniac's

Small jungle streams wind through the abundant vegetation.

taste for Coca-Cola. They also walk into town and raid unattended luggage or storefronts.

The new footbridge over the Napo makes it possible to walk over to the southern bank of the river and down to Jatun Sacha for a visit to the reserve.

Recreation and Tours

One of the best excursions from Misahualli is a **river hike** that starts seven kilometers west of town on the road to Puerto Napo, where a bridge crosses the Río Latas. There are two small signs—one indicating the *cascadas* (falls), and another advertising the Cabañas Gan Eden. Climb the stairs to the snack bar, pay the small entrance fee, and keep going another half hour or so down a slippery, muddy path past smaller falls to the big one with a swimming hole at the base.

Dozens of guides operate out of Misahualli: some reputable, many barely adequate, and a few irresponsible to the point of being dangerous. The following are a few of the best, but shop around—carefully. Remember, the agency is responsible for the trip organization, but in the end, the guide makes or breaks a trip. Fewer tourists come to Misahualli these days, making it harder to put a group together. It's easier to join a group in Tena, and some tours arranged in Tena start in Misahualli.

Expediciones Douglas Clark (no phone, douglasclarkeexpediciones@yahoo.com) has been run by its Ecuadorian namesake for more than two decades and is considered one of the best choices. Operating out of an office on the plaza and at his Hotel Marena Internacional, Douglas runs tours to his Cabañas Sinchi Runa, south of Misahualli at the confluence of the Ríos Arajuno and Puni, as well as to Pañacocha and the Río Yasuní. Some profits are used for conservation efforts, such as purchasing land and helping reintroduce native species.

Ecoselva (ecoselva@yahoo.ec), run by the friendly and highly regarded Pepe Tapia Gonzalez, is another excellent agency. Tours lasting 1–10 days are possible for as low as $30 pp per day, depending on the destination. Pepe speaks English (as does his brother Lenyn) and teaches biology at the Universidad Ecológica in Tena. His office is on the plaza, and he also has an office in Tena.

Hector Fiallos is a highly recommended guide who runs **Sacha Tour** (tel. 6/288-6679 or 6/288-6563) from the Hostal Sacha down on the beach. Up to 10-day trips range as far as Yasuní and Cuyabeno, and some of his guides know a little English (Hector speaks some French). He also uses the name Fluvial River Tours, because other guides have copied the Sacha name. It's best to ask for Hector by name. Tours in the Misahualli area are $35 pp per day. **Viajes y Aventuras Amazonicas** (tel. 6/288-1444) is based at the Hotel La Posada and run by the amiable Carmen Santander. Tours in the Misahualli area are $30 pp for three or four days.

Accommodations and Food

The least expensive hotels and restaurants crowd the plaza. **La Posada Residencial/ Restaurant** serves good food on an open corner porch that monkeys wander into from time to time. Rooms are clean, with private bath, hot water, and fans for $6 pp. Just off the plaza, jungle guide Douglas Clark's **Hotel Marena International** rents rooms with private baths and small refrigerators for $7 pp. The **Hotel Shaw**, part of Ecoselva, has rooms on the plaza for $5 pp with shared bath and fan. There's a popular **Tex-Mex restaurant** on the plaza as well.

About 100 meters up the road toward Puerto Napo, you'll pass the **Albergue Español** (tel./ fax 6/289-0127). Rooms with fans, 24-hour hot water, private baths, and views of the Río Napo cost $8 pp. The hotel owns the Jaguar Reserve (see the *Upper Río Napo* section of this chapter) and organizes day trips for guests. Half a kilometer farther brings you to the hotel **France Amazonia** (tel. 6/289-0009), with a pool and the best accommodations in town for $16 pp, including breakfast.

Keep going and take a right at the fork in the road (straight ahead goes to Puerto Napo), and in just over two kilometers, you'll reach **El Jardín Alemán** (Tomás Bermur 22 and Urrutia, tel. 2/224-7878, fax 2/246-2213, jarnatra@pi.pro.ec). A main lodge with satellite TV, a restaurant, a bar, and laundry facilities sits on 264 acres of primary rainforest on the west bank of the Río Misahualli. Accommodations include five suites and eight comfortable double rooms with fan, terrace, private bath, and hot water. While you're here, you can choose between hikes, jeep trips, and horseback rides into the forest, rafting on the river, or panning for gold. Rates start around $153 pp for three days and $300 for five days; activities with a local guide are included.

The ◖ **Misahualli Jungle Lodge** (Ramiro Dávalos 251, tel. 2/252-0043, fax 2/250-4872, info@misahuallijungle.com, www.misahualli jungle.com) occupies a tranquil clearing in a 145-hectare preserve across the Río Misahualli from town. Fifteen cabins with fans, private baths, and hot water can hold 50 people. Guests are free to wander along well-marked trails into the forest, chat, read, and relax in front of the satellite TV in the central building, or do laps in the pool. Rates are $69 pp, including meals, and transportation can be arranged from as far as Quito. Drop-ins are welcome, and it's worth an afternoon visit from Misahualli. A regular canoe service runs until 9 P.M. for $0.25.

Transportation

Buses from Tena circle the plaza before heading back out of town roughly every hour. The rocky sandbar at the confluence of Ríos Napo and Misahualli is usually occupied by **motor canoes** waiting to depart to lodges and villages downriver. Prices are fixed, but ask in town beforehand to avoid overcharging. Boat service runs to Coca when there are enough passengers.

UPPER RÍO NAPO

From Puerto Napo to Coca, the river is the main artery of life, bringing water and nutrients to the forest, supplies to the colonists, and tourists to the lodges. This stretch is narrower and more wild than the river below Coca, twisting around islands as it rises and falls abruptly in response to rainfall and drought.

Oil prospecting brought the first wave of settlers to the area decades ago, when towns like Misahualli consisted of little more than a crossroads and a general store. Recent roads east from Puerto Napo have opened the region even more to colonization, agriculture, and cattle ranching.

Today, almost all of the rainforest along the first 50 or so kilometers of the river has been disturbed in some way, except for small protected areas around the lodges and Jatun Sacha. The jungle becomes more pristine farther downriver and away from the banks of the upper stretch.

Butterfly Garden

Roughly five minutes downstream from Misahualli is a new butterfly garden opened by Pepe Tapia Gonzalez of Ecoselva. The large mesh enclosure has dozens of species of *mariposas,* with more on the way as appropriate food and cocoon plants are added. To visit the gardens, stop by Ecoselva's office on the plaza in Misahualli to pick up the key and pay your $1 entry fee, then take a boat from the beach (all the drivers know it) for $1.50 one-way. You can pay the driver to wait for you, or have him return at a set time. Some tours include a stop here.

Jatun Sacha Biological Station

Ecuador's premier tropical field research station was begun in 1986 by an Ecuadorian and two North Americans, who gained title to 140 hectares of forest along the upper Río Napo. With the help of various foreign organizations and charities, the nonprofit Fundación Jatun Sacha (Pasaje Eugenio de Santillán N34-28 and Maurián, Urb. Rumipamba, tel. 2/243-2240, fax 2/245-3583, jatsacha@jatunsacha .org, www.jatunsacha.org) was created in 1989 to manage the field station and promote conservation of and education about the rainforest to Ecuadorians and foreigners alike.

Now Jatun Sacha is one of the most prestigious tropical research stations in South America, welcoming scientists, school groups,

canoes ready to go downriver to the jungle lodges

© JEAN BROWN

THE ORIENTE

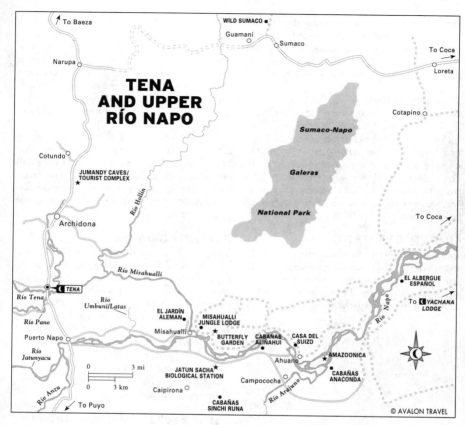

TENA AND UPPER RÍO NAPO

To Baeza

WILD SUMACO ■

Guamaní

Sumaco

To Coca

Narupa

Loreta

Cotapino

Sumaco-Napo

Cotundo

JUMANDY CAVES/
TOURIST COMPLEX

Río Hollín

Galeras

Archidona

National Park

To Coca

Río Misahualli

EL ALBERGUE
ESPAÑOL

TENA

Río Tena

*Río
Umbuni/Latas*

EL JARDÍN
ALEMAN

MISAHUALLI
JUNGLE LODGE

To YACHANA
LODGE

Río Napo

Río Pano

Misahualli

BUTTERFLY
GARDEN

CABAÑAS
ALINAHUI

CASA DEL
SUIZO

Puerto Napo

*Río
Jatunyacu*

Ahuano

AMAZOONICA

0   3 mi

JATUN SACHA
BIOLOGICAL STATION

Campococha

CABAÑAS
ANACONDA

0   3 km

Caipirona

Río Anzu

To Puyo

CABAÑAS
SINCHI RUNA

Río Arajuno

© AVALON TRAVEL

and natural history tours to its 2,000 hectares of protected rainforest. The name means "big forest" in Kichwa, and it rings true: 70 percent of Jatun Sacha's holdings are primary, undisturbed jungle, forming a transitional zone between the lower slopes of the Andes and the true Amazon lowlands farther east.

Jatun Sacha isn't a resort lodge, but independent visitors can spend the night for $30 pp—advance booking is necessary, or pay a day-visit fee of $6 pp. Facilities for visiting scientists and students consist of bunk beds in raised wooden cabins, along with a main building with a dining hall, kitchen, bathrooms, electricity, and a modest library. Well-maintained trails lead to the river and a canopy observation tower. Group reservations should be made at least one week in advance, and prices run $30 pp per day, including lodging and three meals.

Volunteer positions are available in education, station maintenance, and conservation, as well as at the station's Amazon Plant Conservation Center, an experimental medicinal garden completed in 1993. A fee of $450 per month, payable in advance, covers meals and lodging.

Jatun Sacha is 22 kilometers east of the bridge over the river at Puerto Napo; it's marked by a sign on the right-hand side of the road. Buses from Tena headed for the villages of Campococha or Ahuano pass the entrance to the station (look for the Centinela de Tena bus in Tena's main terminal).

Cabañas Aliñahui and Butterfly Lodge

This lodge was operated by Jatun Sacha from 1994 until 2005. A former cattle ranch, it evolved into an ecologically minded lodge that offers eight cabins, comfortably appointed with hammocks and private bath, for a total of 45 people. Three lookout towers provide jaw-dropping views of the surrounding forest and ice-capped volcanoes on the horizon. Rainwater fills the toilets and sinks, solar power provides the electricity, and septic tanks take care of waste. The food is simple and wholesome, and an evening drink at the bar goes well with the muted roar of the forest.

A wide range of activities starts with visits to Jatun Sacha, a few hours by foot along the side of the river. On the way, the vistas of the river and the Andes in the distance show why the cabins are named for the Kichwa word meaning "beautiful view." Aliñahui's other name,

the Butterfly Lodge, probably has something to do with the 750 species of butterflies spangling the trees along self-guided trails that wind through the forest. More than 100 species of orchids have been found nearby. Excursions to native communities and caves can be arranged by canoe or on horseback.

Tours start at $145 pp for three days, rising to $190 pp for five days. Special eight-day native culture tours are also possible for $437 pp (minimum four people), and you can visit Aliñahui on your own for $50 pp per day, meals included. Reservations and information are handled through the Aliñahui office in Quito (Inglaterra 1373 y Amazonas, tel. 2/227-4510, tel./fax 2/227-4947, info@ecuadoramazonlodge.com).

To reach the cabanas, take the road east from Puerto Napo along the south bank of the Río Napo. After 25 kilometers, a turnoff heads north 1.5 kilometers to the bridge over the river. Five or so buses per day leave Puerto Napo heading in this direction, and public canoes from Misahuallí take half an hour and cost $2.

© JULIAN SMITH

THE ORIENTE

ceiba, or kapok, tree

CASA DEL SUIZO

If luxury and service are the most important factors in your choice of lodging, the Casa del Suizo should do nicely. Owned by an Ecuadorian-Swiss partnership, the elegant lodge offers 20 rooms, 30 cabins, and a pool on the Río Napo's north bank near Ahuano. Views from the rooms and the *mirador* (balcony) topping the three-floor main building are superb, as is the buffet-style food. For relaxing, there's a pool and a bar.

The immediate area isn't great for wildlife viewing, so the Casa del Suizo has more of a cultural focus. Visits to a local Kichwa village are one possible activity, as are rainforest hikes. The lodge is also relatively easy to reach, making it the perfect place for those who want to see the forest without much effort or discomfort. Rooms are $79 per night and four-day packages are $350 pp, including everything plus transport from Quito, with a stop in Papallacta. Make reservations through the office in Quito (Julio Zaldumbide 397 and Valladolid, tel. 2/256-6090, fax 2/223-6521, suizh@ecnet.ec, www.casadelsuizo.com).

Cabañas Albergue Español

One of the oldest lodges in the Ecuadorian Amazon is about 1.75 hours downriver from Misahualli. Set on 1,000 hectares of primary forest, this historic place, once known as Jaguar Lodge, has been in business since 1969. It is now owned (and was recently renovated) by the same owners as El Albergue Español. Ten cabins blend wooden beams and clean white walls, and each has a private bath with hot water. Vegetarians will find themselves well looked after at the restaurant, which has a great view over the river.

Thanks to the hotel's relative isolation, primary forest begging to be explored by foot and canoe stretches out in the other direction. Jungle treks and visits to Kichwa villages with local guides are all included in the surprisingly reasonable prices. Visits run $105 pp for two days and $185 pp for four days. Transportation isn't included, unless there are at least four in the group, so factor in another $20 for the trip by private canoe. Reserve through El Albergue Español (tel. 6/289-0004, alb-esp@uio.satnet.net).

Southern Oriente

Macas is one of the least visited jungle towns, while Puyo, its nearest neighbor, is beginning to see an increase in visitors. The latter is connected by paved road to Baños on the eastern slope of the highlands, and the road south to Macas is now mostly paved. The region south of Macas, which sees even less traffic, was the focus of fighting between Ecuador and Peru in the 1980s.

PUYO

The capital of Pastaza Province is also the political capital of Amazonian Indigenous nations, and as such has been growing in importance. The fact that all the access roads from the north, south, and mountains are now either paved or about to be has changed the face of Puyo. The nearby military air base at Shell is also used by missionaries, oil companies, and the local indigenous people as a springboard to the isolated jungle communities. In this growing frontier jungle town (pop. 45,000), stores still buy *oro en polvo* (gold dust), and many streets bear the date of a famous event that happened far away and long ago.

The southern Oriente has started opening up to tourism, and Puyo is poised to take advantage of its direct link to the highlands in one direction and pure forest in the other. The climate here reminds you that you're in the rainforest: the town's name means "cloudy" in a local indigenous language, and hot and wet weather is the norm.

Sights

On the edge of town is the 15.6-hectare **Pedagogical Ethnobotanical OMAERE Park** (8:30 A.M.–5 P.M. Thurs.–Mon., $2 pp), a small botanical reserve described as "superb" for its collection of 1,000 different species of Amazonian plants used by indigenous cultures. A team of Shuar, Sapara, Huaorani, and Kichwa specialists helped establish the gardens which emphasize traditional knowledge. Part of the park is cultivated in nurseries and greenhouses. There is an excellent walk that continues past here and follows the river for a couple of kilometers emerging on the main road to Tena.

Omar Tello has devoted many years to his wonderful collection of orchids and endangered jungle plants. You can visit the spectacular gardens and take a personal tour for $5 pp. Look for the bus to Los Angeles, and ask to be let off at **Las Orquideas,** about a 10-minute ride.

The rescue center **Paseo de los Monos** cares for confiscated and maltreated monkeys on a privately owned reserve, where they are fed and allowed to roam free. Admission is $1.50, and the bus to Arajuno goes right by the entry (look for the sign).

Recreation and Tours

Run by the Sarayaku community, with José Gualinga as the friendly office manager, **Papangu Tours** (27 de Febrero and Sucre, tel. 3/288-7684, www.sarayaku.com) has been recommended for tours to Kichwa and Shuar communities near Puyo. One option for this first-hand look into traditional native culture is a three-day visit to one of the villages closest to Puyo by car and foot ($25 pp per day, three-person minimum). Other, more adventurous trips head farther into the jungle by canoe for a stay of four–six days. Trips can be tailored to the group's interests, but few guides speak English. This option costs $40 pp per day for at least four people and can be shortened by a plane ride, which costs extra.

Diego Escobar, a local environmentalist,

runs **Madre Selva** (Ceslao Marin 668, tel. 6/289-0449, www.madreselvaecuador.com), which offers tours of one to eight days for $35 pp per day. English-speaking, licensed guides are available.

A day trip to **Hola Vida,** with its lovely forest and waterfall, is easy to arrange. You could also visit on the way to **Altos del Pastaza** (tel. 9/853-0616, www.altosdelpastazalodge.com), a new lodge about an hour south of Puyo, in a spectacular setting overlooking the Pastaza river near Pomona. Views of the snowcapped mountains as a backdrop for the jungle and river are breathtaking. Trips include transport from Puyo and cost $198 pp for three days/two nights, $291 for four days/three nights, and $376 for five days/four nights.

THE ORIGIN OF FIRE

Many years ago, the story goes, the Shuar didn't have fire. The only way they could heat their food was with the sun. In all the jungle, only a huge *hombronazo* had fire, and he guarded it jealously in his house. The few Shuar who had tried to steal it from him had been caught and crushed between the monster's huge hands. These fierce blows could be heard in the jungle far away – *tac, tac, tac* – which is why the Shuar called this particular *hombronazo* Takea.

Early one morning, Takea's wife was wandering through her orchard when she found a hummingbird, nearly frozen from the night's cold. The gentle woman took pity on the tiny bird and brought it home and sat it next to the fire. Revived by the heat, the hummingbird suddenly sprang up, grabbed a bit of the fire with his tail, and fled. The bird gave the ember to a Shuar woman, who distributed it to the rest of her village, enabling the Shuar to cook their food, warm their bodies, and light the darkness from that day forth.

– Shuar myth

Puyo's **water park** got a major facelift in 2004. Previously, the swimming pools were underused, but now the the wave pool and spa attract many residents and visitors. Admission is $3 pp, and the park is closed for maintenance and cleaning on Mondays and Tuesdays.

Accommodations

One of the most popular hotels in town for the money is the **Hotel Araucano** (tel. 3/283-3834, fax 3/288-5227), where rooms with private baths and hot water are $8 pp, cheaper on upper floors. Breakfast is included, and you can add a TV for $2 more. The friendly staff is knowledgeable about the area. Please hold the Eagles jokes if you stay at the **Hotel California** (tel. 6/288-5189), where $9 gets you a small but clean and colorful room with private bath. Guests can watch videos in the lobby. **El Colibri** (tel. 3/288-3054, $8 pp) is a short way from the center on Manabi Street, but worth the stroll: rooms are clean and the area is quiet.

The **Hostería Turingia** (tel. 3/288-5180) features alpine-style cabins surrounded by flowers, with a pool, a bar, a patio, and "Sneaky" the boa constrictor. Rates are $22 s, $35 d, including private bath, hot water, and TV.

Several quieter lodging options have opened down by the river, including the small, stylish, and family-run **Posada Real** (tel. 3/288-5887, $25 pp), which includes breakfast; and the **Finca El Pigual** (tel. 3/288-7972, elpigual@hotmail.com, $39 s, $64 d), which offers gardens, a pool, and a restaurant.

Food

Locals say the best of Puyo's scant eating selection is **El Jardín,** down by the river, where main dishes are $4–7. Located next to the Flor de Canela hotel, it recently opened up some attractive rooms ($12 pp). Dozens of *comedores* and cheap restaurants line Atahualpa, as well as 24 de Mayo between 27 de Febrero and 9 de Octubre. For more refined (and expensive) fare, stop by the restaurant at the Hostería Turingia, where almost every entrée, from chili to trout, is around $4. For an authentic Neapolitan pizza or Italian dinner, you can't do better than **O'Sole Mio** (Pichincha and Guaranda, tel. 3/288-4768). For a good traditional breakfast, try **Panadería Susanita's** (Ceslau Marín and Villamil). Special Kichwa foods are often sold off small grills, wrapped in achira leaves and cooked over hot coals. There's tasty wholewheat bread at **Pan de Casa** (Ceslau Marín and 27 de Febrero).

Information and Services

Amazonia Touring (Atahualpa and 9 de Octubre) changes travelers' checks and sells souvenirs. The **Ministerío de Turismo** (on the Y at Atahualpa and Marín) offers a slim selection of maps of the area, and there's a police station one block north of the main plaza on 9 de Octubre. The **post office** is on 27 de Febrero and Atahualpa.

Transportation

The main **bus terminal** is south of the town center and can be reached by buses marked "Terminal," running down 9 de Octubre every 15 minutes. Direct lines go to most major cities in the highlands and on the coast, including Quito ($6, six–eight hours), Baños ($2, two hours), Tena ($3, three hours), Macas ($4, three hours), Ríobamba ($4, four hours), Guayaquil ($8, eight hours), and Ambato ($3, three hours).

A taxi trip within the city limits, including out to the bus station, runs about $1.

MACAS

Half the fun of the southernmost major city in the Oriente is getting there on the new road from Ríobamba. Six buses a day travel this route from the terminal on Cordovez. Only the night buses go all the way through, as work on the bridge and tunnel by Zuñag block the road during working hours. The "Transbordo," a walk from one bus to the other, is about one kilometer across the bridge and through the dripping tunnel. The forest is spectacular—for the best views, sit behind the driver. From the Atillo lakes in the *páramo*, the bike ride

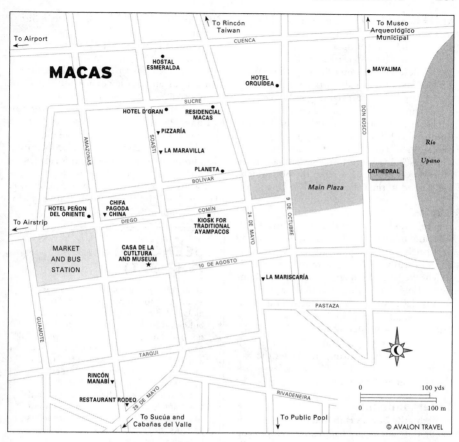

To Airport ←

To Rincón
Taiwan ↑

To Museo
Arqueológico
Municipal ↑

CUENCA

MACAS

HOSTAL
ESMERALDA

HOTEL
ORQUÍDEA

MAYALIMA

SUCRE

HOTEL D'GRAN

RESIDENCIAL
MACAS

AMAZONAS

SOASTI

PIZZARÍA

LA MARAVILLA

PLANETA

DON BOSCO

Río

Upano

BOLÍVAR

CATHEDRAL

Main Plaza

HOTEL PEÑON
DEL ORIENTE

CHIFA
PAGODA
CHINA

To Airstrip ←

DIEGO

COMÍN

KIOSK FOR
TRADITIONAL
AYAMPACOS

24 DE MAYO

9 DE OCTUBRE

MARKET
AND BUS
STATION

CASA DE LA
CULTURA
AND MUSEUM ★

10 DE AGOSTO

LA MARISCARÍA

PASTAZA

GUAMOTE

TARQUI

RINCÓN
MANABÍ

RESTAURANT RODEO

28 DE MAYO

RIVADENEIRA

0   100 yds

0   100 m

To Sucúa and
Cabañas del Valle

To Public Pool ↓

© AVALON TRAVEL

to here compares to any great downhill ride in the world.

Coming to Macas from the north or south, you'll pass scattered Shuar settlements and catch quick glimpses of the forest to the east and mountains to the west. Almost exactly halfway along the road south from Puyo, your bus will cross the Río Pastaza on the new suspension bridge, and from there, the road is paved. The road south is paved beyond Sucua, and work advances toward Logroño.

The rest of the fun comes from the town's combination of a beautiful setting, a mild climate, and friendly inhabitants. Flowers in a range of colors decorate the surprisingly clean town. To the east, the Río Upano meanders through a wide valley separating the Cordillera de Cutucú from the Andes, which loom to the west beyond the airport and the small Río Surumbaino. It's worth a walk to the quiet, residential south end of Macas for a view of the hills and river.

Although it's not readily apparent, Macas (pop. 18,000) has seen its share of action. The original settlement was destroyed at the turn of the 17th century in a Shuar uprising, then rebuilt, only to endure repeated attacks through the 19th century. A foot trail to Ríobamba was

Macas's only link to the outside world until well into the 1800s, and that trail is now essentially the route of the new road.

Macas has been declared the capital of the nearly deserted Morona-Santiago Province, which is gaining inhabitants with the recent discovery of oil. Border fighting in 1995 caused the evacuation of most of the city. Today, the strong military presence is a thing of the past, due to the 1998 peace treaty that decided Ecuador and Peru's border once and for all.

Macas has a more bearable climate than other, lower jungle cities, and the bird-watching is good in the valley of the Río Upano.

Sights

Macas's modern **cathedral** was finished in 1992 and boasts stained-glass windows worthy of a much larger temple. The hallowed image of La Purísima de Macas commemorates a vision of the Virgin that appeared to a local family in 1595, back when the town was called Sevilla del Oro. Five blocks north along Don Bosco, a small ethnographic collection fills the **Museo Arqueológico Municipal,** which sits at the entrance to a pleasant park filled with trees and orchids, offering views over the Río Upano and beyond. It's open weekdays—ask the librarian to let you in.

Entertainment

At night, the **Bar La Habana,** in the basement facing the market, is a happening spot playing everything from reggae to merengue. A well-kept **public pool** (10 A.M.–6 P.M. daily, $0.50 pp) is surrounded by yellow and purple flowers in the COEPRO children's school, about one kilometer south of town on 24 de Mayo.

Recreation and Tours

Planeta (tel. 7/270-1328, planeta.m.s@ hotmail.com), which shares its space with a handicrafts store on Bolívar and 24 de Mayo, runs trips to the village of Yaupi, where you can stay with an indigenous family for $25 per day, including transport and a guide. The company also offers three-day tours to Sangay

($90 pp) and one-day trips to visit Shuar communities.

Rafting trips on the Río Upano are mostly seasonal from November through March and require at least four people. Make arrangements in advance with **Yacu Amu** (Foch 746 y Amazonas, tel. 2/290-4054) in Quito.

To reach the eastern slopes of **Sangay National Park,** head to the town of General Proaño, just north of Macas, where guides are available for hire and for advice on planning trips. From there, a 90-minute bus ride (twice a day, three days a week) can drop you at the trailheads near the village of 9 de Octubre. Plan on a minimum of three–four days for any excursion.

JEENCHAM (THE BAT)

Long ago, the animals of the forest were about to go to war with the birds. The animals called on the bat to fight with them, but he refused. "No, I am not an animal," he said. "I am a bird. See – I have wings." Soon, the birds, looking for allies, also asked the bat to join their side. The bat answered, "No, see that I have teeth and fur. I am not a bird, I am an animal."

The fight began. The bat, seeing that the animals seemed to be winning, went to their side. But the animals spurned his help. As the tide of the battle shifted, the bat ran to the birds and offered his help. The birds also turned him away.

In time, the animals won. As was the custom, the victors held a celebration for everyone involved, animals and birds alike. The bat tried to sneak into the festivities but was discovered. Soon everyone began chasing after the bat, hitting him and shouting at him. And thus the animals and birds together cursed the bat, saying that he would always be a coward who lived in caves and only emerged at night, for fear that he would be caught and killed.

– Shuar myth

Accommodations

Budget travelers should check out the **Residencial Macas** (Sucre and 24 de Mayo), where spare but clean beds with shared bath are $5 pp, and a couple of rooms with private baths run $8 pp. Both the **Hotel Orquidea** (Sucre and 9 de Octubre, tel. 7/270-0970, $9 pp) and the **Hostel Esmeralda** (Cuenca 6–12 and Soasti, tel. 7/270-0130, $8 pp) are spotless and comfortable, with rooms featuring private baths, hot water, and TV. More comfortable and quiet, one kilometer out of town beyond the end of the runway, are **Cabañas del Valle** (tel. 7/270-0226, $12.50 s, $20 d).

Food

Most of the best eateries in town are near the bus terminal. The **Chifa Pagoda China,** a jewel in the jungle, serves generous, tasty portions of *chaulafans* and *tallarines* starting at $4, while any of the nine ways they prepare shrimp will set you back $5. Also highly recommended is **Rincon de Taiwan,** five blocks north on Soasti. **La Mariscaria** (10 de Agosto and 24 de Mayo) is popular for seafood lunches, and the **Rincon Manabita,** at its new location on Amazonas and Tarqui, also attracts faithful local clients. **Mayalima** (Don Bosco and Cuenca) offers traditional foods, including the achira-leaf parcels containing fish and known as *ayampacos.* A new pizza place on Soasti and Sucre is popular in the evenings, and a few doors along from that is **La Maravilla,** where drinks on the weekend may be accompanied by live music.

Information and Services

The helpful folks at the **Casa de la Cultura** on 10 de Agosto can provide information on local sights and recommend guides in the area. There is a small museum on the top floor.

Transportation

The **bus terminal** has a small police branch. Buses run to Quito ($8, eight hours), Puyo ($4, three hours), Guayaquil ($13, 13 hours), Ríobamba ($5, five hours), and Cuenca ($7, seven hours). **TAME** (tel. 7/270-1978) flies to Quito daily except Saturday for $77 pp, with connections to Guayaquil and **Saereo** every day for $70 pp.

SOUTH FROM MACAS

Twenty-three kilometers south of Macas sits the village of **Sucúa,** the center of the Shuar Federation. Vendors sell traditional crafts, and visits to Shuar villages can be arranged through the office of the Shuar Federation (Domingo Comín 17–38), three blocks south of the park. A few meager hotels and restaurants cluster near the central plaza—try the **Hotel Gyna** (tel. 7/274-0926, $7 pp) and the **La Fuente Restaurant,** both on Domingo Comín, for budget prices. For a more special meal, look for **En Chelos** on Carvajal, the street parallel to Domingo Comin. Buses leave for Macas every half hour from dawn to dusk ($0.90, one hour).

The Río Upano guides the road southward passing close to the town of **Méndez,** an attractive and peaceful town with a circular main plaza (much easier for an evening stroll) near the juncture of the Ríos Paute and Zapote. There are several small hostels for around $5 pp. From near here, a side road heads south along the Río Namangoza, then east along the Río Santiago to the remote outpost of **Morona.** The new road to the highlands through Amaluza heads west from here—it has been subject to lots of rain damage and is not always passable, so inquire locally if the buses are going through.

Sixty-four kilometers before Morona is the settlement of **Santiago,** on the shore of the river of the same name, where canoes and guides can be hired to visit **La Cueva de los Tayos** (the Cave of the Oilbirds). These strange nocturnal birds use echolocation—like the clicks of bats and dolphins, except audible to humans—to find fruit by night and locate their nests deep within the earth. The high oil content of the birds' abdominal fat, a side effect of the oily palm fruits they eat, led early settlers and *indigenas* to boil the poor creatures down into an effective lamp fuel. Because it's

THE ORIENTE

85 meters deep and black as night, you should venture into the cave only with a guide. Tour companies in Macas can organize visits.

The main road southwest from Méndez takes 43 kilometers to reach **Limón** (a village saddled with the official name General Leonidas Plaza Gutierrez), where itinerant wanderers can find budget quarters at the **Hotel Dreamhouse** (tel. 7/277-0166, $7 pp) and the **Residencial Limón** (tel. 7/277-0114, $5 pp), both of which have shared baths. A spectacular road climbs west from the town to higher than 4,000 meters before descending to Gualaceo and Cuenca. Two more roads to the highlands leave west from **Gualaquiza**, 80 kilometers farther south, where you can stay at the **Hostal Guadalupe** (tel. 7/278-0113, $3 pp) and eat at the **Cabaña Los Helechos.** The more westerly track follows the Río Cuyes upstream, whereas the other heads more northwest up the Río Cuchipamba to Sígsig, 68 kilometers and 1,000 meters up into the Eastern Cordillera.

KAPAWI ECOLODGE

Deep in a remote corner of the southern Oriente is a lodge that combines luxurious accommodations and service with the highest principles of ecotourism, in the middle of some of the most pristine rainforest in the country.

The Kapawi Ecolodge was begun in 1993, down the Río Pastaza within a stone's throw of the Peruvian border. This is the heart of Ecuadorian Achuar territory, so before Kapawi's parent company broke ground, approval had to be secured from OINAE, the indigenous group's political organization. Three years later, the lodge was able to provide local communities with jobs and ongoing economic support in the form of rent paid for the land. Most of the employees who work for the lodge are Achuar, and Kapawi passed into Achuar management in 2008.

The lodge itself was built entirely with native materials and methods—incredibly, not a single metal nail was used in the construction. Walkways link bungalows that can accommodate 50 people, who may find it easy to forget they're more than 100 kilometers from the nearest city of any size. Everything is first class and completely eco-friendly. One of the largest private solar projects in South America powers the lights, all the trash is recycled, and even the soap is biodegradable. Bottled drinking water and British valet–style umbrellas are provided free of charge.

Two main buildings house a small library, a boutique, a meeting room, and a dining hall, which specializes in exotic jungle fruit and local delicacies. Activities begin after an early breakfast. Silent electric motors power dugout canoes that take you down narrow blackwater streams, where long-nosed bats and Amazon kingfishers launch from the waterside branches. Flocks of blue-and-yellow macaws claim sandbars in the wide Pastaza, and this is the only place in the country where you might spot an orinoco goose.

Hikes ranging from easy to difficult are led by indigenous and biologist guides. Electric-blue morpho butterflies dance down forest trails like living sparks, while troops of squirrel monkeys make huge leaps from branch to bending branch along the river. Indigenous guides demonstrate how forest tribes knock on buttress roots to signal over long distances, and point out plant after plant put to countless uses by the Achuar.

One of the highlights of any stay is a visit to an Achuar settlement. After a traditional

---

SPEAKING ACHUAR

Wiña jai – Good morning/afternoon/ evening
Ja ai – Yes
Atsa – No
Yaitiam – What is your name?
Wiyait jai... – My name is...
Maketai – Thank you
Wea jai – Goodbye

© JULIAN SMITH

Kapawi Ecolodge

greeting by your guide and a brief chat with the owner, your group will be served *nijiamanch* by women in the *tankamash,* or male part of the house. Say *maketai* (thank you, pronounced mah-keh-TIE), and at least pretend to drink the sour beverage, which is made from chewed-up yucca fermented with human saliva—to refuse would be considered an insult. A tour of the small *chakra* where various medicinal plants are cultivated follows.

Visits to Kapawi range from $670 pp for four days to $895 pp for five days, plus $234 for transportation and a small fee for the local Achuar community. Current access means a commercial flight from Quito to Coca, then a charter flight on a small plane. Access to or from Shell may be available on the charter. For more information and to book a visit, contact CEKSA in Quito (Foch E7-38 and Reina Victoria, tel. 2/600-9333 or 2/600-9334, sales1@kapawi.com, www.kapawi.com); in the U.S. contact Canodros (tel. 800/613-6026).

YACUAMBI

This southern town's main claim to fame is that it lies at the end of a traditional Saraguro trail. The three- or four-day hike follows a trade trail still used by the highland Indians to bring cattle to the lush pastures of the upper jungles. Arrange guides in Saraguro, and tell them you want to have time to see the route, or you'll be rushed across the countryside at a cracking pace and arrive in two days. Several buses a day connect with Zamora and Loja, and there are small basic hostels here and in Tutupali. Even with guides, it's nice to have topographic maps of the area for reference.

THE ORIENTE

NORTH COAST AND LOWLANDS

The north and central coast is Ecuador's forgotten quarter, squeezed in by most visitors only if they have time left over after the Galápagos, Oriente, and Sierra. Granted, this may be the least distinctive part of the country, and most of the larger cities aren't particularly inviting. But tiny, isolated fishing villages have a charm of their own, and with a little effort, it's still possible to find deserted beaches washed by warm currents stretching for many unbroken kilometers.

Humid subtropical forests fed by Andean rivers blanket the small portion of the western lowlands that hasn't been cleared for farmland. Mangroves have a similar toehold on the northern coast. The wettest part of Ecuador's shore, this area receives three meters of rain annually,

which makes it one big, wildly successful mosquito-breeding experiment. The central coast is drier, although not as barren as the area near Guayaquil and farther south. Low, thorny hills rise a short distance inland behind Muisne and Cojimíes and near Machalilla National Park.

Ecuador's earliest advanced cultures got their start by the sea, beginning with the Valdivia culture, along the central coast, as early as 3500 b.c. The Manteña-Huancavilca culture counted 20,000 members by the time Pizarro landed near Esmeraldas in 1526. Repeated pirate attacks during the 17th and 18th centuries left a legacy of non-Spanish surnames in pockets throughout the region.

Today, much of the local population is descended from slaves who were either freed or

HIGHLIGHTS

◖ Hacienda Tinalandia: One of the pioneer birding sites in Latin America, these stylish wooden cabins surrounded by hundreds of acres of protected rainforest remain a popular destination for bird-watchers and outdoor enthusiasts alike (page 211).

◖ Canoa: This small surf town offers a welcome alternative to the crowds of more hectic Montañita (page 222).

◖ Bahía de Caráquez: An anomaly on Ecuador's coast, Baháa is a large city that's also tidy and pleasant (page 223).

◖ Puerto López: Word is starting to get out that this is the best place in the country to watch whales June–September (page 231).

◖ Machalilla National Park: Rare coastal forest, archaeology, and the "poor man's Galápagos" of the Isla de la Plata are all reasons to visit (page 233).

LOOK FOR ◖ TO FIND RECOMMENDED SIGHTS, ACTIVITIES, DINING, AND LODGING.

escaped during the colonial era. The Maroon culture, as it's called, remains closely tied to its African heritage through music, dance, and folktales. With its comparatively lenient policies, the *Audencia* of Quito became a haven for escaped slaves from as far away as Brazil, Chile, and Argentina. Even so, frequent uprisings occurred during the colonial period, including in the Autonomous Territory of Gentle Mulattos, which controlled the coast from Canoa to Atacames for a short while, until slavery was abolished in the New World in 1850.

Farms growing everything from rice and coffee to corn and citrus fruits keep the lowlands busy. The oil pipeline from the Oriente dead-ends at Esmeraldas, where lines of tankers wait to carry it around the world. Fishing, both industrial and private, is another major source of income, along with beach and nature tourism.

Mosquito repellent, water, and suntan lotion are essential for any north coast beach getaway, and carrying your own mosquito net is a good idea. Be well aware of the health risks from food—a particular problem in the land of shaved-ice treats and half-cooked seafood. The coast also is one of Ecuador's dicier areas in terms of personal safety. Try to avoid night buses, carry as little of value as possible, and don't trust the lock on your beach cabin to stop a determined thief. Women in particular should not walk alone on secluded beaches, even during the day.

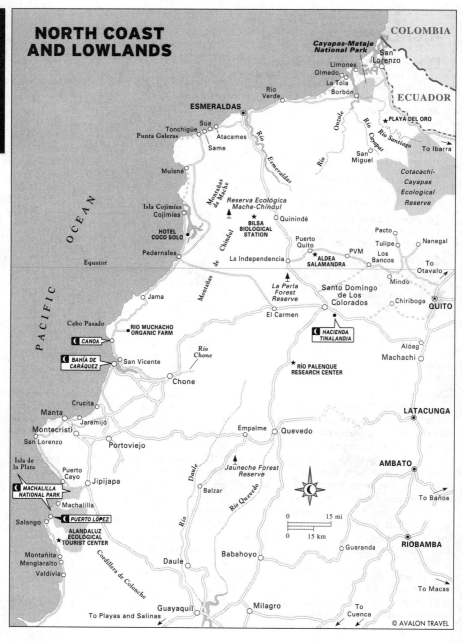

NORTH COAST AND LOWLANDS

COLOMBIA

Cayapas-Mataje National Park

San Lorenzo

Limones
Olmedo
La Tola
Borbón

ECUADOR

Río Verde

ESMERALDAS

Súa
Tonchigüe
Punta Galeras
Atacames
Same

PLAYA DEL ORO

Río Onzole
Río Santiago
Río Cayapas
Río

San Miguel

To Ibarra

Muisné

Cotacachi-Cayapas Ecological Reserve

Montañas de Mache

Isla Cojimíes
Cojimíes

HOTEL COCO SOLO

Pedernales

Reserva Ecológica Mache-Chindul

BILSA BIOLOGICAL STATION

Quinindé

Pacto
Tulipe
Nanegal

Puerto Quito

PVM
Los Bancos

To Otavalo

ALDEA SALAMANDRA

La Independencia

Montañas de Chindul
Montañas de

Río Esmeraldas

Mindo

OCEAN

Equator

Jama

La Perla Forest Reserve

Santo Domingo de Los Colorados

Chiriboga

QUITO

El Carmen

Cabo Pasado

RIO MUCHACHO ORGANIC FARM

HACIENDA TINALANDIA

CANOA

BAHÍA DE CARÁQUEZ

San Vicente

Río Chone

RÍO PALENQUE RESEARCH CENTER

Alóag
Machachi

PACIFIC

Chone

Crucita

Manta
Montecristi
San Lorenzo

Jaramijó

Portoviejo

Empalme
Quevedo

LATACUNGA

AMBATO

Isla de la Plata

Puerto Cayo
Jipijapa

MACHALILLA NATIONAL PARK

Machalilla

Salango

PUERTO LÓPEZ

ALANDALUZ ECOLOGICAL TOURIST CENTER

Montañita
Manglaralto
Valdivia

Daule

Río Daule

Balzar

Jauneche Forest Reserve

Río Quevedo

Babahoyo

Milagro

0   15 mi
0   15 km

To Baños

Guaranda

RIOBAMBA

To Macas

Cordillera de Colonche

Río

Guayaquil

To Playas and Salinas

To Cuenca

© AVALON TRAVEL

PLANNING YOUR TIME

If flying direct to Manta or Portoviejo is beyond your budget, you're stuck with a lengthy but scenic bus trip down from the Andes or up from Guayaquil. Santo Domingo de los Colorados is the major gateway west of Quito, with alternate routes connecting Latacunga with Quevedo, Ambato with Babahoyo, and Riobamba with Guayaquil by way of Milagro.

During the hot, rainy season of December–June, many coastal roads turn into impassable mud bogs. As far as the tourist season goes, holidays bring the largest crowds, especially Carnival, Semana Santa, and the Christmas holidays. June–September is high tourist season, when prices in the few hotels with rooms available can double, as well as the peak of whale-watching season in certain towns. Hotel prices often drop significantly in beach towns midweek.

Depending on how much beach-towel time you need, five–seven days are enough to see the highlights of the north coast. A good home base is **Bahía de Caráquez,** a clean, pleasant place that breaks the stereotype of sweaty coastal cities. Manta is another good place to start, as is Guayaquil. On the small end of the spectrum are places like **Canoa,** popular with surfers. The whale-watching in **Puerto López** is famous throughout the country. **Machalilla National Park** protects dry coastal forest and Isla de la Plata, teeming with wildlife. If you're looking for a place to do some serious relaxing in an eco-friendly way, head to the Alandaluz Ecological Tourist Center north of Montañita, a great place for an extended visit.

Western Lowlands

Ecuador's breadbasket (and banana basket, cacao basket, and palm-oil basket) stretches between the steep western slope of the Andes and the scrubby coastal mountain ranges just before the ocean. Huge agricultural plantations take advantage of the region's rich volcanic soil and abundant water. Profits from this fertile area have traditionally flowed south to Guayaquil.

In this case, however, the cost of development was particularly steep. By the end of the 20th century, more than 95 percent of Ecuador's lowland forests—which rival the Amazon in biological diversity—had been leveled as farms expanded. Add the fact that few of the cities are particularly noteworthy, and you have a region that is usually bypassed or sped through by tourists on their way to the beach. A few small forest reserves provide some respite from the monotonous cultivated fields.

SANTO DOMINGO DE LOS COLORADOS AND VICINITY

The exponentially expanding city in this important agricultural area was recently made into the capital of the new province of the Tsáchilas. Descending into the western lowlands from Alóag (south of Quito) is a balancing act of fascination and fear: The views toward the ocean are stunning, but you're never quite sure that your bus will make it around the next hairpin corner. It's no surprise that the road itself, winding down a lush subtropical river valley, wasn't completed until 1969.

Santo Domingo (pop. 400,000) comes as both a relief (we made it!) and a disappointment (this is it?) to the tired traveler crawling off a bus from Quito or Esmeraldas. This humid, cramped city is one of the fastest-growing in the country, thanks to its position as the main gateway from Quito to the coast and as a transport hub for roads in every direction.

There's not much going on in Santo Domingo. The Colorado *indígenas,* whose name the city commandeered, seldom put on their traditional red *achiote* hair paste, except when someone is paying them (not recommended). Still, Santo Domingo is a popular destination for Quiteños looking for a leafy weekend getaway and for Colombians fleeing

UNCLE TIGER AND RABBIT

One day, Tío Tigre (Uncle Tiger), was walking home with a basket full of fruit and bread. Conejo the rabbit saw him and decided he'd like that food for himself. He hopped through the woods to come out on the road ahead of Tío Tigre, and he lay down pretending to be dead. When Tío Tigre came upon the rabbit in the road, he slowed but kept going, clutching his basket tightly.

Undaunted, Conejo jumped up and took a shortcut that brought him out ahead of Tío Tigre again, where he lay down as before. Once again, Tío Tigre passed by the lifeless body without pausing.

But when Conejo tried his trick a third time, Tío Tigre stopped. Deciding that *three* dead rabbits were too good to pass up, he set down his basket and went back to pick up the first two. And so Conejo tricked Tío Tigre out of his food.

– Maroon folktale

civil unrest in their country. Fans of white-water rafting rush down for the day to enjoy the mostly clean rivers of Toachi and Blanco, before being whisked back up the mountain in the evening.

Entertainment and Events

The **Cine Ambato** shows relatively new films on the big screen, or you can choose your own video for a private screening. Dancers can try the **Mi Tierra** on Pallatanga near Guayaquil. Santo Domingo's **Canonization Anniversary** festival takes place on July 3.

Shopping

Two lively **markets** are crammed into the center of town: one between Guayaquil and Machala along Ambato, and another on the opposite side of 29 de Mayo between Cuenca and Ambato. Both spill into the surrounding streets. Calle 3 de Julio is one long market.

Tours

Turismo Zaracay (29 de Mayo and Cocaniguas, tel. 2/275-0546, fax 2/275-0873, hotelzaracay@porta.net) offers tours to visit the Tsachila communities. Half day tours are $15 per person and full day tours are $25 per person.

Accommodations and Food

Hotels in Santo Domingo are often full, regardless of what day it is. A slew of budget hotels are on the noisy main drag of 29 de Mayo. Of these, the **Hotel Ejecutivo** (tel. 2/276-3305) is the best deal at $7 s, $12 d, with private bath and cable TV. The cafeteria in the second-floor lobby serves a good, cheap breakfast. The **Hotel Caleta** (tel. 2/275-0277) is also a deal at $6 pp with private bath, even without hot water. The **Hostal Jennifer** (tel. 2/275-0577, $7 s, $14 d) has rooms with hot water, private bath, and good showers—the sauna costs extra.

Lots of basic restaurants along 29 de Mayo serve economical *platos del día*, and **La Fornacella Pizzeria,** on the same street, tosses a good wood-oven pie for $4 and up.

More luxurious accommodations and food can be found out of town on Avenida Quito. The first hotel you'll pass is the **Hotel La Siesta** (Quito 12–26 and Pallatanga, tel. 2/275-1013), about half a kilometer away. Classy in a rustic sort of way, La Siesta has a bar and restaurant, along with rooms for $14 s, $20 d. The doubles are a particularly good deal. **Parrilladas Argentinas,** just past the Hotel La Siesta, is recommended for its quality cuts of beef (plates around $6).

Next along Avenida Quito comes the **Hotel de Toachi** (tel. 2/275-4688, $25 s, $35 d). It may look like a U.S.-style motel from the street, but at least the pool is large enough to do laps in. Adjoining the hotel, **Ch' Farina** serves a great pizza with lots of sauce for about $6.

Last but not cheapest, the **Hotel Zaracay** (tel. 2/275-1023, fax 2/275-4535), just past the Hotel de Toachi, is built in a country-estate style with thatched roofs, pleasant landscaping, tennis courts, and a tiny pool. The 70 rooms at this oasis run $49 s, $77 d, with phone, TV, and air-conditioning, including breakfast in the open-air bar/restaurant. Advance booking is advised.

Information and Services
The **post office** is on Tsáchilas and Río Baba, a few blocks north of the plaza on the right.

Transportation
Santo Domingo's **bus terminal** is three kilometers northwest of the center of town. Buses run to and from the terminal regularly, passing north on Tsáchilas and returning west down 29 de Mayo.

From here, buses head to every city connected to Santo Domingo by road. Major destinations include Quito ($3, three hours), Guayaquil ($6, 5.5 hours), Esmeraldas ($4, four hours), Machala ($8, eight hours), Bahía de Caráquez ($6, six hours), and Manta ($7, seven hours), but buses run to most highland cities as well. **Sudamericano Taxis** (Cocaniguas and 29 de Mayo, 2^{ndo} piso, tel. 2/275-2567) runs a shared route to Quito for $13 daily. The taxis take up to four people and can pick you up and deliver you to your hotel on either end.

(Hacienda Tinalandia
Alfredo Garcon named this hotel and estate, about 16 kilometers east of Santo Domingo, after his Russian wife, Tina, when the couple opened it together in the 1950s. Today, Hacienda Tinalandia is run by Tina's heir, Sergio Platanov, a retired helicopter pilot. It's considered one of the hottest birding spots in the country, with more than 350 species identified to date. Ornithological mouthfuls like the rufous-tailed hummingbird, pale-legged hornero, and rusty margin flycatcher flit through 240 acres of protected rainforest along the Río Toachi. Another 600 acres are protected adjacent to the reserve.

Numerous hiking trails branch out from the main cabin complex on the south side of the river toward bird-feeding stations among the trees. Rafting, hiking, and horseback-riding

trips can be arranged, and a seldom-used golf course is marked by flags and untended sand traps. Meals on the porch overlooking the river include homemade delicacies like *naranjilla* ice cream. Temperatures hover around 22°C, and May–September are the driest months.

Sixteen rooms are $122 s, $207 d, including all meals, and the staff can arrange birding guides and transportation from Quito (or use the shared taxi service to Santo Domingo). Make reservations through the hacienda's office in Quito (Urb. El Bosque, Segunda Etapa, Av. Del Parque, Calle 3, Lote 98 #43–78, tel./fax 2/244-9028, info@tinalandia.com, www.tinalandia.com).

SANTO DOMINGO TO GUAYAQUIL
Río Palenque Science Center
This combination reserve and research center contains one of the largest swatches of lowland forest in Ecuador. Almost 200 protected hectares in a crook of the Río Palenque are surrounded by expanses of African palm and banana fields.

Botanist Calaway Dodson has documented one of the highest concentrations of plant diversity on the planet—1,200 species in 100 hectares—at Río Palenque. The reserve's primary forest includes a few stands of Río Palenque mahogany, which used to be the area's most valuable timber tree until overcutting rendered it one of the 10 most endangered plant species in the world. The 360 species of birds are the other main draw: the forest rings with the raucous cries of rufous-fronted wood quail and the liquid tones of the southern nightingale wren. More than 300 species of butterflies have also been identified here.

Facilities are more geared toward researchers than casual visitors. The small field station has a kitchen, generator electricity by day, and private bathrooms with cold showers. Guests pay $5 to visit for the day and $35 s, $60 d, to spend the night.

The reserve is about 40 kilometers southwest of Santo Domingo, shortly past the village of Patricia Pilar. A sign points the way; it's 1.5

kilometers down a side road. For information, contact the Centro Científico Río Palenque (tel. 9/778-0452) or the Wong Foundation in Guayaquil (tel. 4/220-8670, ext. 1350).

Quevedo

Resting on the banks of the wide, brown Río Quevedo, this is a muggy, bustling settlement known as the "Chinatown of Ecuador" for its large Asian population. Most travelers just pass through, stopping off for a meal at one of the many *chifas* before continuing to Guayaquil or Santo Domingo.

The noisy main street, 7 de Octubre, parallels the river and is divided by numbered cross streets. (Although Quevedo is not an especially dangerous place, it's a good idea to stick to 7 de Octubre after dark.) The **main plaza** and **church** (decorated by one of Peli Romarategui's fine mosaics) are on 7 de Octubre between Calles 5 and 6. There are three **markets** on Calle 7 off 7 de Octubre—one to the west and two to the east—and 7 de Octubre is basically one long market in itself.

The **Hotel Ejecutivo International** (7 de Octubre and 4a #214, tel. 5/275-1780 or 5/275-1781, fax 5/275-0596, $12 s, $17 d) is a good value, with air-conditioning and TV. The restaurant is recommended as one of the best in town. An Olympic-size pool and a disco wait at the northeast end of town at the **Hotel Olímpico** (Calle 19 #117 and Roldos, Ciudadela San José, tel. 5/275-0455 or 5/275-0965). Rooms start at $52, and the pool is open to the public for $2 pp. On the whole, Quevedo's *chifas* are dependable and cheap. The **Chifa Pekin** (7 de Octubre and Calle 3) serves a better-than-average *chaulafan* for about $3.

One block north of La Y, a small triangular intersection at the west end of 7 de Octubre with a white statue of a mother and child, is the **post office.**

Like most cities in the western lowlands, Quevedo is a crossroads between the Sierra and the coast. The new bus terminal is in the San Rafael district, a $1 taxi ride from the city center. Major cities served include Quito ($5, four–five hours), Santo Domingo ($2, 1.5 hours), Guayaquil ($4, 3.5 hours), Latacunga ($5, five hours), and Portoviejo ($5, five hours). Many buses pass La Y on their way out of town.

SANTO DOMINGO TO ESMERALDAS
La Perla Forest Reserve

West Virginian Suzanne Sheppard came here in 1949 to start a farm with her husband. After discovering the sad state of Ecuador's coastal forests, the pair decided to establish 250 hectares for the future benefit of visitors and local youth. Since Susan passed away, her children have taken over the administration of this reserve (daily except Sun., $5 pp), which is 41 kilometers north of Santo Domingo. It has minimal facilities, but guides are available by prior appointment. Contact the Bosque Protector La Perla office for information (tel. 2/272-5344 or 9/914-4604).

Bilsa Biological Station

Fundación Jatun Sacha opened this 3,000-hectare field station in 1994, in the middle of what would become the **Reserva Ecologica Mache-Chindul**, which was set aside two years later by the director of the Ecuadorian National Park Service as he left office. Less than 1 percent of this type of coastal tropical wet forest remains in Ecuador, and you'll find most of it here in the low, rugged Mache and Chindul Mountains.

Elevations up to 800 meters lift this island of foggy ridges and muggy forest above the surrounding scrubland. The ecosystem is isolated from the Andes, but rugged enough to trap a dense fog that supports cloud forest flora and fauna that are usually restricted to higher, wetter elevations. The impressive species list includes small, rare jungle cats, jaguars, and mantled howler monkeys, along with 305 recorded species of birds. More than 20,000 plant seedlings are cared for in Bilsa's Center for the Conservation of Western Forest Plants, and an ongoing botanical inventory has uncovered 20 plant species new to science.

Four rustic cabins provide shelter for researchers, students, and natural-history tour groups. Individual visitors should contact the foundation ahead of time for permission to enter. Foreign visitors pay $5 pp to enter the reserve, and $30 pp per day for room and board at Bilsa. Researchers and interns are expected to contribute $450 pp per month to offset lodging and meals. Volunteer opportunities are also possible.

Getting to Bilsa can be an adventure. The nearest town, Quinindé, is where you'll want to find or hire a truck going to the village of Herrera, 25 kilometers from the reserve. In the wet season (January–May), you'll probably only be able to get as far as the intersection known as La Y (accommodations are available at the La Laguna de Cube Cabins, just north of La Y, for $10 pp). During the rest of the year, you might be able to drive all the way to the reserve. Otherwise, it's a three-to-four-hour walk. Contact the Fundación Jatun Sacha in Quito (Pasaje Eugenio de Santillán N34-28 and Maurián, Urb. Rumipamba, tel./fax 2/243-2240, jatunsacha@jatunsacha.org, www.jatunsacha.org) for details on access and reservations.

North Coast

The northern coast has traditionally been one of Ecuador's forgotten regions, lagging behind the rest of the country's economy because of its geographical and political isolation, as well as its proximity to Colombia. Esmeraldas didn't get electricity until 1932, and it wasn't until 1957 that a rail line finally linked San Lorenzo to the outside world (recently replaced by a road). Countless small fishing villages, unchanged for decades, go about their seaside business, as pollution, overcrowding, and disease take their toll on the larger cities. The region calls to mind a peculiar version of the Wild West, with residents carrying machetes and living in stilt houses and a general air of disrepair and lawlessness—it's not for everyone, but it's definitely a distinctive destination. On the up side, the beaches are a big draw, and they get more sunshine than the southern part of Ecuador's coast.

Ecuador fought with its northern neighbor over the border in 1831 and 1916, when the Treaty of Muñoz Vernaza-Suárez established the current boundary. Today, the main sources of friction are smuggling, drugs, and immigration (and the occasional smuggling *of* drugs *by* immigrants).

Visitors to the area should be inoculated against malaria and yellow fever.

ESMERALDAS AND VICINITY

You won't see pictures of Esmeraldas (pop. 95,000) gracing brochures about Ecuador's coast. With a large chunk of the country's entire coastal population scrambling to make a life within its boundaries, the capital of Esmeraldas province hustles and bustles, but certainly doesn't sparkle.

After short rubber booms during the two World Wars, Esmeraldas expanded into the main port city on Ecuador's northern coast in the late 1970s. The country's largest oil refinery—the western end of the trans-Andean pipeline—erupts from the fertile river valley in nearby Puerto Balao like a smoking metal wart. In the city center, a lush central park sidles up to the Orwellian concrete Santuario Nuestra Señora de la Merced.

Esmeraldas is a very poor city, making theft a distinct problem. Be especially careful along the Malecón, even during the day. Much better accommodations and services are available nearby in Olmedo, Atacames, Súa, and Same.

Accommodations

Many basic hotels are located in the center, all fairly close to each other. With seagoing artifacts and flowers in the lobby, the **Hostal El**

Galeón (Piedrahita and Olmedo, tel. 6/272-3820) is a mixed bag. So-so rooms with fan, phone, and private bath run $8 pp, or $12 pp for rooms with air-conditioning and TV. More popular with regular visitors is the **Majestic** (Libertad and O. Lopez, tel. 6/271-4464) where comfortable rooms are $12 pp, including breakfast.

The **Apart Hotel Esmeraldas** (tel. 6/272-8700, tel./fax 6/272-8704) is the best hotel in the center, but at $43 s, $50 d, it isn't a particularly good deal. Rooms have air-conditioning, cable TV, and refrigerators, and suites are also available. The hotel's restaurant is the poshest in the area as well.

In the seaside suburb of Las Palmas, the **Hotel Cayapas** (Kennedy and Valdez, tel. 6/272-1318 or fax 6/272-1319) is probably the nicest hotel in the city. Rooms with TVs go for $33 s, $45 d, with air-conditioning and breakfast in the open-air La Tolita restaurant, the best in town. An extensive menu of pasta, seafood, and meat starts at $4.50, although prices climb as high as $22 for shrimp or paella.

Food

You'll relish the air-conditioned coolness of the **Chifa Asiatica**, on Mañizares between Bolívar and Sucre, where the food actually has some taste compared to many other *chifas*; plates are $4 and up. The **Chifa Oriental** around the corner is also passable. The popular **El Porteñito**, on the corner of Mejía and Sucre, serves coffee and sandwiches at sidewalk tables under a green-and-white awning.

Information and Services

There's a **tourism office** on the second floor of the Consejo Provincial office (enter on 10 de Agosto), but don't expect much help or information. The **post office** is by the *mercado* on Montalvo.

The **Colombian consulate** (8:15 A.M.–12:15 P.M. and 2:15–5 P.M. Mon.–Fri.) in Las Palmas is one block from the Hotel Cayapas, off Kennedy. It's a good idea to stop here if you plan to cross into Colombia by boat at San Lorenzo.

Transportation

Luckily (say some visitors), there are lots of ways to leave this city. There's a new main bus terminal, with buses to Muisne ($3, two–five hours) and Borbón ($4, four–five hours) on **La Costeñita**. Tickets are also sold there to La Tola ($4, four–five hours), where it's possible to catch a boat to San Lorenzo in the mornings. La Costeñita has frequent runs to Atacames ($0.45, 45 minutes), Súa ($0.50, 50 minutes), and Same ($1, one hour).

Panamericano sends the best luxury buses to Quito at 11:45 A.M. and 11:15 P.M. ($6), and to Guayaquil at 11 P.M. ($6). To reach Manta, book with **Reina del Camino,** which offers regular service for $7 and an *ejecutivo* for $9.

Transportes Esmeraldas has numerous buses, both regular and luxury service, to Quito ($5, five–six hours) and Guayaquil ($8, eight hours). It also runs a 5:35 P.M. bus to Huaquillas ($12, 12 hours) and an 8:40 P.M. bus to Machala ($10, 11 hours).

Transportes del Pacífico goes to San Lorenzo ($4, four–five hours) a few times every morning, and **Transportes Zambrano** runs frequent departures to Santo Domingo, plus five per day to Muisne and two to Pedernales. **Cita Express** goes to Ambato ($7, seven hours) and Santo Domingo. Many buses between Muisne, Atacames, and Quito bypass Esmeraldas entirely.

TAME (tel. 6/272-6863) flights to Quito (one daily, with connections to Guayaquil, $59 pp and $100 pp) leave from the **General Rivadeneria Airport,** across the mouth of the river. To get there, it's a 15-kilometer trip upstream to San Mateo, where you cross the river and descend to Tachina. A taxi costs $8 and takes half an hour. Buses to San Lorenzo or other towns to the north pass the airport, but be sure to allow enough time to get there.

ESMERALDAS TO THE BORDER

Ecuador's northernmost coastline dissolves into a tangle of mangroves as it reaches Colombia. Nearly 75 percent of the population in the farthest towns has immigrated—often illegally—from Colombia.

North of Esmeraldas

The road hugs the coast to and past the Río Verde lighthouse, providing ample access to acres of undeveloped sand. Just south in the fishing village of Río Verde is the **Hostería Brisa Oceano** (tel. 6/274-4203), a wonderful beachfront getaway that garners repeat praise. Comfy cabanas with private bath go for $16 s, $28 d. Twenty-two kilometers past the Rio Verde the road divides, left to **La Tola** and **Olmedo** and right, inland to **Borbón.**

Olmedo

This friendly Afro-Ecuadorian fishing village on Punta Lucero, the point northwest of La Tola, has about 150 inhabitants. It's within the boundaries of the **Reserva Ecológico Manglares Cayapas-Mataje** and offers visitors the chance to stay in the **Casa de Manglar** (tel. 6/278-0239), an "eco-cabin" built by a Japanese NGO (nongovernmental organization) in 1999 as part of a locally managed ecotourism project. Five modern rooms are $20 pp per night, including three meals. There's a big veranda deck on stilts with hammocks and dining tables. Guests can explore the mangroves, go clamming or fishing, or just walk along the sheltered beach. Boat trips can be arranged to the archaeological sites of La Tola and up the Cayapas River.

The bus ride from Esmeraldas (with La Costañita or Del Pacífico) is $4 pp and takes about four hours; you may have to change buses at Las Peñas. A boat from San Lorenzo takes four hours and costs $5 pp.

SAN LORENZO

One of the least attractive cities on the coast sits in the mouth of the mangroves in the Cayapas-Mataje Ecological Reserve. Travelers used to come through this town, which was founded in the 18th century by escaped slaves, because it was the destination of the train from Ibarra.

SHAKE, RATTLE, AND FLIRT

The looping rhythms and bouncing melodies of marimba (or *currulao*, as it's called locally) echo down nighttime alleys in cities along Ecuador's northern coast. With its roots firmly in Africa, the music centers around the marimba itself, a xylophone-like instrument with large keys of *chonta* wood mounted over hanging ringers made from split bamboo.

Marimba's heartbeat comes from the *bombo*, a large bass drum made of wood with a head of goatskin or leather, which gives its name to a particular variety of dance. Familiar maracas are shaken, along with *guasas*, made out of dried bamboo stalks filled with *achira* seeds and closed at both ends to produce a sound like a rainstick. Small tambourines called *cununos* are smacked with vigor.

Many varieties of dance and chanting songs accompany the lilting tunes. Watch for the coquettish exchange between male and female dancers before the shaking starts. In one song, the woman sings:

Bolívar, with his sword,
conquered five nations
And me, with my hips,
I conquer all hearts.

Now that the train isn't running, a visit to San Lorenzo is usually warranted only for the festival of Santos Reyes and Santos Inocentes (see below) near the beginning of the year, or the Marimba festivals in July.

Roads connecting San Lorenzo to Borbón and Ibarra were finally completed around 2000; expect to encounter passport checks and luggage searches, because this city sees more than its share of illicit border traffic. Boats can be rented to visit undeveloped beaches on the seaward side of the mangrove islands offshore—most notably **San Pedro.** Otherwise, get ready to slap a few thousand mosquitoes as you wait for your boat or bus to leave.

Shopping, Entertainment, and Events

A small **artesanía** shop on Imbabura, a few blocks north of the train station, sells locally woven baskets. Inquire locally about *salons* where musicians gather in the muggy weekend evenings and beat out marimba music until the wee hours.

Those lilting rhythms also play a significant role in celebrations during the first week in January, when the festival of **Santos Reyes and Santos Inocentes** rolls into town. This event is a reason in itself to visit San Lorenzo: garishly painted residents barely old enough to walk roam the streets, hooting to the Macumba (voodoo) spirits of Africa and the Caribbean, and crossroads are commandeered by *cucuruchos,* self-appointed guardians who collect mock taxes to buy booze.

Accommodations and Food

A few budget hotels are bearable for a night or two—the **Hotel Puerto Azul** (tel. 6/278-0220), right next to the train station, is the best in town. Rooms with private bath, fan, mosquito nets, and satellite TV are $10. If that's full, try the **Hotel Palma de Oro** (tel. 6/278-0214), just off Imbabura, halfway between the train station and the jetty. Rooms are $7 pp with private bath, fan, and mosquito net. No restaurants stand out, but there's a good chance you'll have **seafood** for dinner.

Information and Services

For information on the Cotacachi-Cayapas Reserve, drop by the **Ministerio de Ambiente** office (tel. 6/278-0184), on the main plaza by the jetty. The **post office** (26 de Agosto and Maldonado) is down a side street off the main plaza. If you plan on entering or leaving Colombia, you can get your passport stamped at the Capitanía del Puerto (harbormaster's office) or the police station.

Transportation

Now that the long-awaited road connecting San Lorenzo with Borbón has been completed, a smattering of bus companies has sprung up around the train station, which is slowly falling into disuse. The **train** still leaves daily at 7 A.M. for Progreso (three hours)—you can ride on the roof for kicks—and you can return to San Lorenzo at 2 P.M. ($2 round-trip).

The bus ride to and from Ibarra pales in comparison to the train, but it's still very scenic. Buses leave from the traffic circle along Imbabura near the train station. **Transportes Valle de Chota** buses leave on the hour for the White City (4 A.M.–2 P.M., $5). **Transportes Espejo** also sends buses to Ibarra until 3 P.M., and **Transportes Esmeraldas** sends comfortable coaches all the way to Quito and Guayaquil. All buses out of town either start at or pass the crumbling monument in front of the train station.

If you're into coastal scenery, the boat ride into or out of San Lorenzo can be reason enough to visit. Two boat/bus companies have offices at the pier. **Transportes San Lorenzo de Pailón** sends boats to Limones at 6:30 A.M., 12:30 P.M., and 3:30 P.M. ($4). From there, you can catch another boat to La Tola ($3), which is connected by road to Esmeraldas. **Transportes del Pacífico** offers boat/bus combinations all the way to Esmeraldas leaving every two hours (5:30 A.M.–1:30 P.M., $6 for the bus, same prices as above for the boat sections). In addition, departures to Colombia leave at 7 A.M. and 2 P.M.

Upriver into Cotacachi-Cayapas

Not many visitors enter this sprawling reserve from its downhill side via Borbón. It's a shame, because the brave few who do not only enjoy an incredible lowland jungle, but can also visit the indigenous Cayapas tribes in nearby villages. (For more information on the Cotacachi-Cayapas Reserve, see the *Northern Sierra* chapter.) Borbón is one of the starting or ending points for a trip into the lower regions of the Cotocachi-Cayapas Reserve.

If you have to spend the night in the riverside town of **Borbón,** head to the **Hostal Castillo** (tel. 6/278-6613) or the **Hostal Costa Norte,** both of which have clean rooms with fans, TV, and private bath for $6 pp.

Visitors to the tiny, quiet village of **Santa María de los Cayapas** can choose between the *pensión* of Señora Pastora, dormitory lodging in the local mission, and camping among the trees. **Walter Quintero Torres** is a recommended guide for day trips to nearby Cayapas villages and longer journeys into Cotacachi-Cayapas. Ask for him around the waterfront area in Borbon.

San Miguel, four hours from Borbón by motorized canoe, blends African, Ecuadorian, and indigenous cultures. The village, located almost inside the Cotacachi-Cayapas Reserve, is the main base for excursions into the reserve. Check in at the guard post on the hill for details, and be sure to arrange a spot on the predawn boat downriver the night before leaving.

PLAYA DEL ORO

Instead of a palm-fringed beach where sunbathers sip piña coladas, Playa del Oro (Gold Beach) is a remote village of about 50 Afro-Ecuadorian families who live near the only reserve in the world dedicated to protecting small jungle cats. A visit to this tight-knit community is a wonderful way to combine a rainforest experience with a chance to help support a unique, fragile culture and its surrounding ecosystem.

The tiny settlement is surrounded by roughly 10,000 hectares of community land, mostly primary forest, tucked up against the Cotacachi-Cayapas Ecological Reserve. This stretch of forest between northwest Ecuador and southern Panama, known as the Chocó, is one of the biologically richest and most threatened bioregions in the world. In 1992, the Sustainable Uses for Biological Resources (SUBIR) Project helped the community build a traditional-style lodge near the village. There is no electricity or hot water, but most visitors bathe in the river anyway. Meals combine typical Ecuadorian fare and ingredients from an impressive list of local specialties.

The residents of Playa del Oro run every aspect of the operation, from administration to cooking, under the guidance of the town's youthful president. A few families have opened craft shops in their homes to sell drums, wood-carvings, and toys to visitors to supplement their meager incomes. When not out in the forest, the friendly villagers will soon make you feel like a part of the community. You can join the men for a bit of fishing or football, or tag along with their wives to go panning for gold – the declining but still profitable activity

that gave the village its name. At night, local musicians sometimes turn the lodge's dining room into a dance hall.

Residents also serve as guides to take visitors upriver past an endless succession of waterfalls and into the surrounding forest. Birders can add as many as 330 species to their life lists in the subtropical woodlands, including the endemic scarlet-breasted dacnis and long-wattled umbrellabird.

Best of all, six species of neotropical cats are indigenous to the area: jaguars, pumas, ocelots, margays, oncilas, and jaguarundis. (The village has signed an agreement with the U.S. environmental group Touch the Jungle to protect their communal lands as the **Playa del Oro Reserva de Tigrillos.**) Since they're nocturnal, the cats are rarely sighted, but near the lodge are enclosures with jungle cats rescued from illegal animal traders. After being rehabilitated, these cats are released into the wild. Forest trails range one-four hours, and guests can swim in the river. The area is pristine: no pollution or malaria.

Getting to Playa del Oro requires advance arrangements. A visit to the lodge costs $50 pp per night, including all meals and guide services. It takes six hours by private vehicle to get to Selva Alegre from Quito via Otavalo, and another two hours by boat to the reserve. In Otavalo, Ramiro Buitron, owner of the Hostel Amanecer del Valle (tel. 6/292-0990), can take you to Selva Alegre in a van. It's also possible to get to Selva Alegre by bus via Borbón. A boat ($50 per group each way) must also be arranged in Selva Alegre beforehand.

Occasional **motor launches** connect the various settlements up the Río Cayapas. From Borbón, one daily boat heads to San Miguel around 11 A.M. ($8, four hours). Check locally for the latest word on connecting services between other villages, such as Santa María and Zapallo Grande—the pattern seems to be that they go when they go.

WEST OF ESMERALDAS

This stretch of coast, extending from Atacames to Tonchigile, is one of the more popular beach destinations in the country, due to its proximity to the capital. Resort hotels and Greek-island vacation homes are deserted off-season and jammed during holidays. The towns themselves remain small and modest, and by the time you pass Tonchigüe, you're well out into the boonies. An ant column of buses plies the coastal road.

Atacames

The first resort town west of Esmeraldas sports bright colors and loud music, and on the whole is surprisingly clean. This is the place to have a good time and party with Ecuadorian tourists, especially during the high season and holidays—if you can find space. The wide beach lines a spit of land that is separated from the town by a rank canal. To hit the ocean, take the diagonal road from the main bus stop in town, cross the footbridge, turn right, and follow the sound of surf. Three-wheeled "ecological" taxis cost $0.50 from the beach to the bus stop.

Umbrella hawkers and kids balancing plates of sliced watermelon on their heads ply the Malecón parallel to the ocean. Hotels and restaurants line the strip, with prices dropping in direct proportion to their distance from the beach. Vendors hawk fruit, ceviche, and ice cream, and round, thatched-hut bars each blare a different kind of music on the seaward side.

Take care when walking along the beach, especially at night and on the stretch between Atacames and Súa, because many thefts and assaults have been reported. If you run into problems, there's a police outpost at the west

Bamboo and cade are building materials for the traditional houses.

© JEAN BROWN

end of the bridge in town, half a block toward the beach on the west side. Also beware of the powerful undertow off the beach.

Atacames' beach spreads wide between Isla de los Pajaros to the west and Punta Esmeraldas to the east. Look no further than the Malecón for *discotecas* like **Scala** and **Ludos**. For a quieter drink, head to the homey, unnamed bar with the thatch-and–green metal roof, just before the Hotel Arco Iris.

Atacames has more than 120 hotels. Rates double in the sunny season (December–May), making reservations essential. Otherwise, prices are negotiable, especially on weekdays. On the road to the beach after crossing the footbridge, you'll find the **Cabañas Los Bohios** (tel. 6/273-1089), where two-to-four-person cabins in a walled compound run $10 pp with fan, TV, and a small pool. The nearby **Hostal María Co.** (tel. 6/273-1259) rents apartments with kitchens for $15 pp, up to five persons, or private rooms for the same price. The **Hotel Rodelu** (tel. 6/273-1031) has rooms and cabanas comparable to Los Bohios for $10 pp with private bath and air-conditioning, cheaper with fans. The hotel also has a pool.

Head right (east) on the Malecón for about one kilometer to reach the **(Arco Iris** (tel./fax 6/273-1069, arcoiris@andinanet.net). Nineteen plush cabins with front porches and hammocks line a sandy lane shaded by palm trees and accented with flowers and a pool. Accommodations, which include refrigerators, minibar, kitchen, air-conditioning, and cable TV, cost $18 s, $32 d, with rates doubled during the high season.

More than a dozen cheap hotels cluster at the west end of the Malecón; the **Hotel Miravalle** (tel. 6/273-1138) and **Hotel Guajira** (tel. 6/273-1278) are two of the better ones, with rooms for $8 pp. The upmarket **Hotel Juan Sebastian** (tel. 6/273-1039, $40 s, $59 d), on the Malecón east of Arco Iris, has a good restaurant, plus a night-lit pool and spa facilities that you can use for $10 pp.

A dozen stands on the sand, all under one thatched roof, serve ceviche made fresh in front of you for less than $4 a plate. Choose from *concha* (conch), *langostino* (shrimp), or a *mixto* of the two, and wash it down with fresh-squeezed orange juice. **Gabilos** sells *helados* and a coconut-and-milk sweet called *cocadas manjar.*

Across the street from the Hotel Rodelu, the **(Restaurant Juan Griego** has a wide selection of seafood and meat for around $5 and an excellent *menestra.* The **Ristaurante No Name Pizzeria,** on the Malecón, has been recommended for pizza, and the prosaically named **Mexican Restaurant,** on the Malecón just east of the entrance road, has vegetarian burritos for $3 and shrimp fajitas for $6. There's a **Cuban restaurant** on the Malecón near the center of town with good, filling *almuerzos* for about $2.

The **Farmacia "Su Economica"** by the bus stop will change travelers' checks.

Trans Esmeraldas runs several buses to Quito ($6) and a couple to Guayaquil ($8) from its office on the main plaza. **Aerotaxi,** on Roberto Cervantes by the main bus stop in town, goes to Quito in the evenings.

Súa

Just down the road from the fraternity-house vibe of Atacames is a different world—a small fishing town occupying a tranquil crescent bay. Súa is quieter, cheaper, and much less developed than its neighbors. Hotel reservations are a wise idea on weekends.

Rolling green hills end in cliffs to the west, which can be skirted at low tide. One of these, called "Suicide Cliff," comes complete with a legend: A Spanish captain, so the story goes, fell in love with a princess named Súa, who—upon hearing that the captain had been killed in battle—threw herself off the cliff. But he hadn't died, and when he returned and learned what had happened to his sweetheart, he took the same plunge. It's said that under the full moon, you can see their ghosts wandering the rocks.

Some development has come to this very poor area, but there's still a long way to go. Fishing barely keeps the town above water economically. The west side of town, near the muddy mouth of the Río Súa, still consists of little but rundown shacks where residents tie nets by hand.

Boats range from simple dugout canoes to a few fiberglass launches with outboards. Fishing is done at night, when a bobbing flotilla drifts out under the light of homemade gasoline lanterns. A good catch of 150 kilograms can bring as much as $150. Pregnant *langostinos* (crayfish) are sold to shrimp farms for up to $80.

Look for the sign on the Malecón near the Hotel Clinton that advertises **whale-watching tours** for $20 pp, the cheapest in the country. Tours run June–September when the weather is cool, the sky overcast, and the ocean a little rough.

The **Hotel Chagra Ramos** (tel. 6/273-1006 or 2/244-3822) is a friendly old favorite at the east end of town. Rooms with private baths and fans are $8–10 pp, and the newer cabins and villas spreading up the hill cost the same. Rent a Jet Ski for $48 per hour, or just relax with a cool drink in the restaurant.

At the **Peñon de Súa** (tel. 6/273-4036), located diagonal to the beachfront, double rooms go for $7 pp. All rooms have fans, the restaurant offers seafood dishes for $4 and up, and there is a pool. Nearby, the **Heladería/Pastelería San Luis** serves *batidos* and great fresh bread.

Farther down the short beachfront, the **Hostal Buganvilla** (tel. 6/273-1008) charges $10 pp for rooms with private bath and fan, with prices negotiable in low season. At the **Coffe Bar,** a little west of Buganvilla, you can find a great cup of coffee and some friendly conversation with the perpetually cheerful owner, who insists that he uses only the best beans.

Buses stop along the main road beyond town.

Same

Same (pronounced SAHM-eh) offers the most pleasant developed beach in the area and is actually quieter than Súa—at least for the moment. As the old hotels huddle in the center of the sand, an incredible amount of new building

has been going on—for example, the new **Casa Blanca at Same** (tel. 6/273-3159), a huge condominium and hotel complex with time-share apartments, several restaurants, spa facilities, and a semiprivate beach. Two- and three-person apartments are $100 per night and very in with Ecuadorians. Same is also popular with gringos, so be prepared for higher prices than at Súa or Atacames.

German artist Margaret Lehmann runs the **◖ Seaflower Hostal/Restaurant** (tel. 6/273-3369, $20 p) with her Chilean husband, Luis. Their four rooms, brimming with artwork and seashells, sleep up to five people and have private baths, hot water, fans, and mosquito nets. The homemade food in the restaurant is pricey but delicious, including bread and jam for breakfast, and the owners are always looking for music to add to their collection in the sitting room.

The family-run **La Terraza** (tel. 6/273-3320, $12 pp) has comfy four-person rooms with private baths and hammocks on the front porch with a view of the ocean. The restaurant offers pizza, spaghetti, and seafood for $5–8. You'll have to walk a ways toward the middle of the beach to find the **Hostal El Rampiral** (tel. 2/226-4134). Eleven cabins on stilts with hot water and refrigerators run $49 d, $57 for four people, with prices negotiable in low season. The complex includes a pool and cafeteria.

West of Same

The coastal road splits at **Tonchigüe,** a 20-minute walk from Same. The west branch leads to the lighthouse at **Punta Galera,** with a southern spur to Muisne. Several **Trans Costañita** buses per day run from Esmeraldas to Punta Galera, or you can take a bus to Muisne, get off at the junction, and hitchhike.

Halfway to the lighthouse is the Canadian-run **◖ Playa Escondida** (tel. 6/273-3106), a secluded ecological getaway on 34 hectares of semitropical forest against a cliff-backed beach. This place gets as many rave reviews—the word *paradise* is used a lot—as any destination on the coast. Cabins are $12–18 pp, and camping costs $5 pp. Meals are available. To get here, take one of the Costañita or Pacífico buses from Esmeraldas to Punta Galera, and ask the driver to let you off at the entrance gate, 400 meters from the beach. You can also walk along the beach from Tonchigüe, but only at low tide.

Muisne

As far as beaches go, you can't do much better on Ecuador's northern coast than the seaward stretch on the tip of this stubby peninsula. Although most visitors usually head for the sea, the actual town of "Mui'ne" (lose the *s* to sound like a local) is on the inland side, facing a muddy mangrove estuary at the mouth of the Río Repartadero. The road from Tonchigüe ends at a jetty called *El Relleno,* where you'll take one of the frequent *lanchas* across to the town itself—far from the most picturesque in Ecuador. Fortunately, *tricicletas* wait to pedal you the two kilometers to the beach ($0.50 pp), past cows wading chest-deep in flooded fields.

Muisne's beach is as flat and wide as an airport runway, fading into the palm-fringed distance in both directions. Pelicans skim low over the waves in perfect formation, and the occasional dolphin, turtle, or whale shows its head offshore. An abundance of driftwood becomes bonfire fuel at night. With the edge of civilization at your back and the ocean in front, it's the kind of place some find excruciatingly dull and others can't stand to leave.

Sadly, it seems that you sometimes hear as many horror stories about crime in Muisne as you do raves about its tranquility. Plainclothes police stepped up patrols in 1996, but things are still sketchy away from the hotels and restaurants. Don't walk down the beach alone beyond the buildings in either direction, and never take anything of value with you.

To the left (south) of the road to town are the two best budget hotels. The rustic, friendly **Hostal Playa Paraíso** (tel. 6/248-0192) has 24 beds in 11 rooms and supplies mosquito nets. Rates are $8 pp with private bath. The vegetarian restaurant has plates for $3 and up (all veggies are purified), and a book exchange and hammocks make it hard to leave the main crash-pad room. If you do, there's a volleyball court outside and a bar in back. The owners can arrange horseback-riding trips.

Otavalo *indígenas* own the blue-and-orange **Hotel Calade** (tel. 6/248-0279), two doors to the south. Beds and rooms are clean and spacious with mosquito nets, and they go for $6 pp with private bath, $5 shared. The hotel also has a vegetarian restaurant and can arrange fishing and snorkeling trips and provide information on full-moon parties. Internet service is $1 per hour.

If you're looking for entertainment, try the Hotel Calade's **Robobar,** the **Discoteca Mai Tai** on the north end of the beach, or the **Zulu Bar** in the Hostal Playa Paraíso, open on weekends and holidays. **Boat trips** through the mangroves are organized by FUNDECOL (Fundación Ecológica Muisne, tel. 6/248-0201, fundecol@yahoo.com). Trips are best in the afternoon at high tide and cost $38 for two people for a half day (prices drop rapidly for larger groups). Even better than the fishing is the birding—there are enough frigatebirds, egrets, tanagers, and vermillion flycatchers to keep any enthusiast happy. Many other trips, as well as volunteer opportunities, are available. The foundation's office is off the main street diagonal to the hospital, but it's not easy to find, so take a tricycle taxi or ask around.

You'll find the **post office** in the municipal building on the main plaza, two blocks from the docks. Buses to and from Esmeraldas run often throughout the day. Heading south to **Pedernales,** take a bus to El Salto and change to a southbound bus at the junction. It's still possible to hire a boat to do the trip to Cojimíes; ask around on the dock, and expect to pay about $20 for the two-hour journey. It's a unique opportunity to get wet, seasick, and sunburned all at once, yet fun in its own way.

Trans Esmeraldas runs direct buses to **Quito** ($7, nine hours) at 9:45 P.M. and to **Guayaquil** ($6, 10 hours) at 9 P.M.

Central Coast

The stretch south of Muisne is one of the wilder parts of Ecuador's coast. Several new developments can be visited from the new road. Mompiche, once only accessible by boat or long beach hike, now has several buses a day and offers some lovely hotels. The recently paved—and recently damaged—road from El Carmen to Pedernales has opened up the central part of the coast to many new developments.

Canoa is the main destination before Bahía de Caráquez. Beyond that is the busy shoreside city of Manta, followed by three smaller destinations popular with travelers: Puerto López, the gateway to Machalilla National Park; the Alandaluz Ecological Tourist Center; and the surf town of Montañita.

SOUTH OF MUISNE
Cojimíes to Pedernales

Cojimíes sits at the tip of a sandy peninsula, slowly dissolving into the sea. The only things here are sand and water; you can stay at the **Paraíso de Atardecer** cabins ($5 pp) at the beach entrance to the village and eat at the kiosks at the riverside dock. Rent a boat to tour the local mangroves for $20 per hour.

Cojimíes is also the northern end of one of Ecuador's great drives. Until the construction of an inland road, the only way down this stretch of the coast was a low-tide blitz down the flawless beach itself. It's still possible—and highly recommended—to take the sandy route, where endless ordered rows of coconut palms line the leeward side and rocky cliffs take over farther south. Your hell-for-leather driver will dodge rocks and plow through drifts of shells and sand until the breeze in your face makes you grin like a pilot in a wind tunnel. Along the way lie the rusted hulks of cars that weren't fast or sure-footed enough. Toward the southern end, shrimp fishermen tow nets through the shallows.

About halfway down the peninsula, 20 kilometers north of Pedernales near the village of Cañaveral, is the **Hotel Coco Solo** (tel.

9/940-6048, cocosolo13@yahoo.com), an old museum of a place that would make the perfect setting for a black-and-white movie (*Night of the Iguana*, anyone?) The owners are rightfully proud of the fact that they have no TVs, and they can set you up with a guide to explore the surrounding forest and rivers or point you in the right direction to do it on your own. Bungalows on stilts run $10 pp with breakfast, and campsites are available for $4.

Pedernales

Set on the cliffs, but really looking inland, this town grew as an agricultural center that just happens to be by the beach. The inland road through this area has existed for more than 20 years, but it was open only six months a year, and then not always passable. Once the road had been paved, Pedernales was "discovered" by Quiteños as the closest beach to the capital. Hotels and restaurants in the center of town are still visited by horse-riding farmers shopping for seeds and animal feed. New developments along the beach came into full swing around 2004, with hotels and cabins priced $4–20. The mosaic on the wall of the church is one of the finest works by Romarategui, a Basque artist who embellished many lowland churches with ceramic-and-glass art.

◖ Canoa

This once quiet fishing town sits on a wide stretch of sand—one of the few places on Ecuador's coast where the beach actually grew following the disastrous 1997–1998 El Niño season. With more hammocks per capita than any other coastal town, Canoa is a very *tranquilo* alternative to other, louder beach spots. Luminescent plankton swirl in the water under the new moon, and the surfing is great—there's a big contest here in November.

The clean and friendly **Posada de Daniel** (tel. 5/261-6373) costs $8 pp with private bath. Even though it's a few blocks from the beach, it is popular. The decor mixes bamboo huts and red leather chairs, and there's a bar, a restaurant, a pool, and a boat for snorkeling trips. Friendly owner Daniel Velasco speaks English and arranges surfing lessons.

Cabins and rooms on the beach at the **Hotel Bambú** (tel. 5/261-6370) are $15 pp per night, while dorms with shared bath are $7–12, those with private bath costing more. It has a restaurant, plus surfboards and boogie boards for rent. On the beachfront, the cheery **La Vista** has a restaurant and rooms for $12. Also very popular is **Coco Loco** ($5–12), right on the beach, which offers dorms, private rooms, and a kitchen for preparing your own food.

Seafood eateries line Canoa's beach. **Costa Azul** gets good reviews, but after a few rum-and-cokes, they all seem more or less identical. **El Torbellino** restaurant in town serves good, traditional dishes popular with locals for $2 and up. Grab a drink and shake your tanned rump at the two-story **Coco-Bar Discoteca.**

Vicinity of Canoa

At low tide, head north up the beach (the widest in the country) to a series of natural **caves** frequented by blue-footed boobies and bats. According to legend, a huge emerald belonging to a queen of the Cara tribe was hidden here. Although the caves were somewhat damaged by the 1998 earthquake that hit Bahía de Caráquez, they're still worth a visit, but much care is needed and experienced guides are strongly advised. There have been several incidents where people became trapped overnight by rising tides.

Lots of development is under way on the beaches between Canoa and San Vicente. Already in place are hotels for all budgets, from the **Hostería Canoa** (tel. 5/261-6380, $35 s, $60 d) to **Olmito's** rustic cabins ($7 pp). Other possibilities await at **Briceño.** Buses to Canoa from San Vicente take half an hour ($0.40).

◖ BAHÍA DE CARÁQUEZ

As far back as the 17th century, the Spanish predicted that Bahía de Caráquez, set on a tongue of sand in the mouth of the Río Chone, would be "one of the most beautiful ports in

Surfboards can be rented at several resorts.

© JEAN BROWN

the world." What started as a small port city has evolved into the most pleasant urban area on Ecuador's coast.

Bahía (pop. 20,000), as it's known, is an anomaly. Although many other cities on the coast are sweaty, dirty, and ill-tempered, this town feels like a place you'd visit just to walk the streets. It's long been a retreat for Quiteños, who appreciate its cleanliness and easygoing pace.

The once busy commercial port has given way to a mostly residential city, keeping the white buildings free of the smudges of industry. Generations of residents educated abroad (including former president Sixto Duran Ballén) have returned and invested their money and time into keeping their hometown vibrant through civic improvements, such as the restoration of the waterside Malecón.

A series of natural calamities just before the turn of the millennium almost brought Bahía to its knees. Six months of almost continuous rain during the 1997–1998 El Niño season caused widespread landslides, washing away

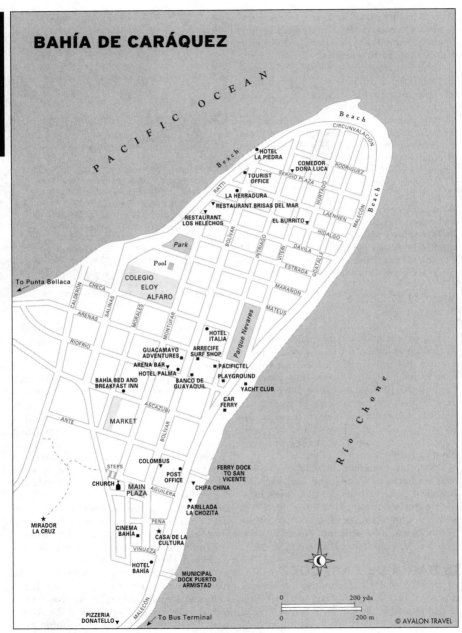

BAHÍA DE CARÁQUEZ

PACIFIC OCEAN

Beach

CIRCUNVALACIÓN

Beach

Beach

HOTEL LA PIEDRA

COMEDOR DOÑA LUCA

RODRIGUEZ

TOURIST OFFICE

SERGIO PLAZA

HURTADO

MALECÓN

LA HERRADURA

RATTI

RESTAURANT BRISAS DEL MAR

LAENNEN

EL BURRITO

RESTAURANT LOS HELECHOS

BOLIVAR

INTRIAGO

VITERI

DAVILA

HIDALGO

Park

GOATALE

ESTRADA

Pool

COLEGIO ELOY ALFARO

MARANON

To Punta Bellaca

CHECA

CALDERON

SALINAS

ARENAS

MORALES

MONTUFAR

MATEUS

RIOFRIO

Parque Nevares

HOTEL ITALIA

GUACAMAYO ADVENTURES

ARRECIFE SURF SHOP

ARENA BAR

PACIFICTEL

HOTEL PALMA

PLAYGROUND

BAHÍA BED AND BREAKFAST INN

BANCO DE GUAYAQUIL

YACHT CLUB

ASCAZUBI

CAR FERRY

Rio Chone

ANTE

MARKET

BOLIVAR

COLOMBUS

STEPS

POST OFFICE

FERRY DOCK TO SAN VICENTE

CHURCH

MAIN PLAZA

AGUILERA

CHIFA CHINA

MIRADOR LA CRUZ

PARILLADA LA CHOZITA

PENA

CINEMA BAHÍA

CASA DE LA CULTURA

VINUEZA

HOTEL BAHÍA

MUNICIPAL DOCK PUERTO ARMISTAD

MALECÓN

0   200 yds

0   200 m

PIZZERIA DONATELLO

To Bus Terminal

© AVALON TRAVEL

many nearby roads. Then, in August 1998, an earthquake measuring greater than 7 on the Richter scale leveled a good portion of the city and left residents (at least those whose homes still stood) without electricity or water for months. At one point, 2,500 of the town's 18,000 residents were living in the streets. Most of the damage has since been repaired.

On a brighter note, Bahía officially declared itself an "eco-city" in 1999, initiating ambitious plans to recycle most of the city's waste and bring it into harmony with its surrounding bioregion. The safe harbor has proved inviting to boat captains, and it's common to see private yachts anchored in the tranquil waters.

Entertainment and Events

Grab your own snack and head to the **Cinema Bahía,** on Bolívar between Peña and Vineuza, for the nightly video at 8 P.M. The showings are almost always in English, and the variety is quite good. At other times, you can watch your own movies in individual DVD rooms.

Bahía has a respectable schedule of annual festivals: **La Candelaria and Los Chiguales** (February 2); **San Pedro and San Pablo** (June 29); **Virgen de La Merced** (September 24); and the city's **canonization** celebration (November 3).

Shopping

Find *artesanías* along the Malecón near the Yacht Club. The wife of the owner of Guacamayo Adventures sells beautiful handmade paper and envelopes with pressed flowers, and the office also stocks T-shirts and a selection of other handicrafts. The city **market** takes up the corner of Morales and Ante and offers a wide variety of fruit, veggies, and seafood.

Recreation and Tours

There's not much in the way of beaches near Bahía (head to Canoa, or south to San Clemente or San Jacinto, for sand). A $2 taxi ride will take you to south Punta Bellaca, where you can walk at low tide. The short hike up to the imposing **Mirador La Cruz** is well

worth it for the view of the bay. Cool off afterward with a dip in the **pool** at the Colegio Eloy Alfaro, which is open to the public. An important regional archaeology collection is housed in the museum at the **Banco Central** (10 A.M.–5 P.M. Wed.–Sat.) on the Malecón at Peña, where other rooms are dedicated to traveling exhibitions.

The entire central coast is the domain of **Guacamayo Adventures** (Bolívar and Arenas, tel./fax 5/269-1412). If the staff can't set you up with information or a tour, they'll find someone who can. They are a good source of general information and have a book exchange. They run excursions to Isla Corazón, an island in the river mouth inhabited by more than 40 species of birds, at high tide the can canoes weave through the mangrove channels. Trips to an ecological farm and education center on the Río Muchacho also get raves—you can ride horses, harvest and roast your own chocolate, and see plenty of wildlife. Tours start at $25 pp per day, and there are half-day tours to nearby tropical dry forests ($12 pp).

Accommodations

The **Bahía Bed and Breakfast Inn** (Ascazubi 316 and Morales, tel. 5/269-0146) typifies a great budget hotel: strong fans, comfortable beds, and cable TV in the lounge, all for $6 pp with shared bath ($8 pp private). The **Hotel Palma** (Bolívar 918 and Riofrio, tel. 5/269-0467) is passable, with rooms starting at $6 pp with private bath. Rooms facing the Río Chone in the **Hotel Bahía** (tel. 5/269-0509) are $8 with bay view and private bath. It's on the south end of the Malecón at Vinueza.

At Hidalgo and Bolívar, you'll find the classy ◖ **La Herradura** (tel. 5/269-0446, fax 5/269-0265). Wagon wheels and iron filigree evoke a snug country club, and the hotel's excellent restaurant facing the ocean has a wide selection of wines and surprisingly few dishes that cost more than $8. Rooms with TV, private bath, air-conditioning, and hot water are $35 s, $65 d, with deals available on the upper floors for $15 pp. Another good value is the

Hotel El Viajero, starting at $10 pp with private bath. Located next door to Guacamayo Tours (Bolívar and Arenas, tel. 5/269-0792), it has been highly recommended recently.

Enjoy a sea breeze on the walkway over the rocks at the posh **Hotel La Piedra** (Malecón and Bolívar, tel. 5/269-0780, fax 5/269-0154). The hotel has a pool and a classy restaurant, and it rents kayaks and bicycles to guests. Rates are $67 s, $69 d, but prices are very negotiable in low season and on weekdays.

Food

Inexpensive meals draw locals and budget travelers to the passenger ferry wharf, where grilled meats range $3–6. In accordance with what seems like national law, Bahía has a **Chifa China,** on the Malecón next to the San Vicente ferry dock. The inexpensive food tastes better than the decor would suggest. For a bit of Italian, head to **Pizzeria Donatello,** on the south end of the Malecón. The **Arena Bar** (Riofrio and Bolívar) offers solid food, service, and atmosphere and caters to vegetarians. Great salads and good seafood can be found at **Colombius** on Bolívar and Ante. Tacos and fajitas are on the menu at **El Burrito,** at Hurtado and Hidalgo.

Itinerant gourmets frequent the restaurants in the more expensive hotels, along with a few others: The **Restaurant Brisas del Mar** (Malecón and Hidalgo) and the **Restaurant Los Helechos** (Malecón and Davila) both specialize in seafood for around $4 a plate. Several other inexpensive seafood places line the Malecón. At the south end of the Malecón is **Puerto Armistad,** on the municipal dock. It's a popular hangout for the "yachties," with good food and happy-hour sundowners.

Information and Services

The **tourist information office** lends a helping hand on the corner of Bolívar and Malecón (tel. 5/269-1044 or 5/269-0372, 8:30 A.M.–1 P.M. and 2–5 P.M. Mon.–Fri.). The local **post office** is also on the Malecón, across from the ferry dock. The **Capitanía de Puerto,** where all incoming yachts must register, is on the Malecón about 100 meters south of the Puerto Armistad.

Transportation

Bahía is an easy and pleasant city to walk around, but for a little diversion, try a **triciclo ride.** These three wheeled, two-passenger, rickshaw-type bicycles, also called eco-taxis, can be found along the Malecón, especially in front of the passenger ferry dock. A short hop shouldn't cost more than $0.50. Drivers also offer a town tour for $2.

Coactur, 800 meters south of the city, sends frequent buses to Manta ($3, three hours) and Guayaquil ($6, six hours). **Reina del Camino,** at the next door down, runs three buses per day to Quito ($8, seven–eight hours), Esmeraldas ($8, eight hours), Santo Domingo ($4, three–four hours), and Guayaquil. Buses to destinations north along the coast leave from the market in San Vicente, across the bay. Construction is underway, in this tranquil town, of a new bridge across the estuary that should be completed in 2011; the new bus terminal south of the city should be ready sooner.

The **passenger ferry** to San Vicente leaves from the dock at Malecón and Aguilera when full (usually every few minutes), about 6 A.M.–11 P.M., for $0.30 pp (10 minutes). A **car ferry** runs every half hour to the airport (only charter flights) at low tide.

MANTA

Ecuador's second-most-important shipping center sprawls across the mouth of the Río Manta. Manta (pop. 183,000) can serve as a handy base or resupply point for excursions to nearby beaches, and it is becoming a visitor destination in its own right with the help of the U.S. military.

A major port since pre-Inca times, Manta was officially established by the Spanish in 1565 as a supply point between Panama and Peru. Repeated pirate attacks drove most inhabitants inland, leaving the city almost empty. Times have changed, though, and today Manta is second only to Guayaquil in the volume of agricultural products exported and

© JEAN BROWN

Maintaining fishnets is an endless job.

manufactured goods imported. The city has become the center of the Ecuadorian tuna industry, and Japanese interests are buying much of the top-quality fish for export.

The arrival of the U.S. military in 1999 brought an economic boom. Nightspots and restaurants now bustle along the Malecón, hotels are being spruced up, and new shopping centers and cinemas have opened. Sun-faded boats brighten the inner harbor, which empties at low tide, and more and more cruise ships anchor farther out on their way between Chile and Peru.

Charlie Tuna welcomes you to Manta along the road from Montecristi, where warehouses and factories sport the logos of fish-export companies. The town center and harbor are north of the Río Manta, with Murcielago beach another two kilometers along. Tarquí beach fronts the tougher section of town east of the river, and the airport lies another three kilometers beyond. Addresses with Avenue and Calle numbers under 30 are in Manta, while numbers over 100 are east of the river in Tarquí. Stay up to date with the help of www.infomanta.com.

Sights and Recreation

Of Manta's two beaches, **Murcielago** is cleaner and wider, with the Manta Surf Club providing lifeguard service and surfing lessons. **Tarquí** beach is seedier, lined with PVC-tube frames that can be covered with a rented cloth to escape the sun. In the early morning, the night's catch is dragged onto the sand—look for sharks, swordfish, red snapper, and the occasional octopus. After dark, head inland to one of the many *discotecas* in the area.

If you have a few hours to kill, stop by the newly built quarters of the **Museo del Banco Central** (10 A.M.–5 P.M., $1 pp, tel. 5/262-6998) on the Malecón and Calle 19, with major exhibits on pre-Inca Manteño culture.

The **Yacht Club,** under the striped blue awnings near the dock at Calle 15, has boats that can be chartered for deep-sea fishing. Several tour companies offer snorkeling at the base of the headland and out at Isla de la Plata; try **Metropolitan Touring** (Av. 4, tel. 5/261-3366, fax 5/261-1277). You can rent a car, mail a letter, and book a tour at **Delgado Travel** (Av. 6 between Calle 12 and Calle 13, 5/262-2813, www.ecuadorpacificosur.com).

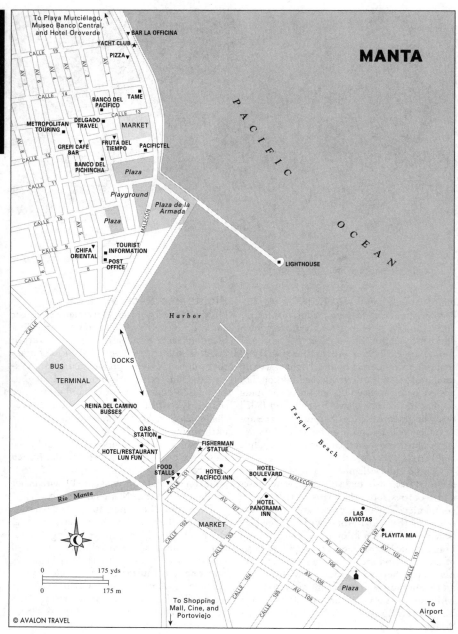

MANTA

To Playa Murciélago,
Museo Banco Central,
and Hotel Oroverde

BAR LA OFFICINA

YACHT CLUB

PIZZA

CALLE 15

AV 6
AV 4
AV 3
AV 2
AV 1

CALLE 14

BANCO DEL
PACIFICO

TAME

CALLE 13

METROPOLITAN
TOURING

DELGADO
TRAVEL

MARKET

AV 8

GREPI CAFÉ
BAR

FRUTA DEL
TIEMPO

PACIFICTEL

CALLE 12

BANCO DEL
PICHINCHA

Plaza

CALLE 11

Playground

MALECÓN

Plaza de la
Armada

CALLE 10

AV 5

Plaza

CALLE 9

CHIFA
ORIENTAL

TOURIST
INFORMATION

AV 6

POST
OFFICE

CALLE 9

8

CALLE

PACIFIC OCEAN

LIGHTHOUSE

CALLE 7

Harbor

BUS
TERMINAL

DOCKS

REINA DEL CAMINO
BUSSES

GAS
STATION

HOTEL/RESTAURANT
LUN FUN

FISHERMAN
STATUE

Tarqui Beach

FOOD
STALLS

CALLE 101

HOTEL
PACIFICO INN

HOTEL
BOULEVARD

MALECÓN

Río Manta

AV 107

HOTEL
PANORAMA
INN

CALLE 102

MARKET

CALLE 103

AV 105

LAS
GAVIOTAS

AV 102

CALLE 107

PLAYITA MIA

CALLE 110

CALLE 104

AV 106

AV 108

AV 108

Plaza

0   175 yds

0   175 m

To Shopping
Mall, Cine, and
Portoviejo

To
Airport

© AVALON TRAVEL

Entertainment and Events

Head west on Calle 14, then right (north) on Avenida 14 or any street beyond that to hit Avenida Flavio Reyes, where some of Manta's newest nightspots are located. Places like **Madera Fina** (Flavio Reyes and Calle 23) and **Tanta** (Flavio Reyes and Calle 20) attract more and less mature crowds, respectively. **Casa de Celi** (Malecón and Calle 19) is a bar that caters to Americans off the base.

The **Feria Agropecuaria** on September 8–9 draws loads of tourists, followed by an **International Theater Festival** in late September and **Manta Day** on November 4.

Accommodations

Rooms at the **Hotel Boulevard** (tel. 5/262-5333) start at $6 per person and include a fan, TV, and tiny but clean private baths. Pay $10 per person for air-conditioning. The neighborhood near Tarquí beach is filled with budget hotels. Two are particularly good deals: the **Hostal Miami** (Av. 102 and Calle 107, tel. 5/262-2055) and the towering **Hotel Pacífico Inn** (Av. 106 and Calle 101, tel. 5/262-3584). Both cost $10 pp with private bath, $12 with air-conditioning, and they have a pool and hydro massage facility across the street.

Within sight of the sand, the **Hotel Miami** (Malecón and Calle 108, tel. 5/262-7823) has rooms for $12 pp with ocean view and air-conditioning ($7 with fan). The **Hotel Panorama Inn** (Calle 103 and Av. 105, tel. 5/262-2996) has accommodations for $27 s, $37 d, with air-conditioning. The **Yara Maria** (Av. 11 and Calle 20, tel. 5/261-3219) overlooks the ocean. Rooms with TVs and air-conditioning run $25 s, $35 d, including access to a whirlpool.

Las Gaviotas (Malecón 109 and Calle 106, tel. 5/262-8840, fax 5/262-0940, $30 s, $49 d) takes the prize for Tarquí's finest. There's a bar/cafeteria (with attached casino), as well as a pool that's nice and cool. Near the bridges over the river is the **Hotel Lun Fun** (tel. 5/262-2966, fax 5/261-0601, lunfunhotel@yahoo.com). The Chinese owners keep the place immaculate and run the highly praised restaurant. Rates are $48 s, $67 d, including breakfast.

For travelers who want international standards and service, the **Oro Verde**, on the Malecón and Calle 23, has it all. Rooms start at $159 s, $170 d (tel. 5/262-9200, ov_mta@ oroverdehotels.com). **Howard Johnson** has also opened another branch of its chain catering to the business community, one kilometer west of town (tel. 5/262-9997, reserves@ hojomanta.com, $116 s or d)

Food

Both beaches are lined with inexpensive, colorful seafood restaurant/bars, specializing in shrimp with rice or a fried *corvina,* plus a pilsner or two to wash it down. The **Chifa Oriental** is a basic Chinese eatery, with *tallarines* for $1. For Japanese, try **Guen-Roku** at Calle 16 and the Malecón.

Pizza (Malecón and Calle 15) serves (surprise!) pizza and Italian food in a faux jungle hut on the way to Murcielago beach. A small pizza with everything is $6. Look for the creeper vines at the intersection of Avenida 3 and Calle 12 to find the **Nashville South Bar.** The pleasant open patio is good for a drink, with seafood plates for around $5. Most of the bars and restaurants along the Malecón have pool tables and a selection of beers. **Fruta del Tiempo,** on the corner of the theater plaza, has a fine selection of sandwiches, juices, and salads. The extra-chunky fruit salad is a steal at $0.60. For a nice meal in lovely surroundings, try **Mantai** (Calle 20 and Av.12A, tel. 5/262-9692), on the hill overlooking the ocean.

Information and Services

You'll find one **tourist information office** (tel. 5/262-2944, 8 A.M.–5 P.M. Mon.–Fri.) on Pasaje Egas between Calles 10 and 11, and another in the Municipio building next to the **post office.**

The **Banco Pichincha** (Av. 2 between Calles 11 and 12) changes foreign currency on the second floor, and the **Banco del Pacífico** (Av. 2 and Calle 13) will change travelers' checks.

CROSS-BORDER CONTROVERSY

The U.S. Southern Command, charged with helping end the Columbian drug trade, expanded an air and naval base near Manta in 1999 to the tune of $80 million. This Forward Operating Location (FOL), sometimes called a "listening post," supported hundreds of personnel and five to eight P-3 surveillance aircrafts flying anti-drug missions over Colombia. The 10-year lease is up for renewal in 2009, and President Correa has already stated that it will be refused. It appears that negotiations with the Chinese government for control of the base are in progress.

Although Pentagon sources deny that funding for the base came from the $2 billion package set aside for "Plan Colombia," the Colombian defense minister and a retired Ecuadorian Army colonel have both said otherwise. Opponents of the plan wonder if the U.S. is on its way to another situation similar to Vietnam and Cambodia in the 1970s, when "mission creep" dragged uninvolved countries into the fighting.

Crime and violence are already spilling over the 370-mile border between the countries, as cocaine laboratories and rival forces in Colombia's mounting civil war flee to their more peaceful southern neighbor. The U.S. military has used the "domino theory" to justify sending troops, advisors, and money to Southeast Asia and Central America to prevent neighboring countries from toppling one after another into communism, and the theory has been proven wrong repeatedly. The U.S. State Department has found it can circumvent restrictions on using U.S. military assistance only to fight drug trafficking by labeling irregular military groups such as the FARC (Revolutionary Armed Forces of Colombia), then invoking the demands of the war on terrorism.

In a much publicized incident in the first days of March 2008, the Colombian army invaded Ecuadorian territory and attacked a FARC campsite, taking out one of the top leaders of the organization. Tension was high and diplomatic relations were broken off. Armaments used for the attack were claimed to be of U.S. manufacture.

Transportation

Manta's main **bus terminal** occupies the southern end of the city center before the bridges to Tarquí. Buses run to Guayaquil ($4, four hours), Esmeraldas ($4, 10 hours), Santo Domingo ($7, seven hours), and Quito ($9, 9–10 hours). **Panamericana** (Calle 12 and Av. 4) runs comfortable buses with bathrooms to Quito and Santo Domingo ($10) at 11 A.M., 9:30 P.M., and 10:30 P.M. **Flota Imbabura,** on the Malecón at Calle 8, has similar bus service at noon and 10 P.M.

TAME (tel. 5/261-3210) sells tickets on the Malecón just north of the theater park (Calle 13). Flights leave for Quito daily from Eloy Alfaro airport, five kilometers northeast of the center of town ($72 pp). The airline also operates daily flights to Guayaquil ($72 pp), as well as daily flights (except Saturdays) to Quito from Portoviejo for $60 pp. **Icaro** (Malecón and Calle 23, tel. 5/262-7327) also

flies to Quito ($58 pp). **Aerogal** (Flavio Reyes between Avenida 20 and 21, tel. 5/262-8899) has daily flights to Quito ($61 pp).

North of Manta

Crucita is an unremarkable fishing town that is fast becoming a busy tourist destination, partly because of its wide and generally clean beach. Visitors come from around the globe to paraglide off the gentle dunes within sight of the sea (many competitions are held here). Diego Castro gives paragliding lessons; ask for him at the **Hotel Voladores** (tel. 5/267-6200), on the south end of the beach. The hotel has rooms with private bath and fan for less than $8 pp. Hang gliding is also popular—ask at El Gordito Parapente Restaurant for details. Crucita has plenty of other restaurants, although none are particularly noteworthy. Buses run often to and from Manta and Portoviejo.

According to archaeological evidence,

residents of the fishing village of **Jaramijo** have been hauling in their catches for more than 4,000 years. Today, Jaramijo is home to the last fishing sailboats in use on Ecuador's central coast. The festivities of St. Peter and St. Paul on August 24 include a unique "miniature U.N." celebration thought to have originated in feudal Spain. Ten "countries" are created and headed by "presidents" chosen from the populace. This honored position entails, among other things, giving speeches on the virtues of one's country and acknowledging pleasantries in return.

Inland from Manta

Montecristi served on multiple occasions as an inland haven for coastal residents fleeing pirate attacks during the 17th century. That was before the *sombrero* industry came to town; as early as 1890, a French visitor noted that "in every hut of these towns were seen a man, woman, or young boy, and sometimes a child at work" weaving the soon-to-be-famous Panama hats. Although the craft is declining, the famous Montecristi *superfinos*—each one requiring up to three months' work—can be bought in town. (Most of the weaving is still done in the countryside.) Shops selling hats and other woven goods line the main street of 9 de Julio.

Portoviejo, climatically the hottest city in Ecuador, has a new museum and historical archive (Olmedo and Sucre, tel. 5/265-2235, 9 A.M.–5 P.M. Mon.–Fri). The market area stocks everything a "Montuvio" farmer could want, from luxurious and fresh kapok mattresses, Mocora straw hats, wooden saddles, and circular fishnets to all the groundbreaking tools you can imagine—and a few more to puzzle over.

Along with the funniest name in the country, **Jipijapa** ("Heepy-happa") claims the title of "Sultana de Cafe" (Sultan of Coffee) because of its location in the middle of a fertile patchwork of coffee, cotton, cocoa, and kapok farms. Fine Panama hats woven in town are sold at the Sunday market.

From Jipijapa, you have the choice of heading straight southeast to Guayaquil or west over the hills to the coast, where the road makes a sharp turn south at **Puerto Cayo** toward the Santa Elena Peninsula. **TAME** operates flights six days a week to Quito at 14:30.

◖ PUERTO LÓPEZ

"The Acapulco of Ecuador" enjoys a wide bay dotted with fishing boats and backed by green hills. Even though most people use Puerto López only as a base for exploring the surrounding area, it's still an enjoyable town with

Puerto López's Malecón

a lovely beach. In the morning, you can watch fishermen bring in and clean their catches, and in the afternoon see them cleaning and repairing their nets and boats. The coastal road serves as the town's long, dusty main street, where it's easy to picture a Wild West showdown taking place at high noon.

Along with its proximity to Machalilla National Park and Isla de la Plata, Puerto López is probably the best-known and most popular whale-watching destination in Ecuador. It can get crowded on weekends during whale-watching season (June–September), so reservations are a smart idea.

Recreation and Events

Understandably, most of Puerto López's activities center around the ocean. **Humpback whales** swimming north from Antarctica can be seen gathering in the calm waters of the bay from late June to early September. You can often spot them from the beach, or choose from about a dozen tour companies in town for close-up viewing from boats. Most of these operations also offer tours to Isla de la Plata and inland parts of nearby Machalilla National Park. All have roughly the same offerings and prices, and sometimes even share tour boats to ensure that the minimum group size is met.

The **Explormar** agency on the Malecón is the best qualified for diving trips; the operator is the PADI rep for the Ecuadorian coast, and services are reliable. Recommendations have also come in for **Perfil Turístico** (tel. 5/230-0147), at the Hotel Pacífico; **Sercapez** (tel. 5/230-0130), on Córdova between the highway and the ocean; and **Machalilla Tours** (tel. 5/230-0154), near Sercapez. Machalilla Tours also rents mountain bikes and organizes horseback-riding tours.

Puerto López hosts the **World of Whales Festival** in June.

Accommodations

The **Sol Inn** (tel. 5/230-0162) and **Itapoa** (tel. 5/984-3042) receive frequent praise. Rooms start at $5 pp with private bath and hot water, along with hammock space and a kitchen. The

friendly owners can point out the best beaches in the area, including Punto Los Frailes to the north.

Tuzco (tel. 5/230-0120, $9 pp), up the hill from the market, is a spotless and cheery place.

The prettiest hotel around is the **⟨ Hostería Mandala** (tel. 5/230-0181, www .hosteriamandala.info), with beautiful gardens near the beach a little north of town. At $18 s, $33 d for one of 21 cabins with hot showers, it's also a good value. The clean **Hotel Pacífico** (tel./fax 5/230-0147) is on the Malecón, a few blocks north of the city center. Rooms are $18 s, $30 d with private bath and fans; air-conditioning costs more. Breakfast is included, and all rooms have hot showers. Hammocks and trees fill the courtyard. **La Terraza** (tel. 5/230-0235) is quiet and immaculate, with great views from the hill, and the German owners are building a pool. Prices start around $15 pp, including breakfast.

Food

If you've been traveling on the coast for more than a few days, you should be able to predict the string of cheap seafood restaurants on the Malecón with uncanny accuracy. **Spondylus** (tel. 5/230-0128) serves some creative maritime breakfasts (try an octopus omelet). **Carmita's** (tel. 5/230-0149), on the beachfront, is another option for a fresh seafood dinner, which you can follow with an evening stroll down the Malecón to walk it off. Both offer main dishes for $4–5 and up.

⟨ Bella Italia (tel. 5/230-0361) on Moncayo is a bit out of the way and hard to find (follow the signs from the Hotel Pacífico), but it serves the city's best Italian dinner Tuesday–Sunday. Prices start around $4. Kevin and Diane own the **Whale Café,** on the south end of the Malecón, which has a large book exchange and several vegetarian options on the menu, as well as home-baked bread and great pizzas ($3.50 and up). The owners know tons about the area. Try the Colombian specialties at **Patacon Pisao,** one block back from the beach, or grab a late-night drink at **Clandestino Bar** at Montalvo and Córdova.

Information and Services

The **Machalilla National Park headquarters**, on the north side of the market, has information on the park and a tiny museum with displays of marine and land fauna. Exchange cash at the **Banco Pichincha** (Córdova and Machalilla). The **post office** is on the Malecón, south of Córdova. Ask at Machalilla Tours about Spanish lessons at the **Costañita Spanish School** (tel. 5/230-0154, fax 5/230-0200, schoolcosta@hotmail.com).

Transportation

All buses to and through Puerto López stop on the main road (Eloy Alfaro) by the market. Buses between La Libertad and Manta are fairly common, so you won't have to wait too long to head north or south along the coast. From the busy transport hub of Jipijapa, you can continue to most of the country. **Transportes Carlos Aray** has a daily 6 P.M. bus to Quito ($10, 11 hours). **Transportes Reina de Camino** also runs a "Pullman" bus to its terminal near Avenida Patria in Quito, which is well worth the extra $1 for the comfort and security.

◉ MACHALILLA NATIONAL PARK

Ecuador's only coastal park protects most of the country's remaining tropical scrub desert and forest, along with a dramatic stretch of coastline and the islands of Salango and La Plata. This hot, arid plant zone once covered an estimated 25 percent of western Ecuador, but today, only about 1 percent is left—most of it here. In all, Machalilla protects 135,000 acres on land and 316,000 acres of coastal waters. If you can't make it to the Galápagos, Machalilla's Isla de la Plata is the next best thing—not to be missed for its fauna above and below the water.

Flora and Fauna

Machalilla is covered with dry forest and coastal scrub vegetation. Many of the tough-looking plants, including opuntia cactus and palo santo trees, will look familiar to anyone who's been to the Galápagos. The fat-trunked ceiba or kapok trees, whose bare branches look like upturned roots, produce a fine, downy fiber that was used in World War II life preservers. Other native plant species include ivory palms, heliconias, and mangroves.

The park is home to at least 230 species of birds, including many Galápagos species, such as frigatebirds, boobies, and waved albatross. The mammal list includes deer, anteaters, armadillos, ocelots, and two species of monkeys. Humpback whales and sea turtles patrol the waters among some 250 species of fish and the only coral formation on Ecuador's mainland coast.

Isla de la Plata

Machalilla's offshore appendix was named for an alleged hoard of silver ingots left by Sir Francis Drake, who stopped here at the end of the 16th century after attacking a Spanish galleon. Today, park rangers and a huge assortment of bird species make their home on this "poor man's Galápagos," a 21-square-kilometer island 24 kilometers out to sea west of Puerto Cayo.

Swimming and snorkeling in Drake's Bay will bring you close to (if not face-to-face with) sea lions and sea turtles. Eleven species of whales pass by June–September.

Archaeology

Traces of cultures up to 3,000 years old have been unearthed in the valley of the Río Buenavista. Agua Blanca, in the northern section of the park, is one of the richest archaeological sites in the country. About 200 stone sculptures show that the area, formerly called Salangome, served as the center of a trading network that sailed as far north as Mexico.

Many of the digs, including others at Los Frailes, López Viejo, and San Sebastián, have been backfilled to protect their contents from looters and the weather, but most of the finer artifacts have been moved to the museum in Salango.

Visiting the Park

Check in at the administrative center in Puerto López (7 A.M.–5 P.M. daily) to enter the park and visit Isla de la Plata. There's a small **museum** in the gateway town of Agua Blanca, five kilometers past the **ranger station** at the entrance near Puerto López. Tracks lead into the hills to other villages, such as Las Peñas. If you go by foot (as opposed to vehicle or rented animal), make sure to take enough water, especially for trips into the drier coastal scrub. Climbing **Cerro San Sebastian** (820 meters) past Agua Blanca takes you through humid forest; a guide is recommended.

The best **beaches**—Los Frailes, Playa Negra, and La Tortuguita—are three kilometers north of the ranger station. You can get here on a bicycle relatively easily from Puerto López (13 kilometers), and—in a full day— you can swing by Agua Blanca to boot.

The entrance fee to the park, including Isla de la Plata, is $20 pp ($12 land only, $15 island only). Numerous tour companies in Puerto López offer guided trips to the park's mainland and offshore sections. If you go to Isla de la Plata, make sure your boat has two motors: it's a long way out there, and getting stranded is no fun.

SALANGO

This sleepy town is home to the small **Museo Salango** (9 A.M.–12:30 P.M. and 1:30–6 P.M. daily, $1), which houses well-designed archaeological displays on prehistoric coastal cultures in Machalilla National Park. You can also hire a fishing boat to take you out to hulking Isla Salango, two kilometers offshore, to see the seabirds. Gary and Coralia Medina run the **Marea de la Plata** tour company (tel. 5/278-0292 or 5/278-0545), with trained, PADI-certified guides to help you visit Machalilla.

Octopus salad ($6) is only one of the seven ways the aquatic cephalopods are served at the **Restaurante Delfin Magico.** Local people drive a few miles to eat the special meals prepared by Victoria and Alfredo. The tasty seafood dishes are made to order, so you can

Museo Salango

stroll over and visit the museum after putting in your lunch requests. *Spondylus* (spiny oyster) in peanut sauce with garlic-tossed *patacones* is another specialty. Alfredo offers transport back to Lopez for groups of diners, or you can stay at the pretty community cabins beside the museum for $8–10; ask at the museum.

Private cabins hold two–five people at the **Hostería Piqueros Patas Azules** (tel. 4/278-0279, $17 pp). It's about three kilometers south of town and has a private archaeological museum, highlighted by numerous in situ burial sites with skeletons encased in large clay jars. The $1 entrance fee gives you access to one of the loveliest beaches on the coast—never crowded and often deserted—as well as a peek at a sizable population of the endangered and colorful *cangrejo azul* (blue crab).

ALANDALUZ ECOLOGICAL TOURIST CENTER

Everything about this luxurious but affordable treehouse resort, between Puerto Rico and Ayampe on the coastal road, is designed to be as healthy, ecologically sound, and self-sustaining as possible. The thatched roofs at **Alandaluz** are set at a 70-degree angle conducive to "inspiration, concentration, and clarity," and the cane and wood used in the traditional construction were cut during the new moon, when the sap level is lowest, making the material more durable and less attractive to insects.

Organic gardens, composting toilets, and a full recycling program minimize the hotel's impact on the fragile coastal environment. Neon tropical flowers surround the sturdy bamboo, stone, and plaster cabins scattered in the bushes around the large main building. Only the infrequent car passing down the coastal road breaks the spell cast by the roar of the ocean, the occasional critter skittering in the bushes, and the nocturnal hum of insects.

Once you've sampled the all-natural meals in the restaurant—try the *corvina* (sea bass) in peanut sauce or the pancakes with *mora* (blackberry) syrup—it's time for some serious lounging on the private beach, from which you can occasionally spot whales and dolphins on the horizon. Just watch out for the undertow.

If you're looking for a little more activity, snorkeling, horseback riding, and bicycling are possible, as are one- and two-day excursions to Machalilla, beaches, and the hotel's Cantalapiedra rainforest wildlife sanctuary on the Ayampe River. They also accept volunteers for a donation of $20 pp per day. Small private cabins and rooms in the main building cost $34 s, $60 d, and you can camp for $5 pp.

Any bus traveling down the coastal road can drop you off at the entrance, just north of Ayampe. From Manta, catch the "Manglaralto" bus ($3, three hours); from Jipijapa, catch the "Libertad" bus ($2, two hours). The hotel also offers private transfers to and from Manta, Portoviejo, and Guayaquil.

For more information, contact Alandaluz directly (tel. 4/278-0690, tel./fax 4/278-0686, info@alandaluzhosteria.com, www.alandaluz.com), or contact the office in Quito (Diego Novoa 216 and Guangüiltagua, tel. 2/224-8604, tel./fax 2/244-0790).

MONTAÑITA AND VICINITY

The small fishing town of Montañita owes its increasing popularity as a seaside hangout to the ocean, which beckons surfers—and surf lifestylers—with the longest right break in Ecuador. Everyone here, it seems, has tan skin and long hair and is either carrying a board or gazing longingly at someone who is. It's not everyone's kind of place: To some, this dense collection of budget hotels, restaurants, surf shops, bars, and tattoo parlors seems sleazy; but to others, it's party heaven. The town lost much of its beach to the 1997–1998 El Niño.

Montañita is tourist-focused and often tourist-filled. Almost every building on the main street is a hotel, restaurant, or surf shop, and you're never more than a longboard's length from Internet access. Vegetarian food and seafood are both common, and you can find surfboards, boogie boards, and bikes for rent all over town. Many hotels rent surfboards, change travelers' checks, and offer Internet access and discounts for longer stays. New hotels are constantly shooting skyward, like the bamboo thickets cut to build them. During Carnival, thousands of tourists descend for the Pan-American surf contest and bikini competition. Things are much more *tranquilo* at the north end of the beach, near the break at Punta Montañita.

Montañita's famous main break skirts the rocks at the north end of the beach. High tides during February and May bring the best waves, but swells of 10 meters can come in June and July. Riptides, jagged rocks, and occasional stingrays merit a watchful eye. The remaining beach is rocky and not particularly inviting (for swimming, head three kilometers to Olon, a half-hour walk north of Punta Montañita), but as long as there are waves and enough sand to build a bonfire, Montañita's reputation will stay more or less intact.

There are about 40 hotels and hostels here in all price ranges. Many will negotiate midweek and for longer stays, but make sure to reserve in advance for Christmas, New Year's, Carnival, and Easter. Be careful when renting surfboards—examine yours for damage before you paddle out.

Punta Montañita

At the entrance to the dirt lane near the break, you'll find the **Cabañas Vitos,** which are as much the sprawling house of a surfer and his family as a hotel. Surfboards and children's toys litter the yard, and there are pool tables inside and a bar on the beach. Surfboards cost $5 to rent for the day, and ragged boogie boards are free for guests. Basic rooms and raised cabins run $8 pp, but you can pitch a tent for even less.

Down the lane on the left, **Tres Palmas Cabañas** (tel. 9/975-5717) offers six rooms facing the ocean for $6 pp with private baths, fans, and hot water. David, the owner, is from San Antonio, Texas, so the Tex-Mex cantina on the beach (recommended for lunch and dinner) is the real deal. Across the lane, the balconies of the clean and pleasant **La Casa del Sol** (tel. 4/290-1302, casasol@ecua.net.ec, www.casasol.com) are covered with hammocks and drying laundry. Rooms with shared bath are $8 ($15 with private bath and hot water), and dorm spaces are $4.

The family-run **Las Olas Restaurant** next door specializes, of course, in seafood. The portions are big and cheap—nothing is more than $5. They also have rooms with shared bath for $8. Farther down the lane, you'll hit **Baja Montañita** (tel. 4/290-1218), a thoroughly modern hotel that seems a bit out of place here. Six-person cabins and rooms cost $35 s, $44 d, and a pool and restaurant face the rocky break.

In Town

A kilometer of empty beach separates the point break from Montañita proper. Here, the three-story **Centro del Mundo** offers dorm rooms for $6 pp and private rooms for $8, all so close to the beach that you can practically fish from the balconies. Prices include breakfast and the use of boogie boards. **La Casa Blanca** (tel. 4/290-1340, casablan@gu.pro.ec), a three-story building situated one block from the sand, is a pleasantly simple *hostal* with rooms for $4–7 pp. All bathrooms have hot water, and the restaurant has satellite TV.

Next door is the huge **Hotel Montañita** (tel. 4/290-1269, $11 pp), with 36 rooms and 90 beds with fans and mosquito nets. Some rooms have balconies and hot water, and hammocks and deck chairs abound. There's a great view of the ocean, satellite TV, and a small pool. Another budget hotel on the same street is the surfer-recommended **Cabañas Tsunami** (tel. 9/714-7344, $8 pp), which doubles as a surf shop.

The **Restaurant Doña Elenita,** on the main drag, garners repeat business for its exotic *empanadas* (banana-and-chocolate is a favorite). The second-floor restaurant **Macchu Picchu,** in the center of town, offers an excellent variety of dishes starting at $4. **Lotus** is an offbeat and inviting watering hole open late, overlooking the beach at the end of Rocafuerte. You'll feel like you're back in Long Beach at the surfer-friendly **Mahalo,** open from sunset on. Places open and close overnight, and prices are usually negotiable midweek or for longer stays, so plan a few days in the sun and surf.

South of Montañita

Fine beaches grace **Olon** and **Manglaralto,** located north and south of Montañita, respectively. Both towns offer limited accommodations and food options, although **La Calderada** in Manglaralto is worth a visit for its tasty traditional dishes. Between Manglaralto and Montañita, on the land of a once famous horse ranch, is **Kamala** (tel. 9/942-3754), with PADI-qualified diving instruction, a pool once used for horse physiotherapy, bamboo cabins ($10 pp), and full-moon parties. Surfers should keep going south to **Punta Brava,** where a consistent left breaks near an air-force base (get permission to enter beforehand).

GUAYAQUIL AND THE SOUTHERN COAST

Even though it boasts the largest city in the country, Ecuador's southern coast—basically the west-facing mouth of the Golfo de Guayaquil—is the part most often bypassed by travelers. But those who skip it risk missing out on the new, improved version of Guayaquil, Ecuador's economic engine (and nightlife trendsetter), as well as a generous helping of unique (albeit small and often out-of-the-way) destinations. Then there are the beaches, from nearly deserted to crowded with fellow vacationers.

Outside of Guayaquil and the "Banana Capital" of Machala, the southern coast is a sleepy, tropical region of fishing villages, scrublands, and farms farther inland. Most of the original forest along this part of the coast has been cut in the last few decades to make room for banana and oil palm plantations, and almost all of the mangrove swamps outside of a few protected areas have been sacrificed for shrimp farming.

PLANNING YOUR TIME

The southern beaches are best visited during the rainy season, December–April, which actually gets the most sunshine. Guayaquil makes the best home base, although Machala will do for visits to Jambelí, Zaruma, and the Puyango Petrified Forest. The string of coastal resort towns west of Guayaquil might be worth another day or two, depending on your recreational tastes.

Leave at least a few days for Guayaquil and a few for the trip to the Peruvian border—more if you plan on visiting a protected area,

© JULIAN SMITH

HIGHLIGHTS

◖ Malecón 2000: A case study in successful urban renewal, Guayaquil's riverside promenade is now one of the most outstanding in South America (page 248).

◖ Parque de los Iguanas: Get up close and personal with a half-tame reptile — and keep an eye out for sloths in the trees (page 252).

◖ Manglares Churute Ecological Reserve: Rare shorebirds nest among the mangroves in this gigantic reserve near Guayaquil (page 262).

◖ Jambelí: Probably the most relaxing beach destination on Ecuador's southern coast, Jambelí can be more or less yours midweek (page 264).

◖ Zaruma: A beautiful setting and fascinating gold-rush history make this town a worthwhile side trip from Macas (page 265).

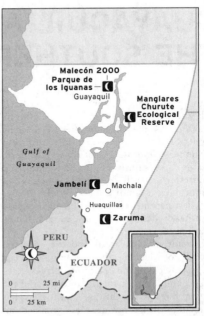

LOOK FOR ◖ TO FIND RECOMMENDED SIGHTS, ACTIVITIES, DINING, AND LODGING.

such as the **Manglares Churute Ecological Reserve,** or heading uphill to the intriguing old mining town of **Zaruma.** In Guayaquil, don't miss a stroll down the gulfside promenade of the **Malecón 2000** or the reptile action in the **Parque de los Iguanas.** For a more mellow outing, head to the beaches of **Jambelí** near Machala.

Santa Elena Peninsula

The scrubby heel of land that forms the Santa Elena Peninsula is now Ecuador's 23rd province, and hands-down the most popular destination for Guayaquileños seeking sun and surf. Families in minivans zip past the cacti and kapok trees to stake out a spot on the sand, preferably within walking distance of their condos. In contrast to the north coast's empty stretches and mellow vibes, the Santa Elena Peninsula bustles with personal watercraft, discos, cell phones, and blinding glass condos so close to the water that the high tide threatens to fill their lobbies. Any of the peninsula's major cities are packed on major holidays and just about any weekend between January and April, so plan your visit accordingly. If you're

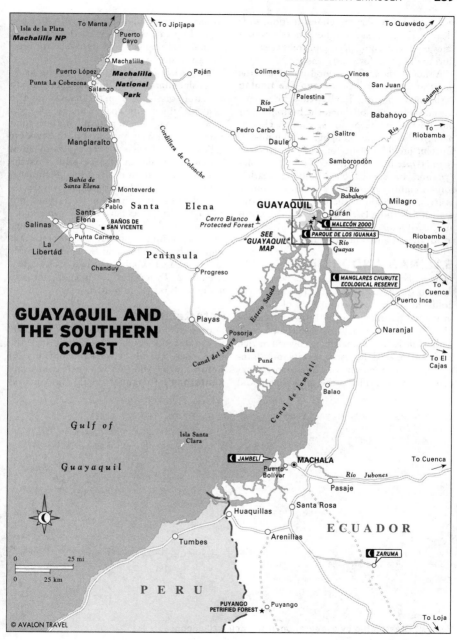

GUAYAQUIL

Isla de la Plata
Machalilla NP

To Manta
To Jipijapa
To Quevedo

Puerto
Cayo

Machalilla
Paján
Colimes
Vinces

Puerto López
Machalilla
San Juan

Punta La Cobezona
National
Park
Río
Daule
Palestina

Salango

Babahoyo

Montañita
Pedro Carbo
Salitre
Río
To
Riobamba

Manglaralto
Cordillera de Colonche
Daule

Samborondón

Bahía de
Santa Elena
Monteverde
Río
Babahoyo

San
Pablo
Santa   **Elena**
GUAYAQUIL
Durán
Milagro

Santa
Elena
Cerro Blanco
Protected Forest
MALECÓN 2000

Salinas
BAÑOS DE
SAN VICENTE
SEE
"GUAYAQUIL
MAP"
PARQUE DE LOS IGUANAS
To
Riobamba

La
Libertád
Punta Carnero
Río
Guayas
Troncal

Chanduy
Peninsula
Progreso
MANGLARES CHURUTE
ECOLOGICAL RESERVE
To
Cuenca

Puerto Inca

GUAYAQUIL AND
THE SOUTHERN
COAST
Playas
Estero Salado
Naranjal

Posorja
To El
Cajas

Isla
Puná

Canal del Morro

Canal de Jambelí
Balao

Gulf of

Isla Santa
Clara

Guayaquil
JAMBELÍ
MACHALA
To Cuenca

Puerto
Bolívar
Río *Jubones*

Pasaje

Huaquillas
Santa Rosa

E C U A D O R

Tumbes
Arenillas
ZARUMA

0   25 mi

0   25 km

P E R U

PUYANGO
PETRIFIED FOREST
Puyango

To Loja

© AVALON TRAVEL

looking for a low-key beach destination, steer clear of the madness and head north. Room rates tend to become negotiable midweek and during the *garua* (overcast) season.

Although the surfing is good at the tip of the peninsula and north of it, **deep-sea fishing** is the main sporting draw. Because the continental shelf is just offshore, the bottom drops out quickly and deepwater species are close at hand. The cool water brought by the Humboldt Current provides plenty of baitfish, which in turn attract billfish like Pacific sailfish, bigeye tuna, and striped, black, and blue marlin, some weighing more 500 kilograms. Bonito, sailfish, and dolphin (the fish, not the mammal) are also popular. The best fishing months are July–October, but make reservations well in advance at any time of year.

SALINAS AND VICINITY

One of the country's best resorts (at least by its own standards) is a sprawling village that holds down the westernmost tip of the peninsula. It's definitely one of the most exclusive places to stay: the beachfront Malecón bristles with white high-rise apartments owned by rich Ecuadorians, and the rest of the city spreads inland in a more typically coastal fashion. Salinas can be crowded during the high season and overpriced year-round, but for stylish sunbathing and upscale discos, you can't beat it. Just about everything you may need or want is on the east Malecón.

The beach is divided into two sections by the posh Salinas Yacht Club, bulging out into the harbor one block from the main plaza. The west side, lined with apartments, is nicer; to the east. you'll have to put up with boats and water-skiers in your horizon. Locals hawk car radios and umbrellas for rent on both sides. Watch for an old set of dock pilings on the eastern side, in front of the Banco Pichincha, lurking just below the surface at high tide.

Addresses are confusing in Salinas: not only do most streets have both a name and a number, but the Avenida numbers also change without warning. For example, Avenida 3 is commonly called General Enriquez, but only east of the Yacht Club—to the west, it's called Avenida 2. To top it off, neither the number nor name is posted in most cases.

Entertainment

During the high season, just follow your ears to the disco of your choice. The rest of the year, there are fewer weekend options. **El Zafari** on the Malecón is a current favorite. **Flintstone's Rockabar** (Gallo and Cuadra)

Sea salt is extracted by evaporation at the Ecuasal lagoons.

© JEAN BROWN

attracts a more eclectic crowd with its pool tables and funky decor.

Recreation and Tours

Various types of **boats** can be rented for toodling or zooming around the harbor, from clunky paddleboats to small motorboats and Jet Skis. **Surfing** equipment and information are available at the **Tropical Surf Shop** and the **Surf and Sport Surf Shop,** both on the Malecón.

Salinas occasionally hosts world **sportfishing** competitions, and several agencies are happy to take up the business in between. **Pesca Tours** (Malecón at Hotel Barceló, tel. 4/244-3365 or 4/277-2391, fishing@pescatours.com.ec) has an office that would have made Papa Hemingway proud, plastered with hundreds of photos of grinning, sunburned clients next to fish larger than they are. Day charters start at $400, lunch or drinks extra.

To take a tour and see the shorebirds that gather at the lagoons left from the Ecuasal salt-extraction plants about five kilometers southwest of town, look for **Ben Haase** at the Oystercatcher Bar (Enriquez Gallo between C 47 and C 50, tel. 4/277-8329). He charges $40 for a morning trip with up to 10 people.

Accommodations

Cheap rooms are few and far between in this resort town, and rates can rise by as much as 50 percent during high season. A double at the **Hotel Albita** (Av. 7 between Calles 22 and 23, tel. 4/277-3211 or 4/277-3042) costs $16 with private bath, fan, and a hammock on the balcony. During the low season, rooms at the **Hostal Las Rocas** (Calle 22 and Av. 3, tel. 4/277-1096) go for as low as $30 for a five-bed guestroom. A second-floor balcony catches the sea breeze, but unfortunately, someone's TV always seems to be on at full volume. **Cocos** on the Malecón (tel. 4/277-4349) offers clean, comfortable rooms with air-conditioning for $15 pp, and it has an attractive restaurant on the ground floor to boot.

The **Hotel Yulee** (Malecón at Calle 16, tel. 4/277-2028) is a family-oriented place that evokes an old mansion, with a courtyard opening onto a plant-filled plaza with umbrella tables. Rooms are $25 s, $50 d in high season with private bath, air-conditioning, and cable TV, and a few rooms with fans are all cheaper out of season. The **Las Olas** (Av. 5 and Calle 17, tel. 4/277-2526 or 4/277-2501) also has spotless lodgings with private bath, TV, and fan for $15 s, $30 d.

For a bit more cash, the **Hotel Francisco 1** (Gallo and Calle 20, tel. 4/277-3544 or 4/277-4106) is small and tasteful. A pool and outdoor bar/restaurant complement rooms with cable TV, air-conditioning, and phone for $37 s, $49 d. **El Carruaje** (Malecón 517, tel./fax 4/277-4282) is known for its excellent restaurant. Fourteen rooms with sea views, air-conditioning, and cable TV run $39 s, $60 d ($31 s, $51 d without the view).

If you have a broader budget, look for the round gate of the **Hotel Calypsso** (tel. 4/277-1992 or 4/277-2425, fax 4/277-1483, calypsso@gye.satnet.net), on the Malecón at Calle 30. Rooms in this luxury high-rise, which includes a pool, gym, and sauna, are $80 s, $98 d.

Food

It should be no surprise that Salinas's Malecón teems with classy seafood restaurants. You can't miss **Mar y Tierra** at the intersection with Calle 37—it's decked out like a pirate ship, complete with cannon ports, a crow's nest, and servers dressed like sailors. Entrées like pasta range $4–15. The **Restaurant Los Helechos** at Calle 23 is less upmarket, but still a popular choice, and a whole meal won't cost more than $5.

Cozoli's Pizza, next to Mar y Tierra, serves pizza by the slice ($1 with a soda), and the **Trattoria Tony Pizzeria** (on the Malecón at Calle 19) makes tasty wood-oven pizzas and pastas for about $4. The **Perla del Pacífico,** on the Malecón at Calle 20, is your basic *chifa* with meals for about $3.

In this equatorial sun, ice cream has never looked so good—so **Il Gelato** and **Pingüino** on the Malecón do booming business, as does **Mardi Gras Frozen Daquiris** (Av. 3 and Calle 19). The **city market** area, along Calles 17 and 18 between Avenidas 3 and 5, features a dozen or so inexpensive eateries frequented by everyone; **La Lojanita** is famous throughout Ecuador. Finally, a few **mini-markets** stock the usual beach supplies, plus a few edible odds and ends.

Information and Services
Try the **Banco del Pacífico** (Av. 3 between Calles 18 and 19) to change travelers' checks and some foreign currencies. For incoming boaters, the **Capitanía del Puerto** is on the Malecón at Calle 30, and the **tourist information office** has a semi-open office in the same area. The **post office** is on Av. 2 and Calle 17.

Transportation
To get to La Libertad or Guayaquil, go to Avenida 7 and flag down a *selectivo*, a type of small bus, or a shared taxi, sometimes called *taxi rutas*. The shared taxis tend to be quicker as they travel only on certain roads to set destinations. The big buses are not allowed into Salinas during the day, so go to Libertad to connect for Guayaquil or the northern beaches.

Punta Carnero
The other walk of life in Salinas lies along the southern side of the peninsula's western tip. Crashing waves and empty sand stretch for kilometers in either direction. Two hotels next door to each other offer very comfortable accommodations overlooking the ocean: the **Hotel Punta Carnero** (tel. 4/294-8057, $49 s, $73 d) and the **Hostería del Mar** (tel. 4/294-8077, $25 s, $40 d). Both have pools, restaurants, discos, and bars.

LA LIBERTAD AND VICINITY
Only slightly more useful from the tourist's perspective than its neighbor Santa Elena, La Libertad still bears the scars of the last El Niño season, when the Malecón washed away. Even though La Libertad is the largest city on the peninsula (pop. 60,000) and its transportation hub, it's still mainly used as a stopover. Although there are a few spots where you could swim, you probably wouldn't want to.

On the whole, the city doesn't feel very safe and has somewhat of a reputation for crime. Fortunately for locals, its busy port and thriving markets keep the economy going.

Accommodations and Food
The **Costa del Oro** (tel. 4/277-9444) has nice rooms ($15 pp) up past the church, toward the new shopping mall and to the right. If your budget is tight, try **Portofino** (Guerra 226 and 9 Octubre, tel. 4/278-5473), with rooms from $7 pp with fans or $12 with air-conditioning. The thatched-roof **Restaurant La Isla**, on the Malecón at Bodero, gets at least the breeze off what used to be the beach. Basic Ecuadorian meals are less than $2. On Avenida 2 is the inevitable **Chifa Taiwan**, with rice dishes for $3–4 and seafood for up to $8.

Transportation
Both CICA (Costa Azul) and CLP (Cooperativa Libertad Peninsular) run a few **buses** to Guayaquil every hour. CLP's are Brazilian-made and especially comfortable. These days, they work in tandem, with departures every 10 minutes at the terminal on the main street, starting before dawn until 10 P.M. Transportes Esmeraldas has evening buses to Quito ($10). To head north along the coast, go about one kilometer south of the center to the "mini" *terminal terrestre* on Montenegro. *Selectivos* (small buses) with various companies drive west on 9 de Octubre toward Salinas.

Baños de San Vicente
If the beach doesn't leave you relaxed enough, try out this small complex of thermal baths (6 A.M.–6 P.M. daily, $1 pp) a few kilometers east of La Libertad. For the full treatment, there's a pool, sauna, and therapeutic mud pit, and half-hour hot-mud massages are $4. Look for the billboard advertising the *baños* east of La Libertad. Accommodations at the **Hotel Florida** onsite are $15 pp with meals.

Museo "Los Amantes de Sumpa"
One kilometer west of Santa Elena, this small complex (9 A.M.–1:30 P.M. and 2:30–5 P.M.

Thurs.–Tues., $1 pp) has a wide variety of displays on five pre-Hispanic coastal cultures. Archaeological exhibits, a full-size traditional *campesino* house, and a Manteño balsa sailboat are all part of the collection. Two hundred sets of skeletons were unearthed in a local cemetery in the 1970s, including the "Lovers of Sumpa," the well-preserved skeletons of a man and woman in an 8,000-year-old embrace. Even though the descriptions are only in Spanish, it's an excellent museum and well worth a stop. A small gift shop sells traditional crafts, such as tagua-nut carvings. Any bus or shared taxi heading east of La Libertad can drop you off nearby.

PLAYAS AND VICINITY

The nearest resort destination to Guayaquil is still a fishing town at heart. Balsa rafts crafted in the ancient style slip into the waves at dusk to ply the waters of the southern point and the Golfo de Guayaquil. Playas is a dusty, very Ecuadorian resort town that's busiest January–April and on weekends year-round. It's less popular than its glitzy cousins to the west, but more bearable as a result. At night, the gazebo in the triangular main plaza is softly lit by lanterns. Robberies and assaults have been reported on the beach at night, so stay inland after sunset.

Playas's layout is a confusing spider web of streets, many of which have more than one name—but everything travelers need is near the main plaza and church at the intersection of Garay and Guayaquil, two blocks up from the beach.

Recreation and Entertainment

The town's gently curving **beach** has showers and changing rooms available for a fee and is popular with surfers. A new Malecón has just been built, and strolling along it during the early evening is a local pastime. For the real low-down on the local wave scene, stop by Restaurant Jalisco and ask for Juan Gutierrez, the president of the Playas Surf Club. He's a friendly guy with a wealth of knowledge, and

he's very patient with those who speak little Spanish.

For even less of a crowd, make your way about five kilometers west along the dirt road to **Punta Pelada,** backed by cacti-studded cliffs. Surfers in search of handmade balsa boards should ask around for Andreas, an ex–Peace Corps volunteer.

D'Alex, facing the Banco Pichincha, is the place to wiggle your hips to salsa, especially on Fridays and Saturdays. **No Santo,** next to the Rincon de Mary, is the hip disco in town; it attracts all the in youngsters. **Oh Sole Mio,** near the Hotel Rey David, has live Latin music nightly under a giant thatched roof, and it really hops on weekends.

Accommodations

Playa's lodging options are slim. The **Hotel Playas** (tel. 4/276-0611), next to the Cabaña Típica on Jambelí near the beach, offers pure drinking water and a restaurant facing the ocean. Rates are $15 d with private bath and fan, and $30 with air-conditioning. Heading one block east brings you to the **Hotel Rey David** (Malecón and Calle 9, tel. 4/276-0024), where good rooms with ocean views, air-conditioning, and private bath cost $25 d.

Food

Don't pass through Playas without eating at one of the seafood cafés strung along the beach. Each is indistinguishable from its neighbors, except for the address and the person it's named after, but the fruits of the ocean can be quite tasty at any of them—try the *ostras* (oysters) and *conchas* (conchs). The rustic **Cabaña Tipica** restaurant on the beach serves great ceviche.

Back in town, the **Restaurant Jalisco** (Paquisha and Av. 7) is a local favorite, with simple Ecuadorian meals and ice-cold drinks for about $3. The **Casa de Marie and Gabriel** has fresh-baked pies, pastries, and cakes, next door to the tumbledown hotel Miralgia. For sandwiches, snacks, and fruit salad, try **Sabory Yogurt,** near the church (burgers are $2). Vegetarians will appreciate Middle Eastern options like falafel and tabouli for $3 at **El**

Rincón de Mary, on Roldos between the beach and the main plaza.

Los Ajos, by far the best place to eat in Playas, with an extensive menu and prices $4–8 (except lobster when it is in season), has relocated next to the "Parque Infantil" and is worth a visit.

Information and Services

The tiny **post office** is on Garay near the bus office, and the **Cabañas Telefonias** on Garay near Guayaquil are available for phone calls. There are a few Internet cafés in the center of town. If you're very patient, the **Banco de Guayaquil** (Guayaquil and Gilbert) will eventually change your travelers' checks, and it also has an ATM.

Transportation

Frequent buses to **Guayaquil** ($2, two hours) leave with Transportes Villamil (Gilbert and Guayaquil) and Transportes Posorja (near the church and main plaza). Cooperativa 9 de Marzo sends rattletraps to **Posorja** from the intersection of Guayaquil and Alexander. The easiest way to travel between Playas and either Santa Elena, La Libertad, or Salinas is to take a Guayaquil-bound bus and change in Progreso.

East of Playas

The road down to the southern tip of the peninsula at Punta Arenas is known as the Data Highway, because it passes through two towns called Data de Villamil and Data de Posorja. For the first 10 kilometers along the coast, the highway is lined with hotel complexes and vacation homes on the shore side, an interesting contrast with the shacks and salt flats on the other side. Signs for public-access lanes to the beach pop up every few kilometers.

Numerous *hosterías* have laid claim to a section of beach for the benefit of vacationers looking to escape Playas. A good example is the **Los Patios** (tel. 4/276-1115), near kilometer 1.5. Rooms are $16 s, $30 d with private bath, air conditioning, and hot water, and the hotel offers a restaurant and private parking. About one kilometer farther along, the Swiss-run **Hostería Bellavista** (tel. 4/276-0600) is more comfortable for $48 s, $60 d with phone, TV, and air-conditioning. This quiet, well-run place has two pools, a squash court, a sauna, and horses available for rent on the weekends for $10 per hour.

The road elbows left at Data de Posorja, near the onion-domed Convento Santa Teresa, before reaching the fishing village of **Posorja.** Looking across the narrow Canal del Morro toward the Isla de Puna, Posorja is a crusty, working-class town dependent on the whims of the sea. Surprisingly homey accommodations are available at the **Hostería Posorja** (tel. 4/276-4115), on the point at the end of town. The terrace over the water and a bar that oozes character might be reason enough to come all the way out here. Rates are $5 pp with private bath and fans. Plans are underway to build an eco-complex on the **Isla de Puna;** meanwhile, there are ferry services, or the local fishermen will take you there to camp on the wide white beaches under the palms. Local women will even cook food for you.

Guayaquil and Vicinity

Once upon a time, the largest city in Ecuador had a bad reputation. Just listen to how Paul Theroux described it in *The Old Patagonian Express:* "Visitors to Guayaquil are urged to raise their eyes, for on a clear day it is possible to see the snowy hood of Mount Chimborazo from the humid streets of this stinking city; and if you look down, all you see is rats." It was not a pleasant place.

But Guayaquil (pop. 4 million) has seen vast improvements since the turn of the millennium. Safety has greatly improved, shopping and nightlife options have greatly expanded, new museums are opening left and right, and the restored Malecón and Las

To Botanical Gardens, Daule, and Manta

PARQUE HISTÓRICO GUAYAQUIL

GUAYAQUIL

BUS TERMINAL

MALL DEL SOL

JARDÍN DE LA SALSA

MI COMISARIATO SUPERMARKET

HILTON COLÓN GUAYAQUIL

Urdesa

AIRPORT

CC ALBAN BORJA

CC POLICENTRO

PLAZA DANIN

Nueva Kennedy

KENNEDY/ ESTRADA

CLINICA KENNEDY

STADIUM

TRAIN STATION

Duran

To Cerro Blanco and Santa Elena Peninsula

STADIUM

Las Peñas

To Machala and Riobamba

SALINAS

MALECÓN DEL SALADO

9 DE OCTUBRE

SEE "GUAYAQUIL CENTER" MAP

SUCRE

PARQUE DE LOS IGUANAS

MALECÓN 2000

MILAGRO

QUITO

PORTETE

AVILES

BUCARAM

Estero Salado

TUNGURAHUA

25 DE JULIO

CENTRO CÍVICO

EL ORO

TRUJILLO

MOSQUERA

VIA PERIMETRAL

JARAMILLO

COMIN

Isla

Santay

Río Guayas

BOSCO

AVE DE LAS ESCUELAS

25 DE JULIO

Estero del Muerto

Estero Santa Ana

COMIN

AGUILERA

PORT AUTHORITY

CALDERON

0   1 mi

0   1 km

© AVALON TRAVEL

VIA PERIMETRAL

ORTIZ

LAS AGUAS

MUNOZ

TOLA

MARENGO

ORELLANA

AVENIDA DE LAS AMÉRICAS

Río Daule

VIA PERIMETRAL

Río Babahoyo

PUENTE DE LA UNIDAD NACIONAL

Río

GUAYAQUIL

Peñas District are among the most successful urban renewal projects in the country. The new Puerta Santa Ana, at the north end of Las Peñas on the site of the old brewery, is a gleaming new development. Restaurants, museums, apartments, and a hotel are in the works, with plans for a yacht marina-this is rapidly becoming the place to be. Guayaquil has officially left the "best-avoided" list and entered the "spend-a-few-days" list.

The vibe is Caribbean here, not Andean—in large part because of the city's diverse racial mix of *indígenas,* Asians, mestizos, and black Ecuadorians—and local priorities include enduring the climate and enjoying yourself.

The city sits on the west side of where the Ríos Babahoyo and Daule meet to form the deep, tidal Río Guayas, only 56 kilometers long, before it empties into the Golfo de Guayaquil. Water in the streets is common, because the city is only an average of four meters above sea level. Various *esteros* (inlets) snake off into the salt flats to the west, outlining countless mangrove-bordered islands.

Guayaquil has always been a prototypical port city, and today, it's Ecuador's most important commercial center and the largest port on this side of South America. Close to half of the country's industry is based here, and almost all of its agricultural products depart for cities around the world.

HISTORY

Guayaquil was founded in 1537 by Francisco de Orellana to replace an original settlement to the east, which had been destroyed repeatedly by native tribes. According to some, the city was named for Santiago de Guayaquil (St. James) because it was refounded on his festival day; whereas the more romantic recall the story of the Huancavilca chief Guayas and his wife, Quil, who killed themselves rather than fall into the hands of the Spanish.

Guayaquil was one of the most important ports in the Spanish South American empire during the 16th and 17th centuries, second only to El Callao near Lima. This fact didn't escape the notice of pirates like Captain Morgan, who obliged by sacking and pillaging at will. By the 18th century, the tropical climate made the area a breeding ground for almost every disease imaginable. Typhoid fever, dysentery, malaria, yellow fever, and even bubonic plague spread quickly through the population, helped by streets that were flooded for months out of the year and an almost complete lack of sanitary facilities. Rats were as common as children in the streets and in many homes, and regular fires raged through the closely packed wooden buildings.

The turn of the 20th century brought some relief, when the United States threatened to withhold traffic from the newly completed Panama Canal if Guayaquil didn't clean up its act. A crack team of doctors sent by the Rockefeller Foundation organized municipal works and sanitation campaigns to make the place more livable.

The second half of the 20th century saw huge numbers of people flow into Guayaquil in response to various economic booms along the coast—most notably the banana blitz of the 1950s. All these people had to find somewhere to live, and because Guayaquil is surrounded by nothing but marshes and salt flats, overcrowding has become a serious problem. Sprawling *suburbios,* poor and squalid settlements, have been staked out on quick-and-cheap landfills covering various inlets and even part of the Río Guayas itself.

ORIENTATION

The city center is all business, with executives crowding the sidewalks and gleaming high-rises facing the river. Occasional colonial housefronts—more common in the barrio of Las Peñas—break this monotony with scrolled grillwork along pastel balconies and latticed windows. Traffic can be a nightmare, so walking is your best bet. Note that some street names change partway along, especially in the northeast section of Guayaquil's center near Las Peñas.

More swank residential suburbs spread north and west, including La Garzota, Sauces, and Alborada. Nueva Kennedy and Urdesa are the two most visited, offering plenty of restaurants, nightclubs, and shopping areas, but little lodging. Most tourists come at night for the action, but the suburbs are a welcome relief from the chaos of the city center. East of the airport, the impressive Puente de la Unidad Nacional spans the Ríos Daule and Babahoyo over to Duran.

CLIMATE

One hotel brochure describes Guayaquil's climate as "deliciously tropical." That isn't exactly the modifier I'd have picked, but I guess "humid as hell" wouldn't sell many tour packages. Temperatures hover around 30°C year-round, so the important variable becomes the amount of moisture in the air. January–March brings 12–15 days of precipitation per month on average. April and May are more bearable, until the sun comes out during the June–December "dry" season. Still, the lack of rain doesn't mean no water in the air; humidity is the rule, regardless of the season.

THE GENERALS MEET

The only time the two greatest leaders in Latin America's independence struggle met was in Guayaquil in 1822. Simón Bolívar and José de San Martín, both celebrated generals, had corresponded during the battle but had never met face to face. Bolívar the Venezuelan operated in the north, whereas San Martín, from Argentina, fought to the south.

Each man had his own issues to settle. San Martín, who requested the meeting, was more concerned with immediate issues, such as the fate of Guayaquil, fought over by Peru and Colombia. Bolívar's thoughts were focused on his precious idea of Gran Colombia, a united South America under one government.

True to style, Bolívar took charge of the meeting from the start. He reportedly rushed from Quito to reach Guayaquil before San Martín, who was on his way north from Peru.

When San Martín arrived, Bolívar welcomed him warmly to "Gran Colombian soil," and at a banquet that night raised a toast to "the two greatest men in South America." What happened at the meeting itself, though, may never be known, because the generals' private aides were not admitted. Because most accounts were written by Bolívar or his supporters, surviving versions of the encounter are probably skewed – but the general consensus is that San Martín, no match for El Libertador's fiery personality, yielded completely.

That night, as Bolívar whirled the ladies at a grand ball, San Martín left the city quietly for Peru. There he resigned his official title of Protector and sailed to Europe, leaving the fate of South America in Bolívar's hands. Today, the largest statue on Guayaquil's riverfront commemorates the meeting.

© JEAN BROWN

La Rotunda commemorates the meeting of the two liberators of South America.

GUAYAQUIL

SAFETY CONSIDERATIONS

With some of the worst poverty in Ecuador, Guayaquil has had serious problems with crime. Don't walk around downtown at night any more than you have to. (Remember, taxis are cheap.)

SIGHTS
C Malecón 2000

Guayaquil's riverside avenue parallels the brown Río Guayas for the entire length of the city center. Starting out as a small port in what is now the Las Peñas neighborhood, Guayaquil's waterfront gained a boost with the construction of its first wharf by president Vicente Rocafuerte. After the Maritime Port was constructed to the south in 1963, the riverfront area stopped being the city's economic and social center and slid into a period of deterioration.

Locals, then, are rightfully proud of the Malecón 2000 (www.malecon2000.com, 7 A.M.–midnight daily), a monumental undertaking that has given the former heart of the city a complete facelift. If you've been here before, you probably won't even recognize it: The 2.5-kilometer pedestrian walkway, now spotless and well-guarded, has been extended out over the river and is decorated with fountains, bridges, and modern sculptures. Shopping centers, crafts markets, restaurants, movie theaters, and an ecological park are all functioning, the South Market Building (a.k.a the "Palacio de Cristal"), built by famed French engineer Gustave Eiffel in 1907, will become a museum and site for tourism fairs. The Banco Central's **Museo Antropológico y de Arte Contemporaneo** (tel. 4/230-9400, 10 A.M.–5 P.M. Tues.–Sat., 11 A.M.–4 P.M. Sun., $1.50), also referred to by its initials (MAAC), has moved its collection here at the northern end close to Las Peñas, while still focusing on archaeology, coastal cultures, and contemporary art.

Next door, the **IMAX movie theater** also houses a historical museum in its circular ground floor. For $2.50, you can listen to the tales of the founding and growth of the city and admire the excellent dioramas.

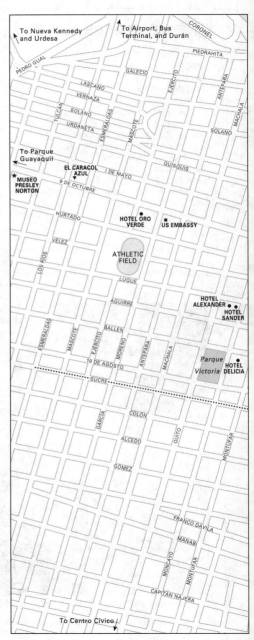

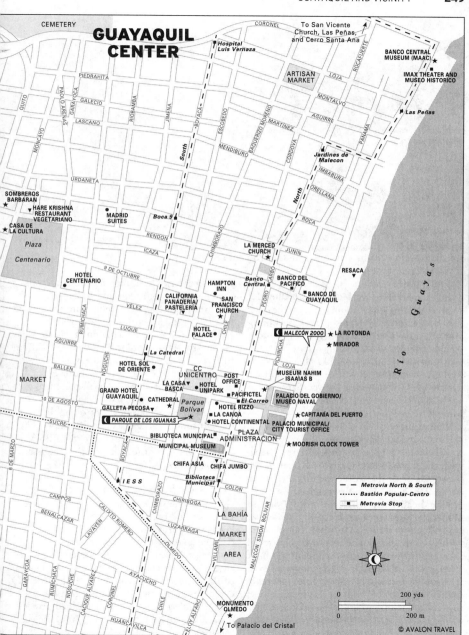

GUAYAQUIL

GUAYAQUIL CENTER

CEMETERY

CORONEL

To San Vicente Church, Las Peñas, and Cerro Santa Ana

Hospital Luis Vernaza

BANCO CENTRAL MUSEUM (MAAC)

PIEDRAHITA

QUITO

PALO Y ABENA

GARAYCA

GALECIO

LASCANO

MONCAYO

RIOBAMBA

JIMENA

South

BOYACA

ESCOBEDO

BAQUERIZO MORENO

MARTINEZ

MENDIBURO

CORDOVA

ARTISAN MARKET

LOJA

MONTALVO

AGUIRRE

PANAMA

ROCAFUERTE

IMAX THEATER AND MUSEO HISTORICO

Las Peñas

Jardines de Malecon

IMBABURA

URDANETA

North

ORELLANA

ROCA

SOMBREROS BARBARAN

HARE KRISHNA RESTAURANT VEGETARIANO

CASA DE LA CULTURA

Plaza

Centenario

MADRID SUITES

Boca 9

RENDON

ICAZA

CHIMBORAZO

LA MERCED CHURCH

JUNIN

RESACA

Río Guayas

HOTEL CENTENARIO

9 DE OCTUBRE

CALIFORNIA PANADERIA/ PASTELERIA

HAMPTON INN

Banco Central

BANCO DEL PACIFICO

PEDRO CARBO

BANCO DE GUAYAQUIL

RUMICHACA

VELEZ

SAN FRANCISCO CHURCH

LUQUE

HOTEL PALACE

CHILE

MALECÓN 2000

LA ROTONDA

MIRADOR

AGUIRRE

La Catedral

PICHINCHA

LOJA

BALLEN

NOGUCHI

HOTEL SOL DE ORIENTE

CC UNICENTRO

POST OFFICE

MUSEUM NAHIM ISAAIAS B

MARKET

10 DE AGOSTO

GRAND HOTEL GUAYAQUIL

LA CASA BASCA

HOTEL UNIPARK

PACIFICTEL

El Correo

PALACIO DEL GOBIERNO/ MUSEO NAVAL

SUCRE

CATHEDRAL

GALLETA PECOSA

Parque Bolívar

HOTEL RIZZO

LA CANOA

CAPITANÍA DEL PUERTO

6 DE MARZO

PARQUE DE LOS IGUANAS

HOTEL CONTINENTAL

PALACIO MUNICIPAL/ CITY TOURIST OFFICE

BIBLIOTECA MUNICIPAL

MUNICIPAL MUSEUM

PLAZA ADMINISTRACION

MOORISH CLOCK TOWER

BOYACA

CHIFA ASIA

CHIFA JUMBO

CHIMBORAZO

IESS

Biblioteca Municipal

COLÓN

CAMPOS

CALIXTO ROMERO

CHIRIBOGA

LA BAHÍA

BENALCAZAR

LAVAYEN

LUZARRAGA

MARKET AREA

VILLAMIL

MALECON SIMON BOLIVAR

GARAYCA

RUMICHACA

NOGUCHE

CACIQUE ALVAREZ

CORONEL

AYACUCHO

OLMEDO

CHILE

ELOY ALFARO

Metrovía North & South

Bastión Popular-Centro

Metrovía Stop

HUANCAVILCA

MONUMENTO OLMEDO

To Palacio del Cristal

0   200 yds

0   200 m

© AVALON TRAVEL

© JEAN BROWN

Malecón 2000 ends by Las Peñas and Cerro Santa Ana.

The southern end of the Malecón's central stretch is marked by the **Monumento Olmedo,** commemorating José Joaquín Olmedo, the city's first mayor and a celebrated poet. Continuing north past the **Centro Commercial Malecón,** you'll reach the unmistakably ornate **Moorish Clock Tower** (8:30 A.M.–4:30 P.M. Mon.–Fri., free) The octagonal structure is the latest incarnation (1931) of an original tower that dated to 1770, and it is being refurbished as part of the Malecón 2000 project.

One of the prettiest sights in the city is the three-masted sailboat *Guayas,* often parked at the Capitanía del Puerto, which shares a berth with the Naval Yacht Club. The boat docks here occasionally between year-round training cruises for Ecuadorian Navy cadets.

The beautiful, white-on-gray **Palacio Municipal** does not resemble most Ecuadorian government buildings: It's ornate but tasteful, with Corinthian columns supporting an arched interior passage with a glass ceiling. It was built 1924–1928 in the Italian Renaissance style. The subdued design is echoed in the **Palacio del Gobierno** to the north, enclosing the model ship collection of the **Museo Naval** (tel. 4/232-4274, ext. 23, 8:15 A.M.–noon and 1–4 P.M. Mon.–Fri., free). Bilingual guides are available.

Between the two buildings, a pedestrian walkway is home to fountains and the pigeon-covered **Monumento Sucre** and forum sculpture celebrating the founding of the city.

Although it's not actually on the Malecón, the **Museo Nahim Isaias B.** (tel. 4/232-4182, 10 A.M.–5 P.M. Mon.–Fri., 10 A.M.–2:30 P.M. Sat., $1.50) is easily reached from the Plaza de la Administracion. It houses well-presented exhibits on colonial art in its deliciously air-conditioned passages. The next stop along the river is **La Rotonda,** at the end of 9 de Octubre. The stately, semicircular monument depicts Bolívar and San Martin's historic meeting (see the sidebar *The Generals Meet*).

Las Peñas and Cerro Santa Ana

Guayaquil's historic heart has been newly restored at the base of Cerro Santa Ana. Las Peñas was part of the original Guayaquil settlement, and the barrio still boasts the largest concentration of historic architecture in the city. A narrow, cobbled street separates beautifully restored wooden houses and gardens. **Calle Numa Pompilio Llona,** lined by cafés and art galleries, was lovingly cleaned up and repainted as part of the Malecón 2000 project, leading to the new Santa Ana project.

© JEAN BORWN

Moorish Clock Tower, gift of the Lebanese residents of Guayaquil

Steps at the entrance lead up to the **Plaza Colón,** where two cannons point mutely at the MAAC (before the expansion of the Malecón, they pointed at the water) to commemorate local resistance to a 1624 raid by Dutch pirates. Las Peñas's **Iglesia de San Vicente** (Rocafuerte and Coronel) is the oldest church in the city, originally founded in 1548. After numerous fatal fires, this version was erected in 1938.

Las Peñas and Cerro Santa Ana are much safer than they used to be—municipal police are all over the place—but it's best to stick to the renovated areas all the same. To get there, take the new Metrovia northbound to the Las Peñas stop, then continue about 100 meters; it's across the Malecón.

The new feather in Guayaquil's cap is this hill, which rises above Las Peñas. Once a dangerous and run-down place, Cerro Santa Ana has been spruced up into a state that's part genuine, part Disney. Brightly painted buildings built of wood and corrugated iron line a 466-step staircase that leads

to the Plaza de Honores, with great views of the city. The restaurants, cafés, nightspots and balconied colonial houses are all quite pretty—look closely, though, and you'll see the judicious use of plastic and the slums still seething beyond the gates and numerous armed guards.

Just below the summit plaza is the **Museo El Fortin de Santa Ana,** which encloses the remains of a fortress built in 1629 to protect the city from pirates. On the plaza is the small **Capilla Santa Ana** and a **lighthouse** that you can climb up to for even better views. The nearby **Historical Museum,** in the basement of the IMAX theater, has a series of well-lit dioramas detailing the development of the city, with push-button commentary in English or Spanish (open daily, $3).

Puerto Santa Ana

At the northern extension of **Calle Numa Pompilio Llona,** and at the foot of Cerro Santa Ana, this bright new development includes three museums. One, built on the site of the country's first brewery, illustrates the history of brewing in Ecuador. Another is dedicated to Ecuadorian football (soccer), telling the tale of the formation of the different local teams—and, of course, the national team, which made it to the World Cup playoffs in 2006. They were eliminated by the English team, but their triumphal return home closed down the city for hours. More recently, in July 2008, the Quito football team known as LIGA defeated the Brazilian team Fulmanense on Brazilian home ground and won the "Copa de los Libertadors" a major shock to the Brazilians. This victory resulted in an all-night party in Quito beginning the afternoon that they returned with the cup. Look for more information on LIGA at the museum as well.

Romantic singer **Julio Jaramillo,** Guayaquil's famous son and father of many, has a museum all to himself (10 A.M.–5 P.M. Wed.–Sun., $1.50). Here, you can cry along with the locals as you listen to the lyrics about broken hearts and lost loves.

◖ Parque de los Iguanas

Not the biggest, but certainly the most interesting, park in Guayaquil, this pleasant plaza is presided over by a monument to Bolívar shaded by 30-meter trees. Almost tame reptiles slither down out of the branches to snap up lettuce and other goodies left by hotel workers around noon each day. Kids especially love the iguanas, squealing as the reptiles joust for scraps and stride down the paths like they own the place. Look carefully, and you might also spot a sloth among the leaves. A fish pond with dozens of turtles and a red squirrel (which can be tempted with patience and grapes) complete the menagerie.

Municipal Museum

The Municipal Museum, located nearby in the Biblioteca Municipal on Sucre between Chile and Carbo (tel. 4/252-4100, 9 A.M.–5 P.M.

Tues.–Sat., free), focuses on the region's history. Its recently renovated collection features everything from archaeology to modern art. Every Saturday, a free two-hour historical tour of the city starts at 11 A.M. and 3 P.M. Tours are also available on weekdays and Saturday afternoons with at least five people and advance reservations.

Plaza Centenario and Beyond

Spanning four square blocks, Guayaquil's main plaza is one of the largest in the country. A **Monument to the Heroes of Independence** includes four statues representing heroism, justice, patriotism, and history. On the west side, at 9 de Octubre, the **Casa de la Cultura** (tel. 4/230-0500) features a museum of Ecuadorian art and archaeology with an impressive collection of gold artifacts, and free educational movies at 7 P.M. on Wednesdays.

OIL AND WATER: QUITO VS. GUAYAQUIL

Like jealous siblings, Ecuador's two largest cities have a long history of sniping at each other over everything from economy to attitude. The rivalry embodies many of the differences – both real and imagined – between the chilly Sierra and the sweltering coast.

Although both cities were founded near the middle of the 16th century, Quito remained the nexus of the country's economic, social, and political spheres well into the 1900s. Once Guayaquil got itself cleaned up enough, its crucial position in the country's economy became undeniable (although residents have always complained about how much of the money earned here ends up in Quiteño pockets). As the seat of government, Quito still runs the country and is the self-proclaimed cultural capital. But although the oil boom has refocused some economic light on the Andean city, Guayaquil is Ecuador's thumping coastal heart.

More pervasive differences can be found in the attitudes of the residents. After a few drinks, an outspoken Quiteño may let on how he considers Guayaquil a dirty, violent, crime-infested town populated by undisciplined *monos* (monkeys). For their part, Guayaquileños simply shrug and call it lack of pretense. Better that, they say, than going through life "polite, prompt, and dull," like their Andean neighbors. Life is short – besides, who'd want to live in a city where the restaurants all close by 10 P.M.? As the saying goes, "Spend your days in Quito and your nights in Guayaquil."

The disparity has been milked by presidential campaigns, from Rodrigo Borja's (Quito) defeat of Abdalá Bucarám (Guayaquil) in 1988 to Sixto Durán Ballén's (Quito) victory over Jaime Nebot (Guayaquil) in 1992. More recently though, Rafael Correa, a native of Guayaquil but more associated with the highlands, has been trying to maintain a balance between the two. The economy also promises to pit the feuding cities against each other in the near future: Quito is currently feeling the advantage of increased oil prices and flower exports, while Guayaquil is enjoying a small agricultural boom in bananas, coffee, and quality chocolate.

Continue west on 9 de Octubre to Carchi, and you'll encounter the new **Museo Presley Norton** (tel. 4/229-3423, free). It celebrates an Ecuadorian entrepreneur, journalist, archaeologist, and bon vivant who, until his death in 1993, worked to raise general awareness of pre-Inca cultures. Continue west again, and you'll arrive at the **Malecón del Salado,** the salty sister of the Malecón 2000. It once bordered a dirty and unsafe district of the city, but after a spectacular cleanup, it's now home to many clubs, bars, cafés, and restaurants— go for the evening, and stay half the night if you wish. Taxis cruise the area until dawn to return you to your hotel.

Other Sights

Guayaquil's **cemetery,** at the north end of the city center, is called the Ciudad Blanca (White City), and even a quick drive past will show you why. Blindingly clean mausoleums make up an ornate city of the dead, sheltering the corpses of the wealthy in better housing than most of the city's living residents could ever hope for. More than 200 marble statues overlook the graves of some 630,000 people. This is another somewhat dodgy area, so try to go during the day and in a group, and don't wander too far from the entrance.

The Ecuadorian Orchid Society opened the **Botanical Gardens** (tel. 4/256-0519, 8 A.M.–4 P.M. daily, $3) in 1989. A significant percentage of Ecuador's lengthy orchid list is represented, planted among shady paths and artificial streams. The five-hectare plot, heading northwest out of town, lies in the Urbanización de Los Orquideas, about 15 kilometers north of the city center. It's most easily reached by a taxi ($7, 30 minutes) or with an organized tour.

On the eastern bank of the Río Daule, in the Cantón Samborondón, the 20-acre **Parque Histórico Guayaquil** (tel. 4/283-3807, www .parquehistorico.com, 9 A.M.–4:30 P.M. Wed.– Sun., $3, $4.50 Sun. and holidays) re-creates life—both human and animal—near the turn of the 20th century. A raised walkway leads visitors through the endangered wildlife zone, where you might spot one of 50 species of birds, mammals, or reptiles. Deer, tapirs, monkeys, sloths, wild cats, and harpy eagles all avoid the midday sun, making morning and afternoon best for visits. Displays in the reconstructed rural hacienda and 19th-century suburb show the crafts and crops of the coastal zone a century ago. Tours are available in Spanish and English, and visitors can peruse the museum, restaurant, and cafeteria at their leisure. Samborondón is a natural extension of Guayaquil between the two rivers: New developments include an equestrian club, a hippodrome with regular races, and motocross and carting arenas.

ENTERTAINMENT AND EVENTS
Nightlife

Guayaquil offers plenty to keep locals and visitors busy after dark. Countless **discos and bars**—mostly concentrated in the outer neighborhoods—hum into the early hours with every kind of crowd imaginable. Las Peñas is a relatively new addition to the local scene, with its recent renovations and increased police presence. (If the atmosphere where you are doesn't suit you, try next door.) Many larger hotels, like the Oro Verde and Unihotel, have discos and **casinos** as well.

The **Centro de Eventos El Jardín,** on Avenida de Las Americas north of the airport, can—and sometimes does—hold 5,000 gyrating dancers. **Resaca** on the southern end of the Malecón near Junín, is a good place to grab a drink with views of the waterfront.

Other popular discos include **Chapos,** at Estrada and Las Monjas, and **Santé,** on Orellana next to the Hilton Colón. The intriguingly named **Ojos de Perro Azul** ("eyes of the blue dog") is in the growing district known as the *Zona Rosa* (surrounding Montalvo between Rocafuerte and Panama), where LGBT clubs and nightlife raves last till the wee hours. Guayaquileños move with the time, and their favorite spots change quickly. Take a tip from the locals and check www.farras.com, a bustling website with information on all the latest nightlife.

GUAYAQUIL

Cinema and Theaters

Listings for close to a dozen **movie theaters** appear in *El Telegrafo* and *El Universo*, Guayaquil's two major papers (see the sidebar *Guayaquil's Movie Theaters*). This is also where you'll find information on theatrical performances at the **Centro Cívico**, along 25 de Julio south of the city center. **Centro Cultural Sarao** (Ciudadela Kennedy) has innovative dance and theater performances on Fridays and Saturdays. Several other cultural centers also advertise in the local papers.

The Malecón is now home to the only **IMAX theater** (tel. 4/256-3069, www.imaxmalecon2000.com) in South America. Large-format movies are shown in Spanish daily.

Festivals

Carnival in Guayaquil includes the usual melée of flying water, paint, and mud. July 24–25, **Bolívar's Birthday** combines with the **Foundation of Guayaquil** for one of the city's largest celebrations, including the "Pearl of the Pacific" beauty contest and various cultural events. Another combination celebration occurs October 9–12 for the **Independence of Guayaquil** and **Columbus Day/Día de La Raza.**

SHOPPING

Guayaquil's **main market** is technically bordered by 10 de Agosto, Ballén, 6 de Marzo, and Garzacocha, but new regulations are forcing it indoors. (This is an area where caution is wise, especially at night). **La Bahía,** near the Malecón north of Olmedo, is more of a black market. All kinds of goods, from shoes to refrigerators, arrive in a tax-free, semi-legal way.

Various **shopping centers** cater to more choosy browsers. Unicentro is north of the Parque Bolívar in the city center. Urdesa has the Centro Commercial Río Centro, and Nueva Kennedy has two malls named Policentro and Plaza Quil. The Unicentro mall borders the Parque Bolívar, and the popular C.C. Alban Borja is north of Urdesa. The only thing more exciting to Guayaquileños than the Malecón 2000 is the **Mall del Sol,** a gigantic American-

style mall—the largest in the country—that boasts 150 shops, a food court, and a 10-screen cinema. It's four kilometers north of downtown in the Vernaza Norte suburb, near the airport. It is so successful that there many other popular malls have followed: Take a taxi to **Mall del Rio, Mall del Sur, Mall San Marino, Riocentro Los Ceibos,** or **Riocentro Entre Rios,** which all have restaurants, cinemas, and the compulsory air-conditioning.

For *artesanías* like paintings and sculpture, try the Las Peñas district. An **artisan market** occupies the block south of Loja between Moreno and Córdova. Out of 250 or so shops, a handful sell quality items, including woven hats and bags and leather work. It's not Otavalo, but the selection is good. It's open 9:30 A.M.–6:30 P.M. daily. Other

---

GUAYAQUIL'S MOVIE THEATERS

- **Cinemark:** Mall del Sol, tel. 4/269-2015

- **Cinemark:** Mall del Sur, tel. 4/208-5110

- **IMAX:** Malecón 2000, tel. 4/256-3078

- **Maya:** Las Lomas and Dátiles, tel. 4/238-6456

- **Metro:** Boyacá, tel. 4/232-2301

- **Supercines:** C.C. Plaza Mayor, tel. 4/224-4986

- **Supercines:** 9 de Octubre and Rumichaca, tel. 4/252-2054

- **Supercines:** Riocentro Entre Ríos, tel. 4/283-1234

- **Supercines:** Riocentro Los Ceibos, tel. 4/285-2790

- **Supercines:** San Marino, Orellana y Plaza Dañin, tel. 4/208-3268

- **Supercines Sur:** Riocentro Sur, tel. 4/243-9290

Otavalan goods are sold in many shops and stalls around the San Francisco church. There's another artisan market at the southern end of the Malecón.

Sombreros Barbaran, on 1 de Mayo half a block west of the Parque Centenario, sells Panama hats made in Montecristi. If you'd like to pick up a Guayasamín painting while you're here, head to the **Man-Ging Art Gallery** (111 Cedros), just off Estrada. Its excellent work is worth a visit, even if you're just browsing.

TOURS

In addition to trips aboard the *Galapagos Explorer II,* **Canodros** (Urb. Santa Leonor, Solar 10, tel. 4/228-5711, U.S. tel. 800/613-6026, fax 4/228-7651, canodros@canodros .com, www.canodros.com) arranges visits to its celebrated Kapawi Ecolodge in the southern Oriente.

Galasam (9 de Octubre 424 and Córdova, Ed. Gran Pasaje, tel. 4/230-4488, fax 4/231-1485, www.galasam.com.ec) sells some of the city's least expensive tours to the Galápagos. Galasam can also take you, deep-sea fishing, scuba diving, and to the Manglares Churute reserve, as well as just around town.

Chasquitur (Acacias 605 and Las Monjas, tel. 4/288-8988, fax 4/238-8987, chasquitur@ yahoo.com) is recommended for earth-friendly trips, including visits to Manglares Churute Ecological Reserve and bird-watching in several locations around Guayaquil. Whale-watching tours are available July–September, and dolphin-watching is possible in the mangroves year round.

Several other companies offer the standard mix of Galápagos, Sierra, and Oriente ventures: **Kleintours** (Alcivar, Mz. 410, Solar 11, Kennedy Norte, tel. 4/268-1700, fax 4/268-1705), **Ecuadorean Tours** (9 de Octubre 441 and Chile, tel./fax 4/232-6670), and **Metropolitan Touring** (Calle 11 NE 103 and Av. 1 NE, tel./fax 4/228-6565).

You can book half-day tours of the Botanical Gardens and the Parque Histórico Guayaquil through the Hotel Sol de Oriente for $20.

The Municipalidad (tel. 4/253-1691 or 4/252-4200) offers free tours of the city's historic sites. A small fleet of roofless, double-decker "Visión" **tourist buses** make the rounds of the Malecón, Las Peñas, and the major parks and plazas. Ninety-minute tours leave every two hours from the Plaza Calderón, at the south end of the Malecón, on weekends and holidays for $5 pp. You can buy tickets onboard at the three Malecón stops.

ACCOMMODATIONS
Under $10

For the largest city in the country, Guayaquil has a sad dearth of decent budget hotels. The well-run **Hotel Delicia** (Ballén 11–05 and Montúfar, tel. 4/232-4925) is one of the most popular, which explains why it's usually full. Clean rooms run $8 with fan and $12 with a/c, including private bath and TV.

A bit out of the center of town, but worth the trip, is the **Ecuahogar Youth Hostal** (tel. 4/224-8357, fax 4/224-8341). Shared rooms in the four-floor building are $20 s, $25 d, dorms $10 pp including breakfast (ISIC discount). Try to get a room on the top floor for the views. The hostel has cable TV and a VCR, and it runs city tours. It's on Avenida Isidro Ayora near the airport; to get there, take a taxi or bus 2 from the bus terminal. Also popular is **Dreamkapture** (Alborada 12th Etapa, Mz. 02, v 21, tel. 4/224-2909). It's a little hard to find, but located on a quiet street with a plunge pool in the garden. Rooms with either fans or air-conditioning run $10–18 pp.

$10-25

Rooms with private bath, TV, and fans at the **Hotel Sander** (Luque 1101 and Moncayo, tel. 4/232-0030 or 4/232-0944) are $12 s, $15 d. It's clean and well-run. One of the best values in this category is the **Madrid Suites** (Quisquis 305 and Rumichaca, tel. 4/231-4992), a safe, inexpensive and clean place with air-conditioned rooms for $15 pp.

The **Hotel Centenario** (Vélez 728 and Garaycoa, tel. 4/251-5578, fax 4/232-8772) overlooks a park of the same name. Rooms with air-conditioning and cable TV are $11–15 pp. It has a popular restaurant and disco.

$25-50

The **Hotel Alexander** (Luque 11–07 between Moncayo and Quito, tel. 4/253-2000 or 4/253-2651, hotelalexander@hotmail.com) is a good value at $30 s, $37 d, with in-room phones, cable TV, and air-conditioning. At the **Hotel Rizzo** (Ballén 319 and Chile, tel. 4/232-5210, fax 4/232-6209), all 60 rooms have air-conditioning, TV, and phone, and they include a continental breakfast for $36 s, 40 d.

The **(Tangara Guest House** (Sáenz and O'Leary, Ciudadela Bolivariana, Bloque F, Casa 1, tel. 4/228-4445 or 4/228-2828, fax 4/228-4039) is the first real standout in this midprice category. Operating under the slogan "Budget Accommodations for Upmarket Travelers," the friendly Perrone family runs the tastefully appointed place as if guests were staying in their own home. Six rooms run $39 s, $56 d (10 percent SAE discount), and a fully equipped kitchen is available. It's between the airport and the bus station; ask your taxi driver to head for Ciudadela Bolivariana.

$50-75

An Asian motif winds through the **Hotel Sol de Oriente** (Aguirre 603 and Escobedo, tel. 4/232-5500 or 4/232-8049, fax 4/232-9352). Accommodations ($59 s, $69 d) include buffet breakfast, and the Great Wall restaurant is open to all.

$75-100

The renovated **Hotel Palace** (Chile 214–216 and Luque, tel. 4/232-1080, fax 4/232-2887, info@hotelpalaceguayaquil.com.ec) provides good security and travel assistance for $94 s, $120 d. Its restaurant receives repeat applause. Tucked behind the cathedral **Grand Hotel Guayaquil** (Boyacá 1600 and 10 de Agosto, tel. 4/232-9690, U.S. tel. 800/989-0025, fax 4/232-7251, grandhot@grandhotelguayaquil .com, www.grandhotelguayaquil.com) has it all: 180 luxury rooms with cable TV, a sports complex with two air-conditioned squash courts, a lushly landscaped pool, and two restaurants. Rates are $90 s, $96 d, suites $150.

$100-200

Guests at the elegant **(Unipark Hotel** (Ballén 406 and Chile, tel. 4/232-7100, U.S. tel. 800/447-7462, fax 4/232-8352, unipark@oroverdehotels.com) can amuse themselves for days without ever leaving the building. It's attached to the Unicentro shopping mall, which features a casino and video arcade. The Unipark has El Parque French restaurant, the Unicafe, and the upstairs Unibar, which specializes in sushi and sports a view of the Parque Bolívar. You'll also find a gym with a hot tub and sauna. Reception is on the second floor. Rates for the 139 rooms are $134 s, $146 d.

At **Hotel Oro Verde** (9 de Octubre and Moreno, tel. 4/232-7999, fax 4/232-9350, reservasgye@oroverdehotels.com), guests enjoy 192 rooms and 62 suites with air-conditioning, satellite TV, and VCR. There's also a gourmet deli, a casino, three restaurants, a piano bar, a fitness center, and a partridge in a pear tree (not really). Rates start at $146 s, $152 d.

There are three top-notch restaurants at the **Hotel Continental** (Chile and 10 de Agosto, tel. 4/232-9270, U.S. tel. 800/333-1212, fax 4/232-5454). One of them, El Fortin, has won international gourmet awards. Rooms go for $182 s, $194 d.

Over $200

A 10-story atrium is only the beginning of Guayaquil's newest luxury digs, the **Hilton Colón Guayaquil** (tel. 4/268-9000, fax 4/268-9149), five minutes from the airport on Orellana in the Ciudadela Kennedy Norte. It also has 274 rooms and 20 suites with climate control and noise-insulated windows, cable TV, and phones. Downstairs there's a casino, a gym, a pool, five restaurants, and a 24-hour café. Rates are $364, and reservations can be made in the United States (tel. 800/445-8667).

FOOD

Most of Guayaquil's best restaurants are in the ritzy suburbs and the more expensive hotels in the city center. Breakfast can be difficult to locate: The most popular morning meal in the city seems to be an *empanada* and carrot juice from a sidewalk vendor. You can also try the extensive breakfast buffet at the Pepa de Oro in the Grand Hotel Guayaquil ($6.50), or one of the small places on 9 de Octubre across from the U.S. Embassy. The website www.quecomoahora.com helps Guayaquileños choose their restaurant for the night. It features most of the best restaurants in town, with menus and sometimes prices, and updated addresses and telephone numbers assure that diners arrive without hassle.

Asian

Sucre and Chile is Guayaquil's *chifa* corner. The **Chifa Jumbo** and **Chifa Asia** are your usual budget eateries with nothing on the menu more than $7. For slightly more money, you can't top the ambience—shark-fin soup and cats in the potted plants—at the **Gran Chifa** (Carbo 1016 near Sucre). Entrées here are $2–5. You'll spot lots more *chifas* in this area. **Tsuji** (Estrada 813 and Guayacanes in Urdesa) is the classiest Japanese establishment in town. A meal will set you back around $15–20, and you can stick around for karaoke afterward.

Ecuadorian

Restaurant 1822 at the Grand Hotel Guayaquil comes recommended as a within-reason splurge, with a classy atmosphere and fantastic plates, including steak and seafood starting at $6. **Lo Nuestro** (Estrada 903 and Higueras) offers midpriced Ecuadorian fare in Urdesa for $5–15, with Italian entrées on the inexpensive side. **La Canoa** (Chile between 10 de Agosto and Ballén), near the Hotel Continental and the Oro Verde's **El Patio,** also offers Ecuadorian fare at slightly higher prices. **Café de Teri** (Hermano Miguel and Rolando Pareja) only serves Ecuadorian breakfast, but a huge variety of them—keep eating until lunchtime if you wish. You can get a huge, fresh bowl of ceviche for a hangover, or try the *bolones de verde* to really fill an empty stomach.

Lunch and Snacks

On the ground floor of the Unicentro mall, the cheerful **Unicafe** has lunch plates in the $4–7 range. If you want, you can choose your own *trucha* from the live tank. The **Pepa de Oro** coffee shop/cafeteria in the Grand Hotel Guayaquil serves a wide range of juices and empanadas.

The **Galleta Pecosa** bakery, at 10 de Agosto and Boyacá turns out some of the best pastries you'll find in Ecuador; try an $0.80 *borrachita* ("little drunkard"), a chocolate truffle-style pastry moist with raisins and liquor. For bread and other treats, stop by the **California Panadería/Pastelería** on Urdaneta, between Jimena and Boyacá or Velez and Escobedo.

Seafood

Gourmets swear by one of Guayaquil's most expensive eateries, the Chilean **El Caracol Azul** (9 de Octubre 1918 and Los Ríos). Here on the coast, **crab houses** *(casas de cangrejo)* are a way of life, brimming with beer and hungry patrons up to their elbows in crustaceans. Ask at your hotel for the current favorites. The **Red Crab** (Estrada and Laureles in Urdesa) is a high-class place with prices to match, but you can still get ceviche for just $5. **Sushi No bar** in the Centro Comercial San Marino comes highly recommended as the best place for good rolls.

Steak Houses

The huge ◖ **La Parillada del Ñato** (Estrada 1219 and Laureles in Urdesa, tel. 4/238-7098) is famous throughout Ecuador for its mammoth portions and is always packed. Filet mignon is $7, and vegetarians can get a great pizza for $3.50.

Vegetarian

For a healthy, inexpensive meal, try **Hare Krishna Restaurant Vegetariano** (tel. 4/230-5862), on the northwest corner of the Parque Centenario. It serves a variety of Ecuadorian, Chinese, and Western plates for $3–4.

A shawarma is just over $3 at **Maalik Al Shawarma** (811-B Estrada in Urdesa), and falafel is only $1.50 Almost across the street is the **Café al Sindibad** (Estrada and Guayacanes), featuring shawarma ($3) and water pipes with flavored tobacco.

Other International

The 🄲 **Trattoria de Enrico** (Balsamos 504 and Ebanos in Urdesa, tel. 4/238-7079) has received multiple awards from a national gastronomic club for being the best restaurant in the country. Don't be scared off by the waterfall and fish ponds at the entrance—you can get pasta here for as little as $6, although an entire meal can run up to $30. The ambience is hard to beat, making this Italian star worth a splurge.

A good wine selection and reasonably priced Spanish delicacies set apart **La Tasa Vasca,** a restaurant and tapas bar at Baquerizo Moreno and 9 Octubre. A *paella de Valencia* goes for $6–7, as do most other dishes on the restaurant's constantly evolving menu.

Fans of French cooking should inspect the award-winning **Le Gourmet** at the Hotel Oro Verde, where dinner will set you back at least $15. Mexican favorites at **Viva Mexico** (Estrada and Datiles in Urdesa) run $4–6 per plate. Dinner, tapas, cocktails, or just a nice glass of wine or whisky are all available, along with a great river view, at **Arturo's,** at the northern end of Calle Numa Pompilio Llona in Las Peñas.

INFORMATION AND SERVICES
Money

Head to Pichincha and Icaza near the Malecón to find the **Banco del Guayaquil** and the **Banco Pichincha,** both of which have ATMs and offer credit-card cash advances. **Cambiosa** (9 de Octubre 113 and Malecón) will change travelers' checks at a high commission, although it's better than what you'll find at the airport. You can also change money at **Delgado Casa de Cambio,** between Chimborazo and Chile.

American Express (tel. 4/239-4984) is on the second floor at 9 de Octubre 1900 and Esmeraldas, and **MasterCard** (tel. 4/256-1730)

has an office in the Edificio San Francisco at Córdova and 9 de Octubre. There's a 24-hour **Western Union** office (Guillermo Pareja Rolando 56, tel. 800/937-837) in the Edificio de Bronce in the Alborada neighborhood, as well as a branch in the Centro Comercial Malecón.

Communications

The **post office** is in the building bordered by Ballén, Aguirre, Carbo, and Chile. **Internet cafés** are everywhere, especially in malls like Unicentro, along Estrada in Urdesa, and along 9 de Octubre downtown.

Health

The **Clínica Kennedy** (San Jorge between 9a and 10a, Nueva Kennedy, tel. 4/228-6963) is the hands-down first choice among Guayaquil's foreign community for its specialists and emergency services.

Other Services

The **immigration office** out by the bus terminal (tel. 4/229-7004 or 4/229-7197) can give extensions on visas and answer other border-related questions. The **Ministry of Tourism** (Orellana in Ciudadela Kennedy, across from the World Trade Center, 9 A.M.–5 P.M. Mon.–Fri.) is staffed by helpful English-speaking employees. There's also an office at the airport with friendly staff. The **city tourist office** (tel. 4/252-4100, www.guayaquil.gov .ec, 9 A.M.–5 P.M. Mon.–Fri.) in the Palacio Municipal stocks more general information about the city and area.

For maps, stop by the **Instituto Geográfico Militar** (Quito 402 and Solano, tel. 4/239-3351).

TRANSPORTATION
Land

If you're feeling left out because you haven't been ripped off by an Ecuadorian **taxi** driver yet, you can solve that within a few hours in Guayaquil. Trips within the downtown area should cost about $1, and don't pay more than $4 to go to Urdesa, the airport, or the bus

GUAYAQUIL CONSULATES AND EMBASSIES

Most Guayaquil consulates and embassies are open 9 A.M.-noon or 1 P.M. Monday-Friday.

- **Austria:** Circunvalación Sur 718, tel./fax 4/238-4886
- **Belgium:** Avenida de las Ameritas s/n y Joaquin Orrantia, Edif. TC Television, piso 3, tel. 4/283-3374
- **Bolivia:** Cedros 100 and V.E. Estrada, Urdesa, tel. 4/288-5790
- **Brazil:** Av. del Periodista 312 and 3 Este, Nueva Kennedy, tel. 4/228-0846, tel./fax 4/229-3046
- **Canada:** Joaquin Orrantia y J. Tanca Marengo, Ed. Nobis Centro Ejecutivo, tel. 4/229-6837
- **Chile:** 9 de Octubre 100 and Malecón, Ed. Banco Previsora, piso 23, of. 3, tel. 4/256-2995
- **Colombia:** Orellana, Edif. World Trade Center, Torre B, piso 11, tel. 4/263-0674
- **Denmark:** Córdova 604 and Mendiburu, tel. 4/230-8020
- **Finland:** Urdaneta 212 and Córdova, tel. 4/256-4268
- **France:** José Mascote and Hurtado, tel./fax 4/284-8314
- **Germany:** Las Monjas and Arosemena, km 2.5, Ed. Berlin, tel. 4/220-0500

- **Holland:** Quisquis 1502 y Tulcan, piso 1, tel. 4/228-0156
- **Israel:** 9 de Octubre 729 y Boyaca, piso 4, tel. 4/232-2555 or 4/232-2000
- **Italy:** Icaza 423 y B. Moreno, Ed. Banco de Machala, tel. 4/256-8358
- **Japan:** Km 11.5 via a Daule, tel. 4/225-3055
- **Norway:** Malecón del Salado 106 and Todos los Santos, tel. 4/238-9610
- **Panama:** Mz208.V28 M.H. Alcivar y J. Rolando Coello, tel./fax 4/228-5984
- **Peru:** Orellana, Edif. Porta, piso 14, tel. 4/228-0114
- **Spain:** 9 de Octubre 100 y Malecon, piso 29, tel. 4/256-1340
- **Sweden:** Km 6.5 via a Daule, tel. 4/225-4111, fax 4/225-4244
- **Switzerland:** Tanca Marengo Km 1.8 and Castillo, Edif. Conauto, piso 5, tel. 4/268-1900, ext. 034
- **United Kingdom:** Córdova 623 and Solano, tel. 4/256-0400
- **United States:** 9 de Octubre 1571 and García Moreno, tel. 4/232-3570
- **Venezuela:** Chile 329 and Aguirre, piso 2, tel. 4/232-6579 or 4/232-6566

GUAYAQUIL

terminal, except at night. Ask at your hotel about how much you should expect to pay to your destination before hopping into a cab.

Traffic downtown makes **local buses** worth it only for journeys out of the downtown area. All buses have fares (usually about $0.25) and numbers posted in the front window, and most post the destination in the window. Bus number 52 heads north up the Malecón to Urdesa frequently, and number 2 passes the same way for the airport and bus terminal. Numerous buses pass the Centros Commerciales Policentro and Alban Borja and the Mall del Sol. Bus number 13 also goes to the malls.

A new rapid transit system whisks commuters across town in its own private lane, passing the crawling traffic during rush hours and leaving even the weaving taxis in the dust. The northern terminus of the shiny new **Metrovia** is across six lanes of speeding traffic from the new bus terminal—just like the locals, take your life in your hands and sprint across when the lights are red. (Plans for a bridge or underpass are a long way off. "Not this year" is what the Foundation Coordinator told me, and probably not next year either.) This first line runs right through the downtown area, with regular station stops, then runs along beside the immaculate Barrio Centinario and into the Guasmo, where three-wheeled motorbike taxis rumble over the ruts in the unpaved streets. A second Metrovia line is under construction; it will also whisk passengers out of the congested heart of the city, but in a westerly direction on Calle Sucre.

Guayaquil's new combination **bus terminal** and shopping mall is just north of the airport. It's clean, efficient, and the pride of the city. Buy your ticket at one of the 80 windows and head up the escalator to the gate to catch your bus. Rides depart for just about every city in the country. Quito is eight hours and $8 away. CIFA buses direct to Piura and Sullana, Peru, leave four times a day for $9 (nine hours). Ormeño buses direct to Lima, Peru, leave daily at 11:30 A.M. from Avenida de Las Americas at Centro Comercial El Terminal Bahia Norte, oficina 34 (tel. 4/229-7362). Oroguayas taxis offers direct service to Machala from Ballén between Carbo and Chile for $10 pp (four can fit in one taxi).

Renting a car in Guayaquil is expensive, starting at around $50 per day before insurance, tax, or gasoline. If you find that a car is absolutely necessary, however, some major companies include: **Avis** (Av. Kennedy and Av. de Las Americas, C.C. Olímpico, tel. 4/228-5498, fax 228-5519), **Budget** (Av. de Las Americas 900 and Andrade, tel. 4/228-4559), and **Localiza** (Francisco Boloña 713, tel. 4/239-5236). All three also have airport offices, along with several other companies: **Avis** (tel. 4/216-9092) **Budget** (tel. 4/228-8510), **Expo** (tel. 4/216-9088), **Localiza** (tel. 800/562-254), **Rentauto** (tel. 4/390-4520), and **Seretur** (tel. 4/216-9184).

Air

Head north of the city center on Quito to Avenida de las Americas to reach the new **Jose J. Olmedo International Airport** (tel. 4/216-9000). Tickets for international flights are available from any of the numerous travel agencies in the city or at the airline offices. The international departure tax is $25 pp. The new

the new rapid transit Metrovia terminal

© JEAN BROWN

facilities include luggage storage where you can leave you bags for up to five hours for $3.

TAME flies to Quito 10–12 times daily ($87 one-way); to Cuenca daily ($66); to Loja daily except Saturdays ($80); to Esmeraldas daily ($100); to Lago Agrio Monday–Saturday ($120); to Macas via Quito daily except Saturdays ($120); to Tulcán via Quito on Monday, Wednesday, and Friday ($120); to Manta twice a day except Saturdays ($72); to Baltra twice daily ($312–355); and to San Cristóbal, in the Galápagos, on Tuesday, Friday, and Sunday ($312–355). Note that only Galápagos residents can buy one-way tickets.

Aerogal flies to Quito daily ($67); to Cuenca daily ($60); to Baltra daily ($312–355); and to San Cristobal on Monday, Thursday, Saturday, and Sunday ($312–355). **Icaro** flies to Quito daily ($66) and operates the Galápagos charter flight on Saturdays. **Vipsa** operates a smaller plane to Quito weekdays and to Salinas on Tuesday, Friday, and Sunday.

About two kilometers south of the main airport is the small aircraft terminal, where other airlines, air taxis, and charters leave for coastal cities like Bahía de Caráquez, Machala, and Esmeraldas.

GUAYAQUIL AIRLINE NUMBERS

- **Aeca:** tel. 4/228-8110
- **Air France/KLM:** tel. 4/216-9068, reservations 4/216-9050
- **American Airlines:** tel. 4/256-6458
- **Avianca:** tel. 800/003-434
- **Continental Airlines:** tel. 800/222-333
- **Copa:** tel. 4/230-3211
- **Delta:** tel. 800/101-060 or 4/600-5300
- **Iberia:** tel. 4/232-9558 or 4/232-9382
- **Japan Airlines:** tel. 4/288-9789, reservations 4/238-5108
- **Lan:** tel. 4/259-8500, reservations 800/101-075
- **Lufthansa:** tel. 4/259-8060
- **Santa Barbara:** tel. 4/216-9108 or 4/216-9109
- **TACA/Lacsa:** tel. 800/008-222, reservations 4/232-1007
- **TAME:** tel. 4/256-0728, reservations 4/256-0778
- **United Airlines:** tel. 4/256-0822
- **Varig:** tel. 4/229-0429, reservations 4/229-5153

Water

The **ferry to Durán** has been discontinued until the train is rehabilitated, but if you want to go out on the river, the boat **Pirata Morgan** (located a few of blocks north of the Palacio de Cristal on the Malecón) takes customers for rides up and down the river in front of the Malecón. On weekends, there are regular sailings to the **Isla de Puna** at the mouth of the Guayas river, departing from the **Puerto Fluvial** facing the bus terminal—across the same six lanes of speeding traffic that separate the Metrovia, but on the river side. Isla de Puna was an original settlement of the pre-Colombian Huancavilca tribe and is still thought of by many as a haunt for modern-day pirates.

NEAR GUAYAQUIL
Cerro Blanco Protected Forest

This may well be the only nature reserve you'll ever encounter that owes its existence to the enlightened attitude and conservation efforts of a cement plant. Only 15 minutes southwest of downtown Guayaquil, Cerro Blanco (tel. 4/287-1900, 8:30 A.M.–5 P.M. daily, $4 pp, $3 to camp) protects 6,000 hectares of tropical dry forest in the Chongón-Colonche hills under the auspices of the El Cemento Nacional, which in turn profits off the plentiful limestone in the area.

The almost 200 species of birds in Cerro Blanco include many waterfowl and the endangered great green macaw, the symbol of the reserve. Its nests (the first of which was found in 1994) are closely guarded by park personnel. Morpho butterflies flash their iridescent turquoise wings by day, howler monkeys earn their name in the evenings, and crab-eating raccoons dip into water pools by night.

An interpretive center stands next to well-furnished campgrounds and the starting point for two trails: the short loop, Quebrada Canoa; and the longer, scenic Buenavista path. Hiring a park guide ($7–12) is required on three of the four trails, which range one–four kilometers. The only one you can do on your own is the short Avenida de los Aves, leading to a butterfly garden. There's also a rescue center for injured animals near the plant nursery.

To get to Cerro Blanco, take any bus to Chongón or toward the Santa Elena Peninsula from the main terminal. Look for the large sign just before the cement plant, about 15 kilometers from Guayaquil near the community of Puerto Hondo. It's a short walk from there to the information center. You can also drive yourself or take an expensive taxi ride.

◖ Manglares Churute Ecological Reserve

This coastal reserve 45 kilometers south of Guayaquil safeguards 50,000 hectares of mangroves from the ravages of shrimp farming. The tangled plants cover 67 percent of the park's area, and along with the surrounding salt flats provide shelter for a wide range of shorebirds, such as laughing gulls, roseate spoonbills, ospreys, herons, egrets, and ibis.

Manglares Churute (8 A.M.–6 P.M. daily, $10 pp) is one of the few places in Ecuador to see horned screamers (the feathered kind). January, when water levels in the many shallow *lagunas* are highest, is the best time to view waterfowl. Inland stretches of dry tropical forest in the coastal Cordillera de Churute shelter white-fronted capuchin and mantled howler monkeys, along with the occasional agouti, tigrillo, and armadillo.

At the park's **information center,** you can view videos and arrange for maps and guides for walks into the reserve. Four relatively short trails lead downhill to the mangroves and up into the dry peaks of the Cerros El Mirador and Masvale. Guides ($5) are required, and they speak only Spanish. Boats to explore the mangroves, with room for up to 12 people, can be hired for $12 per day.

The road between Guayaquil and Machala passes the entrance to the reserve. Look (or ask) for the administrative center on the west side, near the pueblo of Churute, 26 kilometers south of where the road splits at Boliche (itself 26 kilometers east of Durán). Not all drivers know it, so make sure yours knows exactly where you want to go, or you may get dropped off in the middle of nowhere. Alternatively, you can book a tour of Manglares Churute through Chasquitur in Guayaquil.

Zoo El Pantanal

Once a private menagerie, this zoo (tel. 4/226-7047, zooelpantanal@hotmail.com, 9 A.M.–5 P.M. daily, $3 pp) is now open to the public. The collection includes at least 60 species, many of which are endangered, with enough crocodiles to satisfy any budding herpetologists. The zoo is located 23 kilometers north of Guayaquil on the road to Daule.

DURAN

Once important because of its position as the end of the Quito and Guayaquil Railway, this rather dismal town still provides a large part of the workforce for Guayaquil. Thousands commute daily across the two bridges that span the confluence of the rivers Daule and Babahoyo. Each year in September, Duran hosts an international fair that showcases new products and ideas. Each evening during the fair, concerts draw thousands of Guayaquileños across the river to salsa dance or be serenaded by famous Latin American artists and bands.

Machala and Vicinity

Sometimes it seems as if every major human settlement has its claim to fame, from the City of Brotherly Love to the Largest Ball of Twine East of the Mississippi. The capital of El Oro Province proclaims itself the Banana Capital of the World—and it's easy to see why, with *El Bananero* (a statue of a giant banana grower) welcoming you to town. Acre after acre of neatly planted fronds wave in the coastal breeze, and every morning, the beach writhes with freshly caught fish. It seems as if everyone in town turns out to help clean them.

After its founding in 1758, Machala (pop. 205,000) enjoyed a cacao boom in the early 20th century that resulted in most of the economic development of the southern coast, before the yellow torpedo took over in the 1930s. Even the rise of shrimp farming in the 1980s didn't shake the banana's hold—more than one million tons of the fruit leave annually through

Puerto Bolívar, seven kilometers west. Over the decades, these agricultural bonanzas have made El Oro's capital one of the most prosperous and well-kept cities on Ecuador's coast.

Aside from being a place to change buses on your way into or out of the country, Machala offers access to the beaches of Jambelí, along with a wider choice of hotels than in the border town of Huaquillas. It's also the closest large city to the Puyango Petrified Forest, and if you're coming north from Peru, it's the quickest way to get into the Ecuadorian highlands via Cuenca.

ORIENTATION

Machala's streets are oriented diagonally, running northeast–southwest and northwest–southeast. The main thoroughfare, 9 de Octubre, runs along the northeast side of the **Parque Central** and the city's **cathedral.** Head north one block along 9 de Mayo, and you'll find the main **outdoor market.** About five blocks southeast of the market on Olmedo is the **Parque Colón,** and **Parque de los Héroes** is five blocks northwest of the Parque Central.

ENTERTAINMENT AND EVENTS

Machala's **World Banana Fair** slides into town the third week in September, but movies are shown all year round at the **Cine Popular** (Sucre between Guayas and 9 de Mayo). The film selection varies, so you'll probably find better pickings at the **Unioro Mall** on the northeast edge of town, where relatively recent movies are often shown with Spanish subtitles. Take bus number 1 from the Parque Central, or a taxi for about $2. The **Peña de Machala,** on Guayas just north of the Parque Central, has live music every night.

ACCOMMODATIONS

Many travelers crossing the border prefer to spend the night here rather than in Huaquillas, and with good reason—Machala is a much more pleasant place. Budget rooms with private baths and air-conditioning have been recommended at the friendly **Hostal Mercy** (Junín between Olmedo and Sucre, tel. 7/292-0116) for $6 pp with fan, $7 with a/c; and at the **Hotel Mosquera Internacional** (Olmedo between Guayas and Ayacucho, tel. 7/293-1752) for $14 s, $22 d with a/c and cable TV.

The **Hotel Ecuatoriano** (9 de Octubre and Colón, tel. 7/293-0197 or 7/296-2077) has large rooms with private baths and air-conditioning for $15 s, $26 d. Accommodations at the **Hotel Rizzo** (Guayas 2123 and Bolívar, tel. 7/293-3651) run $30 s, $55 d. It has a pool, disco, restaurant, casino, and private parking.

Luxury travelers should steer toward the **(Hotel Oro Verde** (Circunvalación Norte and Calle Vehicular V7, tel. 7/293-3140, fax 7/293-3150, ovmachala@oroverdehotels.com), surrounded by tropical gardens in the Unioro suburb 10 minutes out of town. It has 58 rooms and 12 suites for $120 s, $134 d. Gourmands can sample La Fondue Swiss restaurant, as well as a café and gourmet deli.

FOOD

In Machala itself, **Don Angelo** (9 de Mayo at Rocafuerte) scores points for its breakfasts and large portions, and for being open 24/7. Seafood and pasta dishes average around $3. Also try the **Chifa Central** (Tarquí between 9 de Octubre and Sucre), where the air-conditioning is set on "arctic" and nothing will cost you more than $5; and the **Cafetería Americana** (Olmedo between Guayas and Ayacucho), which serves reasonably priced Ecuadorian food.

Chesco Pizzeria (Guayas 1050, tel. 7/293-6418), half a block north of the Parque Central, has good pizzas starting at $4. (It also delivers.) Full *almuerzos* are only $2 at **El Paraíso de la Vida** (tel. 7/293-0218), a vegetarian restaurant on Ayacucho at 9 de Octubre.

The short hop to **Puerto Bolívar** is well worth it for the wide selection of fresh seafood. When three places right next to each other all advertise the "best ceviche in the world," it can be hard to choose—but hey, that also makes it hard to go wrong. It's a five-minute cab ride ($3) or a 10-minute bus ride ($0.25) from the Parque Central.

INFORMATION AND SERVICES

Exchange travelers' checks at **Delgado Travel,** on 9 de Mayo near the plaza. There's also a **Banco del Pacífico** (Rocafuerte and Junín) and half a dozen other banks along the Parque Central. For border matters, stop by the **Peruvian Consulate** (Urb. Unioro, Mz 14, v 11, tel. 7/293-7040) in the Unioro neighborhood. For questions about Manglares Churute Reserve, the **Ministry of the Interior** has an office on 9 de Mayo and Pichincha (tel. 7/293-2106).

Machala's **post office** is on Bolívar 733 and Montalvo. Enter the local **tourism office** (9 de Octubre between 9 de Mayo and Montalvo, tel. 7/293-2106, 8 A.M.–12:30 P.M. and 1:30–5 P.M. Mon.–Fri.) through a boutique on the first floor.

TRANSPORTATION

Machala's airport is about one kilometer southwest of the center along Montalvo. From there, you can fly small air taxis to Guayaquil. **TAME** (Montalvo between Pichincha and Bolívar, tel. 7/293-0139) reinstigated direct morning and evening flights to Quito daily except Sundays ($104) in March 2008.

There's no main long-distance bus terminal—just pick your destination and head to the respective *cooperativa* office, concentrated between Junín, Sucre, Colón, and Bolívar. CIFA (Bolívar and Guayas) leaves every 20 minutes throughout the day for **Huaquillas** ($2, 75 minutes). For buses to **Guayaquil** ($4, four hours), visit Ecuatoriano Pullman (9 de Octubre and Colón). CIFA also goes to Guayaquil from 9 de Octubre 627 and Tarquí. Transportes Occidentales (Buenavista and Olmedo) and Panamericana (Colón and Bolívar) both go to **Quito** ($10, 10 hours), and Transportes Loja (Tarquí 1813 and Rocafuerte) heads for **Loja** ($6, six hours).

Cuenca ($5, 4.5 hours) is also a destination for Rutas Orenses and Transportes Pullman

Sucre and Azuay, both on Sucre between Junín and Tarquí. Cooperativa TAC (Colón 1819 between Rocafuerte and Bolívar) sends buses hourly throughout the day to **Zaruma** ($3, three hours).

Oroguayas taxis run an efficient service to Guayaquil for $10 pp: In three hours, they will deliver you to the door of your hotel in Guayaquil or to the airport. They leave hourly from Guayas and Pichincha (tel. 7/293-4382) as early as 5 A.M. Pay in advance, and they'll collect you from your hotel, too.

NEAR MACHALA
◖ Jambelí

Facing the Golfo de Guayaquil from the northern tip of the Archipelago de Jambelí, this beach resort becomes crammed with Machala's hard-working residents during weekends and holidays. There's little shade on the beach, one of the few south of Guayaquil, but the mangroves and palm trees make it an agreeable spot to stick your toes in the sand.

Jambelí is almost deserted midweek, when you'll have it pretty much to yourself, although many businesses are closed. Inexpensive restaurants and hotels cater to locals and the few foreign tourists who visit. There aren't any cars, and electricity and hot water are not that dependable, but that's part of the charm of the place.

Stay at **Maria Sol** for $8 pp (you can also eat there, plates $3–5). Another food option is **El Niño Turista,** open daily on the main street, with entrées for $3–6. Otherwise, interchangeable kiosks and open-air restaurants line the beach on weekends.

About 10 canoes leave daily from the old pier in Puerto Bolívar, departing every 30 minutes (or when full on weekends) until noon on weekdays and 3 P.M. on weekends and holidays. The trip ($3 pp) through the estuary affords birders some small relief from the brackish heat, with the chance to view a rufous-necked wood rail or yellow-crowned night heron. It costs $0.25 to get onto the island itself.

Puyango Petrified Forest

The largest petrified forest outside of Arizona hides in a small section of the Río Puyango Valley, only seven kilometers from Peru. Trunks of the *Auracaria* trees, whose cellulose has been replaced over millennia by minerals, can reach 20 meters long and almost three meters around. Worm holes are clearly visible in the stone giants, and if you look closely, you can find many other species of Triassic period plants and ferns trapped in surrounding rocks.

A dirt road runs south from Arenillas through Palmales and La Victoria before reaching the village of Puyango 50 kilometers later. Transportes Loja buses from Machala make the trip twice a day ($3, 2.5 hours). There's a visitors center in the village, where you can pay the entrance fee ($5 pp) before crossing the bridge to the reserve (8 A.M.–5 P.M. daily). Buses only go as far as the turnoff; from there, it's an hour's walk to the reserve, or you can arrange transportation with one of the pickup trucks there on weekends. Grabbing a snack in town, you can take the opportunity to ask for directions to a good campsite near the Río Chirimoya.

◖ Zaruma

If you're heading east toward Loja, a short detour via Piñas to the mining country around Zaruma provides a glimpse into the southern Sierra's ancient heart of ore. Spanish King Felipe II decreed the establishment of this town in 1549 to serve as a base for gold extraction, which provided an easy choice of the eventual name for the province itself—El Oro (the gold). With its narrow streets and charming wooden houses, this remote town is one of the prettier places in the southern half of the country.

The lodes have been picked almost clean by now, but visits to the mines can still be arranged—you'll marvel and cringe at the almost prehistoric equipment. Locals can point out a set of **thermal springs** and several orchid gardens in the nearby hills. Lodgings are available at the excellent **Hotel Roland** (tel. 7/297-2800,

$12 pp), which has a swimming pool and great views. The best coffee in Ecuador (or so they say) is freshly roasted in a small shop on the main street into town—just follow your nose. Buses run to Machala often.

Huaquillas

Ecuador's largest southern border town sits across the Río Zarumilla from Aguas Verde in Peru. Peruvians once crossed here regularly to take advantage of lower prices on the Ecuadorian side—now, with inflation and Ecuador's adoption of the dollar, the situation is reversed. Smuggling and bribes are the sport of choice here, and the local police act accordingly, so travelers are advised to pass through this place as quickly as possible and to keep a sharp eye out as they do.

Facilities are marginal, but at least everything is on or near Avenida La República, the main street. The **Grand Hotel Hernancor** (tel. 7/299-5467, 1 de Mayo and Hualtaco, $14–17) is the best bet if you have to spend the night, and **La Habana** (Córdovez and Santa Rosa) serves all meals daily for $3–4 apiece.

To cross the border, get your exit stamp at the Ecuadorian immigration office 4–5 kilometers outside of town. From here, you can cross freely into Aguas Verdes, as the Peruvian side is called. Complete the entrance formalities in the Peruvian immigration office a few kilometers beyond the bridge; taxis waiting to take you farther into Peru will stop here.

Panamericana runs a handful of direct buses to Quito daily ($14, executivo $20, 14 hours), and Ecuatoriana Pullman leaves regularly to Guayaquil ($5, five hours). CIFA has frequent departures direct to Machala ($2, 75 minutes), and now operates four buses a day direct from Guayaquil to Tumbes, Sullana, and Piura in Peru via Huaquillas ($9, nine hours).

If you have the option, the smaller border town of Macará, southwest of Loja (detailed in the *Southern Sierra* chapter) is a much less chaotic place to enter and leave Peru.

SOUTHERN SIERRA

As you head south through the Avenue of the Volcanoes, the topography gradually grows less forbidding, but no less wild. Snowy peaks become less common, the horizon less jagged, the uninhabited stretches between cities longer. By the time you reach Cuenca, Ecuador's "Third City" after Quito and Guayaquil, you'll find that its old-world character fits the scenery perfectly.

The southern highland provinces of Cañar, Azuay, and Loja contain few peaks higher than 4,000 meters, but they still enclose some of the most rugged and diverse landscapes in the country. Ecuador's long-running border dispute with Peru (settled in 1998) centered around the forbidding Cordillera del Condor in the southernmost Amazonian province of Zamora-Chinchipe, and it was the region's inaccessibility (one river was discovered only in 1947) that, along with decades of political posturing, made it almost impossible to determine where one country ended and the other began.

Because of its historical isolation from the rest of the country—major highways didn't connect Cuenca to Quito and Guayaquil until the 1960s—the southern Sierra has held firmly onto its roots. Cuenca's colonial heart still beats strongly after centuries, and older ruins within the city tie it to its pre-Columbian past. Indigenous groups, such as the Saraguros and descendants of the Cañaris, retain traditions that predate even the Inca.

Although the southern Sierra lacks the

HIGHLIGHTS

◖ Catedral Nueva: Cuenca's central park is flanked by the unmistakable sky-blue domes of the cathedral, decorated with beautiful stained glass and a gilded altar (page 272).

◖ El Cajas National Park: Easy access to stunning alpine scenery is only an hour from Cuenca (page 282).

◖ Ingapirca Ruins: Ecuador's most outstanding set of Inca ruins is highlighted by grazing llamas and a sweeping view (page 285).

◖ Podocarpus National Park: This park, near Loja, protects a stunning swatch of the country, from rainforest to *páramo* (page 295).

◖ Vilcabamba: A visit to Ecuador's fabled "Valley of Longevity" may or may not help you live longer, but it will help you unwind, with its hiking trails, cabins, and spas (page 297).

LOOK FOR ◖ TO FIND RECOMMENDED SIGHTS, ACTIVITIES, DINING, AND LODGING.

immense national parks and protected areas of its northern neighbors, outdoor enthusiasts can still get their fill here, from ancient Inca roads to highland lakes and cloud forests.

PLANNING YOUR TIME

Give yourself at least five–seven days to do the southern Sierra justice. **Cuenca's** churches alone are worth almost a full day, and the city itself demands at least a few nights to soak in the venerable ambience. The vistas of lakes and misty hills in **El Cajas National Park** rival any in the country, and intrepid hikers will uncover unique treasures farther south in **Podocarpus National Park,** which stretches from the cloud forest to the upper Amazon. The three-day hike along the lofty Inca Trail south from Achupallas ends at **Ingapirca,** Ecuador's premier set of Inca ruins. All three of these can be visited on your own for the day, but overnight guided trips are also possible.

Cuenca, the obvious travel hub for the region, can be reached by bus from Riobamba (quite a haul, albeit a scenic one) or on the less popular uphill route from Machala. Daily flights connect Cuenca with Quito and Guayaquil. The road connecting the beautiful, tranquil city of **Loja** with the Oriente via Zamora is used even less, but passes through some of the least visited areas in the

SOUTHERN SIERRA

To Guayaquil

Alausi → To Riobamba

Achupallas

Manglares
Churute
Ecological
Reserve

Inca Trail

LOS
PAREDONES
RUINS

Río Paute

To Mendez

Tambo

Cañar

INGAPIRCA RUINS

Naranjal

LAGUNA
TOREADORA
VISITORS CENTER

Biblián

AZOGUES

Isla Puná

EL CAJAS
NATIONAL PARK

CATEDRAL
NUEVA

Paute

Bulcay

Gualaceo

CUENCA

Chordeleg

SOLDADOS
GUARDPOST

San
Bartolome

Sígsig

Río
Gualaceo

Golfo de
Guayaquil

Girón

Jima

Jambeli

MACHALA

PANAMERICANA

Río Zamora

Puerto Bolívar

San Miguel
de Cuyes

Gualaquiza

Pasaje

Huaquillas

Santa
Rosa

Oña

To
Tumbes
and Peru

Arenillas

Saraguro

Cordillera Cordoncillo

24 de Mayo

Saracay

San Lucas

Zaruma

Puyango

El Cisne

Santiago

Yantzaza

PUYANGO
PETRIFIED FOREST

Alamor

Nambija

Celica

Catamayo

LOJA

ZAMORA

Catacocha

CAJANUMA
RANGER
STATION

BOMBUSCARA
RANGER STATION

Río
Catamayo

VILCABAMBA

PODOCARPUS
NATIONAL PARK

Utuana

Sozoranga

Macará

La Tina

Cariamanga

ECUADOR

Zapotillo

To
Sullana

Río Mayo

Amaluza

Las Lomas

Río

PERU

Zumba

Las
Basas

0   15 mi
0   15 km

© AVALON TRAVEL

country. South of Loja, the laid-back village of **Vilcabamba** is about as far from Quito as you can get and still be in the Sierra, but for fans of quiet hikes by day and massages in the evening, it's well worth the distance.

The southern Sierra is usually your first or last glimpse of Ecuador if you're traveling overland via Peru. Huaquillas on the coast and Macará southwest of Loja are the main places to cross the border, and there are smaller, infrequently used border posts at Zapotillo, Amaluza, and Zumba.

Cuenca and Vicinity

Like a trio of siblings, Ecuador's three largest cities have distinct personalities. Eldest Quito is the successful one, dressed up and ready for business. Guayaquil lazes on the coast and stays up late, but somehow makes more money than anyone. Cuenca takes its studies seriously, keeps its pants creased, and always makes the grandparents proud.

The capital of Azuay Province is a pious, dignified city with the most intact colonial character in the country. What some would call stuffy, others call stately—either way, Cuenca seeps reverence from every pore. To dispel any lingering doubt, consider the city's municipal motto: *Primero Díos, Después Vos* ("First God, Then You").

With more than 400,000 inhabitants, Cuenca still has a surprisingly small-town feel—nuns stroll down narrow, cobbled streets, and everyone seems to know everyone else. The so-called Athens of Ecuador also boasts seven universities and was the first regular meeting place of poets in Latin America. Things close early, and there's not all that much to do after dark, but that leaves the evenings free for wandering and enjoying the play of sunset light on the famous New Cathedral—entertainment enough for the poetically inclined.

Cuenca has become popular with travelers looking for a quiet, scenic city to settle down in and study Spanish for a few weeks or months. It's an ideal city for strolling, whether along the banks of a river or among its many outstanding churches, theaters, and museums. And despite its attachment to history, it's also a surprisingly progressive place: Phone and electric cables are buried, broadband Internet abounds, and the tap water is safe to drink.

Cuenca is also home to Jefferson Pérez, who became Ecuador's first Olympic medalist in 1996 by taking the gold in speed walking. At age 22, he was also the youngest ever Olympic walking champion, and he set the world record for the 20-kilometer walk. His silver medal in Beijing in 2008 was Ecuador's second Olympic medal ever. You might see Cuencanos practicing race-walking in Parque Calderón, which has been nicknamed the "Chochodrome" in honor of Luis Chocho, Pérez's first trainer. Chocho's academy in Cuenca has trained generations of champion speed walkers.

HISTORY

Cuenca began as a Cañari settlement called Guapondelig, meaning "valley of flowers." The Incas moved in against fierce resistance in the 15th century and transformed the site into the palatial Tomebamba, a favorite residence of Huayna Capac and the ruling hub of the Quitosuyo, the northern reaches of the Inca Empire. Its grounds and buildings, suitably fit for a king, were said to rival Cuzco itself.

In the civil war that followed the sudden death of the ruling Inca, his son Atahualpa was briefly imprisoned here by his half brother with the help of the local Cañari *indígenas*. After a narrow escape (supposedly by turning into a snake), Atahualpa defeated his brother and razed the city in revenge, putting its entire population to death.

Spanish lieutenant Gil Ramirez Dávalos refounded the city of Santa Ana de los Cuatro Ríos de Cuenca (*cuenca* means "river basin")

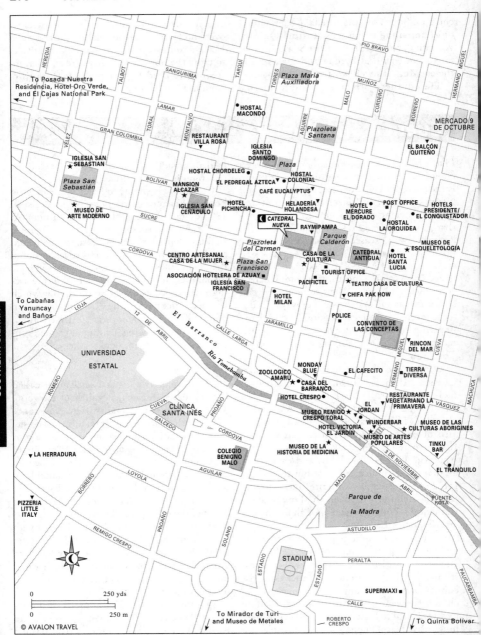

To Posada Nuestra Residencia, Hotel Oro Verde, and El Cajas National Park

HEREDIA

TALBOT

SANGURIMA

TARQUÍ

TORRES

Plaza María Auxiliadora

PÍO BRAVO

MUÑOZ

MALO

CORDERO

BORRERO

HERMANO

MIGUEL

LAMAR

MONTALVO

GRAN COLOMBIA

TOBAL

HOSTAL MACONDO

AGUIRRE

Plazoleta Santana

MERCADO 9 DE OCTUBRE

EL BALCÓN QUITEÑO

VÉLEZ

RESTAURANT VILLA ROSA

IGLESIA SANTO DOMINGO

Plaza

IGLESIA SAN SEBASTIAN

BOLÍVAR

HOSTAL CHORDELEG

EL PEDREGAL AZTECA

HOSTAL COLONIAL

Plaza San Sebastián

MANSION ALCAZAR

CAFÉ EUCALYPTUS

MUSEO DE ARTE MODERNO

SUCRE

IGLESIA SAN CENÁCULO

HOTEL PICHINCHA

HELADERÍA HOLANDESA

CATEDRAL NUEVA

HOTEL MERCURE EL DORADO

POST OFFICE

HOTELS PRESIDENTE/ EL CONQUISTADOR

HOSTAL LA ORQUIDEA

CÓRDOVA

RAYMIPAMPA

Parque Calderón

MUSEO DE ESQUELETOLOGIA

CATEDRAL ANTIGUA

HOTEL SANTA LUCIA

Plazoleta del Carmen

CENTRO ARTESANAL CASA DE LA MUJER

Plaza San Francisco

CASA DE LA CULTURA

ASOCIACIÓN HOTELERA DE AZUAY

IGLESIA SAN FRANCISCO

TOURIST OFFICE

PACIFICTEL

TEATRO CASA DE CULTURA

CHIFA PAK HOW

To Cabañas Yanuncay and Baños

LOJA

12 DE ABRIL

El Barranco

CALLE LARGA

HOTEL MILAN

JARAMILLO

POLICE

CONVENTO DE LAS CONCEPTAS

RINCON DEL MAR

CUEVA

UNIVERSIDAD ESTATAL

ROMERO

Río Tomebamba

MONDAY BLUE

EL CAFECITO

HERMANO MIGUEL

TIERRA DIVERSA

MACHUCA

ZOOLOGICO AMARU

CASA DEL BARRANCO

CUEVA

CLÍNICA SANTA INÉS

SALCEDO

HOTEL CRESPO

MUSEO REMIGO CRESPO TORAL

EL JORDAN

RESTAURANTE VEGETARIANO LA PRIMAVERA

VÁSQUEZ

WUNDERBAR

MUSEO DE LAS CULTURAS ABORIGINES

CÓRDOVA

PROAÑO

HOTEL VICTORIA EL JARDIN

MUSEO DE ARTES POPULARES

TINKU BAR

LA HERRADURA

COLEGIO BENIGNO MALO

MUSEO DE LA HISTORIA DE MEDICINA

EL TRANQUILO

BORRERO

LOYOLA

AGUILAR

MALO

3 DE NOVIEMBRE

12 DE ABRIL

PUENTE ROTA

PIZZERIA LITTLE ITALY

PROAÑO

Parque de la Madra

REMIGO CRESPO

SOLANO

ESTADIO

ASTUDILLO

STADIUM

ESTADIO

PERALTA

SUPERMAXI

0   250 yds

0   250 m

CALLE

© AVALON TRAVEL

To Mirador de Turi and Museo de Metales

ROBERTO CRESPO

PAUCARBAMBA

To Quinta Bolívar

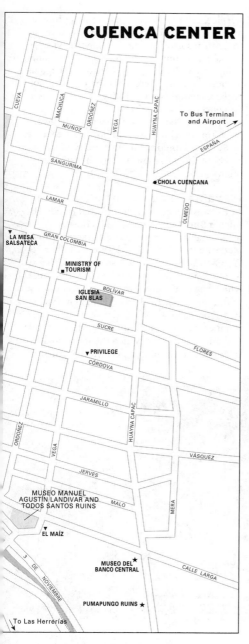

CUENCA CENTER

To Bus Terminal and Airport

CHOLA CUENCANA

LA MESA SALSATECA

MINISTRY OF TOURISM

IGLESIA SAN BLAS

PRIVILEGE

MUSEO MANUEL AGUSTÍN LANDIVAR AND TODOS SANTOS RUINS

EL MAÍZ

MUSEO DEL BANCO CENTRAL

PUMAPUNGO RUINS ★

To Las Herrerías

Streets: CUEVA, MACHUCA, ORDÓÑEZ, VEGA, HUAYNA CAPAC, MUÑOZ, ESPAÑA, SANGURIMA, OLMEDO, LAMAR, GRAN COLOMBIA, BOLÍVAR, SUCRE, FLORES, CÓRDOVA, JARAMILLO, HUAYNA CAPAC, ORDÓÑEZ, VEGA, VÁSQUEZ, JERVES, MALO, MERA, 3 DE NOVIEMBRE, CALLE LARGA

in 1557, according to precise planning guidelines issued by the Spanish crown. Alongside Quito and Guayaquil, it served as a capital of one of the three provinces that made up the territory of Ecuador. Growth over the following centuries was slow because of Cuenca's isolation from the northern Sierra. The 1739 French equator-measuring expedition provided the most excitement in years. The 19th century saw a local economic boom, as Cuenca became a major exporter of Panama hats, quinine, and other goods.

It wasn't until the mid-20th century that decent roads connecting Cuenca to the rest of the country were completed, transforming it from a sleepy market center into a modern city with the requisite factories, suburbs, and clamor. Luckily for visitors, it still retained enough of its colonial character that its historical center, preserving much of the original orthogonal town plan, was declared a World Cultural Heritage Site by UNESCO.

ORIENTATION

Four rivers feed the fertile Tomebamba Valley that cradles Cuenca. The Ríos Tomebamba and Yanuncay drain El Cajas National Park to the west, joining with the Ríos Tarquí and Machángara to form the Río Cuenca on their way east to the jungle. The Tomebamba divides the city center into two sections: to the north, the historical center has changed little since colonial times, whereas gleaming glass buildings and modern suburbs are visible to the south.

On the whole, central Cuenca is safe to walk around in until 10 P.M. or so, although it's wise to take care in the market areas, particularly the Mercado 9 de Octubre.

SIGHTS

Cuenca's wealth of religious architecture makes it easy to believe the saying that the city has a church for every Sunday of the year. Many are attached to convents (self-contained worlds of sacrifice and austere beauty preserved over centuries). The churches of San Sebastian and San Blas once marked the city's boundaries.

◖ Catedral Nueva

Tall palms and taller pines fill **Parque Calderón,** Cuenca's central park. On its west side sits one of Ecuador's architectural wonders—the massive Catedral de la Inmaculada, usually called simply the Catedral Nueva (New Cathedral). Begun in 1880 by an ambitious local bishop who decided the old cathedral wasn't big enough, it was originally planned as South America's largest church, with room for 10,000 worshippers. Work stopped in 1908 because of "architectural miscalculations," leaving the twin square towers unfinished. The pink travertine facade and blue domes (covered with tile imported from Czechoslovakia) are unmistakable.

Inside, the Catedral Nueva is even more awe-inspiring, humbling patrons into reverence with its pink shadows and stained glass from Belgium and Germany. Services fill the nave with voices chanting prayers in Latin and Spanish. Even if you're feeling burned-out on churches, this one is not to be missed.

The Catedral El Sagrario, also known as the **Catedral Antigua** (Old Cathedral), is the city's oldest building, begun in 1557 with stones from the ruins of the Inca palace of Pumapungo. The

steeple was used by La Condamine's group as one of the fixed points in measurements of the equator, inspiring a Spanish scientist visiting in 1804 to comment that this spire was more famous than the Egyptian pyramids. Religious services were held here until the construction of the Catedral Nueva. Today, it is often used for concerts.

Opposite the Catedral Nueva, at the intersection of Sucre and Malo, the **Casa de la Cultura** contains an art gallery, museum, and bookshop. Exhibits by local artists change often.

Plaza San Sebastian

At the western edge of the colonial center, the **Iglesia San Sebastian** occupies the north side of this park. Facing it is the **Museo de Arte Moderno** (Sucre 15–27 and Coronel Talbot, tel. 7/283-1027, 8:30 A.M.–1 P.M. and 3–6:30 P.M. Mon.–Fri., 9 A.M.–1 P.M. Sat.–Sun., free), which began as a Casa de Temperancia (House of Temperance). In the late 19th century, the story goes, a local bishop returning home one night came across a victim of the devil's drink laid out in the street. When the sot turned out to be a priest, the bishop decided that Cuenca's

Cuenca's Catedral Nueva on Parque Calderón

© M. JOAN KROLL

drunks needed a place to sleep it off, and he began the House of Temperance in 1876. Cells used to house the inebriated were later used for criminals when the building became a jail.

After passing through various incarnations as a home for beggars, children, and the insane, the stately old structure was barely saved from destruction by the famous Ecuadorian painter Luis Crespo Ordóñez and was inaugurated as a museum in 1981. The setup is excellent, with lots of white space (notice the thick colonial walls) and long, flower-filled courtyards setting off intricate modern sculptures and paintings.

Plazoleta del Carmen

Flower vendors in new kiosks fill this tiny square plaza, also called the Plaza de las Flores, with colors and scents every day. The twin spires of the **Iglesia El Carmen de la Asunción,** founded in 1682, rise behind a small fountain. Stones carved in Spanish baroque style frame the main entrance. A handful of nuns inhabit the **Monasterio del Carmen,** spending their days in prayer and contemplation completely cut off from the outside world, except for a small festival on July 16 in the adjoining plaza. The nuns do not even accept medical attention, but locals can leave offerings in a tiny chapel near the entrance. A painted refractory includes colonial masterworks by Caspicara (Manuel Chili) and Miguel de Santiago.

Museo del Banco Central

You can't miss the smoked-glass edifice of the Banco Central, with the best archaeological collection in the southern Sierra next door in its museum (Larga and Huayna Capac, tel. 7/283-1255, ext. 502, 9 A.M.–6 P.M. Mon.–Fri., 9 A.M.–1 P.M. Sat., $3 adults, $1.50 children). Much of the pre-Columbian pottery and many of the figurines were collected by Padre Carlos Crespi, a local friar who believed devoutly in the theory that coastal Ecuador was settled by the Phoenicians. Antique musical instruments, local art, time-faded photos of Cuenca, and libraries share the building, and the entrance

fee includes access to the **Pumapungo ruins** out back.

Pumapungo, Huayna Capac's palace-away-from-home, had already fallen into ruin in 1547 when Spanish chronicler Pedro Cieza de León rode through. "These famous lodgings," he wrote, "were among the finest and richest to be found in all [the viceroyalty of] Peru, and the buildings the largest and best.... Today all is cast down and in ruins, but still it can be seen how great they were." Many Pumapungo stones found their way into the foundations and walls of buildings in Cuenca's colonial center.

German archaeologist Max Uhle rediscovered the ruins in 1922. Along with a temple to Viracocha, the Inca creator-god, Uhle uncovered the skeleton of a man in a specially widened section of wall, evidence of the pre-Columbian custom of burying a man alive in the foundation of a new wall to give it strength. Shattered jars, widespread scorching, and rooms filled with ash gave silent witness to Pumapungo's violent end.

More Churches and Convents

Cuenca's richest religious art collection is housed in the museum of the **Convento de las Conceptas** (Hermano Miguel 6–33 and Jaramillo, tel. 7/283-0625, 9 A.M.–6:30 P.M. Mon.–Fri., 10 A.M.–1 P.M. Sat.–Sun., $2.50), which occupies the block between Córdova, Jaramillo, Borrero, and Hermano Miguel. (The entrance is on Miguel.) In the late 17th century, one Doña Ordóñez dedicated one of the finest houses in the city to serve as the convent, on the condition that her three daughters would be accepted (the house also served as their down payment to enter, a common practice in colonial times). The doors were shut in 1682, leaving a holiday on December 8 as one of the few times the Conceptor nuns are allowed to glimpse the outside world. Twenty-two rooms of sculpture and painting include many treasures from the Sangurima school of colonial art, along with crucifixes dating to the 17th century.

The Virgen del Rosario is the most precious icon in the **Iglesia Santo Domingo** (on Colombia between Torres and Aguirre). Gold and jewels donated by Cuenca's wealthiest women encrust the Virgin's crown. The modest exterior of the **Iglesia San Francisco** (on the plaza of the same name) belies a lavish baroque altarpiece inside, which is intricately carved and covered with gold leaf.

More Museums

A stroll along Calle Larga takes visitors past five museums (and close to several more), many lovely hotels, restaurants, and lots of new nightspots. One interesting stop is the **Museo del Sombrero** (Calle Larga 10–41 and Torres, tel. 7/283-1569, 9 A.M.–6 P.M. Mon.– Fri., 9:30 A.M.–4 P.M. Sat., 9:30 A.M.–1:30 P.M. Sun., free), where the process of Panama hat making and finishing is explained. Huge old machines used to form the hats are on display, as well as good descriptions of the different stages of production.

The **Museo Remigio Crespo Toral** (Larga 7–27 and Borrero, tel. 7/283-3208, 9 A.M.–1 P.M. and 3–6 P.M. Mon.–Fri., 9 A.M.–1 P.M. Sat.–Sun., free) reopened its doors in April 2008 after a long period of restoration. It contains a sparse but high-quality collection. Religious sculptures, paintings, archaeological relics, and *artesanías* fill the wooden building overlooking the Río Tomebamba.

The impressive private collection of a local doctor is on display at the **Museo de las Culturas Aborigines** (Larga 5–24 and Cueva, tel. 7/283-9181, 8:30 A.M.–6:30 P.M. Mon.–Fri., 9 A.M.–1 P.M. Sat., $2). Some 5,000 pre-Columbian pieces span every Ecuadorian culture up to the Spanish conquest. Optional guides speak English, Spanish, and French.

In 1970, workers clearing a small park between Larga and Avenida Todos Santos unearthed a confusing jumble of rocks. Careful digging revealed layers of cultures: large, crude blocks of Cañari origin, finer Inca stonework with characteristic trapezoidal niches, and a Spanish watermill using both of the previous styles as a foundation. The **Museo Manuel Agustin Landivar** (Larga and Vega, tel. 7/282-1177, 8 A.M.–1 P.M. and 3–6 P.M. Mon.–Fri., $1, guides available in English, Spanish, and Mandarin) entrance to the site of Todos Santos Ruins is through the museum.

At the bottom of the steps of La Escalinata (a continuation of Hermano Miguel) along the river is the **Museo de Artes Populares** (Hermano Miguel 3–23 and Larga, tel. 7/282-9451, 9:30 A.M.–1 P.M. and 2–6 P.M. Mon.– Fri., 10 A.M.–1 P.M. Sat., free), with a museum of folk art, library, and excellent crafts shop run by the Interamerican Center for the Development of Popular Arts (CIDAP). It has a very good collection of crafts and clothing from across Latin America.

Even fans of the macabre will consider the **Museo de la Historia de la Medicina** (9 A.M.–noon and 1–5 P.M. Mon.–Fri., $0.50) one of the most bizarre collections they have ever seen. Everything that had anything to do with the old military hospital whose grounds it occupies is on display at the Medical History Museum, from ledger books and bedpans to an X-ray machine that would make Dr. Frankenstein proud. As if to make the collection even more unsettling, everything is displayed in stark white rooms either in bright yellow cases or just lying on the floor—including the corpses. (Modern-art fans will notice an uncanny similarity to the works of Damien Hirst.) This is one place that really needs to be seen to be believed. It's across the river on 12 de Abril.

The **Museo de los Metales** (Solano 11–83 between 10 de Agosto and Tres Puentes, tel. 7/281-1302, 10 A.M.–noon and 3–5 P.M. Mon.–Fri., free) is near Rio Yanuncay in southern Cuenca.

Examine the internal architecture of Ecuador's vertebrates at the **Museo de Esqueletología** (Bolívar 6–57 and Borrero, tel. 7/282-1150, 10 A.M.–1 P.M. and 4–7 P.M. Mon.–Fri., 10 A.M.–2 P.M. Sat., $1), and ogle the country's multitudinous snakes, reptiles, and fish at the **Zoologico Amarú** (Benigno Malo 4–64 and Larga, tel. 7/282-6337, 9 A.M.–1 P.M. and 3–6 P.M. Mon.–Fri., 10 A.M.–5 P.M. Sat.–Sun., $2).

Architecture and Green Space

The round portico of the **Banco del Azuay,** at Bolívar and Borrero, features Doric columns supporting a cupola of rose-colored travertine and forms the elegant entrance to another space for visiting art exhibits. The same material decorates the imposing three-story facade of the **Palacio de Justicia** on the southeast corner of Parque Calderón, originally built for use as the University of Cuenca.

The district of Las Herrerias, with its ancient houses, is across the bridge at the southern end of Huayna Capac, below the Pumapungo ruins. Cuencanos come here to buy the traditional ornate crosses that adorn the roofs of finished homes; the wrought-iron-working shops make a great variety of other useful items, too. Nearby is an exuberant sculpture of the god Vulcan breaking free of the ground.

The grassy slopes of the Río Tomebamba, known as **El Barranco,** make an afternoon meander down 3 de Noviembre one of the more enjoyable in the country. Colonial houses and modern apartments spill down from Larga almost to the riverbank, where generations of indigenous women have laid out their wash to dry.

West of the city at the Quinta Balzain, you can find the excellent *Orquidario* (orchid garden, $1 pp), a beautiful collection that's well worth a taxi ride.

ENTERTAINMENT AND EVENTS
Nightlife

Cuenca's local papers, *Tiempo* and *El Mercurio,* list what's showing at Cuenca's movie theaters—at least those still surviving since the opening of the six-screen **Multicines** in the Millenium Plaza (Peralta and Merchán), and another set at Mall del Rio beside the Rio Tarqui. The **Teatro Casa de la Cultura** (Cordero 7–42 and Córdova), not to be confused with the Casa de la Cultura on Sucre and Aguirre, occasionally hosts movies and houses the popular Cinema Café (tel. 7/282-2446).

Head down the steps of La Escalinata (south from Miguel) to reach **Wunderbar** (Hermano Miguel 3–43 and Larga, tel. 7/283-1274), a small, cave-like place with German beers and occasionally live music. Like its sibling in Quito, **El Cafecito** (Vásquez 7–36 and Borrero) is a *hostal* by day and a cozy, candlelit bar by night. It's popular with backpackers and features music on the weekends.

La Mesa (Gran Colombia 3–55 and Ordóñez) is a fun (and small) *salsateca* open Wednesday–Saturday. **Privilege** (Córdova 100-14 and Vega) was until recently called Blue Martini (some still use the old name). Whatever you call it, it's a glossy place with more modern music and another good spot to get your groove on.

For the younger side of Cuenca nightlife, head to the intersection of Remigio Crespo Toral and Borrero, behind the State University, or follow Gran Colombia west toward Cajas, near the shopping malls.

The area around Calle Larga between Aguirre and Machuca has blossomed with restaurants, café bars, and nightspots. Look for **Monday Blue** on Larga and Cordero, **Sankt Florian** (opposite), and **La Parola,** a little further down with a terrace view of the river. Another couple of blocks down is **Tinku,** in a traditional house facing Puente Rota; and last, continuing on Larga, you'll find **Del Tranquilo.** Two other very popular spots are **Julian Matadero,** by the river behind Hotel Crespo, and **Eucalyptus,** on Gran Colombia 9–41 and Malo.

Festivals

Cuenca's main festivals include **Corpus Christi,** nine weeks after Easter (usually June), when firecracker-studded towers are ignited in Parque Calderón for nights on end as flocks of paper hot-air balloons rise toward the stars. The **Foundation of Cuenca,** April 10–13, is another excuse to cut loose, and the celebrations for **Cuenca's Independence** on November 3 are combined with All Souls' and All Saints' Days (November 1 and 2) for a three-day festival of theater, art, and dancing.

Cuenca's **Christmas festival** is one of the most famous in the country. The Pase del

Niño Viajero—said to be the best holiday parade in Ecuador—begins on the morning of Christmas Eve. *Indígenas* from villages for kilometers around throng the streets. Symbols of prosperity, including strings of banknotes, poultry, and bottles of alcohol, are both carried and worn in the hope of arranging for even more of the same over the next year. The procession winds from the Iglesia San Sebastian to the cathedral, and the festivities don't stop until the next day.

SHOPPING

Coaches for the upcoming Leisure Olympics—where the main events are Strolling and Shopping—couldn't ask for a better training camp than Cuenca. Vendors specialize in the unusual, the finely wrought, and the expensive: custom jewelry, handmade ceramics, pre-Columbian-style *ikat* textiles, and enough antiques and religious icons to stock a dozen castles.

Ceramics magician Eduardo Vega sold off his major factory and accompanying **Artesa** outlets, but they still sell many of his designs and ceramics. Vega has since opened a private workshop and gallery in the gardens of his house 60 meters below the **Turi** lookout, which focuses on more individual designs. **Galería Pulla** (Jaramillo 6–90 and Borrero) is named after another famous Ecuadorian artist whose paintings and sculptures fill the showroom.

Jewelry can be expensive, but it's worth shopping around for the occasional deal. Most comes from nearby crafts villages. *Joyerías* (jewelry shops) are concentrated on Cordero near Colombia and along Colombia between Aguirre and Cordero, and jewelry stands fill the Plazoleta Santana on the corner of Lamar and Malo. Leonardo Crespo's Joyería Turismo, a Cuenca institution, has changed both its location and its name. It's now the **Relicario de las Artes** (Borrero 9–64 and Gran Colombia) and carries paintings as well as jewelry.

Many antiques stores surround Las Conceptas. The **Cafe Galería** (Córdova 7–54) and **Laura's** (Miguel 7–16) both have good selections. **Productos Andinos** (Colombia between Malo and Cordero) sells the usual Andean artifacts. Both **El Tucán** (Borrero 7–35) and **Collecciones Jorge Moscoso** (Cordero and Córdova) have a little of everything—for the right price. The **Centro Artesanal Casa de la Mujer** (across from the Plaza San Francisco Market on General Torres) is a mall with more than 100 vendors selling just about every type of *artesanía* imaginable, from baskets and balsa sculptures to Panama hats and paintings. Here, you will find **Mama Kinoa,** the indigenous organization that runs a restaurant with traditional foods; and **Cushihuari,** which is part of an organization promoting community tourism and cultural exchange programs.

Some of Ecuador's finer Panama hats are made in the southern Sierra by families who have woven the *toquilla* straw for generations. The family behind **Homero Ortega Padre e Hijos** (tel. 7/280-9000, www.homeroortega.com) export sombreros around the world from their shop on Dávalos 3–86 behind the *terminal terrestre.* (You know Ecuador has entered the 21st century when its Panama hat weavers have websites.) **Aurelio Ortega** sells hats at Malo 10–78, and you can also try Alberto Pulla and his store/workshop, **La Casa del Sombrero** (Tarquí 6–91 and Córdova). For a wider selection, stop by the Thursday morning hat market at María Auxiliadora Plaza.

Markets

Cuenca's main market day is Thursday, with smaller spreads on Saturday and minimal vending the rest of the week. The **Mercado 9 de Octubre** sees the most goods changing hands, including crafts, clothes, and *cuyes* (guinea pigs). Witch doctors cure true believers and the gullible on Tuesdays and Fridays. The flower and plant market in the **Plazoleta del Carmen** is one of the most photogenic in the southern Sierra.

Otavalo textiles and everyday goods are sold in the **Plaza de San Francisco** and the **Plaza Rotary,** and a local market fills the small plaza fronting **Las Conceptas.** Panama hat weavers sell directly to wholesalers in the **Plaza María Auxiliadora.**

RECREATION AND TOURS

Contact the **Club Andinismo Sangay** (Gran Colombia 7–39 and Cordero, tel./fax 7/283-6758, adinismosangay@yahoo.com) for information on climbing courses and hikes into El Cajas. Group hikes happen most Sundays, with a bus leaving Parque Calderón at 8 A.M. ($3 for the trip). You can rent camping gear at **Acción Casa Deportiva** (Bolívar 12–70 and Montalvo, tel. 7/283-3526).

Ecotrek (3 Noviembre 2–47 and Jacarandar, tel. 7/283-4677) is probably the best-known adventure travel operation in Cuenca. The knowledgeable and experienced guides are specialists in rock climbing. **Terra Diversa** (Herman Miguel 5–42 and Vásquez, tel.

ANDEAN GENETIC ADAPTATIONS

A research project in Peru by scientists from the University of British Columbia made some surprising findings among the highland Quechua. Not only do the high-altitude *indígenas* have larger lungs and hearts up to one-fifth bigger than normal – pumping two quarts more blood through their bodies than lowlanders – but their muscles also operate differently.

When you and I push our muscles to the point of anaerobic metabolism (relying on stored-up energy, rather than oxygen from the outside air), they produce lactic acid that eventually builds up and causes cramps. With such little oxygen at high altitude, you'd think that Quechua muscles would produce a lot of this acid, but instead they accumulate *less* lactate byproducts.

It might have something to do with their preference for carbohydrates (i.e., grains) rather than fats as body fuel, but their muscles act the same when they're brought down to sea level, suggesting an actual genetic adaptation. Researchers hope to use this information to help people survive the temporary lack of oxygen caused by strokes and heart attacks.

7/282-3782) was opened by two experienced guides, Juan Heredia and José Saltos, and offers the best selection of tours out of Cuenca. The staff speaks English, and their information center is open daily. **Expediciones Apullacta** (Gran Colombia 11–02 and General Torres, Of. 111, tel. 7/283-7815, info@apullacta.com, www.apullacta.cedei.org) runs day trips to El Cajas, Ingapirca, and surrounding artisan villages, including English- or Spanish-speaking guides and lunch.

Hualambari Tours (Borrero 9–67 and Colombia, tel./fax 7/284-2693) has day trips to El Cajas, Ingapirca, and nearby villages ($35 pp) that are reportedly excellent. Guides speak English, Spanish, German, French, and Italian. Cuenca tour operators got together and organized a cooperative for their most popular tours—by running shared tours, they can offer trips with more frequency and maintain standard prices and high levels of service. Trips to El Cajas and Ingapirca each cost $35 pp with any operator.

ACCOMMODATIONS

Hotels in Cuenca are generally of a higher standard than those in the rest of the country. All have private baths and hot water, unless otherwise noted. Cuenca's best rooms for the money fall in the $20–90 range. Many are converted colonial houses, with shady courtyards ringed by interior balconies.

Under $10

El Cafécito (Vásquez 7–36 and Cordero, tel. 7/283-2337, cuenca@cafecito.net, www.cafecito.net) is a funky, comfortable, little place with a twin in Quito. It's attached to a popular café that features live music on weekends. Rooms are $9 pp in the dorm and $13 with private bath.

A veritable clutch of dubious looking hotels and hostels can be found near the market on Sangurima close to Huaynacapac, and on adjacent side streets. Prices range $4–8. Some are passable if you're on a tight budget, but others fall into the Ecuadorian category of *mala muerte* (bad death)—be sure to inspect your room before signing on. The other area where several budget hotels cater to backpackers is around Calle Larga and Hermano Miguel. The secure **Hotel Pichincha** (Torres 8–82 and Bolívar, tel. 7/282-3868) is an immense building run like clockwork by *dueña* Sara Muñoz. With rooms for only $6.50 pp, it's justifiably popular with the backpacking set.

$10-25

Near the river, the **Casa del Barranco** (Larga 8–41 and Cordero, tel. 7/283-9763, casadelbarranco@yahoo.com) has an open courtyard, wood floors, and rooms with private bath and TV for $15 s, $28 d.

The colonial **Hostal Macondo** (Tarquí 11–64 and Lamar, tel. 7/284-0697, fax 7/283-3593, macondo@cedei.org) is a wonderful spot to park yourself for a few days or a week. It offers kitchen facilities for guests and an interior garden. Rates are $21 s, $30 d, with private bath and breakfast. The friendly and well-informed owners offer city tours and day trips.

For $18 s, $24 d, the quarters at the **Hostal La Orquidea** (Borrero 9–31 and Bolívar, tel. 7/282-4511, fax 7/283-5844) are a bargain. Each has a TV and phone, and there's a good restaurant on the premises. The **Hotel Milan** (Córdova 9–89 and Aguirre, tel. 7/283-1104, hotmilan@etapaonline.net.ec) is another fine value at $15 s, $22 d. It runs day tours in the surrounding area and offers mountain bikes to rent for $6 per day, including helmets.

At the **Hostal Colonial** (Gran Colombia 10–13 and Aguirre, tel./fax 7/284-1644, hcolonial@cue.satnet.net), rooms around a pleasant courtyard are $16 s, $26 d, including TV and refrigerator. The restored colonial antique home also houses a good restaurant.

The colonial **Hostal Chordeleg** (Colombia and Torres, tel. 7/282-4611, fax 7/282-2536) offers rooms with TV, phone, and private baths for $20 s, $34 d, including breakfast.

Centrally located, the newly renovated and newly named **Majestic** (Cordero 11–29 and Lamar, tel. 7/284-3502) has new beds and stunning old colored ceiling tiles. Rooms are $20 s,

$35 d, and very open to negotiation, and there's free tea and coffee available at any hour.

Behind a private house southwest of the city center are the **Cabañas Yanuncay** (Cantón Gualeco 21–49 between Loja and Las Américas, tel. 7/288-3716). Two cabins in a garden are yours for $15 pp, including breakfast and a gurgling river. Other homemade organic meals are available, and the owner speaks English. A taxi is the easiest way to get there, or else take a Baños-bound bus and get off at 1ero de Mayo and Loja; cross the river on the right and turn left. Or just call ahead for a free pickup. People traveling with campers can find space here, with power and services connections in the garden.

$25-50

Numerous travelers recommend the **《 Posada Nuestra Residencia** (Los Pinos 11–00 and Ordóñez Lazo, tel. 7/283-1702, fax 7/283-5576, 2carrion@etapa.com.ec), a quiet bed-and-breakfast west of the city center. Bilingual owners Rafael and Lucía Carrión are gracious hosts and offer guests eight comfortable rooms with cable TV for $37 s, $51 d, including breakfast. One room has a kitchenette, and there's a garden, fireplace, and outdoor barbecue for everyone to enjoy.

If you stay at the **Hotel Casino Presidente** (Colombia 6–59 and Miguel, tel. 7/283-1066 or 7/283-1341, hotelpresidente@yahoo.com), try to get a room on one of the upper floors for the best views. Rates are $34 s, $46 d, including breakfast.

Beautiful rooms with wall-to-wall windows overlooking the Tomebamba are available at the **Hotel Victoria** (Larga 6–93 and Borrero, tel. 7/282-7401, santaana@etapaonline.net.ec, $43 s, $55 d) in the newly renovated building that also houses the restaurant El Jardín.

$50-75

The **Hotel El Conquistador** (Colombia 6–65 and Borrero, tel. 7/283-1788, fax 7/283-1291) offers lodging for $53 s, $64 d, including cable TV, refrigerators, a breakfast buffet, and airport transportation.

The classic **Hotel Crespo** (Larga 7–93 and Cordero, tel. 7/284-2571, $73 s, $85 d, includes breakfast) has rooms with views over the river, as well as some cheaper interior rooms.

$75-100

The **Hotel Oro Verde** (tel. 7/283-1200, fax 7/283-2849, ov-cue@oroverdehotels.com) is three kilometers west of the city center on the way to El Cajas, on Avenida Lasso along the Río Tomebamba. For all the usual luxuries, along with a Swiss restaurant considered one of the best in the city, visitors pay $91 s or d, including breakfast and airport transport. There's a more casual restaurant as well, along with a bar, deli, outdoor pool, gym, and sauna. Llamas, peacocks, and parrots grace the outdoor lagoon near the trout stream and herb garden.

A pair of recently renovated colonial mansions have been converted into two of the loveliest city hotels in the country. The (**Hotel Santa Lucía** (Borrero 8–44 and Sucre, tel. 7/282-8000, $76 s, $113 d) is centrally located and run by the Vintimilla family, with three generations of experience in hotels and restaurants. The building was built by the Azuay's first provincial governor in 1859, and it also houses an attractive café in the front and a lovely Italian restaurant in the central patio.

The (**Mansion Alcazar** (Bolívar 12–55 and Tarquí, tel. 7/282-3918, $98 s, $159 d) surpasses just about anything in Ecuador with its sumptuous rooms full of antiques and its late-19th-century ambience. (The prince of Asturias came here on his honeymoon.) Also in the heart of the city, the hotel features 14 rooms and suites, a gourmet restaurant (Casa de Alonso), bar, and library. It was completely restored in 2001, and it now glitters with crystal chandeliers and locally crafted art and furniture.

Over $100

In the city center, the **Hotel Mercure El Dorado** (Colombia 7–87 and Cordero, tel. 7/283-1390, fax 7/283-1663, ventas@mercu-reeldorado.com.ec) is a modern place offering a disco, gym, and a piano bar up on the seventh floor. For $110 s or d, guests enjoy satellite TV, a minibar, a free continental breakfast, and transportation to and from the airport.

FOOD
Cafés and Sweets

The café at the **El Cafecito Hotel** is always packed, partly because the hamburgers, pasta, and Mexican entrées are around $3. A local institution for a few years running is the **Café Austria** (Malo and Jaramillo), with a wide-ranging international menu, plus coffee and cakes.

The **Heladería Holandesa** (Malo and Bolívar) satisfies any sugar cravings with its cakes, fruit salad, and abundant ice cream.

Continental

Vying for the title of Best Restaurant in Cuenca are **El Jardín** (Larga 693 and Borrero), in the Hotel Victoria, where prices range from $5 for ceviche to $24 for lobster; (**Villa Rosa** (Colombia 12–22 and Montalvo), with slightly lower prices and a more intimate setting; and **Casa de Alonso**, a delightful conservatory in the garden of Mansion Alcazar, where exquisitely presented plates tempt the eyes and taste buds. At El Jardín, you'll enjoy wonderful views over the river and international cuisine prepared from scratch—the service is accordingly very slow. Most entrées are $6–12, and there's a good wine selection.

Restaurante El Mirador earns its name from its spot on the ninth floor of the Hotel Presidente. It's fancy but affordable, with entrées like breaded sea bass and filet mignon in mushroom sauce for around $4. Breakfast starts at $3.50. Great views of Cuenca are included. Seafood specialists take friends and family to **La Casa del Marisco** (Paukarbamba and Luis Moreno Mora, tel. 7/288-3677).

International

(**El Pedregal Azteca** (Colombia 10–33) has the most authentic Mexican fare this side of the Yucatán, down to a stained-glass likeness of Catinflas and the dish of *mole* on the table. Portions are tasty but not huge for $4–9. Not to be confused with El Jardín next door, the restaurant **El Jordan** (Larga 6–111 and Borrero, tel. 7/285-0517) serves Middle Eastern food in a beautiful setting overlooking the river. Prices are reasonable: $3.50 for entrées and $5–8 for main dishes, with many vegetarian options.

The **Chifa Long Yung** (Sucre 9–014 and Malo) is one of the city's best but still reasonably priced—plates average $3. The **Chifa Gran Muralla** (Gran Colombia 22–282 and Unidad Nacional) comes highly recommended for Chinese as well.

Local Favorites
Authentic local meals can be had in the yellow house called **El Maiz** (Larga 1–279 and Vega), where prices start at $2 and dishes are creative.

Raymipampa (Benigno Malo 859), under the arcade on the west side of Parque Calderón, has been popular with tourists and locals for years, with a view of the park and a bright, café-style atmosphere. Entrées, including crêpes, fall in the $3–5 range.

You'll find *parilladas* aplenty on Remigio Crespo, west of the stadium. Locals recommend **La Herradura Grill,** on Romero just off Remigio Crespo. For seafood at local prices (mostly less than $3), try the **Rincon de Mar** on Miguel, diagonal from the Convento de la Conceptas. The *trucha con menestra* is a tasty mix of the coast and the Sierra.

Pizza
When Cuencanos order their pies, chances are they call the **Pizzeria Little Italy** (Cueva 6–17 and Remigio Crespo, tel. 7/288-5674), where a small cheese pizza is $3. You can also eat in. **New York Pizza** is moving, soon to be on Tarqui and Lamar (tel. 7/286-6914). Previously located across from the Iglesia Santo Domingo, it's the real thing—slices are $2.50 and family-size pizzas are $9–15. Everything else on the menu, from ravioli to *churrasco,* is less than $6. They also deliver.

Supermarkets
To stock up for yourself, there's a **Supermaxi** on Avenida de las Americas just north of Ordóñez Lazo, west of the center; and another on Calle, east of the stadium. You can also go to the new malls (Millenium Plaza or Mall del Rio).

Vegetarian
Cuenca's health-conscious citizens steer toward **Vegetariano El Paraiso,** which has two locations (Ordóñez at 10–45 and 5–66), for the fruit salads, soy-meat sandwiches, and $1.50 set lunch.

INFORMATION AND SERVICES
Tourist Information
The **Ministerio de Turismo** (Córdova between Aguirre and Malo, tel. 7/282-2058) has an office with maps and brochures on the second floor of the Edificio San Agustín. In the bus terminal, you'll find the **Camara de Turismo del Azuay** (tel. 7/286-8482), with city maps and a waiting room with leather couches and cable TV. It's open daily from 8 A.M.

There's also a well-staffed **tourist information office** (Sucre between Cordero and Malo, tel. 7/285-0521) on Parque Calderón, in the municipal offices. Here you can also pick up a free copy of the useful *Agenda Conmemorativa,* published every month and packed with information, cultural events, exhibitions, concerts, photos,and much more.

For information and maps of El Cajas, stop by the office of the **Ministerio del Ambiente** (Bolívar 5–33 and Miguel), on the third floor of the MAG office.

Money Exchange
Most *casas de cambio* are found east of Parque Calderón. **Vaz Cambios** has a branch at Gran Colombia 7–98 and Cordero, with Western Union money-transfer service available.

If you'd rather deal with a bank, the **Banco del Pacífico** (Malo 975 and Gran Colombia) gives cash advances on credit cards. Most

CONSULATES IN CUENCA

- **Brazil:** Ramirez Davalos 1434 y Turuhuaico, tel. 7/287-1870
- **Chile:** Paeso 3 de Noviembre 2406 y Escalinata, tel. 7/284-0061
- **France:** T. Torres 1-92 y Aguilar, tel. 7/282-5298
- **Germany:** Bolívar 9-18 y Malo, tel. 7/282-2783

banks also have **ATMs** for up to $500 daily in cash withdrawals.

Communications

Cuenca's **post office** is in the center of town on Borrero and Gran Colombia.

Spanish Schools

Cuenca is a very popular city in which to study Spanish for extended periods, which explains the many high-quality language schools in town. The **Centro de Estudios Interamericanos** (B. Malo 10-70 and Lamar, tel. 7/283-9003, info@cedei.org, www.cedei .org) offers classes for $6 per hour, as well as courses in Kichwa, colonial Latin America, and Andean literature. It can also arrange positions teaching English.

Nexus Lingua y Culturas (3 Noviembre 2–47 and Jacarandar, tel. 7/283-4677) offers Spanish classes for $5 per hour, plus positions teaching English locally. The **Centro Cultural Ecuatoriano-Norteamericano Abraham Lincoln** (Borrero 5–18 and Vasquez, tel. 7/284-1737, tel./fax 7/282-3898, rboroto@cena.org .ec) is recommended at $7 per hour. It can also arrange homestays with local families.

The **Si Centro** language school (Aguirre 9–43, tel. 7/282-0429) comes recommended by readers as well. **Fundacion Amauta** (Miguel and Cordova, tel. 7/284-6206) is highly recommended by the tourist office, as it also works with communities and development. **Escuela Simon** is a branch of the frequently recommended school in Quito (Cordero 12–25 and Gran Colombia).

Health Care

The 24-hour **Clínica Santa Inés** (tel. 7/281-7888) is just across the river from *el centro* and employs a few English-speaking doctors.

TRANSPORTATION
Buses

Cuenca's *terminal terrestre,* probably the most orderly and pleasant in the country, is two blocks northeast of the traffic circle at España and Huayna Capac. Several bus companies have luxury service to Guayaquil ($5, five hours), as well as most cities between and beyond, including Quito ($10, 9–10 hours) and Macas ($9, 9–10 hours). Panamericana (5–24 España) has an office just beyond the bus station and sends luxury buses to Quito daily at 10 P.M. ($12). Buses to Loja ($5, 5.5 hours) run via Saraguro, and Transportes Cañar has direct service daily to Ingapirca at noon, 1, and 2 P.M. daily ($2). Local city buses cost about $0.20. Buses to the small towns and villages out of Cuenca leave from Terminal Sur, close to the Feria Libre on Avenida de las Americas.

Taxis and Car Rental

The minimum taxi fare in Cuenca is $1.25, which will get you just about anywhere in town (taxis don't have meters). The bus station and airport are each a $2 ride from the city center. To hire your own wheels, try **Localiza** at the airport (tel. 7/286-0174).

Air

Planes leave from Cuenca's Mariscal Lamar airport, two kilometers northeast of the town center on Avenida España. It's a 10-minute walk from the *terminal terrestre,* or a short hop by taxi or local bus.

TAME has offices in town (Astudillo 2–22, tel. 7/288-9581) and at the airport (tel. 7/286-6400). Flights leave for Quito

CUENCA AIRLINE OFFICES

- **Aerogal:** España 1114, tel. 7/286-1041 or 7/280-4444
- **American Airlines:** Hno. Miguel 8-63 y Bolívar, tel. 7/283-1699
- **Continental:** Aguirre 10-96 y Lamar, tel. 7/284-7374
- **Copa:** Lamar 989 y Aguirre, tel. 7/284-2970
- **Lan:** Bolívar 9-18 y Malo, tel. 7/282-2783
- **Lufthansa:** Bolívar 9-18 y Malo, tel. 7/282-2783
- **TACA:** Sucre 7-70 y Cordero, tel. 7/283-7360
- **TAME:** Astudillo 2-22, tel. 7/288-0051

Monday–Saturday ($85) and for Guayaquil Monday–Saturday ($66). For similar prices, **Icaro** and **Aerogal** also fly to Quito daily and to Guayaquil daily except Saturdays.

VICINITY OF CUENCA

Head four kilometers south of Cuenca's center along Avenida Solano, and you'll crest at the **Mirador Turi,** a lookout with a view all the way to the peaks of El Cajas on a clear day. Match the painting of Cuenca with the real city below. Processions from Cuenca on Good Friday lead to the white Iglesia de Turi. "Turi" buses leave from 12 de Abril and Solano ($0.25), or a taxi will cost you about $3.

Not to be confused with the larger tourist mecca to the north, the *pueblito* of **Baños** sits eight kilometers southwest of Cuenca. Similar to its eponymous sibling, hot springs are the draw here, burbling up from 3,000 meters to surface at more than 86°C. A few cheap *residenciales* provide lodging, as does the colonial-style **Hostería Durán** (tel. 7/289-2485, $56 s, $80 d). This full resort boasts tennis and racquetball courts, a gym, water slides, private hot springs, and plush rooms with all the amenities. The best hot springs are near the *hostería;* **Rodas** has the hottest thermals for $3 pp per day.

Take a taxi from Cuenca or catch a local bus at the intersection of 12 de Abril and Solano, south of the river, which then passes the Plaza San Francisco on Cordova. Buses also leave from outside the bus station and head down Muñoz. Buses run from Cuenca to the top of the hill, where a baby-blue church with tiled domes is worth a look. The Hostería Durán is a short distance below, surrounded by a billiards hall, discos, and plenty of restaurants.

◖ EL CAJAS NATIONAL PARK

Some of the most varied and spectacular scenery in the country fills this reserve, whose proximity to Cuenca—only one hour's drive west—helps make it one of the most popular outdoor destinations in the area. El Cajas's 70,000 acres shelter everything from cloud forest to rocky lunar landscapes, but it's the lakes (more than 200 of them), scattered among jagged peaks, that best characterize the reserve. Despite its proximity to Cuenca, it's an easy place to find a surprising amount of solitude, whether you're here for the **hiking** or **trout fishing.**

Most of El Cajas lies above 3,000 meters, with *páramo* covering most of the rugged terrain. Frost and ice above 4,000 meters try their best to deter the thriving of hardy vegetation, such as the tiny *quinua* tree, which clings to life higher than any other tree in the world. Look for these 200-year-old specimens tucked up against hillsides in pockets of primary forest, clothed in a green palette of mosses and ferns and fighting each other for sunlight.

Visitors stand a good chance of seeing the wild llamas that were reintroduced to the park in the late 1990s. The park's other animal inhabitants, such as the spectacled bear, puma, and tigrillo, are more elusive. A long bird list counts hummingbirds, toucans, and Andean condors.

Archaeology

Fragments of Inca roads throughout the reserve link numerous *tambos* (ruins of way stations along the royal highway, which is said to have run through here all the way to the coast. Traces of the roads connect Lagunas Luspa and Mamamag, and Lagunas Ingacocha and Ingacarretero. The area near Molleturo Hill has the highest concentration of ruins in El Cajas, where great views of Chimborazo and El Altar give evidence of the Inca skill at picking sites that were both scenic and easily defended. Other ruins can be found near Lagunas Toreadora and Atugyacu.

Visiting the Park

The main route to El Cajas from Cuenca starts as Avenida Gran Colombia before turning into Avenida Ordóñez Lazo as it nears the Hotel Oro Verde. After eight kilometers, the road passes the village of Sayausi before reaching Laguna Toreadora **visitors center** (6 A.M.–5 P.M. daily) after 34 kilometers.

Buses heading to Guayaquil from Cuenca's main terminal take about 45 minutes to reach the *laguna* ($1.50). They run about every hour during daylight and return just as often. Ask to be let off at the *refugio,* where you can pay your entrance fee ($10 pp) and sleep for $2 pp. There are kitchen facilities and electricity but no hot water, and a small restaurant is open irregularly on weekends.

El Cajas is full of hiking trails, from day hikes to multiday outings. One popular day hike is the trail from the Tres Cruces hill, four kilometers west of the information center, up over the continental divide (4,103 meters) and past Lagunas Larga, Tagllacocha, and Luspa. The loop around Laguna Toreadora takes a few hours, and Cerro San Luis (4,200 meters), on the opposite side, can be climbed in a day. The trail from Laguna Toreadora past Laguna Totoras and Laguna Patoquinuas (told you there were a lot of lakes here!) takes about six hours.

Guides are a good idea all the time, and they may be required for overnight hikes.

These include a trek to the Inca ruins by Lago Osohuayco and the hike from Miguir to the southern park guard post at Soldados. Be warned that trails have a tendency to peter out, and the weather can turn on you in a minute. Nighttime temperatures can drop below freezing, and deaths from exposure have occurred here. Bring waterproof clothing, maps, a compass, and possibly rubber boots. Also consider fishing gear and a compass if you plan to wander far afield, which you certainly should. Four IGM 1:50,000 maps cover the area: *Cuenca, Chaucha, San Felipe de Molleturo,* and *Chiquintad.* The tourist office also has an excellent illustrated map that covers the whole park area.

The August–January dry season is the best time to visit, promising the most sun and regular but short-lived rain showers. The rainy season February–July has the highest average temperature but more precipitation. High altitudes make acclimatization a good idea—hike high, sleep low.

Tour companies in Cuenca organize excursions to El Cajas.

EAST OF CUENCA

The hills above Cuenca to the east shelter several crafts villages that are well worth a detour. Sunday is market day, but it's possible to visit all the main ones on any day of the week and be back in Cuenca by night. Buses run every few minutes between each town and its neighbors, usually from the main market plaza, and numerous tour companies in Cuenca offer tours by private bus or car. If you'd prefer to take your time, there are numerous lodging options and a network of trails connecting the towns, similar to the area around Otavalo in the northern Sierra.

Gualaceo

On the banks of the Río Gualaceo, 34 kilometers from Cuenca, this small town hosts the largest indigenous market in the area every Sunday. Three separate markets—fruits and vegetables, crafts and clothes, and produce and household goods—blend effectively into one. Tourists come for the fine woven and embroidered textiles, such as the *macana* shawls with macramé fringe, in nearby Bullcay, and for the bucolic scenery that has earned Gualaceo the nickname "the Garden of Azuay."

The **Hotel El Molina,** a few blocks south of the center, is $12 pp. In the town center, two blocks north of the church plaza, is **Carlos Andres,** which has clean rooms for $6 pp.

Restaurant Don Q, on the northwest corner of the main plaza, gets high marks for its food and ambience, serving typical Ecuadorian fare for about $4 a plate. **El Dragon Restaurant,** one block north of the bus station, serves Ecuadorian and Chinese food. Gualaceo's **Peach Festival** in early March features exhibitions of flowers and crafts.

The road from Cuenca (45 minutes, $0.50) is plied by buses that leave every 15 minutes from Cuenca's *terminal terrestre.* Gualaceo's bus station is on the east side of Roldos between Cordero and Reyes, southeast of the main market plaza. A shortcut down into the Amazon heads east through the Macas Pass (3,350 meters) after 24 kilometers before dropping to Limón.

Bullcay

North of Gualaceo, this small town suffered a difficult period after the "La Josefina" landslide, which wiped out part of the village and the access road to Cuenca. People are returning and the road is open again, many of the weavers of Macanas are once again producing wonderful *ikat* shawls and belts using the traditional methods and indigo dyes. Several families will give you a demonstration of the process. Also at the entrance to the village is a lovely orchid garden—ask for Jose Partilla. The **Peñon de Cuzay** (tel. 7/220-3815) offers comfortable rooms, plus use of the spa and pool for $12 pp.

Chordeleg and South

This smaller village lies five kilometers downhill from Gualaceo, a pretty one-to-two-hour walk if you're so inclined. The Sunday market here is more oriented to tourists, with flashier merchandise and higher prices. Chordeleg has been a jewelry center since before the Inca arrived, and today a couple of handfuls of *joyerías* (jewelry shops) around town turn out finely wrought silver and gold. A small community museum on the main plaza has displays on the history and techniques of this and other local crafts, including ceramics, hat weaving, and textiles.

A smaller, more indigenous Sunday market is held in **Sigsig** (26 kilometers south of Gualaceo). Panama hats made in town are usually for sale. The Chaquiñan (walking road) southeast to Gualaquiza in the Amazon lowlands makes a good two-to-three-day hike. Ten kilometers to the south of Sigsig are the famous pre-colonial caves of Chobshi and some nearby Inca ruins.

This trip can be done as a loop, returning through the hillside village of San Bartolomé, where generations of craftsmen have handmade guitars, then crossing over the *paramos* to El Valle and Cuenca.

NORTH OF CUENCA
Cañar

The nearest major town to the Ingapirca ruins is the home of descendants of the Cañari *indígenas* who were defeated and assimilated by the Inca. The Cañari fill the streets with their brightly colored ponchos and white felt bowlers, chatting in Kichwa sprinkled with a few words of their own ancient tongue. They're known for their double-sided weavings sold in town and at the vibrant Sunday market. The best place to buy them is at the local jail, half a block up Colón from the main plaza, where prisoners make and sell them from behind a metal fence. They don't come cheap, nor is bargaining with the inmates easy, as you can probably imagine. They will, however, happily tell you the stories of their incarceration—I bought one from a man serving five years for killing a thief.

Residencial Monica (tel. 7/223-5486, $5 pp)

is on the plaza. At the Monica 2 (no sign—ask at the plaza), rooms with private bathrooms and hot water are $8 pp. Buses leave every 20 minutes from the east side of town ($1, ask for directions) for the village of Ingapirca (not the ruins), taking almost one hour. Transportes Cañar has departures every 15 minutes to Cuenca ($1.50, two hours) from its office on 24 de Mayo, a few blocks east of the plaza. Buses also go to Ingapirca regularly. A few head north from Cañar, but locals recommend going out to the Pana or El Tambo and flagging one down.

◀ INGAPIRCA RUINS

Ecuador's only public and easily accessed Inca structure—not to mention its most impressive pre-Columbian ruins—survived the Spanish invasion more or less intact. The classic fine masonry perched on a picturesque hillside makes the 10-kilometer detour from the Pana a definite must-do day trip.

History

The Cañari were the first to build here, calling their temple/observatory Cashaloma, meaning "place where the stars pour from the heavens." The Incas came steamrolling through at the end of the 15th century, erecting the current structure before being flattened themselves by the Spanish. Archaeologists are still unsure as to the site's specific function—most likely it was a religious settlement, with a distinctive oval temple and attached convent for ritual maidens (many female skeletons have been unearthed). Other guesses range from a military fortress and grain depository to a *tambos,* or rest spot, along the Inca highway. Most likely, Ingapirca was a combination of all of the above.

In the centuries since the Incas departed, many Ingapirca stones were carted away to provide the foundations of buildings, especially churches, in the immediate area. In 1966, the site was opened to the public, and nine years later responsibility for the ruins' upkeep and administration fell to the local Cañari *indígenas.*

THE INCA TRAIL TO INGAPIRCA

One of Ecuador's most popular multinight hikes follows an ancient Inca road through the southern tip of the Avenue of the Volcanoes. Mountain vistas and great trout fishing make the three-day journey enjoyable, but campsite thieves can do the opposite. (Avoid this by hiring locals with mules to carry your luggage.)

Keep in mind that you'll be hiking at higher than 3,000 meters the whole way, and that the trail follows a river, so it can get muddy – take it slow and bring rubber boots. The IGM 1:50,000 maps *Alausí, Juncal,* and *Cañar* cover the area and should put the trip within range of even weekend hikers – with a compass. Alternatively, book a spot on a guided trek with tour companies in Quito or Cuenca.

First make your way from Alausí to Achupallas, a one-hour taxi ride ($12) or tiring 25-kilometer hike. Leave Achupallas to the south past the elementary school, cross the Río Azuay, and reach the west bank of the Río Candrul after passing through a natural hole in the rock. From here, the trail heads clearly south between the Cerros Mapahuña and Pucará. There's a good campsite on the south side of the Laguna Tres Cruces at 4,200 meters, 14 kilometers and six-seven hours from Achupallas.

Day two takes you below the peak of Cerro Quilloloma to the west, which is the highest point along the hike (4,400 meters). Ríos Sansahuín and Espíndol join the Candrul near here. Although it would be possible to push to Ingapirca in one long second day, most hikers choose to spend the night among the graffiti of Los Paredones (Big Walls) ruins, east of the Lago Culebrillas and 10 kilometers from the Laguna Tres Cruces.

The worn stone path eventually disappears past Los Paredones, but the rooftops of Tambo come into view soon after. Pass under a power line on the way down to and across the Río Silante before ascending to Ingapirca.

The Site

Five hectares of low stone walls and grassy slopes are anchored by the famous rounded temple. Grazing llamas add a picturesque touch to the scene, which, aside from the temple, is mostly just a vague outline of what once stood here. The small **Pilaloma** complex on the south side marks the original Cañari settlement, next to a pointy-roofed replica of an Inca house and round depressions called *colcas* that were used to store food.

A fragment of Inca road called the **Ingañan,** better engineered than many modern Ecuadorian highways (notice the drainage channel), leads past *bodegas* used for food storage to an exterior plaza called **La Condamine** after the French scientist's visit in 1748. These were the nobles' living quarters, including the *acllahuasi*—dwellings of ceremonial virgins. Don't miss the V-shaped rock at the entrance, supposedly used for beheadings. Next to it is a larger stone with 28 holes that was thought to be used as a lunar calendar; the holes caught rainwater that told the date by reflecting the moon's light differently throughout the month.

Across the **main plaza** sits the **Temple of the Sun,** also known as El Castillo (The Castle). If you've been to Peru, you'll recognize the mind-boggling stonework that forms the two-story structure, too tight to fit even a piece of paper between the blocks. The elliptical shape, pocketed with trapezoidal niches, is unique in Inca ruins. The entire structure is exactly three times as long as it is wide, leading some archaeologists to envision three adjoining circles representing the three phases of the sun: *anti* (dawn), *inti* (noon), and *cunti* (sunset).

The collection in the well-done **site museum** includes a mummy, pottery, and ancient textile fragments set under a magnifying glass to show the amazing craftsmanship. Guidebooks to the site are available in different languages, and a room upstairs contains examples of traditional indigenous dress. An **artisan shop** next door sells regional crafts; *cafeterías* and public toilets are across the way.

Visiting Ingapirca

The ruins (tel. 7/221-5115, kurinti@cue.satnet.net, 9 A.M.–5 P.M. daily) can be reached from the Pana via either El Tambo or Cañar, by car, bus, or foot (a scenic but mostly uphill three-hour hike). The entrance fee for foreigners ($6 pp) includes a free tour; tips, as always, are appreciated.

About one kilometer before the ruins is the village of Ingapirca, where the family-run **Residencial Inti Huasi** (tel. 7/221-5171) has clean rooms with hot water and private bathrooms for $6 pp, as well as a popular restaurant where good Ecuadorian fare goes for about $3. If the restaurant is full, as it often is, **Restaurant El Turista** a few doors down will do.

The newly extended **Posada Ingapirca** (tel. 7/221-5116 or 7/283-1120) has 22 fancy but still rustic rooms with private baths, hot water, and breakfast for $55 s, $67 d. Set in a restored farm building, this place can make you feel as if you've stepped back a century. The antiques-filled dining room is the haunt of tour groups, but if you come just for the $8 lunch, views of the Temple of the Sun and heat from the fireplace are included.

Trans-Cañar buses run direct from Cuenca's *terminal terrestre* at 9 A.M., noon, 1 P.M., and 2 P.M. daily ($2.50 pp), returning at 1 and 4 P.M. Most tour companies in Cuenca offer organized excursions.

SOUTH TO LOJA

The Pana splits 15 kilometers south of Cuenca. On its way downhill to Machala, the west branch reaches **Girón** after 27 kilometers, with great hikes in the surrounding cloud forest to waterfalls and rivers teeming with trout. Another 30 kilometers brings you to the **Yunguilla Valley** and just beyond to **Santa Isabel.** The climate here is considered ideal by the Cuencanos who travel down to this warm area to their weekend homes, or to stay at one of the lovely *hosterías* with swimming pools and other outdoor activities. The residents of Machala drive up to this deliciously cool climate to escape the coastal heat. **Fundacion Jocotoco** bought several adjoining parcels of land here to protect the dusky brush finch, which was severely endangered and now seems to be reproducing well.

Jima

This small village about 20 kilometers southeast of Cuenca bills itself as a "hiker's paradise" and is the starting point for a three–four-day hike to the Amazon. Small, clean **Hotel Carlos Aguilar Vazquez** (tel. 7/229-0681) offers beds for $4 pp and friendly service. Ask here for trail maps detailing day hikes to the top of numerous forested peaks that rise to 3,300 meters. Guides are also available for the overnight hike through San Miguel de los Cuyes and La Florida, about three days' walk from Jima, where you can catch a bus to Gualaquiza in the Oriente.

Peace Corps volunteers have helped set up a nonprofit, community-based tourism organization called the **Fundación Turística Jima,** through which you can hire local guides and mules for hikes. The **Tambillo Protected Forest** is a protected cloud forest 45 minutes from town toward the Oriente, where the bird list counts over 200 species. (Trucks can be hired in town to get there, and a small entrance fee is charged.)

The annual **Festival de la Chicha de Jora,** held on the first Saturday in October, includes a *chicha*-judging contest (sign me up!) and dance competitions. Five Transportes Jima buses leave Cuenca every couple of hours 8:30 A.M.–5 P.M., boarding opposite the Feria Libre outdoor market on Avenida Americas (two hours, $2). Six buses return to Cuenca 6 A.M.–5 P.M. daily.

Saraguro

The eastern branch of the Pana threads the Tinajilla Pass (3,527 meters) crossing high *paramo* and desert canyons before reaching this village, which is home to the *indígenas* of the same name. Almost everything of import is located on the main square, including several craft vendors (who, for a small fee, will teach you how the beadwork is done), and the restaurants **Reina Cisne,** where a filling

---

THE SARAGUROS

Indigenous Saraguros, whose name means "corn worm" in Quechua, thrive in Saraguro and the nearby mountain villages of Oñacapa, Lagunas, Quisuginchir, and Tuncarta. Numbering about 30,000, the Saraguros have held onto their cultural identity particularly well since being moved here from Peru by the Inca.

Both sexes wear white hats with wide, flat brims, and the predominance of black in their wardrobes is thought to reflect perpetual mourning for their betrayed Inca, Atahualpa. Men wear a sleeveless shirt called a *cushma,* along with a poncho and knee-length black or blue wool pants held up by a leather belt decorated with silver. A double shoulder bag called an *alforja* is hung over one shoulder, and long hair is worn braided. Special occasions call for white wool chaps called *zamarros.* Women wear black wool shawls, embroidered blouses, and pleated black skirts called *anacus.* Glass bead necklaces and silver earrings provide some sparkle, and silver shawl pins called *tupus* are often family heirlooms.

The financially successful Saraguros began as crafts makers, but they've since moved on to herding cattle as far as the Amazonian province of Zamora-Chinchipe in search of grazing land.

For more information on the Saraguros, visit www.saraguro.org.

---

almuerzo is $1.50; and **Mama Cuchara,** where traditional meals are washed down with *horchata,* a refreshing pink drink made with 19 herbs and flowers. **Turu Manka,** a walk up the hill on Calle Loja, offers international cuisine at affordable prices—a filet mignon with all the trimmings is available for lunch or dinner for $5.

Buses to Loja and Cuenca pass roughly every half hour and stop in front of their offices on Calle Azuay; some also loop through the plaza before leaving. Catch a bus here to Loja (two hours) or Cuenca (3.5 hours). The **post office** has moved northeast a couple of blocks and shares a building with the local radio station Buen Pastor. A municipal museum is planned to house some of the Inca rocks (see the sidebar *Inca Supermen*) and other cultural artifacts from the area. The design was scheduled for completion in June 2008—it will be on Calle Loja, a few hundred meters from the center.

Simple accommodations are available in town. The best of the bunch is **Samana Wasi** (tel. 7/220-0315, $8 pp). The **Residencial Armijos** (tel. 7/220-0306) and the **Residencial Saraguro** (tel. 7/220-0286), both northeast of the plaza, have rooms for about $5 and hot water in the mornings (or so they claim). The latter has a flower-filled courtyard.

Just on the outskirts of town toward the peak is the very best place to stay in the whole area: **Achik Wasi** receives rave reviews for its clean, comfortable rooms, really hot showers, and balconies with views over the town—at $20 pp, including breakfast, it's worth every penny.

For a small town high in the Andes, Saraguro has plenty to do. For starters, stop by the **Sunday-morning market** or one of the many indigenous artisan shops. Ask directions to the home workshop of **Manuel Encarnacion Quishpe,** who weaves dozens of different kinds of textiles on 12 upright looms. His wife and daughters make jewelry.

Suggested **hikes** nearby include the Hizzikaka (Sinincapa) Caves, the Virgen Kaka Waterfall, Puglla Mountain, and the Washapamba Cloud Forest. Many side tracks lead off into the hills all along this section of the Pana into some of the most remote regions of the Ecuadorian Sierra. Local guides are available to lead the three–four-day traditional hike to the jungle, as well as many other hikes. The community tourism organization (www.turismocomunitario.com) arranges family homestays for $18 pp, including meals, and can set up visits to other places. Also try the route through **Nabón** from La Ramada north of Oña, or either of the east–west roads from Saraguro. From here, the southbound Pana inches over four more passes before descending to Loja.

Loja and Vicinity

The gateway city to the southern Amazon enjoys the pleasant climate of the Cuxibamba Valley (meaning "cheerful flowery garden"), which helps account for its tranquil character. It's one of the oldest cities in the country, founded in 1546 to the west before being moved to its present location two years later. The only event of note in Loja's history occurred in 1897, when a small hydroelectric project just west of the city center lit the first lightbulbs in Ecuador.

Today, Loja (pop. 150,000) is a quiet, clean, pretty city of little distinction. Gold finds to the east and west have brought in money over the years, but the city still has a very middle-class air, enjoyable and relaxed. A national university, two technical colleges, a music conservatory, and a law school make the capital of Loja Province a center of learning on Ecuador's southernmost tip. Ríos Zamora and Malacatus bracket the city center, intersecting just north of it before heading east to add more water to the jungle. Ecuadorians consider the Loja accent to be the best in the country, claiming the city's inhabitants almost sing when they speak Spanish.

In 2001, Loja won Best in Criteria of Community Involvement in the International Awards for Livable Communities, and a few hours in town will show you why. There are no beggars on the streets, the drinking fountains work, and many old buildings have been attractively painted. There's little garbage, because just about everything is recycled.

Loja is a good hub for accessing the Peruvian border, the southern Amazon, Podocarpus Reserve, and the ever popular Vilcabamba.

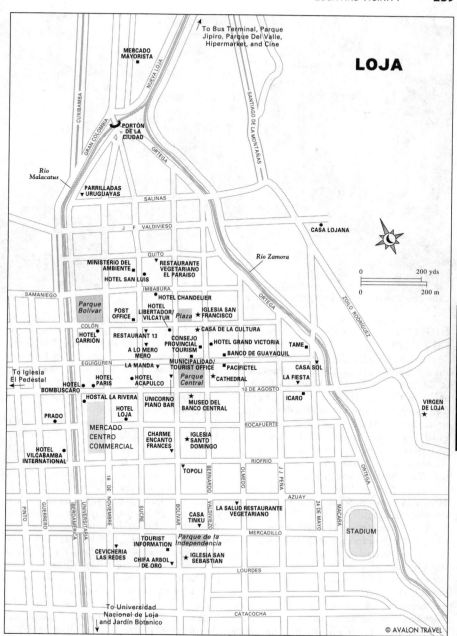

LOJA

To Bus Terminal, Parque Jipiro, Parque Del Valle, Hipermarket, and Cine

MERCADO MAYORISTA

PORTÓN DE LA CIUDAD

Río Malacatus

PARRILLADAS URUGUAYAS

CASA LOJANA

Río Zamora

MINISTERIO DEL AMBIENTE
RESTAURANTE VEGETARIANO EL PARAISO
HOTEL SAN LUIS

HOTEL CHANDELIER
Parque Bolívar
POST OFFICE
HOTEL LIBERTADOR/ VILCATUR
Plaza
IGLESIA SAN FRANCISCO

HOTEL CARRIÓN
RESTAURANT 13
A LO MERO MERO
CONSEJO PROVINCIAL TOURISM
CASA DE LA CULTURA
HOTEL GRAND VICTORIA
BANCO DE GUAYAQUIL
TAME

LA MANDA
MUNICIPALIDAD/ TOURIST OFFICE
PACIFICTEL
CASA SOL
LA FIESTA

HOTEL PARIS
HOTEL ACAPULCO
Parque Central
CATHEDRAL

HOTEL BOMBUSCARO
To Iglesia El Pedestal

HOSTAL LA RIVERA
UNICORNO PIANO BAR
MUSEO DEL BANCO CENTRAL
ICARO
VIRGEN DE LOJA

HOTEL LOJA
PRADO

MERCADO CENTRO COMMERCIAL

HOTEL VILCABAMBA INTERNATIONAL

CHARME ENCANTO FRANCES
IGLESIA SANTO DOMINGO

TOPOLI

CASA TINKU
LA SALUD RESTAURANTE VEGETARIANO

TOURIST INFORMATION
Parque de la Independencia

CEVICHERIA LAS REDES
CHIFA ARBOL DE ORO
IGLESIA SAN SEBASTIAN

STADIUM

To Universidad Nacional de Loja and Jardín Botánico

0   200 yds
0   200 m

SOUTHERN SIERRA

© AVALON TRAVEL

Street labels: CUXIBAMBA, GRAN COLOMBIA, NUEVA LOJA, ORTEGA, SANTIAGO DE LA MONTAÑAS, SALINAS, J F VALDIVIESO, QUITO, SAMANIEGO, IMBABURA, COLÓN, EGUIGUREN, ZOILO RODRIGUEZ, 10 DE AGOSTO, ROCAFUERTE, RIOFRIO, BERNARDO, OLMEDO, J J PEÑA, AZUAY, 18 DE NOVIEMBRE, SUCRE, BOLIVAR, VALDIVIEZO, MERCADILLO, 24 DE MAYO, MACARA, ORTEGA, PINTO, GUERRERO, IBEROAMÉRICA, UNIVERSITARIA, LOURDES, CATACOCHA

SOUTHERN SIERRA

Calle Lourdes is part of a city restoration project.

© JEAN BROWN

SIGHTS
City Center

At the north end of the city center, where the rivers intersect, the castle-like **Portón de la Ciudad** (City Gate) is handsomely lit up at night. On the east side of Loja's **Parque Central** stands the city **cathedral,** which hosts the Virgen del Cisne icon (see *West of Loja*) from late August to the beginning of November. Across from the Municipal Building is the **Museo del Banco Central** (tel. 7/257-3004, 9 A.M.–1 P.M. and 2–5 P.M. Mon.–Fri., free), with small exhibits of archaeology and works by local artists in a restored colonial building.

As in Cuenca, many of Loja's old buildings have recently been restored, making a random stroll through the city center a rewarding experience. The stretch along Lourdes between Sucre and Bolívar is particularly attractive. Loja's independence was declared on November 18, 1820, in the aptly named **Parque de la Independencia** (a.k.a. Plaza San Sebastián), five blocks south of the central plaza. All of the buildings around the plaza have been given facelifts, making it one of the most beautiful plazas in Ecuador. Dance and music performances are occasionally held here in the shadow of the clock tower on weekday evenings.

At the end of 2006, the **Museo de Arte Religioso** opened its doors to the public in the Monastery of the Madres Conceptas (10 Agosto 12–78 and Bernardo, tel. 7/256-1109, 9 A.M.–noon and 2–5 P.M. Mon.–Fri., $1). Housed in spare surroundings, the ornate religious pieces make quite a contrast.

Loja has always been famous for its musicians and singers, so the **Museo de la Musica,** which opened in 2003 in the patio of Colegio Bernardo Valdivieso (Bernardo between Riofrio and Rocafuerte, tel. 7/256-1342, 8.30 A.M.–12:30 P.M. and 3–7 P.M. Mon.–Fri., free) was long awaited. The collection is small, but the presentations by local artists on Thursdays draw a goodly number of visitors.

Loja's best views are from the **Virgen del Loja** statue, east and uphill on Rocafuerte, and the **Iglesia El Pedestal,** also called the Balcón de Loja (Balcony of Loja), west of the city center on 10 de Agosto.

Outside the Center

Head a few kilometers north of the center to reach **Parque Jipiro,** a fantasy world for young and old on an island in Río Zamora. The park's most famous landmark—a miniature, slide-filled Saint Basil's Cathedral—is only part of a huge playground filled with equipment that would send American liability lawyers into convulsions. There's a video room in the European castle and a planetarium in the mosque. Other diversions include a pool with water slides, a skate park, paddleboats, and a small avian zoo. A small extra charge is levied for some activities. To get there, take a taxi or a bus north from Universitaria.

South of the center spreads the campus of the **Universidad Nacional de Loja.** Go just to see the **Jardín Botánico Reindaldo Espinosa** (tel. 7/264-2764, 9 A.M.–4 P.M. Mon.–Fri.), a large botanical collection with more than enough flowers and bizarre plants to make the trip worthwhile for floraholics and bird watchers alike. The actual entrance is 150 meters south of where you will surely assume it is. Across the highway is the **Parque Universitario La Argelia** (with a network of well-maintained trails leading up into the piney woods). The park is open from dawn to dusk, but it's hit or miss when the visitors center will be open. Excellent views of the city await from the *mirador,* half an hour's walk from the entrance. Southbound buses marked "Argelia Capuli" pass the garden and park.

ENTERTAINMENT AND EVENTS
Nightlife

The so-called Musical Capital of Southern Ecuador has a depressingly limited range of evening options. Most are of the drinks-and-taped-music variety, such as the **Unicorno Piano Bar** (Bolívar 763 and 10 de Agosto), with a dim, red-velvet interior on the west side of Parque Central. You'll find live music and lively company at the **Casa Tinku** (Mercadillo

clock tower in Plaza San Sebastian

between Valdivieso and Bolívar), a candlelit bar decorated with artwork. You can get your groove on at **La Fiesta** (10 de Agosto between Juan José Peña and 24 de Mayo), or stop by the **Casa de la Cultura** (Colón and Valdivieso) to see if anything interesting is on the schedule.

Festivals

Loja comes alive during the first few weeks in September, when the **Virgen del Cisne** rolls into town. Huge processions and a produce fair in Parques Del Valle and Jipiro liven up this otherwise mild city. The **Independence of Loja** is celebrated on November 18, and the **Feast of San Sebastian** on December 8 coincides with the *fiesta* commemorating the **Foundation of Loja.**

SHOPPING

Unlike its larger neighbor to the north, Loja is not a great shopping city, but the **Mercado Centro Comercial** was rebuilt in 1991 into perhaps the cleanest and best-organized indoor

INCA SUPERMEN

Chronicles written at the time of the Spanish Conquest relate a tale of an Inca palace built in Cuzco, Peru and carried into Ecuador. Many archivists who have read these stories were convinced that the Incas were simply boasting to impress the Spaniards.

As the Inca tale goes, Huayna Capac, Sapa Inca of the Inca empire, decided that a fine palace should be constructed in the newly conquered northern territories. The rocks were quarried from one of the sources of fine rock near Cuzco, and stonemasons cut and finished the giant stones and assembled them. The buildings were then dismantled and the rocks sent to Ecuador. The rocks made their way along the spine of the Andes to Ecuador, climbing over high mountain passes and into deep river valleys.

After crossing one of the high passes in a storm, a bolt of lightening struck the main door lintel, a massive faced stone, and sundered it. The Inca decided that it was a very bad omen, and the exhausted travelers simply dropped all their rocks and headed home. There the tale ends – well, at least for 500 years. Archivists, archaeologists, and anthropologists passed over this tale as pure fabrication and got on with their research in other areas.

"The church in Paquishapa is Inca," was a statement heard many times by ex-Peace Corps volunteer Jim Belote. He hiked over to take a look and saw fine colonial fluted columns and an obviously post-colonial construction – definitely not Inca! However, Dennis Ogburn, an archaeologist from the USA working in Saraguro, went to investigate deeper into the ancient myths and legends after speaking with both ex- and current Peace Corps volunteers. In 2004, they explored the area and Dennis sampled the blue-grey andesite rocks found in the foundations of many local buildings, including the Paquishapa church. The samples were geo-chemically analyzed, and yes, they came from the Rumiqolqa Quarry near Cuzco! To date over 450 rocks have been located and positively identified in Saraguro and the surrounding area.

Four people are needed to lift even the smallest of these rocks, which can weigh up to 700 kilograms. Yet these rocks were carried at least 1,600 kilometers! This was an incredible undertaking, especially for a people who never had draft animals nor used the wheel for transport.

market in Ecuador. It's a good place to spot visiting Saraguro *indígenas,* as is the **Mercado Mayorista,** on Nueva Loja just north of the river confluence.

RECREATION AND TOURS

Vilcatur (tel./fax 7/258-8014, vilcatur@impsat .net.ec) operates out of the Hotel Libertador, offering tours to Puyango Petrified Forest for $50 pp (two-person minimum) and birdwatching in Podocarpus for $35 pp. Tours also go to Saraguro, El Cisne, and other destinations nearby. English-speaking guides are available, as are rental cars.

Aratinga Aventuras (Lourdes 14–80 and Sucre, tel./fax 7/258-2434, aratinga@loja.telco-net.net) specializes in well-recommended bird-

watching tours to Podocarpus ($50 pp with two people), but owner/guide Pablo Andrade can also set up trekking and camping trips. He rents equipment as well. **Biotours** (Bernardo between Eguiguren and Colón, tel. 7/257-9387, biotours_ec@yahoo.es) also does natural history, bird-watching, and cultural tours in the area.

ACCOMMODATIONS
Under $10

Several recommended budget hotels have good deals on rooms with private bath. Try the colonial **Hotel Loja** (Rocafuerte 15–27 and Sucre, tel. 7/257-0241, $8 pp) or the newer **Hotel Chandelier** (Imbabura 14–82 and Sucre, tel./ fax 7/256-3061, $9 pp).

$10-25

Rooms with private bath, cable TV, and phone are $11 pp at the **Hostal La Riviera** (Universitaria and 10 de Agosto, tel. 7/257-2863, tel./fax 7/257-7302). The **Hotel Acapulco** (Sucre 7–61 and 10 de Agosto, tel. 7/257-0651) has rooms for $14 s, $26 d, with cable TV, private bath, and phone. Other choices include **Hotel Paris** (10 de Agosto 16–49 between 18 de Noviembre and Universitaria, tel. 7/256-1369, $13 pp) and **Hotel Carrión** (Colón 16–36 and 18 de Noviembre, tel. 7/258-4548, $11 pp).

$25-50

◖ **Hotel Libertador** (Colón 14–30 and Bolívar, tel. 7/257-0344) offers guests racquetball courts, a gym, and a pool. Rooms cost $50 s, $61 d, with a presidential suite for $66. Across the river, the **Hotel Vilcabamba Internacional** (Iberoamérica and Riofrio, tel. 7/225-26339, $25 s, $33 d) has rooms of comparable quality, along with its own La Bastilla Restaurant.

Over $50

Casa Lojana (Paris 0008 and Zoila Rodriguez, tel. 7/258-5984) was opened a few years ago with the idea of providing Loja with a first-class hotel where students of tourism would be able to take part in running the facilities. It is attached to the university faculty and has comfortable, elegant rooms for $73 s, $98 d, including breakfast. The **Grand Victoria Boutique Hotel** (Bernardo 6–50 and Eguiguren, tel. 7/258-3500) was custom-built in fake republican style. Its 38 rooms and suites provide the most upscale accommodations in the province. Rooms begin at $110 s and include a buffet breakfast and spa and pool facilities. The elegant restaurant is open to the public and offers reasonably priced, well-presented meals from $4.50–12.

FOOD
Cafés and Health Food
La Salud Restaurante Vegetariano (Azuay 12–08 and Olmedo) satisfies vegetarians in the south end of town with a $1.50 *almuerzo,* and **Restaurant Vegetariano El Paraiso** (Sucre and Imbabura) does the same for patrons in the north with its $2 *menú del día.*

Juice and healthy snacks fill the short menu at **La Manda** (Eguiguren between Sucre and Bolívar). The corner café **Topoli** (Riofrio and Bolívar) features tasty breakfasts and yogurt in the morning and burgers, hot dogs, and falafel in the afternoon—all for less than $3. **Restaurant 13** (Colón 14–66 and Sucre, tel. 7/256-1586) is a quiet place for coffee or fruit juice and a good breakfast on the upper terrace of a well-maintained colonial house. Inside, rooms with antique wallpaper are used to host lunch and dinner weekdays and lunch on weekends.

International
Visit the **Casa China,** next to the Hotel Paris, for a taste of the Orient, southern-Sierra style; or try **Chifa Arbol de Oro** (Lourdes and Bolívar), with slightly higher prices. **Parilladas Uruguayas** (Salinas and 18 de Noviembre) is a good, inexpensive grill.

colonial Casa Sol restaurant terrace

© JEAN BROWN

SOUTHERN SIERRA

In the spirit of variety—and to enjoy its a mouthful of a name—try ◖ **Charme Encanto Frances** (Riofrio and Bolívar), which does a little French, a little Italian, and a little Ecuadorian for $4–7. Inexpensive Mexican food is on the menu at the family-run **A Lo Mero Mero** (Sucre 6–22 and Colón).

Local Food and Seafood

Loja is not particularly known for fine dining, but prices are lower than other provinces for decent meals. The **Cevichería Las Redes** (18 de Noviembre and Mercadillo, tel. 7/257-6977) is modest but good. Dishes start at $2.

At **La Castellana,** in the Hotel Libertador, one of the fanciest in the city, beef tenderloin in "caviar sauce" (go figure) is $6.50.

Locals eat a set lunch for $1.75 at **Casa Sol,** a charming old building with an upper terrace next to the Rio Malacatos (Ortega and Eguiguren). The traditional Loja plantain soup called *repe* is often on the menu.

INFORMATION AND SERVICES

The **tourist information center** (tel. 7/257-0407, ext. 219 or 220, 8 A.M.–1 P.M. and 2–6:30 P.M. Mon.–Fri., 9 A.M.–1 P.M. Sat.), in the Municipal Building on Parque Central, stocks maps and information on activities in the region. Around the corner in the **Consejo Provincial** (facing the Grand Victoria hotel), the tourism office on the ground floor has plenty of information about the rest of the province.

Banco de Guayaquil, on Eguiguren just east of Parque Central, will change travelers' checks. Assorted shops on 10 de Agosto will also change money—look for **La Moneda** and **Compraventa.**

Loja's **post office** is at Colón 15–09 and Sucre. Information on entering the country to the south can be found at the **Peruvian consulate** (Rodriguez 03–05 and Carrión, tel. 7/257-9068).

If you're thinking of visiting Podocarpus National Park, check in with the **Ministerio del Ambiente** (Sucre between Quito and Imbabura, tel. 7/257-1534 or 7/258-5421, 8 A.M.–12:30 P.M. and 1–4:30 P.M. Mon.–Fri.), up on the third floor. The **Fundación Arco Iris** (Buganvillas 24–22 and Gobernacion, tel. 7/258-8680, direccion@arcoiris.org.ec) administers the San Francisco Cloud Forest adjoining Podocarpus National Park and can provide information on the park as well.

TRANSPORTATION

Like its market, Loja's *terminal terrestre* is clean, modern, and organized. It's a 10-minute bus ride or a 20-minute walk north of the city center on Cuxibamba. Local buses run north on Universitaria and back down Iberoamérica/Aguirre every few minutes. A new integrated service has raised stops and is a fast, efficient north–south route. Panamericana has luxury overnight buses for Quito leaving at 5:15 P.M. for $15 (14–15 hours). Normal buses to Quito are $14, and you can also get to Cuenca ($7.50, five hours) and Zamora ($2, two hours). Transportes Loja and a Peruvian bus line go to Piura, Peru, four times a day ($8, eight hours).

Vilcabamba Turis buses leave for Vilcabamba every half hour from the terminal. Just as convenient, quicker, and less inexpensive—albeit less comfortable—are the *taxi rutas* leaving from Iberoamérica and Chile, half a kilometer south of the city center. Local buses heading south on Iberoamérica pass nearby—just tell the driver where you're going. They cost $1 pp and leave when full; it's 45 minutes to Vilcabamba.

Flights with **TAME** (24 de Mayo and Ortega, tel. 7/257-0248) and **Icaro** leave from the airport called La Toma in nearby Catamayo (see *West of Loja*).

EAST OF LOJA

The southern gateway to the Ecuadorian Amazon follows Río Zamora northeast from the town of Zamora. This little-used back door to the Oriente is perfect if you'd like to go where none of your friends have been. The road from Loja is one of the most scenic in the country, making the bus ride alone worthy of a day trip. Leaving Loja, the route twists and turns so much that you'll find yourself still staring down at the city half an hour after you've left. It climbs up to a 2,500-meter pass before snaking through deep wooded valleys and past waterfalls. The road is in good condition most of the way, so it would also make an excellent bike ride (even if you cheat and have a bus take you up to the pass).

Zamora

The powerful sun that hits you as you step off the bus reminds you that Zamora, at 1,000 meters elevation, is definitely on the tropical side of the country, both geographically and culturally. This rough-and-tumble frontier town 65 kilometers east of Loja succumbed to continual raids by local indigenous tribes after its founding in 1550. Rebuilt in the 19th century, it became the capital of the newly founded (and similarly undeveloped) province of Zamora-Chinchipe in 1953; it was another decade before the city saw its first motor vehicle. The rediscovery of gold in nearby Nambija has injected some life into the dusty streets, but Zamora still seems like the kind of town where the mail arrives by stagecoach and the bars don't serve drinks with umbrellas.

On Tamayo, a block uphill from the park, the **Tzanka Ecological Refuge** (tel. 7/260-5692) has a small zoo with Amazonian animals, an orchid garden, and a one-room museum with a random but interesting collection. The refuge also offers a small restaurant and rooms for rent ($15 pp, including breakfast), as well as jungle tours.

Zamora's other lodging options serve as a reminder that this isn't a tourist town. The most comfortable is the **Orillas de Zamora** (Diego de la Vaca and Alonso de Mercadillo, tel. 7/260-5565, hotel_o_zamora@hotmail .com), with well-maintained rooms overlooking the river for $14 s, $24 d. **Hotel Gimyfa** (tel. 7/260-5024), on Diego de Vaca one block east of the plaza, is also good for $9 s, $15 d, with TV, private bath, and hot water.

Ceviche is $3.50 at the open-air **Cevichería Bart's Cave,** on the northwest corner of the plaza near the **King Burger.** More than a dozen restaurants in and around the bus station serve basic Ecuadorian fare. One block south of the bus station on Sevilla de Oro is **Cheers,** a good place for a beer. A block west is **Restaurant Don Pepe,** serving *comida típica* across the street from the hospital for $3 and up.

The **post office** sits a few doors east of the plaza on Sevilla de Oro, although you would hardly know it from the faded sign. For information on Podocarpus, stop by the **Ministerio del Ambiente** office (tel. 7/260-6606, 8 A.M.– 12:30 P.M. and 1:30–4:30 P.M. Mon.–Fri.), across from the cemetery a short distance out the road to Loja. There's a **tourist office** (tel. 7/260-5996, 8 A.M.–12:30 P.M. and 2–5 P.M. Mon.–Fri.) with maps and local information on the third floor of the Municipal Building on the main plaza.

The **bus terminal** is a few blocks east of the plaza, across Amazonas from the **market.** Buses and *rancheros* head out to various small towns where locals will stare at you as if you fell out of the sky—even more than in Zamora. Gualaquiza is $5 and five hours away.

Near Zamora

Bird-watchers will delight in **Cabañas Ecológicas Copalinga** (tel. 9/347-7013, jacamar@impsat.net.ec), a farm halfway down the road to Podocarpus National Park. Catherine Vits and her husband, Boudewijn De Roover, can accommodate small groups in lovely cabins ($30 s, $45 d, $50/70 with all meals). Student cabins are available for $14 pp, or $24 with all meals. They both guide and speak several languages. Advance notice is advisable. Look for the black iron entrance gate three kilometers from Zamora on the right-hand side.

█ PODOCARPUS NATIONAL PARK

Ecuador's southernmost national park is a hidden gem. Large tracts of virgin forest shelter a bewildering array of climates and residents, and some of the most spectacular scenery lies within easy access of Loja and Vilcabamba. Even as poaching, illegal colonizing, and especially mining take their toll, the relatively few tourists who visit Podocarpus come away knowing they've seen something special—whether it's the fairy-tale high-altitude forest or one of the flashier of the park's hundreds of bird species.

Natural History

Stretching unbroken from the high Andes to low-altitude rainforest, Podocarpus's 360,000 dripping hectares encompass countless microclimates, many found nowhere else in Ecuador. The park is roughly divided into a *zona alta* (high zone) to the west, rising up to 3,600 meters in the Nudo de Sabanilla mountain range; and a *zona baja* (low zone) to the east. Most of Podocarpus lies between 2,000 and 3,000 meters, consisting of hillsides covered with moist cloud forest and waterfalls. Four separate watersheds, including that of Loja, depend on Podocarpus for their moisture. More than 100 small Andean lakes left in glacial depressions dot the landscape, fed and drained by waterfalls and rushing streams.

More than 40 percent of the park's thousands of plant species are endemic. Podocarpus takes its name from having the country's largest contingent of the Podocarpus or *romerillo* tree, the only conifer native to Ecuador. Although many of these trees have been cut down for their high-quality wood, some old 40-meter giants can still be appreciated in remote tracts of cloud forest. Once the world's only source of quinine to fight malaria, the cascarilla tree *(Chinchona succirubra)* is common on the western slopes. Other common plants include orchids, bromeliads, palms, and tree ferns.

Podocarpus is by far the most important animal sanctuary in Ecuador's southern Andes. Along with attractive but seldom-seen species, such as the spectacled bear, mountain tapir, ocelot, puma, and deer, the park is home to enough avian variety to make birders ecstatic: 600 species have been recorded so far.

The main entrance at Cajanuma has been called one of the best spots in the world, in terms of variety and easy access, for viewing Andean birds. The list goes on and on: 61 species of hummingbirds, 81 different tanagers, and the endangered bearded guan *(Penelope barbata)* are only the beginning. Endemic species, such as the neblina metaltail *(Matallura odomae)*, also make a strong showing. **Fundacion Jocotoco** took its name from the call of a new species of antpitta that was discovered on the park boundaries in 1998—its call sounds like a cross between an owl's hoot and a dog's bark. International funding has allowed the foundation to purchase tracts of land adjacent to the park to protect the second-largest known antpitta in the world.

Visiting Podocarpus

Podocarpus has two main gateways. To access the *zona alta*, head 14 kilometers south of Loja to the turnoff for the **Cajanuma ranger station.** Buses to Vilcabamba can drop you off here, but it's another nine kilometers uphill to the *refugio*, opened in 1995 with the help of the Nature Conservancy, the World Wildlife Fund, and the Peace Corps. (It's sometimes possible to hitch a ride with park employees.) It has space and facilities for up to 20 people. Book your spot with the Ministerio del Ambiente in Loja beforehand.

Grab a map and hit one of the many marked *senderos* (trails) that wind off into the woods, ranging from the 400-meter-loop Sendero Oso de Anteojos (Spectacled Bear Trail) to the two-day hike to Lagunas del Compadre. The Sendero al Mirador takes three–fours hours to reach a lookout point at 3,050 meters.

The **San Francisco Cloud Forest,** administered by the Fundación Arco Iris and the Ministerio del Ambiente, is west of Loja on the road to Zamora. Here, you can hike the Sendero los Romerillos (four hours round-trip) to a grove of ancient Podocarpus trees and stay in a simple but comfortable **lodge** with hot showers and kitchen facilities for $8–10 pp. (Book in advance with the Ministerio or Arco Iris in Loja.)

Reach the *zona baja* by way of Zamora. Six kilometers south of the city (walk or take a taxi), down the west side of the Río Bombuscara, is the **Bombuscara ranger station.** After a dip in the river, try one of the numerous short trails and keep your eyes open—maybe you'll see a gray tinamou, coppery-chested jackamar, Ecuadorian piedtail hummer, one of a whole spectrum of tanagers (paradise, orange-eared, blue-necked, bay-headed, green-and-gold, and spotted), or a white-breasted parakeet *(Phyrrura albipectus).* The Sendero Higuerones is the longest path here, taking three–four hours round-trip.

The **entrance fee** is $10 pp for the *zona alta* and $20 pp for the *zona baja,* paid at the Ministerio del Ambiente offices in Loja or Zamora. Ask at one of those offices for information about cabins ($3–5 pp) inside the park, which are preferable to camping, due to the unpredictable high-altitude weather.

For most of the park, October–December are the driest overall months, with February–April seeing the most rain. Temperatures vary from a 12°C average in the high Andes to 18°C in the rainforest. Raingear is a must. The west side of Podocarpus is covered by the IGM 1:50,000 maps *Río Sabanilla* and *Vilcabamba* (or the 1:100,000 *Gonzanamá*), and the east side falls within the 1:50,000 *Zamora* and *Cordillera de Tzunantza* maps. Tour companies in Loja, Zamora, and Vilcabamba offer trips.

WEST OF LOJA

Catamayo, 31 kilometers west of Loja, is the site of **La Toma Airport.** TAME has flights to Quito daily ($83) and Icaro Sunday–Friday ($76), and to Guayaquil Monday–Saturday ($72). Reserve your seats beforehand.

A short spur north from Catamayo ends at **El Cisne,** where the **Santuario de La Virgen del Cisne** is kept in a grand old church. The icon was carved in the late 16th century and is one of the most venerated in the Ecuadorian Andes. A five-day festival starting August 15 clogs the road to Loja with crowds of pilgrims bearing the image on their shoulders. Some make the entire trek on foot. The Virgin arrives in Loja on the 20th, where it stays until November 20. There's lovely walking in the area, and several small hotels offer accommodations for $4–5 pp with beautiful views. You can camp at the pilgrims' house for $2. Avoid weekends and the month of August for a quiet retreat.

Macará

In 1995, Ecuador's second-largest gateway to Peru saw gunfire across the bridge over the Río Macará. Since the signing of the border agreement in 1998, thankfully, things have quieted down. Because fewer tourists come this far out, the border crossing at Macará (pop. 15,000) is simpler than at Huaquillas to the north, and thus preferable. Besides, the mountain scenery is better here.

The hotel **Terra Verde** (tel. 7/269-4585, $8 pp), on the hill behind the bus stop at the north end of town, is the only place in town with air-conditioning and cable TV. The **Hotel Espiga de Oro** (Ante and 10 de Agosto, tel. 7/269-4405, $8 pp with fan, $12 pp with a/c), between the plaza and the market, is also good. Grab some seafood at **Dragón Dorado** on Calderón or a *plato del día* at **Restaurant D'Marco's** (Calderón and Veintimilla).

Direct your border-crossing questions to the **Peruvian consulate** (Bolívar and 10 de Agosto, tel. 7/269-4030, 9 A.M.–1 P.M. and 3–5 P.M. Mon.–Fri.). **Cooperativa Loja** and **Cariamanga** both send buses to Loja ($4, five-six hours).

Crossing the border: The Pana rolls southwest from the center of town for 2.5 kilometers to a bridge at the Peruvian border. Taxis and trucks make the trip to *la frontera* often, or you can walk it in less than an hour. Get your exit stamp at the Ecuadorian immigration office, then cross the bridge into La Tina, Peru, where you can get your entry stamp in the Peruvian immigration office in the building on your right. (Both are open 24 hours.) *Colectivos* run from the Peru side to Suyo (20 minutes), Sullana (two hours), and Piura (35 minutes more).

◖ VILCABAMBA

This small town, nestled in one of Ecuador's most pristine corners, gained some fame when word began to spread that residents lived longer—sometimes *much* longer—than usual. Although further study has somewhat debunked the Valley of Longevity theory, Vilcabamba wouldn't be a bad place to grow

VILCABAMBA'S CENTENARIANS

Vilcabamba has long held a reputation as the Valley of Eternal Youth – but not for nearly as long as some of its residents have been alive. The jury is still out on whether or not there really is something special here that scares off the Reaper. Even scientists agree, however, that you could choose a much worse place to live out a long, healthy life.

Since scientists began visiting the area in the 1970s, reports have conflicted concerning if and why Vilcabamba has more than its share of very old residents, and exactly how many there are. Exact numbers are few and far between. A 1971 survey found 819 townspeople older than 100 – a little over 1 percent, or 1 per 100. In comparison, the United States at the time had one per 330,000.

But seven years later, an anthropological research team from universities in Wisconsin and California concluded that nobody in Vilcabamba was older than 96. In 1988, a local hospital administrator claimed that there were 39 Vilcabambans alive who were born in the 19th century. Theories for the overestimations include lying for higher social status (age is revered in Latin America), the exodus of younger residents leaving an age-heavy population, and the use of identical names by a few interrelated people.

In rural Ecuador, the most reliable way to confirm age is through birth, baptismal, and marriage records kept by the Catholic church. Passports and letters, albeit rare, also come in handy. More suspect are memories of historic events – which, though fascinating if true, are easily fabricated – and word of mouth. Visiting in 1970, a Harvard researcher was introduced to Miguel Carpio as the oldest person in the village at 121. Four years later, the same scientist returned and was introduced once again to Carpio – then said to be 132.

I'LL HAVE WHAT HE'S HAVING

Scientists have long lists of theories of how people older than 100 pull it off. All agree that clean water and air are two fundamental building blocks. Next comes lots of physical activity – well into old age – to increase cardiovascular fitness. Heart attacks may still strike a great-great-grandpa in good shape, but they may be "silent" and go unfelt and ineffectual.

Diet is also crucial. The average Vilcabamban over 50 eats a daily diet of 1,200 calories (versus the 2,400 suggested in the United States for folks over 55), including 35-38 grams of primarily animal protein (versus 65 suggested in the United States) and 12-19 grams of fat, mostly from vegetables. Such healthy, spartan fare may head off atherosclerosis (fatty buildup in the arteries). It's thought that high levels of magnesium in Vilcabamba's water may help break up saturated fats and prevent arteriosclerosis.

Next step: Stay happily married. Along with the companionship and psychological support of a healthy relationship, researchers have concluded that the benefits of marriage don't stop at the dinner table. A Japanese TV team filming in Vilcabamba in 1980 reported that one citizen was still having sex at 117. Locals still tell with reverence the story of one man in the 1950s who allegedly married for the third time at 105 and went on to father two more children. "A good bed is the secret of longevity," said Albertano Roa, supposedly 119 years old in 1994.

Geneticists point to the "unhealthy" lifestyles led by some centenarians – smoking, drinking, and raising (limited) hell – in espousing their version. Lack of "bad" genes that lead to fatal disease may also be a key. Perhaps a small group of individuals genetically predisposed to longevity settled here long ago, starting a pocket of descendants who would reap the benefits of long life for generations to come. Then there's always the theory that Vilcabamba is bombarded with "toxin-killing radiation from magnetic sun storms." Whatever the cause, the town's reputation has caught on abroad – a Texas-based company has marketed a "Vilcabamba formula" multivitamin modeled on the mineral content of the local water.

old, and its gorgeous setting and tranquil pace of life have taken over as its main draws. Set at the intersection of five valleys, Vilcabamba enjoys clean air, mild weather, and hiking, biking, and horseback-riding options in every direction.

Since the days of hippie guru Johnny Love Wisdom's failed University of Life, Vilcabamba (pop. 10,000) has had to make room for legions of wanderers drawn by the undeniably healthy atmosphere. The 20th century arrived a little late here—horses are still as common as cars in the streets—and as a result, the town has had to cope with significant changes in the last few decades. Along with electricity, running water, and sewage systems, Vilcabamba has seen a rise in crime, along with health problems like cancer and heart disease. In a sad irony, residents of Ecuador's Valley of Eternal Youth are dying younger than ever before.

Add to that the legions of backpackers who scribble Vilcabamba next to Otavalo, Baños, and Montañita on their must-see lists, and you have a beautiful place balanced on the edge. It's one of those spots that travel writers hesitate to describe too lovingly, lest it become loved to death. By all means, come and inhale the air, ride a horse, and leave a little healthier—just please tread lightly.

Recently designed websites promoting retirement homes and gated community living, have encouraged a large influx of moneyed retirees, who, unlike earlier arrivals, do not particularly want to integrate into the community, or even learn the language. Life in this sacred valley is changing fast.

Entertainment and Events

Vilcabamba isn't the after-hours center of southern Ecuador. **Iguana** (on Montalvo) is—fortunately—the only nightclub in town.

Wherever you find yourself after hours, that glazed look in the eyes of your fellow partiers might not just be too much *aguardiente,* but rather the hallucinogenic (and illegal) effects of the endemic San Pedro cactus, which was once one of the town's main draws for the mood-altering-inclined.

In late February, Vilcabamba's annual **festival** brings visitors from throughout southern Ecuador for a long weekend of music, dancing, horse-riding competitions, and general revelry.

Recreation and Tours

The best and cheapest recreation option in Vilcabamba is **hiking.** A good place to start is one of the three drinking-water plants in town, where Vilcabamba's reputation for longevity is bottled for those unfortunates in less balmy climes. Along with Vilca Vida and Kastal, Vilcagua spring water is said to have beaten out Perrier and Evian in an international tasting competition.

Maps and trail descriptions for various hikes, including a day hike along the Río Uchima, are available at the tourist information. That oddly shaped peak that dominates the valley to the west is called Cerro Mandango (Tripe Mountain). To climb it, head south out of town past the bus station and the *cooperativa* sign. A trail leads uphill to the right—you're on the right track if you have to pass through a gate. Ask for the *sendero al cumbre de Mandango* (trail to Mandango peak). One hour uphill through forest and cow pastures brings you to a hilltop cross overlooking the town, but you won't reach the real summit for another hour. Afterward, it's possible to descend north into the valley of Río Vilcabamba, then head east toward Madre Tierra and the main road.

Other trails lead to the Agua de Hierro Springs and viewpoints on the eastern side of the valley. To get into the forest, head to the Cabañas Rio Yambala (Charlie's cabanas), where you can climb to viewpoints, swimming holes, and waterfalls on your way to Las Palmas Reserve and Podocarpus National Park. The IGM 1:50,000 *Vilcabamba* map covers the area.

Day-long **horseback rides** are one of the most popular diversions in Vilcabamba. They usually cost $5–10 pp for a four-hour trip and up to $75 per day for three-day excursions, and should be arranged at least the day before. Trips can be set up through most hotels or through one of the many private guides in town.

Resettled Kiwi Gavin Moore runs **Caballos Gavilan** (Sucre between Vega and Agua de Hierro, tel. 7/264-0158, gavilanhorse@yahoo .com) and offers excursions ranging one–three days to his cloud forest cabin for about $30–35 pp per day. His tours have received enthusiastic kudos.

Many hotels have **mountain bikes** for guests to use (check the brakes before heading down a hill), or you can rent them by the hour ($2) or day ($10). The proprietor of **El Chino,** on the corner of Vega and Toledo, does his own maintenance, so his bikes are in good condition.

After two decades guiding in the Galápagos, **Orlando Falco,** of the Rumi Huilco Ecolodge (tel. 7/267-3186, ofalcoecolodge@yahoo.com, www.vilcabamba.org/rumihuilco.htm), moved to Vilcabamba and began leading trips into the wilds of the southern Sierra. He's an ecologically minded, knowledgeable naturalist guide who leads trips of different lengths and difficulty into the rainforest and Podocarpus National Park. He provides English-speaking guides and transportation for $25 pp per day, including lunch and the park entrance fee. **Avetur** (tel. 7/258-0686, www.vilcabamba .org), in the Hostal Valle Sagrado, organizes local guides for two-to-three-day eco-tours to a *refugio* in Podocarpus.

Accommodations in Town

Vilcabamba's cheapest rooms are at the **Hotel Valle Sagrado** (tel. 7/264-0686, $3 pp), on Calle Sucre in the main plaza. Currently the front part of the hotel is being rebuilt, so enter from the back, a block below the bus station. When the work is finished, prices will probably rise. The **Hostal Mandango** (Huilcopamba and Montalvo, $5 pp) is a close runner-up for budget lodgings, but receives mixed reports. It has an inner courtyard with hammocks and an open-air rooftop bar. Both places see a lot of traffic and are comfortable for the price.

Just off the main plaza is the cheerful **Jardín Escondido** (tel./fax 7/264-0281, hiddengarden@yahoo.com), a combination *hostal* and Mexican restaurant. Bright, simple rooms cost

$12 pp with private bath, including breakfast, and guests can use the pool and kitchen facilities and wash their own laundry or have it done. There's a pool and Jacuzzi for guests, as well as satellite TV and DVDs in the lounge.

The **Hosteria La Posada Real** (tel. 7/264-0904) sits on the edge of the fields at the northeast corner of town on Agua del Hierro. A wide balcony around the raised first floor gives it an almost Victorian feel, by way of the Amazon. Seven large rooms are $7 pp with private bath and hot water, and limited *cafetería* and kitchen facilities are available.

A welcome addition to Vilcabamba's lodging scene is **Le Rendez-Vous** (Diego Vaca de la Vega 06–43, sergisa@yahoo.com or rendezvousecuador@yahoo.com). Cabins in pretty gardens have hammocks and hot showers; rates are $10 pp, including a tasty breakfast. Owners Isabelle and Sergio Ruhard speak three languages: English, French, and Spanish.

Accommodations Outside Town

Vilcabamba's most luxurious lodgings, in the traditional sense, are at the **Hostería Vilcabamba** (tel. 7/264-0271, fax 7/264-0273), a short distance before the town center on the road to Loja. You'll find guests sunning on the terrace facing the great mountain view after enjoying the elegant pool and spa (also open to the public for $3 pp). Rooms are $34 s, $50 d and have private baths with bathtubs. The *hostería* has a bar and a small café.

A whole different kind of crowd congregates at the (**Hostería Madre Tierra** (tel./fax 7/264-0269, madretierra@vilcanet.net, www .madretierra1.com, $39 s, $69 d), one of the loveliest places to stay in Ecuador. Rooms have private baths, and guests can choose among the small rock pool, steam room, nightly videos, or the hammock strung up among the birds and flowers. Prices include a delicious communal breakfast and dinner. The owners have opened a spa uphill from the main building, where you can immerse yourself in every bodily luxury, from massages and mud baths to herbal wraps and colonics.

© JEAN BROWN

morning journal writing at Hostería Izhcayluma

About two kilometers south of Vilcabamba on the road to Yangana is the **Hostería Izhcayluma** (tel. 7/264-0895, info@izhcayluma .com, www.izhcayluma.com), owned by a pair of German brothers. They've installed a pool and a restaurant with spectacular views of the Vilcabamba Valley, and they offer everything from trekking tours to Spanish courses at the La Cumbre language school in town (lacumbre_vilcabamba@yahoo.de, www.cumbrevilcabamba.com) for $5 pp per hour. Three cabins are $15 s, $20 d, with showers and private baths. A taxi from the plaza is the best way to get here.

Out into the countryside to the east, you'll find the **⟨ Cabañas Río Yambala** (tel. 7/264-0299, rio_yambala@yahoo.com, www.vilcabamba.cwc.net), also known as Charlie's Cabañas. Rooms and cabins in a beautiful riverside setting five kilometers from town range $5–14 pp, depending on which cabin you choose and whether or not you want breakfast. With its balconies, hammocks, and newly finished sauna, Charlie's is a favorite retreat for budget-conscious travelers looking to relax in solitude and quiet—the only sounds are running water

from the nearby river, bird calls, and the wind in the trees. The owners also arrange hikes and horseback rides to a cloud forest refuge in the foothills of Podocarpus National Park. They've set up a marked trail system nearby and run guided day trips on horseback. The cabins are a one-hour walk from the town center; a taxi costs a few dollars, or book in advance and use Charlie's free transfer service.

Alicia and Orlando Falco, naturalist guides with experience in the Galápagos and the Amazon, run the **Rumi Huilco Ecolodge** (tel. 7/267-3186, ofalcoecolodge@yahoo.com, www .vilcabamba.org/rumihuilco.htm) in a nature reserve of the same name a 10-minute walk from town. It's a rustic, secluded place set up on stilts at the edge of the Río Chambo, with cooking facilities and rooms in adobe and bamboo cabins starting at $5 pp. There's a kitchen, hot showers, and room for bonfires next to the river. A fridge and blender mean you can make fresh *jugos* from the fruit in the garden. The lodge is a seriously relaxing place, but if you're up for some activity, try the hiking trails in their 40-hectare reserve. The Falcos also organize nature walks in Podocarpus.

Food

Interesting places to eat crowd the plaza and nearby streets. On the east side on Bolívar below the plaza is **Vilcabamba Natural Yogurt,** which specializes in homemade yogurt, juices, and inexpensive breakfasts ($2). Try the tempeh burgers. At the northwest corner, the small **Restaurante Huilcopamba** serves a good selection of fresh juice to accompany plates in the $2 range, including some vegetarian options. At the northeast corner, **La Terraza** serves excellent Mexican, Thai, and Italian food on the plaza for $3–4; the chicken fajitas are recommended. There is a popular vegetarian restaurant one block from the plaza on Calle Sagrado. Several restaurants offer tempeh and other excellent soybean products as meat replacements.

The restaurant **El Punto,** on the southeast corner, serves up tasty crêpes and a good pancake breakfast. It also has a daily happy hour 6–7 P.M. and hosts a small-stakes poker game some evenings. **Shanta's Café-Bar,** on Diego Vaca de la Vega across the rivers, is good for pizza and spaghetti by day ($3), and drinks on the saddle-barstools by night. Further up the hill **Piccola Italia** (tel. 8/876-6849, lunch and dinner Thurs.–Sun.) serves authentic Italian food by an Italian chef.

Don't miss the whole-grain bread, cookies, granola, and energy bars made by ☾ **Martha Clayton,** an American woman who resettled in Vilcabamba. Ask for her at the Cabañas Río Yambala.

Information and Services

The **tourist office** (tel. 7/264-0890, 8 A.M.–1 P.M. and 3–6 P.M. daily) on the main plaza is helpful and stocks maps and information on what to do in the valley. Avetur's website (www.vilcabamba.org) is also a good source of information. The **post office** shares the **police** building one block north of the plaza.

Something about the Vilcabamba Valley soothes the soul, so it seems only natural to let someone soothe your body with a **massage.** Fanny Santin (Valle Sagrado and Diego Vaca de la Vega) gives great massages and provides natural spa treatments as well. The masseuses at the Hostal Madre Tierra's spa can also knead away your cares.

Spanish lessons are available through the Hosteria Izhcayluma's La Cumbre language school.

Transportation

Several bus companies go to Loja: **Sur Oriente, Cariamanga,** and **Vilcabamba Turis** are the most frequent. They leave roughly every hour from the terminal at Jaramillo and Eterna Juventud, or they stop in front if they are coming from the frontier (90 minutes, $1). **Taxi Ruta** at Avenida 24 de Mayo crams four people into one car for the run to Loja, which costs a bit more ($1.50) but takes half the time.

Since the opening of the Peruvian border, more and more travelers are heading south from Vilcabamba to cross into Peru at the newest crossing south of **Zumba** to take a shortcut to the Chachapoyas ruins. Eleven buses a day serve Zumba, where the best of the basic accommodations (La Choza) costs only $2 pp. Take the early Transportes Union Cariamanga bus to see the amazing scenery and cross the frontier the same day. It leaves Loja at 5:30 A.M. and passes Vilcabamba at about 6:30 A.M.; have a quick lunch and take the 1 P.M. *ranchera* to La Balsa and the new frontier bridge. Pickups on the Peruvian side wait to take you to San Ignacio. If you're in a hurry, take one of the four night buses (leaving between 11:30 P.M. and 1 A.M.) and cross in the morning. All the buses originate in Loja, so you have to flag them down on the road in front of the Vilcabamba bus station.

THE GALÁPAGOS ISLANDS

You don't often come across a place that's unique in the world. All too many "must-sees," no matter how glowingly they're described by guidebooks and friends, seem to pale in the harsh light of reality. But the Galápagos Islands exist truly without parallel, and I have yet to meet a disappointed visitor. Huddled far out in the Pacific Ocean, the archipelago protects a bubble of life like nowhere else on earth.

Initial impressions of the islands certainly don't promise much—the bleak, plant-stubbled landscape carries all the impact of a cheap movie set at first glance. But within a day or two of beginning your tour, you'll see things you'd never have believed existed: tortoises the size of armchairs, iguanas that swim, and birds with huge blue feet that are all completely nonplussed by your presence. By the end of your stay, you'll have gotten a taste of what the earth was like well before the human race showed up and started throwing its weight around. You'll go home understanding how a short visit to the islands more than a century ago sparked one of the greatest scientific insights in history.

Galápagos wildlife is often described as tame, but I disagree. It's not that the animals are tame, it's that they just don't care that you're there. In a self-enclosed world that has existed for millennia with no major predators, human beings are still just another large, curious-looking thing, about as threatening as a tree. The feeling of looking at acres of wild animals that don't flee at your arrival—a place where you actually have to be careful not to step on anyone as you walk down the trail—is nothing short of amazing.

HIGHLIGHTS

◖ **Charles Darwin Research Center:** Researchers at the research station in Puerto Ayora are working to help giant tortoises – including the infamous Lonesome George – to survive (page 344).

◖ **Punta Espinosa:** On Fernandina Island, watch flightless cormorants dry their useless wings in the sun near more marine iguanas than you'll ever see anywhere else (page 360).

◖ **Post Office Bay:** On Floreana Island, leave a postcard in the barrel like a whaler of yore, and see if some kind stranger delivers it in person – and vice versa (page 362).

◖ **Punta Suárez:** Waved albatrosses and an abundance of boobies are the highlights of this spot on Española Island, one of the islands' best visitors' sites (page 364).

◖ **Wolf and Darwin Islands:** These far-off islands are known as one of the best dive spots in the world (page 365).

LOOK FOR ◖ TO FIND RECOMMENDED SIGHTS, ACTIVITIES, DINING, AND LODGING.

You'll hear the Galápagos described as a "laboratory of evolution," which, along with all the other talk about species, adaptations, and 19th-century naturalists, is enough to make any nonscientist's head spin. What's going on? In a nutshell, the archipelago is as close to a perfect laboratory experiment on evolution as any place ever discovered. Nobel laureates couldn't have designed a better test if they tried—take a few species, stick them out in the middle of nowhere for a few million years, and see what happens. The result is many unique species, perfectly adapted to their difficult environment, and a few only halfway through the evolutionary process thrown in for good measure.

In part because of how special they are, the Galápagos Islands face a host of problems that threaten its singular ecosystems. The causes are nothing new—human overcrowding, exploitation of resources, too many tourists "loving" the islands to death—but the results could be tragic. If you're interested in helping, tax-deductible **donations** for research, conservation, and environmental education can be sent to the **Charles Darwin Foundation** (407 N. Washington Street, Ste. 105, Falls Church, VA 22046, tel. 703/538-6833, darwin@gala-pagos.org, www.darwinfoundation.org) or the **Galápagos Conservation Trust** (5 Derby Street, London, W1Y 7AD, tel. 44/020-7629-5049, gct@gct.org, www.gct.org).

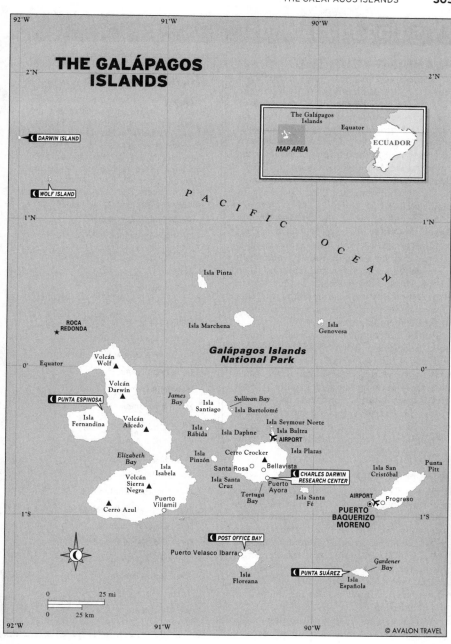

THE GALÁPAGOS ISLANDS

The Galápagos Islands

Equator

MAP AREA

ECUADOR

P A C I F I C   O C E A N

DARWIN ISLAND

WOLF ISLAND

Isla Pinta

ROCA REDONDA

Isla Marchena

Isla Genovesa

Galápagos Islands National Park

Equator

Volcán Wolf

Volcán Darwin

PUNTA ESPINOSA

James Bay

Isla Santiago

Sullivan Bay

Isla Bartolomé

Isla Fernandina

Volcán Alcedo

Isla Rábida

Isla Daphne

Isla Seymour Norte

Isla Baltra

AIRPORT

Elizabeth Bay

Isla Pinzón

Cerro Crocker

Isla Plazas

Volcán Sierra Negra

Isla Isabela

Santa Rosa

Bellavista

CHARLES DARWIN RESEARCH CENTER

Isla San Cristóbal

Punta Pitt

Isla Santa Cruz

Puerto Ayora

Cerro Azul

Puerto Villamil

Tortuga Bay

Isla Santa Fé

AIRPORT

Progreso

PUERTO BAQUERIZO MORENO

POST OFFICE BAY

Puerto Velasco Ibarra

Isla Floreana

PUNTA SUÁREZ

Gardener Bay

Isla Española

0   25 mi

0   25 km

© AVALON TRAVEL

Visiting the Islands

PLANNING YOUR TIME

Since most visitors come here on packaged tours, the idea of planning your time in the Galápagos is somewhat moot. A tour of at least five days is recommended, and eight or more is better, including a half day each way to come and go. You can also come here on your own and find a tour in the islands, or take day tours out of Puerto Ayora on Santa Cruz or Puerto Baquerizo Moreno on San Cristóbal, although this is less common. (See *Choosing a Tour* for more details.)

Almost all tours visit the **Charles Darwin Research Center** in Puerto Ayora, where giant tortoises are raised from eggs, and Lonesome George may have finally found a mate. On Floreana, whose history could (and has) filled a book, check if any postcards in the barrel in **Post Office Bay** are heading in the direction of your hometown; if they are, tradition says to deliver them in person.

Punta Suárez on Española Island boasts both "Boobieville"—that would be the birds—and one of the two waved albatross breeding sites in the world. Experienced divers must not miss the underwater menagerie at **Wolf and Darwin Islands**, northwest of the main group. The largest colony of marine iguanas in the islands awaits at **Punta Espinosa** on Fernandina, next to the scraggly nests of flightless cormorants.

WHEN TO GO

High tourist season in the Galápagos occurs near the winter holidays (December–January) and during the northern hemisphere's summer (June–August). In those months, it can be hard to find space on a tour unless you book well ahead. Then again, fewer boats operate during the off-season, which can make spots scarce as well. Many boats are dry-docked for repairs and maintenance during September and October.

As far as weather is concerned, during the dry season (June–November) the islands become

ISLAND NAMES

Almost every island in the Galápagos boasts at least two names, and some have three or more, including English, Spanish, and nicknames. I've followed the lead of Michael Jackson (the author, not the singer) in selecting the names used in this book, listed here alphabetically and followed by any variations. All names are official, except Floreana and Santiago, whose official names follow in boldface.

- Baltra (South Seymour)
- Bartolomé (Bartholomew)
- Beagle
- Cowley
- Darwin (Culpepper)
- Enderby
- Española (Hood)
- Fernandina (Narborough)
- Floreana (**Santa María;** Charles)
- Genovesa (Tower)
- Isabela (Albemarle)
- Marchena (Bindloe)
- Pinta (Abingdon)
- Pinzón (Duncan)
- Plazas
- Rábida (Jervis)
- San Cristóbal (Chatham)
- Santa Cruz (Indefatigable)
- Santa Fé (Barrington)
- Santiago (**San Salvador;** James)
- Seymour Norte (North Seymour)
- Sin Nombre (Nameless)
- Tortuga (Brattle)
- Wolf (Wenman)

brown and sere as dormant vegetation waits for the rains. Skies are often cloudy but little rain falls, and the water is somewhat colder for swimming. Rains come during the wet season (January–April), alternating with hot and sunny days. The islands turn green, and sea turtles lay their eggs. November and April may well be the best overall months to visit—not too hot or cold, and not too many tourists.

The Galápagos are one hour behind mainland Ecuador (six hours behind GMT).

WHAT TO BRING

Aside from shorts and T-shirts, bring a light jacket or sweater and a pair of long pants for chilly mornings and evenings, plus a rain jacket for visiting the damp highlands. Sturdy boots are essential for the rough lava, and a hat and sunglasses keep the impact of the equatorial glare to a minimum. Bring a water bottle and refill it onboard with boiled or purified water. Sunblock and seasickness pills or wristbands should go in with your toiletries. The latter is crucial if you're prone to motion sickness; the open waters between the islands can be surprisingly rough, especially in smaller boats, although trips are rarely canceled because passengers can't stand the constant nausea. A day pack and water bottle make shore visits easier, and a bathing suit and good snorkeling equipment guarantee that you won't be caught with your trunks down in the water.

If you have any money left after booking your tour, spend it on photography equipment. Even if you're only a casual photographer, you'll feel like a pro in this wildlife photographer's nirvana. Grab close-ups with a telephoto lens—at least 200 mm, preferably 300 or even larger—and bring UV and polarizing filters to help cut the midday glare. Water protection for your gear, even if only sturdy freezer bags, is a must for *panga* rides. Finally, bring twice as much film or digital memory as you think you'll need, and then some more on top of that. You'll be amazed how quickly frames fly by, and film prices on ships and in the islands are ridiculously high.

GETTING THERE

Transport to the islands is not generally included in the coast of a tour. **TAME** and **Aerogal** both have two daily flights from Quito to Baltra for Santa Cruz via Guayaquil, leaving Quito between 7:30 and 9:30 A.M. The trip costs $407 pp round-trip (slightly less in the low seasons, May–mid-June and mid-September–end of October), and round-trip fares from Guayaquil are around $50 lower. Both carriers also operate flights to San Cristobal daily, with two flights on Sunday between 9–9:45 A.M. for the same prices. Discounts are available during high season for students with ISIC cards, available only in person on weekdays at least one day before departure at the central TAME office in Quito. Check-in is at least 90 minutes before departure. The flight takes about three hours from Quito, and you're allowed to bring one main piece of luggage up to 45 pounds.

If you booked your flight independently, make sure you're flying to the correct island at the correct time to begin your tour *before* booking your boat trip. The ticket counter in Quito is a madhouse, with tour agents checking in large groups as everyone else jostles in line. All flights originate in Quito and stop over in Guayaquil for at least one hour, where everyone often has to get off while the fuel tanks are topped off. Tours should reconfirm for you both ways—don't duplicate the reservation yourself, or the computer will erase you. If you wish, you can check a few days before departure and make sure your name is on the passenger list, not the waiting list (*lista de espera*).

The **National Park entrance fee** is $100 pp for foreigners, payable in cash only at the airport upon arrival. Keep your receipt, because your boat captain will need to record it. The new migratory control card costs $10 and is for Ecuadorians and visitors alike. Don't loose it—you'll need to surrender it upon departure.

Tour groups are met at both airports by smiling, sign-waving guides who will direct you to the bus to take you to the dock and your

THE GALÁPAGOS ISLANDS

waiting boat. If you're arriving without being booked on a tour, getting from Baltra to Puerto Ayora is a bit more complicated. The journey has three stages: a free bus ride to the Itabaca canal between Baltra and Santa Cruz (don't take the bus to the "muelle"), a short ferry across the channel, and another bus up and over the Santa Cruz highlands and down to Puerto Ayora. The whole trip takes about 1.5 hours. To get back to the airport from town, catch a taxi ($1) to the bus terminal on the edge of town in the morning. (The Baquerizo Moreno airport on San Cristobal is within walking or taxi distance of town.)

CHOOSING A TOUR

The only way to visit the Galápagos is by boat with a tour group; beyond that, your choices are limited to what kind of boat and, for some, whether to sleep aboard or not. Prices vary widely, as does service: When shopping around for a tour, remember that in the Galápagos—perhaps more than most destinations—you get what you pay for. Visiting the Galápagos is probably the most expensive thing you'll do in Ecuador, but if you plan it right and luck out with good weather, a good guide, and friendly companions, it can easily be one of the most amazing things you ever do.

Tour boats are organized into five classes—economic, tourist, tourist superior, first, and luxury—and trips range four–eight days, with occasional special charters of 11 and 15 days. Unless you're really strapped for cash or time, five days should be the minimum length of time you consider. Prices range from less than $750 pp for a five-day economy-class trip to $5,000 for eight days on a luxury-class vessel. (Arrival and departure days are counted as tour days.) It may lessen the sting to know that these prices include food, accommodations, transfers to and from your boat, trained guides, and all your shore visits. You'll have to pay extra for airfare to and from the islands, insurance, gratuities, souvenirs, and alcoholic or soft drinks on board.

Itineraries are strictly controlled by the National Park Service to regulate the impact of visitors on the delicate sites. This means sticking to a tight schedule, so if you sometimes feel as if you're being herded, well, you are—in theory, for the good of the islands. The only valid reasons on most boats for altering an itinerary are medical emergencies and bad weather.

Economy Boats

Prices for boats in the economic class range $1,000–1,250 pp per week, or a little less for special last-minute deals or tours that spend the nights ashore. Guides are usually not as well trained as those on luxury boats, and accommodations and food may likewise be underwhelming. Because most economy boats are small (8–16 passengers), you'll get to know your fellow travelers well—perhaps too well—and your boat will toss more on rough seas.

Certain security measures should be heeded for any economy boat tour in the Galápagos (or Ecuador, for that matter). Be sure the boat has adequate safety equipment: fire extinguishers, life jackets, and flares.

Economy-class boats, on the whole, are the best (or only) option for those on a limited budget or time frame. If you plan well and negotiate your dollars and days carefully, your trip can turn out great—even a bit of an adventure.

Moderately Priced Boats

Tourist-class and tourist superior–class boats are the most common in the islands. They're usually medium-size sailboats or motorboats holding 10–16 passengers. Accommodations are a step up from economy class, but the cabins in most are still small, with bunk beds, and the toilets are pumped by hand. Some would argue that the food in tourist class is the best, because the cooks are generally excellent and only have to cook for a small group. Guides range from mediocre to outstanding—generally, the better the boat, the better the guide.

Tourist Superior boats frequently include Genovesa in their itinerary.

Costs range $1,300–1,550 pp per week for tourist class and $1,600–1,950 pp per week for tourist superior class.

First-Class Boats

Not all but most first-class boats include a visit to the western islands of Isabela and Fernandina. These destinations are confined to the better class of boats, which can sail faster, having larger engines and fuel tanks. Most of these boats take 16–26 passengers, accommodated in comfortable cabins or staterooms with beds rather than bunks. Several are beautifully maintained sailing ships (don't expect to sail to the longer overnight destinations) and all have guides with a reputation for excellence. Prices here range $2,000–3,800 pp for a week.

Luxury Tours and Cruise Ships

If your tastes run to crisp linens and mimosas in the morning, reserve a berth on a luxury liner like the 292-foot *Celebrity Xpedition.* Boats in this class maintain a standard of luxury matching the finest hotels on the mainland. Cabins, food, and service are all top-notch, and accoutrements include things like exercise rooms, spas, and salons. For guests of Lindblad Expeditions' 47-passenger *Islander,* massages are administered on a floating, glass-bottomed pontoon in a secluded cove.

Everything is organized by loudspeaker announcement, from shore visits to buffet lunches and sit-down dinners. Guides are the cream of the crop—multilingual fluency and university degrees are the norm. Since there are several guides, groups can be split up to match guests with similar interests and energy levels. Because these boats are the largest ones plying the archipelago, they're able to visit far islands like Fernandina, Isabela, and Espanola, which lie beyond the range of smaller, slower boats. Sea rolling is minimized, although still a factor.

The short list of minuses includes a lack of intimacy with all the passengers (you can't meet them all in eight days). Everything is planned to the minute, and flexibility is restricted to the options of "go" or "not go" for any visit or landing. Luxury-class tours start at $3,800 pp per week and climb to around $5,000.

Shore-Based Tours

Those especially troubled by seasickness may be glad to hear that a few options allow you to sleep on shore. However remember that time will be wasted traveling to and from the islands every day (on smaller boats that do roll with the ocean), and many of the farther islands will remain completely out of reach. Budget travelers can find accommodations in Puerto Ayora or Baquerizo Moreno and arrange a string of day tours.

Guides

Next to a boat that doesn't sink, a good guide is the most important factor in your visit. All Galápagos guides are trained and licensed by the National Park Service. They qualify in one of three classes, in ascending order of quality: Class One, usually on economy boats or handling land-based tours; Class Two, on tourist- and tourist superior–class boats; and Class Three, on first-class and luxury boats. All guides are supposed to speak at least two languages, but Class One guides often speak little besides Spanish. Every guide has to pass rigorous examinations every three years and complete a training course on the islands every six years to keep his or her certification.

When booking a tour, ask about your guide's specific qualifications and what language he or she speaks. In general, the more expensive the tour, the better the guide.

Booking and Payment

Tours can be arranged by phone from your kitchen table in your home country, but keep in mind that the farther from the boat you set things up, the more you're paying for legwork you could conceivably do yourself. To book a cruise from abroad, a deposit of at least $200 pp (via wire transfer or Western Union) is required. Ecuador does not permit the use of credit cards for any payments by Internet or telephone, so these can't be used without the owner, the card, and the passport being present in Ecuador. Even so, only a handful of boats accept credit cards for payment in person, and these still require partial payment in cash or travelers' checks. You can pay for your flights with credit cards, albeit only when there is at least one full working day between purchase and departure.

Many travel agencies in Quito advertise tours, so shopping around is the way to go. The best deals often come when agencies are desperate to fill the last few spaces on a tour, so some judicious holding out may help save you 5–50 percent—although it could leave you stranded as well. (The best last-minute deals are on the better classes of boats.) Beyond the list included here, Safari Tours in Quito and the South American Explorers are the best sources for up-to-date information on recommended boats. Deposits range 10–50 percent, depending on the boat and tour operator. You are normally required to have paid in full 30 days before sailing, unless you're getting a last-minute deal.

Puerto Ayora is the place to go for booking a tour in the Galápagos, although this applies mainly to budget tours and not in busy season. While you're negotiating the price and itinerary, keep a few things in mind: Try not to include sites you could visit yourself, like the Darwin Center and the Santa Cruz highlands, and be sure to get the entire agreement down on paper—vouchers provided by the boat companies normally have the itineraries preprinted on them. Direct all complaints concerning tours, before or after, to the port captain (Capitanía del Puerto) if you booked in the islands, and to the agency directly if you booked in Quito or outside the country.

LIFE ON BOARD
Daily Routine
The day of arrival in the islands, you'll be

shown to your boat and cabin. Don't worry if it's small (and most are, except on the cruise ships); you'll have something to keep you busy during most of the day, and any spare minutes you have, you'll probably want to spend on deck or socializing in the common area/dining room. Your guide will introduce him or herself and the rest of the crew and spend a few minutes explaining the park rules, your itinerary, and the day-to-day schedule during your stay.

Every day after that, you'll be rousted out of bed at 6 or 7 A.M. to find breakfast waiting. Chances are the boat will be in a different location—maybe even a different island—than when you went to bed, after sailing or motoring most of the night. The morning visit takes two–three hours, including the *panga* ride to shore. Your guide will direct the group along the path or down the beach, explaining what you're seeing and filling in relevant natural history details as you go.

If your guide seems overly concerned about keeping the group together and making everyone stick to the trail, try not to let it bother you. After all, these people herd thousands of tourists a year past the same sites, and a surprising number of folks think that, because they paid so much money to come here, they shouldn't have to follow orders once they arrive. This is simply not true. Better too strict than too lax, for the sake of the islands. The same sentiment applies when your guides insist that you wear a lifejacket during *panga* rides; they face fines and jail time if they're caught with passengers not wearing one.

Back on board, you'll find your cabin clean and lunch ready. The midday meal is casual—a buffet on cruise ships and fixed menus on smaller vessels. Your guide will announce the departure time for the afternoon excursion. There's usually time for a short break of an hour or so to rest, digest, or update your journal. Occasionally, the boat will travel between sites by day.

The afternoon visit runs much like the morning, except now the best light for photos comes with the setting sun. If you have the opportunity to **snorkel,** don't miss it. Where else can you swim with sea lions and turtles, along with the usual gorgeous fish and marine life? Wetsuits are handy, especially in the cold season, but not necessary in the warm season; wearing just a swimsuit, most people can last about half an hour in the water before getting chilled.

There should be some time before dinner to wash up and relax. Dinner is the most significant meal of the day; on cruise ships, it's a formal, sit-down affair with invitations to the captain's table and all that jazz. Your crew might surprise you with fresh lobster or fish, such as *pargo* (red snapper) or *bacalao* (cod). After the meal, your guide will give a talk on what you saw today and where you'll be visiting tomorrow.

An evening's post-dinner entertainment ranges from dancing on cruise ships to swapping tall tales over beers on sailboats. Remember that drinks are not included in the tour price, so be ready to pay the piper the day of departure. A day in the equatorial sun takes a lot out of you, though, so don't be embarrassed to make a beeline from the dinner table to bed.

Tipping

Giving a gratuity at the end of the voyage is customary and should be factored into the cost of your Galápagos trip. Your crew and guide work hard, as they'll probably remind you—beyond that, any tip should reflect the level of service, so use your best judgment. Cash and travelers' checks are both welcome. The usual procedure is to tip the guide separately from the rest of the crew. Crew tipping should be done through a tip box or given to the entire group at once to minimize the chances of anyone getting short-changed. As an example, on the tourist and tourist superior boats, the average tip is around 5 percent of the cost of the cruise; on the first-class and luxury boats, 10 percent is more normal, with the total divided between crew and guide.

Safety and Annoyances

All this talk of natural history seems to fuel some biological urge to breed, or at least try to, since complaints of male guides hitting on female passengers are so common. If an island tryst wasn't in your plans, decline politely, and if it persists, report him to the tour operator.

Smoking is prohibited on any of the uninhabited islands and at all the visitors sites on the inhabited islands. Most boats have no-smoking policies as well.

DIVING IN THE GALÁPAGOS

You must be getting tired of superlatives by now, but heed at least one more: The Galápagos are among the most spectacular dive destinations in the world. The islands' underwater riches have been known since the New York Zoological Society's Oceanographic Expedition sent divers with lead boots and hand-pumped air hoses in 1925. In 1998, the long-awaited Special Law for the Galápagos extended the protected marine zone to 40 nautical miles from the shores of the islands. At last count, there were more than 60 marine visitor sites throughout the archipelago, many on islands closed to visitors above the surface.

Diving in the Galápagos is not for beginners. Cold waters make a wetsuit essential, and the best marine life usually keeps to areas of strong currents—up to 3.5 knots in places. Visibility is poor, ranging 10–25 meters (half that of the Caribbean). Many dives are in open water, making holding onto coral not only permitted, but essential. Luckily, there is a decompression chamber in Puerto Ayora.

If you have the necessary skills, though, the Galápagos Islands offer a world-class diving experience, with schools of fish so thick that the water seems alive. Sea jacks arrive in boisterous groups, while cod wait farther down. Active volcanic vents keep things interesting, but not nearly as much as a school of sharks circling in a tornado of teeth. The list goes on from there: whale sharks, manta rays, sperm whales, marine iguanas, and penguins all make appearances, and the animals below the surface are as approachable as those on land.

Live-aboard charters are the usual way to go. Most large Galápagos tour agencies can book dive trips aboard the small number of boats that are equipped for it. Many companies require a certain level of experience: an open water certification and a minimum number of dives (usually 25), and sometimes a medical certificate.

The best diving is during the hot season (roughly December–May), with water temperatures 20–25°C, making a three-millimeter wetsuit adequate. Temperatures drop to 15°C in the cold season, when a six-millimeter wetsuit with hood, booties, and gloves becomes necessary. Other than your own wetsuit, you'll also want to bring a mask, dive alert whistle, and sausage or scuba tuba. Boats supply tanks, air, and weights. You can rent gear at Galápagos Sub-Aqua or Scuba Iguana in Puerto Ayora, but since tours go straight to the boat from the airport, this can be complicated.

A full day's sail north of the main island group, the **Wolf** and **Darwin Islands** aren't even on most maps of the Galápagos. But they should be, because the diving here is some of the best on the planet. Schools of hundreds of hammerheads can be seen off Wolf, and gigantic whale sharks cruise slowly by between June and November. Bottlenose dolphins are common at Darwin's Arch.

Day dive trips are available through the several agencies in Puerto Ayora to nearby dive sites, including Academy Bay, Santa Fe, Gordon Rocks, Daphne Minor, Mosquera Islet, Seymour, and Cousins. Occasional dives from the regular cruise boats have been outlawed with the introduction of tighter park regulations in 2007.

Because most visitors depart by plane, plan on leaving a day free at the end of your dive trip to avoid possible pressurization problems. (Most dive tours spend the last day on Santa Cruz.)

Dive Agencies

Fernando Zambrano of **Galápagos Sub-Aqua** (tel. 4/230-5514 or 4/230-5507 in Guayaquil, tel. 5/252-6350 or 5/252-6633 in Puerto Ayora, www.galapagos-sub-aqua.com) was the first scuba guide on the islands and boasts two decades of diving experience. His outfit has a good safety record. Eight-day live-aboard trips are $3,000–4,500 pp. They also have an office in Puerto Ayora, where they offer day dives for $100–160 pp per day.

Also in Puerto Ayora is **Scuba Iguana** (tel. 5/252-6497, info@scubaiguana.com, www.scubaiguna.com), run by dive master Matias Espinosa, who was featured in the *Galápagos* IMAX movie. Daily dive prices start at $100 pp for two dives in Academy Bay and rise to $160 pp for other destinations. They also book live-aboards.

The **Aggressors I & II** (www.aggressors.com) operate top-of-the-line dives to Darwin and Wolf. Prices start around $3,800 pp, rising to $4,700 pp for a week.

HISTORY

The Galápagos Islands' inhospitable nature has saved them for much of their history. In the middle of the ocean, with hardly a drop of fresh water, the islands left visitors unimpressed for centuries before permanent settlers managed to scrape a toehold in the volcanic soil. The world eventually became aware of the treasure secreted among the barren-looking islands, just as early visitors were beginning to permanently alter the islands' natural balance.

Early Visitors

Pre-Inca *indígenas* from the coast of Ecuador were probably the first to visit the islands, as evidenced by fish bones and food remains uncovered in various spots. Blown out to sea by storms and swept west by the Humboldt Current, these hapless sailors often made one-way journeys of discovery. In 1572, the Spanish chronicler Miguel Sarmiento de Gamboa reported that the Inca Tupac Yupanqui had visited the archipelago on the advice of a seer who flew ahead to scout the way. However, this account is generally considered a legend, since the Incas weren't seagoing people.

In 1535, a ship carrying Tomás de Berlanga,

Bishop of Panama, stood becalmed off the coast of what would become Colombia on its way to the Spanish settlements in Peru. The Panama Current pushed the helpless vessel southwest for weeks before washing it among the Galápagos. The thirst-maddened crew chewed cactus pads for moisture before stumbling across pools of rainwater. Setting sail once more, the ship and crew spent almost a month at sea before the Bahía de Caráquez came into sight.

In a subsequent letter to the Spanish king, Berlanga described the islands' unique and fearless wildlife, but concluded that they weren't fit for colonization. He described the giant tortoises as having shells like riding saddles (called *galápagos* in Spanish), and the description stuck. On the 1574 *Orbis Terrarum*, the map of the known world, a small cluster of dots off the South American coast bore the label *Insulae de los Galopegos*.

That same century, the Spanish conquistador Diego de Rivadeneira landed in the Galápagos after 25 days at sea. On his return to Guatemala, Rivadeneira tried to claim discovery of the islands, calling them Las Islas Encantadas (The Enchanted Islands) after their supposed tendency to drift on the ocean, coming and going in the enshrouding mist. Half a century later, English pilot Sir John Hawkins wrote: "Some fourscore leagues to the westward of the Cape lyeth a heape of Ilands the Spaniards call Illas de los Galápagos; they are desert and beare no fruite."

Pirates and Whalers

During the 17th century, Dutch, English, and French pirates turned the Galápagos into a base for attacks on coastal ports and Spanish galleons laden with treasure for Madrid. Sir Francis Drake was among the buccaneers who attacked rich port cities like Guayaquil before retreating to the islands to escape pursuers. The pirate William Ambrose Cowley made the first working map of the Galápagos, naming them after British royalty. Floreana and Santiago Islands were originally dubbed Charles and James, respectively, after British monarchs, and Isabela

was once called Albemarle after a duke of the same title.

Pirates were the first to realize that the islands' giant tortoises could be stored aboard to provide fresh meat for long voyages, a practice that was honed to deadly perfection by 18th-century whalers. In 1841, Herman Melville visited the Galápagos on one of hundreds of whaling ships plying the rich waters around the archipelago, inspiring his account entitled *Las Encantadas*. By then, it was apparent that the Galápagos were worth something, so on February 12, 1832, Ecuador beat out halfhearted attempts by the United States and Great Britain to claim the archipelago officially. ("A harmless and even comical opinion," muses Kurt Vonnegut in his novel *Galápagos*, about as significant as if the country "had annexed to its territory a passing cloud of asteroids.")

Darwin's Visit

Charles Darwin's visit aboard the H.M.S. *Beagle* in 1835 gained renown with the publication of *The Origin of Species* in 1859. Although the visit itself didn't actually give the budding naturalist an instant lightning-strike of inspiration, it did provide crucial evidence for Darwin's later theories and culture-shaking publications. (See the sidebar *Charles Darwin and the Galápagos*.)

An isolated penal colony established on Floreana in the 1830s began a proud Galápagos tradition that continued throughout the 19th and 20th centuries. The brainchild of Galápagos governor-general José Villamil, the first colony was home to Ecuadorians whose death sentences were commuted to a life of toil on the islands. Almost 300 convicts made a meager living growing a native lichen for dyes and selling produce to passing ships. Englishman Colonel J. Williams, the infamously cruel governor of the colony (1839–1841), was driven out in an uprising that left only 80 convicts behind. Other penal colonies, on San Cristóbal in the 1890s and Isabela in the 1960s, have also begun to enter the realm of legend.

THE GALÁPAGOS ISLANDS

CHARLES DARWIN AND THE GALÁPAGOS

The man who would make the Galápagos famous with what some have called "the greatest idea anyone has ever had, anywhere" was born in 1809 into an upper-middle-class British family. Throughout his childhood and youth, Darwin was fascinated by nature, constantly collecting specimens to study. He was thrilled to accept the post of unpaid naturalist onboard the *H.M.S. Beagle,* a small sailing vessel which left Plymouth, England, on December 27, 1831.

During the voyage, Darwin befriended Captain Robert Fitzroy, who shared his cabin and saw the young landlubber through the seasickness that plagued him the entire trip. The *Beagle* landed twice off the coast of Africa before crossing the Atlantic and beginning a two-year exploration of South America's eastern coast. Darwin roamed the forests near Bahía, Brazil, and rode alongside *gauchos* in the high plains of Uruguay. In 1834, the *Beagle* rounded Cape Horn and headed up the western coast of Chile and Peru.

Darwin had already noticed things along the way that challenged the biblical theory of creation. Dinosaur bones in Argentina and fossilized sea shells at 4,000 meters in the Andes proved to him the theories of slowly changing land masses put forth in Charles Lyell's groundbreaking *Principles of Geology.*

During a five-week stay in the Galápagos Islands, Darwin managed to visit San Cristóbal, Floreana, Santiago, and Isabela. The naturalist filled his time by collecting samples, observing the animals, and taking notes. What he discovered provided crucial clues that led to the gradual birth of the theory of evolution through natural selection. From the tortoise shells and finch beaks, shaped differently from island to island, Darwin began to ponder the idea of separate species evolving from a common ancestor. The fearlessness and beneficial adaptations of the iguanas, cormorants, and penguins all added pieces to the puzzle.

Before returning home to England, the *Beagle* crossed the Pacific and Indian Oceans, stopping at New Zealand, Australia, and Mauritus before rounding the tip of Africa. The ship sailed into Falmouth Harbor on October 2, 1836. Darwin was never the same after the voyage. His studies took on an intensity they never had before.

When the *Beagle* set sail, Darwin was still a firm believer in the biblical story of creation and the immutability of life on earth. But after witnessing the animals on different islands, similar enough to be related but different enough to be separate species, he slowly began to change his mind.

However, it would take another two decades before Darwin was ready to publish his theories. He spent much of this time worrying about the impact his work would have on England's highly evangelical society. Further, he also could have faced criminal charges of sedition and blasphemy. In the end, only the threat of someone else publishing the theory first – which Alfred Russel Wallace was about to do in 1858 – finally spurred Darwin to act. That same year, friends arranged for Darwin and Wallace to read a joint paper to the Linnean Society of London, formally presenting evolution to the public for the first time.

On November 24, 1859, Darwin published ***On the Origin of Species by Means of Natural Selection,*** a work that would forever change the way we view ourselves and our place in the world. In a nutshell, the book proposed a **theory of evolution,** in which separate groups of animals change over time in response to their environment.

In the *Origin of Species,* Darwin proposed an idea so simple that it was almost sublime: that groups of organisms changed over time in response to the challenges their individual members faced every day. Perhaps gazelles hadn't always been fleet of foot – perhaps they hadn't even always been gazelles! The ability to run, along with countless other qualities, such as a long neck to reach tree leaves up high, thick fur to stay warm in winter, or a nervous disposition to make an animal bolt when danger threatened, could have developed over time in response to pressures from the surrounding world.

Perhaps, Darwin suggested, these traits – called **adaptations** – were not the whims of an almighty being, but rather the result of some spontaneous natural process that could be quantified and studied.

One germ for the idea was the Galápagos finches, which displayed a wide array of beak shapes and sizes to take advantage of different types of food, but still closely resembled each other. Darwin wondered if one sort of finch arrived at the islands long ago, then had somehow become all these different kinds in the interim.

To explain the process, Darwin proposed a mechanism called **descent with modification.** He based it on observations of animals and plants in captivity, which produced many more offspring than their environmental "niche" could possibly support. Only the ones best-suited to their environment survived to reproduce.

This idea became the cornerstone of the process of **natural selection:**

As many more individuals of each species are born than can possibly survive; and as, consequently, there is a frequently re-curring struggle for existence, it follows that any being, if it vary however slightly in any manner profitable to itself, under the complex and sometimes varying conditions of life, will have a better chance of surviving, and thus be natu-rally selected.

If somehow these "selected" organisms could pass on the qualities that made them suc-cessful to their offspring, then the members of that particular line, logically, would even-tually out-reproduce their less "fit" competi-tors and spread their successful selves over the landscape – hence the book's subtitle, *The Preservation of Favoured Races in the Struggle for Life*.

The process could even work in "reverse," leading to the loss of adaptations that were suddenly no longer beneficial. On an island with no predators, and hence no need to fly to safety, wings might eventually just get in the way. Birds that could somehow forgo growing them would be able to swim after fish more efficiently and have more energy left over for other things – such as reproduc-ing – than their fellows. Thus the flightless cormorant.

Darwin was the first to admit that his theory was still full of holes, and that he was not the first to suggest this concept, having drawn on the work of a long list of scientists, including Jean-Baptiste Lamark, Charles Lyell, Thomas Malthus, and Darwin's own grandfather, Eras-mus. In Darwin's words, this process of **evolu-tion** was "clumsy, wasteful, blundering, low, and horribly cruel," characterized by inef-ficiency, lifelong struggle, and probable ex-tinction – surely not the method employed by sublime Nature.

Although it's as well documented today as any phenomenon in science (and therefore to many a "fact," not a "theory"), the ideas in the *Origin of Species* caused an uproar in Vic-torian England, just as its author had feared. The clergy especially had a problem with it: Evolution implied that what might have once been created by God must have been in need of improvement.

But Darwin's evidence was overwhelming, and his argument fit the 19th-century spirit of exploration and discovery (and, conveniently, the contemporary attitude of more "ad-vanced" cultures colonizing and dominating more "primitive" ones). Darwin tried his best to stay out of the furor his theory caused, pre-ferring to leave that to other scientists, such as his friend and "bulldog," English biologist Thomas Henry Huxley. Darwin's theories grad-ually became accepted among scientists and the general public.

The naturalist who was now known world-wide spent the last decades of his life writing up his notes, studying plants, and living in the Downe countryside with his wife and their 10 children. He died on April 19, 1882, and was buried in honor next to Sir Isaac Newton in Westminster Abbey in London.

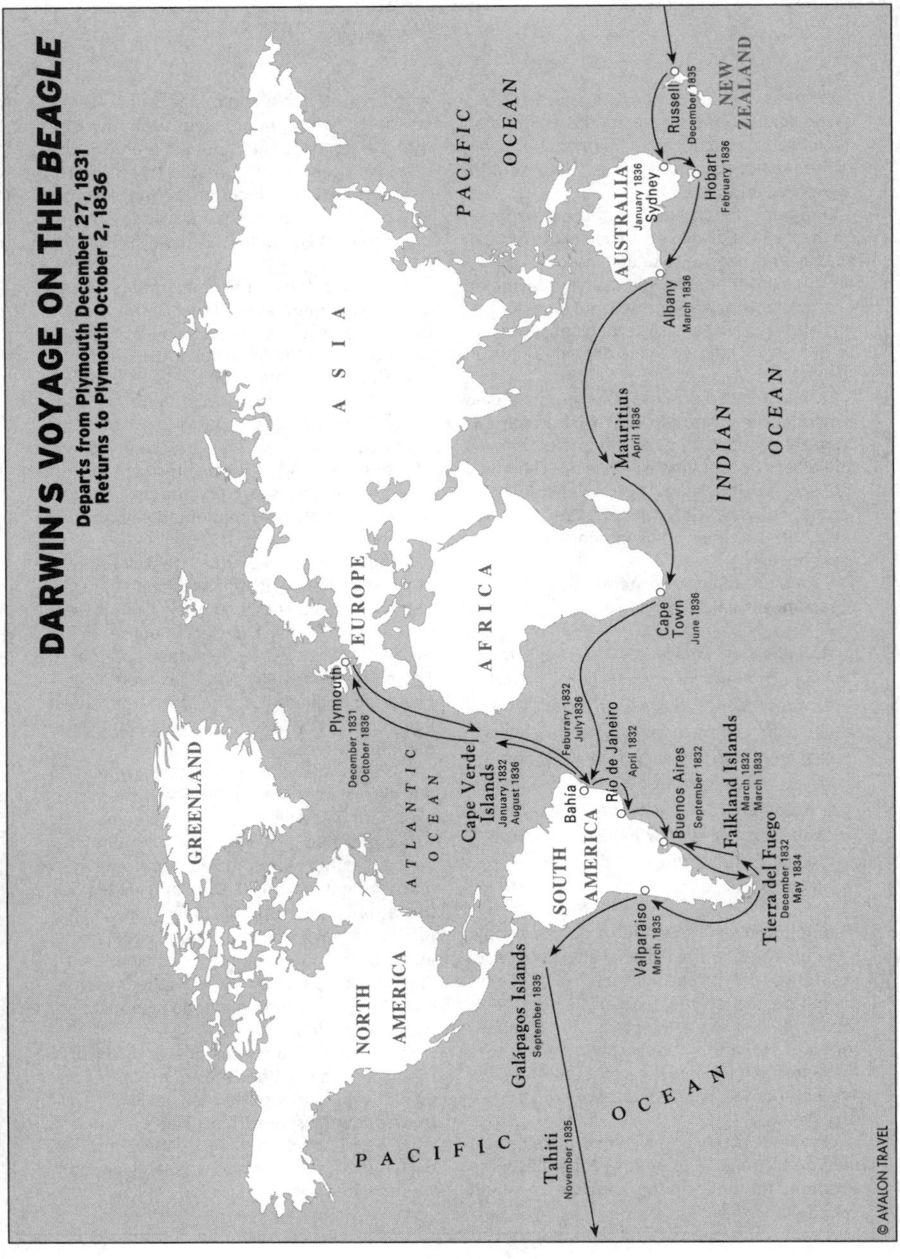

DARWIN'S VOYAGE ON THE BEAGLE

Departs from Plymouth December 27, 1831
Returns to Plymouth October 2, 1836

NORTH AMERICA

GREENLAND

EUROPE

A S I A

ATLANTIC OCEAN

AFRICA

PACIFIC OCEAN

INDIAN OCEAN

SOUTH AMERICA

AUSTRALIA

NEW ZEALAND

Plymouth
December 1831
October 1836

Cape Verde Islands
January 1832
August 1836

Feburary 1832
July 1836

Rio de Janeiro
April 1832

Bahia

Buenos Aires
March 1832
September 1832

Falkland Islands
March 1832
March 1833

Tierra del Fuego
December 1832
May 1834

Valparaíso
March 1835

Galápagos Islands
September 1835

Tahiti
November 1835

Mauritius
April 1836

Cape Town
June 1836

Albany
March 1836

Sydney
January 1836

Hobart
February 1836

Russell
December 1835

PACIFIC OCEAN

© AVALON TRAVEL

First Settlers

The islands' strategic location stirred serious foreign interest during the early 20th century. The U.S. offered to lease the Galápagos to protect the entrance to the new Panama Canal, finished in 1914, and the U.S. Navy trained in the waters of the archipelago during World War I. During World War II, the Ecuadorian government allowed the U.S. Sixth Air Force to set up a station on Baltra and a few other islands to protect the Panama Canal and to monitor Japanese activity in the South Pacific. The airport built on Baltra was given to Ecuador after the war.

William Beebe's book *Galapagos: World's End,* published in 1924, helped change the public's image of the islands from a strange, forbidding place to a starkly beautiful sanctuary with a unique ecology. A healthy dose of weirdness remained, though, and seemed to attract outcasts and settlers with more fancy than practicality, especially on Floreana (see *Floreana* for more details). Norwegians arrived to catch and smoke fish, whereas others came simply for the isolation and freedom.

Recent Conservation Efforts

The islands were declared a national park in 1959. The Charles Darwin Research Center in Puerto Ayora, opened in 1964, was followed four years later by the Galápagos National Park Service, signaling the start of an earnest effort to study the islands and conserve them for the world. Tourism began in the 1930s, when wealthy boaters stopped off for a few days to paint their ships' names on the rocks and admire the giant tortoises over martinis and pâté. Metropolitan Touring began operating some exclusive tours in the 1960s. A monthly ship from Guayaquil was the only other way to

THAR SHE BLEW

When the British whaler *Rattler* began the first reconnaissance of the Galápagos in 1793, its crew quickly realized what a gold mine they had found. Between starting the Post Office barrel on Floreana and making the first workable charts of the islands, the *Rattler's* crew marveled at the pods of sperm, humpback, and fin whales on almost every horizon.

When word reached Europe and North America, the hunt began. The second whaler to visit the islands, the British ship *William,* took 42 sperm whales in 18 days – and that was just the beginning. The first half of the 19th century brought an onslaught of traffic to the islands. In addition to attracting attention for the numerous whales, the Galápagos made a perfect stopover on the way to the even richer grounds of the South Pacific Islands. The Galápagos provided a safe harbor where wood and water could be found inland.

Most important, the islands supported a seemingly endless supply of animals that did everything but hop into the pot and cook themselves. Giant tortoises in particular were almost wiped out because it was discovered that they could survive unaided for months in ships' holds, providing fresh meat well into a long ocean voyage. It became a wholesale slaughter: In nine days, the USS *Moss* took 350 tortoises, only to be outdone by the USS *Uncas,* which captured 416 in five days. More than 15,000 tortoises were taken from Floreana alone, leading to the extinction of that island's endemic species (later joined by those of Santa Fe and Rabida). Since an estimated 1,000 ships visited the archipelago during the 19th century – almost every one of which took between 60 and 90 tortoises – the total count is thought to approach 100,000.

As icing on the cake, whaling ships introduced black rats to the islands, a species that remains a major problem today. By the mid-1800s, though, the Galápagos had earned its reputation for *dry cruising,* because most of the whales in the vicinity had been hunted out. The discovery of petroleum in the late 19th century spelled the end of the whaling industry – not a moment too soon for the islands' inhabitants.

reach the Galápagos until regularly scheduled air service began in the early '70s.

Meanwhile, unrestricted immigration to the islands increased the discontent of island residents with their situation and the government on the mainland. Friction continues to this day, as settlers led by false preconceptions pour in and find much less than they expected. Water and electricity are scarce, and money is tight; the government is accused of concentrating on tourism at the expense of its own citizens. For its part, the government, in the uniform of the National Park Service, struggles to protect a fragile ecological balance from a 6 percent annual immigration rate and close to 171,000 visitors per year.

The archipelago was among the first 12 regions in the world to receive UNESCO protection in 1978. The 1986 Galápagos Marine Resources Reserve, which bestowed National

---

INTRODUCED SPECIES

By far the most serious threats to the ecosystems of the Galápagos are the descendants of the animals and plants left by settlers and visitors over the centuries. Only two of the major islands are free of exotic species, while the plants and animals on the rest of the islands are largely defenseless against 500 species of feral intruders. The most noxious intruders include 13 species of mammals and 10 species of birds. Hundreds of flora species pose a threat to native flora and fauna. Introductions still occur: The Norway rat arrived in 1983 and has spread to at least two islands already. Fruit flies recently arrived in San Cristóbal.

INTRODUCED ANIMALS

Most introduced species began as domestic animals that escaped into the wild. **Donkeys** can exist in lower, drier elevations, where they eat through cactus-tree trunks to get at the juicy pulp, killing the plant in the process. Scattered **horses** and **cattle** roam the highlands, and feral **pigs** gobble down turtle eggs, sometimes as quickly as the turtle lays them. Groups of **wild dogs** have reportedly staged inexplicable, bloodthirsty attacks on land iguana colonies. Hundreds of corpses have been left to rot on both Isabela and Santa Cruz.

Cats revert to the wild almost instantly (just ask any cat owner) and are a major threat to bird chicks on many islands. **Rats** and **mice,** present since the first whaling ship came ashore, are among the most difficult species to control, as well as the most destructive. Almost every giant tortoise hatchling on Pinzon in the last century has fallen prey to black rats, leaving an elderly population with little hope of reproducing. House mice began in settlers' homes and soon spread to many islands.

Because their permeable skin makes it impossible for them to survive a long, dry ocean voyage, amphibians were the only one of five classes of vertebrates that hadn't colonized the Galápagos – that is, until 1998, when a small species of **tree frog** was first captured on Isabela and Santa Cruz. Scientists think the frogs arrived in cargo ships and were able to establish sustainable breeding populations during the particularly wet 1997-1998 El Niño season.

Of all the introduced animals, **goats** have been the most serious threat. Thanks to their ability to eat almost anything (they can survive on seawater during droughts), goats can bulldoze their way across an island in no time. The tough animals eat plants down to the ground, leaving nothing for native animals to eat and causing severe erosion. Add to this mix the reproductive capabilities of a copying machine and you have a recipe for disaster; three goats left on Pinta in the late 1950s had generated more than 40,000 descendants by 1970. Today, only San Cristóbal and Santa Cruz have remnant goat populations.

INTRODUCED PLANTS

Not as obvious but just as deadly, introduced plants steal sun, water, and nutrients from native species. Introduced species have skyrocketed from 77 in 1971 – many brought by early settlers for food, medicine, and building ma-

Park status on the waters around the islands as well, was received particularly poorly, since it included a ban on unrestricted fishing in the local waters. Strikes and protest culminated in a group of machete-wielding sea-cucumber fishermen seizing the Darwin Center and threatening the life of tortoise Lonesome George. The Ecuadorian government backpedaled in response, opening the waters around the archipelago to limited commercial fisheries in 1995.

The most recent installment in the saga occurred in March 1998, when the Ecuadorian National Congress approved the long-awaited Special Law for the Galápagos. Aimed at conserving the islands' biodiversity while encouraging and regulating sustainable development, the law addresses the threat of introduced species through eradication and quarantine programs. It also restricts immigration and promotes local environmental education

---

terials – to almost 500 in 1997 (compared to only 560 native species). Today, vines such as the passionfruit and blackberry grow quickly into impenetrable thickets, and trees such as the guava and red quinine take over entire hillsides. It's estimated that the guava species *Psidium guajava* alone covers 50,000 hectares in the Galápagos.

SOLUTIONS

The Ministry of the Environment, the Ecuadorian National Park Service, and the Charles Darwin Research Center are joining efforts to rid the islands of introduced species. Each method has its drawbacks: hunting, the simplest solution, is difficult in the broken terrain; traps and poison may kill native species as well; and fencing is expensive and effective only with larger animals.

The SICGAL organization now checks all luggage and packages entering the islands or moving between islands for organic materials of any kind. This has discouraged many new importations and led to confiscations of animals, plants, and seeds. Families wishing to keep pets in their towns must register their neutered animals and produce health certificates; unregistered animals are destroyed.

The hard work is paying off. In 2002, a four-year campaign by the National Park Service and the Charles Darwin Research Center succeeded in ridding Santiago Island of 25,000 feral pigs. The 300,000 goats that infested Isabela have suffered a similar fate. After ground-pounding hunters reduced goat populations, a number of "Judas goats" were fitted with radio-tracking collars and brightly painted horns and released into the wild. When the naturally gregarious animals found a herd, they were located from the air, all the other animals shot and left to rot, and the process began again. As of 2003, some 125,000 goats had been killed this way, and the technique helped reduce Pinta's goat population from 30,000 to next to nothing. In 2006 goats were eradicated from Isabela and Pinta.

The disastrous El Niño of 1982-1983 actually helped an eradication campaign on Santiago by weakening goats and pigs. Park employees were able to kill 20,000 out of 100,000 goats and half of nearly 10,000 pigs. Black rats have been eliminated from Seymour North, fire ants eradicated from Marchena, and wild dog populations are being controlled.

Floreana's dark-rumped petrel is an encouraging success story. Formerly, large populations of petrels had been decimated by dogs, cats, rats, and pigs. (At one point, pigs ate so many petrels that farmers noticed their pork tasted faintly of fish from the contents of the seabirds' stomachs.) One study in the 1960s showed that only 4 out of 92 nests produced young. A predator-control program involving poisoned bait and traps has turned things around – today, four out of five petrels survive chickhood, instead of one out of five, as before.

Plans to re-introduce the endemic Floreana mockingbird to Floreana from Champion islet, where they are currently reproducing well, are also underway.

programs. The percentage of tourist revenue going to the park itself has been increased to 40 percent, and other badly needed funds are being redirected to the islands' inhabitants, earmarked for increased conservation efforts.

The law's most controversial section is proving to be the expansion of the Galápagos Marine Reserve from 15 to 40 nautical miles into the waters around the islands. Within these new boundaries—at 133,000 square kilometers, the country's second-largest marine reserve—only tourism and *"artesanal"* (i.e., local traditional) fishing are permitted.

Illegal fishing ships are still being caught and impounded, and some protests continue. In one instance, the Ecuadorian Marines had to be flown in. As a result, the Ecuadorian government has once again backed down, increasing lobster quotas and extending the fishing seasons. Emboldened fishermen are pushing for even more concessions.

On January 16, 2001, the captain of the Ecuadorian-registered tanker *Jessica* misjudged his entry into Shipwreck Bay on San Cristóbal Island. The ship ran aground and began leaking diesel fuel. Despite international cleanup efforts, approximately two-thirds of the ship's 240,000-gallon cargo, originally meant for tour boats, found its way into the pristine waters.

Fortunately, favorable winds and tides carried much of the fuel to the north and away from the islands. Small stretches of beach and some animals were contaminated, but on the whole, shoreline damage was kept to a minimum. The long-term effects of the spill on ocean-floor algae, the foundation of the islands' entire food chain, have yet to be determined, but the director of the National Park said he expected the ecosystem to recover fully within three–four years. The ship captain was sentenced to 90 days in jail. Currently, an insurance settlement of $3.375 million is under discussion.

The end of 2001 brought much better news: In December, UNESCO designated 133,000 square kilometers of marine reserve around the islands as a World Heritage Site. (It's also been labeled one of the Seven Underwater Wonders of the World by conservation groups.) Residents weren't universally thrilled, fearing it would hinder fishing and other sea-based businesses.

The oil spill did have one positive outcome: it spurred Ecuador to sign an accord with environmental groups to move toward clean, renewable energy systems in the islands. A wind-energy project has been installed on San Cristobal, providing around 60 percent of the island's power needs and replacing a diesel-powered plant; small boats are now required to replace polluting outboard motors with cleaner versions; and recycling systems are working in the towns.

The Natural World

Take five-and-twenty heaps of cinders dumped here and there in an outside city lot; imagine some of them magnified into mountains, and the vacant lot the sea; and you will have a fit idea of the general aspect of the Encantadas, or Enchanted Isles.

– Herman Melville, *Las Encantadas*, 1854

Life in the Galápagos is defined by geology, which here can be barren, beautiful, and busy in equal measure. The 13 volcanic islands of the province of Galápagos lie scattered over 60,000 square kilometers in the eastern Pacific Ocean. Actually the tips of underwater volcanoes, the islands become younger and higher to the west. Isabela, the largest island of the group (4,275 square kilometers), consists of six volcanic peaks joined by old lava flows. One of these, Cerro Azul, is the highest point in the archipelago at 1,689 meters. Sixteen tiny islets and almost 50 rocks complete the archipelago's 8,000 square kilometers of land. Land and sea meet in more than 1,350 kilometers of coastline.

Most residents live on Santa Cruz Island, where Puerto Ayora is the largest city. Sleepy Puerto Baquerizo Moreno on San Cristóbal serves as the provincial capital, and Puerto Villamil on Isabela is the islands' third largest town.

VOLCANIC ORIGINS

The Galápagos sit directly over a hotspot in the Pacific crust plate, where underlying magma bulges much closer to the surface than usual. Millions of years ago, molten rock began to bubble up through the crust, cooling in the seawater and piling into mountains that eventually poked above the surface.

As the Pacific crust plate slowly grinds its way southeast under the Nazca plate, which supports the South American mainland, the volcanoes were carried along as well. New volcanoes quickly formed to take the place of older ones and were slowly worn away by the sea and weather, resulting in a rough chain of islands trailing off toward the mainland. (The Hawaiian Islands are also hotspot volcanoes.)

All of this slow bubbling and sliding produced a few interesting side effects. The islands that currently make up the archipelago are about 3.5 million years old—geologic newborns—but the entire process has been going on for much longer. This means that many more volcanoes have come and gone, weathered away to nothing beneath the seas to the east, than remain visible today (a crucial clue in an evolutionary puzzle concerning the iguana). The islands will eventually disappear, as the Nazca plate drives them under the continent faster than the hotspot can push out new ones. Don't worry, though—we're only talking a few centimeters per year, and the whole process will take about 50 million years.

VOLCANIC ACTIVITY

Clues to the Galápagos's volcanic origins are everywhere, and new scars form daily. Beaches

pahoehoe lava

© JULIAN SMITH

of volcanic minerals and jagged spires of tuff (compacted volcanic ash and debris) dot the coast, whereas farther up in the highlands, you can visit collapsed calderas and lava tunnels, which formed when lava continued flowing within a hardened outer layer.

On more recent flows, such as the one in Sullivan Bay, it's possible to distinguish the two main types of basaltic lava found in the islands. Ropy pahoehoe (pa-HOY-hoy) lava, from the Polynesian word for "calm sea," is formed when a cooled surface layer wrinkles over a liquid base like the skin on cooling hot chocolate. Jagged a'a (AH-ah) lava contains more silicates and starts out stickier, cooling quickly and completely into a super-stucco surface that's tricky to negotiate on foot. The name comes from the Polynesian word for "choppy sea," but it's more easily remembered as the sound you'd make walking over it in bare feet.

The islands of Marchena, Pinta, Isabela, and Fernandina, farthest north and west, are the youngest and most geologically active. Isabela

lava gulls

AN IGUANA MYSTERY SOLVED

Scientist Vincent Sarich raised an interesting question in his 1983 scientific paper, "Are the Galápagos Iguanas Older Than the Galápagos?" While the current estimate for the age of the archipelago is between two and three million years, naturalists were sure that marine and land iguanas must have needed at least 15 million years to diverge so completely from their common mainland ancestor. In short, the islands weren't nearly old enough to have given endemic species sufficient time to evolve into their present state.

Careful analysis of the ocean floor to the east yielded an answer. Six hundred kilometers from the mainland to the east of the archipelago, the remains of old, sunken islands were found, formerly part of the Galápagos group. Before plate drift had carried them east and erosion had reduced them to undersea nubs, these islands may have been around for as long as the Galápagos hot spot has been active (more than 80 million years). Present species would then have had ample time to arrive, evolve, and move to the present islands.

and Fernandina blew off steam, and occasionally much more, well into the 20th century. In 1954, a passing film crew noticed a strange new white beach in Urbina Bay on the west coast of Isabela. On closer investigation, they found that an entire stretch of shoreline—coral, fish, and all—had just been raised six meters above sea level by volcanic pressure underneath. Fernandina's latest eruption in 1995 lasted three months and sent a 100-meter-wide flow of lava five kilometers into the sea.

THE SEA

The islands are pushed and pulled by several ocean currents, which are stirred by trade winds dragging over the water's surface and intensified by the earth's rotation. The Peru (or Humboldt) Current, one of the world's grandest, sweeps north along the coast of Chile and Peru, bringing cold waters into the Equatorial region. Subdivided into coastal and oceanic currents, the Peru Current parts from the coast near the equator to flow west and wash the Galápagos with its cool waters. The Panama Current flows down from Central America, turning west toward the archipelago near the coast of mainland Ecuador.

West of the islands, the warm Equatorial Current (split into northern and southern

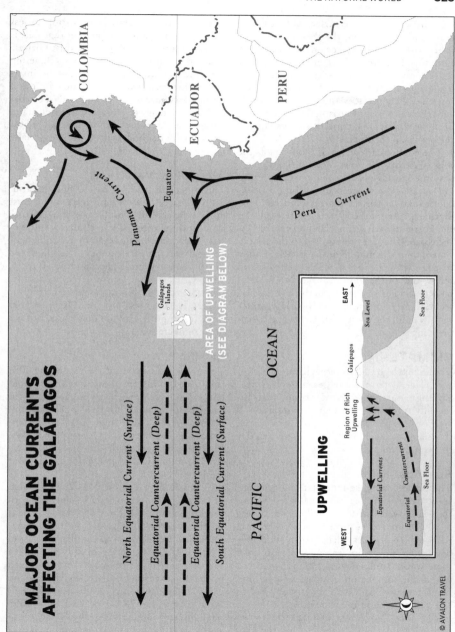

MAJOR OCEAN CURRENTS AFFECTING THE GALÁPAGOS

COLOMBIA

ECUADOR

PERU

Panama Current

Equator

Peru Current

Galápagos Islands

AREA OF UPWELLING (SEE DIAGRAM BELOW)

PACIFIC OCEAN

North Equatorial Current (Surface)

Equatorial Countercurrent (Deep)

Equatorial Countercurrent (Deep)

South Equatorial Current (Surface)

UPWELLING

WEST

EAST

Sea Level

Sea Floor

Galápagos

Region of Rich Upwelling

Equatorial Currents

Equatorial Countercurrent

Sea Floor

© AVALON TRAVEL

sections) continues the surface thrust of the Peru Current west into the Pacific. Deep beneath the water's surface, meanwhile, the Equatorial Counter Current—also called the Cromwell Current—rushes toward the Galápagos from the west. Upon encountering the westernmost islands in the archipelago, the countercurrent is deflected upward, bringing with it cool, nutrient-rich water from the depths of the Pacific.

The countercurrent isn't as constant as the other currents—it flows more during the dry season—but it's possibly the most important one of all. The western upwelling, 5–10°C cooler than the surface waters, is crucial to the marine habitat of the islands. Algae thrive on the nutrients, attracting fish and marine invertebrates that are more suited to the coastal waters than the middle of the Pacific. Larger marine mammals such as whales and dolphins follow these fish, and terrestrial animals and birds depend on the bounty of the surrounding sea. Galápagos penguins and flightless cormorants wait for the countercurrent to begin their breeding season.

CLIMATE

The archipelago's subtropical climate is almost completely determined by sea currents, whose varying temperatures bring seasons that differ only in cloud cover and the amount and type of precipitation. Smack on the equator, the islands enjoy 12 hours of sunlight per day throughout the year.

Seasons

The hot or **rainy season,** late November–June, arrives when the Panama Current warms the nearby waters to 26°C. Daily showers bring 6–10 centimeters of precipitation per month. Although there is less chance of a completely dry day during the hot season, you'll encounter more warm, sunny days per month than you will in the cool season. Average temperatures climb into the 30s, with February and March the warmest and sunniest months.

The June–November **dry season** arrives with the colder (20°C) waters from the Peru

Current. Average temperatures drop to less than 27°C, and any precipitation that falls is usually in the form of *garúa,* a misty drizzle that gathers in the highlands. This lingering fog forms at the inversion layer—the intersection between lower ocean-cooled air and warmer air above it—at around 400–600 meters. There are fewer chances of outright rain, but overcast days are common. Lower elevations remain dry and dead-looking, especially from August to November.

Altitudinal Variations

The climate at sea level can be hot and arid. Rain is scarce, with minor drizzles and mist during the cool season. Average temperatures drop into the teens as you climb to 500 meters, where the climate begins to resemble subtropical and temperate zones. The highlands on the larger islands (Fernandina, Isabela, Santa Cruz, and San Cristóbal) bear a distinctive type of cloud forest, complete with mist, mosses, lichens, grass, and trees. Temperatures up here, amplified by the dampness, can get downright chilly.

El Niño

There was a time toward the end of the 20th century when it seemed as if everything from heat spells to failed marriages was being blamed on this mysterious climatic phenomenon. Named for the Christ child because of its tendency to appear near the Christmas holidays, El Niño (and its climatic cousin, La Niña) arrives periodically to create havoc throughout the Pacific basin.

When El Niño is in town, December–March in certain years, warm waters from the north surge suddenly and force the Peru Current south for anywhere from 6 to 18 months. Ocean temperatures rise, clouds gather, and 6–10 centimeters more rain falls per month than average. The extra moisture is welcomed by the thirsty islands, but occasionally El Niño brings too much of a good thing. Extreme El Niño seasons in 1982–1983 and 1997–1998 wrought havoc on the archipelago's fragile ecosystem, causing high mortality among marine

THE INCREDIBLE SHRINKING IGUANAS

Although the 1997-1998 El Niño didn't hit the Galápagos as hard as it did mainland Ecuador, it still had a large effect on the island's inhabitants. One of the most curious results was reported in the journal *Nature* by Martin Wikelski, professor of ecology, ethology, and evolution at the University of Illinois at Urbana-Champaign.

In examining data collected since 1987, Wikelski and his coworkers noticed that marine iguanas shrank when the marine algae they feed on died during the El Niño season, then regrew to their original size when food became plentiful again. The study was the first conclusive finding of a shrinking adult mammal, and it countered an unofficial dogma among scientists that animals, well, just don't do that.

On one island, Wikelski found that some iguanas lost not only half their body weight but also a quarter of their length during the 1997-1998 El Niño season. They're not sure how exactly the iguanas managed it, but the scientists hypothesized that the animals may have somehow absorbed part of their skeletons. By becoming smaller, an iguana would increase its chances of survival by making it easier to forage and be warmed by the sun. When food became plentiful again, the iguanas started growing back to their original size to increase their odds of winning territories and reproducing. "You want to be the largest one during the non-El Niño years," summed up the report, "and then you want to be the smallest one during the El Niño years."

The ability to control the loss and recovery of bone mass may eventually have significant implications in human health care. The U.S. national expenditure for osteoporosis – a medical condition in which bones become brittle and break easily, especially in the elderly – was estimated at $10 billion in 1987, and astronauts are known to lose bone density during extended periods in space.

iguanas, sea lions, waved albatrosses, penguins, and boobies.

FLORA AND FAUNA

Life in the Galápagos is a study in extremes. These parched, rocky islands spread under the equatorial sun are surprisingly rich in life. The only way to survive here, it seems, is to adapt, which means a high level of **endemic species**—those found nowhere else on earth. The Galápagos has 1,900 endemic species out of 5,000 total: 32 percent of the plants, almost half of all birds, half of all shore fish and insects, and 90 percent of the reptiles have become so specifically adapted to life in the islands that they hardly resemble their original mainland ancestors at all.

In contrast, the fragility of the Galápagos ecosystem shows itself in a low level of **diversity:** There aren't as many different species as one would expect. This paucity of species has created a delicate balance—certain species, both plant and animal, are completely dependent on others.

Colonization

By now, you've probably asked yourself the most obvious question about the islands' inhabitants: How did they get there? The Galápagos were never connected to the mainland, and 1,000 kilometers of open water is a long swim. As impressive as it seems, though, most species arrived more or less under their own power. Fish and marine mammals cruising the currents might have bumped into the islands and decided to stay, whereas land birds blown off course wouldn't have known the way back to the mainland even if they had wanted to leave. Seabirds and migrant species, knowing a good fishing spot when they saw one, might have returned to breed year after year. Insects and plant seeds could also have been carried from the South American continent by high winds, whereas other seeds were probably excreted by birds or arrived stuck to their feet.

As for terrestrial reptiles and rats, the generally accepted explanation involves the large rafts of vegetation that still wash down

Ecuador's ocean-bound rivers. Any animals or plants that happened to be aboard, provided they could survive the journey, stood a slim chance of riding the currents all the way to the Galápagos. (Some rafts are even large enough to support living trees—another colonization possibility.) With their ability to slow their own metabolism, reptiles are particularly suited for such a long, difficult journey. On the other hand, large mammals would tend to die of dehydration, and amphibians would dry up during the trip, which explains why there weren't any of either group on the islands before the arrival of humans.

Marinelife

The Galápagos are every bit as spectacular beneath the water's surface as above it. A staggering diversity of life inhabits a wide range of marine habitats, from mangrove estuaries to lava-rocky tide pools, volcanic beaches to the sandy bottom. About 50 marine species are endemic, in a percentage comparable to endemic numbers on land. All of this is a result of a few climatic factors—a combination of warm and cold currents and the El Niño phenomenon, which warms things drastically every so often—that have turned the Galápagos into a natural marine reserve in the middle of the Pacific.

Because the ravages of hunting have not, for the most part, reached far below the surface, the same animal fearlessness is found beneath the waves as on land. Sea turtles sleeping near the surface will only steer casually away upon being awakened. Sea lions almost treat you like one of the pack—just stay out of the way of the territorial bulls. And in the deep, it's almost as if you weren't there at all, as huge schools of fish engulf divers in living clouds of silver.

Taxonomy

A brief explanation of taxonomy (the scientific classification of living things) should help neophytes better appreciate the natural history of the islands. Every single organism ever discovered has been given a unique spot in the hierarchy of taxonomic divisions, pinpointed by a lengthy label of Latin and Greek terms. The term you'll hear over and over again in talk of the Galápagos ecology is **species,** the fundamental taxonomic unit that's loosely defined as a group of organisms sharing many common characteristics (abbreviated "sp" or "spp"). Species usually live in a specific area and are only able to successfully reproduce with each other. The next two categories above species are genus and family.

Plants and animals are most often referred to by their **common name,** as well as their **scientific name,** usually written as the genus and species. Animals in the Galápagos also have Spanish names, of course, only some of which are related to their common (English) names. For example, the blue-footed booby (common name) is called the *piquero patas azules* in Spanish (blue-footed lancer) and saddled with the scientific name *Sula nebuoxi* (genus Sula, species nebouxii).

REPTILES

The reptiles of the Galápagos define the islands more than any other group of animals. Here, reptiles still rule the earth, giving a taste of what the rest of the planet may have been like tens of millions of years ago. More than 90 percent of the reptile species in the Galápagos are endemic, a testament to their ability to enter a state of hibernation-like torpor that would have allowed their ancestors to survive the long ocean crossing. In addition to the reptiles described below, the Galápagos harbors five endemic species of **gecko** and three species of **Galápagos snake.**

Giant Tortoise

These creaking giants, with skin like the world's oldest leather jacket, are the largest in the world. They're found only here and on a few islands in the Indian Ocean, notably in the Seychelles off the coast of Tanzania. The Galápagos species, *Geochelone elephantopus,* can reach 250 kilograms and nobody knows how what age. Dependable records top out at 100 years, but some stories have turtles lasting more than 200 years. During your visit to the Darwin Center in Puerto Ayora, notice the smooth domes of the tortoises in captivity, and think how long it must have taken to wear those huge shells down.

The shell of a giant tortoise reveals which island, or at least what type of island, its owner hails from. Saddle-shaped shells, high in front and the back, evolved on low, arid islands where tortoises must lift their heads as high as possible to browse tall vegetation. (The tortoises' necks and legs are also longer on these islands.) Semicircular domed shells come from higher, lusher islands with vegetation that grows low to the ground. Males have larger and longer tails, with a concave plastron (bottom plate) that helps them mount females during mating.

During mating season, the only time tortoises make any noise, unearthly groans echo for kilometers as males joust for dominance—a relatively simple showdown in which the higher head wins. When her eggs are ready to hatch, the female softens the soil with urine before digging a nest for as long as five hours. A single layer of tennis-ball-sized eggs is covered with six inches of packed earth that soon dries hard. The nest is a surprisingly delicate system: The top layer of mud must keep the heat and moisture levels within a narrow range, because a temperature difference of a few degrees Celsius decides whether the offspring will be male, female, or stillborn. Broods hatch during the first months of the year.

Tortoises spend much of their lives in a state of torpor, when their metabolism and body temperature slow significantly. This ability allows them to survive dry periods on the island with a minimum of food and water. But when the rains do come, look out—on Alcedo Volcano on Isabela, the wet season is greeted by a slow-motion orgy of eating, drinking, mating, and wallowing in new pools of water. By nighttime, everyone ends up in the mud, snoozing contentedly in large groups.

When the islands were first discovered, there were as many as 250,000 tortoises, and 14 islands each had their own species. Today, there are only about 15,000 left, and three of those species (Santa Fe, Floreana, and Fernandina) are extinct. The Pinta species is represented by one surviving member named Lonesome George. Whalers were once the tortoises' main enemy, but today the danger comes from introduced animal species. Pigs can dig up dozens of nests in no time, hatchlings fall prey to cats and rats, and larger tortoises can be killed by dogs. Even if they do survive to adulthood, tortoises often have to compete with burros, goats, and cattle for food.

Marine Iguanas

The only true marine lizard in the world, *Amblyrhynchus cristatus* evolved from a terrestrial species that took to the water to survive. In a short time, evolutionarily speaking (only two–three million years), marine iguanas have adapted well to feed on coastal seaweed. A flattened snout allows closer munching, a vertically flattened tail propels better in the water, long claws grab underwater rocks firmly, and a pair of salt-eliminating glands in the nostrils cleanse sea salt from their system. As a result, they're prodigious divers that are able to stay under for well more than an hour by lowering their heart rate by half.

Anywhere from 200,000 to 300,000 marine iguanas inhabit the Galápagos. Males can reach a little more than one meter in length and weigh up to 20 kilograms, with the average size increasing toward the western islands. Bright colorings attract females during the dry season; Espanola's iguanas are particularly colorful. Despite their prehistoric appearance (one was used as a model for the updated version of *Godzilla*), the iguanas are harmless.

Marine iguanas feed on shallow-growing seaweed, shunning the tough, brown stuff for tender green and red morsels. This inconspicuous but surprisingly nutritious plant grows like, well, a weed—a one-kilometer patch can quintuple its mass in less than two weeks and support up to 3,000 iguanas at once. Marine iguanas feed for about an hour every day, always at low tide. Basking in the sun helps each iguana generate enough heat to digest a bellyful of cellulose.

Regulating body heat is a prime concern, especially after a long dive. Like all reptiles, marine iguanas are ectotherms, meaning their internal body temperatures are at the mercy of outside temperatures. Males prefer to dive during the hottest part of the day to keep cool. On shore, the trick becomes not warming back up too much: Lava-rock temperatures can climb more than 40°C, and iguanas die if their body temperature rises above 45°C. To remedy this problem, iguanas face the sun, exposing as little surface area as possible, and raise their bodies off the ground to allow air to circulate underneath. On cold days and at night, iguanas congregate into huge piles to conserve heat.

Marine iguana populations fell slightly over the years as a result of hunting by early visitors, but recent El Niño seasons in the 1980s and 1990s struck much more deeply. Abnormally warm waters killed the shallow-growing algae, spelling doom for those animals not strong enough to dive to reach deeper algae. Since then, in a handy example of evolution in action, marine iguanas have become slightly larger, and females breed every year instead of every two as before.

Land Iguanas

The seven subspecies of land iguana (*Conolophus* spp.) in the Galápagos have evolved a pale yellow coloring, in contrast to their mainland ancestors' arboreal green. Land iguanas evolved from a similar species as their seagoing relatives—the difference being that by the time land iguanas' ancestors arrived at the islands, enough ground vegetation had grown that they didn't have to take to the water to survive.

Land iguanas live in dry areas, where they spend the night in dugout burrows to conserve heat. Their menu is mostly vegetarian: any plant within reach gets chomped, including berries, flowers, fruits, and cactus pads, spines and all. Land iguanas get much of their water from food. After digging their way out of the nest, tiny newborn iguanas must avoid hawks, owls, and introduced predators until they're large enough to defend themselves. Males can reach 13 kilograms and live more

CHARLES, LEAVE THE IGUANAS ALONE

The father of evolutionary theory would have been booted from the Royal Society for the Prevention of Cruelty to Animals because of his own accounts of tormenting, eating, and expressing general negativity toward the Galápagos's inhabitants during his visit. In the *Voyage of the Beagle*, he wrote of dining on giant tortoises: "The breast-plate roasted . . . with the flesh on it, is very good; and the young tortoises make excellent soup; but otherwise the meat to my taste is indifferent."

He went on to describe the marine iguana as "a hideous-looking creature, of a dirty black colour, stupid, and sluggish in its movements." One hapless iguana Darwin repeatedly threw into the ocean kept returning to the same place on shore. This "singular piece of apparent stupidity" caused the naturalist to wonder about the animal's response to predators: "Urged by a fixed and hereditary instinct that the shore is its place of safety, whatever emergency there may be, it there takes refuge" – meddling naturalist or not.

Land iguanas fared little better. "Like their brothers the sea-kind," he noted, "they are ugly animals, of a yellowish orange beneath, and of a brownish red colour above: From their low facial angle they have a singularly stupid appearance." Even in the dinner pot, the land iguana just couldn't measure up: "These lizards, when cooked, yield a white meat, which is liked by those whose stomachs soar above all prejudices." After watching one land iguana dig a nest hole "for a long time," Darwin proceeded to yank it back out by the tail.

"At this it was greatly astonished," he wrote, "and stared me in the face, as much as to say, 'What made you pull my tail?'"

than 60 years. Maturity comes between ages 10 and 15, when adult males begin a career of vigorously defending a specific territory, with head-nodding threats that often end in battle.

As a result of hunting and introduced species, the land iguana species on Santiago and Baltra have become extinct, and those on other islands are in trouble. A captive-breeding program at the Darwin Center attempts to maintain threatened populations at viable levels. Only Fernandina's iguanas have avoided outside intrusion, and they're among the largest in the islands.

Sea Turtles

The eastern **Pacific green turtle** *(Chelonia mydas agassisi)* is the most common species in the islands. Called *tortugas negras* (black turtles) in Spanish, Pacific greens depend on the Galápagos for nesting beaches. Beyond that, it's not known whether they live here year-round or migrate periodically to the mainland. Green sea turtles average around 100 kilograms and can often be spotted sleeping on shallow sandy bottoms or mating in open water. Awkward at or above the surface, sea turtles glide gorgeously beneath, where they can hold their breath for hours. They're often seen coming up for air alongside anchored boats.

Also present in the islands, although rarely seen, are the **Pacific leatherback** *(Dermochelys coriacea)* and the **Indo-Pacific hawksbill** *(Eretmochely imbricata).*

Lava Lizard

Seven species of the ubiquitous lava lizard *(Tropidurus albemarlensis)* scurry over sand and rock on almost every island. Larger males can reach 30 centimeters, and females can be identified by red throat patches. Lava lizards feed democratically, gulping down insects, plants, and even each other. In turn, they're pursued by many larger birds, who are only occasionally fooled by the lizards' break-away tails.

Like soldiers at boot camp, male lava lizards do pushups constantly, to the point that their Spanish name *(lagartija)* has become a slang term for pushup. The pattern of ups and downs

is different for different island species and is thought to defend territory, as well as regulate body temperature.

MAMMALS

Only six species of mammals originally called the Galápagos home, and four of those arrived by swimming or flying. The long ocean crossing (at least two weeks by floating raft) is too long for most mammals to survive; in fact, Galápagos rice rats set a world record for long-distance colonization.

Galápagos Sea Lion

Somehow feline and canine at the same time, the Galápagos sea lion *(Zalophus californianus wollebacki)* is a smaller cousin of the California sea lion. (Males in the Galápagos reach only 250 kilograms in size.) Their charming snouts, whiskers, and dark eyes belie a voice that sounds like the winner of a belching contest—even a newborn pup can bleat like a Billy goat coughing up a hairball.

© JULIAN SMITH

Galápagos sea lions

THE GALÁPAGOS ISLANDS

Some 50,000 sea lions sprawl over beaches and rocks throughout the islands—prolonged snoozing helps replenish oxygen used up during long, deep dives after fish. Sharks and killer whales are the sea lion's chief predators. Sea-lion bulls defend beach harems—short stretches of sand filled with females and pups—by patrolling loudly just offshore. Any male who is careless enough to approach the boundary is confronted immediately; the winner is usually the one who can raise his snout higher. Although most of this posturing is harmless, sea lion attacks are the most common cause of animal injury in the Galápagos. Steer well clear of patrolling males, especially when snorkeling.

Galápagos Fur Seal

With its small external ears and strong propulsive forward flippers, the Galápagos fur seal (*Arctocephalus galapagoensis*) isn't really a true seal (family Phocidae) at all. Like the larger Galápagos sea lion, the fur seal is a member of the eared-seal family Otariidae. Fur seals are smaller than sea lions, with a thick, furry coat that traces their ancestry to the cold coasts of Peru and Chile.

This luxurious coat almost led to the fur seal's extinction in the 19th century. The warm, two-layered pelt was in high demand in Europe and the United States, leading to unchecked slaughter at the hands of hunters. One ship in 1823 reported a take of 5,000 skins in two months. By the turn of the 20th century, the seal was thought to be extinct—a California Academy of Sciences expedition in 1905 found only one seal in an entire year.

Fortunately, the fur seal has made a comeback, despite a low birth rate of one pup every two years. Today, 30,000–40,000 fur seals inhabit the northern and western islands of Pinta, Marchena, Santiago, Isabela, and Fernandina.

Whales and Dolphins

Several cetaceans (completely aquatic mammals) can be seen around the islands. Those without teeth use hairy plates of baleen in their jaws to strain gallons of tiny creatures from the water. The **blue whale,** the largest animal in the world, is an occasional visitor to the archipelago, and the more common **humpback whale** (*Megaptera novaeangliae*) can reach 16 meters. The sight of one of these giants breaching completely out of the water—most often seen west of Isabela and Fernandina—is awe-inspiring. Smaller baleen species include finback, Sei, Bryde's, and Minke whales.

Toothed cetaceans eat larger prey, including fish and squid. Black-and-white **killer whales** (*Orcinus orca*) are the true lions of the sea. The sight of a tall, black dorsal fin is enough to clear a beach of sea lions in an instant. A population of **sperm whales** (*Physete macrocephalus*) is slowly recovering from the depredations of 19th-century whalers. Three resident species of **dolphin** surf the bow waves of cruising ships with unmistakable glee. Schools of up to 100 can be seen leaping in unison through the waves.

Bats and Rats

Two endemic species of bats made the long crossing—probably by accident—to make their home in the Galápagos. Two species of rice rats are left from an original seven. The rest were driven to extinction by the Norwegian black rat *(Rattus rattus),* which was introduced by visiting ships and is now a major threat to native species.

SEABIRDS

With nothing but water in every direction, the Galápagos are a perfect stopover for wide-ranging seabirds. Estimates range as high as 750,000 in the islands at any one time. Because they can come and go freely, seabirds have evolved fewer endemic species in the Galápagos compared to other types of birds. Out of the 19 species of seabirds on the islands, only five are endemic: the Galápagos penguin, flightless cormorant, waved albatross, lava gull, and swallow-tailed gull. Of these, only the last three can fly.

Boobies

Named after the Spanish word *bobo* (clown), boobies are the awkward but endearing mascots of the Galápagos. They belong to the same family as gannets (Sulidae), whom they resemble, with their large webbed feet, round heads, and long pointed beaks. All boobies catch fish with astounding plunges into the water from midair. You'll see blue-footed boobies doing this most often near the shore—a crash into the water inches from the base of rocky cliffs, a second of silence, then a pop to the surface, and *gulp*—down goes a fish. Air sacs in their skulls diffuse the shock of impact, and closed-beak nostrils keep salt water out. Boobies typically lay two or three eggs to ensure that at least one (and often only one) chick survives to adolescence. This brutally effective evolutionary insurance policy often involves larger chicks killing their smaller siblings.

Blue-footed boobies *(Sula nebouxii)* symbolize the Galápagos in the minds of much of the world, helped by countless T-shirts, hats, postcards, and posters. About 30 percent of the world's population nests in the islands—close to 10,000 pairs—where they feed close to shore. Males and females both have the famous neon-blue feet, so the only way to tell the sexes apart is by the size of their pupils (smaller in males) and the sound of their calls (females honk, males whistle). Males show off their feet during the courtship dance, a high-stepping ritual designed to show off sexual maturity and good genes—the bluer, the better. This strange ceremony is both comic and thought-provoking. As Kurt Vonnegut writes in his novel *Galapagos,* it "seems to have absolutely no connection with the elements of booby survival, with nesting or fish. What does it have to do with, then? Dare we call it 'religion?' Or, if we lack that sort of courage, might we at least call it 'art?'"

Blue-foots nest on the ground, where they scrape a shallow depression that becomes surrounded by a white ring of guano. Lacking the usual avian incubating pouch, parents keep the eggs warm on top of their feet, which are richly veined with warm blood vessels. After hatching, any chick that ends up outside the nest ring is as good as dead, ignored by its parents and pecked at by its siblings if it tries to reenter.

© JULIAN SMITH

blue-footed boobies

There are more **red-footed boobies** (*Sula sula*) than any other booby species in the Galápagos (a quarter of a million pairs), but they're also the least often seen. Although the world's largest colony of red-foots nests on Tower Island, its inhabitants are usually feeding far out to sea. Red-footed boobies are the smallest on the islands and have blue bills and brown plumage (a few have white feathers). Their relatively small feet, tipped with small claws, allow them to nest in trees.

The beautiful **masked boobies** (*Sula dactylatra*) nest on cliff edges because, as the largest booby species, they have a harder time taking off from level ground. Most of the masked boobies in the world nest in the Galápagos, giving you a good opportunity to see their stunning plumage: one of the purest whites in the animal kingdom, with a black eye mask and black wing edges.

Waved Albatross

Nearly the entire world population of the waved albatross (*Diomedea irrorata*)—some 12,000 pairs—nest on Española Island. Bulging white eyebrows atop cream-colored feathers give albatrosses a refined yet slightly comical appearance (think Groucho Marx in a nice suit). As graceful as it is soaring on its two-meter wings, the waved albatross is a duck out of water on land, waddling around like a sailor after too long at sea. The air-to-land transition seems to be a bit of a problem, too, as landings often end in a flailing tumble of feathers and squawks. Granted, many albatrosses have been cruising the thermals of the South Pacific for as long as three–four years without landing. The most successful albatross launch is a seaward leap off a cliff into a headwind.

For a long time, waved albatross couples were thought to mate for life, which can mean a 50-year commitment. The pair bond is reinforced through an elaborate courtship display, an ecstatic ritual that peaks in October and is worth scheduling a visit around. Bills clatter, circle, and point at the sky as participants perform an exaggerated version of their normal swaying walk.

Recent research, however, has cast some doubts on this astounding display of fidelity. One study recorded 1,724 matings among some 300 albatrosses over 40 days—one female mated 85 times with 49 different males—and found through DNA testing that one out of every four chicks was not actually sired by the bird that acted as its "father." Practices such as adoption, adultery, and even rape have been observed among the graceful seabirds.

After going on long hunting junkets, parents stuff chicks to bursting with up to two liters of a predigested mixture of fish and squid. Researcher Bryan Nelson described the result: "For the first four months of its life the chick is hardly more than a great, oil-filled skin, covered in matted brown down. It is grotesque with the fascination of the truly ugly."

Galápagos Penguin

Short-listed for the Cutest Endemic Species award, the Galápagos penguin (*Sheniscus mendiculus*) seems as out of place in the hot, dry islands as a polar bear at a beach party. At 35 centimeters high, it's one of the smallest penguin species. Having evolved from the Humboldt penguins that inhabit the Patagonian coasts of Peru and Chile, the Galápagos penguin is the only penguin found north of the equator. Because they still retain much of their original insulation, Galápagos penguins have to struggle to stay cool in the hot sun. The classic wings-out pose lowers a bird's temperature, but it occasionally comes down to a choice between the cooking of the nest eggs (which must be continually shaded by day) or the parents (who are forced to jump into the water). With only 3,000–5,000 breeding pairs, Galápagos penguins are one of the rarest species of seabirds in the world.

Frigatebirds

The bad boys of the Galápagos are notorious for making a living stealing food from other species. This type of feeding, called kleptoparasitism, is the reason frigatebirds were named after fast colonial-era warships. A forked tail, backswept wings, and extremely low weight for their size make them faster and more maneuverable then anything else in the air. They can often be seen harassing a booby returning with fish for a chick until the parent disgorges its meal; the frigatebird will then scoop its pilfered food out of the air. They're not above stealing food right out of a chick's mouth on the ground, either. This light-fingered lifestyle has evolved partly because these birds can't dive for their own food—with only vestigial preening glands, a frigatebird can't waterproof its feathers, and it sinks like a stone if it becomes waterlogged.

The males' distinctive red throat pouch is inflated to attract females. Once they go to the bother of pumping it up with air, they'll leave it inflated all day. A female drifting over a group of males during the mating season elicits waves of pouch-waving, bill-rattling, and calling meant to attract her to particular nests. Pairs mate for life, and chicks take up to one year to learn the thieving acrobatics of survival.

The male **magnificent frigatebird** (*Fregata magnificens*) has a purple-tinged nape and a white patch on the breast conveniently shaped like an M. An all-white breast and greenish neck and chest distinguish the male **great frigatebird** (*Fregata minor*).

Flightless Cormorant

You'll have to make it out to Fernandina and western Isabela to see some of the 2,000 pairs of flightless cormorants (*Nannopterum harrisi*), one of the few bird species in the world that has lost the ability to fly. The aquatic birds are a study of evolution in action from their steel blue eyes to their asymmetrical feet. Millennia of diving after fish, eels, and octopi on the near-shore bottom, combined with a lack of predators on land, have allowed the cormorants' wings and tail to atrophy to vestigial nubs. The typical avian keeled breastbone—a solid anchor for strong flying muscles—has vanished in flightless cormorants, whereas their long snakelike necks, strong kicking legs, and huge webbed feet make them experts at pursuing fish underwater. Flightless cormorants still haven't forgotten their roots, though, and they

stand patiently to dry their ragged wings every time they emerge from the water.

Cormorant nests are an impressive conglomeration of flotsam and twigs that are in use year-round by breeding pairs. The nests are often set precariously close to the waterline, and many eggs are washed away by high spring tides.

Endemic Gulls

Close to 15,000 pairs of **swallow-tailed gulls** (*Creagrus furcatus*) nest throughout the islands. They're one of the prettier gulls around, with a charcoal-colored head and white and gray body highlighted by red feet and a distinctive red eye ring. Unlike most other gulls, swallow-tails feed out to sea at night, pointing boat captains the way toward land in the morning. The **lava gull** (*Larus fuliginosus*) is thought to be the rarest gull in the world, consisting of only about 400 mating pairs nesting in the Galápagos. Their dark gray plumage blends into the lava rocks they prefer, but their obnoxious chortle gives them away immediately.

Other Species

A distinctive chattering call signals the return of the **red-billed tropicbird** (*Phaethon aethereus*) from feeding far out to sea. If they make it past the frigatebirds, their next task is to pull off a swooping landing into the windy cliffside nests they prefer. Tropicbirds have a fragile beauty, with a gray and white body and long, flowing white pintails capped by a red bill and a black mask.

If you've spent any time near the coast, you'll undoubtedly recognize the **brown pelican** (*Pelecanus occidentalis*), groups of which are often seen at sunset skimming regally in formation, inches above the water. It's one of the largest and most commonly seen Galápagos seabirds, but actually one of the smaller species of pelican. It may not seem designed for it, but this ungainly-looking seabird plunges into the ocean over and over to capture food. After filling its 14-liter beak pouch with water on impact, the pelican filters out the fish and gulps them down.

The western cliffs of Isabela are home to the **brown noddy** *(Anous stolidus)*, a tern-like bird that nests in caves and dark niches. Noddies bring a classic beauty to the Galápagos, with an avian tuxedo of smart gray plumage punctuated by a white forehead and eye patches. You'll occasionally see them waiting on pelicans' heads for scraps.

If you happen to see a small black bird skimming the water for fish, it could be one of a few species. Both the **Audubon's shearwater** *(Puffinus l'herminieri)* and the larger **dark-rumped petrel** *(Pterodroma pharopygia)* have black backs and white fronts. The latter, also called the Hawaiian petrel, is nocturnal and highly endangered—more so in Hawaii than the Galápagos.

White rump patches decorate three types of storm petrels: the **white-vented** or **Eliot's storm petrel** *(Oceanites gracilis);* the nocturnal **Madeiran storm petrel** *(Oceanodroma castro);* and the day-feeding **Galápagos storm petrel** *(Oceanodroma tethys).*

COASTAL BIRDS

While they're not quite as distinctive as their seagoing cousins, the islands' coastal birds make the most of their niche between water and land.

Herons and Egrets

Five species of herons inhabit the islands. All hunt small reptiles, mammals, insects, and fish by waiting motionless, then spearing their prey with a quick jab of their long beaks. The **great blue heron** *(Adrea herodias)* stands 1.5 meters high as it poses one-legged among the mangroves. You might be surprised by one standing silent and fearless in a Puerto Ayora back alley. The smaller **yellow-crowned night heron** *(Nyctanassa violacea)* feeds by night. Its hunched shoulder and furtive, yellow-eyed glance give it a cloak-and-dagger look, capped by a bright yellow sweep of feathers atop the head. Lava rocks hide the small, gray **lava heron** *(Butorides sundevalli)*, the only endemic species of heron. They hunt fish, crabs, and lizards in rocky tide pools.

Greater Flamingos

About 500 of these pink, leggy birds *(Phoenicopters ruber)* wade through brackish lagoons around the archipelago. Punta Cormorant on Floreana, Red Beach on Rabida, and near Dragon Hill on Santa Cruz are good places to see them feeding on brine shrimp by filtering through the salty ooze. Listen closely and you can hear the quiet splooshes as the birds, heads upside-down, push the water through their hairy beak filters similar to whale's baleen. Here's a cocktail-party fact for you: flamingos are actually white, but they turn pink from the carotene pigments in the shrimp they eat.

Waders, Paddlers, and Beach Stalkers

The **American oystercatcher** *(Haematopus ostralegus)* looks like a bad drawing of a bird: head too small, red bill too large. Only 150 or so pairs of these bright-eyed birds live in the islands, where they comb intertidal areas for food. Along with flamingos, inland bodies of water are home to the **white-cheeked pintail duck** *(Anas bahamensis)*, also known as the Bahamas duck, along with the **common stilt** *(Himantopus mexicanus)*.

Galápagos shorelines and beaches are patrolled by **whimbrels** *(Numenius phaeopus)*, **sanderlings** *(Crocethia alba)*, **ruddy turnstones** *(Arenaria interpres)*, **northern phalaropes** *(Lobipes lobatus)*, and **semipalmated plovers** *(Charadrius semipalmatus)*.

LAND BIRDS

The only way that land birds could have reached the Galápagos was to have been blown far out to sea by a storm, which is why only 29 species inhabit the islands today. Those that arrived survived by adapting, eventually dividing into 22 endemic species. A greater variety of the endemic species can be found on islands with higher elevations, which have more vegetation zones, and thus, more ecological niches.

Darwin's Finches

The Galápagos' 13 species of finches, made

famous by Charles Darwin's work, all look more or less alike. Don't worry about trying to tell them apart; just being aware of their significance is enough. After all, as one researcher noted, "it is only a very wise man or a fool who thinks he is able to identify all the finches which he sees."

The key to the finches, as Darwin quickly noticed, is the beak. Different types of finches have beaks of different sizes and shapes, allowing them to gobble many different kinds of food. Short, thick beaks enable **ground finches** to crack hard seeds, whereas longer, slimmer bills allow other species to probe crevices for insects and munch cacti or flowers. The finches, it seems, evolved to fill a wide range of ecological niches left vacant by the lack of other terrestrial birds—a process ecologists call **adaptive radiation.** At the same time, they remained similar enough to have obviously come from a common ancestor. Darwin noticed all this, writing: "The most curious fact is the perfect gradation in the size of the beaks in the different species. One might really fancy that from an original paucity of birds in this archipelago, one species had been taken and modified for different ends."

The eating habits of a few finches are worth special mention. **Woodpecker** and **mangrove finches** use a cactus spine or small twig to get at a fat, tasty grub burrowed deep in a tree branch, making them one of the few animals to use and modify tools. The sharp-billed ground finch goes one step farther—this unremarkable brown bird pecks at the base of a boobie's tail until a trickle of blood starts flowing, which the finch drinks without much protest from its victim. These "vampire finches," as they have been nicknamed, also roll other birds' eggs—some nearly as big as themselves—over lava rocks until they crack, then eat the insides.

Mockingbirds

Like the finches, the four species of mockingbirds endemic to the Galápagos seem to have filled a niche usually taken by other animals. In this case, small land mammals were absent, leaving the mockingbirds free to pick up insects, small reptiles, and various scraps. The birds exhibit an interesting family bonding, in which related groups guard territory and share in the responsibilities of raising juveniles.

The ranges of the four species are separated onto different islands. The **Galápagos mockingbird** (Nesomimus parvulus) is the most widespread, found on Isabela, Floreana, Santa Cruz, Santiago, and Santa Fe. San Cristóbal is home to the **Chatham mockingbird** (Nesomimus melanotis), and on Española, you'll find the inquisitive **Hood mockingbird** (Nesomimus macdonaldi), with its long, curved beak. The **Charles mockingbird** (Nesomimus trifasciatus) once ranged over the Floreana area, but today is limited to a few nearby islets.

Other Land Birds

Because it has no natural enemies, the **Galápagos hawk** (Buteo galapagoensis) is known for its fearlessness. Darwin noted that "a gun here is almost superfluous; for with the muzzle I pushed a hawk out of the branch of a tree." This endemic scavenger is actually a type of buzzard. Through an unusual mating system known as cooperative polyandry, up to four males may mate with a single female and cooperate to help her raise the young, regardless (and ignorant) of whose offspring they are.

It's a tossup as to which land bird is the prettiest. In the running is the **Galápagos dove** (Zenaida galapagoensis), whose plumage combines pink, gray, and white with red feet, an aqua-blue eye ring, and green iridescent patches on either side of the neck. Because many of these birds were hunted for food by early visitors, Galápagos doves aren't as tame as they once were, hiding under bushes and eating the opuntia cactus. The male **vermillion flycatcher** (Pyrocephalus rubinus) looks like a small fireball in the trees, with its brilliant red coloring set off by a black eye stripe, wing, and tail. It typically catches insects in the highlands, along with the bright **yellow warbler** (Dendroica petechia), whose liquid song echoes on most islands.

Early morning and evening are the best times to catch the **short-eared owl** (Asio flameus) out after chicks, rodents, and insects. The endemic **Galápagos barn owl** (*Tyto punctissima*) is nocturnal, so there's less chance you'll glimpse this moon-faced bird on the prowl.

Cattle Egrets (*Bubulcus ibis*) have been expanding their range around the globe, and were first reported in Galapagos in 1960. Since then, their numbers have increased. While not introduced by humans, they have spread through the islands, posing a dilemma for scientists and the National Park. Evolution is not static, but this self-introduced species has expanded its range from the agricultural areas, putting pressure on some of the longer-established species.

INSECTS AND ARTHROPODS

Few insects make their home in the Galápagos, because of the islands' isolation and short growing season. Those that do live here are usually dull-colored and come out only at night to escape the heat. As a result, many flowers are light-colored, so their insect pollinators can find them even in low light.

The **carpenter bee** (*Xylocopa darwini*) is one of the most important pollinators in the archipelago. Rocks and sand hide the endemic **Galápagos scorpion** (*Centruroides exsul*), a favorite prey of lava lizards. Also hunted by lava lizards, the bright **painted locust** (*Shistocerca melanocera*) wears a carapace decorated with red, yellow, green, and black. All of these insects are abundant in the lowlands.

FISH

Waters around the Galápagos shelter a strange mix of cold and warm-water species. The variety differs, depending on where and when you're in the water. Currents and seasons bring water as cold as 15°C and as warm as 30°C to the islands, and the waters on different sides of the same island at the same time can vary as much as two–three degrees. Lava rocks serve as aquatic condos in place of coral reefs. Such a wide range of habitats allows more than 300 regular fish species to inhabit the surrounding ocean. Almost one-quarter of these are endemic—every one of the 15 fish Darwin brought back to England was identified as a new species.

Even snorkelers can enjoy a colorful show in the shallows. The **moorish idol** (*Zanclus cornutus*) trails a long dorsal fin over a body banded with black, yellow, and white, and the **blue parrotfish** (*Scarus ghobban*) wears pastel green, blue, and pink. The **harlequin wrasse** (*Bodianus eclancheri*) is one of the most colorful fish around, covered with spatters of orange, red, black, and white. This type of wrasse is called a protogynus hermaphrodite, meaning it can spontaneously change sex from female to male.

Lava rocks hide the **hieroglyphic hawkfish** (*Cirrhitus rivulatus*), colored in complicated patterns of brown, yellow, and gray. It seems as if the **red-lipped batfish** (*Ogcocephalus darwini*) was made from leftover parts, with a forehead horn, long snout, and stiff pectoral fins it uses as makeshift legs. True to its name, the bizarre-looking batfish sports a bright-red mouth and is usually seen on night dives. Even stranger is the mottled **four-eyed blenny** (*Dialommus fuscus*), which can breathe air temporarily as it travels up to 30 meters from the water in search of insects and crabs. Its eyes are each split into two parts, enabling it to see above and below the surface simultaneously.

One of the biggest thrills while diving in the Galápagos is to be engulfed by an opaque school of fish that seems to go on forever—veteran divers describe being blinded by fish for 20 minutes or more. Deep-sea schoolers include **amberjacks** (*Seriola rivoliana*), **yellow-tailed surgeonfish** (*Prionurus laticlavius*), **steel pompanos** (*Trachinotus stilbe*), and **barracudas** (*Sphyraena idiastes*).

Sharks and Rays

Stingrays frequent sandy beaches—your guide should warn you when it's wise to shuffle your feet to keep from stepping on one and getting stung. Formations of **golden rays** (*Rhinoptera steindachneri*) and the beautiful **leopard-spotted eagle ray** (*Aetobatus narinari*) often slip through the shallow waters of mangrove lagoons. These last two, as well as **manta rays** up to six meters across, frequent open water as well.

© JULIAN SMITH

Sally lightfoot crab

White-tipped sharks and **black-tipped sharks** are also seen near shore. Both have dorsal fins tipped with their respective color. Farther out to sea, large schools of **hammerhead sharks** provide divers with enough excitement or terror (or both) for a week of normal diving. **Whale sharks** up to 20 meters long drift after schools of plankton, trailing remoras from their flanks. These last two are most often seen by divers at Wolf and Darwin Islands.

MARINE INVERTEBRATES

No slide show of a Galápagos trip is complete without at least a handful of pictures of the **Sally lightfoot crab** (*Grapsus grapsus*), which are named for their ability to skip across water for short distances. The crabs' brilliant reds and yellows stand out perfectly against dark volcanic rocks, making for countless photo opportunities.

In shallow waters, snorkelers come across **golden sand dollars** while foraging along sandy bottoms dotted with **pencil-spined sea urchins** and many neon-colored species of **starfish.** Gulf stars have bright red and/or white spiny backs, whereas the blood star is, naturally, pure red. Black sun stars fold their

legs under their body during the day, and fragile stars seldom have five legs of equal length.

Many divers consider **scallops** to be the most beautiful marine invertebrate. The 15-centimeter shells of the magnificent scallop (*Lyropecten magnificus*) snap shut when divers approach, so you'll have to sneak up slowly to see the beautiful crimson and violet of the inner mantle, lined with golden tentacles and blue eye spots. **Slipper lobsters** (*Lyropecten magnificus*) venture out at night to avoid predators—an option the heavily hunted and less mobile **sea cucumber** doesn't have.

The waters off the islands are too cold for true reef-building coral, but other types are found in the depths. **Pebble coral** (*Cycloseris mexicana*) lies loose on the bottom beneath masses of endemic **yellow-black coral** (*Antipathes galapagensis*). The electric-orange **cup coral** (*Tubastraea tagusensis*) is thought to have been wiped out by the 1982–1983 El Niño.

On the reefs, you'll find the **leopard-spotted sea anemone** (*Antiparactis*), along with **golden sea fans** (*Muricea*), made up of thousands of tiny individual polyps held together by eight arms. In the shadows lurk **squid** and **octopi,** blending in perfectly with their surroundings by expanding and contracting colored skin cells called chromatophores. **Nudibrachs,** shell-less members of the snail family Gastropoda who have taken to the water, come in a range of bright colors. These beautiful floating slugs eat other invertebrates, such as anemones and jellyfish, each of which probably dies surprised that its stinging cells (nematocysts) didn't protect it. The nudibrachs digest their prey and store the stinging cells for their own use later on.

FLORA

"All the plants have a wretched, weedy appearance," wrote Darwin in *The Voyage of the Beagle,* "and I did not see one beautiful flower." Although it may be uninspiring at times, the flora of the Galápagos is worth a second look. True, most of it is desert or semidesert vegetation, and in certain seasons the lower parts of the islands look about as lush as a vacant lot. But they're unique dead-looking plants—of the Galápagos's 550 native species, about 34 percent are endemic (42 percent when all subspecies and varieties are included).

Many species, such as opuntia and *scalesia,* have evolved from a single original colonizer species on one island to more than a dozen species endemic to different islands today. And there are even regions of true, wet green in the upper altitudes of the higher islands, distinguished from their tropical mainland counterparts only by an abundance of endemic species.

Vegetation in the Galápagos is divided into three areas by altitude and climate. The coastal or littoral area that surrounds each shoreline is delimited by the meeting of fresh highland water with oceanic salt water. The semideserts of the dry areas receive the most visitors, whereas the lush, humid area is the smallest, continually dampened by the *garúa* mist.

Coastal Areas

Tangled walls of **mangroves,** ringing many islands like a woody mat of uncombed hair, are good examples of plants' adaptations to salty conditions. Able to grow only in brackish waters, mangroves weave themselves into the sand and marshes by sending down prop roots from limbs and sending up small breathing roots called *pneumatophores.* Long, pendant seedlings drop into the water, where they either stick vertically into the bottom or float until they lodge somewhere suitable for sprouting.

Mangrove species can usually be distinguished by their leaves. The red mangrove (*Rhizophora mangle*) has larger, pointier, shinier leaves than the white mangrove (*Languncularia racemosa*). Also found in the archipelago are the black mangrove (*Avicennia germinans*) and the less common button mangrove (*Conocarpus erectus*).

The creeping stems of the **beach morning glory** (*Ipomoea pes-caprae*) support the plant's beautiful, funnel-shaped flowers. The lavender blossoms are among the largest in the islands, and the vine is important in stabilizing sands along the coast. The **lava morning glory** (*Ipomoea habeliona*) also has long, tubular blossoms. The fleshy leaves of the **sesuvium** species, common throughout the archipelago, change from bright red in the dry season to green in the wet season. Land iguanas love them, despite their salty taste. Leaves of the **saltbush** (*Cryptocarpus puriformis*) are even brinier.

Dry Areas

Most of the shrubs in this intermediate region are usually prickly and uninviting (the better to ward off predators), and almost all are xerophytic (tolerant of dry conditions). The **palo santo** (*Bursera graveolens*) is the most visible species, blanketing entire hillsides with its lifeless gray forms during the dry season. The tree, a relative of frankincense and myrrh, is burned as incense in churches for its fragrant (and insect-repelling) smoke. Its name, meaning "holy wood," comes from its habit of flowering near Christmas.

The other plants you'll remember best from your visit are the **cacti,** the most distinctive flora of the islands. Like their mainland cousins, Galápagos cacti bristle with protective spines (actually leaves adapted for defense and water retention) and fat stems to store water. The prickly pear cactus (*Opuntia spp.*) provides a lesson in evolution in itself. Fourteen separate species have evolved on different islands from a common ancestor. All have large, flat pads but vary widely in height and armor. On islands with land iguanas and tortoises, the plant's major predators, opuntia have evolved a tall, woody trunk and tough spines for protection. Cacti on Santa Cruz, for example, can grow 12 meters high. On islands with no large predators, on the other hand, opuntia grow low to the ground. These species have spines that are soft enough to allow birds to nest among them—and, with luck, to pollinate the cactus in return.

Other Galápagos cactus species include the endemic lava cactus (*Brachycereus nesioticus*), a small, chunky plant that's often the first thing to grow in new lava flows, and the candelabra cactus (*Jasminocereus thouarsii*), whose slim cylindrical trunks can support candelabra branches up to seven meters across.

Members of the **Scalesia** genus may not be as distinctive as their prickly neighbors, but they've got them beat in diversity, with 15 species and six subspecies spread throughout the islands. The woody shrubs, relatives of the daisy and sunflower, also stem from a single pioneer species and range up into the humid area. The newest species, *Scalesia gordilloi*, was only discovered on Santa Cruz in 1986.

The thorny **palo verde** ("green wood") grows 2–10 meters high. Its scientific name, *Parkinsonia* genus, refers to the plant's tendency to shake like someone with Parkinson's disease during periods of drought. This motion drops the plant's tiny leaves, which would otherwise let too much water evaporate. Four endemic species of **tiquilia** grow low, gray, and ugly in volcanic ash. Even more unappealing is the **amargo** plant (*Castela galapageia*), a shrub so bitter that even goats won't touch it. The nasty little fruit of the **manzanillo** (*Hippomane mancinella*) is poisonous, and its sap can cause severe skin reactions. Steer clear of this 10-meter-high tree, also called the "poison apple," and its small, green leaves and flowers.

It's hard to believe, but the fruit of the tiny, wild **Galápagos tomato** (*Lycopersicon cheesmanii*) contains about 40 times more vitamin A and beta-carotene than its supermarket cousin. Cross-bred varieties are being developed for commercial distribution.

Humid Areas
The moist highlands of Santiago, Santa Cruz, San Cristóbal, and Floreana support dense forests of **lechoso** (*Scalesia pedunculata*). Garlands of mosses, ferns, and liverworts festoon the tall trees' branches, along with orchids and clumps of Galápagos mistletoe (*Phoradendron henslovii*). Some 90 species of **ferns** are found in the higher reaches, including the three-meter fern tree (*Cyathea weatherbyana*) on Santa Cruz.

Cacotillo, or cat's claw (*Miconia robinsonia*), gives its name to a humid area subregion. The shrub, which is endemic to Santa Cruz and San Cristóbal, sports colorful purple and pink flowers. Charles Darwin even had a flower named after him—the tiny white blossoms of the endemic **Darwin's aster** (*Darwiniothamnus tenuifolius*) peek from the highland grasses.

Santa Cruz and Nearby Islands

The geographic and economic center of the Galápagos, Santa Cruz (pop. 12,000) is almost a visit in itself. Actually, if you're short on time or money (or both), that's not a bad idea—much of the island can be seen independently or with a guide hired in Puerto Ayora, and many of the best Galápagos sites are within day-trip range.

PUERTO AYORA AND VICINITY
The largest city in the Galápagos is small by any standards. Brightly colored houses line streets made of sole-scouring volcanic cobblestones, and front yards lined with flowering vines are more likely to have a boat up on blocks than a car. With the highest standard of living in the islands, Puerto Ayora is a tourist

THE GALÁPAGOS ISLANDS

marine iguana and pelicans checking the quality and freshness of the catch

town where travel agencies, hotels, restaurants, and souvenir stores compete for the flood of dollars released from cruise ships. Everything here is more expensive than on the mainland, especially film, food, and batteries. Residents will tell you that the only things lacking on Puerto Ayora are enough fresh water and a good hospital (most medical emergencies are handled in Quito).

Entertainment and Events

La Panga downstairs and **Bongo Bar** up-stairs don't complete with the Seventh Day Adventist church next door on the bend in Charles Darwin. A handful of mellower bars are scattered around town; try **Limón y Café,** on the corner of Darwin and 12 de Febrero.

Shopping

Throw a rock in the air in Puerto Ayora, and you'll probably hit a T-shirt or souvenir stand. There has to be a shop in Puerto Ayora named after every animal in the Galápagos.

Most sell stamps, postcards, and T-shirts and offer mail services, but for the last, the post office is more dependable—plus, collectors can sometimes obtain colorful stamps with Galápagos themes. A few shops have book exchanges. Remember to steer clear of buying anything made of endangered black coral or shells.

The Charles Darwin Center has two good gift shops whose profits go to the National Park and the Darwin Foundation. The **Galápagos Gallery** has a high-quality selection of souvenirs, including many wood carvings.

Recreation and Tours

Snorkeling gear is available for rent on almost every corner, but the best equipment comes from the dive shops. Book local snorkeling trips on a glass-bottomed boat with **Aqua Tours** (tel. 2/252-6234). Two good spots in Darwin Bay are Las Grietas, across from the docks, and off the beach near the Charles Darwin Research Center (watch for *pangas*).

© JEAN BROWN

PUERTO AYORA

LAUNDRY ■

To Galápagos National Park Office and **C** *CHARLES DARWIN RESEARCH CENTER*

CEMETERY

ISLA FLOREANA
LAS PIQUEROS
LAS FRAGATAS
SANCHEZ

GALÁPAGOS GALLERY

RED MANGROVE INN

■ SCUBA IGUANA

HOTEL SILBERSTEIN ★

CAFE DEL MAR ▼
NAUTI DINING ▼

AVE CHARLES DARWIN

To Ingala Office, Highlands, Ferry to Baltra and Bus Terminal →

12 DE NOVIEMBRE
RABIDA

▲ AEROGAL

■ MERCADO MUNICIPAL

TINTORERAS ▼
MAINAO INN ▲ GALÁPAGOS SUB-AQUA ▼
EL CHOCOLATE ▼
ANGELIQUE GALLERY ▼
B&B PEREGRINA ●

■ DOCK

Academy

NAVIEDA
LARA

HOTEL SANTA CRUZ ●

INDEFATIGABLE
AV.
BALTRA

CÁMARA DE TURISMO ★

BANCO DEL PACÍFICO ■

Bay

TROPIC BIRD CAFÉ ▼
MOONRISE TRAVEL AGENCY ●

● HOTEL SOLYMAR

★ LA GARRAPATA RESTAURANT
★ LA PANGA DISCOTECA & BONGO BAR
● ESTRELLA DEL MAR

PACIFICTEL ■

12 DE FEBRERO
LOS AMIGOS ●

TAME ●

● POLICE STATION

RESIDENCIAL FLAMINGO ▼
HOTEL SALINAS ▼

LIMÓN Y CAFÉ ▼
DOLCE ITALIA ▼
THE ROCK ▼

LOBO DEL MAR ●

FOOD STALLS ▼
FOOD STALLS ▼

CHARLES BINFORD
TOMÁS DE BERLANGA

HOTEL LIRIO DEL MAR ▼

AVE CHARLES DARWIN

MILITARY BASE

To Tortuga Bay ←

CHARLES BINFORD

COOKING SCHOOL RESTAURANT ▼
VEGETARIAN RESTAURANT ▼

HERNÁN CAFÉ BAR RESTAURANT ▼

PORT CAPTAIN ●

BRITO

CAFETERÍA SUNRISE ▼

GRAN HOTEL FIESTA ●

HOSPITAL ●
WC ■
CHURCH ★
HOTEL NINFAS ●

Park

LOS COLONOS

Las Ninfas

HOTEL CASTRO ●
RESTAURANT SALVAVIDAS ▼

SUPERMERCADO PRO-INSULAR ■

CARGO DOCKS AND WATER TAXIS

TOURIST JETTY

To Angermeyer Point, Waterfront Inn, and Finch Bay

0   500 yds
0   500 m

© AVALON TRAVEL

Rent bicycles from $12 per day at several agencies.

The **Moonrise Travel Agency** (tel. 5/252-6403, yennydivine@hotmail.com) is great for last-minute bookings aboard boats in the area. Tours of four to eight days are available, and day tours to Santa Fé, South Plaza, Seymour Norte, and Bartolomé are available from $65 pp per day. **Galaven** (tel. 5/252-6359) operates the *Galápagos Adventure I* and *II* and the *Esmeraldas III* for day tours. Guayaquil-based **Galasam** (tel. 5/252-6126) owns several boats and has a helpful office staff. **Gala Travel** (tel. 5/252-6581) runs mostly smaller economy boats. All are on Darwin near the town park.

Accommodations

Most of Puerto Ayora's budget hotels are afflicted with brackish water, and many don't have hot water. A friendly family runs the **Bed and Breakfast Peregrina** (Darwin and Indefategable, tel. 5/252-6323) out of their home. Five rooms with private baths run $22 pp, including breakfast. There's a shady terrace and garden, and laundry service is available.

Los Amigos (Darwin and 12 de Febrero, tel. 5/252-6265) has rooms with shared bath for $15 s, $20 d. The small, friendly **Hotel Santa Cruz** (Baltra and Indefategable) has six rooms with shared bath for $10 pp. The **Hotel Salinas** (Naveda and Berlanga, tel./fax 5/252-6107) is central and clean, with a small garden, communal cable TV, a restaurant, and rooms for $35 with private bath. Rooms at the recently upgraded **Lobo de Mar** (12 de Febrero and Darwin, tel. 5/252-6188, fax 5/252-6569) are $75 s, $99 d, with private bath, air-conditioning, and balconies.

Forty dollars will get you a single with private bath and hot water at the **Hotel Castro** (Los Colonos and Malecón, tel. 5/256-5089, fax 5/252-6113, $60 d). It's recommended as a clean, quiet place with fans, a terrace, a restaurant, and a bar. The **Estrella del Mar,** around the corner on 12 de Febrero (tel. 5/252-6427, $46 s, $66 d), is often recommended for its ocean views. Several new hotels have opened and others have been remodeled, mostly within one or two blocks of Charles Darwin. They are all in the $80–130 price range. To find a double, look for **Fernandina, Fiesta, Mainao** and **Red Booby.**

Muted orange path lights lead you through the mangroves to the **Red Mangrove Inn** (Darwin and Las Fragatas, tel./fax 5/252-6564, info@redmangrove.com, www.redmangrove .com), the hippest place in the islands. Opened in late 1994, this small hotel is as cozy as a California artist's weekend home (no shoes inside), with wine bottles in the walls decorated with batiks and tiles made by one of the previous owners. The dining room opens onto a deck and hot tub overlooking Darwin Bay. Rooms at the Red Mangrove cost $125–260 s, $155–290 d, with mountain bikes, sea kayaks, and windsurfing equipment available on request. The owners also offer tours of Santa Cruz by mountain bike, kayak, and horseback. The restaurant Red Sushi has you-know-what, plus other seafood dishes.

Behind El Pelicano restaurant sits the ◖ **Hotel Silberstein** (Darwin and Los Piqueros, tel./fax 5/252-6277, $100 s, $180 d), a beautiful place surrounding a tropical courtyard. Every spacious room has a fan and private bath with solar-heated water, and those on the second floor open onto terraces over the swimming pool. The owners speak Spanish, English, and German and can arrange day tours.

Angermeyer's Waterfront Inn is the latest addition to gracious living. Accessed by water taxi near Angermeyer's Point, it was the home of Gus Angermeyer and has been fully

© JEAN BROWN

Angermeyer's Point

remodeled by his son Teppy into a lovely, spacious hotel overlooking the bay. Prices for doubles with breakfast range $134–218, plus tax.

A water taxi and short walk from town is the recently remodeled ◖ **Finch Bay Eco Hotel** (tel. 2/250-8810, ext. 2810, www.ecuadorable.com, $250 d), one of the plushest options around. The 21 rooms have soft beds, and guests can enjoy a secluded beach for sunbathing, and snorkeling. Also in the highlands is the ◖ **Hotel Royal Palm Galápagos** (tel./fax 5/252-7408, info@royalpalmgalapagos.com, www.royalpalmhotel.net), a palatial spread with 10 villas, four veranda studios, and three suites, all with satellite TV, Internet access, and sweeping views of the highlands. There's a fine-dining restaurant and a piano bar, and for fun a pool, spa, gym, and tennis courts. Prices start at $420 per night.

Food

Start your day off with a filling traditional breakfast of *bolon,* eggs, beef stew, and juice or coffee—or just a regular American breakfast—at the **Descanso del Guia** on Darwin. It also has good, inexpensive set lunches. Several small kiosks along Binford east of Baltra are open in the evening (and some in the afternoons), serving traditional dishes that are prepared well and served fresh and cheap. The **Kiosco William** offers tasty *encocado de langostino* (lobster in coconut sauce).

On the corner of Darwin and Binford, the **Tropicbird Cafe** (next to Moonrise travel agency) is perfect for people-watching. Homemade cakes and breads are on the menu, with sandwiches and salads for $5–11. The **Hernan Café Bar Rest** facing the park has two open-walled bars, walls of lava stone, and lamps made of dried cacti. Breakfast is $3.50–5.50, pizzas are $6 and up, and pasta, fish, and meat dishes are $6–12. Coffee drinks cost $2–4.

I like **La Dolce Italia:** it's air-conditioned, and pasta dishes such as spaghetti puttanesca with fish and black olives are $6–11. **Tintorera** (Floreana and Darwin) serves good breakfasts and organic salads starting around $4–12. Try

the cakes and fruit pies. **Café de Mar,** up the block, offers good pies (which sell out quickly). Sandwiches are $5 and up, and pizzas range $6–20. **The Rock** (Darwin and Naveda) is the new place to eat. Friday night is sushi night, and its tasty lunches and dinners keep the crowds coming.

For seafood, try ◖ **Restaurant Salvavidas** by the docks, the most authentically nautical in decor and location. It's popular with tourists and locals alike, who will tell you it's the best seafood place in town. Fish dishes are good and inexpensive, starting around $4.50. The open-air tables at ◖ **La Garrapata** are always packed after sundown, because it's the longest-running quality restaurant in Puerto Ayora. Good music and an attractive setting go well with the excellent *parillada de pescado.* Lunches are $4, à la carte dishes run $7–15, and it has great fresh juice and occasional live music in the evenings.

Angermeyer's Point may not have air-conditioning, but it's got sea breezes, an unbeatable position, and excellent food. Take a water taxi for a romantic fairy-lit supper, or join the "get away from the crowd" lunchers for a seafood feast.

Information and Services

Steer your tourist questions to the **Cámara de Turismo** (Darwin and Binford, tel. 5/252-6206) or the **Galápagos National Park Office** (tel. 5/252-6511) near the Darwin station. Both offer maps and information in English.

Puerto Ayora's **Banco del Pacífico** is probably one of the few in the country that actually overlooks the Pacific. It changes travelers' checks, but lines are often long. Internet access is available around town, but it's slow. Both **Porta** and **Movistar** offer cell phone coverage in much of the islands.

Monyfri Laundry, on 12 Noviembre next to Hotel Fernandina, will get your togs clean and dry in a few hours for $0.75 a pound.

Transportation

CITEG and **Transgalapagos,** both based at the new bus terminal, send eight buses to

© JULIAN SMITH

Marine iguanas claim a dock in Puerto Ayora, on Santa Cruz Island.

the airport between 6:30 and 9:45 A.M. The whole trip costs $1.80 pp each way and is much quicker now that the road has been paved. Buses can stop on the way out of town anywhere in the highlands, but they're often full coming back from the airport.

The interisland boat service is a series of "Fibras" departing in front of Restaurante Salvavidas at 2 P.M., making the trip ($30 one-way) to Puerto Baquerizo Moreno on Santa Cruz or Puerto Villamil on Isabela. The ride can be quite rough for those prone to seasickness.

Camionetas (pickup trucks) are available for hire all around town; most destinations are $1. **Water taxis** wait at the dock to shuttle passengers to boats waiting in the harbor ($0.60 pp by day, $1 at night). Just go down to the dock, yell "Taxi!" and tell the pilot which boat you're on. You can also wave down taxis from your boat to go into town, or call on radio channel 14.

Interisland flights with **EMETEBE** (Los Colonos and Darwin, tel. 5/252-5177) can get you to Isabela or San Cristóbal in half an hour for $90–100 pp each. The office is on the top floor overlooking the harbor, in what could pass for a control tower. **TAME** has an office at Darwin and 12 de Febrero (tel. 5/252-6165), and **Aerogal** (tel. 5/244-1950) has an office at Rodrigues Lara and San Cristobal.

Tortuga Bay

One of the most beautiful beaches in the Galápagos is a 45-minute walk from Puerto Ayora. Take Binford out of town to the west, up the steps, and past the National Park guard post. Follow the moderately rough trail straight to the beach. Tortuga Bay beach is wide, flat, and usually empty, and around the iguana-patrolled rocky point is a calm mangrove inlet that's perfect for swimming.

◖ Charles Darwin Research Center

The main arm of the Charles Darwin Foundation for the Galápagos, the Darwin Center (tel. 5/252-6146, info@darwinfoundation.org, www.darwinfoundation.org, 7 A.M.–6 P.M. daily) was begun in the 1960s as a research and breeding center for endangered native species. It's on every tour itinerary.

The visiting area includes the tortoise breeding and rearing center, where endangered subspecies are hatched and cared for until they're old enough to protect themselves in the wild. The program started in 1965 with the Pinzón island tortoise, and it has since expanded with the aim of reproducing 50 of each subspecies each year.

Lonesome George, the last surviving member of the Pinta Island subspecies (*Geochelone elephantopus abindoni*), has been the most famous resident of the center since he arrived in 1971. Find a female Pinta tortoise and claim the $10,000 reward that's still standing. In August 2008, eggs that appear to be fertile were recovered from Lonesome George's corral, which he inhabits with two females of closely related species. This has aroused great excitement in the scientists at the research center. Farther down the trails are research facilities and offices, near an iguana rearing center that's closed to the public because of the animals' shyness. A beach is open 7 A.M.–6 P.M. daily.

For those interested in keeping up with events on the islands, the foundation publishes the *Galápagos Bulletin* twice a year. Check the website for information on volunteer opportunities.

SANTA CRUZ HIGHLANDS

Because 100 meters of altitude difference in the Galápagos has the same effect on the vegetation as a 600-to-700-meter variance on the mainland, your surroundings change quickly as you climb into the heights of Santa Cruz. Before you know it, you've left the dry, rocky coast for misty forests edging up against fields and pastures.

Seven kilometers above Puerto Ayora are the small towns of **Bellavista** and **Santa Rosa,** from which several trails lead into the hills. The peaks of **Media Luna,** five kilometers from Bellavista, can be climbed in four–five hours, and three kilometers beyond it is **Cerro Crocker,** a journey of seven–eight hours. Guides are advised, but not required.

You can also visit two sets of **lava tunnels** near Bellavista, one called the "Tunnel of Love" for the heart-shaped hole in its ceiling.

© JULIAN SMITH

Galápagos tortoises at Charles Darwin Research Center

Entered through collapsed roof sections, the tunnels stretch into the earth wide enough to drive a semitrailer into and sometimes continue for miles. Admission is charged to enter the tunnels, which are on private land.

Steve Devine's Butterfly Farm, between Bellavista and Santa Rosa, is another regular stop on tours of the highlands. The combination cattle ranch/restaurant offers lunch and dinner with prior notice and has camping spaces. Giant tortoises graze in the wet grass among the cattle, while pure white cattle egrets *(Bubulcus ibis)* strike at bugs like feathered serpents. The tortoises plod through here from the tortoise reserve to the southwest, giving visitors perhaps their only chance to see the giant reptiles in a semi-wild setting. Yellow warblers follow the tortoises picking off parasites, and vermillion flycatchers frequent the trees.

The **El Chato Tortoise Reserve** claims the entire southeast corner of Santa Cruz Island as a habitat for the endemic giant tortoise subspecies. The seven-kilometer journey from **Santa Rosa** can be made by foot or horse. Up the road from Santa Rosa are **Los Gemelos,** twin pit craters formed when large caverns left empty by flowing lava collapsed on themselves. Galápagos hawks, barn owls, and vermillion flycatchers flit through the damp *scalesia* forests surrounding the craters, which lie just off the road to Baltra, a few kilometers past Santa Rosa.

OTHER SANTA CRUZ VISITORS SITES
Bachas Beach

Named for the remains of some wrecked WWII barges that have all but rusted away, this is one of the first sites most cruisers visit. The white-sand beach is a sea turtle nesting site, and at certain seasons, it attracts marauding frigatebirds looking for hatchlings for breakfast, lunch, or supper. The lagoons behind the beach are home to many flamingos, and marine iguanas and sea lions laze around near the waterline.

Black Turtle Cove

Just west of the Canal de Itabaca between Santa Cruz and Baltra, this shallow mangrove lagoon

© JULIAN SMITH

a *panga* ride among the mangroves in Black Turtle Cove, Santa Cruz

extends far inland. The visit is just a slow *panga* float, leaving you free to admire the abundant birdlife. Lava and great blue herons, lava gulls, frigatebirds, and boobies all nest in the tangled branches of red and white mangroves.

Life beneath the surface is just as active. Spotted eagles and golden rays glide by in slow, silent formation, and a watery snuff sound alerts you to green sea turtles coming up to breathe. Pencil-spined sea urchins and starfish litter the bottom near a shallow rocky neck—navigable only by small craft—where white-tipped sharks sleep swimming against the current.

Cerro Dragon

This new visitor site on the west side of the island has a dry or wet landing, depending on the tide. Within the first few minutes of landing, you'll pass blue-footed boobies propped on the rocks, marine iguanas sunning themselves on the beach, and two lagoons that, depending on the season, may be filled with flamingos. The two-kilometer trail eventually leads to the top of Cerro Dragon, a modest climb with good views, which is named for the land iguanas that congregate nearby.

DAPHNE MAJOR

Biologist Peter Grant spent decades studying finches' beak adaptations on Daphne Major, one half of a pair of tiny islands between Santa Cruz and Santiago. The results, which are considered the first measured study of evolution in action, are described in his book *Beak of the Finch*. Daphne Minor is closed to the public, and visits to Daphne Major (considered a scientific research area more than a visitor site) are strictly limited by the Galápagos National Park Service.

If you're one of the select few visitors, a difficult dry landing will lead you to a steep trail up to the rim of one of the island's two sunken craters. Masked boobies nest on the way up, and blue-footed boobies can be seen inside the crater. The trail continues along the rim to the lip of the second crater, with red-billed tropicbirds visible along the way.

SANTA FÉ

A short sail from Puerto Ayora (two hours) or Puerto Baquerizo Moreno on San Cristóbal (three hours) brings you to the beautiful anchorage off Santa Fé, a shallow bay where

opunita cactus, a favorite food of land tortoises

sea turtles and manta rays are dark shadows against the sandy bottom. After a wet landing, you'll begin a short loop trail starring a local variety of land iguanas. Members of this endemic species are pale yellow with well-defined scales and can grow more than 1.5 meters long. Santa Fé's species of opuntia cactus have grown up to 10 meters high and developed tough, woody stems for defense. Galapagos hawks often sit in the cactus forest, watching and waiting for a meal to present itself.

SEYMOUR NORTE

Volcanic uplift raised this small dot at the end of Baltra. It's a small, crowded island with a loop trail reached by a tricky dry landing. Walking the trail takes 1–2 hours, winding through gray groves of palo santo and opuntia cactus set low to the ground. Because many day trips from Santa Cruz come here, the island can become crowded with people.

Swallow-tailed gulls nest in the rocks near the landing, often with fuzzy chicks. A large colony of blue-footed boobies nests along

the inland part of the loop. Magnificent frigatebirds, part of the largest colony in the Galápagos, nest farther in. At just about any time during the year, you can see the males displaying their bright red air sacs and chattering seductively to females soaring overhead. Marine iguanas and sea lions have claimed the beach along the coastal section of the walk.

SOUTH PLAZA

Just off the east coast of Santa Cruz, a pair of tiny uplift islands curve toward each other like parentheses. At only two square kilometers, South Plaza is one of the smallest islands you'll visit. The distinctive bright yellow of the local land iguanas stands out among the cacti, as the lizards feed on cactus fruit and opuntia pads.

The loop trail begins near one of the largest sea lion colonies in the Galápagos—about 1,000 individuals—and climbs through a surprisingly colorful landscape. During the dry season, South Plaza's *sesuvium* turns bright red, contrasting with the gray and white rocks, green cacti, and turquoise ocean. (The plants become bright green during the rainy season.) Birds barnstorm the cliffs at the far end of the trail, sometimes trying to land three or four times before finally hitting the nest. Audubon's shearwaters, red-billed tropicbirds, boobies, frigatebirds, and swallow-tailed gulls all live near South Plaza's cliffside.

photographing sea lions on Seymour Norte

THE GALÁPAGOS ISLANDS

San Cristóbal

Nothing could be less inviting than the first appearance. A broken field of black basaltic lava, thrown into the most rugged waves, and crossed by great fissures, is every where covered by stunted, sunburnt brushwood, which shows little signs of life.

– Charles Darwin,
The Voyage of the Beagle

Darwin must have landed on San Cristóbal near its northern end, an area covered by lava and eroded volcanoes that give it away as one of the oldest islands in the archipelago. The bottom half of this easternmost island in the Galápagos shelters the provincial capital, Puerto Baquerizo Moreno, below green highland slopes and a freshwater lake.

HISTORY

Near the end of the 19th century, Ecuadorian entrepreneur Manuel J. Cobos began a penal colony in the San Cristóbal highlands. The brutal settlement, named El Progreso (Progress), was intended to make money from sugarcane harvesting, but 14-hour workdays starting at 4 A.M. soon took their toll. For the slightest offense, the 400 prisoners were lashed, executed, or marooned on deserted islands. The penal colony ended in an uprising in 1904. Cobos, who was 67 years old, was shot dead while standing on a porch in his underwear.

Six decades later, a group of more than 100 people from the northwestern United States tried to found a utopian fishing community near Puerto Baquerizo Moreno. The ill-conceived project collapsed within 14 months from a combination of disease, lack of skill, and poor planning. A scheme to catch lobsters and sell them to the U.S. market failed when it was discovered that no one knew how to catch the spiny crustaceans, which were in short supply to begin with.

PUERTO BAQUERIZO MORENO

The capital of the Galápagos Islands is smaller and poorer than Puerto Ayora. It's also less dependent on tourist dollars, because most of the populace fishes for a living or administrates in one of the government offices. Sea lions sleep on dinghies at anchor in the amazingly clear harbor. Prices are generally lower here than in Puerto Ayora.

Sights

The high point of any visit to Baquerizo Moreno is a stop at the town's **Interpretation Center** (tel. 5/252-0358, 7 A.M.–5 P.M. daily, free) down Alsacio Northia past the Cabañas de Don Jorge. It's better than anything in Puerto Ayora outside the Darwin Center, with views of the ocean, wooden walkways, and exhibits on the human and geological history of the islands and, of course, the plants and animals.

Giant windmills adorn a south facing hill in the highlands and generate 60 percent of the

traditional wooden house in Puerto Baquerizo Moreno

© JEAN BROWN

THE GALÁPAGOS ISLANDS

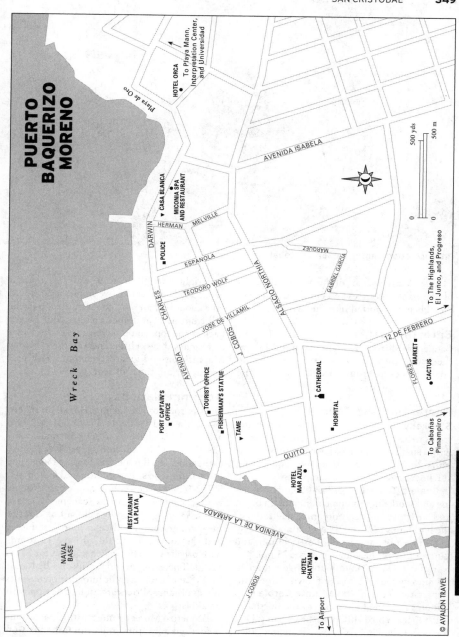

PUERTO BAQUERIZO MORENO

Wreck Bay

Playa de Oro

HOTEL ORCA
To Playa Mann, Interpretation Center, and Universidad

AVENIDA ISABELA

CASA BLANCA
MICONIA SPA AND RESTAURANT

DARWIN
HERMAN
MELVILLE
POLICE
ESPANOLA
TEODORO WOLF
CHARLES
JOSE DE VILLAMIL
AVENIDA
J. COBOS
A SACIO NORTH IA
MARQUEZ
GABRIEL GARCIA

To The Highlands, El Junco, and Progreso

12 DE FEBRERO
FLORES MARKET
CACTUS

PORT CAPTAIN'S OFFICE
TOURIST OFFICE
FISHERMAN'S STATUE
TAME
CATHEDRAL
HOSPITAL
QUITO

To Cabañas Pimampiro

HOTEL MAR AZUL

RESTAURANT LA PLAYA
AVENIDA DE LA ARMADA

NAVAL BASE

J. COBOS
HOTEL CHATHAM

To Airport

0   500 yds
0   500 m

© AVALON TRAVEL

THE GALÁPAGOS ISLANDS

© JEAN BROWN

Interpretation Center on San Cristóbal

island's electricity, part of the plan to make use of renewable resources and cut the quantity of diesel being imported into the islands.

Entertainment

Baquerizo Moreno by night features drinks at the **Scuba Bar,** near the pier; and music and board games at **Iguana Rock,** on Juan José Flores near Quito.

Recreation and Tours

Sharksky (tel. 5/252-0349) is open daily and seems to be where the action is. The proprietors have a small café on the Malecón and offer day tours, diving, bike rental, snorkel equipment, surfboards. All prices are competitive.

Chalo's Tours (tel. 5/252-0953) rents diving and snorkeling equipment, mountain bikes, and surfboards. It can organize day tours of the highlands ($25 pp), Playa Chino ($30 pp), Leon Dormida and Isla Lobos ($45 pp), and Punta Pitt and the Galapaguera ($75 pp).

You can reach **Playa Mann** in less than 10 minutes by foot; it's north of town near the interpretation center. **Playa Punta Carola** is 15 minutes past the lighthouse to the north. To reach **Frigatebird Hill,** pass the Cabañas Don Jorge and the University San Francisco, then

turn right through the stone wall near the end of the road after about five minutes. It should take about half an hour to reach the top of the hill from here, and once you get your breath back at the top, you'll be rewarded with views of beaches, bays, cliffs, and the town below. Magnificent and great frigatebirds both nest here at certain times of year.

Accommodations

On the road to the airport **Hotel Chatham** (Northia and Armada Nacional, tel./fax 5/252-0137, chathamhotel@hotmail.com) has rooms with fan, hot water, TV, private bath, and a small pool, starting at $15 pp. The **Islas Galapagos** (Esmeraldas and Colon, tel. 5/252-0203) is newer and also clean. Rooms with the same amenities (except TVs) are $20 s, $30 d. The friendly folks at **Los Cactus** (near the telephone office at Juan José Flores and Quito, tel. 5/252-0078) have 13 rooms with private bath, hot water, and fan for $15 s, $20 d. There are several family-run bed-and-breakfast places—ask for information upstairs at Casa Blanca. Prices are around $15 pp with breakfast.

Baquerizo Moreno's most distinctive accommodations are at the family-run **Cabanas Don**

Playa Mann is close to town and popular on Sundays.

Jorge (tel. 5/252-0208, cabanasdonjorge@ hotmail.com), on Alsacio Northia east of town. Four unusual cabins have lava-stone walls, high ceilings, bunk beds, and lofts, and one has a fridge and kitchenette. Each cabin also has a fan and a private bath with hot water. Rates are $25 pp and monthly rates run around $550, not including food—in high season, they don't offer short-term rentals. An eating area, bar, and living room fill the main house.

Miconia, along the north end of the Malecón, is the best in town at $59 s, $85 d. Breakfast and use of the spa and gym are included. The restaurant of the same name on the ground floor is open all day except Sundays, when it opens only for dinner.

Overlooking the town are the **Cabanas Pimampiro** (Quito and Tulcan tel. 5/252-0323), with three cabins and three family suites around the pool. Prices start at $60–98, including breakfast.

Food

Grab a quick snack and a drink on the outdoor patio of **Casa Blanca,** beyond the Pocita at the shorter pier. For dependable lunches, locals head to **Perla Pacifico** (Villamil and Charles Darwin) and the **Cebicheria El Langostino**

(Melville and Hernandez). Rustic **Albacora** (Northia and Española) is recommended by locals for its seafood and big breakfasts; generous *platos* run $4–6.

A favorite of the international yacht crowd, **Restaurant Rosita** (Hernandez and Villamil) has been around for 50 years. It has lots of character and an extensive menu, with set meals around $3. **La Playa,** close to the entrance to the naval base, is popular with tourists and locals for a special supper.

Information and Services

There's a **CAPTURGAL** tourist information office (tel. 5/252-1124, 8 A.M.–noon and 2–5:30 P.M. Mon.–Fri.) on Darwin near Wolf, and telephone cabins at several locations. The **post office** is at the western end of Darwin, past the Municipal Building.

Transportation

Buses leave from the Malecón half a dozen times daily for El Progreso in the highlands. **Taxis** to El Progreso cost about $3. The interisland boat service departs at 7 A.M. each morning to Santa Cruz ($30 pp); for Isabela, continue from Santa Cruz after lunch for another $30 pp.

THE GALÁPAGOS ISLANDS

© JEAN BROWN

pink flamingo at San Cristóbal's airport

settlement of Soledad, near an overlook at the southern end of the island, and east to Cerro Verde and Los Arroyos. On the way to Cerro Verde is the **Laguna El Junco,** one of the few freshwater lakes in the islands. The collapsed caldera is fed by rainwater, and it shelters wading birds and seven species of Darwin's finches. El Junco is 10 kilometers past El Progreso; follow the highway and take a right onto a steep dirt track to get there. A narrow trail encircles the rim, offering views of almost the entire island.

Trails continue from Cerro Verde along the length of the island. Destinations include **Puerto Chino,** a beach on the south coast 30 minutes downhill; **La Galapaguera** to the north, where San Cristóbal tortoises reside in the wild; and **Hobbs Bay** and **Punta Pitt** at the far north end of the island. The southbound track near El Junco leads to Jatun Sacha's center where volunteers can live and work eradicating invasive (unwanted) plant species and replant with native endemics.

OTHER VISITORS SITES

All sites on San Cristóbal are within day-trip range of Puerto Baquerizo Moreno. Around the western point of the island, directly south of the airport, is **La Lobería.** Half an hour by boat will bring you within sight of sea lions, blue-footed boobies, and the endemic San Cristóbal mockingbird. It's possible to walk here from Baquerizo Moreno in half an hour, or you can hire a taxi. **Isla Lobos,** 30 minutes north of Baquerizo Moreno by boat, also takes its name from sea lions. Blue-footed boobies nest on the tiny islet, but because the dry landing and hike are both difficult, the site is not that popular.

Visits to sites on San Cristóbal's north coast are often combined with a stop at one of the beaches near Isla Lobos, including **Playa Ochoa, El Muerto,** and **Playa El Manglesito.** Farther north is **Puerto Grande** (also called Sapho Cove), a beach facing one of the Galápagos's most famous

EMETEBE (tel./fax 5/252-0036) has flights leaving most mornings at 8 A.M. for Baltra ($90 pp one-way, 30 minutes) and Isabela ($100 pp, 45 minutes). San Cristóbal's **airport** is at the end of Alsacio Northia past the radio station.

SAN CRISTÓBAL HIGHLANDS

You don't need to be part of a tour group to visit San Cristóbal's highlands, although it does occasionally help with transportation. Avenida 12 de Febrero climbs north out of Baquerizo Moreno to El Progreso, a notorious former penal colony that's now a quiet farming village. Here you'll find the **Casa del Ceibo** (tel. 5/252-0248), a house in a huge ceibo tree that you can rent for $15 pp per night. You'll have to provide your own food, but it's a good way to avoid the heat of the lowlands. The casa offers *parilladas* and other typical foods on weekends. The **Quinta D'Cristhi** also has food on weekends, along with football and volleyball games.

Tracks continue north from here to the

© JEAN BROWN

Kayaks provide a quiet ride in the bay.

landmarks, **Kicker Rock.** Called León Dormido (Sleeping Lion) in Spanish, this leaning bolt of volcanic tuff stands 146 meters high a short distance from the coast. If your captain feels adventurous and sails through a narrow split in the rock, you'll see blue-footed and masked boobies nesting near frigatebirds on the rocks.

Just past Kicker Rock, the beach at **Cerro Brujo** provides a relaxing stop of swimming and snorkeling. The northeastern tip of San Cristóbal is named **Punta Pitt,** where a great visitors site was opened in 1989. A wet landing and long hike bring you inland to the only place you can see red-footed boobies in the Galápagos besides Tower Island. Other seabirds find the spot equally enticing, including masked and blue-footed boobies, frigatebirds, storm petrels, and swallow-tailed gulls.

Santiago and Nearby Islands

SANTIAGO

The Galápagos's fourth-largest island once had the distinction of harboring one of the archipelago's largest and most destructive herds of feral goats. The four goats left on the island in the early 1800s multiplied to more than 100,000 by the middle of the 20th century. Recent backbreaking efforts by the Park Service and the Charles Darwin Research Center reduced the population, and in 2006 goats were successfully eradicated.

Sullivan Bay

This site on the east end of Santiago near Bartolomé sounds like one of the dullest—an hour-long walk over bare lava—but it can be one of the most enchanting. An eruption in 1897 left the area covered in mesmerizing patterns of black lava. Frozen blorps and squirts punctuate the endless expanse of smoky chaos frozen in stone, which is rough on the shoes but captivating to the eyes. The lava's glassy, almost ceramic feel comes from its high silicate

THE GALÁPAGOS ISLANDS

content. This may have been one place Darwin had in mind when he wrote, ". . . immense deluges of black, naked lava, which have flowed either over the rims of the great caldrons, like pitch over the rim of a pot in which it has been boiled, or have burst forth from smaller orifices on the flanks."

Buccaneer Cove

A freshwater source just inland made this cove a haven for pirates during the 17th and 18th centuries. Today, tour boats sail past under impressive cliff faces spotted with a millennia's worth of guano from nesting birds and dark volcanic sand beaches lead to hillsides.

James Bay

An easy wet landing sets you on the black beach of **Puerto Egas,** home to a dozing posse of sea lions. Snorkelers will enjoy exploring the rocks to the right. A two-kilometer, three-hour loop trail leads inland past the rusted remains of a 1960s salt operation. Cruise-ship crews

have built a makeshift soccer field nearby. (Your guide might tell you about a National Park guard who was forgotten here in the 1950s for nearly eight months, instead of the usual three—legend has it that he was taken off the island in a straitjacket.) Overhead soar Galápagos hawks, while on the ground, you may spot Galápagos doves, mockingbirds, and even a Galápagos scorpion under a rock.

Farther down the trail are the famous fur-seal grottoes, where the heaving ocean fills a series of pools and underwater caverns that are occupied by seals, sea lions, and crabs. It's a shame that visitors are no longer allowed to swim here, although it's understandable: the long trail is often crowded with as many as six tour groups at once. A wealth of marine life teems in the tidal pools. Bright Sally lightfoot crabs crawl over marine iguanas the color of lava, and yellow-crowned night herons, oystercatchers, and sandpipers hunt among the crevices. Four-eyed blennies and numerous marine invertebrates lurk underwater. Lavender sea-

wave-sculpted scenery at James Bay, Santiago

© JULIAN SMITH

urchin spines blanket the beach near the end of the trail.

A second, little-used path from the landing ascends **Sugarloaf Volcano,** about 1,000 feet high. **Espumilla Beach,** a second beach slightly north of Puerto Egas, is the start of a trail through mangroves to a lagoon populated by Galápagos flamingos and other wading birds. Sea turtles nest on the sand near the mangroves, and snorkeling and swimming off the wide beach are possible.

BARTOLOMÉ ISLAND

Most boats anchor under Pinnacle Rock on the southwestern end of Bartolomé Island. From here, it's a short *panga* ride to the mangrove-fringed beach, one of the island's two visitor sites. This is a relatively relaxed site—most guides will let you do your own thing for an hour or two, then herd everyone on to the climb. Don't miss this chance to snorkel: In addition to hosting the usual spectacular underwater sights, this is one of your best opportunities to swim with Galápagos penguins. Keep your eyes open, and you'll probably see one of the stubby black torpedoes shooting past after a school of fish. It may not be able to fly, but the Galápagos penguin sure can swim—at speeds up to 40 kilometers per hour.

Back on shore, a trail heads through the mangroves to a beach on the other side of the neck. You can't swim off this beach (white-tipped sharks and stingrays aplenty), but between December and March, you may glimpse female sea turtles waiting for night to come ashore and lay their eggs. Birders should keep their eyes open for Galápagos hawks, herons, and oystercatchers near the mangroves.

The other site on Bartolomé begins with a tricky dry landing on a rock jetty that is usually guarded by sea lions, sleeping as often as not. The 30-minute climb to the top of the island is made easier by a wooden staircase winding up the blasted volcanic face. It's a real moonscape up here, scarred by lava chutes and parasitic spatter cones (offshoots of the main lava tube).

The incredibly light lava rocks come in a rainbow of pastel colors, from creams, grays, and browns to almost floral hues of rose and lime. Pioneer species such as *tiquilia* and lava cactus are only beginning to gain a foothold on the jagged landscape.

The famous view from the 108-meter summit is worth the hot climb. In front of you stretches the neck of Bartolomé, green with mangroves and punctuated by 40-meter Pinnacle Rock. Santiago Island covers most of the horizon—notice the Sullivan Bay lava flow to the left and how it enveloped offshore islands like viscous black water until they became welded to the mainland.

RÁBIDA ISLAND

The exact geographic center of the Galápagos sits off the southern coast of Santiago. A wet landing drops you onto a rust-colored beach filled with dozens of sea lions stretched out moaning and snoring as if it were the morning after the world's biggest sea-lion party. As you make your way down to the section of beach with grains the size and texture of Grape Nuts cereal, you'll come upon a colony of brown pelicans nesting in the salt bushes. Pelican chicks have a mortality rate of 60–70 percent during their first year of life; hence the numerous corpses scattering the sand. The live ones more than make up the difference, though, filling the air with their pterodactyl-like cries for food.

A salt pond on the other side of the bushes provides food for Galápagos flamingos and yellow-crowned night herons. It's a good spot to find a Galápagos hawk perched on a tree branch, stoically watching the assemblage of young and old sea lions who have claimed the shores of the lagoon as a combination nursery and retirement colony. Newborn pups suckle loudly and bleat for more between rolls in the shallow mud.

The snorkeling near the landing is excellent—just watch out for male sea lions. From here, a trail leads up and over the hillside for a view of the salt pond and the steep cliffs on the other side of the spit. If you're visiting during the dry season, notice how the palo santo trees on the far hillside turn vaguely green at mist level, about halfway up.

SOMBRERO CHINO

The aptly named "Chinese Hat" island, off the east end of Santiago just south of Bartolomé, is open only to boats carrying 12 people or fewer. A wet landing onto a rough coral beach begins a short walk through a broken volcanic landscape, ending above the ocean on the far side. The snorkeling off Sombrero Chino is excellent—just watch the strong current.

Western Islands

Isabela and Fernandina, the largest and least disturbed islands in the Galápagos, respectively, are on most week-long itineraries. A double feature of Tagus Cove and Punta Espinosa makes for an unforgettable day of touring.

ISABELA ISLAND

The largest island in the Galápagos consists of five different volcanoes joined together over the eons by repeated lava flows. From north to south, they are: Wolf (1,646 meters), Darwin (1,280 meters), Alcedo (1,097 meters), Sierra Negra (1,490 meters), and Cerro Azul (1,250 meters), and all remain at least partially active. The 130-kilometer-long island harbors a wide range of habitats and a correspondingly large variety of animal species. It fits most people's mental image of a Pacific island: palm trees, pure white beaches, rocky cliffs, mangroves, and an easy pace of life in the settlements that's interrupted by few tourists. About 1,500 people live on the island, mostly in Puerto Villamil.

Isabela's moist higher altitudes provide an ideal habitat for giant tortoises, and five separate subspecies of tortoise have evolved here, one on each volcano. Volcán Alcedo is home to the most—more than 35 percent of all the tortoises in the archipelago—and Darwin and Wolf together shelter another 15 percent. The cool upwelling waters off Isabela's west coast wash in enough nutrients to support large populations of flightless cormorants and Galápagos penguins, with whales and dolphins common offshore. With so much food available, Isabela's marine iguanas are the largest in the Galápagos.

Some of Isabela's older tortoises have seen the deadly days of the whalers replaced by modern threats. Feral goats, once the plague to tortoises and iguanas, have finally been eradicated, a monstrous task that never received the accolades it deserved. In 1984, an accidental fire on Sierra Negra raged for five months and destroyed much of the volcano's tortoise habitat.

History

Isabela's traffic began arriving in the 18th century, when whalers plied the rich waters to the west, stopping off to gather a few hundred tortoises along the way. The names of some of these ships are still etched into the rocks at Tagus Cove.

In 1946, a penal colony was built on the Sierra Negra's southern slopes, a brutal place filled with the worst offenders from the mainland. Hours were spent on pointless, dangerous tasks to fill the time: The lava-rock *muro de las lagrimas* (wall of tears), still standing near Puerto Villamil, was stacked by countless hands in the hot sun.

Many prisoners are thought to have died at the hands of guards, although the truth may never be known. It's said that one police chief reported to a navy officer, upon receipt of a month's supplies: "Commander, nothing to report. Thirty prisoners fewer." The notorious jail was closed in 1959 after numerous escape attempts and campaigns by local residents to shut it down.

Normally teeming with birds, the lagoon at Villamil is deserted in the late afternoon.

Puerto Villamil

About 1,500 people live in this settlement on the southern slope of the Sierra Negra Volcano. Various projects have kept the local populace busy since the towns were founded at the turn of the 19th century, including sulfur mining, lime production, coffee farming, and fishing. The tourist infrastructure here is still basic, but those who visit can enjoy the area's beautiful beaches, bird-filled lagoons, and highland hikes.

Isabela Tours (tel. 5/252-9207) is on the plaza and can arrange day trips. Antonio Gil, at the Hotel San Vicente, is one of several people who arranges highland tours ($45 pp). Travel by van to the highlands, then horse-ride to the volcano and hike into the crater. It's a half-hour walk into the uplands west of town to reach the **Centro de Crianza** (La Galapaguera), where Galápagos tortoises are being bred and repopulated to their original areas. Fifteen minutes farther out by car is the *muro de las lagrimas,* in the remains of the penal colony. The **beaches** west of town are good for surfing, and you can snorkel among the mangroves and rocky inlets east of town.

Budget rooms can be found at **San Vicente** (Cormorant and Las Escalacias, tel. 5/252-9140, $23 pp), with breakfast, private bath, air-conditioning, and hot water. It's often full of groups, and the restaurant offers set meals for $6. **Tero Real** (Tero Real and Opuntia, tel. 5/252-9195) has six cabins with private bath, fans, and refrigerators for $15 s, $20 d. Meals are available at both on request. The lovely new **Albermarle** is on the beach facing the pier. Rooms are $122 s or d, including tax and breakfast on the terrace, and the British owner personally meets his guests.

At the east end of town was the Hotel Ballena Azul, which has just changed hands and was being remodeled as of May 2008. Upon completion, the six double cabins on the beach will have a deck and an outdoor cooking area facing the ocean. It will join the Red Mangrove chain with a new name, **Red Mangrove Sierra** (tel. 5/252-9238, www.redmangrove.com), and prices will be $100 d, including breakfast.

Just a few doors down is **La Casa de Marita** (tel./fax 5/252-9030, info@galapagosisabela .com, www.galapagosisabela.com), a beautiful beachfront place that has seven rooms with kitchenettes, hot water, and private baths for $50 s, $85 d, including breakfast. It also has an elegant family-style restaurant. Keep going a little farther to **Wooden House** (tel. 5/252-9484, www.thewoodenhouse.com), where a

© JEAN BROWN

EMETEBE interisland flights

shady garden and pool invite you to lounge outside. Rooms all have air-conditioning and cable TV and cost $37 pp, including breakfast.

Backpackers should walk to the western end of the village and beyond the bend, where they will find **La Jungla.** Spacious tents with good mattresses can be rented for $5 pp, and small rooms with fans cost $10 pp.

El Encanto de la Pepa is considered the best restaurant in town, with good food in an attractive setting on the plaza. Meals start at $5. On either side, find daily specials at the **La Choza** or the friendly **Yolita.** Enjoy a cold beer out on the pier and watch the surfers on the beach.

The **police station** is on the plaza, and the **National Parks** office is one block away. There is no bank, ATM, or post office—bring cash, because it's next to impossible to change travelers' checks or pay with credit cards here.

Buses leave daily on the 48-kilometer round-trip into the highlands. They depart at 7 A.M. and noon by the market, returning about two hours later. **Trucks** can be rented to spots around town or in the highlands. **EMETEBE** (tel. 5/252-9155) has flights to San Cristóbal and Baltra for $90–100 pp one way. *Lanchas* (speed boats) sail for Puerto Ayora daily at 6 A.M. from the main dock ($30 pp one-way, three hours).

Isabela Highlands

High above the town of Santo Tomás towers the **Sierra Negra Volcano,** Isabela's oldest and highest. It can be visited in a day trip by horse from Santo Tomás, or a three-to-five-hour hike will bring you to the edge of the huge caldera, 10 kilometers in diameter, where you'll see fumaroles—evidence of the last eruption in 2005. Volcán Chico, another four kilometers away, last erupted in 1979. **Alcedo Volcano,** to the north, has been closed to visitors since 1995. It's recuperating after the goat-eradication program.

Punta Moreno

The first stop here, north of Cerro Azul, is a *panga* ride along the sea cliffs and into a grove of mangroves in search of penguins and great blue herons. Then a three-hour hike takes you from the coast—with its penguins, flightless cormorants, and marine iguanas—to a handful of brackish ponds frequented in season by white-cheeked pintails and flamingos.

Elizabeth Bay

Slightly farther north, in Isabela's elbow, Elizabeth Bay is explored only by *panga*. The scattered islands at the mouth of the bay support small populations of flightless cormorants, penguins, and marine iguanas. A peaceful drift brings you into shallow mangrove lagoons stocked with rays, turtles, and small sharks.

Urbina Bay

In 1954, a volcanic eruption lifted a sizable chunk of seabed six meters above the water's surface so suddenly that a visiting group of scientists found fish still flapping in puddles of seawater. Now visitors can get a slightly surreal look at a coral community, littered with the bones of marine animals and the shells of as many as 30 sea turtles. Flightless cormorants and marine iguanas have moved in already.

Tagus Cove

Centuries of graffiti decorate the rocks above this popular anchorage in the Bolívar Channel, directly across from Fernandina. The older records from whalers and sealers are carved into the rock (one reads 1836), while more recent crews have added the names of their vessels in paint. At three kilometers, this is the longest walk (aside from volcano ascents) in the islands and strenuous in places.

The first 200-meter section above the dry landing follows a steep gully, fragrant with sea-lion droppings, up to the base of a wooden staircase. A short hike beyond the top of the stairs brings **Darwin Lake** into view, filling an eroded crater 12 meters deep in the center. A white ring around the edge is evidence of the lagoon's high salinity, which is too much for most creatures besides the occasional visiting Bahama duck.

Scientists once wondered how the lake filled with water, because it was too saline for rainwater and too permanent to be filled by the occasional wave washing over the narrow wall between the lake and the bay. The answer? Seawater filters in through porous lava rocks beneath the surface, keeping the water level in the lagoon even with the ocean outside. The small, round pebbles covering the trails began as raindrops that collected airborne volcanic ash and hardened before hitting the ground.

The trail peaks at a lookout over the entire extent of Isabela, including a large lava flow from the Darwin Volcano. Your guide should point out how new plant species began to appear near the top, forming thickets inhabited by the Galápagos flycatcher, finches, and mockingbirds.

A *panga* ride along the cliffs makes up the second half of the visit. Good snorkeling along the rocky northern shore may reward you with close encounters with sea turtles, Galápagos penguins, and sea lions, and handsome noddy terns nest in the caves and shadows. The ocean reaches into the rock itself, forming long caves where you might glimpse the so-called gringo fish—pink on the back, like a sunburned tourist.

FERNANDINA ISLAND

The westernmost island in the Galápagos is one of the most pristine island ecosystems in the world. No foreign species have been introduced, despite heavy traffic nearby during the whaling heyday of the 19th century. Fernandina is many guides' favorite island, and for good reason: if your tour makes it out this far, you'll get to experience a very special place, where a lizard walking across a shattered field of lava seems like a scene from the dawn of time.

Fernandina is the youngest volcanic island in the archipelago (only one million years old), as well as the most active. Eruptions in the wide caldera continued well into the 20th century; one, in 1968, collapsed the entire 30-square-kilometer caldera more than 300 meters. Glowing plumes of lava from a 1991 eruption were captured on videotape by observers.

> *Our ears were suddenly assailed by a sound that could only be equalled by 10,000 thunderers bursting upon the air at once; while the whole hemisphere was lighted up with a horrid glare that might have appalled the stoutest heart.... At the time, the mercury in the thermometer was at 147 [°F], but on immersing it into the water, it instantly rose to 150. Had the winds deserted us here, the consequences must have been horrible.*
>
> Benjamin Morrell, describing the 1825 eruption of Fernandina

◖ Punta Espinosa

Fernandina's only visitors site lies on the island's northeast corner across from Isabela's Tagus Cove. After a dry landing in a grove of white mangroves, you'll come to a sandy point that's partly covered by rough lava from recent flows. The largest colony of marine iguanas in the Galápagos nests nearby, sneezing like the cold ward in a hospital. As you proceed single-file down the beach (to avoid stepping on buried nests), you'll see shells and bleached mangrove trunks littering the sand, evidence of recent volcanic uplifts.

Sea lions fill the pools among the jagged rocks, females and pups playing while males patrol. At the tip of the point waits the highlight: the flightless cormorant nesting site. Each nest—a ragged witch's mop of seaweed and twigs—supports a female sitting regally while her mate hunts for fish. Keep your eyes open for returning males, who offer a seaborne trinket to the female before drying their stubby wings in the ocean breeze.

Back near the landing site. you'll take a detour over the jagged lava, spotted with short, squat *brachycereus* lava cacti. Brilliant vermillion flycatchers often sit in the mangrove branches. A *panga* ride out into the straights where the Cromwell current upwells may reward you with sightings of the strange deepwater sunfish or a school of dolphins.

Southern Islands

South of Santa Cruz, the main attraction of Floreana is its fascinating history. Other highlights include checking your mail at Post Office Bay, snorkeling around the "Devil's Crown," and spotting sea-turtle hatchlings at Punta Cormorant. Punta Suárez on Española is widely considered one of the top visitors sites in the islands.

FLOREANA ISLAND

Floreana's turgid story begins in the 18th century, when the island was bequeathed to an Ecuadorian officer as a reward for bravery in battle. The officer soon held the island's 80 residents in a state of near-slavery, using giant mastiffs as police and bodyguards. An island-wide rebellion eventually forced the Dog King of Charles Island to flee to the mainland.

Life on Floreana got really interesting in the early 20th century. William Beebe's book *Galápagos: World's End* captured the imagination of readers everywhere, particularly in Europe, with its portrayal of the islands as a strangely beautiful "lost paradise." Among these readers were Dr. Friedrich Ritter, a holistic doctor and philosopher, and his lover Dora Strauch, a former patient left crippled by multiple sclerosis. In 1929, the starry-eyed couple left their native Germany and respective spouses to start a new, natural, naked life in the Galápagos.

Ritter and Strauch chose Floreana for its reliable water supply and relatively rich soil, and they named their settlement Friedo, a contraction of their first names. Ritter's accounts of gardening and nudism in the exotic islands

© JULIAN SMITH

marine iguanas and Sally lightfoot crab

caused a stir when published back in Germany, and the island began to attract passing yachters and more settlers. Friction between the couple began early, though, as Ritter's cold personality and misogynistic Nietzschean philosophy began to wear on his no-longer-blushing bride.

Three years later, the Wittmer family arrived: father Heinz, pregnant wife Margaret, and their 12-year-old son, Harry. Although inspired to come by Ritter's articles, the staunch German family kept to themselves. Later that same year (1932), the most colorful immigrants yet arrived: Eloise Wagner de Bosquet, a self-styled "baroness" with a shady past, along with her two companions, Rudolf Lorenz and Robert Philipsson. Straight out of an S&M fantasy—complete with black boots, crop, riding britches, and pearl-handled revolver—the baroness settled her enclave in Post Office Bay, where she began causing trouble almost at once.

From the start, the baroness acted as if the entire island belonged to her, even to the point of bathing in the main water source, a large cistern near Post Office Bay. She talked of plans to build a luxury hotel on the island while rifling through mail and supplies intended for

the Wittmers and Ritter and Strauch. Her relationship with Lorenz and Philipsson was the subject of much speculation. Other residents began to see her as a vindictive, manipulative sex maniac who tormented her "love slaves" for the sheer fun of it. Lorenz began to show signs of physical abuse at the hands of the baroness and Philipsson, and Ritter and Strauch's relationship continued to sour.

By now, the inhabitants of Floreana were known around the world, and luxury yachts stopped by regularly to visit and deliver mail and supplies. A severe drought in March 1934, with temperatures soaring to 50°C, pushed things over the edge. One afternoon, the baroness and Philipsson suddenly left by boat, saying only that they were headed for Tahiti, as if the island were next door instead of halfway across the Pacific. Almost all of their possessions were left behind in the abrupt departure, including the baroness's beloved copy of *The Portrait of Dorian Gray*, sitting on a night table. The pair were never seen again.

Eyebrows lifted during a search of the baroness's house when Ritter allegedly commented, "She won't return. You have my word on it." Lorenz also began exhibiting an ominous new calm, wandering off alone and breaking into abrupt fits of crying for no apparent reason. In July 1934, he left the islands aboard the small boat *Dinamita,* bound for Guayaquil. Within weeks, the boat was reported missing.

Six months later, Ritter—supposedly a vegetarian—became gravely ill from eating spoiled chicken cooked by Strauch. Later, Margaret Wittmer recalled how he cursed Dora with his dying breath, trying to kick her when she approached his bedside. That same month, the mummified bodies of Lorenz and the captain of the *Dinamita* were found on the parched beach of Marchena Island, dead of thirst and starvation. Lorenz's desiccated corpse weighed less than 10 kilograms.

Theories still simmer about what exactly happened among Floreana's unlucky colonizers. Dora Strauch returned to Germany, where she lived until 1942. The Wittmers alone remained to tell the tale. Margaret died at 95 in 2000, leaving the mysteries unsolved, and her descendants still live in Puerto Velasco Ibarra and operate a small guesthouse. Margaret's son Harry was killed in a boating accident in 1951, but her other son, Rolf, the first native resident of the Galápagos, opened a successful tour company that still runs ships around the islands.

Several books tell the story of Floreana, including Margaret's own *Floreana, Isle of the Black Cats* and *Curse of the Giant Tortoise.*

Puerto Velasco Ibarra

A dry pier landing welcomes you to this unofficial visitors site, a small settlement of 80 inhabitants near the original infamous colony. Floreana's isolation makes it ideal for anyone looking to escape the outside world, and agony for anyone addicted to a fast pace of life. There aren't any banks, the electricity is on for just part of the day, and the only mail service is through the Post Office Bay barrel. On top of that, there's only one phone on the island, at the **Pensión Wittmer** (tel. 5/252-0150 or 5/252-1026). Rooms and bungalows all overlook the beach and cost $30 s, $50 d, with fans,

private baths, and hot water. Three meals are $20 more pp.

Buses leave for the highlands early every morning. It's a half-hour drive or a three-hour walk eight kilometers into the highlands to the **Asilo de la Paz,** the island's only water source. Since most of the three-day dive trips out of Puerto Ayora stop here, it may be possible to find passage on one back to Santa Cruz.

Punta Cormorant

After a wet landing at Punta Cormorant, you'll set foot on a beach with a noticeably greenish tinge. Take a closer look, and you'll see bits of olivine, a volcanic material, mixed with the dark sand. From here, a trail leads up and over the neck of the point. Along the way, you'll stop at an overlook above a brackish inland lagoon populated by occasional flamingos and other wading birds, such as white-cheeked pintails, stilts, and gallinules. Floreana's environment, slightly less forbidding than other islands its size, encourages several endemic plants. Along this trail, you might happen across the velvet daisy *(Scalesia villosa)* or the cut-leaf daisy *(Lecocarpus pinnatifidus).*

At the end of the trail awaits the so-called organic beach, covered with an incredibly fine white sand straight out of a Caribbean advertising executive's dream. Powdery enough for an hourglass, the sand is said to be a byproduct of marine life nibbling away at coral (although some scientists disagree). Stingrays and spotted eagle rays are common near the beach, so shuffle your feet if you walk in the water, which is stained the color of cream by the flourlike sand. Sea turtles nest here November–February, but you might see a confused hatchling struggling toward the ocean even in the off-season. Bleached driftwood and the green vines of beach morning glory make this the most beautiful beach on the islands.

◖ Post Office Bay

The practice of leaving mail in a barrel began in 1793, when ships bound for the Pacific whaling grounds would leave letters here to be picked up by homeward-bound ships whose crews would deliver the mail by hand. Today, the barrel has evolved into a wooden box on a pole surrounded by a fascinating assortment of junk: driftwood, bones, T-shirts, business cards, luggage tags, even email addresses scratched into the wood. Tradition dictates that if you find a letter addressed to someone near where you live, you're supposed to take it home with you and deliver it in person. Feel free to leave a postcard or letter yourself (no postage is necessary).

Just a few meters beyond the barrel are a lava tunnel and the rusted remains of a Norwegian fish operation dating to the 1920s.

Corona del Diablo

Actually a marine visitor site, the Devil's Crown is the unmistakable circle of jagged rocks situated offshore from Post Office Bay. The nooks and crannies of the forbidding islet offer great snorkeling, either outside the ring or in the shallow inner chamber, which is reached through a side opening or an underwater arch.

Sea lions and the occasional hammerhead make things interesting from time to time, but you'll almost definitely see colorful tropical species like parrotfish, angelfish, and damselfish. The current on the seaward side can be strong and the water cold.

ESPAÑOLA ISLAND

The southernmost island in the Galápagos is also one of the oldest, weathered down until it pokes just above sea level. It's often the first stop for tours leaving from San Cristóbal, and what an introduction—many different seabirds use the island as a stopover or nesting site. The visitors sites can be crowded, because the island is within reach of day tours from San Cristóbal.

Gardener Bay

A wet landing deposits you on this beautiful, one-kilometer-long crescent beach on the northeast side of Española. While the site is a bit mundane—no hikes, just beach—the snorkeling is excellent. Some of the dozens of sea

© JEAN BROWN

resting after a morning of fishing

lions sprawled on the sand might join you in the water, along with the occasional stingray or white-tipped shark. The beach is an important nesting site for marine turtles, so you might be lucky enough to come across one in the process. Turtle Rock, a short *panga* ride offshore, shelters legions of bright topical fish like moorish idols, damselfish, and parrotfish.

Landlubbers can follow the guide's example and relax or read a book. Notice the endemic Hood mockingbirds, inquisitive little buggers often found squabbling over territory on the beach. In this type of behavior, rare in land birds, two family groups face each other down over an invisible line in the sand and set about displaying—bending down to the ground with tails spread in the air—and screeching.

◖ Punta Suárez

Almost one hour by boat from Gardener Bay on the western tip of Española waits one of the most outstanding visitors sites in the Galápagos. After a wet landing, you'll head out on a trail that loops toward cliffs on the south side of the point. Along the way, you can't miss Boobieville, a major blue-footed booby colony. In fact, you'll have to be careful not to step on any of the nests, parents, or young that sit in the middle of the trail like feathery toll attendants. Guano-stained rocks as far as the eye can see are peppered with boobies in all stages of life, from fuzzy newborns to mangy-looking teenage equivalents (adolescence is kind to no beast). Everyone who's not a parent is demanding to be fed.

Farther along the trail nest almost all of the waved albatrosses on the globe. Between April and November, about 10,000 breeding pairs nest on Punta Suárez, one of only two breeding sites in the world. (The other is the Isla de la Plata off mainland Ecuador.) You might even be lucky enough to see the elaborate courtship dance, or at least hear the bill-clattering from behind a bush. You'll almost surely witness take-offs and landings, worth a wince or two at best. The soaring giants aren't all that graceful within range of the earth, making landings more an exercise in quick braking and luck. The nearby cliff face makes take-offs a little easier—the birds simply inch to the edge and leap.

Many other seabirds soar over the impressive cliffs at the end of the loop, including the Galápagos hawk, Galápagos dove, and swallow-tailed gulls. Down below, a blowhole sends spray 50 feet into the air with every crashing wave. Española's male marine iguanas, spread on the rocks at the base of the cliffs, boast brighter mating colors than anywhere else in the Galápagos. Neon turquoise spreads over their back and front legs, thought to be the result of eating algae particular to this island. Scientists also hypothesize that they may be a separate species.

Northern Islands

Since they're relatively far from the rest of the archipelago—most boats need an overnight voyage to reach them—the northernmost islands of the Galápagos are visited less frequently. Scuba divers would be foolish to forgo the crossing, though, as Wolf and Darwin Islands are considered "dive-before-you-die" kinds of places.

GENOVESA

Genovesa, also known as Tower Island, provides a jumping-off point for seabirds in the far northeast corner of the archipelago. It's eight hours by boat from its larger neighbors, meaning that the long, rolling crossing is usually done at night (stock up on seasickness remedies). The collapsed caldera that forms the low island opens to the sea to the south—boat captains navigate the tricky entrance to Darwin Bay by lining up the metal towers on shore.

Darwin Bay Beach

Keep an eye on the murky shallows on the way to the wet landing, and you can spot white-tipped sharks. Graffiti recording the names of visiting ships decorates the rocks next to the organic beach. Trails from the beach head into the saltbushes filled with the nests of red-footed boobies and frigatebirds. Huge, hapless chicks stare out from the greenery on every side as their parents compete overhead for nest materials and food. Masked boobies and swallow-tailed gulls also nest here, and you may spot a storm petrel or its nemesis, the short-eared owl.

Another branch of the trail leads over rough rocks next to a series of tidal pools. Yellow-crowned night herons sit on the rocks, half-asleep by day, as lava gulls hover above. Notice how soft the opuntia cactus spines have become here, because the plants don't have to defend against anything more dangerous than a bird's nest.

Prince Philip's Steps

Named in honor of a royal visit in the 1960s, this site near the tip of Darwin Bay's eastern arm is limited to boats of 16 people or fewer. First a *panga* ride along the bottom of the cliffs lets you look for frigatebirds and red-billed tropicbirds. Next, a steep-railed stairway takes you to a trail along the top of the cliffs. Masked and red-footed boobies nest near great frigatebirds among the palo santo trees, as storm petrels swoop overhead.

◖ WOLF AND DARWIN ISLANDS

These tiny islands, around 135 miles northwest of the main group, are visited only by diving tours, which endure a full night at sea to experience some of the best diving in the world. Clashing currents beneath unmistakable **Darwin Arch** bring schools of sharks and barracudas past "cleaning stations" where smaller fish nip off parasites. June–November, whale sharks glide by like spotted buses, and geothermal activity makes bubble streams from the ocean floor.

© JULIAN SMITH

Wolf Island

BACKGROUND

The Land

Tucked up on the northwestern shoulder of South America, Ecuador is really three countries in one—or four, if you count the Galápagos Islands. The Andes run like a knobby spine down the middle, with the Pacific coast to the west and the Amazon jungle to the east. Each region is distinct from its neighbors, but all are so close that you can easily travel from one to another in less than a day. At 269,178 square kilometers, Ecuador is the second smallest Spanish speaking country in South America—about the size of Colorado. Colombia lies to the north and Peru to the east and south, and the equator skewers the country just north of Quito.

GEOGRAPHY
The Sierra

The Andes and their foothills fill about a quarter of Ecuador's land area, thrusting 10 of the country's 24 provinces skyward. Two parallel mountain ranges run north to south. The Cordillera Occidental (Western Range) and Cordillera Oriental (Eastern Range) together support 22 peaks higher than 4,200 meters. The result is one of South America's most scenic drives: south of the capital lies the Avenue of the Volcanoes, where a dozen snow-capped volcanoes loom on either side of the Pan-American Highway.

© JEAN BROWN

Intermountain basins called *hoyas* are divided by east–west foothills called *nudos*. The 10 main basins average 25 kilometers wide and 2,100 meters high. Nearly every one cradles its own large city, including the capital, Quito, and altogether they contain half the country's population. Farms reach high into the foothills, surrounded by forests, grassy slopes, and rocks. Even higher are the harsher climates of the prickly *páramo* and bare, icy mountaintops. Meltwater and rain feed the headwaters of rivers spilling east and west.

The Coast

With 2,237 kilometers of coastline, the coastal lowlands stretch from the foothills of the Andes to the Pacific Ocean, encompassing some low mountain chains such as the Mache and Chindul near the middle and the Colonche near Guayaquil. None climb higher than 1,000 meters. Tropical rainforests fade into dry, thorny scrublands toward the south. Mangrove-choked estuaries and sandy beaches—some lined with palms, others with cliffs—face the water.

Two main rivers drain the lowlands. To the north, Río Esmeraldas flows for 320 kilometers before emptying into the Pacific. Farther south, Río Guayas—only 60 kilometers long between its genesis at the junction of Ríos Babahoyo and Daule and its mouth at the Gulf of Guayaquil—is the widest river on the Pacific coast of the Americas. Isla Puná sits in one of the richest deltas in the hemisphere.

The Oriente

Ecuador's Amazon takes up the other half of the country, spilling east from the gentle eastern slope of the Andes into lush northern Peru. The rainforest continues all the way to the Atlantic coast of Brazil, at such a gentle slope that its rivers drop less than 500 meters over the entire 2,200 kilometers. The Andes give a few last gasps before giving up completely, sending up peaks like Sumaco (3,732 meters), east of Baeza. To the south, the rugged Cordillera del Cóndor was the center of a long-running border dispute with Peru.

The Oriente's rivers are its highways. In the north, Ríos Coca and Aguarico feed into Río Napo, Ecuador's longest river at 855 kilometers. Río Pastaza drains Pastaza Province and lies just north of Río Zamora, which becomes Río Santiago in Peru.

GEOLOGY

Ecuador's gorgeous mountain scenery comes at a high price. The country sits smack on the Pacific "Rim of Fire," where two tectonic plates grind together. The Nazca Plate under the eastern Pacific is slowly shoving itself under the American Plate, which supports mainland South America. The result is the upthrust of the Andes, as well as a host of unpleasant side effects.

Approximately 65 of Ecuador's peaks began as **volcanoes,** and five or six are still smoking. Cotopaxi last erupted in 1877, but it's still considered one of the tallest active volcanoes in the world (a title some ascribe to Chile's Tupungato). Sangay is one of the most active on earth, with a constant pool of lava burbling in its crater. Antisana, El Altar, and the Pichinchas were active in the 20th century, and Guagua Pichincha, Tungurahua, Reventador, and Sangay all erupted in the late 1990s and early 2000s. Most cities in Ecuador's northern highlands, for some reason, are built within range of an active volcano. Ecuador's history books are filled with horror stories of entire cities being leveled in a heartbeat by lava and mudslides.

Along with the creeping magma and scalding smoke, most volcanic eruptions are accompanied by **earthquakes.** A major tremor in 1987 destroyed 40 kilometers of the oil pipeline from the Oriente to the Sierra, killing hundreds of people, and Bahía de Caráquez is still reeling from a 1998 quake that measured 7.1 on the Richter scale.

It gets worse: **Lahars**—catastrophic avalanches of melted ice, snow, mud, and rocks—can reach 80 kilometers per hour when careening downhill. A heavy rain is often enough to induce a **landslide** in the steep Andes or the muddy Oriente. ("The approach of rain is enough to make the hair stand up on any countryman's neck," wrote Henri Michaux, "knowing as he does how rain can make a mountain split and go under.")

CLIMATE

Here on the equator, there are only two real seasons: a hot and wet period called *invierno* ("winter"), and a dryer and cooler period called *verano* ("summer"). Temperatures often vary more in a single day than they do from month to month, especially at higher altitudes. (For information on weather in the Galápagos, see the *Galápagos Islands* chapter.)

The Sierra

The mid-Andes climate strikes a balance between the icy reaches of volcanic peaks and the sweltering extremes of lower altitudes, resulting in a pleasant, comfortable "eternal spring." Days warm quickly and cool just as fast at night, varying as much as 15°C between day and night. Daytime temperatures average around 21°C year-round, with nights at 7–8°C.

The rainy season occurs October–May, with overcast skies and precipitation peaking near April. The dry season runs June–September, with a short resurgence around December. Daily rainfall is mostly confined to brief afternoon showers.

The Coast

The wet and dry seasons are more sharply defined on the coast, and ocean currents influence weather patterns more than anything else. The Peru (Humboldt) Current flowing up from Chile brings cool, dry weather May–December, making that the best time to travel but the worst time for lying on the beach, since skies are usually cloudy. Dominated by the warmer Equatorial Counter Current from the north, January–April is hot and rainy with daily downpours. Roads are often flooded and impassable. When it's not raining, though, the sun blazes and daytime temperatures average 31°C. For half the year, hardly any rain falls in Ecuador's southern coast at all.

Every few years, the famous **El Niño** weather pattern brings abnormal amounts of rain from the end of the year to April or May, causing flooding and landslides along the coast and wreaking havoc with wildlife dependent on stable ocean temperatures. (See the *Galápagos Islands* chapter for more details on this phenomenon.)

The Oriente

Weather forecasters in the Amazon have it easy: "Hot and wet today, with continued hotness and wetness through this time next year." Calling the seasons rainy and rainier pretty much sum things up. Most precipitation falls June–August, and September–December is drier. Daily highs average 30–32°C, with the nighttime low reaching 20°C.

Up to five meters of rain fall annually in certain spots, usually arriving in the afternoon in one of the country's most dramatic climatic displays: Around 1 or 2 P.M., the air grows quiet suddenly and heavily, as the sky starts to gray. Temperatures drop quickly, just before you hear a muted roar approaching. Then, *boom!*—it's time to break out the scuba gear. After half an hour or so of brutal downpour, the sky quickly clears, preparing for yet another spectacular sunset.

The Natural World

For a country with only two-thousandths of the earth's surface, Ecuador's landscape is almost unbelievably lush and varied. The numbers alone can be overwhelming: 10 percent of all plant species on earth grow here, including nearly 5,000 species of orchids. South America boasts a third of the world's estimated 9,000 species of birds, and of these, roughly half live in Ecuador. That means this tiny country is home to one-sixth of all bird species on the planet. On the whole, Ecuador is rightly considered one of the most species-rich countries in the world.

Along with the stunning range of habitats described below, however, Ecuador has an equally long list of threats to its natural world. Some ecosystems are close to disappearing completely, and far too many once-plentiful species are down to only a handful of individuals. If done right, tourism can help as much as anything else to preserve the country's wildlife; but in the end, the only true solutions will germinate among those who live with the natural world every day.

CLOUD FORESTS

The rainforest's lofty cousin covers the transition zone between the high Andes and lowland jungle. Nicknamed the *cejas de las montañas* ("eyebrows of the mountains"), cloud forests have a delicate, misty appearance, with moss-draped trees set along cold rushing streams. Annual precipitation comes in the form of clouds and fog as often as it does in raindrops, and temperatures drop much lower here than in the Amazon.

Flora

Cloud-forest vegetation is similar to that of the rainforest but sparser, more sturdy than lush. Up to 60 percent of all plants are **epiphytes,** which live off airborne moisture and nutrient particles as they grow far above the soil, depending on other plants for support. Many of these are **orchids,** which thrive at moist, moderate-to-high altitudes. The largest family of flowering plants (with more than 30,000 identified species), orchids range from pinhead-size buds to three-inch flowers suspended on branches of up to three meters. The woody trunks of **tree ferns** reach heights of five–eight meters, topped by a crown of giant fronds. Huge stands of **bamboo** go to seed and die all at once, and every available surface is covered with **mosses, lichens,** and **brachens.**

Fauna

Startling red feathers make the **Andean cock-of-the-rock** a birder's favorite. These birds prefer vertical cliffs and gather in courtship clearings called *leks*. **Golden-headed quetzals** have bright turquoise plumage and live in tree cavities next to vivid **tanagers** and top-heavy **toucans.** Dozens of species of **hummingbirds** have the best names of all: collared Inca, gorgeted sunangel, booted racket tail, and the green violetear, to name a few. Temperatures in the cloud forest fall too low for most large mammals to handle, but there are still a few around. **Mountain tapirs,** one of three Ecuadorian species have elongated snouts that betray their relation to the rhinoceros. Most likely, all you'll see is their rear ends crashing off into the underbrush and their tracks in the mud (look for three toes on the rear foot and four on the front).

The **Andean spectacled bear,** named for white patches around its eyes, is the only bear native to South America. Males can grow two meters long and range through the cloud forest and *páramo* from Venezuela to Bolivia. Ecuador has one of the largest populations of this highly endangered animal, which is poached for its meat and supposed medicinal value—the paws are said to protect one from evil, and its fat is used as a healing ointment.

PÁRAMO

These high-altitude grasslands stretch between the temperate montane valleys and the inhospitable snows of the highest peaks. Chill mists, dark lakes, and tussocks of sharp grasses make the *páramo* a surreal and beautiful environment to explore.

Flora

Thick, waxy leaf skins covered with fine, insulating hairs help the low, spongy ground cover to survive high levels of ultraviolet light and wet, often freezing, conditions. Plants stick low to the ground to escape the wind and temperature variations, and often grow their leaves in a circle to make sure none shade any of the others.

The distinctive *frailejón* (*Espeleta hartwegiana*) is characteristic of the northern *páramo* near the Colombian border. With its crown of yellow leaves covered with insulating down, the plant is actually a member of the sunflower family. *Frailejones* range through the Andes from Ecuador to Venezuela, just as their namesake friars did in colonial times. At higher altitudes, *frailejones* grow closer together for mutual protection against the elements.

The thistlelike **chuquiragua** (*Chuquiragua insignis*), regarded as the national flower, has jagged leaves and orange flowers and is used by *indígenas* as a liver, kidney, and urinary-tract cleanser. Its name means "sword of blood" in Quechua, and it's one of the few flowers found at this altitude. The **lycopodium** (*Lycopodium crassum*) club-moss also brightens the dreary landscape with its tubular red and orange stalks. **Caspivela** plants have flat, bushy branches that resemble evergreens. Also called candlewood, this waxy bush is so flammable that it will burn in the rain.

Fauna

Hummingbirds (*colibrís* in Spanish) are characteristic of Ecuador's higher altitudes. Blurring wingbeats allow them to hover and move backward, and at night most can enter a state of semihibernation called "torpor," in which their body temperatures and metabolism drop significantly. Their iridescent feathers were once sewn into cloaks for Inca rulers. Listen for the buzz of the buff-colored tawny-bellied hermit, the endemic Ecuadorian hillstar, or *oreotrochilus chimborazo*, with its blue head and white breast. The sword-billed hummingbird totes around a 10-centimeter snout.

Torrent ducks, white-capped dippers, and **torrent tyrannulets** gather near running water. **Andean lapwings** have an unmistakably grating call and a gaudy, white-and-brown-striped wing pattern. Cotopaxi National Park is the best place to see the **carunculated carara,** the largest member of the falcon family, with its bright red face, yellow bill, and black body.

Cotopaxi is also a good place to spot the **Andean condor,** which is related to the California condor and almost as endangered. Actually a vulture (*Vultur gryphus*), the condor is the world's largest flying bird, with a wingspan of more than three meters. Mature condors have glossy black plumage with white upper flight feathers, a fuzzy white neck ruff, and a hooked beak. The red head and neck are naked of feathers to keep the bird clean as it digs into a tasty mess of carrion, its meal of choice. Fewer than 100 mating pairs remain alive because of habitat destruction and a mistaken fear among *campesinos* that the giant scavengers will carry off livestock and children.

South America's high-altitude relatives of the camel—**llamas, vicuñas,** and **alpacas**—were once domesticated by the Incas for meat, wool, and hauling cargo. Since the arrival of the Spanish, these animals have become extinct in the wild, but reintroduction programs in the Chimborazo Fauna Reserve and Cotopaxi National Park are promising. Chances are slim that you'll spot an **Andean deer, puma,** or small *páramo* **cat.**

COASTAL FORESTS

Northwestern Ecuador falls within the Chocó bioregion, which extends from the Andes to the Pacific and into Colombia. The **tropical forests** in this area are some of the most biologically diverse on earth, in part because they acted as warmer refuges during various ice ages, saving countless species of plants and animals from extinction. They're also incredibly wet, thanks to the union of the warm Panama Current just offshore. Up to one-fifth of the plants in some areas are endemic (found nowhere else in the world). Sadly, less than 5 percent of the original tree cover has survived colonization, agriculture, and the timber industry.

Even less of the **tropical dry forests** remains undisturbed—as little as 1 percent by some estimates. These forests stretch from the middle coast of Ecuador south to the Peruvian border, a region with well-defined wet and dry seasons. Machalilla National Park and the Chongón Hills west of Guayaquil shelter some of the largest tracts of this increasingly rare ecosystem.

Plant life consists of species more suited to the desert: water-stingy varieties include the palo santo tree common to the Galápagos, ceiba and balsa trees, and the tagua palm, whose nuts can be carved like ivory. Birds such as the vermilion flycatcher, Pacific pygmy owl, and long-tailed mockingbird make their homes among the dry hills, accompanied by armadillos, opossums, and small cats called *tigrillos.*

Large, tangled groves of **mangroves** grow in brackish conditions where fresh water meets the ocean. The red mangrove is the most common, each with an extensive network of stilt limbs sent up from roots and down from branches. Mangroves are good colonizers, providing homes for seabirds in their branches and sea creatures among the roots. Once again, protected areas such as Manglares Churute near Guayaquil are all that stands between this ecosystem and the spread of civilization. Here, the main threat is the shrimp industry, which bulldozes mangrove swamps to build shrimp ponds.

RAINFORESTS

Compared to the common preconception of the jungle—an impenetrable Tarzan backdrop filled with strange cries in the sweltering mist—the reality is often surprising. It's unexpectedly quiet, cooler than you would imagine, and spacious, with little undergrowth below the high, closed canopy. During the day, the hum of insects and the occasional cry of a bird overhead are the only sounds in the still ocean of green. At night, both bugs and stars come out in astonishing profusion.

Rainforests are defined by low altitude (up to 1,000 meters), high temperatures (25–28°C), and daily rainfall that varies widely over the year. The annual norm is two–three meters of rain. The result is a warm, humid environment as perfect for unbridled growth as any on earth. Among the oldest of all ecosystems, rainforests are also among the least known because of difficult access and scientific interest that has only recently blossomed. Large percentages of Ecuador's Amazonian plants and animals were only discovered within the last few decades.

Species Richness

Scientists are just beginning to understand the incredible biological diversity of Amazon forests, where 3,000 different types of beetles have been found in study plots of 12 square meters, and 87 species of frogs and toads were found in one hectare. Aside from having near ideal conditions for life, rainforests have also had time on their side. In some cases, plants and animals have had hundreds of millions of years to evolve into each one's particular "niche," a vague ecological term that essentially means an individual's role in the overall grand production of life—the space it occupies, the food it consumes, the ecological elbow room it needs. Over the eons, species become more and more specialized, leaving room for other species to find equally narrow, but slightly different, niches often only a few millimeters to one side.

The theory of Pleistocene forest refugia holds that during cool, dry periods far in the past, isolated patches of rainforest served as islands in the midst of huge expanses of grasslands. These refuges eventually reconnected, complete with thousands of new, unique species that had evolved in isolation. Most of eastern Ecuador falls within the Napo Refuge, which has been one of the largest and most stable refuges throughout history, and thus one of the most biologically diverse.

Shallow Basement

As any Amazon settler who's tried to start a farm will tell you, rainforest soil is surprisingly thin and poor. In contrast with temperate forests and their rich, deep layers of humus, rainforests have most of their nutrients suspended in the vegetation itself—in both living and dead matter—instead of the ground. In fact, less than 1 percent of forest nutrients are thought to penetrate deeper than five centimeters into the soil. As a result, when rainforests are cleared, the thin topsoil washes away in a few years to reveal an impenetrable layer of clay on which little can grow.

Death takes on a whole new importance in an ecosystem where so little is siphoned away through the ground. Countless bacteria, fungi, and insects are crucial in breaking down dead matter quickly enough to return the nutrients to the pool of life. Thriving fungi give the rainforest its characteristic rich, organic odor.

Hydrology

Blackwater rivers, unique to tropical forests, get their tealike color from tannins, the substances used in winemaking and leather tanning, which are leached out of the tropical forests. Even algae can't grow in these highly acidic waters. Look near the shallows for the beautiful reddish-brown color. Sediment from the Andes gives **white-water rivers** their milky appearance and neutral pH.

Oxbow lakes are formed when a bend of a meandering lowland river is cut off from the main flow. The resulting U-shaped *cocha* (lake) slowly fills in with a succession of plants until it becomes indistinguishable from the rest of the forest.

Flora

"Tropical vegetation has a tendency to produce rhetorical exuberance in those who describe it," writes Paul Richard in *The Tropical Rain Forest.* It's easy to see why, with such a varied tangle of growth surging upward toward the precious sunlight. Ecuador is home to more than 20,000 species of vascular plants, more than in all of North America, and most of them live in the Amazon. Although temperate forests in North America may contain six tree species in abundance, a plot of rainforest 10 meters on a side may shelter 25 different species.

Primary forest, undisturbed by humans, has a high, tight canopy layer that blocks out most sunlight, keeping undergrowth to a minimum. This is where you'll find the best example of **emergent trees,** up to 50 meters high and 5 meters across at the base. Roots like rocket fins keep the towering giants upright—most of the time—and were used by indigenous tribes to signal over long distances (bang on one to see why). The smooth branches on the **ceiba**—look more like upside-down roots, each covered with characteristically thick, smooth, oval leaves with tapered ends to shed heavy rainfall.

Each large tree in the rainforest supports a veritable zoo of aerial plant life, starting with huge, woody **lianas** that climb host trees to reach the sun. One kind of liana, contrary to all plant logic, initially grows toward darkness to find the base of the largest nearby tree to start climbing. Large lianas can loop several trees together, so that if one tree falls, several neighbors follow.

Epiphytes, aerial plants that get all their nutrients and water from the air, include **bromeliads,** which resemble the tops of pineapples (they're in the same taxonomic family). Inside each bromeliad's leafy crown, a small puddle of rainwater can support hundreds of insects, amphibians, and even other epiphytes. Epiphytes grow aerial roots to trap dust and falling debris for food, which can accumulate to half a meter thick on the tops of larger branches.

Supporting so much life has its drawbacks. **Strangler figs** of the *Ficus* genus are called *matapalos* ("tree killers") in Spanish for good reason. Starting as a small airborne seed, the fig eventually sends down woody roots that can encircle the host tree completely and squeeze it to death. By then the fig, a tree in its own right, has established roots of its own. Their wood isn't good for lumber, so figs are often the only trees left standing in cleared plots, but birds and animals love the sweet fruit.

All this added weight can easily cause even a large tree to collapse, so the hosts have developed several defensive strategies. Some trees shed their outer bark periodically, leaving a smooth surface that epiphytes can't cling to. Other plants produce repulsive chemicals. Nonetheless, **tree falls** are surprisingly common, even if no one is around to hear them, and actually serve a crucial role in the life of the forest. Every large tree in a patch of forest can fall in as little as 100 years, each one producing a vital light gap that allows smaller plants to spurt upward in the hope of becoming canopy members themselves.

Translated as "vine of death" in Quechua, **ayahuasca** is a type of vine well known to almost all Amazon tribes. *Banisteriopsis caapi* can grow up to eight centimeters in diameter and sprouts white, yellow, or red flowers. Its hallucinogenic properties come from an orchestra of alkaloids that give ayahuasca its intense yellow-brown color when cut. In carefully controlled ceremonies, tribe members use the vine to speak with dead ancestors, discover the causes of sickness, and communicate with the forest itself.

Other survival tactics are more ingenious. One type of tree has worked out an arrangement with a particular type of ant that clears the branches and the surrounding forest floor of competing plants and attacks any creature foolish enough to take a bite of a leaf. In return, the ants (which taste like lemon—honest!) get to make their home in special hollow stems. Stinging spines on the roots and trunks of other trees discourage larger creatures from climbing, scratching, or otherwise hurting the tree.

Chemical defenses often have beneficial side effects for humans. An incredible array of **medicinal plants,** long known to native cultures, have only recently begun to be appreciated by modern science. Many substances you're already familiar with were discovered this way—among them nicotine, caffeine, strychnine, novocaine, and quinine, the first effective medicine against malaria.

Pollination strategies can be just as complex. Because other plants of the same species may be situated kilometers away, wind and luck may not be enough to get seeds or pollen to a receptive host. Large, white nocturnal flowers attract bats with their rich pollen, and hummingbirds love small, reddish flowers filled with sugar-rich nectar. In both cases, pollen (microscopic male seeds) is attached to the unwary creature and transported to the next plant. Seeds hidden inside tasty fruit are designed to pass through the digestive systems of monkeys, rodents, fish, and birds unharmed and grow wherever they are dispersed—some won't germinate otherwise.

Insects are the most common pollinators and are deceived to no end by plants, often gaining little or nothing in return. Some orchids have parts that mimic female tachnid flies to lure males, or provide fragrances that male orchid bees collect and store to lure females. Fig wasps lay their eggs in fig flowers, from which the larvae eventually eat their way out and emerge covered in pollen. Some flowers smell like rotting meat to attract scavengers, whereas others mimic a mammalian ear, down to reddish veins and a musky odor, to lure mosquitoes.

Birds

It's said that 80 percent of the animal life in the rainforest lives above eye level, and most of that, it seems, is on the wing. Birds are by far the most abundant animal life you'll see: Ecuador alone has nearly 1,600 identified species, compared to 700 in the U.S. and Canada combined. You'll have the best luck spotting them along the border of clear-cut areas and rivers, near a fruiting tree, at a salt lick, or from the lodge's canopy towers and walks. Different species often forage together in mixed flocks for added protection from predators.

Of the thousands of different species, a few stand out. **Hoatzins** are unmistakable, with their Mohawk crest, ungainly body, and prehistoric squawk. These beauty-school dropouts have been called a missing link between birds and reptiles, since chicks are born with claws at the outer joints of their wings to help them climb back into the nest after they fall or jump out to escape predators. The hoatzin is one of the few birds that actually eats leaves, which it digests in a large, heavy crop that makes it almost impossible for the bird to fly gracefully. The smell of decomposing leaves gives these birds the nickname "stinky turkeys."

The liquid call of an **oropendula** is unmistakable—like a large drop of water falling into a deep well—and their long, woven nests are commonly seen dangling from tree branches. Oropendula chicks are a favorite prey of botfly larvae, so the birds often hang their nests near the nests of wasps to help keep the flies away. Parasitic species such as cuckoos lay their eggs in other birds' nests, leaving the unwitting parents to raise chicks that are often larger than themselves.

Every species of **kingfisher** found in South America lives in Ecuador, including the ringed, green, Amazon, and the rare green-and-rufous American pygmy. **Harpy eagles** use their daggerlike claws to snatch monkeys out of tree branches. These eagles, which are South America's largest bird of prey, are revered by indigenous tribes.

Twenty species of **toucans** have huge, hollow bills for reaching and opening fruit and seeds in the canopy. Forty-five species of **macaw,** including the blue-and-yellow and the chestnut-fronted, mate for life.

Mammals

Large mammals are rare, partly because so many plant defenses have prevented the evolution of large herbivores that would have served as prey. Seventeen species of **monkeys** belong to the arboreal New World group (Platyrrhina), as opposed to the ground-dwelling Catyrrhina of the Old World, which include ourselves. Capuchins have white-and-black coats and faces like angry little old men. Red howlers are named after the roaring call—audible for kilometers—that males produce with a specialized bone in their throat. Squirrel monkeys follow larger species to fruiting trees and lack a prehensile tail. At the bottom of the scale are silky-furred pygmy marmosets, who eat tree sap and are among the smallest primates in the world.

Adorable **sloths** come in two- and three-toed varieties. Both hang from branches with their long claws and move so slowly that algae grow in their dense hair. A host of insect species also nest in sloth fur, including one type of moth that only lays its eggs in sloth feces (carefully buried at ground level once a week). More than 100 species of **bats** flit through Ecuador's jungles in search of insects, small animals, fruit, and blood.

Piglike **tapirs** and **peccaries** root among leaves for tasty morsels, accompanied by the dog-sized **capybara,** the largest rodent in the world. Hunted for their coats, nocturnal jungle cats such as the **jaguar,** the aquatic **jaguarundi,** and the **ocelot** are rarely seen. Murky waters hide endangered **manatees** and pink **river dolphins,** descendants of Pacific species cut off from their ancestors by the upward thrust of the Andes. These rare dolphins often feed where rivers join to produce clashing currents that confuse fish.

Reptiles and Amphibians

More than 400 species of **frogs and toads** fill the night with their sounds, giving Ecuador the highest frog and toad diversity per unit area of any country in the world, and almost as many species as the entire United States contains. Poison-arrow frogs raise their tadpoles in cups of water trapped in bromeliads. Their neon reds, blues, and greens warn potential predators of some of the most potent toxins in the animal kingdom. Indigenous groups use the frogs' secretions on their arrow and dart points to bring down large game.

Semi-aquatic **anacondas** can grow up to 10 meters long, but even trained experts find it hard to locate most snakes. Flashlight beams will catch the glittering eyes of **caimans,** the smallest crocodilians in the New World.

Fish

Amazon catfish, called *bagre* in Ecuador, are the largest freshwater fish in the world, often topping 200 kilograms. Fear of **piranhas** shouldn't keep you out of the water completely; these small fish do have a potent set of choppers, but they rarely attack an animal that isn't bleeding already. Some species feed solely on fruit. Tales of "feeding frenzies" probably come from occasions when large groups of piranhas, trapped in small pools of water, are driven wild by the scent of blood.

Watch out for **stingrays,** though, which hide in muddy shallows and can inflict an excruciating sting with a barb on the end of their whiplike tail. Shuffle your feet when you can't see the bottom. Even more fearsome is the **candirú catfish,** a narrow little fish with a propensity for warm, dark openings. After following a warm water current into the gills of fish, they attach themselves to feed by extending a

© JULIAN SMITH

Galápagos land iguana

sharp dorsal spine. A stream of urine can attract these little guys as well, and a urethra can be mistaken for a gill in muddy water, so don't swim naked.

Insects

Some estimates say insects make up 80 percent of all animal species in Ecuador. Because they reproduce so often, insects can evolve quickly: scientists estimate that the thousands of species they've already cataloged are still only a small fraction of what's out there. Insects are also easier to spot than most other creatures—just turn on a light after dark, and you'll be swarmed within minutes.

Some insect species have evolved close relationships with certain plants to the point where each couldn't survive without the other, an arrangement called **obligatory mutualism.** *Heliconius* butterflies live months instead of weeks when they eat the nutritious vine pollen of the cucumber vine *(Psiguria),* which in turn gets cross-pollinated as the insects travel from one plant to the other. **Leafcutter ants** live in huge colonies of up to several million individuals. Small bits of leaves carried back to the nest are chewed up, fertilized with ant feces, and set in carefully tended gardens to grow a particular type of fungus the ants then eat. The fungus can't survive on its own, and the ants can't eat anything else.

Other times, the relationship isn't as mutually beneficial. The same *heliconius* butterflies love the vine leaves of the passionflower, which tries to discourage them by growing barbed hairs, changing the shape of its leaves, and sprouting warts that deceive female butterflies into thinking that another butterfly has already laid eggs on the leaves. But the butterflies keep adapting, covering the lethal hairs with soft webs and learning to detect the plant by its scent instead of its appearance. The result is the continual evolution of new species of butterfly and plant.

The papery nests of **termites** are a common sight, made of digested wood cemented together with droppings. Termites play a crucial recycling role in the rainforest by digesting dead wood with the help of microbes living in their gut. Inexorable columns of **army ants** are followed by antbirds, which eat the insects the army ants scare up. Three-centimeter **conga ants** forage alone for other insects and plant nectar. These horror-movie extras are known as *veinte-quatros* ("twenty-fours") for the day-long pain of their potent bite. Electric-blue **morpho butterflies** are one of the most eye-catching creatures in the forest, drifting lazily through patches of light on their way down forest trails or waterways.

Environmental Issues

PROBLEMS

Ecuador has the second-highest rate of deforestation in Latin America. Every year, more than 323,000 hectares of forest—close to 2.5 percent of the country's total—are cut down, including almost 81,000 virgin hectares from the half of the rainforest that remains undisturbed. In the highlands, many native plant species have been replaced by fragrant stands of **eucalyptus** *(Eucalyptus globules)* brought from Australia in the 19th century for timber.

The fast-growing trees, whose long, shallow roots suck up lots of water, have spread like weeds.

Pressure from the highest population density in South America is the clearest engine for deforestation. More and more people need land for cultivation and cattle grazing, and wood for cooking, heating, and building. A short-term economic vision encourages Amazonian settlers to "improve" their land by clearing and planting it. Timber harvesters are paid on the basis of sheer volume, not on the amount of useful wood cut.

Today, many of the primary western cloud forests are threatened by mining companies, many registered in Canada and Ecuador under phoenix-style (i.e., frequently changing) names. The search for copper and other precious metals has caused rifts in local communities, as proposals for huge opencast mines come with offers of schools and dubious employment benefits. The use of chemicals in the extraction processes will pollute many of the pristine water sources in these areas.

Meanwhile, the Galápagos Islands are in danger of being loved to death. Organized tourism, which began with 4,500 visitors in 1970, has blossomed to close to 100,000. Immigration rates are soaring to 10 percent annually in response to unemployment on the mainland and a common misconception that life is easier on the islands. In the Oriente, nature reserves are also feeling the strain of overcrowding. Cuyabeno National Park saw 5,000 visitors in 1996, as compared to 500 a decade before, and more than 12,000 settlers received title to Amazon lands between 1964 and 1982. Oil companies tap the country's economic jugular, but in so doing push indigenous tribes out of their ancestral homelands and leave thousands of hectares polluted by oil spills. Overgrazing on the coast encourages erosion, washing precious soils into the ocean.

SOLUTIONS

Even in the face of all these problems, there is hope. Reforestation programs in the Andes have planted hillsides with fast-growing Monterey pines. Debt-for-nature swaps, in which foreign conservation groups buy off part of the country's foreign debt in exchange for the protection of threatened areas, are another positive move. In a 1989 swap, the Nature Conservancy, the World Wildlife Fund, and Ecuador's Fundación Natura joined forces to raise $10 million, enlarging the Cotacachi-Cayapas and Cayambe-Coca Ecological Reserves. Environmental groups can also outbid logging companies for

forest concessions—an expensive but effective arrangement. The nonprofit Fundación Jatun Sacha is currently trying to raise money to buy a section of the Mache-Chindul coastal rainforest. The group purchased 1,400 hectares in the mid-1990s but needs more money to buy the rest.

Sustainable Development

Both economists and settlers have recently begun to realize that a tract of forest can be more valuable left alone than stripped for lumber and agriculture. The key is renewable rainforest products, which can bring in as much or more money over the long haul than logging, farming, oil drilling, or cattle ranching can in the short term. Along the way, environmentalists must debunk the age-old belief that the only good forest is a cleared forest, and make sure that the profits go directly back to the people who generate them, so they'll continue what they're doing.

Conservation International's Tagua Initiative is an excellent model of sustainable development. The oblong white seeds of the tagua palm (which resemble Brazil nuts) are soft enough to carve when raw but become as hard as ivory when dried. They once accounted for one out of every five buttons used in the United States, but demand plummeted after the advent of plastics. Today, the Tagua Initiative is trying to resurrect this trade in Peru, Bolivia, Colombia, and Ecuador, where artisans are being trained to carve buttons, jewelry, and figurines from the seeds for export. One community in Ecuador employs more than 1,000 workers and exports enough raw material for the production of 25 million buttons.

Other sustainable rainforest-friendly products include chocolate, manioc, quinine, and natural rubber from trees. In this age of patent medicine, the health benefits alone from rainforest products can be worth their weight in gold. It's become almost a cliché to say that a cure for cancer may be hiding in the last representative of a rainforest plant species right in the path of a bulldozer, but with all the medicines that have been found here already, it's probably not pure hyperbole. International pharmaceutical companies send expeditions into the rainforest to tap the wealth of native healing knowledge, and even cosmetics firms are studying the possible uses of local fruit in their shampoos.

Agroforestry, in which native species are left growing among introduced food crops, anchors the soil and ensures a wider mix of nutrients for all plants involved. Indigenous tribes have been doing this for years—just visit any Achuar *chakra*—but modern colonists often still try to grow just one crop, quickly exhausting the soil's supply of key nutrients.

Eco-Tourism

Defined as "responsible travel that conserves natural environments and sustains the well-being of local people," eco-tourism has been a rising wave in travel since the 1990s. There's a difference between eco-tourism and simple "nature tourism," in which the natural world is used only as a draw; true eco-tourism promotes conservation among travelers and locals alike, educating and inspiring both to continue conservation efforts even after the tour.

Some purists claim that even eco-tourism is too much, arguing that any amount of traffic erodes trails, compacts soils, leaves litter, and disturbs animals. Imagine cruise ships on the Napo River, or Jet Skis buzzing around the Galápagos.

In fact, the islands are a good example of both the pluses and the minuses of eco-tourism in Ecuador. Early management plans were well-intentioned but set somewhat arbitrary limits on the number of visitors per year. A second airport was built as more and more concessionaires and tour operators vied for a piece of the pie, gradually bumping the visitation limits higher and higher. Worst of all, the animals began to suffer. Today, Galápagos tourism treads a fine line between conservation and exploitation. More visitors are arriving

than ever before, but the park service is doing its best to strictly supervise the impact of tour groups and the legality and qualifications of tour operators.

ASECUT The Ecuadorian Eco-tourism Association (Calle Pedro Basan N35-86 and Manosca, Quito, tel. 2/224-1893) is a federation of tour operators, hotels, and government agencies that are happy to provide a list of eco-friendly tour operators in Ecuador. Also try the award-winning **Planeta.com**, a great starting point for information on eco-tourism in Latin America.

Parks and Reserves

Since the Ecuadorian park service, INEFAN, disbanded, 16 different conservation units have fallen under the administration of the Ministerio del Ambiente (Ministry of the Environment) in Quito. Not all is rosy in these protected areas, which cover an estimated 11 percent of the country. Parks are often understaffed and underfunded, and squatters, poachers, and mineral exploitation are very real threats.

On a hopeful note, in January 1999, President Jamil Mahuad declared Cuyabeno-Imuya and Yasuní National Parks off-limits to oil drilling, mining, lumbering, and colonization. The 2.7 million protected acres, twice the size of the state of Delaware, are home to at least 10,000 members of tribes like the Huaorani, who have violently but often futilely resisted the encroachment of modern society. Government sources reported that "friendly tourism" will still be allowed.

A host of private reserves, often associated with private lodges, have their own legal right to administer the land, buy more, and interact with local communities. Many of these reserves are seeking official national protected status through the auspices of the Corporacion Nacional Bosques Privados del Ecuador (Network of Private Forests, www.geocities.com/redbosques).

History

History—what do the French say of it again?—is a fable agreed upon. Here, the fable is bloody and colorful, with violent incident, with gold, Incas, treachery, and a scoundrel unmatched—at least until recently unmatched—I am speaking of Pizarro. But we also have handy things, lovely memories, good names, and deeds to remember.

— Ludwig Bemelmans, quoting an
Ecuadorian in *The Donkey Inside*

EARLIEST CULTURES

The first humans to gaze on the "New" World were nomadic hunter-gatherers who wandered across the Bering land bridge from Siberia up to 18,000 years ago. They gradually made their way south, arriving in South America 12,000–15,000 years ago. Close to the Panamanian isthmus, Ecuador was one of the first areas to be settled. In fact, the oldest pottery yet found in all of the Americas was unearthed in Ecuador, dating to the **Paleoindian period** (11000–4000 B.C.), when small family groups roamed the area.

Andean

Coastal merchants found a new market for salt in three major kingdoms that had developed in the Sierra. The **Cara** got their start on the coast near A.D. 900, conquering the Bahía de Caráquez area before following Río Esmeraldas upstream to settle near Quito. The Shyri family dynasty ruled this sun-worshiping culture, built observatories to track the seasons, and believed that people inhabited the moon. Around A.D. 1300, a prince of the Puruh, a famous warrior tribe, married a Shyri princess to unite the groups into the **Quitu** kingdom, which dominated the Sierra until the arrival of the Incas and spawned many of today's indigenous groups, including the Otavaleños.

A loosely organized federation of 25 tribes formed the **Cañari** nation in the southern Sierra and coastal lowlands. These ferocious fighters would prove to be the Incas' toughest opponents in centuries to come. Even after many of them were relocated to Peru, the rest allied with the Spanish to fight against their former Inca overlords. According to oral history, the Cañari sacrificed 100 children every year to the god of corn and buried their chiefs with an entire retinue of wives and servants put to death for the purpose.

Coastal

Cultivation of corn, pumpkins, and beans began around 6000 B.C. near the Santa Elena Peninsula. By the **Formative period** (4000–300 B.C.), organized settlements had begun growing crops, making pottery, and trading goods in earnest. The shiny red shell of the spiny oyster *(Spondylus calcifer)*, still a traditional material in the necklaces of Otavalan women, was especially valued as a symbol of fertility. The **Valdivia** culture thrived along the dry coastline of Manabí and Guayas province during the early part of the period, followed by the **Machalilla** and **Chorerra** cultures.

The period of **Regional Development** (300 B.C.–A.D. 700) saw more coastal cultures building *tolas,* huge pyramids of earth topped with wooden temples. Hierarchical societies, such as the **Jama-Coaque** and **Bahía** in Manabí, grew into communities of thousands clustered around ceremonial centers like San Isidro and Isla de la Plata. The **La Tola** culture, which spread from La Tola island in northern Esmeraldas into southern Colombia, was the first in history to work platinum, a complex technique requiring temperatures of 1,000°C that wasn't discovered in Europe until the 19th century. Bizarrely beautiful feline images became a trademark of the La Tola, and their sun-mask emblem is the symbol of the Banco Central.

Coastal cultures reached their peak during the period of **Integration** (A.D. 700–1460). The **Manteña-Huancavilca** civilization, stretching from the Bahía de Caráquez to the Peruvian border, counted 20,000 members by the time the Spanish arrived. Master seamen took advantage of favorable winds and currents as they piloted balsa rafts as far as Mexico to trade precious metals, mother-of-pearl, textiles, and ceramic figurines.

The Oriente

With a lack of major archaeological sites and an environment better suited to burying the past than preserving it, the Amazon region was once thought to be historically infertile. Historians have started to change their tune, however, theorizing that large settlements well into the thousands populated the jungle and the eastern slopes of the Andes almost as early as the coast and Sierra were originally settled. Manioc root, still a jungle staple, is known to have been domesticated at least 8,000 years ago and may have been instrumental in supporting Andean and coastal societies, along with corn imported from Central America. Clay pottery began to make an appearance around 4000 b.c.

THE RISE AND FALL OF THE INCAS
Conquest

The empire of the "Children of the Sun" began ignominiously near the shores of frigid Lake Titicaca, between Peru and Bolivia, in the 11th century. Soon the Inca empire began to expand from its capital in Cuzco, Peru. By the 14th and 15th centuries, the empire they called Tahuantinsuyo stretched from northern Chile to the edge of Ecuador.

In 1463, the ruling Inca, Tupac Inca Yupanqui, began the push into Ecuador from Peru. As they advanced into the Sierra, Inca armies met fierce resistance from local tribes. Spears, slingshots, and war clubs flew in screaming melees where combatants wore cloth armor or nothing at all. The Cara were defeated only after 17 years of resistance. Thousands were slaughtered in retribution, including thousands who were killed at the edge of Lago Yahuarcocha (Bloody Lake) north of

Ibarra. A new northern Inca outpost called Tomebamba, decked out in enough splendor to rival Cuzco itself, was built on the ruins of the Cañari capital in present-day Cuenca.

By 1500, Ecuador was under the thumb of Huayna Capac, the son of Tupac and a Cañari princess. Huayna grew up in Ecuador and spent much of his time suppressing local uprisings.

Life under the Incas

Ecuador's new overlords ruled for less than half a century but made their mark with surprising speed. The Inca emperor, revered as a living god, imposed an iron fist on the Quitosuyo—as the section of the empire from Ecuador to Cuzco was known—from his base in Cuzco. Ongoing local resistance made military rule a necessity. Workers built fortifications called *pucarás* at dozens of strategic lookouts, bridges, and mountain passes. Populations that refused to pay tribute to the divine authority of the Incas were moved in their entirety as far as Chile, and a *mita* system of collective work and annual tribute fueled the empire's expansion and filled the coffers in Cuzco with riches.

The Incas imposed the Quechua language (not to be confused with the Quechua people, who spoke and continue to speak their own language) on conquered cultures. Agriculture was collectivized under the watchful eye of the state, as new crops such as sweet potatoes and peanuts were grown on terraced fields watered by complicated systems of irrigation. Spring plowing was forbidden until the ruling Inca had broken the ground at Cuzco with a ceremonial golden hand-plow.

Records were kept through an intricate system of knotted, colored cords called *quipus*, which could be used to keep track of populations, seasons, and food supplies. Buildings in the famous Inca masonry style—blocks weighing tons fitted perfectly together—housed collections of intricately woven textiles, utensils made of precious metals, and musical instruments made of clay, shells, and human bones.

An incredible network of roads, perhaps the Incas' most impressive achievement, tied everything together. Eight meters wide and paved with stone, the highways boasted trees planted for shade and a ditch of fresh water running alongside. Teams of runners could make the 2,000-kilometer journey from Cuenca to Quito along the Capacñan (Inca Highway) in eight days, crossing suspension bridges over at least 100 rivers and resting in roadhouses along the way. A second highway ran 4,800 kilometers along the coast from Santiago, Chile, to Guayaquil, and was connected to the Inca Highway by roads climbing into the Sierra.

Things Fall Apart

Huayna Capac died suddenly in 1526, leaving a power vacuum contested by Huáscar, the legitimate heir in Cuzco, and Atahualpa, the offspring of Huayna and a Quitu princess. Civil war began almost immediately, as Atahualpa established his headquarters in Cuenca after defeating Huáscar's finest general and making a *chicha* cup out of his skull. That same year, an exploratory mission led by Spaniard Bartolomé Ruiz de Estrada waded ashore in northern Ecuador.

The drama began in earnest in 1532, when Atahualpa defeated his half brother and took him prisoner, after a major battle near Riobamba that still inspires a mild dose of nationalistic pride in Ecuadorians (Atahualpa, after all, was the Ecuadorian Inca). The Inca empire was thus completely divided and ravaged by war when the conquistador Francisco Pizarro arrived that same year.

THE CONQUISTADORES ARRIVE
The Spanish Conquest Begins

Most conquistadores (literally, "conquerors") were low-ranking Spanish noblemen heading to the New World for wealth, fame, and adventure, in that order. Francisco Pizarro, the central figure in the conquest of the Incas, was an illiterate and illegitimate fortune-seeker from the Extremadura region of southern Spain. A decade after he accompanied Vasco Nuñez de Balboa across the Panamanian isthmus to discover the Pacific Ocean, Pizarro received permission from the Spanish crown to explore the west coast of South America with fellow adventurer Diego de Almagro.

Two voyages in 1524 and 1526 failed miserably, but the next year, Pizarro—acting against royal orders—landed in northern Peru with 13 men. After returning to Spain to plead for money and authority from King Charles I for another voyage, Pizarro once again arrived in the New World with the title of Governor and Captain-General of Peru. In 1531, he landed in the Bay of San Mateo near Manabí with Almagro (who was jealous of Pizarro's title and authority), 180 men, 27 horses, his brothers Gonzalo and Juan Pizarro, and two half-brothers.

Atahualpa's Fate

In November 1532, Atahualpa, having just captured his half-brother Huáscar, met with Pizarro's group in Cajamarca in the mountains of northern Peru. The ensuing scene would have been fascinating to witness: two leaders meeting in the sun-baked central plaza under the eyes of dozens of Spanish soldiers and thousands of Inca warriors, with tension resonating in the air. Accounts about the events that followed differ, but most witnesses agree that Atahualpa refused the Spanish chaplain's order to submit to Spain and the Catholic god, throwing a Bible to the ground in disgust.

At a prearranged signal, Spanish soldiers fired cannons and charged their horses into the heart of the astonished Inca garrison. Within two hours, 7,000 Inca soldiers lay dead, the Sun King had been taken captive, and the fate of South America's greatest empire had been sealed. Among the Europeans, only Pizarro was wounded as he rushed to grab Atahualpa. For the record, Atahualpa later admitted that he had had a similar plot in store for the conquistadores. They just beat him to it, adopting the headlong charge that would prove brutally effective against native foot soldiers in the years to come.

During the nine months of his imprisonment, Atahualpa learned Spanish, chess, and cards while retaining most of his authority.

Attendants still dressed and fed him, burning everything he touched. Thinking that Pizarro planned to depose him in favor of Huáscar, Atahualpa ordered his captive half-brother killed. When it became clear that his own life hung in the balance, Atahualpa offered to buy his freedom with the wealth of his entire kingdom. He is said to have reached high on the wall of a room five meters wide by seven long, offering to fill it once with gold and twice with silver. The ransom—one of the largest the world has ever known—was assembled and on its way to the capital when Atahualpa was baptized Francisco, put on trial for polygamy, idolatry, and crimes against the crown, and strangled on August 29, 1533. The ransom, quickly hidden en route from Cuzco, has never been found (see the sidebar *The Inca's Ransom* in the *Central Sierra* chapter).

The Conquest Is Completed

In November 1533, Cuzco fell to Pizarro and Hernando de Soto, and the Inca empire was finished. The victors were welcomed as liberators by many native tribes, who had resented and fought against the yoke of the Incas. A few battles remained to be fought: In May 1534, Sebastian de Benalcázar (Pizarro's second-in-command) found himself facing 50,000 Inca warriors under the guidance of Rumiñahui, the greatest Inca general, who had deserted and burned Quito rather than surrender it to the invaders. Benalcázar, aided by Cañari soldiers, defeated "Stone Face," whose capture, torture, and execution signaled the end of organized native military resistance.

By 1549, fewer than 2,000 Spanish soldiers had defeated an estimated 500,000 natives. Although these numbers seem unbelievable, they can be explained by a combination of battle tactics, epidemiology, and luck. In the 16th century, Spanish soldiers were among the best in the world, almost invulnerable to attack from the ground when mounted on their fierce war horses in full battle armor. A dozen mounted soldiers could hold off and even defeat hundreds of Inca foot soldiers. In addition, European diseases, to which the

natives had no immunity, killed them by the thousands.

As much as anything, the incredible timing of the conquest sealed the Incas' fate. If the Spanish had arrived as little as a year or two earlier or later, things might have worked out much differently. As it happened, though, they showed up exactly at the moment of greatest vulnerability, the Inca empire split by a civil war that already had many local tribes itching to throw off their newly acquired masters. The conquistadores, especially Pizarro, manipulated the situation brilliantly. They installed puppet rulers to pacify the masses, and always acted with brutal decisiveness, as if they weren't actually months from reinforcements and thousands of miles from home.

The End of the Conquistador Era

Infighting among the Spanish began as soon as the Incas were out of the picture. In 1538, Diego Almagro contested Pizarro's right to govern the new territory of Peru. Almagro was defeated, tried, and sentenced to death in Lima. Francisco himself was assassinated in 1541 by the remaining members of Almagro's rebel army.

The Spanish crown tried to step in by imposing the New Laws of 1542, aimed at controlling the unruly conquistadores and ending the enslavement of the indigenous peoples, already a widespread practice. A new viceroy sent to oversee the budding colonies was fought and killed by Gonzalo Pizarro near Quito in 1544. Pizarro, in turn, was defeated by royal troops in 1548 and hung for treason.

THE COLONIAL PERIOD

From 1544 to 1720, Ecuador existed as part of the Viceroyalty of Peru, one of the divisions of Spain's New World colonies. During two centuries of relative peace, settlers replaced the conquistadores, and female immigrants evened the balance of the sexes.

Farms and Slaves

Without the mineral wealth of Peru or Bolivia, Ecuador had to earn its keep from its soil. Soon the rich volcanic earth of the Andean highlands bore bumper crops of wheat, corn, and potatoes, which thrived in the mild climate. Cattle, horses, and sheep grazed on endless fields of grass.

The most common form of land tenure was the *encomienda* system, in which Spanish settlers were given the title to tracts of the best land, along with the right to demand tribute from any indigenous people who happened to live there. In exchange, the *encomendero* agreed to develop the land and convert its inhabitants to Christianity. The Spanish crown strove to impose strict rules governing the treatment of the *indígenas*, but the system was hard to regulate and usually resulted in virtual slavery. By the early 17th century, about 500 *encomenderos* controlled vast tracts of the Sierra.

Another important source of income was textile *obrajes* (workshops), where *indígenas* were forced to turn out cotton and wool cloth from dawn to dusk, often chained to their looms. Agriculture along the coast was hampered by rampant tropical diseases like malaria and a frustrating lack of natives to enslave. Bananas, cocoa, and sugarcane filled lowland plantations, and shipping and trade kept ports such as Guayaquil in business. The coast north of the Manta area received the most of the few African slaves that were imported to Ecuador. There they intermarried with indigenous tribespeople and occasionally escaped into fortified communities of runaways.

A sweltering climate, impassable terrain, and fierce indigenous groups kept most settlers out of the Oriente, beyond a few brave (and often martyred) missionaries.

The Holy Scorecard

The Catholic church was a cornerstone of life during the colonial period for natives and immigrants alike. By a majority vote, the Vatican had decided that indigenous peoples actually did have souls, making their conversion a worthwhile endeavor. Every town had a church operated by either Franciscans, Jesuits, or Dominicans, all competing for souls like soccer teams vying for points. A strict tithing system made the church the largest landowner in the colonies. Jesus and the Virgin Mary were blended with the old gods of the sky and mountains in ceremonies in remote villages.

The Racial Pot Simmers

Over everything lay the subtle but pervasive gauze of race. Europeans, born in Spain *(peninsulares)* or the New World *(criollos),* stood at the top of the social ladder. They ran the sweatshops and owned the *haciendas* (farm estates), raking in money as others labored in the sun.

Mixed-blood *mestizos* were in the middle, keeping the urban machinery going as shopkeepers, craftsmen, and skilled laborers. This middle class, aspiring to wealth and status as they looked down on the native masses, was politically unstable and easily provoked by fiery rhetoric—a ready source of fuel for the spark of independence.

The indigenous peoples that remained after the Spanish conquest made up most of colonial society, ranging in number from 750,000 to one million by the 16th century. Countless had died of imported diseases like smallpox, measles, cholera, and syphilis, to which they had no natural immunity, especially on the coast. Others were forced onto *reduciones,* hastily assembled townships that made it easier for the Spanish to collect taxes and demand labor.

Forced labor systems had *indígenas* working months to build roads and buildings. The debts they accumulated along the way far outweighed the pittance they earned, if anything, resulting in a system of peonage in which debt was handed down from generation to generation. Some *indígenas,* luckily, were left more or less alone, since much of the land inhabited by native groups was inaccessible or otherwise of little interest to the Spanish.

INDEPENDENCE FROM SPAIN
First Sparks

Just as things had settled into a comfortable pattern in the colonies, a series of events unfolded that would eventually shake the continent to its foundation. Scientific visitors started to bring news of the outside world and new ideas in science and philosophy. From 1736 to 1745, the French mission to measure the equator (see the sidebar *Measuring the Earth* in the *Northern Sierra* chapter) spread ideas of rational science and personal liberty, courtesy of the Enlightenment. In the early 19th century, German explorer and scientist Alexander von Humboldt and aspiring naturalist Charles Darwin both helped diffuse the latest scientific findings around this mostly forgotten corner of the globe. Revolutions in the United States (1776) and France (1792) set the stage for the wars of Independence in South American countries.

In Ecuador, the physician and writer Eugenio Espejo was born in 1747, growing up to become a liberal humanist who demanded freedom and a democratic government for the colonies. Thrown in jail repeatedly and even exiled for his books and articles, Espejo died in Quito in 1795 and is hailed as one of the fathers of independence. Elsewhere in the country, uprisings among both *indígenas* and *mestizos* protested colonial treatment at the hands of Spain and its regime in the New World.

The final straw came in July 1808 when Napoleon invaded Spain, deposed King Ferdinand VII, and installed his brother Joseph Bonaparte on the throne. Monetary demands on the colonies—always a source of friction—skyrocketed as Spain sought funds to fight for

EL LIBERTADOR

Revered and despised, triumphant and frustrated, El Libertador (The Liberator) embodied all the contradictions and potential of the continent he helped set free from the colonial yoke of Spain. One thing is true: whether as the heroic liberator of South America or the tyrannical despot chasing an impossible vision of continental unity, Simón Bolívar made his mark on history. At his death, his dream remained only half fulfilled: he had freed his beloved land, but he couldn't unify it.

Born in Caracas on July 24, 1783, to a wealthy family of planters, Simón Antonio de la Santisima Trinidad Bolívar y Palacios saw both his parents die before his 10th birthday. Relatives and friends helped raise him in the cultured circles of the New World's upper class. "His chest was narrow," according to a friend, "his legs particularly thin, his hands and feet were small – a woman might have envied them." But he also had a dark side: "His expression, when he was in good humor, was pleasant, but it became terrible when he was aroused. The change was unbelievable."

Bolívar's early teenage years were spent in military school, where his records reveal his innate martial talent. His studies continued in Europe; he divided his time between aristocratic parties and studies of history, art, and the classics. His attention was soon captured by the rising star Napoleon Bonaparte, who had just crowned himself emperor of France for life. As he soaked up the rhetoric of philosophers such as Rousseau and Voltaire, advocating the sacred duty of a monarch to protect the common man by means of the law, Bolívar was solidifying his own ideas for South America.

From his European experiences, Bolívar came to believe that the best way to organize the struggling republics would be through a strongly centralized, even dictatorial government. At the helm would preside a lifetime ruler with limitless power who would labor for the greatest good, instead of abusing his position – in other words, a "moralistic monarch."

By 1807, Bolívar was back at his estate in Caracas and a member of the growing independence struggle. Napoleon's deposition of Ferdinand VII of Spain gave the revolutionaries their chance: Venezuela proclaimed its independence on July 5, 1811, and declared war on Spain soon after. Although the campaign did not fare well initially, Bolívar soon established his military reputation. Two years later, ecstatic crowds greeted him in Caracas, where he was formally titled El Libertador and given complete dictatorship over the country.

the deposed Ferdinand, and the colonists decided enough was enough.

Early Uprisings

On August 10, 1809, a group of Quito's elite threw the president of the Quito *audencia* (colonial government) in jail and seized power in the name of the deposed king of Spain. Ironically, the Quiteño Rebellion, the first declaration of independence in the Spanish colonies, took place in support of the Spanish king and ended abruptly. All the main players were executed by troops loyal to Bonaparte. In December 1811, a junta declared the *audencia* independent and sent troops off to fight the Spanish, who mauled them to a man. In October 1820, the city of Guayaquil declared its own independence under a junta led by poet José Joaquín Olmedo.

The Heat of Battle

By then, the New World's fight for independence was in full swing. Two main armies were led by Venezuelan Simón Bolívar (see the sidebar *El Libertador* below) in Colombia and Venezuela, and Argentine José de San Martín to the south. The fight for Ecuador began in earnest in May 1821, when brash young general Antonio José de Sucre arrived in Guayaquil at Bolívar's orders. After winning the first few battles, Sucre's army was whipped by loyalist troops near Ambato. Fourteen hundred fresh

---

Spain struck back with crushing force, occupying Caracas in 1814. Ironically, the defeat of his political role model at the battle of Waterloo provided crucial aid to Bolívar's revolution. Having declared "war to the death," Bolívar quickly snapped up the surplus arms and soldiers and turned them to his cause. Meanwhile, he was busy organizing the Congress of Angostura, which in 1819 made his dream of Gran Colombia real, with Bolívar as dictatorial president.

Nowhere else did Bolívar's contradictions seem more apparent than in his political philosophy. The same man who admired the United States so much that he described the North American democracy as "a government so sublime that it might more nearly benefit a republic of saints," also wrote to a friend how he was "convinced that our America can only be ruled through a well-managed, shrewd despotism." Perhaps Bolívar was demonstrating a ruthless practicality. Latin America, in his eyes, was simply not ready for democracy. "Do not adopt the best system of government," he said, "but the one that is most likely to succeed."

Spain's hold over Venezuela had finally been broken, but the battle for a united South America was far from won. Even before Bolívar freed Ecuador and Peru, finally eliminating the

Spanish threat to the New World, his dream of Gran Colombia began to falter. Bolívar knew the worst was yet to come – and it was in peace that the newly freed nations would eventually disappoint him. His noble-minded revolution soon dissolved into a bloody struggle between disparate political, regional, and racial factions. In a last-ditch attempt to reconcile the warring populations, Bolívar organized a peace congress in Panama in 1826. His effort was in vain – only four countries showed up.

Bolívar succumbed to tuberculosis early in the afternoon of December 17, 1830, in a small town on the Colombian coast. He never answered the question of whether a South America unified under a monarch would have prospered, or if he simply would have re-created in the New World the system he fought to dispel. Shortly before he died, the fiery general seethed with bitterness at what he saw as the betrayal of both himself and his dream: "There is no good faith in America, nor among the nations of America. Treaties are scraps of paper; constitutions, printed matter; elections, battles; freedom, anarchy."

Even on his deathbed, though, his thoughts were full of hope for his beloved federation: "Colombians! My last wishes are for the happiness of our native land."

soldiers sent from Peru by San Martín soon put them on another winning streak, which culminated on May 24, 1822, at the Battle of Pichincha, a decisive victory on the slopes above Quito. Within, hours the *audencia* belonged to Sucre, and Ecuador was free.

A pair of additional victories in Peru sealed South America's independence. The Battle of Junín on August 7, 1823, was fought by so many cavalrymen that it was called the "Battle of the Centaurs." The night before the Battle of Ayacucho in 1824, men from both sides crossed into the opposing camps to bid farewell to friends and brothers. The next day, fewer than 6,000 patriots defeated more than 9,000 royalists, who had them outgunned by a factor of 10. Spain was beaten and withdrew its administrative apparatus from the Americas, with its tail between its legs.

In August 1830, Ecuador withdrew from Gran Colombia, Bolívar's ill-fated confederation that had succumbed to regional rivalries. Suddenly, 700,000 people found themselves citizens of a new country, with nowhere to go but up.

EARLY YEARS OF THE REPUBLIC

Ecuador's childhood as a nation was marked by power struggles among *criollo* elites, in particular aristocratic conservatives from Quito and free-enterprise liberals from Guayaquil. Meanwhile, the new republic had little effect on most of the country—the poor, in other words, stayed poor.

Juan José Flores held power 1830–1845, either directly as president or through puppet figures. Most of his power came from Quito, but widespread discontent by 1845 forced him to flee the country. The period 1845–1860 saw 11 governments and three constitutions come and go, as the economy stagnated and the military's influence in politics grew. By 1860, the country was on the brink of chaos, split by provincial rivalries and tension over border disputes with Peru and Colombia.

The Moreno Era

In 1860, a new player rose to the top. Gabriel García Moreno embodied devout Sierra conservatism—so much so that some historians have dubbed his regime a theocracy. He grew up during the chaos of the preceding decades and was determined that that kind of anarchy would never happen in his Ecuador—not if he and the church had anything to say about it.

Conservatives loved him, citing his many social programs as proof that he saved the country from disaster. An improved school system now accepted women and *indígenas*, new roads connected the coast to the highlands and Quito to the rest of the country, hospitals and railways were built, and exports jumped from $1 million to $10 million 1852–1890. Liberals saw him as a religious nut who consecrated the country to the Sacred Heart of Jesus, renamed army battalions "Guardians of the Virgin" and "Soldiers of the Infant Jesus," and established Roman Catholicism as the official state religion, with membership a prerequisite for citizenship and voting. Free speech was tightly controlled and political opposition squelched.

In 1875, six years after establishing the official Conservative Party, Moreno was shot on the steps of the Capitol. (Tour guides still point out the bullet holes on the wall.) Liberal Ecuadorian journalist Juan Montalvo rejoiced from his exile: "My pen has killed him!"

INTO THE 20TH CENTURY

Two decades of jousting between the Liberal and Conservative Parties ended with the ascension to power of General José Eloy Alfaro. In two terms as president, 1897–1901 and 1906–1911, Alfaro embodied the Radical Liberal Party as much as Moreno once typified conservatism. Alfaro toppled the Catholic church from its pinnacle at the top of daily life by seizing church lands, instituting freedom of religion, and secularizing marriage and education. But sure enough, on January 28, 1912, Alfaro was killed by a government-instigated crowd in Quito. His body was dragged through the streets and burned in Parque El Ejido.

Musical Presidents

Between 1925 and 1948, Ecuador had no fewer than 22 heads of state, each of whom tried to ride out a series of economic slumps that culminated in the 1929 Wall Street crash, which caused exports to fall by two-thirds. In 1934 began the celebrity of José María Velasco Ibarra who said, "Give me a balcony, and I will become president!" and was elected over and over. The first to appeal to both liberals and conservatives, Ibarra was nonetheless overthrown four times during his five terms between 1934 and 1961.

Early Border Struggles

The border between Ecuador and Peru, outlined only roughly by the colonial *audencia* in Quito, has been a bone of contention since Ecuador became a country. Boundary talks broke down into skirmishes in 1938, and three years later, Peru launched an all-out invasion of Ecuador's southern and easternmost provinces. Fearing a coup, president Carlos Alberto Arroyo del Río kept the best troops in Quito during the border fighting, but a cease-fire was arranged within two months.

The January 1942 Protocol of Peace, Friendship, and Boundaries (also known as the Río Protocol) quickly became a national disgrace to Ecuadorians. Not only did Ecuador have to sign away more than 200,000 square kilometers of territory rich in oil and gold deposits to her hated larger neighbor, but the country also lost the Amazon river port of Iquitos, her main river access to the Atlantic, in the bargain. Ecuadorians quickly looked for someone to blame beyond the guarantor countries of the United States, Chile, Argentina, and Brazil, who were more interested in the recently erupted World War.

Ups and Downs

A period of relative political stability in the mid-20th century proved too good to last. Ecuador sided with the Allies in World War II, during which the United States built a naval base in the Galápagos and tried to kick all German settlers off the archipelago. After the war, Ecuador enjoyed a resurgence of democracy and its attendant freedoms. Even old Velasco Ibarra was finally able to finish a full term—his third—in 1952.

When a wave of disease ravaged Central America's banana crop, Ecuador stepped in to supply the huge U.S. demand, with the help of the United Fruit Company. Exports jumped from $2 million in 1948 to $20 million in 1952, and Ecuador's position as world banana king became official.

By the late 1950s, however, the banana boom was over. Ibarra, who was reelected in 1960, began a proud Ecuadorian political tradition by renouncing the Río Protocol in his inaugural address, to the delight of the crowd. His left-leaning policies proved ill-timed, however, coming as they did at the height of the Cold War. A gunfight in the Congressional chamber proved how bad things had gotten at the top. In November 1961, the military removed Ibarra from power; and two years later, it replaced his successor with a four-man junta.

Ecuador's first experiment with outright military rule was short-lived, barely managing to pass the well-intentioned but ultimately ineffectual Agrarian Reform Law of 1964 before succumbing to concerns over another economic slump. Ibarra was reelected in 1968 for the fifth time with barely a third of the popular vote. For two years he enjoyed military support as he dismissed Congress and the Supreme Court, suspended the Constitution, and dictated harsh but necessary economic measures designed to get the country back on its feet.

By 1972—the same year in which Ecuador was found to have the third-largest petroleum reserves in Latin America—another military junta was back in power. In response to widespread concern that the newfound wealth would be squandered by a corrupt civilian government, the junta instituted a firm strategy of modernization. Industrialization leapt forward, and the middle class grew in numbers and power, but further attempts at land reform met the stone wall of the landholding elite. Not surprisingly, the poor suffered from the oil-boom inflation without reaping the attendant benefits.

Democracy at Last

Coups in 1975 and 1976 caused splits within the military, and in January 1978, a national referendum voted for a new constitution, universal suffrage, and guaranteed civil rights. Jaime Roldós took office in 1979, finding himself at the wheel of a country unfamiliar with democracy, but with a government budget and per capita income increased more than 500 percent by the oil windfall. His center-left government began programs of improving rural literacy and housing—but less than two years later, Roldós was killed in a plane crash, along with his wife and minister of defense.

RECENT HISTORY

The early 1980s brought a cluster of crises. Border fighting with Peru flared up in January 1981, December 1982, and January 1983, and the disastrous 1982–1983 El Niño weather phenomenon caused $640 million in damage from drought and floods, ruining rice and banana crops along the coast. Sudden declines in petroleum reserves left the country with a foreign debt of $7 billion by 1983, when inflation hit an all-time high at 52.5 percent.

Conservative León Febres Cordero beat out eight other candidates for the presidency in 1984. A pro-U.S. foreign policy and economic austerity plan brought him into conflict with Congress and the country. In January 1987, Cordero was kidnapped by air force troops under orders from a mutinous general in prison. Only by granting the general amnesty was he able to secure his own release after 11 hours in captivity. That same month, an earthquake in Napo Province killed hundreds and ruptured the all-important oil pipeline, causing Ecuador to suspend interest payments on its $8.3 billion foreign debt.

In 1992, Christian Socialist Sixto Duran Ballén assumed the presidency. Further economic austerity measures, including a privatization law that left 100,000 public employees without jobs, helped curb inflation but prompted widespread demonstrations, bombings, and a general strike in May 1993. Ballén's administration was also clouded by a scandal involving vice president and economic guru Alberto Dahik, who fled to Costa Rica in a private plane after being accused (correctly, as it turned out) of embezzling millions of dollars in state funds. A government cover-up, which involved the seizure of Central Bank vaults that held incriminating microfilm, led to the resignation of ministers and the impeachment of one Supreme Court judge. The fallout left many convinced that the country would be better off under an authoritarian regime like that of Peruvian president Alberto Fujimori.

Tensions with Peru erupted into outright war in January 1995. Six weeks of combat over the headwaters of Río Cenepa ended only after the intervention of a multinational team of observers. The fighting cost Ecuador $250 million in damage, plus untold more in lost commerce and tourism, but Ballén's popularity rating soared to greater than 90 percent.

El Loco

In 1996, the same year Jefferson Pérez became Ecuador's first-ever Olympic medalist by winning a gold in speed walking in Atlanta, a political circus began with the presidential election of Abdalá Bucarám Ortiz, a former mayor of Guayaquil and one of the least boring politicians in recent memory. Of Lebanese descent, Bucarám campaigned under the moniker "El Loco" (The Crazy One) and promised to lead Ecuador's vast army of the poor to newfound prosperity, and to curb inflation by stabilizing the sucre and selling off state-owned enterprises. The urban poor propelled Bucarám to victory in the second round of elections.

From the start, it was clear that El Loco wasn't firing on all cylinders. His inaugural address was described as a two-hour "hysterical diatribe." One day he was raising money for charity by shaving his moustache on live TV; the next he was having lunch with Ecuadorian-American Lorena Bobbitt of tabloid-surgery fame. The president released an album entitled

A Madman in Love and crooned at beauty contests.

Accusations of corruption and political favoritism, along with the fallout from a strict austerity package passed in January 1997, proved to be El Loco's undoing. A general protest strike paralyzed the country, and on February 6, Congress surprised even themselves by voting the president "mentally incompetent" and unfit to govern by a 44–34 margin. Bucarám holed up in the presidential palace, saying he'd rather die than step down in disgrace.

Vice president Rosalia Arteaga stepped into the presidency, becoming Ecuador's first female leader. Thousands of demonstrators surrounded the presidential palace, demanding that Bucarám leave office. When the military withdrew its support, Bucarám left the country, fuming that "Congress is not a psychiatrist." (Amazingly, Bucarám still lurks in the wings of Ecuadorian politics.)

When the smoke cleared, former Congressman Fabian Alarcon had assumed the title of president from Arteaga, and he wasted no time in repealing the austerity measures that got the ball rolling in the first place.

Into the Millennium

Ecuador rode into the 21st century on a wave of upheaval. Another round of El Niño hit the country badly in 1998, washing out roads, devastating the country's farming and fishing industries, and killing off wildlife in the Galápagos. In August, an earthquake measuring 7.1 on the Richter scale hit near Bahía de Caráquez, knocking out water and electricity supplies and even more roads.

Meanwhile, former Quito mayor Jamil Mahuad claimed the presidency by a margin of less than 5 percent in a hotly contested election. The Harvard-educated political centrist took office in August, just in time to lay to rest the long-standing border dispute with Peru. Guagua Pichincha and Tungurahua both erupted in late 1999, forcing the evacuation of thousands from Quito and Baños, and Sangay erupted in January 2004.

A mounting economic crisis caused the sucre to slide drastically in value. In 1999, Ecuador because the first country to default on its Brady bonds, and Mahuad likened the situation to the sinking of the *Titanic* in a state-of-the-nation speech. He may not have been surprised, then, when 10,000 mostly indigenous protestors shut down much of the country in a general strike in 2000 to protest one of Ecuador's worst financial crises in history. Opponents charged that the president's plan to make Ecuador the first country in Latin America to adopt the U.S. dollar as its official currency would further impoverish poor citizens who have their savings in sucres, instead of stabilizing the economy. Filanbanco, the country's largest bank, folded, taking $1.2 billion in public funds with it.

Hundreds of indigenous protestors occupied the Congress and Supreme Court buildings in Quito and declared a new government. Violent protests in Guayaquil followed, and Mahuad was deposed by a three-man military junta in a bloodless coup. Mahuad had no choice but to hand over the reins to his vice president, Gustavo Noboa Bejerano, a university professor from Guayaquil. No sooner had Ecuador faded from the global spotlight than an oil spill in the Galápagos Islands in early 2001 focused world attention on the country once again. (See *The Galápagos Islands* chapter for more details.)

In 2002, the leader of the coup that disposed Mahuad was himself elected president. Colonel Lucio Gutiérrez campaigned on an outsider platform that painted him as a friend of the downtrodden. His ascent was seen as one more signal of a general leftward political shift in Latin America, but it didn't last long. In April 2005, Gutiérrez himself was sent packing by Congress and was replaced by his vice president, Alfredo Palacio.

On the positive side, the country's economy grew by 7 percent in 2004, in part due to higher oil prices, which helped the government post a fiscal surplus for the first time in decades.

Recent trends in Latin America, seen as a rejection of Neo-Liberalism, saw popularist

President Rafael Correa take office in January 2007. One of his proposals was to write a new constitution (the twentieth), and an assembly was elected by national vote to review existing laws. Of the 130 members, 80 are with the presidential party, a reflection of the massive support the country has given him.

The new constitution was presented in July 2008, and a half-day national holiday was declared. It will now have to be passed into law and officially adopted. Meanwhile, Congress has been suspended until the new constitution is official. The differences it will make to life and trade in Ecuador remain to be seen.

Government and Economy

POLITICS

For much of its history, Ecuador has been anything but politically stable. The first 160 years after independence saw 86 governments and 17 constitutions come and go. The 19th constitution faced a referendum in September 2008. Of the few administrations that resulted from popular election, not many were free of fraud. Citizens became understandably disenchanted with the system. "We have a revolution here every Thursday afternoon at half-past two," said one Ecuadorian in Ludwig Bemelmans's book *The Donkey Inside*, "and our government is run like a nightclub."

At the same time, Ecuador has managed to avoid many of the pitfalls its neighbors have fallen into. Democracy has been in place in name since 1948, and in reality since the end of military rule in 1979. Recent political fireworks have shaken many Ecuadorians' faith in the system and scared away a few tourists, but in the end, the message has been reassuring: The military hasn't wanted to take over, as it has in other Latin American countries, and political problems are usually corrected with surprising speed and little bloodshed. Ecuador was one of the first countries in Latin America to return to democracy after a wave of dictatorships in the 1960s and 1970s, and the political system seems more entrenched every day.

The traditional rivalry between liberal, trade-happy coastal residents and conservative, landholding Sierra elites has spilled over into politics, with the presidency often alternating between the two interests. Sometimes the transition isn't smooth: In 1988, outgoing president Febres Cordero, a Guayaquileño, refused to hand over the presidential sash to his successor, Rodrigo Borja from Quito.

Organization

Under the 1979 constitution, reformed in 1998, Ecuador is a representative democracy with compulsory suffrage for all literate citizens over age 18. An executive branch consists of 14 ministers, a vice president, and a president elected by majority vote every four years. Presidents must be elected by at least a 50 percent majority, leading to frequent run-off elections. They cannot be reelected for a consecutive term.

The Congreso Nacional (National Congress) has 100 seats filled by national and provincial deputies who serve four-year terms. The regional voting system gives less populated provinces, such as those in the Oriente and the Galápagos, disproportionate representation, since each deputy needs fewer votes to be elected. Congress in turn appoints 32 justices to form the judiciary branch of the Corte Suprema (Supreme Court), whose members serve for life.

Twenty-four *provincias* (provinces)—the newest, Santo Domingo de los Tsachilas and Santa Elena, were formed in 2007—are ruled by governors who oversee 219 *cantones* (counties) and around 1000 *parroquias* (parishes).

Parties

About 35 different political parties keep elections interesting. The traditional extremes of the Conservative Party (PC) and the Radical

© JEAN BRONW

The prickly pear cactus is harvested in the highlands.

Liberal Party (PLR), with power bases in Quito and Guayaquil, respectively, have grown stale through the 20th century. Today, the left is the realm of the Democratic Left (ID), formed in 1977 by Rodrigo Borja and supported by younger reform-minded professionals. The Social Christian Party (PSC) and the Ecuadorian Conservative Party (PCE) claim the center-right. The populist left is the domain of the Roldosist Party (PRE), the Popular Democratic Movement (MPD), and the Concentration of Popular Forces (CFP). Pachakutik, the mostly indigenous political party, is an important political force. It helped overthrow Jamil Mahuad and elect Lucio Gutiérrez, and can organize nationwide strikes involving thousands of members.

No one party is strong throughout the country, making coalitions an important factor in national elections. The Catholic church's political strength has waned, and the military usually chooses to stick to the sidelines. Student unrest flared in the 1960s, causing military crackdowns on university campuses, but has since mellowed considerably.

ECONOMY

Ecuador's economy balances between relatively small agricultural enterprises, businesses in the Sierra, and monster export projects along the coast. Oil and export agriculture are the country's two main pillars. Natural resources abound, but a large foreign debt hampers development, and unemployment and inflation are both high. Informal craftspeople and vendors make up close to 40 percent of the workforce.

As with many developing countries, Ecuador's wealth is concentrated in a few people at the top of the social ladder, with little trickling down to the rest. A large gap separates the haves from the have-nots; the sight of a Nissan Pathfinder driving past a dirt hut is jarring but common. In 1994, 35 percent of the country's population was estimated to live below the poverty line, and the monthly minimum wage stood well below the cost of living for a family of four.

Agriculture

The conquistadores never realized it, but Ecuador's true wealth lies in its soil and the people who work it. Agriculture is the primary industry in the Sierra, followed by livestock trading and crafts. Despite agrarian reform laws established in 1964 and 1974, the land remains unevenly distributed: Three-quarters of all farms work less than 10 percent of the arable land. Tiny farms of less than two hectares can't support families, leading many people to emigrate to the cities and the coast in search of work.

The rich river flood plains on the coast have seen their share of booms and busts. At the turn of the 20th century, cocoa beans provided funds for the Quito–Guayaquil railway, and coffee and rice took off in the 1930s. Today, coffee is the nation's second most valuable crop, grown on 20 percent of all farms. Rich shrimp farms along the coast made Ecuador the world's largest shrimp exporter in 1986. Bananas slid onto the scene in the 1940s, becoming Ecuador's leading export crop by 1947. One Ecuadorian in 10 is dependent in some way on the banana industry, which generated $827 million in 2001, nearly 5 percent of the country's GDP. Flower exports exploded in the 1990s and are now the country's fourth-largest export (see the sidebar *Flower Exports: To Russia with Love* in the *Central Sierra* chapter).

Industry

One-quarter of Ecuador's gross national product (GNP) has some catching up to do—the country still leans toward the export of raw materials and the import of finished products—but the situation is better than in many other developing countries. Factories process food and manufacture textiles, wood products, chemicals, plastics, metal goods, and timber. In 1997, Ecuador's $3.4 billion in exports were split between petroleum (30 percent), bananas (26 percent), shrimp (16 percent), cut flowers (2 percent), and fish (2 percent).

Recent mining strikes, including 700 tons of gold discovered in the Nambija region in southern Zamora Chinchipe, have some experts predicting that Ecuador will soon become the biggest gold producer in Latin America. Large international companies are already vying for mining permits to over a sixth of the country.

The biggest moneymaker, though, is oil—the "black gold" that brought the Oriente into the national economy and Ecuador to the attention of the world. Natives in the Amazon once dug pits that filled with a dark, sticky substance, which they would let evaporate and use to caulk canoes and make torches. Modern drilling in the Amazon had to wait for decades after the invention of the internal combustion engine, because most of the Oriente was still inaccessible.

Major strikes in 1967 near Lago Agrio got the sticky black ball rolling. In 1971, a pipeline was built from Lago Agrio through Quito to Esmeraldas, and Ecuador began to export petroleum. One year later, Ecuador was found to have the third-largest reserves in Latin America, and a symbolic barrel of oil was paraded around the country. Ecuador joined OPEC (the Organization of Petroleum Exporting Countries) in 1974, and the economic focus of the country began to shift away from agriculture. The government's coffers filled, allowing the construction of new roads and factories. Foreign countries began to see Ecuador as a credit-worthy nation, and export earnings quintupled 1971–1975.

Oil and mining averaged 12.1 percent of Ecuador's GDP 1997–2001. But along with the economic windfall, a downside has appeared. Such a dependence on oil makes the country highly subject to fluctuations in world oil prices. Government borrowing against future revenues and increased subsidies led to economic instability in the 1980s and ran the foreign debt up to $13.6 billion by 2001, compared to the country's overall GDP of $18 billion, leaving continued production as the only hope to avoid bankruptcy. Earthquakes occasionally disrupt the pipeline, severing the source of Ecuador's lifeblood. The damage to the Amazon's ecosystems and indigenous groups by foreign oil companies is only beginning to be understood. Current reserves are estimated to be exhausted soon, forcing the underdeveloped country to further expose itself to international oil firms with the ability to search for more deposits.

Recent Turmoil

A dependence on world oil prices recently dragged Ecuador into its worst recession in almost a century. A period of economic stagnation and labor trouble in the mid-1990s followed several government privatization measures and austerity programs aimed at compensating for depressed oil prices. The damage caused by the 1997 El Niño season dug the pit deeper. When citizens began draining their bank accounts for fear that their dollar-based savings would be confiscated, the government shut down much of the banking system.

In 1998, the government radically devalued the sucre, sparking widespread demonstrations, strikes, and protests and undermining public confidence in the country's economy. By 1999, the economy had shrunk by more than 7 percent, making it one of the worst performers in Latin America. At one point, the inflation rate topped 60 percent. Foreign reserves were drained

and foreign debt mounted. President Mahuad's emergency measures, including cutting the budget, raising taxes, and declaring emergency bank holidays with limited withdrawals, only made things worse. Massive strikes and protests brought the country to a halt, as residents protested rising gas and utility prices that weren't reflected in stagnant salaries.

By freezing the sucre at 25,000 to the U.S. dollar and making the dollar Ecuador's official currency in early 2000, Mahuad hoped to halt inflation and stabilize the economy. By the end of that year, confidence in the economy was rising, along with oil prices, cocoa exports, and tourism, and inflation was slowing. While only 10–20 percent of businesses paid taxes before the crisis, the government began to crack down on tax collection to the point of shutting down establishments that are slow in paying.

The attacks in the United States of September 11, 2001, caused tourism to drop off, and it was still recovering in 2008. High oil prices in 2004, though, helped the country's economy grow by 7 percent.

The People

DEMOGRAPHY

Ecuador's 12.5 million inhabitants are packed tight. Even with large, empty tracts of Amazon rainforest, the country still has the highest population density in South America. This overcrowding situation is visibly apparent along the coast and in the Sierra, where most of the land outside of parks, reserves, and jagged mountains is built on, planted, or otherwise occupied. The country doesn't feel that crowded—you can drive for kilometers through hills and fields without seeing more than a handful of people—but the people are here, and the land strains to support them.

Ecuador's population is growing despite government attempts at family planning. It's a Catholic country to the core, so birth control is frowned upon, when it is an option at all. Large families are preferred for several reasons: more

hands to help in daily labor, a sign of the father's virility, and proof of God's favor. Women marry young and have children quickly. Death rates are decreasing, especially infant mortality, which has been cut by more than half in the last three decades.

On the other hand, there are signs of slowing growth. Family-planning efforts have begun to bear fruit—at least in the awareness of contraceptives, if not their use—and more women are working outside the home, making it more difficult to have and support a large family. The direct relationship between education and a lower birthrate is becoming apparent. Women (and men) who finish their basic schooling have fewer children than those who do not. Ecuador's annual birthrate fell from 33 per 1,000 in 1990 (versus a world average of 27.4, and second only to Bolivia in South

America) to 22 per 1,000 in 1999, giving it an overall population growth rate of 1.8 percent. Fertility rates have dropped from almost seven children per woman in the early 1960s to 2.5 in 1996.

Nonetheless, Ecuador has a steep hill to climb. The cone-shaped population curve, with 35 percent of all Ecuadorians under 15 years old in 1999, foreshadows a boom in women of child-bearing age and huge pressures on the already strained school systems and job market. The country's population is estimated to double every 27 years.

Distribution

Until the middle of the 20th century, the Sierra was Ecuador's most populated area. Between 1950 and 1974, though, a large shift to the coast in response to a land crunch in the highlands and an expanding coastal economy left the populations of the two regions roughly equal. Another countrywide shift from rural areas to the cities resulted in millions of people stranded in slums ringing urban centers. Ecuador's eastern forests still support only 3–5 percent of the country's population. Immigration into the Río Napo region was so heavy that in 1989, it was split into two provinces, Napo and Sucumbíos.

Racial Breakdown

With such a subtle spectrum of racial mixtures, numeric divisions are always off by more than a few percentage points. Mestizos—people of mixed Spanish and indigenous heritage—make up the largest sector (40–65 percent), with indigenous citizens coming in second at 20–25 percent. The remainder of Ecuadorians are Caucasians of direct Spanish descent, along with a small population of blacks descended from colonial slaves (about 500,000), and immigrants from the Middle East, Asia, Europe, and elsewhere in Latin America.

Emigration

Ecuador's recent political and economic troubles have prompted one–three million of the country's inhabitants to try their luck elsewhere. Most live in the United States, Spain, and Italy, and many of them are in those countries illegally. Lines for passports stretch around the block in Quito, and high-quality fake documents are often caught, along with their owners, at the transit sections of the Miami and Houston airports. Many of those that make it send back millions of dollars to relatives and families in Ecuador every year.

INDIGENOUS GROUPS
The Sierra

Most of Ecuador's indigenous population inhabits the northern and central Andes. About 800,000 of the **Runa,** or "the people," as the Quechua-speaking descendants of the Incas call themselves, live in tightly knit communities where kinship bonds are paramount, and everyone helps in voluntary communal work events called *mingas.* The *cabildo* (town hall), which is run by the *alcalde* (mayor), keeps things running smoothly. Artisanal work and subsistence agriculture bring in the most money, with private and community-owned plots planted with maize, barley, and potatoes. Festivals of Catholic patron saints are combined with ancient Inca harvest ceremonies.

Imbabura Province is home to the famously successful **Otavaleños,** as well as smaller groups of **Caranquis,** and **Natabuelas.** Traditional dress persists here, with different groups represented by different colors and patterns. Cotopaxi Province is home to special celebrations of Corpus Christi, along with important pilgrimages to sanctuaries in Baños and El Quinche.

Many indigenous men from Bolívar Province descend to the coast for work. Back home, the number of bands on their felt hats indicates their marital status: two means single, three married. Chimborazo Province has more highland *indígenas* than any other province, while Cañar is home to the ancient **Cañari** tribe, and Loja to the successful cattle-raising **Saraguros.**

The Coast

The **Tsachilas,** also known as the Colorados, inhabit the western foothills of the Andes near Santo Domingo de los Colorados. A handful of small communities contain about 2,000 members who make their living farming tropical crops and raising livestock. Modern clothing and hairstyles have mostly replaced the traditional dress and red hair-painting. They are famous for their knowledge of natural medicine—the governor-general is also the head *pone* (curer), who is adept in the use of medicinal plants, as well as ceremonies to drive away evil spirits, attract good fortune, and look into the future.

The tropical river country of the western Cotacachi-Cayapas Ecological Reserve is home to the **Chachis,** also called the Cayapas. Tradition holds that they came from Quito in a series of migrations under pressure from Spanish settlers. Today, the Chachis number about 4,000 and practice slash-and-burn agriculture, fishing, and hunting. Traditional open-sided, one-room homes covered by thatched roofs are built by entire communities.

About 1,600 **Awá-Kwaiker** live between the Mira and San Juan Rivers in the province of Carchi near Colombia, as well as in Imbabura province. The Awá owe their continued existence to a flagship program begun by Ecuador and Colombia in 1986, in which three protected areas, including 100,000 hectares in Ecuador, are being managed for environmental and cultural longevity.

The Oriente

Of the 17 distinct ethnic groups that lived in the Amazon before European contact, only eight are left today. Animistic religions practiced in the Oriente center around the idea of transmigration of souls from one form to another—the animal you kill today was probably a person in another life, and you may come back as a plant, so treat them all with equal respect. Shamans serve as intermediaries between the terrestrial and spiritual world, curing diseases, overseeing initiation ceremonies, and

preserving oral traditions. Crafts include basket-weaving, pottery, and colorful ornaments of wood, feathers, beads, and insect parts. Foreign demand for animal parts has encouraged some native groups to kill endangered species.

Although contacted much later than groups in the highlands and coast, Oriente tribes have had to deal with tens of thousands of settlers because of a huge push from the Ecuadorian government to populate the area, as well as the pollution and development that have accompanied oil exploration. Disease, clear-cutting, and slaughter of game animals are all part of the mess, which has encouraged the formation of strong-willed tribal groups to fight for indigenous rights.

Lowland Quechuas, or Kichwas, are the largest group of Amazonian *indígenas,* counting 30,000–40,000 members. Two distinct subgroups, the Napu (Quijos) and the Canelos, fill western Napo and northern Pastaza Provinces. Patrilineal groups of extended families called *ayllus* live in widely dispersed, permanent settlements that raise cattle and grow crops in communal *(llactas)* and family *(carutambo)* plots. Men hunt, fish, clear the land, and tend the cattle, while women weed, harvest, and care for the home *(huasi)* and garden plot *(chakra).*

Women also make the famous lowland Quechua pottery, an art that is passed down from mother to daughter. One subgroup, the Sarayacu, is especially well-known for creating striking white, red, and black images of gods such as Quilla Runa, the moon, who was banished to the sky for committing incest with his sister; and Pasu Supai Huarmi, the beautiful forest goddess with long dark hair, black lips, and teeth stained red from drinking the blood of her enemies.

The second-largest indigenous group in the Ecuadorian Amazon is actually two related tribes. United by language to each other and tribes across the border into Peru, the **Shuar-Achuar** once sent fear into the hearts of children worldwide, when they were known as the Jivaro, "savages" who shrunk the heads of their enemies. For centuries, the two closely related tribes have earned their tough reputation by protecting their rugged, isolated territory between the Pastaza and Marañón Rivers east of Cuenca. Their resistance started in 1527, when they sent Huayna Capac packing after his attempt to invade the Amazon; the Inca leader was forced to buy time with gifts as he fled. Soon after the first contact with the Spanish, the Achuar decided that the Europeans' desire for gold was a disease. After capturing the town of Logroño, they poured molten gold down the governor's throat to satisfy his thirst for the metal.

Salesian missionaries helped the Shuar-Achuar found the first ethnic federation in the Ecuadorian Amazon in 1964. Today, the groups, under the Shuar Federation and the Organization of Ecuadorian Achuar Nationalities, are among the best organized in the country. One reason for this was the ongoing border war with Peru, which pitted indigenous battalions against members of their own tribes across the border. They're still not to be trifled with: A survey of the Achuar in 1993 found that 50 percent of tribe members' male ancestors had died from gunshot blasts, usually administered by other members. This gave them one of the highest murder rates of any population group in the world and still helps explain the traditional Achuar greeting, *"Pujamik"* ("Are you living?)"

Many Shuar-Achuar live in the traditional oval house called the *jea*, separated into male *(tankamash)* and female *(ekent)* zones. Crops such as yucca, papaya, sweet potato, and pineapple fill the gardens. The ceremonial process of creating *tsantstas* (shrinking heads) has faded, although the occasional unlucky sloth is still targeted. The fine-tuned Achuar calendar predicts everything from the rainy season to the breeding time of jungle insects. It's timed around the movement of the Pleiades, which the Shuar-Achuar view as seven mythical orphans called the Musach, who fled their despotic father for the heavens. The Pastaza River serves as the axis of the traditional Shuar worldview of the earth as hemispheres of earth and sky surrounded by water.

The **Huaorani,** or Waorani, entered the headlines for their fight against oil exploration. They were one of the last groups contacted in the Ecuadorian Amazon, and they remain one of the least westernized. Most of the tribe's 1,300 or so members live in a special reserve created for them in the shadow of Yasuní National Park, from the Napo River to the Curaray River. The Huaorani have started to abandon their nomadic ways and settle in small enclaves grouped by clan.

Men once wore only a *komi,* a small cord tying the penis to the belly, but western clothing has become popular. Both sexes still stretch their earlobes with balsa plugs, called *dicago,* up to five centimeters around. The Huaorani have a reputation for defending their isolated autonomy with a fierceness equaled only perhaps by the Shuar. They speared five Summer Institute of Linguistics missionaries to death in 1956, and as recently as 1987, a Roman Catholic bishop visiting the tribe on a government-sponsored mission to open the way for the oil companies was found with 17 spears in his body.

About 1,000 **Siona-Secoya** live a seminomadic existence along Ríos Aguarico, Eno, Shushufindi, and Cuyabeno in Sucumbíos and eastern Napo Province. The two groups, related in language and history to neighboring tribes across the border in Colombia, merged during the 20th century but have recently begun to maintain distinct ethnic identities. After oil exploration began to devastate their territory, the Sionas and Secoyas sued Texaco (now ChevronTexaco) in 1993 for more than $1 billion for environmental abuses. The case was unsuccessful in U.S. courts but has entered the Ecuadorian system.

The **Cofán** are the smallest remaining group, with about 600 members left (down from 20,000 at the time of the Spanish conquest). They live along the Bermejo River in western Sucumbíos Province. Randy Borman, the son of an American missionary couple, grew up among the tribe and has become their de facto headman, leading them in their fight against oil exploration and encroachment by settlers.

Recent anthropological studies have shown that the **Zapara,** once thought extinct, have actually partially integrated with some of the **Lowland Quechuas** living in isolated parts of the central jungles. Funding from international NGOs is helping to preserve their language and culture.

Culture

RELIGION

Since the first conquistador planted a cross in honor of God and the king of Spain, Roman Catholicism has been a linchpin of Latin American culture. Although it once rivaled the government in its wealth and control of daily life, especially in education, the church's role has been moderated somewhat.

One of the most significant shifts occurred in the 1960s, when a wave of liberation theology swept through Latin America. Priests who once encouraged the poor to accept their lot in life and hope for better treatment in heaven began to urge them to improve their current situation instead. Missionaries instituted literacy campaigns and helped fight for land reforms and social justice, to the horror and opposition of the more conservative elements of society.

Aside from masses and annual festivals, the church's influence is still felt in education, social services, and important occasions such as marriage, funerals, baptisms, and *quinceañeras,* a girl's coming-out celebration on her 15th birthday.

Protestantism continues to make inroads, particularly among evangelical sects in the more remote areas of the country. Missionaries have been instrumental in contacting isolated tribes in the Amazon and recording their language and cultures—at the same time inevitably altering them. Indigenous religions are still firmly entrenched, although usually mixed with Catholicism, creating an intriguing combination of faiths. Other religions such as Mormonism (Church of Jesus Christ of Latter-day Saints), Judaism, and Baha'i have small enclaves.

LANGUAGE

Spanish is Ecuador's official tongue. Many residents of the Sierra still speak dialects of Quichua (the language of the Inca), and in the farther reaches of the Oriente, several indigenous languages are still in use. English is often spoken on the established tourist trail, as well as other European languages, albeit less frequently.

Nine times out of 10, even a modest knowledge of Spanish is enough to get by as a traveler. Ecuadorians are patient with foreigners and appreciate any efforts you make to speak their language. They also speak relatively slowly and clearly, making cities like Quito, Baños, and Cuenca popular for studying Spanish.

EDUCATION

In theory, primary schooling up to the age of 14 is free and compulsory. Many children in rural areas, however, lack the money for school supplies, without which they can't attend school. (This makes pencils a good present to hand out to begging children, if you must give something.) Secondary schools are often private and/or religious, exist only in urban centers, and focus on foreign languages. A dozen state universities along the coast and in the Sierra are free, and there's a Catholic University in Quito. Private universities and technical schools have a tighter focus.

Ecuador has the highest literacy rate in South America—compulsory schooling was introduced here even before it was in Great Britain. In 2001, Ecuador's literacy rate was estimated at 93 percent, helped by government programs in rural areas where Spanish is often secondary to indigenous languages such as Quechua. Government spending on education has increased over the last few decades, and enrollment and retention rates have followed. Still, a frighteningly small percentage of rural children complete even primary schooling—only about a third in some areas. Despite a tenfold increase in the number of professors 1960–1980, qualified teachers are still in demand. Many Ecuadorians seek higher education abroad.

ARTS AND ENTERTAINMENT
Visual Arts

Early colonial sculptors and painters remained anonymous, remembered only by their gloomy but heartfelt images of the Virgin and Gothic-style saints. Indigenous influences began to emerge with the onset of the Renaissance and baroque styles, allowing artists like Gaspar Sangurima, Manuel Chili (a.k.a. Caspicara), and Miguel de Santiago more freedom for personal expression in their works.

The Quito School, spanning the 17th and 18th centuries, typified a new realism in Ecuadorian art. Only the extreme would convince the faithful: Jesus had to suffer more than average citizens in everyday life, and Mary had to be more radiant than any living woman. The 19th century brought "popular" art to the fore. Concerned with the secular as much as the holy, it consisted of intense colors and naturalistic images of landscapes and common people. This was followed in the 20th century by the reverberations of Impressionism and Cubism.

Powerful representations of the dignity and suffering of Ecuador's original inhabitants dominated the work of Ecuadorians Eduardo Kingman (1913–1999), Camilio Egas (1889–1962), Olga Fisch (1901–1990), and Manuel Rendón (1894–1982). Oswaldo Guayasamín (1919–1999) is probably Ecuador's most famous modern artist. His tortured, distorted figures, heavily influenced by Cubism, led people to call him an "Americanista Picasso," while his landscapes of Quito and his series of mother-and-child works are among the most beautiful in Quito's museums.

A school of "naïve" painting, centered in the Tigua Valley in the central Andes, began with images painted on ceremonial drums. Now the miniature paintings are made on animal skin stretched over a wood frame. Quality varies widely, but the better ones are true works of art—vibrantly detailed depictions of everyday life in the *campo.*

Music

The haunting melodies and wistful lyrics of the Ecuadorian Andes are played by groups throughout the highlands, from brass bands to guitar trios and lone crooners on street corners. Flutes were considered holy by the Inca, who provided the original set of instruments and tunes for modern-day Andean music. The *quena,* a vertical flute once made from condor leg bones, is used to play the melody, along with panpipes such as the *rondador* and *zampoña.* Bass drums made from hollow logs or clay are used to keep the beat, with the help of various rattles and bells.

The colonial Spanish tried their best to suppress indigenous music, but in the end only succeeded in adding a host of new instruments. Relatives of the guitar include the 10-stringed *charango,* originally from Bolivia and made from armadillo shells. The *charango* is strummed lustily next to *bandolinas* (15 strings) and familiar-looking *guitarras* with six nylon strings. Violins, clarinets, accordions, harmonicas, mandolins, and brass instruments were used to join in the fun along the way, and modern influence has added electric amplifiers, microphones, and the rhythms of salsa, merengue, and rock.

Along the coast, you'll find some of the most African-influenced music on the continent. Rhythms like marimba and the Caribbean-flavored *cumbia,* from Colombia, make it almost impossible not to move your hips while listening, especially to bands along the northernmost coast and up the valley of Río Chota into the northern

Sierra. Half the fun is the attitude: During the bottle dance, young women gyrate in front of male partners with an open bottle of liquor on their heads—without spilling a drop.

Literature

Ecuadorian writers of the 20th century have focused on realistic social themes of injustice and race. Jorge Icaza's *Huasipungo* (*The Villagers*, 1934) is considered one of Ecuador's best novels, vividly portraying the hardships of everyday life in an indigenous village. *Cumandá*, written by Juan León Mera in the 19th century, is still popular with book buyers as well.

Philosopher and essayist Juan Montalvo wrote *Los Siete Tratados* and *Capitulos Que Se Le Olviadaron a Cervantes* (*Chapters Cervantes Forgot to Write*), and José Joaquín de Olmedo eulogized the struggles for independence in *The Victory of Junín* and *Song of Bolívar*. Adalberto Ortiz's *Juyungo* (1942) deals with the lives of poor blacks in Esmeraldas. Jorge Carrera Andrade, from Cuenca, is one of the country's best-known poets for his *Place of Origin*. The bilingual selection *Ten Stories from*

Ecuador, available at the Libri Mundi bookstore in Quito, gives good insight into modern Ecuadorian writers. Current writers, such as Abdon Ubidia, whose *Wolf's Dream* is available in English, or Gabriela Aleman, who was voted one of "Latin America's 40 most promising writers under 40", help keep Ecuador well-represented on bookshelves.

Festivals and Public Holidays

Sometimes it seems like you could hop around Ecuador from fiesta to fiesta for an entire year. Historical and political holidays commemorate famous generals, battles, and independence anniversaries, and they can range from nationwide parties to special days for individual towns. Religious holidays combine the solemnity of Catholic processions and services with *chicha*-for-everyone blowouts.

Many of the better festivals are worth scheduling a visit around, such as San Lorenzo's Santos Reyes and Santos Inocentes during the first week in January, or Cuenca's solemn Christmas processions. Most major holidays consist of up to a week of blowing off steam

woven baskets for sale at the Guamote market

© JULIAN SMITH

PUBLIC HOLIDAYS & MAJOR FESTIVALS

- **January 1:** New Year's Day – Six days of post-holiday festivities include dancing and fireworks.

- **January 6:** Epiphany

- **February/March (weekend closest to new moon):** Carnival weekend – celebrated with parades and abundant water throwing.

- **February 27:** Patriotism Day – Speeches, parades, flag-waving.

- **March/April (40 days after Ash Wednesday):** Easter Week – Religious parades, beginning on Palm Sunday.

- **May 1:** Labor Day – Workers' parades

- **May 24:** Battle of Pichincha – Commemorates Battle of Liberation from Spain in 1822.

- **May/June (9th Thursday after Easter):** Corpus Christi – Honors the Eucharist. Heavy indigenous influence in the Central Sierra.

- **June 24:** San Juan parades and traditional dances, especially in Otavalo.

- **June 29:** San Pablo parades, dances, and singing, with Inti Raymi, Cayambe, and Tabacundo, as well as San Pablo and San Pedro on the coast.

- **July 24:** Simón Bolívar's Birthday – Continent-wide celebration.

- **September 29:** San Miguel parades and bullfights in San Miguel, Salcedo, Chugchilan, combined with Equinox observation.

- **October 9:** Independence of Guayaquil – Parades and fireworks.

- **October 12:** Columbus Day – Celebrates the "discovery" of the New World – or in spite of it – under the name Día de la Raza (Day of the Race). Celebrated by indigenous peoples.

- **November 1:** All Saints' Day

- **November 2:** All Souls' Day – also known as Day of the Dead. Indigenous and traditional families bring food, flowers, and offerings to the graves of loved ones.

- **December 24:** Christmas Eve – midnight Misa del Gallo (Rooster's Mass).

- **December 25:** Christmas – Includes Paseo del los Niños (Children's Parade).

- **December 28:** All Fools' Day – Masquerades and clowns.

- **December 28-31:** New Year's Eve – Life-sized effigies of prominent figures and the outgoing year called Años Viejos (Old Years) are ridiculed and burned at midnight. Minor roads are blocked with revelers after 4 P.M. Travelers need lots of small change to pay the "tolls" collected by party makers.

and generally celebrating life, as well as the only acceptable occasion for cross-dressing in this hypermasculine culture. Parades march to the beat of brass bands, as entire towns dance in the street. Special food is cooked, fireworks lit, and beauty queens picked in between serious religious processions and private celebrations in homes. Hotels and restaurants often fill to overflowing and jack up their prices. During national holidays, it can be difficult to find space on a bus—or to find a bus, period. Most businesses close on the public holidays, so make reservations and exchange money beforehand.

The Catholic church's most festive season revolves around **Easter,** which technically occurs on the Sunday after the full moon of the vernal equinox. **Carnival,** in February or March, is the huge party before the 40 days of fasting and penance known as **Lent,** which begins on **Ash Wednesday. Holy Week** (Semana Santa) occurs just before Easter. **Palm Sunday** kicks things off, with parishioners bringing palm fronds or corn stalks to church. Four days later, **Holy Thursday,** similar to the Day of the Dead in November, precedes the solemn processions on **Good Friday** and elaborate nighttime masses on **Holy Saturday.** Businesses not closed already will close on Saturday. Easter

INDIGENOUS MARKET DAYS

- **Sunday:** Cajabamba, Cañar, Cayambe, Chugchilán, Cuenca, El Quinche, Guangaje, Machachi, Peguche, Pujilí, Sangolqui, Santo Domingo, Sigchos

- **Monday:** Ambato, Guantualo

- **Tuesday:** Latacunga

- **Wednesday:** Cumbe, Cusubamba, Pujilí

- **Thursday:** Cuenca, Guamote, Riobamba, Salcedo, Saquisilí, Tulcán

- **Friday:** Latacunga, Salaron

- **Saturday:** Guaranda, Latacunga, Otavalo, Peguche, Riobamba, Suscal, Zumbahua

morning mass signifies the end of the deprivations of Lent and the holiday cycle.

FOOD AND DRINK

Ecuador isn't known for gourmet food, but it does have a wide range of tasty dining options. "Traditional" Ecuadorian cuisine *(comida típica)* borrows from the country's indigenous and Spanish heritage, and often caters to a poor majority with dishes that can be described in two words: cheap and filling. For the most part, *comida típica* isn't health food, so vegetarians and the health-conscious should consider preparing their own food occasionally or heading to one of the many vegetarian restaurants or *tiendas naturistas* (natural-food stores) found throughout the country. More expensive restaurants serve just about every major world cuisine and often offer surprising quality and value.

Food from outdoor markets and supermarkets can be less expensive and better tasting, provided you have access to a kitchen or at least a knife and plate. Prepare fruits and vegetables by peeling and washing them in purified water or with a concentrated food bactericide like Vitalin, available in supermarkets. Ubiquitous *víveres* stores, found in every last town in the country, stock a little bit of everything, from simple food and drinks to batteries and machetes.

Staples

Inexpensive, carbohydrate-rich foods like rice, potatoes, plantains, yucca, and corn are staples for most of the country. Grains include wheat, barley, and native *quinua*, which was once sacred to the Inca and is now being recognized globally as an incredibly nutritious food with many of the same complete proteins as meat. Grains are popular in soups. Bread such as empanadas are often filled with meat, cheese, or vegetables.

Maíz (corn) is eaten whole or smashed and fried into tortillas. Roasted *choclo* (corn on the cob) is often served with fresh cheese and mayonnaise, and small bowls of watery *mote* (hominy) come with most meals. Sweet *humitas,* corn flour steamed in plantain leaves, are a popular afternoon snack with coffee.

Meats include *lomo* (beef, also called *res* or simply *carne,* "meat") and *chancho* (pork),

© JEAN BROWN

toasting turnovers

served *a la parilla* (roasted) or *asada* (grilled). *Chorizo* is a spicy pork sausage, and *chuletas* are pork chops. Set meals often include a *seco*, literally a "dry" stew, but often just a piece of meat served with rice and a side of vegetables. Choose between beef, *pollo* (chicken), *chivo* (goat), or *cordero* (lamb).

It's easy to remember the name of the hot pepper sauce that sits on almost every table in the country: *ají* is also the sound you'll make when you put too much of it on your food. It comes in handy to flavor up bland dishes, leading to the saying, *"Comida buena con ají es más plena; comida mala con ají resbala"* ("With *ají*, good food is better; with *ají*, bad food slips by").

When your plate is clean, treat yourself to a pan dulce (sweet bread), *helado* (ice cream), or flan (a sweet custard made with eggs). Toasted coconut sweets called *cicadas* and *bocadillos*, peanut nougat with honey, are also popular.

Specialties

Fanesca, a whole grain dish including everything from peanuts and fish to squash and onions, is eaten at Easter and is a leading contender for the Ecuadorian national dish. *Salchipapas* are the archetypal Ecuadorian snack: a plastic bag of half-cooked french fries topped by a chunk of hot dog and smothered with ketchup, mayonnaise, and mustard.

Dozens of varieties of potatoes have been grown in the Andes for centuries since they were first domesticated near Lake Titicaca between Peru and Bolivia. In some places, they're cultivated as high as 4,000 meters. Potatoes figure prominently in piping hot soups: *Caldos*, including *caldo de patas* (pig's foot soup) are thinner, whereas thick *locros* are made with potatoes, corn, and cheese. *Llapingachos* are fried potato cakes that originated in Peru.

Coastal delicacies start with fish, but don't end there. Delicious *encocadas* are seafood dishes cooked with coconut milk. Ceviche consists of seafood (often raw), onions, and coriander marinated in lemon or lime juice, served with a dish of popcorn on the side. When shrimp is used in ceviche, it's cooked

beforehand, but those made with raw *pescado* (fish) or *concha* (clams) may pose a health risk. *Patacones,* small pieces of plantain mashed flat and fried crispy, originally hail from Colombia.

Dishes made with *trucha* (trout), *pargo* (red snapper), *corvina* (white sea bass) or *atún* (tuna) are served *frito* (fried), *apanada* (breaded and fried), or *a la plancha* (filleted and baked, literally "on the board"). *Camarones al ajillo* (shrimp in garlic sauce) is popular countrywide, for good reason. Other shellfish include *cangrejo* (crab), *calamare* (squid), *ostione* (oyster), and *langosta* (lobster or jumbo shrimp).

In the Amazon, you might be treated to piranha (more bones than meat), but you'll definitely sample a huge *bagre* (freshwater catfish), which often takes two or more people to drag from the muddy rivers. The small heart of the *chonta* palm, called *palmito*, makes a tasty side dish, even though it kills the entire plant to harvest. Most are grown on farms.

Eating Out

A restaurant filled with locals usually means the food is good. These come in subcategories such as *parilladas* (steakhouses) and the ever present *chifas* (Chinese restaurants), where quality varies widely but there's always an excellent volume-to-price ratio. *Chaulafan* (fried rice) and *tallarines* (noodles) can be mixed with meat or vegetables. A set meal *(menú del día)* is the cheapest and most filling option for budget travelers in any restaurant.

Breakfast *(desayuno)* isn't big, often just enough to hold you over to lunch. For a dollar or so, you can get a continental breakfast consisting of *tostada* (toast) or simply piping fresh *pan* (bread) with *mantequilla* (butter) and *mermelada* (jam), *cafe* (coffee), and *jugo* (juice) to wash it down. It'll cost a little extra for a *desayuno Americano* (American breakfast), which adds *huevos* (eggs) served *fritos* (fried), *tibos* (soft boiled), or *revueltos* (scrambled). A bowl of fruit, yogurt, and granola is another popular breakfast option.

At lunch *(almuerzo)*, the largest meal of

the day, everyone comes home from work or school to eat and relax during the hottest part of the early afternoon. Set lunches *(almuerzos)* include a *sopa* (soup), a *segundo* (main dish, usually some sort of meat with rice), a *verde* (small side salad or vegetable), and a *postre* (dessert). Dinner *(cena)* is eaten from 8 P.M. on. A set evening meal is called a *merienda*.

A GRINGO'S GUIDE TO SOUTH AMERICAN FRUIT

- **babaco:** Resembles a skinnier green-yellow papaya and has pronounced ridges that form a star in cross-section. Soft, juicy flesh is lightly sweet with a citrus tang.

- **banana:** The wide variety includes *guineos* (familiar, long, and yellow), *magueños* (red and stubby), and *oritas* (finger bananas).

- **chirimoya:** Also known as custard apple or sweetsop, fist-sized with green, dimpled skin and sweet flesh.

- **granadilla:** Smooth, round crust six-eight centimeters in diameter, with yellow, red, or green colors and a short stem. Crack it open to enjoy the delicious insides with the disgusting texture.

- **guanabana:** Football-sized and vaguely pear-shaped, dark green outside, with stubby spines. Spongy, white flesh has lung-like consistency, almost artificially sweet.

- **mango:** Smooth and fist-sized, in yellow, orange, green colors. Ripe when soft. Peel off the skin to uncover the stringy flesh around a large seed. Sweet, tart, a delicious mess: Slice off sections of skin and eat from those.

- **maracuyá:** (passionfruit): Pale yellow baseball-sized rind is similar to granadilla, but crust is tougher and orange insides are more tangy.

- **mora:** South American native in the blackberry family, delicious source of ice cream and juices.

- **naranjilla:** Yellow-orange, bright and shiny, five-seven centimeters in diameter, with stem. Tart citrus taste is best in juice. Grown only in Ecuador and Colombia.

- **papaya:** Dark greenish-orange skin, 20-30 centimeters in diameter, 20-100 centimeters long, heavy, and slightly soft when ripe. Inside is smooth, pink-orange flesh great for *batidos*. Scoop out seeds and cut off skin to eat. Skin has peppery taste.

- **pepino:** Yellowish oval about 10 centimeters long, with dark stripes and/or spots. Sweet vegetable taste similar to cucumber. Just wash, cut open, and eat.

- **plátanos:** These green cooking plantains look like large bananas. They turn sweet when baked (served with cream), or crunchy when fried.

- **taxo:** Elongated yellow-orange fruit 10 centimeters long, with peach-like skin. Soft when ripe. Tightly packed flesh packets with orange seeds inside. Sweet and tangy, similar to maracuyá.

- **tomate del arbol:** The tree tomato is sweet, but still definitely a tomato. Good in juice.

- **tuna:** Cactus fruit (prickly pear) is two-four centimeters long and green, yellow, and red, with spine stumps. Mildly sweet.

- **uvilla:** Small, round, yellow/orange fruit comes wrapped in its own papery protection and looks like a Chinese lantern. A specialty in Chota Valley.

- **zapote:** Solid and fist-sized, with brown peach-fuzz skin and an acorn-like stem cap. Bright orange pulp surrounds four or five large seeds. Lightly sweet vegetable taste. Suck the stringy pulp off the seed, then go floss.

Drinks

Delicious *jugos* can be made from just about any type of fruit available. They're often mixed with *agua* (water) or *azúcar* (sugar) but can be ordered *puro* (pure). *Batidos* are made with milk, juice, and often sugar. Instant **coffee** (Nescafé) is surprisingly common, but more and more places in tourist areas are serving *tinto*, the real brewed stuff.

Chilean **wines** yield the best value for the money, because Ecuadorian vintages tend to be poor. Local **beers** such as Pilsner (large bottles) and Club (small bottles and cans) are ubiquitous. U.S. and European imports of both wine and beer are available but much more expensive. Microbreweries are slowly appearing, including the Turtle's Head in Quito.

Chicha is a fermented Sierra home brew made with corn, yeast, and sugar. In the Oriente, it's still made the old-fashioned way: Women chew up yucca, spit it into water, and wait a day or so for the enzymes in the saliva to start fermentation. ¡*Salud!*

Sugarcane liquor, also called *aguardiente*, *trago de caña,* or simply *trago,* is the rocket fuel of choice in most of rural Ecuador. Heated and mixed with cinnamon and sugar, the potent concoction is called *canelazo.* With honey and *naranjilla*, a relative of the tomato, it becomes an *hervida*, served hot at fiestas. In any form, it can make a grown man cry. If you get too *borracho* (drunk) the night before, you may wake up *chuchaqui*, a Quechua word meaning "hungover" that proves even the Incas knew the perils of the morning after.

Sports and Recreation

MOUNTAINEERING

There aren't many countries where you can leave the capital, climb an ice-capped volcano, and be back in your hotel the next day. In Ecuador, you can do that with 8 of the country's 10 highest peaks, including one higher than 20,000 feet, as long as you're prepared and lucky with the weather. It's a great country to gain experience in high-altitude mountaineering without the usual toll in sweat and tears.

Guiding services are numerous, and competition keeps prices down. With plenty of easy routes, several difficult ones, and even a few new routes waiting to be tackled, Ecuador is a climber's playground.

Beginning mountaineers will find the country an excellent training ground for higher, more difficult ascents elsewhere, but there's still enough challenging climbing to keep veterans busy for years. Most of the major peaks

MOUNTAIN REFUGES

Mountain	Cooking Facilities	Storage	Toilets	Sleeping Spaces
Cayambe	Yes	Yes	Yes	25
Chimborazo	Yes	Yes	Yes	45
Cotopaxi	Yes	Yes	Yes	70
Guagua Pichincha	Yes	No	Yes	10
Ilinizas	Yes	No	No	13

along the Avenue of the Volcanoes have roads leading close to or even partway up their bases, and the ascents themselves are usually straightforward. Modest technical gear will do for the big three—Chimborazo, Cotopaxi, and Cayambe—whose huts and summits overflow with climbers during busy weekends in the peak season. Other peaks aren't as welcoming. El Altar, probably the most difficult in the country, wasn't climbed until 1963. Even the "easy" ones can turn deadly in an instant. An avalanche on Easter Sunday in 1996 buried the shelter on Cotopaxi, killing 11 visitors. Never underestimate the mountains.

In the end, though, there is no substitute for **up-to-the-minute information** and the services of a **trained guide.** An overwhelming majority of climbers killed in Ecuador were climbing without a locally trained guide. Conditions and routes vary drastically from year to year, or even day to day. If you're hesitant, be sensible and hire a qualified guide—or at the very least, arm yourself with the latest reports on the mountain you plan to tackle. Remember: Many climbers fall victim to not knowing when to turn back.

Climbing Weather

Although climatic conditions differ among regions, December and January are generally the best months to climb. Coastal weather patterns influence the Western Cordillera, making June–September dry, clear, and perfect for climbing. December and January tend to have good snow conditions and weather as well. February–May are the wettest months in the Western Cordillera. Warm air from the Oriente brings heavy precipitation June–August to the Eastern Cordillera, including El Altar, Antisana, Sangay, Tungurahua, and Cayambe. This side of the Andes is driest in December and January, and occasionally passable as early as October and as late as February.

Training Climbs

Several peaks are good starters for acclimatizing and getting into shape with a minimum of special equipment or training. Pasochoa, Guagua Pichincha, Imbabura, Cotacachi, Corazón, and Atacazo can all be done in a day. Iliniza Norte requires a night in the refuge, but can often be done in hiking boots. Rumiñahui occasionally requires snow-climbing equipment and may involve spending the night on the way up, depending on whether you have your own transportation or not. Tungurahua is off limits until it stops erupting.

Equipment

Specialized mountain gear, such as hard plastic boots, crampons, rope, helmets, and ice axes, can be rented from various shops in Quito. An ice hammer, ice screws, and snow stakes are necessary for the glaciated peaks. Refuges make tents unnecessary, but bring your own sleeping pad and a 20°C sleeping bag. For warmth,

Running Water	Price (pp)	Contact
Yes	$20.15	Alta Montaña (Quito), tel. 2/225-4798
Yes	$10	Alta Montaña (Riobamba), tel. 3/294-2215
Yes	$20.15	Alta Montaña (Quito), tel. 2/225-4798
Yes	$5	Defensa Civil (Quito), tel. 2/246-9009
Yes	$10	Vladimir Gallo, tel. 2/231-4927

a down jacket can't be beat when combined with a balaclava, gloves, and thermal underwear. Waterproof outer layers, gaiters, and dark climbers' glasses with side light-guards complete the outfit.

Because snow climbing is done at night, when the snow is hardest, a headlamp is essential, as are ski poles for balance and support. All huts have stoves for cooking. Your medical kit should include a low-reading thermometer for hypothermia, glacier cream or zinc oxide for the high-altitude sun, and inflatable splints or at least Ace bandages for falls and sprains. Topographical maps are available from the Instituto Geográfico Militar in Quito.

Guides

An experienced, responsible guide can make the difference between success and failure—and life and death—in the thin air and unpredictable conditions of Ecuador's highest peaks. It's easy to underestimate the task at hand or overestimate your own abilities, twin errors that kill novice and veteran climbers alike around the world. A guide is essential for your first few ascents of snow-capped mountains.

Guided climbs typically include any necessary equipment, transportation to the base, meals in a hut, and a guide who will take you to the peak or decide if conditions merit a hasty retreat. For all that, you'll pay $170 pp and up, depending on the mountain, the season, and how many people are in your group. Pay less, and you're probably looking at less experienced guides and lots of extra costs, like equipment rental.

Always go with a licensed and qualified guide. Several organizations handle licensing, including groups set up by the tourism board, university groups, and **ASEGUIM,** the Ecuadorian Mountain Guide Association (tel. 2/222-2954, fax 2/223-4109, 3–6 P.M. Mon., Tues., Thurs., www.aseguim.org). (ASEGUIM membership had fallen and it is now being restructured to improve services.) A ratio of two or three clients per guide is recommended, although larger groups allow more of a chance to rearrange rope teams if some people need to turn back.

The most up-to-date information is available from the South American Explorers' Quito clubhouse, climbing clubs in Quito, or guides themselves. See individual city listings for local guides (nationwide operators are listed in the *Quito* chapter), and see *Suggested Reading* for recommended climbing guidebooks.

HIKING AND CAMPING

With boots, a backpack, a tent, and a sleeping bag, you're ready to explore just about any part of Ecuador's spectacular countryside. Even if all you brought is tough footwear, it's amazing how much lies within reach of a day hike, even near major cities. Longer trips can bring you to places accessible only by foot in the high Andes and remote jungle.

Parks and reserves are the most popular areas for camping, and the only ones with organized, maintained campsites. Park entrance fees range $5–20 on the mainland (the Galápagos cost $100 to enter). Information is available from many branches of the Ecuadorian National Park agency or from local guide companies.

Outside the reserves, you'll have to find your own campsites, often on private property. This is usually no problem, so long as you ask permission first. Camping near a house may discourage thieves. Avoid military zones, especially in the Oriente and along the coast, and always keep valuables close at hand. You may be able to find shelter in a *tambo,* one of many small thatched huts used by *campesinos* for emergency shelter in the Andes. (Try to secure permission from the owner beforehand.)

Bring everything you think you need from home; camping and hiking equipment in Ecuador tends toward high prices and low quality (good hiking boots like Hi-Tec and Timberland are available at various shopping centers in Quito and Guayaquil). Water purification is essential, either through a filter or iodine tablets. Even day hikers should always carry one–two liters of water, snacks, warm and waterproof layers of clothing, a flashlight, at least a minimal first-aid kit, and either a map or compass (better yet, both). Never leave for a trip without telling someone where you're going, your approximate route, and when you expect to be back; don't forget to confirm your safe return.

RAFTING AND KAYAKING

River running is starting to take off in Ecuador, and you'd be hard-pressed to find a better country for it. Experienced paddlers describe the rafting and kayaking as some of the best they've seen anywhere, waxing rhapsodic about wide, brown rivers that wind through thick, green foliage and precipitous gorges before suddenly erupting into rapids. The water is warm, the scenery is gorgeous, and the rivers are easily accessible.

Guides in Quito, Baños, Quijos Valley, and Tena can take you on day trips or weeklong expeditions. With some experience and your own equipment, you may be able to tackle many of the country's best runs on your own. The upper section of rivers in the Andes offer difficult, technical Class V runs best left to expert kayakers. As they flow downward and pick up volume, the flows become mellower, but the rapids can still be continuous, requiring sustained effort ("cardiovascular kayaking," as one paddler put it) to manage the hours of Class III and IV white water. The eastern slope of the Andes is less polluted and more remote than the western slope.

Rafting and kayaking are nascent sports in Ecuador, without any official safety or training regulations for guides and tour operators. Most of the better companies have applied international standards to the training of their guides, and trip leaders all have Wilderness Advanced First Aid qualifications. (As of 2008, a guide licensing system was being planned by the Ministry of Tourism.) When shopping around, look for experienced guides and new equipment in good condition. Ask about guides' rafting, rescue, and first-aid training, and make sure each trip has safety and first-aid equipment. Safety kayakers and on-river emergency communications are recommended on many rivers.

The more reliable companies in the country tend to be run by foreign or foreign-trained Ecuadorian guides, such as Steve Nomchong's Yacu Amu in Quito.

Rivers

The **Río Blanco** is the most frequently run in Ecuador, in part because it's so close to the capital. Many of the 100 kilometers of raftable white water in the Blanco valley can be done in a day trip, which often starts in the Toachi. After navigating the technical Class III–IV run, including the notorious El Sapo Canyon, rafters enter the lower Río Blanco to ride its big Class III rapids. The upper Río Blanco offers 47 kilometers of sustained Class III–IV rapids in four hours—probably the most white water you'll ever hit in a day. If they're still hungry for more, kayakers can take on Ríos Mindo (Class III–IV), Saloya (IV–V), Pilaton (IV–V), and the upper Toachi (IV–V), depending on the time of year and their ability.

Within a 30-minute drive of the town of El Chaco, the "white-water playground" of the **Río Quijos** offers everything from Class III white water near the Antisana Reserve to steep Class IV–V streams as it drops through narrow rock canyons. Rafters, including the world's top racers, head for the main Quijos (Class III–V), and kayakers tackle the Papallacta (V), Cosanga (III–IV), and Oyacachi (IV) tributaries.

As it runs from Puerto Libre to Lumbaquí, the upper **Río Aguarico** has large Class II–III rapids within two hours of Lago Agrio. To the south, the clear **Río Due** tributary flows off Volcán Reventador in Class III–IV rapids.

Near Tena, the **Río Napo** and its tributaries offer enough variety to let you paddle a different river every day for a week. The most popular trip in the area is the Class III Upper Napo, but the Class IV **Río Misahualli Bajo** is considered the prize. It's subject to sudden, extreme changes in water level, but still draws paddlers with its jungle setting and the hairy portage around Casanova Falls. For seekers of nonstop Class IV action, trips on the steeper and more technical Río Misahualli Alto are also offered during the rainy season, April–September.

Kayakers have a longer list of possibilities, including parts of **Ríos Misahualli, Jondachi, Anzu, Piatua** and **Hollin,** which tend to stick around Class IV–V when there's enough water to ride. The **Río Patate** is run out of Baños, but pollution, the eruption of Volcán Tungurahua, and the death of four tourists here in the late 1990s have lessened its popularity. Some expert kayakers have called the **Río Topo** (Class V) the best steep creek run in Ecuador, and they talk in hushed tones about the magnificent Namangosa Gorge of the **Río Upano** (Class IV), lined with primary rainforest and 100-meter waterfalls. Dozens of new rivers have been opened for Kayak trips the last two years on both the Western and Eastern flanks of the Andes.

When to Go

The Toachi, Blanco, and Upper Napo Rivers are run year-round. The commercial companies run the bigger jungle rivers (Quijos, Lower Misahualli, Upano) during the dry season, October–February, when air temperatures are comfortable and water levels are reasonable but still challenging. The rainy season, March–September, brings high flows and continuous white water that are more suited to expert kayakers.

Resources

In addition to local tour operators, a few foreign-based companies organize raft and kayak trips in Ecuador. **Small World Adventures** (P.O. Box 1225, Salida, CO 81201, tel. 800/585-2925, info@smallworldadventures .com, www.smallworldadventures.com) organizes trips starting at around $1,500 pp per week. It also publishes the small but detailed *Kayaker's Guide to Ecuador* ($20), available by mail order or at Crossroads hotel in Quito. For more information, visit www.kayakecuador.com.

SURFING

With 2,237 kilometers of Pacific coastline, Ecuador's western fringe offers plenty of tasty waves. Santa Elena Province has the most well-known breaks, especially the area around the tip of the Santa Elena Peninsula and north. The 2004 World Surfing Games were held at Salinas, and good breaks arrive west of Playas. Even though it lost a sizable chunk of its beach to the 1997–1998 El Niño, Montañita is still the biggest surfer hangout in the country, although it's anything but mellow. For that, head to Canoa, Mompiche, or San Mateo. Manta and Bahía de Caráquez in Manabí province also see some action, whereas Esmeraldas Province to the north is less explored.

The best months for large swells and little wind are December–May. Warm shore currents mean wetsuits aren't necessary, but footwear is a good idea to protect your feet against lava rocks and spiny creatures. A few shops rent and sell boards, but bring your own if you have one. Some breaks in Guayas province are on military land; if you're polite and show your passport, you shouldn't have a problem.

FISHING

Take some fishing tackle on your hikes into the high Sierra, and with minimal effort and luck, you'll reel in some of the rainbow trout that have been introduced throughout the highlands, with an as-yet-unknown impact on native ecosystems. In the Oriente, a simple line and hook baited with meat is enough to catch the infamous piranha, a small, bony fish with nasty chompers. It'll take a bit more to bring in a 90-kilogram *bagre* (catfish) from the muddy rivers, but the delicious meat makes it worth it. Deep-sea charters off the central coast yield black marlin, sailfish, tuna, and bonito.

BIRDING

Ecuador is one of the premier countries for birding in the world, hands down. With almost 1,600 recorded species of birds—twice as many as all of Europe—Ecuador has the highest avian diversity of any region its size on the continent. An incredible range of habitats shelter many endemic species (those found nowhere else).

It's almost futile to list the best regions in the country, because they're all great. It's almost guaranteed you'll see new species every day anywhere in the Oriente. The western slope of the Andes is especially diverse, including the area around Mindo near Quito and the northern lowlands near the Hacienda Tinalandia and the Río Palenque Science Center. Southwest Ecuador, including Podocarpus National Park, is rich in endemic and endangered species.

Many parks and lodges offer checklists for nearby species. Guides to Ecuadorian birds are listed in *Suggested Reading*. Cornell University Press published Greenfield and Ridgely's two-volume *Birds of Ecuador* in 2001. Another good source for bird books and bird-call tapes on Ecuador and the Galápagos is the **Los Angeles Audubon Society Bookstore** (7377 Santa Monica Blvd., West Hollywood, CA 90046-6694, tel. 888/522-7428 or 323/876-0685, fax 323/876-7609, books@laaudubonorg, www .laaudubon.org).

Some of the tour companies listed in the *Quito* chapter have birding tours, particularly those that operate in the Mindo area. Swede Jonas Nilsson and American Charlie Vogt run **Andean Birding** in Quito (Salazar Gómez E14-82 and Eloy Alfaro, tel./fax 2/224-4426, info@andeanbirding.com, www.andeanbirding.com). They promote responsible tourism, contributing a portion of their profits to conservation and ornithological research. Birding trips of 5–14 days start at $750 pp.

Several foreign tour companies also focus on birds. The leading agency is **Victor Emanuel Nature Tours** (2525 Wallingwood Drive, Ste. 1003, Austin, TX 78746, tel. 512/328-5221 or 800/328-8368, fax 512/328-2919, info@ventbird.com, www.ventbird.com), which offers highly regarded birding tours throughout Ecuador. As an example, the 10-day trip to the Napo Wildlife Center in the Amazon runs $2,495 pp from Quito.

Wings (1643 N. Alvernon, Ste. 105, Tucson,

AZ 85712, tel. 888/293-6443, 520/320-9868, or 520/320-9373, wings@wingsbirds.com, www.wingsbirds.com) has been leading international birding tours for almost 30 years. The company offers four tours to Ecuador, including a 15-day trip to southern Ecuador for $3,480 pp. **Field Guides, Inc.** (9433 Bee Cave Rd., Bldg. 1, Ste. 150, Austin, TX 78733, tel. 512/263-7295 or 800/728-4953, fax 512/263-0117, fieldguides@fieldguides.com, www .fieldguides.com) offers a 13-day tour of southwestern Ecuador for $3,225 pp.

JUNGLE TOURS

It's possible to find yourself in a primeval world of overwhelming richness in the Ecuadorian Amazon for surprisingly little money and effort. From community-run cabanas to luxury lodges, Ecuador's *selva* offers one of the easiest ways to experience the rainforest in South America.

As always, you get what you pay for: Smaller operators and freelance guides are more flexible and cheaper, and they may surprise you with their expertise; whereas larger, more expensive companies have the facilities, training, and staff to correct problems or solve them before they occur. A good guide, like a good schoolteacher, makes all the difference.

Most travelers book Amazon tours in Quito, in Baños, or online. These usually cost $50 pp per day and up, not counting airfare to the gateway town. Booked on the spot, guides alone cost $30 pp per day and up. Check to see if guides are licensed and speak your language, or at least one you can understand. Companies often have their own lodges in the forest, but make sure you're not taken to zoos or other "prefab" sites during your stay. A book of glowing comments from past participants may or may not be useful as an indicator of quality, but recommendations from friends or the South American Explorers are usually objective and accurate.

Some indigenous communities are starting to arrange visits themselves, which provides much-needed income by employing locals as guides and support staff. The best visits happen when villagers simply take a few minutes to chat with you about their lives and yours and show you around their homes.

Jungle lodges are the most comfortable and most expensive way to go. Guides at places such as Kapawi, La Selva, Sacha, and the Napo Wildlife Center are top-notch, and the amenities often approach those of luxury hotels back in "civilization." Packages start at $500 pp for four days/three nights and climb from there.

Naturally, the farther from human settlement you go, the more undisturbed the forest and its inhabitants are. The trade-off is how long it will take you to get there—a full day in some cases—and the expense of the luxury lodges, which are your only option that far out. If you're limited on time, you might not be able to go farther than the parts of the upper Río Napo near Tena and Misahualli. This area has been the most disturbed by development, leaving little primary forest and few mammals, but it is good for cultural visits and rafting and kayaking. Similarly, the region near Lago Agrio and Coca suffers from settlement and oil exploration. But if these are your only options, don't let it dissuade you: Even secondary jungle is beautiful.

Farther down the Napo and south into the provinces of Orellana and Pastaza lie the largest areas of completely undisturbed rainforest. Small planes give access to the most pristine jungles.

When to Go

Although it rains just about every day in the Amazon, June–August has the most precipitation, making many roads impassable. Less rain falls September–December. No matter when you go, don't make any important plans (especially connecting flights) for the first day or two after you're due back, since the vagaries of climate and airplane mechanics can easily cause delays.

What to Take

Leave your hiking boots at home—rubber boots (botas de caucho) are essential in the sodden rainforest. They're available at hardware stores in larger cities and come in handy if your tour doesn't provide them, or if you need an usually large size (U.S. size 10 and up for men). It's also essential to bring insect repellent with as high a percentage of DEET (see Health and Safety) as possible. Careful, though—a high concentration of this stuff is potent enough to melt plastic. Even the U.S. Army has conceded to the mysterious insect-repelling properties of Avon Skin-So-Soft. Hanging mosquito screens for beds (mosquiteros) are available in most jungle cities. It's now possible to buy clothing treated with insecticide.

Bring your passport for frequent military checkpoints, and make sure you have enough cash, since it's hard to find places in the Oriente to exchange travelers' checks, and the rates are bad. A cheap plastic rain poncho or even an umbrella allows more air to circulate than waterproof jackets and pants. Plastic garbage and resealable Ziploc bags will protect your things from the insidious dampness.

Activities

Every tour includes guided hikes along forest paths, ideally with an indigenous guide to spot and explain different species of plants and animals along the way. Often the sound of branches shaking overhead is your clue to troops of capuchin, squirrel, or saki monkeys moving through the treetops. (Don't let your guides hunt animals during the trip, even for food—this is illegal and hurts animal populations that have already been severely diminished.)

Canoe trips are another staple of rainforest tours. On large water stretches, you may hear the huff of pink river dolphins surfacing to breathe, or spot the dark head of a river otter. Nocturnal hikes will show you how much more active and noisy the forest is after dark. Listen for the soft, quick fluttering of bats swerving to miss your flashlight beams. Along the shore, your light might catch the iridescent eyes of caimans or, if you're very lucky, a jaguar coming down to drink.

FOREIGN TOUR COMPANIES

- **Cheeseman's Ecology Safaris** (20800 Kittredge Rd., Saratoga, CA 95070, tel. 408/867-1371 or 800/527-5330, fax 408/741-0358, info@cheesemans.com, www.cheesemans.com): Smaller, more intimate trips led by a husband-and-wife team of biology professor/wildlife photographer and birder. Two weeks in the Galápagos for $4,990 pp plus airfare.

- **Holbrook Travel, Inc.** (3540 NW 13th St., Gainesville, FL 32609, tel. 800/451-7111, travel@holbrooktravel.com, www.holbrooktravel.com): Galápagos tours, field courses, and custom tours. Ten days in the Galápagos for $2,900.

- **Journey Latin America** (12 & 13 Healthfield Terr., Chiswick, London W4 4JE, tel. 020/8747-8315, fax 020/742-1312, tours@journeylatinamerica.co.uk, www.journeylatinamerica.co.uk): Trips all over Latin America, including many in the Ecuadorian Sierra, Amazon, and Galápagos.

- **Mountain Travel-Sobek** (1266 66th St., Emeryville, CA 94608, tel. 888/687-6235 or 510/594-6000, fax 510/594-6001, info@mtsobek.com, www.mtsobek.com): Adventure tours range from Galápagos cruises to hiking the haciendas in the Sierra.

- **Myths and Mountains** (976 Tee Ct., Incline Village, NV 89451, tel. 800/670-6984, fax 775/832-4454, travel@mythsandmountains.com, www.mythsandmountains.com): Educational tourism combines classroom and hands-on study of religion, folk medicine, crafts, and natural history with fieldwork among indigenous communities in the Sierra and Oriente.

- **Nature Expeditions International** (7860 Peters Rd., Ste. F-103, Plantation, FL 33324, tel. 954/693-8852 or 800/869-0639, fax 954/693-8854, info@naturexp.com, www.naturexp.com): Educational adventure travel for older active guests. Tours of the Galápagos and the Sierra starting at $2,650 pp.

- **Wilderness Travel** (1102 9th St., Berkeley, CA 94710, tel. 510/558-2488 or 800/368-2794, fax 510/558-2489, www.wildernesstravel.com): Tours of the Sierra, including haciendas, along with visits to the Galápagos and destinations in Peru, start at around $2,700 pp.

- **Wildland Adventures** (3516 N.E. 155th St., Seattle, WA 98155-7412, tel. 206/365-0686 or 800/345-4453, fax 206/363-6615, info@wildland.com, www.wildland.com): Honored in 1994 by *Condé Nast* as one of the 18 top ecotourism travel companies in the world. Visits to La Selva, the Galápagos, and highland haciendas can be customized for families and honeymooners, starting at $1,775 pp.

A visit to an indigenous village can easily be the high point of a tour. Some tours are based around cultural encounters, but even if it's only for an afternoon, the chance to see how people eke out a living in the rainforest is not to be missed. Rest assured that they'll be as curious about you as you are about them; electronic cameras and blowguns can be equally fascinating, depending on your upbringing. You may be invited to lend a hand in the manioc field, learn how to thread a bead necklace, or get your face painted and watch a traditional dance, complete with macaw feathers and gourd rattles.

It's up to you how large a grain of salt to take it all with. Sure, they probably wouldn't be dressing up and dancing if you weren't there, and the crafts are often made solely for the tourist trade. But if you consider yourself as much a cultural ambassador as the wide-eyed tribe members in front of you, you'll realize that exploitation can be a very relative term.

OTHER RECREATION

Ecuador's tortured topography makes **cycling** an arduous but rewarding way to experience the country. Various tour companies and private operators in major cities rent bikes and organize cycling trips in the Sierra. The vertical landscapes are conducive to **paragliding,** a sport that has recently taken off in the Sierra.

Before the introduction of cars and trains, everyone who could afford it got around on **horseback.** Today, many people still do, and renting horses on your own or in a guided trip is a great way to see the countryside up close. Guided horseback tours cost approximately $25–50 for four hours.

The incredible marine life of the Galápagos makes the islands among the world's best spots for **scuba diving** and **snorkeling.** A few agencies in Puerto Ayora offer diving certification and rent snorkeling gear, an indispensable part of any island tour. Machalilla Park's Isla de la Plata is one of the few places to snorkel off the mainland.

SPECTATOR SPORTS

Soccer *(fútbol)* is a Latin American passion and Ecuador's national game. Informal matches pop up on makeshift fields in the most improbable places: at the edge of a steep drop-off in the Sierra, for instance, or on a patch of cleared jungle with bamboo goalposts in the Amazon. Players on local teams compete fiercely for the chance to rise into the big leagues and play internationally.

Ecuavolley, the local version of volleyball, gathers larger afternoon crowds than just about any other sport in the country. Another sport particular to Ecuador is *pelota de guante* (glove ball), a strange-looking game played with a rubber ball and spiked paddles of heavy wood. Some authorities say the game has its roots in the Basque regions of Spain, whereas others say it has been played in Ecuador since well before the Spanish arrived.

Even small towns have pits for **cockfights** *(pelea de gallos),* whose participants defend the sport by rationalizing that at least the losers end up in the cooking pot. Fiestas are the best times to catch **bullfights** *(corrida de toros),* which are held in *plazas de toro* (bullrings) throughout the highlands. Be warned that inexperienced local matadors often lack the skill to make a clean kill. Other more pedestrian pastimes include **basketball** *(basquet),* **golf, polo,** and **billiards** *(billares).*

ESSENTIALS
Getting There

BY AIR
A wide range of airlines offer flights into Ecuador's two international airports, located in Quito and Guayaquil. Tracking down the cheapest fare is more of a problem than finding a flight in the first place.

General Air Travel Suggestions
Make your reservations as early as possible, and *reconfirm your flight* more than once, or make sure your travel agency does it for you. Otherwise, you may find that your seat mysteriously vanishes right before your eyes.

It may be less expensive to fly to other cities in South America than directly to Ecuador, depending on where you're coming from and how much time you have to complete the trip to Ecuador overland. Caracas, Venezuela, is the cheapest city in South America to fly to from the United States, and Lima, Peru, is a travel hub for the northwestern section of South America.

Published fares to Latin America can vary much more than flights within the United States—up to 30–40 percent from airline to airline. Comparing prices among various airlines can pay off in spades. Flights to Latin America aren't cheaper if you buy them ahead of time, but planes may be full for months in advance of the peak season during the North

© JEAN BROWN

American summer and December–January. Ask about "open-jaw" flights, meaning you can fly out of a different city than you flew into, but don't consider one-way tickets unless you plan on staying more than a year.

It's usually much cheaper to book a round-trip ticket and change your return date if necessary, instead of buying a return ticket once you're in Latin America, where ticket prices are much higher. Tickets valid for 30 days, called "bulk tickets," are almost always the cheapest. Stopovers are common among Latin American airlines, which tend to drastically overbook flights—always reconfirm flights two or three days before departure and arrive at the airport early to make sure you get your seat.

The travel agency **eXito** (tel. 800/655-4053, info@exitotravel.com, www.exitotravel.com) specializes in flying to Latin America and has useful information on its website. It organizes guided tours in Ecuador, Peru, and Bolivia; sells airpasses; and can set you up with language schools in many different countries. Other good general resources for inexpensive globetrotting by plane include *The Worldwide Guide to Cheap Airfares,* by Michael McColl (Insider Publications, 1998) and *The Practical Nomad: How to Travel Around the World,* by Edward Hasbrouck (Avalon Travel Publishing, 2000).

Charters and consolidators, called "bucket shops" in the U.K., are legal discount ticket brokers who often advertise in the classifieds and travel sections of major city newspapers. In exchange for a lower price, you may have to buy your ticket quickly before the particular fare is sold out, or put up with a narrow travel window.

Student, Teacher, and Youth Fares

If you're under 26 and/or enrolled in some sort of school, you're eligible for a host of discounts. **STA Travel** (tel. 800/781-4040 or 800/385-9808, www.statravel.com) is the world's largest youth and student travel organization, with offices in 85 countries. Customers have access to worldwide emergency assistance, and

STA issues the handy **International Student Identity Card** (ISIC) for $22, which can save you a great deal on airfare, lodging, and activities in Ecuador and other countries. The ISIC carries basic accident/sickness insurance coverage, as well as access to a 24-hour travelers' assistance hotline offering legal and emergency medical services. Teachers can purchase an **International Teacher Identity Card** (ITIC), and nonstudents under 26 are still eligible for an **International Youth Travel Card** (IYTC)—both offer similar discounts and insurance for the same price. The cards are also available directly from the **International Student Travel Confederation** (www.isic.org), a worldwide network of organizations devoted to promoting travel, study, and work exchange opportunities for students, young people, and academics.

Airpasses

Ask a travel agent about the **All America Airpass,** which covers almost 30 airlines flying to and within Latin America. Choose from an unlimited combination of flights throughout the region, with fares that depend on the route and carrier. LAN (www.lan.com), an alliance of LanChile and LanPeru, is part of the **One World Visit South America Airpass,** good for travel in Argentina, Brazil, Bolivia, Chile, Colombia, Ecuador, and Peru. Other airlines participating in the One World program include American Airlines, British Airways, Iberia, and Qantas.

Courier Flights

Anyone looking for inexpensive airfare from the United States, after checking with the various discounters and student travel agencies, should consider a courier flight. Usually the cheapest flying option, these legal operations will give you a greatly discounted ticket in exchange for your baggage allotment in the belly of the plane. It's a trade-off: While tickets can go for as low as $200 round-trip, you can't take any baggage beyond what you can carry, and your stay is often limited to a few weeks (courier flights are always round-trip, and you're obligated to use the return ticket). Because most flights pass through Miami, plan on adding $20–30 in departure taxes to whatever taxes and/or membership fee the agency charges. Some courier flights also leave from New York, Los Angeles, or other major hubs. Excess personal luggage will cost extra, up to $80–100 and beyond.

A good place to start is the **International Association of Air Travel Couriers** (www .courier.org), which publishes the monthly *Shoestring Traveler* newsletter.

Baggage Restrictions
These restrictions vary by airline, usually hovering in the neighborhood of two checked bags per person, weighing 20–30 kilograms each. Fees for more luggage add up quickly. A customs duty is sometimes charged when leaving Ecuador with any checked bags beyond the first two.

Leaving Ecuador
A $41 **exit tax** is levied at Marisal Sucre International Airport in Quito (leaving from Guayaquil costs $25). The current **duty-free** allowance includes one liter of alcohol, 200 cigarettes or 50 cigars, and a "reasonable quantity" of perfume and gifts totaling no more than $200.

To and From the United States
American Airlines (tel. 800/433-7300, www .aa.com) has daily flights to Ecuador (Quito tel. 2/226-0900) from most major U.S. cities via Miami or New York. **Continental** (tel. 800/222-333, www.continental.com) shuttles its planes through Houston and New York, and some stop over in Panama. **Delta** (tel. 800/101-060, www.delta.com) has daily flights from its Atlanta hub. All these airlines offer quality service and can bring you to either Quito or Guayaquil. Newer routes are offered by **Copa** (www.copaair.com) through Panama and by **LACSA/TACA** (www.taca .com) through Costa Rica. **Aerogal** (www .aerogal.com.ec) and **Lan** (www.lan.com) are competing with new flights to Miami. Round-

trip prices vary, but expect to pay $500–800 for a round-trip ticket.

To and From Canada
Most flights from the Great White North connect through gateway cities in the United States. **Travel Cuts** (www.travelcuts.com) is Canada's discount student travel agency, with more than 60 offices throughout the country.

To and From Europe
Of the major European carriers, only **KLM** (www.klm.com) and **Iberia** (www.iberia .com) fly their own planes to Ecuador. **Air Comet** and **Air Europa** are new competition from Europe. All others make connections in Caracas, Bogotá, or the U.S.

A cutthroat discount travel market in the U.K. keeps prices low. Good reports have come in on **South American Experience** (47 Causton St., Pimlico, London SW1P 4AT, tel. 020/7976-5511, fax 020/7976-6908, info@ southamericanexperience.co.uk, www.south-americanexperience.co.uk) and **Journey Latin America** (12 & 13 Healthfield Terrace, Chiswick, London W4 4JE, tel. 020/8747-3108, fax 020/8742-1312, flights@journey-latinamerica.co.uk, www.journeylatinamerica .co.uk).

To and From Latin America
Although major airlines connect Quito and Guayaquil with most other capitals in South America, it's usually cheapest to cross borders by bus, because international flights are highly taxed. For prices and flight times, check in the various capitals for the national airline or a branch of an Ecuadorian airline in: **Argentina** (Aerolineas Argentinas), **Bolivia** (Lloyd Aero Boliviano), **Brazil** (VARIG), **Chile** (LanChile), **Colombia** (Avianca and TAME Calí), **Peru** (LanPeru and Aero Continente), and **Venezuela** (Santa Barbara).

Airlines that offer flights within Central America and the Caribbean include LACSA/ TACA in **Costa Rica,** CUBANA in **Cuba,** and COPA in **Panama.** The least expensive air route between Central and South America is via Colombia's tiny Caribbean island of San Andrés, connecting to Cartagena and beyond.

BY CAR OR MOTORCYCLE

To drive a vehicle into Ecuador, you'll need your passport, your driver's license from your home state, and full registration papers in the driver's name. If someone else holds the title, bring a notarized letter signed by the owner authorizing you to use the vehicle. As of this writing, a *libreta de passage* or *carnet de passages en douanes* was not required to enter the country, but be sure to double-check, because this requirement tends to change from year to year. Hold on to all documents you are given, so you can leave with a minimum of hassle.

Until the Pan-American Highway penetrates the jungles of the Darién Gap between Panama and Colombia, driving from Central to South America will remain impossible. Shipping companies in Panama City will transport your vehicle around the gap by ferry, and some go all the way to Ecuador.

Driving in Ecuador can be hair-raising, especially in large cities. In the countryside, road signs are infrequent or nonexistent, and gas stations are few and far between in the mountains. A four-wheel-drive vehicle is ideal, especially those that run on diesel, because diesel is the cheapest and most accessible fuel. For driving in bad weather on the coast and in the Oriente, extra tire traction is essential. Two-wheel-drive automobiles should have high clearance. When preparing your vehicle, think of Mad Max. The more problems you're able to diagnose and fix yourself, the easier life on the road will be. Take every tool and spare part you can, and know how to use them. Security is equally important: Two antitheft devices, the more visible the better, are a good idea.

BY SEA

One interesting way to get to Ecuador is on a **freighter.** Few people know that these floating warehouses usually carry passengers along with cargo, and those who have taken freighters comment on the first-class service (amenities often include TV/VCR, swimming pool, and officer's-mess dining) and the chance to stop in different countries along the way. The biggest drawbacks are the itineraries, which can change at the last minute, and being cooped up on a ship for weeks at a time. As an example, the 207-meter **CSAV Hamburgo** stops in Guayaquil on its 42-day journey from New York to Chile and back. One double cabin or three single cabins go for $3,780.

The **Travltips Cruise & Freighter Travel Association** (P.O. Box 580188, Flushing, NY 11358, tel. 800/872-8584, info@travltips .com, www.travltips.com) publishes a newsletter on worldwide freighter travel. **Freighter World Cruises** (180 South Lake Ave., Ste. 335, Pasadena, CA 91101-2655, tel. 626/449-3106 or 800/531-7774, info@freighterworld.com, www.freighterworld.com) is a freighter travel agency.

Getting Around

BY CAR OR MOTORCYCLE

Driving in Ecuador should not be taken lightly. Although many roads have been improved in recent years, the range of hazards still includes potholes big enough to swim in, ice in the upper elevations, cows on the low roads, and a frightening lack of road signs and traffic lights.

On the whole, Latin Americans drive much more aggressively than most North Americans. Vehicles spend more time passing each other than in the driving (right-hand) lane, turn signals are unheard-of, and red *pare* (stop) signs seem to elicit the same response as a matador's cape. It's even worse for pedestrians, as explained by Richard Poole in *The Inca Smiled:*

"Crossings exist but they mean nothing, except that if you put your faith in one, you are more likely to die there than anywhere else."

Police and military checkpoints, especially in the Oriente, are common. As a gringo in a rental or foreign car, you may just be waved through, but be prepared to stop and show your passport and documents. Gasoline ranges from unfiltered fuel siphoned out of drums in the Oriente to quality high-octane unleaded. With so many trucks hammering the highways, diesel is common.

Drivers should carry a driver's license from their home country, along with the title to the vehicle and a temporary import permit given at the border (if applicable). This should be enough to satisfy any official. Guard all of these documents like gold.

Roads

The Pan-American Highway (Panamericana, or usually just "Pana") is the country's main artery, running through the Andes from Tulcán to Machala. Side branches lead east and west: The Oriente can be reached from Julio Andrade, Quito, Baños, Riobamba, Guamote, Azogues, Cuenca, or Loja, and roads run to the coast from Ibarra, Quito, Aloag, Ambato, Riobamba, Latacunga, Cuenca, Alausi, Cañar Tarqui, and Loja. Road numbers exist but are seldom used or even indicated. Most secondary roads are dirt tracks. Towns of any significant size will most likely have paved roads, smaller towns may have cobbled roads, and remote villages have only dirt roads.

Safety and Security

In case of an accident, keep a level head and don't leave the scene or move anything or anyone, especially if they are damaged or hurt. Summon an ambulance or doctor if someone is injured, and wait for the police to arrive. Gather any and all relevant information about the other car and witnesses, and get a copy of the *denuncia* (report) for insurance and possible legal tangles. Be warned that drivers are often assumed guilty until proven innocent, and may be put in jail until things are sorted out.

© JEAN BROWN

Obstacles to driving around Ecuador are many and varied.

In case of a breakdown or flat, try to flag down help or a ride to the nearest repair shop (*mecánica automotriz*). Hundreds of *vulcanizadoras* (tire repair shops) line major roads, most no more than a wooden shack with an old tire hanging out front. It's fascinating to watch tires be repaired with brute force and the crudest of tools.

Try not to drive at night, if possible. Road hazards materialize out of the darkness, and thieves have been known to stop vehicles with roadblocks. To discourage thieves, never leave anything of value in a parked car; take everything with you, and leave the glove compartment open and empty.

Street parking spaces may have a self-appointed guardian, often a scruffy child who will look after your vehicle for 50 cents. You might not have much choice in the matter, so it's best to go along with it.

Car Rental

You'll have to shell out as much or more than you would back home to enjoy the freedom of driving yourself around Ecuador. Drivers must be at least 25 years old and have a credit card. A hefty deposit is charged on the card to ensure that the car is returned in one piece. Prices vary widely, but don't expect to pay much less than you would in the U.S. During the high tourist season, cars are more expensive and harder to come by without reservations.

Before driving your rental car off the lot, check the vehicle carefully inside and out, recording all dings and blemishes on the checkout form. Try to spot any missing parts, such as a radio antenna or windshield wipers; once you leave the lot, the company may hold you responsible for any lost article not noted on the form. Make sure a jack and inflated spare tire are included, and check fluid and pressure levels.

Rental agency branches overseas often have nothing in common with their namesake agencies back home, so be sure to get everything about the rental in writing, including prices, insurance, taxes, discounts, and where and when you're supposed to return the vehicle. Read the contract carefully, so you'll notice any extra charges that happen to turn up on the final bill.

Taxis

Cabs in Ecuador are cheap by most standards, seldom charging more than $1–2 for cross-town trips in the provinces. Taxi drivers are legally required to use a meter in the larger cities, although you'll often hear that *"el métro está" roto* ("the meter is broken"), or simply *"no hay"* ("there isn't one"), even if this is obviously untrue. In that case, there are two schools of thought on how to proceed. You can wait until you get to your destination before negotiating a fare, since by then you'll have some automatic bargaining leverage, or you can agree on a fare before leaving to avoid any unpleasantness. Whichever tactic you choose, it's a good idea to ask a store owner, hotel employee, or policeman for a ballpark figure to where you want to go, so you have a legitimate number to bargain with. Nights and weekend trips are always more expensive, and a small tip is appreciated.

This isn't to say that all taxi drivers are scam artists. I've gotten to the point where I'll give a driver a tip simply for *not* trying to overcharge me, and I've found that if you act like you know where you're going and how much it should cost, you'll be fine most of the time. Don't be afraid to get out and look for another taxi.

Longer trips of a half or entire day can be an economical, efficient alternative to renting a car, especially if a group of people splits the cost. You'll find that some drivers are also knowledgeable, friendly local guides.

Hitchhiking

I won't recommend it as a safe or reliable alternative to waiting for the bus, but in a pinch, hitching may be the only option. Even though *ir al dedo* ("thumbing it") means the same in Latin America as it does elsewhere, here you'll have to wave down passing cars for them to stop. Truck drivers, often bored and lonely, are a good bet. But for this reason (among many others), women alone or even in a group should not consider hitchhiking. It's common to offer a token sum for the service: Just ask *"¿Le debo algo?"* ("Do I owe you anything?") when you're dropped off.

BY BICYCLE

Crossing Ecuador by bike will put you in intimate contact with the land, people, and weather. Along the way, you'll experience well-paved highways, muddy tracks, and cobblestone roads populated by drivers whose idea of sharing the road is somewhat short of ideal.

Mountain bikes are the best for the terrain—the most important concern—even though they're heavier and less aerodynamic. Touring bikes are more delicate, but also more comfortable over long distances. Their higher speed can be a blessing until the first major pothole warps your wheel.

Toe clips, bar ends, and a big granny gear make high-altitude grinds less of an ordeal. To carry your gear, you'll need to invest in panniers (bags that attach to special frames on your bicycle) or a tow-behind trailer like the BOB Yak. Other extras to include are two water-bottle cages, a quality pump, an odometer, a rearview mirror, a U-lock, and a flashing red taillight or three. Also consider an ultrasonic dog zapper, fenders, a dust mask, and a tube or two of Slime to protect tubes against punctures.

Carry as many lightweight tools and replacement parts as you think are practical—the only ones available regularly in Ecuador are tubes, spokes, and cables. Although there are *talleres de bicicletas* (bike repair shops) in most moderate to large towns, mechanics may lack the experience to repair complicated modern mechanisms.

Safety and Security

Always yield to traffic, whether you have a choice or not. Paved shoulders are rare, so be ready for the unexpected, which could pop out in the road ahead of you at any moment: people, cars, animals, potholes, oil slicks, or debris. Buy a good, comfortable helmet and *always* wear it.

Lock both tires and the frame to a solid object every time you park, and keep a photo of the bike, its serial number, and a photocopy of your bill of sale in a safe place in case of theft. Because panniers are the most visible and accessible target for thieves, lock them securely or take them with you. Always take bicycles inside at night.

Transporting Bicycles

Most airlines will accept bicycles as checked baggage. Bike stores will usually give you a box that new bicycles come in. Take off the wheels and pedals, deflate your tires to keep them from exploding, and pad your bike well before entrusting it to the baggage handlers.

Lock your bike to the roof rack on buses, and remove anything that can be taken or shaken off. Some buses may have room inside in the back for the entire bike, but this is rare.

Resources

Tour operators in various cities offer guided trips lasting from one to several days. The bikes supplied are often high-quality imports, and support vehicles and guides take some of the burden off novice riders. The Mountaineers publish two excellent books on cycling in Latin America: *Latin America by Bike,* by Walter Sienko, and *Two Wheels and a Taxi,* by Virginia Urrutia.

BY BUS

The sight of a rattletrap old bus huffing its way uphill in a cloud of exhaust fumes inspires fond and not-so-fond nostalgia in anyone who's spent much time in Latin America. Ecuador's network of bus routes ties the country together like a spider's web, allowing the poorest *indígena* down the farthest dirt lane in the Sierra to reach the capital with relatively little expense and inconvenience. Bus travel is how most people get around here, and if you want to do any traveling on your own, you'll get to know Ecuador's buses well.

Most cities have a central *terminal terrestre* (bus terminal), or at least a park or intersection from which buses come and go. Some companies also have their own office/terminal for arrivals and departures. With so many people to carry, long-distance schedules are strict and competitive. Local schedules are looser, allowing drivers to leave early if the bus is full or circle around to gather up more people before they depart.

Comfort levels vary as widely as the buses themselves. Usually, the longer the trip, the better the bus—all the way up to sleek, ultramodern vehicles with air-conditioning, toilets, reclining seats, and hostesses. Some luxury routes depart in the evening and drive by night, saving you money on a hotel room but leaving your neck bent in strange angles by morning (an inflatable travel pillow makes life easier).

Shorter trips are handled by shoddier buses that might seem strangely familiar to North American riders (ever wonder where old school buses go to die?). Smaller *colectivos* and *busetas* make inner-city runs, and *camionetas* (pickups) and *rancheros* (wooden buses with open sides) ply rural areas. Drivers load buses to capacity, and then some—you may find yourself crammed among crates of chickens, sacks of *quinua,* and the obligatory motion-sick child.

Riding on the roof is permitted and recommended for the views and fresh air; just hold on tight, bring warm and waterproof layers for higher altitudes, and watch for low branches and wires.

Ecuadorian bus drivers seem to have the same relationship to silence that vampires do to light. Foam earplugs are worth their weight in gold to block out the constant, screeching music. Most buses have VCRs and TVs, but as far as the movie selection goes, let's just say that after a few long trips, you'll be intimately familiar with the entire Jean-Claude Van Damme oeuvre. Long-distance buses stop for meals, and vendors climb aboard in most towns selling sodas, ice cream, and snacks, but you might want to bring along something more substantial.

Occasionally, you'll have to disembark to pass a landslide or washed-out bridge on foot to another bus waiting on the other side, especially during the rainy season. Keep an eye on your bus at military checkpoints, where you have to get off and register with the authorities in person, to make sure it doesn't leave without you. Be especially careful of thieves and pickpockets in terminals and on buses. Try to avoid the cramped back seats in older buses, whose rear suspensions are often shot. To get off along the way, yell *¡pare!* (stop!), *¡a la esquina!* (at the corner!), or simply *¡gracias!* (thanks!).

Baggage

If your luggage is small enough, it's best to keep it inside the bus with you—either next to you or on your lap, not in an overhead rack. Don't let the bus company charge you for the extra seat your backpack may take up—it's their responsibility to find a place for bags, even if they have to put them on the roof. If yours does wind up on the roof, get out the protective covering and lock everything to the roof rack.

Cost

On average, buses cost about $1 per hour. Prices climb slightly higher for longer luxury rides. It's possible to buy tickets a day or so ahead of time to reserve a seat, which never

hurts. Watch for a "gringo tax," charged when buying your ticket on the bus itself—pay attention to how much everyone else is charged, or ask at the station for the correct price. Cheaper fares usually mean older, less comfortable buses. You should pay less if you're only going partway—something you may need to remind the ticket collector. Don't forget to collect your *cambio* (change), even if you have to wait until the collector has gathered enough coins from everyone else.

International Buses

A few companies run buses as far as Lima or Bogotá, but it's always less expensive to take an Ecuadorian bus to the border, cross overland, and get on a Peruvian or Colombian bus on the other side.

BY TRAIN

Latin America is a gold mine of classic railroads, and Ecuador is—or at least was—the mother lode. Steam engines half a century old still puff along a network that includes one of the most impressive pieces of railway engineering in the hemisphere south of Alausí. Sadly, Ecuador's railways hang on by the barest of threads. The iron horse that cut two-week mule journeys down to 12-hour jaunts has been swept aside by frequent landslides, courtesy of El Niño, dwindling government subsidies and passenger demand, and an improving road system. Now its chief function is to ferry foreign tourists (for many times the normal price) through scenery that remains some of the best you'll ever see from the roof of a train—all the more reason to hop aboard quick, while there's still time.

For years, the roof was considered by many travelers to be the best seat, as long as you didn't mind breathing some fumes and remembered to duck in the tight tunnels. Following the death of two Japanese tourists in 2007, railway authorities have forbidden roof riding. Vendors hop aboard at the frequent stops and roam around inside the cars selling snacks and drinks.

Routes

The rail line that once connected Quito to Guayaquil has been reduced to a short ride from Riobamba through the short but hair-raising section downhill from Alausí. This section includes the Alausí Loops, built on a 5.6 percent grade, and the famous switchbacks at the foot of the Nariz del Diablo (Devil's Nose), which took nine years to build and actually force the train to run backward for a short distance. The weekend train from Quito to the edge of Cotopaxi National Park is as good a way as any to spend a day.

BY AIR

Flights within Ecuador that originate in Quito and Guayaquil are relatively cheap and convenient; many travelers prefer them to long bus rides. Another option is to take buses on the way out, then fly back once you've gone as far as you want.

TAME, Ecuador's military-run airline, offers domestic flights, including to the Galápagos. Booking seats can be a chore: Flights are often overbooked and delays are common, though thankfully less so than outright cancellations. Reconfirmation is essential. On some flights, seats aren't even reserved, turning boarding into a first-come, first-served elbowfest.

Air prices have gone up in recent years. Tickets, payable up front and refundable only with time and patience, cost more for foreigners than for Ecuadorians to the Galápagos and the Amazon. Most flights within mainland Ecuador cost $50–90 one-way per person. It'll cost you $310–410 to get to the Galápagos, depending on the time of year and whether you fly from Quito or Guayaquil. Students under age 26 can get discounts on high-season prices—apply weekdays at the main TAME office on Colon. AEROGAL also flies to the Galapagos, landing at both Baltra or San Cristobal. Prices vary from TAME's within a couple of dollars, but proceed with caution: Tickets are not transferable between airlines, and boats will meet only one flight per day. A few smaller air companies, such as Icaro, Saereo, and Vipsa, have limited national flights. Flight schedules don't change often, but ticket prices rise a few times every year.

Visas and Officialdom

Tourist Visas

Most travelers entering Ecuador are given a stamp in their passport and a stamped **tourist card** (also called a T-3) upon entry. As of June 20, 2008 the duration of your visa is 90 days. If you're given less time, request that the duration be corrected in accordance with the presidential decree. If you overstay your visa without trying to extend it, you'll have to pay a $200 fine.

To enter Ecuador, all travelers must have a passport that is valid for more than six months from the date of entry, a return ticket, and "proof of economic means to support yourself during your stay," which is loosely defined and may just involve showing a sheaf of travelers' checks to the immigration authority. The latter two requirements are seldom invoked, and only then by a harried border official to someone who's really annoying. Hold onto your stamped visa card, because you'll need to turn it in when you leave.

Tourist visas may be extended beyond the original 90 days, often for a month at a time, at the discretion of the migration official. The upper limit is typically 180 days. Extensions beyond 90 days are handled in Quito at the Jefatura Provincial de Migración in Quito (Isla Seymour 1152 and Río Coca, tel. 2/224-7510, 8 A.M.–12:30 P.M. and 3–5 P.M. Mon.–Fri., 8 A.M.–noon and 3–6 P.M. Sat.).

Longer Stays

Other types of visas include student visas, good for up to one year and renewable; professional or government visas, good for variable periods; religious or volunteer visas, good for two years; cultural exchange or teaching visas, good for one year; and business or tourism visas, good for 90–180 days. It's hard to get a visa in Ecuador, so you're much better off dealing with this at home. Ecuadorian law says that a tourist visa cannot be changed to any other type of visa inside the country, so one option is to come with a six-month business visa (12-IX), then change it.

To obtain a visa, call the Ecuadorian consulate nearest you to check on what you'll need (everything from bank statements to negative HIV tests have been required in the past), and follow the instructions. Start this process early, because it may take a while. For initial questions, check with the U.S. Passport and Information Service (tel. 800/225-8472). If you're pressed for time, try an expeditor service, such as **A Briggs Passport and Visa Expeditors** (1054 31st St. NW #270, Washington, DC 20007, tel. 800/806-0581, fax 202/464-3006, www.abriggs.com) or **Travisa** (1731 21st St. NW, Washington, DC 20009, tel. 202/463-6166 or 800/222-2589, fax 202/293-1112, www.travisa.com).

If you're staying longer than six months, you'll need a **censo,** the temporary residence card that can save you lots of money entering Ecuador's national parks (the Galápagos are $25 with a *censo,* as opposed to $100 for foreigners). To get one, register your visa in Quito at the **Dirección de Extranjería** (6 de Diciembre and San Ignacio) and pay the $10 fee at the bank indicated. Then get your *censo* on the ground floor of the **Dirección Nacional de Migración** (Amazonas and Repùblica). If the visa is for more than one year of residence, a *cedula* is then issued at *Registro Civil*

(Amazonas and Naciones Unidos). There is a 30-day time limit in which this must be completed; otherwise there will be a fine of $200.

Because visa rules change often, including which office handles what, it's a good idea to check in at the South American Explorers' Quito clubhouse (corner of Plaza and Washington, tel. 2/722-5228, 9 A.M.–5 P.M. Mon.–Fri.) for a recent update.

Leaving Ecuador

Tourists with 90-day visa cards simply turn them in at the border and get an exit stamp in their passports. Those with longer visas must present their *censo* and their passports at the airport when leaving.

Customs

It's prohibited to bring firearms, ammunitions, or illegal drugs into Ecuador. Importing plants or animals requires prior permission from the Ministerio de Agricultura y Ganadera (Ministry of Agriculture and Livestock). Exportation of any kind of plant or animal product or archaeological artifact is forbidden. Check with your country's customs office for details of what you can bring home legally.

Border Towns

The major crossing points into and out of Ecuador are at **Huaquillas, Macará,** and **Zumba** on the Peruvian border, and **Tulcán** on the Colombian border. Two newer crossings into Peru are now open daily at **Amaluza** and **Zapotillo.** It's also possible to cross at other points along the border, such as in the Oriente at Nuevo Rocafuerte, and Morona on the Rio Santiago, but there is little regular traffic as of yet.

Conduct and Customs

Visitors from North America and Europe will sense it right away, although perhaps unconsciously at first: that slight undercurrent of looseness lying just beneath the surface in Latin American culture. It's the feeling of *"así es la vida"* ("that's life"), which emphasizes going with the flow, even if things aren't always on your side—in contrast with the stubborn gringo reliance on rules, regulations, and schedules.

Punctuality isn't nearly as ingrained here as it is in northern cultures. Showing up hours late for appointments is common (although this is changing—see the sidebar *Sorry I'm Late . . .*), and business hours owe more to the whim of the proprietor than the numbers written in the window.

Bureaucracy, usually in the form of the arbitrary enforcement of rules by a low-ranking official, is the biggest downside of South American culture. Even Edward Whymper noticed it in the 19th century: "It is indeed true that nearly everything may be obtained in Ecuador. It is also true that we often had great difficulty obtaining anything." Richard Poole delivers a gratifying rant on the problem in *The Inca Smiled,* describing how Ecuador is "divided into two clearly defined groups, those with authority and those without, and the former instinctively abuse the latter.... The tyrant behind the counter can only be appeased. He cannot be reasoned with, much less challenged."

Blowing your top won't help—in fact, it will often make things worse. The best strategy is to play along, but be persistent. If you find yourself up against a wall, smile and say, "Well, what can we do about this?" *("¡Pues, qué podemos hacer?"),* and you might be surprised to find that things shift in your favor.

Politeness

Latin Americans are much more physical in day-to-day interactions than their northern

SORRY I'M LATE . . .

In late 2003, Ecuador embarked on a great national quest of introspection and self-improvement. At noon on October 1, Jefferson Pérez, the country's only Olympic medalist, led his compatriots to synchronize their watches to inaugurate a **national punctuality campaign** aimed at getting people to show up on time.

In the era of split-second business decisions and just-in-time manufacturing, a *mañana* (tomorrow) attitude just doesn't cut it. The civic group behind the campaign estimated that a tendency to tardiness costs Ecuador some $724 million per year in lost labor. Other studies put that figure in the billions.

The government has distributed posters to offices and schools urging people to show up on time, and has recommended that dawdlers be barred from meetings. Signs have appeared across the country saying, "Do not enter: the meeting began on time."

It's going to be an uphill battle. Half of all public events in Ecuador don't start on time, and two-thirds of the appointments at the Ministry of Education are said to start late. Keeping people waiting is an easy way for bureaucrats and businesspeople to assert their power, and Latin American culture is notoriously averse to strict timekeeping.

More than anything, change will have to be a collective effort. If more people start showing up at the right time, then foot-draggers will become as out of place as dinner guests showing up exactly on time are today. But it's going to be a tough transition: when a spokesman went on TV to announce President Lucio Gutiérrez's support for the program, he arrived at the studio several minutes late.

neighbors. Although public pawing is not acceptable, you'll soon get used to the *abrazo,* a platonic hug and peck on the cheek when being introduced to a female. (Men forgo the kiss when meeting other men.) Even complete strangers are always greeted with *"Hola, como está?"* ("Hello, how's it going?") or *"Buenos días/ tardes/noches"* ("Good day/afternoon/night") when passed on the street. Latin American politeness is very nonconfrontational, occasionally to the point of suppressing personal feelings: You'll rarely see one Ecuadorian ask another to stop smoking, turn down a radio, or control a rampant child.

Hospitality

Henri Michaux said it best: "The Ecuadorian is not simply hospitable in an unheard-of style. He actually enjoys giving. On a boat, the Ecuadorian will treat the whole ship to a drink. And it hurts him very much not to be able to invite by radio all the ships going in his direction to draw up alongside." The trick for foreigners lies in determining when the invitation is "real" or firm, in a non-Latin sense. Ecuadorians will ask you left and right to come to their homes, meet their families, and stay for as long as you like—and if you show up, they'll make good on the offer. But this doesn't always mean they expect you to show up, which may lead to slight social strain when offers are taken too literally. You'll have to suss out and set your own limits for accepting hospitality, and try to think of the offers as polite rather than false.

Gender

Latin American culture is very sexually polarized. Men tend to be the traditional heads of the household, and women manage the home and raise the children. Recently, though, Latin American women have begun to assert themselves and claim new freedoms in work and daily life.

Feminism came late to Ecuador: In 1979, president Jaime Roldos's wife, Martha, was the first prominent Ecuadorian feminist and the first woman to serve in the country's cabinet. The challenges women face are clear: Female beauty is overwhelmingly emphasized, women receive lower salaries than men and none at all for housework, and male dominance runs through society from top to bottom. Women find themselves in a split position in Latin society—both elevated on a platform as the saintly wife/mother figure, and looked down upon and protected as the "weaker sex." Equal rights, recognition of the value of running the household, and advancements in family planning and reproductive choice are among the many goals of feminism.

The culprit? Machismo, which manifests itself in ways ranging from subtle to blatant. Whistles and catcalls are seen as harmless, a double standard of marital fidelity accepts sneaking around by men but condemns it for women, and spousal abuse is often swept under the carpet. Men find themselves having to prove their manhood in their posturing, driving, and womanizing.

Dealing with machismo as a foreigner can be tricky. Realize that it's a part of the culture, but don't let it pass unchallenged. Women may be frustrated that silence is often the best weapon, whereas men will find that confronting another man about his sexist worldview may provoke a thoughtful response.

Tips for Travelers

OPPORTUNITIES FOR STUDY AND EMPLOYMENT
Language and Cultural Studies

Intensive Spanish instruction attracts students of all ages to Ecuador for anywhere from a week to a year. A host of schools, both foreign and national, offer language courses and programs in ecology, literature, and Latin American culture. Optional excursions to the Galápagos, Amazon, or out into the Andes are part of some curricula.

Ask beforehand if insurance and airfare are included in the price. Are there any prerequisites, such as a minimum grade point average or previous Spanish instruction? How large are the classes? What's the refund policy? Can you transfer credit to a college back home? Past participants are your best source for first-hand recommendations; most programs will supply you with a list.

Volunteering in Ecuador

Conservation and cultural organizations, like Fundación Golondrinas, Jatun Sacha, and the Charles Darwin Foundation, accept volunteers for various lengths of time. Duties vary from the mundane to the fascinating—before you sign up, try to get a description of what you'll be doing. You may be asked to contribute some money toward room and board. The South American Explorers organization has information on volunteer programs in and out of Quito.

Volunteers for Peace (1034 Tiffany Rd., Belmont, VT 05730-0202, tel. 802/259-2759, fax 802/259-2922, vfp@vfp.org, www.vfp.org) runs 2,800 low-cost volunteer programs in more than 90 countries, including Ecuador. The group's *International Workcamp Directory* is available on the organization's website. **JustAct** (3307 26th St., San Francisco, CA 94110, tel. 415/431-4204, fax 415/431-5953, info@justact.org, www.justact.org) promotes global justice by linking students and youth in the United States to organizations and grassroots movements working for sustainable and self-reliant communities around the world. **WWOOF** (www.wwoof.org) is an international organization encouraging the exchange of work for room and board on organic farms around the world.

Working in Ecuador

Teaching English is the most common job for foreigners. Regardless of your position, you'll need a work visa (see *Visas and Officialdom*). Your employer should be able to arrange this, ideally before you enter the country. *International Educator* (P.O. Box 513, Cummaquid, MA 02637, tel. 508/362-1414, fax 508/362-1411, tie@tieonline.com, www.tieonline.com) lists teaching jobs worldwide. The paper is published five times a year for $35.

Project volunteers put their machetes away at the end of the day.

© JEAN BROWN

TEACHING ENGLISH IN QUITO

If you're interested in supporting yourself during an extended stay in Ecuador, teaching your native language is one of the surest ways to do it. Demand for teachers is high, so getting a position can be easier than you think. It's also possible to receive Spanish instruction in exchange for teaching English: check the bulletin boards at the South American Explorers' Quito clubhouse and the Catholic University language department in Quito. (There are also opportunities to teach French, German, Dutch, and Chinese at international schools associated with these respective countries.)

Requirements vary from school to school. Teachers who can speak Spanish are usually preferred, and you may be asked to provide an English teaching certificate – Teaching English as a Foreign Language (TEFL) or Cambridge RSA – or sign an extended contract (and show up dependably). A CV or résumé listing any previous teaching experience is standard, as is a personal interview. The pay is enough to live on modestly – but some teachers have reported problems getting paid, so it's a good idea to go with a reliable, recommended institute, like those listed below.

Teacher training ranges from plenty to next to nothing, and contracts can be on a day-to-day basis or last six months or more. Private lessons offer higher wages and more flexible hours.

LANGUAGE INSTITUTES

Centro de Educación Continua of the Escuela Politecnica Nacional (Reina Victoria and Baquedaño, Ed. Araucaria, tel. 2/250-0068, fax 2/235-3605, guytobar@access.net.ec): Requires B.A. degree or equivalent; experience preferred.

The Experiment in International Living (Hernando de la Cruz N31-120 and Mariana de Jesús, tel. 2/255-1937, fax 2/223-3528, eilecua@access.net.ec): Teaching English as a Foreign Language (TESL) degree pre-ferred, but inexperienced conversation teachers OK.

Fulbright Commission (Almagro 961 and Colón, tel. 2/256-3095, fax 2/250-8149, fulbright@fulbright.org.ec): Native speakers with TESL certification and experience preferred.

Harvard (10 de Agosto and Riofrio, tel. 2/256-8870, fax 2/290-1878)

Princeton International Language Institute (Colón 1133 and Amazonas, tel. 2/252-8291, tel./fax 2/254-7944, princetonec@hotmail.com): Native speakers with TESL preferred.

South American Spanish Institute (Amazonas N-2659 and Santa María, tel. 2/254-4715, fax 2/222-6348, info@southamerican.edu.ec): Six-month or one-year contracts offered.

HIGH SCHOOLS

These international or bilingual schools offer extended contracts and may require teachers to instruct in other subjects besides languages.

Academia Cotopaxi (de las Higuerrillas and de las Alondras/Monteserrin, tel. 2/246-7411, fax 2/244-5195, cotopaxi@cotopaxi.k12.ec): Teaching certificate, B.A. degree, and three years' international teaching experience required.

Colegio Albert Einstein (Diego de Contreras km 4.5, tel. 2/247-7901, tel./fax 2/247-0144, einstein@einstein.k12.ec): September–July contract.

Colegio Americano de Quito (Manuel Benigo Cueva N80-190, Urb. Carcelén, tel. 2/247-2974, fax 2/247-2972, dirgeneral@fcaq.k12.ec).

Colegio Menor de la Universidad de San Francisco (Cumbayá via santa y net, tel. 2/289-3391, mcalderon@mail.cmsfq.edu.ec): Bachelor's and master's degrees required.

ACCOMMODATIONS

The entire spectrum of accommodations is represented in Ecuador, from luxury international hotels to places you'd hesitate to use as storage space. Here are a few tips to have the best stay possible.

- Prices vary depending on the season and the whim of the owner, so bargaining is possible in less expensive hotels.

- Two people can share one *cama matrimonial* ("marriage bed").

- A 22 percent tax is levied in more expensive hotels (added into prices when applicable in this book), along with a 10–20 percent surcharge for paying by credit card.

- Electric showers in less expensive places can be dangerous if improperly wired; *don't* turn them on or off when you're soaking wet. Remember that *C* stands for *caliente* (hot) and *F* means *frio* (cold).

- The plumbing in Ecuador can't handle toilet paper, so be sure to throw it in the garbage instead of flushing it down the toilet.

- Motel rooms are always available by the hour—wink wink, nudge nudge.

- If you find yourself stuck in the middle of nowhere without camping gear, you might be able to wrangle a spare room in a private house, school building, community center, or jail. Police officers *(policía)*, the local mayor *(alcalde)*, the town headman *(jefe)*, and the village priest *(cura)* are good people to ask. Inquire around for *"la posada,"* which can mean simply a place to sleep.

Homestays

One of the best ways to get under the skin of a country is by staying with a local family. By stepping outside the normal world of hotels, restaurants, and hanging out with fellow travelers, you can gain firsthand knowledge of another culture, as well as its language.

The largest and most experienced international homestay network is **Servas** (11 John St., Room 706, New York, NY 10038, tel. 212/267-0252, fax 212/267-0292, helpdesk@usservas.org, www.servas.org), which has 14,000 members in 130 countries. Travelers must be at least 18 years old and pay a yearly membership fee. Once you're interviewed and accepted, you are loaned lists of hosts who have agreed to provide up to two nights' room and board with prior notice. Servas has members throughout South America, including three in Ecuador, and also gives you the option of becoming a host for foreign travelers at home.

Many Spanish schools in Ecuador set up students with local families. In Quito, check with **South American Explorers** (Jorge Washington 311 and Plaza, tel./fax 2/222-5228, explorer@saec.org.ec, www.saexplorers .org) for a recent list of families offering homestay arrangements.

Haciendas

Throughout the Sierra, you'll find these relics of former huge estates that often date back to the 16th and 17th centuries, when the king of Spain handed out parcels as big as the thousands of hectares. Recent land reforms have broken up most of the largest estates, which once served as social, political, and commercial centers for entire provinces. Nowadays, flower farms, organic gardens, and computer technology have infiltrated the sprawling grounds, but legions of caretakers and housekeepers are still needed to keep everything running smoothly.

If you can afford it, staying in a hacienda is an experience not to be missed. The settings are invariably the most beautiful around, and accommodations and service are of the highest quality. Home-cooked meals by a roaring fire, thick white-washed walls hung with antique portraits and worn leather saddles, and lush flower gardens all create the feeling of stepping back in time. Hiking, horseback riding, and shopping for locally made crafts are among the many recreational opportunities.

Reservations can be made directly through the haciendas or through tourism agencies, such as Safari Tours or Metropolitan Touring in Quito. Ride Andes (tel. 2/223-6237 or 9/973-8221, rideandes@rideandes.com, www.rideandes.com) will take you from hacienda to hacienda on horseback. Also check out Ecuador Explorer's hacienda listings at www.ecuadorexplorer.com/html/haciendas.html.

ACCESS FOR DISABLED TRAVELERS

Travelers with disabilities shouldn't expect many concessions. Wheelchair ramps are rare on buildings and sidewalks, Braille is nonexistent, and seeing-eye dogs need at least a rabies vaccine to enter the country. For more information, contact **Mobility International, USA** (45 W. Broadway, Ste. 202, Eugene, OR 97401, TTY tel. 514/343-1284, fax 514/343-6812, info@miusa.org, www.miusa.org) and the online **Global Access Disabled Traveler Network** (www.globalaccessnews.com).

Travelers with disabilities have a range of options for travel-planning assistance, including the **Information Center for Individuals with Disabilities** (P.O. Box 750119, Arlington Heights, MA 02475, fax 781/860-0673, contact@disability.net, www.disability.net) and the **Access-Able Travel Source** (www.access-able.com). Health escorts can be arranged through **Travel Care Companions** (Box 21, Site 9, RR1, Calahoo, Alberta, Canada T0G 0J0, tel. 888/458-5801 or 780/458-2023, tc@travelcarecompanions.com, www.travelcarecompanions.com).

WOMEN TRAVELING ALONE

Whistles, comments, honks, and catcalls are an ingrained part of Latin American culture. Thanks to pop culture stereotypes, foreign women—especially North Americans and *especially* blondes—get the most attention. Follow the lead of Ecuadorian women and simply

ignore it. After all, a response is what they're after—the more vehement, the better.

Physical boundaries are a different story. Pinches and outright grabs should be dealt with immediately and unequivocally. Just make sure there are other people around. Also on that note: Don't go anywhere alone at night.

This doesn't mean that women can't travel alone; many do with no problems at all, despite repeated disbelief from Ecuadorians. You just need to take extra care.

TRAVELING WITH CHILDREN

Children are considered life's greatest reward in Latin America, so parents traveling with children will enjoy compliments and assistance across the continent. Products for children and babies are available in department stores in larger cities.

GAY AND LESBIAN TRAVELERS

Technically illegal and condemned by traditional Catholic edicts, homosexuality exists far underground in Ecuador. Attitudes have begun to change over the years—the August 1998 constitution recognized "the equality of all before the law without discrimination against age, sex, ethnic origin, color, religion, political affiliation, economic position, sexual orientation, state of health, incapacity, or difference of any kind"—but on the whole, Latin American society is anything but welcoming to the gay and lesbian lifestyle. Gay and lesbian travelers are advised to keep a low profile.

The only real way to join the community is to meet someone already inside. The few gay bars and discos in Quito and Guayaquil are often members-only. Stop by the **Gay Guide to Quito & Ecuador** (http://gayquitoec.tripod.com) for a listing of gay/lesbian clubs and gay-friendly businesses in Quito and Guayaquil.

SENIOR TRAVELERS

Age is respected in Ecuador, but there aren't any senior associations or travel organizations in the country. Make sure you can handle the physical demands of tours and lodges (some of the Galápagos hikes are steep and strenuous), and bring along a printed medical history and enough prescription medications for the entire trip, plus extra.

The **American Association of Retired Persons** (tel. 888/687-2277, www.aarp.org) offers a Purchase Privilege Program for discounts on airfares, car rentals, and hotels. **ElderHostel** (tel. 877/426-8056, www.elderhostel.org) is a 25-year-old nonprofit that offers educational adventures for adults older than 55.

Health and Safety

PREPARATION

Travelers to tropical (i.e., northern) South America must take a number of specific health concerns into consideration. There are diseases here you've probably never heard of, although most are rare and/or preventable. Don't worry, though—with proper precautions, you shouldn't have any problems.

Major hospitals and those attached to universities in your home country usually have **traveler's clinics** or **occupational medicine clinics** that can recommend and administer pre-travel shots. The *International Travel Health Guide* (see *Suggested Reading* in the *Resources* chapter) has a list of clinics in the United States. Also check with your local Department of Public Health for an **immunization clinic.** If you're sufficiently informed, you might just be able to walk in with a list of the shots and pills you want.

Recommended Vaccinations

Vaccinations are recorded on a yellow **International Certificate of Vaccination,** which you should bring with you to Ecuador. You may be asked to show this document to prove your immunizations, especially in the case of a yellow fever outbreak. Take care of these vaccinations as soon as possible, since some shot series take a few months to take effect. Your doctor should know which ones not to mix with others (especially immune globulin), so as not to decrease their effectiveness.

See your doctor at least four–six weeks before you leave to allow time for immunizations to take effect.

Viral hepatitis A: The new Havrix vaccine confers complete protection for 20 years after two shots spaced 6–12 months apart. Otherwise, immune globulin (IG) provides short-term protection.

Typhoid fever: Recommended if you plan on venturing into rural areas, this can be administered as a live oral vaccine or through two injections taken at least four weeks apart.

Yellow fever: This vaccination is necessary when entering Ecuador from Peru or Colombia (both officially infected countries), but a good idea in any case.

Routine immunizations: Any trip is a good time to update the following: diptheria-tetanus, influenza, measles, mumps, poliomyelitis, and pneumococcus.

Other Concerns

Travelers who plan to spend extended periods in remote areas and come into frequent contact with local people and/or animals should also consider vaccines against **rabies** and **hepatitis B.** Although **cholera** is a problem, the vaccine against it isn't recommended, because it's only partially effective, short-lived, and possibly dangerous.

Try to get a **dental checkup** before you leave on a long trip, stock up on any prescription medication you require (including oral contraceptives), and bring copies of prescriptions for eyewear and birth control pills (just in case).

WHILE ON THE ROAD

The best you can do while traveling—besides taking any prescriptions you brought along—is to wash your hands often, pay attention to what you eat and drink, and be on the lookout for any unusual symptoms. In the end, nothing can take the place of qualified medical attention, both at home and in Ecuador.

Sunburn

It's easy to forget the amazing power of the equatorial sun when you're shivering in the Andes, but unexposed parts of your body can fry just as badly under a sweater as under a swimsuit. Sunscreen (SPF 30 and above), lip balm, and proper clothing—especially a wide-brimmed hat—will help protect you.

Diseases from Food and Water

If you're going to get sick while traveling, it will be through contaminated water and/or food. Minimize your chances by remembering this mantra: Cook it, peel it, wash it, or forget it. Get in the habit of washing your hands at least two or three times a day, preferably before every meal. Be careful with salads—some restaurants wash their vegetables in purified or chemically treated water and will definitely advertise this. Otherwise, steer clear. Undercooked eggs and meats are a health risk.

Fruit juices are occasionally mixed with unpurified water or unpasteurized milk, and ice cubes can be a risk as well (ask for drinks *"sin hielo,"* "without ice"). Even though it's handy and often tasty, food from street vendors should only be eaten at your own risk. Purify water with a camping filter, by boiling (a few minutes is sufficient), or with a chemical treatment. Iodine tablets like Potable Aqua or five drops of tincture of iodine per gallon will kill any bacteria in 10 minutes.

No one is safe from **traveler's diarrhea,** although most cases are mild. Bloody stool or anything beyond mild diarrhea, gas, cramps, nausea, or fever may be cholera or dysentery, which require medical attention. Treat a low-grade case of the runs with Imodium A-D or Pepto-Bismol, which can also be used as a preventive measure in modest doses (two tablets twice a day). Drink plenty of noncaffeinated fluids like fruit juice and ginger ale. More

serious cases may require antibiotics and an oral rehydration solution (one teaspoon salt and two–three tablespoons sugar or honey in a liter of water will work).

Cholera is an intestinal infection caused by bacteria. Luckily, the risk is low and symptoms are often mild. About 5 percent of sufferers lose enough liquids through severe diarrhea and vomiting to require medical attention. Otherwise, a rehydration mixture should do the trick.

Typhoid fever is also a bacterial infection courtesy of *Salmonella typhi.* Early symptoms resemble the flu: fever, chills, aches, and loss of appetite. Diarrhea, constipation, and rashes are less common. Seek medical attention, since a quarter of all cases may be fatal.

Hepatitis A, which attacks the liver, is transmitted by contaminated food or water or contact with an infected person. It's the most common type of hepatitis and present in Ecuador's rural areas. Symptoms appear two-six weeks after exposure and include nausea, vomiting, aches, fatigue, fever, loss of appetite, dark urine, and jaundice (a yellowing of the whites of the eyes). Once you catch it, there's no treatment; the best treatment is resting, drinking a lot of fluids, and avoiding fats, alcohol, and unnecessary medications.

Diseases from Insects

You can triumph in the eternal fight against bug bites by taking a few simple precautions. Repellents include DEET (diethylmethyltoluamide), permethrin (sprayed on clothing), and pyrethrin (sprayed on surfaces). Higher percentages of the chemicals on a small area are more effective, but also more caustic to humans. Camping stores and mail-order catalogs carry mosquito netting to cover beds. It's also available in Ecuador at fabric stores.

Malaria gets its name from the Italian for "bad air," since it was once thought to be spread by infected winds. Now we know it's caused by the *Plasmodium* parasite, which is spread by the bite of the *Anopheles* mosquito, but that doesn't keep the *P. falciparum* strain from killing three million people worldwide each year. Fortunately for travelers to Ecuador, the nonlethal *P. vivax* strain is much more common—found in up to 95 percent of the insects in some areas—and 9 out of 10 malaria cases occur in sub-Saharan Africa. Ecuador's Oriente and northern coast have the highest number of cases, but malaria is a risk anywhere below 1,500 meters. Symptoms don't necessarily appear right away, but they are unmistakable: dark urine and alternating cycles of chills and fever. A prophylactic drug regimen suppresses the symptoms, but nothing can kill the parasites but your own immune system.

Yellow fever is also spread by mosquitoes. Symptoms include jaundice, fever, headaches, chills, and vomiting. No treatment exists, but the disease is rarely fatal. Even so, seek medical attention.

Dengue fever, transmitted by the *Aedes* mosquito, is most common in coastal urban areas. Flulike symptoms, such as nausea, bad headaches, joint pain, and sudden high fever, are often misdiagnosed as other tropical diseases. Severe cases leading to shock syndrome or hemorrhagic fever are rare. The only treatments known so far are rest, fluids, and fever-reducing medications. Medical attention is necessary, if only for diagnosis.

Chagas' disease is caused by the *Typanosoma cruzi* parasite found in the bite of the nocturnal reduviid, or "kissing" bug, common to rural coastal regions. The insect usually bites near the mouth (hence the name) after dropping from the ceiling. Only a small percentage of victims show symptoms beyond a hard swelling around the bite area. Even if you escape the fever, swollen lymph nodes, vomiting, diarrhea, and rash, you're not in the clear yet. Over decades, the untreated disease attacks the heart, making it one of the leading causes of heart disease in Latin America. Apply insect repellent and use netting when camping along the coast, especially inside adobe buildings with thatched roofs. Seek medical attention if symptoms develop; a vaccine is in the works.

Leishmaniasis arrives aboard the tiny *Phlebotomus* sandfly. One of the world's most common parasitic diseases, it occurs throughout Ecuador. Small, itching red bites develop into skin lesions that affect the mucous membranes. Once the disease spreads to the internal organs, death follows quickly. Netting must be extra-fine (more than 10 holes per square centimeter) to keep these buggers out. Keep an eye on any particularly annoying insect bites, and see a doctor if they don't heal.

Onchocerciasis, also known as "river blindness," occurs near rivers in Esmeraldas province. Tiny roundworms spread by the bite of a black fly cause itching, rash, and inflammation of the eye. Less than 10 percent of cases result in blindness. No vaccine is available, but a simple complete blood count (CBC) test reveals the disease.

Other Diseases

Human Immunodeficiency Virus (HIV) is transmitted by direct contact with the bodily fluids of an infected person, most often through blood transfusions, intravenous injections, or sexual contact. It's a serious problem in Latin America, but easy to prevent: Do not have unprotected sex, share needles, or accept a blood transfusion that isn't 100 percent safe. To be extra careful, take and use your own syringes. There is no cure yet for HIV or the AIDS virus. Other types of **sexually transmitted diseases (STDs),** such as chlamydia, gonorrhea, syphilis, and herpes, reveal themselves through various types of genital pain, discharge, and sores. These are even more common than HIV—another reason to practice safe sex. Some can be treated by antibiotics.

Hepatitis B, like its cousin A, is a viral infection of the liver, but it is spread through exchange of body fluids, such as the blood or semen of an infected person. Chances of complete recovery and subsequent lifetime immunity are excellent. Practice the same precautions as you would to prevent contracting HIV, and seek medical attention in cases of infection. Once commonly spread by body lice, **typhus** is on the way out worldwide. Symptoms include pounding headaches, a dark rash on the upper body, fever, and delirium. Medical facilities should have tetracycline drugs to cure it.

Animals

Any mammal bite leads to a risk of contracting **rabies,** which is fatal if left untreated. Immediately wash the wound with soap and hot water, disinfect it with alcohol or iodine, and try to capture or kill the animal—within reason. Treat any dog bite as a possible risk, and see a doctor in all cases.

The most dangerous creatures (to humans) frequent the water. Portuguese man-of-war jellyfish, sea wasps, and stingrays can each inflict a painful, even fatal, sting requiring quick medical attention. Male sea lions are the most dangerous animals in the Galápagos—don't approach one, and back off if it looks like it wants you to.

Ecuador's collection of potentially harmful **arthropods,** including scorpions, centipedes, black widows, and brown recluse spiders, ranges from one end of the country to the other. Pay attention to any bites to notice if unusual symptoms develop. **Poisonous snakes** are more frightened of you than you are of them. Even if you've been bitten, there's a good chance that no venom was injected. If swelling, pain, numbness, or loss of consciousness occur, however, immobilize the bitten area and find a doctor. Try to bring the snake along for identification, if possible.

Mountain Health

High-altitude illnesses can be prevented by proper acclimatization. Spend a week in Quito and climb a few 4,000-meter peaks before tackling any higher ones, eat a diet high in carbohydrates, drink plenty of fluids, and avoid caffeine and alcohol. Altitude sickness can strike even the prepared and experienced, so mountaineers should be able to recognize the symptoms.

About one in four climbers suffers some degree of **acute mountain sickness (AMS),** which feels like the world's worst hangover: headache, nausea, fatigue, insomnia, and loss of appetite. The drug acetazolamide (Diamox) can lessen the odds of getting AMS, and analgesics can handle some of the aches. **Pulmonary edema** occurs when fluids start accumulating in the lungs, causing shortness of breath and a rattling cough that eventually brings up blood. **Cerebral edema** is fluid in the brain, which is accompanied by severely impaired mental functioning and poor judgment. Each of these conditions is less common than the one before it, and all should be treated by immediate descent to a lower altitude. Edemas require medical attention.

Hypothermia occurs when your body loses more heat than it can produce. Wet clothing, wind, and an exposed head are the most common culprits. Always be prepared in the Andes, even on short hikes, with raingear and warm layers for your body, head, and hands. Watch your companions during climbs for signs of dropping body temperature. Severe shivering reveals mild cases, where the body temperature doesn't drop below 33°C (90°F). Get the person warm and dry, and encourage her to move around to generate heat. Shivering actually ceases as the body temperature drops, followed by loss of coordination, impaired judgment, fatigue, and eventually death.

Pain in the extremities isn't necessarily the surest indicator of **frostbite,** when part of the body becomes frozen. Numbness is often the first symptom, followed by the area's becoming hard and white, then black. Often the area has become wet or the person is exhausted. Keep extremities warm and moving, especially the toes, fingers, ears, nose, and cheeks. A little numbness is normal, but if it lasts longer than half an hour, you'll want to loosen tight clothing, stamp your feet, or warm your chilly parts against a friend's body. Do not rub afflicted areas with snow. If frostbite has taken hold, special rapid rewarming techniques become necessary. There's no particular hurry to start this excruciating process, since frostbitten fingers and toes can, in effect, hibernate for days.

You'd be surprised at all the places sunlight bouncing off the snow can cause **sunburn** (inside your nose, for one). Spread high-SPF sunscreen, glacier cream, or zinc oxide everywhere you can reach. Reflected sunlight can also cause agonizing **snow blindness,** a temporary condition that only dark glacier goggles with side baffles can prevent. The goggles are a good investment if you plan to do several high-altitude snow climbs; you can buy them in Quito. **Cavities** can hurt like hell at high altitude because of a pressure difference between the inside of the tooth and the outside.

If Something Happens

Because many locals can't afford the services of a doctor, **pharmacists** *(farmacéuticos)* tend to be more proactive in Latin America. Provided you speak some Spanish, they can usually be trusted to recommend treatments and medicines for minor ailments that require a prescription back home. If you are hospitalized, try to talk to an English-speaking doctor before agreeing to any procedures. Be ready to pay up front, even if you have insurance coverage. Make sure to get a detailed, comprehensive receipt—in English, if possible—for insurance repayments.

Back Home

If you're taking any medical regimens, such as malaria pills, make sure to continue taking them for as long as you're supposed to, even after you return home. Pay close attention to your health for at least six months after your trip, since many exotic diseases have long incubation periods. Symptoms may resemble other illnesses, such as the flu, causing doctors unfamiliar with tropical medicine to misdiagnose. If you have any mysterious symptoms, tell your doctor where you've been—a fever in particular should call for a malaria blood test. A post-travel checkup with blood and stool exams is a good idea in any case, as well as tests for STDs, particularly HIV, if you've had sexual contact with unfamiliar partners during your travels.

RESOURCES

The **U.S. Centers for Disease Control and Prevention** (tel. 877/394-8747, www.cdc.gov/travel) has an extensive website with up-to-date information on health issues around the world. The **Pan American Health Organization,** or PAHO (525 23rd St. NW, Washington, DC 20037, tel. 202/974-3000, www.paho.org), is the Americas branch of the World Health Organization. PAHO's website has country health profiles for travelers and information on many health topics.

The nonprofit **International Association for Medical Assistance to Travelers** (1623 Military Rd. #279, Niagara Falls, NY 14304-1745, tel. 716/754-4883, info@iamat.org, www.iamat.org) is one of the best general travelers' health resources. For free or a small donation, the organization sends you tons of information on health risks abroad, including an immunization chart and a membership card that allows you access to its worldwide list of English-speaking doctors who operate for a fixed fee.

The **Traveler's Emergency Network** (P.O. Box 668, Millersville, MD 21108, tel. 800/275-4836, fax 888/258-2911, www.tenweb.com) has membership programs starting at $129 per person, per year that offer worldwide medical assistance, 24-hour medical consultation, referral to English-speaking doctors, and emergency sickness or injury evacuation.

Travel Medicine (351 Pleasant St., Ste. 312, Northampton, MA 01060, tel. 800/872-8633, travmed@travmed.com, www.travmed.com) and **Chinook Medical Gear** (P.O. Box 1736, Edwards, CO 81632, tel. 800/766-1365, fax 970/926-9660, chinook@vail.net, www.chinookmed.com) both sell medical supplies and books for travelers.

Excellent travel health books include Avalon Travel Publishing's own *Staying Healthy in Asia, Africa, and Latin America,* by Dirk Schroeder, ScD, MPH (5th ed., 2000); *International Travel Health Guide,* by Stuart Rose, M.D. (Northampton, MA: Travel Medicine, 1998); *A Comprehensive Guide to Wilderness & Travel Medicine,* by Eric A. Weiss, M.D. (Adventure Medical Kits, 1998); and *The Pocket Doctor,* by Stephen Bezruchka (Seattle: The Mountaineers, 1999). The last three are available from Travel Medicine and Chinook Medical Gear.

AVOIDING CRIME

"Violence is never far from the surface in Latin America," writes Tina Rosenberg in *Children of Cain* (Viking Penguin, 1992), her excellent study on the subject. "It is a culture of violence and has been ever since the Spaniards arrived, and, in some cases, well before." No exception to the rule, Ecuador does have crime problems, but it isn't nearly as dangerous as its neighbors. There's no more crime, on the whole, than in a large city back home. The same caveat applies here as it does in health matters: Remember that the list of potential problems illustrates worst-case scenarios. A few simple precautions and the right attitude will go a long way toward keeping your trip trouble-free.

General Concerns

At the turn of the millennium, incidents of crime were increasing as the country's economic situation deteriorated. Muggings, burglaries, purse-snatchings, and encounters with pickpockets were on the rise, even in broad daylight, and armed gangs or rural protestors occasionally stopped buses. Most of these crimes were nonviolent—in many cases, the victims didn't even know they were targeted until well after the criminal had moved on—but the incidences of knives or guns being used were also increasing.

Kidnappings near the northern border showed that Colombia's problems were spilling over onto its southern neighbor. The U.S. Embassy (always the mother hen) advises against travel in certain parts of Carchi province and has restricted its personnel from visiting Sucumbios province after five U.S. citizens were kidnapped near the Colombian border in the late 1990s.

Now for the good news: As the switch to the U.S. dollar brings stability, things are getting better. As a traveler, you won't have to worry about many common types of crime, such as carjackings and home burglaries. Traffic accidents are still the primary hazard to foreigners (motorcycles kill more Peace Corps volunteers than anything else), followed by opportunistic crimes such as casual theft or purse-snatching.

Armed mugging, assault, and rape do occur, though not often.

Staying Safe

As simple as it sounds, the best defense is to keep one eye open at all times and to look like you know what you're doing. Insecurity attracts criminals, and inattentiveness gives them a window of opportunity. You won't be able to prevent all crimes, but you can cut down the odds drastically. Pay attention to your gut instincts: If something tells you not to walk down that dim alley, don't. Lock expensive items in the lockbox *(caja fuerte* or *caja de seguridad)* available in most hotels, along with your passport, tickets, and money. Get a receipt for the exact contents.

Make copies of your passport, plane tickets, and travelers' checks. Keep one copy of these at home, along with a list of expensive items you're bringing and their model and serial numbers, and take one copy with you separate from the originals. Find out if and what your insurance covers while abroad, and how to file a claim. Leave extraneous valuables at home, especially jewelry.

Some travelers carry an emergency wad of money in their shoes or sewn into a piece of clothing. Velco strips sewn across pockets will slow down pickpockets. A small canister of mace or pepper spray may give you added confidence. Although you can't fly with one, you can buy canisters at *ferreterías* (hardware stores) in major cities. Take a few practice squirts *(outside)*.

Money

Don't carry your wallet in your back pocket. Most secure is a pouch worn under or as part of your clothing, like a money belt or nylon leg or neck pouch. One trick is to wear a neck pouch with the string around the waist and the pouch down the front of your pants—nobody's going to try to get in there. It's a bad idea to carry all your money in one place. Leave most of it locked in a secure place, and keep a few dollars separate from the rest.

Try to insist that all credit-card imprints are

made in front of you. Tear up any incomplete or void imprints yourself, and make sure you know the whereabouts of all carbons.

Luggage

Small locks for outside pockets and zip closures are available in most stores at home, or in Ecuador on the street and in hardware stores. Cable locks are useful for securing your bag to the roof of a bus, or to something hefty in your room while you go out. These locks won't stop a determined thief, but they will at least slow things down long enough to prevent a casual theft. Discourage bag slashers and snatchers by carrying purses and day packs in front of you, securely held in place with one arm. Keep hold of a strap when you put a bag down, and never leave anything hanging on the back of a chair.

One of the best ways to secure your belongings is with a **Pacsafe** from Outpac Designs (tel. 800/873-9415, www.pac-safe.com). These lightweight but sturdy steel-mesh sacks fit snugly over backpacks and duffel bags and lock closed, making it impossible for someone to open your bag without a key. You can use them to lock your bags to anything sturdy as well. Outpac also makes the Travel Safe, a small, lockable nylon pouch reinforced with steel mesh.

Where and When to Be Careful

Airports and bus stations are the favorite haunts of bag snatchers. Pickpockets and bag slashers prefer city buses and jostling crowds, particularly in markets. Walk briskly and look like you know where you're going (or better yet, *actually* know where you're going), particularly at night and after coming out of a bank or money-exchange office. Everyone should be exceptionally vigilant after dark. For women, certain precautions can decrease your odds of assault: Travel by day as much as possible, travel with men or in a group, and avoid situations where you could be cornered in an out-of-the-way spot.

Use your judgment if someone other than a good friend offers you food or drink; druggings

are known to happen. If you decide not to accept what someone offers, the best strategy is to feign illness or allergy. Traveling in pairs allows one person to dig in and the other to decline.

Robbery, assault, and rape have occurred in the backcountry, especially on popular climbs like Pichincha and Tungurahua. Try to go in a group, and never leave gear unattended in mountain huts. Everyone should avoid deserted beach areas after dark.

Scams

The most common scams involve one person distracting you momentarily while another cleans out your money or slashes your bag. Someone might "accidentally" spill or squirt something on you, or start an argument with you or someone else nearby. There have been reports of people being handed babies and having their pockets cleaned out as they stand there confused.

I've heard enough reports of strangle muggings—in which two or three people sneak up behind you and put you in a headlock until you pass out—to always be wary of running footsteps behind me.

Drugs

Even though Ecuador's drug situation is much better than that of Peru or Colombia, controlled substances still top the list of things you don't want to get mixed up in as a foreigner. Most of the foreigners in jail in Ecuador are there for drug offenses. Drug sales are often setups, and police can be in cahoots with informants. If you're caught, don't expect much support from your embassy or the Ecuadorian legal system. Jails are far from comfortable, the judicial process can take years, and penalties are steep. Steer clear.

Officialdom

Being stopped and asked to show your papers is often a new experience for foreigners, but it happens occasionally in Ecuador—just smile and comply. Police searches of cars and rooms can happen. Make sure you're present, and request a *testigo* (witness). Because civil servants are paid next to nothing, corruption does occur among police. Some are even outright criminals, or criminals posing as police or drug enforcement agents. Be wary of anyone posing as a plainclothes police officer. Insist on seeing his identification—for more than a brief flash—and don't go anywhere with him if none is produced, especially not into a vehicle. Even if everything seems on the level, insist on walking to the nearest police station in public.

If Something Happens
In the police station, you'll have to fill out a *denuncia* to report a crime. Get a receipt, for insurance purposes if nothing else, and ask for temporary identification papers if yours were stolen. Your embassy may be able to help arrange the wiring or emergency funds, or even (in rare cases) a reimbursable loan in the interim. The embassy can also help find a lawyer if you're thrown in jail.

In the unfortunate event of rape, women's health clinics (*clínicas de la mujer*) in larger cities can provide specialized treatment and gather evidence for the police report. Don't expect too much help from local police, but fill out a report as soon as possible in any case. A high dose of oral contraceptives (also known as the morning-after pill) lowers the odds of an unwanted pregnancy and is available at most

farmacias. Every woman's emotional response to such a traumatic event will be different. For some, continuing their travels may be the best antidote, whereas others may prefer to end the trip early.

Travelers' checks and credit cards each have their own emergency numbers in case of loss or theft. Notify your travelers' insurance carrier, if applicable. In the case of a lost airline ticket, you'll probably have to buy a new one and wait until you get home to be reimbursed for the old one. Ask at the local airline branch for details. Your embassy will tell you what to do in case your passport goes missing.

Resources for U.S. Travelers
The **Bureau of Consular Affairs** of the U.S. Department of State (2201 C St. NW, Washington, DC 20520, tel. 202/647-5225, www.travel.state.gov) publishes Travel Advisories on individual countries, available by mail, fax, or on its website. Publications such as *A Safe Trip Abroad, Travel Warning on Drugs Abroad,* and *Tips for Travelers to Central & South America* are available online as well. U.S. citizens can register with the Department of State for free before leaving home (http://travelregistration.state.gov/ibrs), so that information is on file in case of an emergency.

Information and Services

MONEY
Currency
In September 2000, Ecuador officially laid the beleaguered old *sucre* to rest and replaced it with the **U.S. dollar.** While the reasons for this switch were clear, opinions differ on whether or not it was a good idea—most Ecuadorians I've talked to seem to think not.

Travelers carrying dollars from home, of course, will be happy they don't have to worry about exchanging money. The flip side of this convenience is that prices have risen significantly. Once one of the cheapest Latin

American countries for traveling, Ecuador is now in the middle of the price list.

Outside of major cities, **cash** is the easiest—and often only—form of money to use. Ecuador's coins are equivalent to U.S. cents (100 to one dollar): nickels ($0.05), dimes ($0.10), quarters ($0.25), and half dollars ($0.50), although they have different symbols and faces than their U.S. counterparts. Finding small change is always a problem; it's best to bring small bills as most places don't accept bills over $20. Keep an eye out for **counterfeit** bills, which can often be spotted by their smoothness (real bills are printed with faint impressions), limpness (real bills are crisp), and sloppy presidential portraits.

You could carry the bulk of your money in **travelers' checks,** which can be refunded if lost or stolen, but they are becoming steadily more difficult to change outside of major cities, and commissions are usually charged. U.S. dollars are best; Canadian and British pounds, Japanese yen, and euros are very difficult to change. American Express and Visa travelers' checks are the most widely accepted, but Thomas Cook and Citibank checks also pass. Always try to have some cash on you—the farther you get from Quito and Guayaquil, the more of a commission you pay to change travelers' checks, especially on weekends. Commissions are often 2–5 percent, and sometimes depend on the amount changed.

Be sure to keep the serial numbers and the number to call if your checks are lost or stolen in a separate place from the physical checks. Exchange houses (*casas de cambio,* an almost extinct species nowadays) and some banks change travelers' checks to cash dollars, but only some businesses will let you pay with travelers' checks—usually those near the high end. Most tellers are very picky with signatures, so if your chicken scratch doesn't match the one on the check, it may be rejected. If this happens with American Express checks, the office in Quito will issue you new ones immediately.

Credit cards are accepted in many higher-end shops, hotels, restaurants, and travel agencies. Although it's technically illegal, most businesses pass the 10 percent service charge for credit-card transactions straight on to the customer. Some don't—most notably the Supermaxi supermarket chain and the South American Explorers—and many others offer discounts for cash payments. It's generally best to pay with cash whenever possible and save your credit cards for emergencies or ATM use. MasterCard and Visa are the most widely accepted, and cardholders can draw cash advances. American Express, Diner's

Club, and Discover are much harder to use. ATMs mostly have a $500-per-day limit, so carrying an extra card from another account can be useful.

Note that interest rates on **cash advances** are often compounded daily, and they may even carry a maintenance fee. These are available in Ecuador only at the credit-card's head offices, listed in the *Quito* chapter. American Express members can buy AmEx travelers' checks at the office in Quito, using a personal check from your account for a 1 percent fee (gold card members don't even need the personal check).

Keep the customer service number in a separate place from any credit card, in case the card is lost or stolen. Just because an establishment sports a credit-card sticker doesn't mean it necessarily takes them. Always ask.

Automated teller machines (ATMs) are becoming more and more common in Ecuador. Almost all credit cards can now issue you a personal identification number (PIN) so you can use the card to withdraw cash advances at ATMs. (Ask for a four-digit PIN, since five-digit ones don't work in Ecuador.) Machines accept ATM cards on the Plus and Cirrus networks, as well as MasterCard and Visa cards that have been assigned a PIN—call your card issuer for information on setting this up. Most ATMs have a daily withdrawal limit of $300–500 or less, which you can sometimes subvert by visiting multiple machines. Don't count on getting more than $500 in a single day. Check with your bank about any transaction charge. Cash advances are available from the main office of Banco del Pacifico in Quito and other cities.

Money transfers are probably the least cost-effective way to get funds, but in a pinch, they're often the only fast and sure way to get your hands on cash. Ask at your home bank about direct bank-to-bank transfers. Find out before your trip which banks in Ecuador, if any, your bank deals with, and how long the transaction takes. **Western Union** has offices all over the country.

Tipping

A *propina* (tip) isn't required or expected, but it usually doesn't take much out of your pocket and can make someone's day. Better restaurants add 10 percent for *servicio* (service) and 12 percent *IVA* value-added tax; if they don't, charge 10 percent consider leaving it anyway. For cheaper restaurants, porters, hairdressers, taxi drivers, and guides, 5–10 percent will do. See the *Galápagos Islands* chapter for advice on tipping naturalist guides in the islands.

Taxes

Shops, hotels, and restaurants must charge a 12 percent **IVA** (value-added tax), which should be noted separately on the *cuenta* (bill). More expensive restaurants and hotels add 10 percent for *servicio* (service) to their bills. Upon leaving the country, you'll be slapped with an **airport departure tax** ($41 in Quito and $25 in Guayaquil).

Budgeting

No longer the travel steal it once was, Ecuador is still a comparatively inexpensive place to visit. Serious budget travelers can get by for under $20 pp per day by taking advantage of cheap buses, $5–8 hotel rooms, and $2–3 set meals. A more comfortable budget of $20–30 per day will leave you room for a movie, museum, and a *cerveza* or two when the day is done. (While researching this book, my budget fell around $30–40 per day). Planning $40–50 per person, per day allows you to factor in quality hotels, national plane flights, and day tours, whereas any figure above that enters the realm of luxury hotels and rental cars.

COMMUNICATIONS AND MEDIA
Mail

With the arrival of the Internet and email, "snail mail" systems around the world are shrinking in volume and rising in price. Airmail postcards and letters under 20 grams cost about $1.55 to North and South America ($1.80 to Europe, $2.40 elsewhere). For mail weighing 20–100 grams, you will pay $3.71 to North and South America, $4.29 to Europe, and $5.28 to anywhere else. Don't mail any objects of value, as things go missing quite often from Ecuador's postal system, especially incoming packages. It's better to use a private courier company like DHL or Federal Express.

To receive mail via general delivery *(poste restante)*, have items marked "Firstname LASTNAME, Lista de Correos, Quito, Ecuador, South America." Pick it up at the new post office at Eloy Alfaro and 10 de Agosto. When asking the person at the post office any poste restante mail has come for you *(¿Hay algo para mi en el poste restante?)*, have them check under both your first and last name. The South American Explorers' Quito clubhouse, American Express, and various Spanish schools can receive and hold mail for members.

Telecommunications

Compared to the postal service, the national telephone system functions well under the auspices of the national phone company. It's currently called Andinatel in the Andes and Pacifictel along the coast, although you'll still see old EMETEL signs in distant towns. Almost every town has its own office, but service varies; national calls are no problem, but international calls may be impossible. (Some offices will charge you for calls if the phone rings more than eight times, even if no one answers.) Connections to the Galápagos and some parts of the Oriente and the coast are sometimes congested and tenuous at best. New *cabinas* have sprung up in towns and villages all over the country: **Allegro, Movistar,** and **Porta** provide excellent service, meaning that it is no longer necessary to search out the **Andinatel** office to make a call in any city or town.

National calls cost about $0.15 per minute. All calls cost up to 20 percent less on weekdays after 7 P.M. and from 7 A.M. Saturday to 7 A.M. Monday. Calls from hotels are always more expensive, and many businesses will let you use their phone for national calls for a small charge. Hotel management will sometimes try to charge you, even if you use a calling card or call collect.

TELEPHONE PREFIXES

Prefix	Province(s)/Specialty	Major Cities
1	Services	
2	Pichincha, Santo Domingo de los Tsáchilas	Quito, Santo Domingo
3	Bolívar, Cotopaxi, Chimborazo, Pastaza, Tungurahua	Guaranda, Latacunga, Riobamba, Puyo, Ambato
4	Guayas, Santa Elena	Guayaquil, Salinas
5	Los Ríos, Manabí, Galápagos	Babahoyo, Quevedo, Manta, Portoviejo, Santa Cruz
6	Carchi, Esmeraldas, Imbabura Napo, Orellana, Sucumbíos	Tulcán, Esmeraldas, Ibarra, Tena, Coca, Lago Agrio
7	Azuay, Cañar, El Oro, Loja, Morona-Santiago, Zamora-Chinchipe	Azogues, Cuenca, Loja, Macas, Machala, Zamora
8 & 9	Cell phones	

To make long-distance calls within Ecuador, dial a 0 followed by the regional prefix code and the seven-digit phone number. Drop the 0 within the same region. Cellular phones are everywhere; their numbers begin with 09 or 08. For directory information, dial 104; for help with national long distance, dial 105; and for international long distance, dial 116 or 117. Numbers beginning with 800 are toll-free.

If you bring your own cell phone from home, you can take it into a service shop and purchase a chip for local use at minimal cost.

Although it's possible to call other countries through the normal telephone network, Internet phone connections are so much cheaper that it's almost not worth it. It will cost you about $1 per minute to talk on a normal connection through the national telephone system or one of the pay phone companies. Different countries have different codes for reaching an international operator. All codes are preceded by 999. Codes for some countries include: Canada, 175; Italy, 164/174; Spain, 176; United Kingdom, 178; Switzerland, 160; France, 180; U.S., 170 for MCI, 171 for Sprint/NYNEX, 119 for AT&T USA Direct.

To call Ecuador from the United States, dial the international access code (011), the country code for Ecuador (593), the province/cell phone code (02–07, 08, or 09), and the seven-digit local number—that's 15 digits in all. **Language Line** (tel. 877/886-3885, info@languageline.com, www.languageline.com) has translators available around the clock for a moderate per-minute charge.

Two competing cellular companies, Movistar and Porta, offer public pay phones. Porta seems to have better coverage in the mountains, and each system takes its own type of calling card (*tarjeta telefónica*), which you can buy in various denominations just about anywhere. Phones display the amount left on your card; national calls cost about $0.17 per minute.

Internet

Along with volcanoes erupting, governments mutating, and a whole new system of money, the most remarkable change in Ecuador in the late 1990s was the arrival of the Internet. Perhaps a dozen places in the country offered access in 1997; three years later, you could hit that many with a rock from some street corners in Quito. Instantaneous and inexpensive, email *(correo electronico)* makes it easy to keep in touch with friends back home.

Most Internet cafés are open daily 7 A.M.–10 P.M. and charge $1 or less per hour. Almost all cafés offer Internet phone services that allow you to dial phone numbers worldwide and talk through the computer using a microphone and headset. This setup is much cheaper than normal long-distance calls ($0.10–0.20 per minute from Ecuador to the United States). Most Internet cafés also have instant messaging programs with webcams, scanners, printers, fax services, and word-processing programs. If you plan to use the Internet to stay in touch, you can set up a free email account through services like Hotmail (www.hotmail.com), Yahoo! (http://mail.yahoo.com), or Gmail (www.google.com/gmail). Digital photographers can burn images onto CDs for $2–3 at many Internet cafés.

Since Internet cafés open and close with surprising speed, it doesn't make much sense to list specific ones in cities outside of Quito. Rest assured that just about wherever you are, you'll find an Internet café within a block or two. In addition, many hotels and restaurants have Wi-Fi service included, so travelers can bring their own laptops.

Newspapers and Magazines

Local publications include national Spanish-language newspapers, such as *Hoy, El Comercio,* and *El Universo.* International editions of *Time* and *Newsweek,* along with the foreign edition of the *Miami Herald,* are available in larger cities. It's often just as easy to keep up to date online.

Television and Radio

Latin American television consists of three things: soccer, slapstick, and soaps. *Telenovelas* are archetypal Latin soap operas in which poor Cinderellas from the *barrio* struggle for love against the wickedness of the rich.

Because they're inexpensive and not

© JULIAN SMITH

riding on top of the train through Devil's Nose

limited by mountainous terrain (as phone lines are), transistor radios are the only connection between much of Ecuador and the outside world. They're the first thing plugged in when electricity is installed, and they are seldom turned off—or even down—from then on. Stations, mostly AM, broadcast music, news, and educational programming in Spanish and indigenous languages.

MAPS AND TOURIST INFORMATION
Maps
International Travel Maps (530 West Broadway, Vancouver, BC V5Z 1E9, Canada, tel. 604/879-3621, fax 604/879-4521, itmb@itmb.com, www.itmb.com) has 150 of its own maps and distributes 23,000 more by other publishers. Its 1:700,000 Ecuador map ($13.95) is without peer. In the United States, maps of Ecuador and South America are available from **Maplink** (30 South La Patera Ln., Unit 5, Santa Barbara, CA 93117, tel. 805/692-1394, fax 805/692-6787, custserv@maplink.com, www.maplink.com).

Travel Resources
The **South American Explorers** organization has its headquarters in the United States (126 Indian Creek Rd., Ithaca, NY 14850, tel. 607/277-0488, explorer@samexplo.org, www.samexplo.org) and clubhouses in Quito, Cusco, and Lima. See *Information* in the *Quito* chapter for more details on this valuable travel clearinghouse.

ELECTRICITY
As in North America, electricity in Ecuador is a 100-watt/60-cycle alternating current. Flat-prong outlets seldom have a third grounding hole. Plug in expensive electronic equipment, such as computers, using a three-to-two-prong adapter/surge protector available at U.S. hardware stores.

Power outages are common, even in major cities. Electricity is often shut off in rural areas after dark, and far-flung lodges usually operate on electric generators or solar panels, limiting usage even further.

TIME
The mainland is five hours behind GMT, which is the same as U.S. eastern standard time. The Galápagos Islands are one hour behind the mainland (six hours behind GMT, the same as U.S. central time). Because days and nights on the equator are the same duration year-round, there's no need for daylight saving time in Ecuador.

BUSINESS HOURS
Hours of operation change with amazing rapidity, often at the whim of employees or owners. Long lunch breaks are the norm, and they last longer (up to three hours) in hotter areas, such as the coastal region. A good strategy is to come 10–20 minutes before something reopens after the lunch break to guarantee your spot at the front of the line.

Typical business hours are Mon.–Fri. 8 or 9 A.M.–5 or 6 P.M., with a lunch break 12:30–2 P.M. Saturdays are often half days ending at noon or 1 P.M. Banks operate weekdays 9 A.M.–1 P.M., occasionally in the afternoons, and on Saturday. Government offices and embassies often close by early afternoon. Restaurants tend to stay open later, in typical Latin American fashion. Dinner usually starts at 9 or 10 P.M.

LAUNDRY
Self-service laundry machines are few and far between. Many inexpensive hotels, though, have a *pila* (scrubbing board) and a clothesline out back. Water basins are often used for drinking water, so scoop water out instead of washing directly in the basin. Hotels generally frown on guests washing clothes in sinks. Packets of *detergente* are available at general stores.

Laundry services wash clothes by the piece or the kilogram. This can be expensive in high-end hotels, and it may take a day or two for everything to air dry. Laundromats (*lavanderías*) can usually have your things back the same day or the next morning. Dry cleaning (*lavaseco*) is available in larger cities.

RESOURCES

Glossary

abrazo a platonic hug given when introduced to someone of the same sex

alimentador feeder bus (or chicken feeder)

allullas doughy cookies served with cheese

almuerzo lunch

artesanías handicrafts

botas de caucho rubber boots

brujo/a witch, practitioner of magic

buseta mini bus

caliente hot

camioneta truck, often public transport

campesino/a rural resident

casa de cambio money exchange business

centro comerciale mall

chifa Chinese restaurant

chugchucara a fried dish with pork skins, bananas, corn, potatoes, and empanadas

cine movie theater

colectivo public bus or truck

curandero/a medicinal healer

fanesca a dish served during Lent that includes nine different grains, squash, rice, and dried fish, served with hard-boiled eggs, onions, and sliced hot peppers

frio cold

helado ice cream (*helados de paila* is a type of sherbet, an Ecuadorian specialty)

hostería inn

indígena indigenous person

invierno "winter," a relatively hot and wet season

lancha small boat

lavandería launderette

lavaseca dry cleaner

maíz corn

menú del día plate of the day

mosquitero hanging mosquito screen for beds

obraje textile workshop

panadería bakery

panga small boat

páramo high-altitude grasslands

parillada restaurant specializing in grilled meat

paseo stroll or walk, often in the evening

peña nightclub

policía police

propina tip

quinua grain native to the Andes

ranchero wooden bus with open sides, also known as *chiva*

salchipapas french fries topped with a chunk of hot dog and smothered with ketchup, mayonnaise, and mustard

salsateca Latin dance club

selva jungle

tambo a small, thatched hut used for emergency shelter in the Andes

terminal terrestre bus terminal

tienda shop

tróle trolley

verano "summer," a drier and cooler season

Spanish Phrasebook

Your Ecuadorian adventure will be more fun if you use a little Spanish. Ecuadorians, although they may smile at your funny accent, will appreciate your halting efforts to break the ice and transform yourself from a foreigner into a potential friend.

Spanish commonly uses 30 letters: the familiar English 26, plus four straightforward additions: *ch*, *ll*, *ñ*, and *rr*, which are explained under *Consonants*.

PRONUNCIATION

Once you learn them, Spanish pronunciation rules – in contrast with English – don't change. Spanish vowels generally sound softer than in English. (Note: The capitalized syllables below receive stronger accents.)

Vowels

a   like ah, as in "hah": *agua* AH-gooah (water), *pan* PAHN (bread), and *casa* CAH-sah (house)

e   like ay, as in "may:" *mesa* MAY-sah (table), *tela* TAY-lah (cloth), and *de* DAY (of, from)

i   like ee, as in "need": *diez* dee-AYZ (10), *comida* ko-MEE-dah (meal), and *fin* FEEN (end)

o   like oh, as in "go": *peso* PAY-soh (weight), *ocho* OH-choh (eight), and *poco* POH-koh (a bit)

u   like oo, as in "cool": *uno* OO-noh (one), *cuarto* KOOAHR-toh (room), and *usted* oos-TAYD (you); when it follows a "q," the **u** is silent; when it follows an "h" or has an umlaut (ü), it's pronounced like "w"

Consonants

b, d, f, k, l, m, n, p, q, s, r, t, v, w, x, y, z, and **ch** – pronounced almost as in English; **h** occurs, but is silent – not pronounced at all.

c   like k, as in "keep": *cuarto* KOOAR-toh (room), Tepic tay-PEEK (capital of Nayarit

state); when it precedes "e" or "i," pronounce **c** like s, as in "sit": *cerveza* sayr-VAY-sah (beer), *encima* ayn-SEE-mah (atop).

g   like g, as in "gift," when it precedes "a," "o," "u," or a consonant: *gato* GAH-toh (cat), *hago* AH-goh (I do, make); otherwise, pronounce **g** like h as in "hat": *giro* HEE-roh (money order), *gente* HAYN-tay (people)

j   like h, as in "has": *Jueves* HOOAY-vays (Thursday), *mejor* may-HOR (better)

ll   like y, as in "yes": *toalla* toh-AH-yah (towel), *ellos* AY-yohs (they, them)

ñ   like ny, as in "canyon": *año* AH-nyo (year), *señor* SAY-nyor (Mr., sir)

rr   like a Scottish rolled r. This distinguishes *perro* (dog) from *pero* (but) and *carro* (car) from *caro* (expensive).

Note: The one small but common exception to all of the above is the pronunciation of **y,** when used as the Spanish word for "and," as in "Ron y Kathy" (Ron and Kathy). In such cases, pronounce it like the English ee, as in "keep": Ron "ee" Kathy.

Accented Syllables

The rule for accenting, or putting relative stress on given syllables within a given word, is straightforward. If a word ends in a vowel, an n, or an s, accent the next-to-last syllable; if not, accent the last syllable.

Pronounce *gracias* GRAH-seeahs (thank you), *orden* OHR-dayn (order), and *carretera* kah-ray-TAY-rah (highway) with stress on the next-to-last syllable.

Otherwise, accent the last syllable: *venir* vay-NEER (to come), *ferrocarril* fay-roh-cah-REEL (railroad), and *edad* ay-DAHD (age).

Exceptions to the accent rule are always marked with an accent sign: (á, é, í, ó, or ú), such as *teléfono* tay-LAY-foh-noh (telephone), *jabón* hah-BON (soap), and *rápido* RAH-pee-doh (rapid).

BASIC AND COURTEOUS EXPRESSIONS

Most Spanish-speaking people consider formalities important. When approaching anyone for information or any other reason, do not forget the appropriate salutation – good morning, good evening, etc. Standing alone, the greeting *hola* (hello) can sound brusque.

Hello. *Hola.*
Good morning. *Buenos días.*
Good afternoon. *Buenas tardes.*
Good evening. *Buenas noches.*
How are you? *¿Cómo está usted?*
Very well, thank you. *Muy bien, gracias.*
Okay; good. *Bien.*
Not okay; bad. *Mal* or *feo.*
So-so. *Más o menos.*
And you? *¿Y usted?*
Thank you. *Gracias.*
Thank you very much. *Muchas gracias.*
You're very kind. *Muy amable.*
You're welcome. *De nada.*
Goodbye. *Adios.*
See you later. *Hasta luego.*
please *por favor*
yes *sí*
no *no*
I don't know. *No sé.*
Just a moment, please. *Momentito, por favor.*
Excuse me, please (when you're trying to get attention). *Disculpe* or *Con permiso.*
Excuse me (when you've made an error). *Lo siento.*
Pleased to meet you. *Mucho gusto.*
How do you say . . . in Spanish? *¿Cómo se dice...en español?*
What is your name? *¿Cómo se llama usted?*
Do you speak English? *¿Habla usted inglés?*
Is English spoken here? (Does anyone here speak English?) *¿Se habla inglés?*
I don't speak Spanish well. *No hablo bien el español.*
I don't understand. *No entiendo.*
My name is . . . *Me llamo . . .*
Would you like . . . *¿Quisiera usted . . .*
Let's go to . . . *Vamos a . . .*

TERMS OF ADDRESS

When in doubt, use the formal *usted* (you) as a form of address.

I *yo*
you (formal) *usted*
you (familiar) *tu*
he/him *él*
she/her *ella*
we/us *nosotros*
you (plural) *ustedes*
they/them *ellos* (all males or mixed gender); **ellas** (all females)
Mr., sir *señor*
Mrs., Madam *señora*
Miss, young lady *señorita*
wife *esposa*
husband *esposo*
friend *amigo* (male); *amiga* (female)
sweetheart *novio* (male); *novia* (female)
son; daughter *hijo; hija*
brother; sister *hermano; hermana*
father; mother *padre; madre*
grandfather; grandmother *abuelo; abuela*

TRANSPORTATION

Where is . . . ? *¿Dónde está . . . ?*
How far is it to . . . ? *¿A cuánto está . . . ?*
from...to . . . *de...a . . .*
How many blocks? *¿Cuántas cuadras?*
Where (Which) is the way to . . . ? *¿Dónde está el camino a . . . ?*
the bus station *la terminal de autobuses*
the bus stop *la parada de autobuses*
Where is this bus going? *¿Adónde va este autobús?*
the taxi stand *la parada de taxis*
the train station *la estación de ferrocarril*
the boat *el barco*
the airport *el aeropuerto*
I'd like a ticket to . . . *Quisiera un boleto a . . .*
first (second) class *primera (segunda) clase*
round trip *ida y vuelta*
reservation *reservación*
baggage *equipaje*
Stop here, please. *Pare aquí, por favor.*
the entrance *la entrada*
the exit *la salida*

the ticket office *la oficina de boletos*
(very) near; far *(muy) cerca; lejos*
to; toward *a*
by; through *por*
from *desde*
the right *la derecha*
the left *la izquierda*
straight ahead *derecho; recto*
in front *en frente*
beside *al lado*
behind *atrás*
the corner *la esquina*
the stoplight *el semáforo*
a turn *una vuelta*
right here *aquí*
somewhere around here *por acá*
right there *allí*
somewhere around there *por allá*
street; avenue *calle; avenida*
highway *carretera; pana*
bridge; toll *puente; peaje*
address *dirección*
north; south *norte; sur*
east; west *oriente (este); occidente (oeste)*

ACCOMMODATIONS
hotel *hotel*
Is there a room? *¿Hay cuarto?*
May I (may we) see it? *¿Puedo (podemos) verlo?*
What is the rate? *¿Cuál es el precio?*
Is that your best rate? *¿Es su mejor precio?*
Is there something cheaper? *¿Hay algo más económico?*
a single room *un cuarto sencillo*
a double room *un cuarto doble*
double bed *cama matrimonial*
twin beds *camas gemelas*
with private bath *con baño*
hot water *agua caliente*
shower *ducha*
towels *toallas*
soap *jabón*
toilet paper *papel higiénico*
blanket *corbija; manta*
sheets *sábanas*
air-conditioned *aire acondicionado*

fan *ventilador*
key *llave*
manager *gerente*

FOOD
I'm hungry *Tengo hambre.*
I'm thirsty. *Tengo sed.*
menu *carta; menú*
order *orden*
glass *vaso*
fork *tenedor*
knife *cuchillo*
spoon *cuchara*
napkin *servilleta*
soft drink *refresco*
coffee *café*
tea *té*
drinking water *agua pura; agua potable*
bottled carbonated water *agua mineral*
bottled noncarbonated water *agua sin gas*
beer *cerveza*
wine *vino*
milk *leche*
juice *jugo*
cream *crema*
sugar *azúcar*
cheese *queso*
snack *botana; refrigerio*
breakfast *desayuno*
lunch *almuerzo*
daily lunch special *el menú del día*
dinner *cena*
the check *la cuenta*
eggs *huevos*
bread *pan*
salad *ensalada*
fruit *fruta*
mango *mango*
watermelon *sandía*
papaya *papaya*
banana *plátano*
apple *manzana*
orange *naranja*
lime *limón*
fish *pescado*
shellfish *mariscos*
shrimp *camarones*

meat (without) *(sin) carne*
chicken *pollo*
pork *chancho*
beef; steak *res; bistec*
bacon; ham *tocino; jamón*
fried *frito*
roasted *asada*
barbecue; barbecued *ala parrilla; al carbón*

SHOPPING

money *dinero*
money-exchange bureau *casa de cambio*
I would like to exchange travelers' checks. *Quisiera cambiar cheques viajeros.*
What is the exchange rate? *¿Cuál es el tipo de cambio?*
How much is the commission? *¿Cuánto cuesta la comisión?*
Do you accept credit cards? *¿Aceptan tarjetas de crédito?*
money order *giro*
How much does it cost? *¿Cuánto cuesta?*
What is your final price? *¿Cuál es su último precio?*
expensive *caro*
cheap *barato; económico*
more *más*
less *menos*
a little *un poco*
too much *demasiado*

HEALTH

Help me, please. *Ayúdeme por favor.*
I am ill. *Estoy enfermo.*
Call a doctor. *Llame un doctor.*
Take me to . . . *Lléveme a . . .*
hospital *hospital; clinica*
drugstore *farmacia*
pain *dolor*
fever *fiebre*
headache *dolor de cabeza*
stomachache *dolor de estómago*
burn *quemadura*
cramp *calambre*
nausea *náusea*
vomiting *vomitar*
medicine *medicina*

antibiotic *antibiótico*
pill, tablet *pastilla*
aspirin *aspirina*
ointment; cream *pomada; crema*
bandage *venda*
cotton *algodón*
sanitary napkins use brand name, e.g., Kotex
birth control pills *pastillas anticonceptivas*
contraceptive foam *espuma anticonceptiva*
condoms *preservativos; condones*
toothbrush *cepilla dental*
dental floss *hilo dental*
toothpaste *crema dental*
dentist *dentista*
toothache *dolor de muelas*

POST OFFICE AND COMMUNICATIONS

long-distance telephone *teléfono larga distancia*
I would like to call . . . *Quisiera llamar a . . .*
collect *por cobrar*
station-to-station *a quien contesta*
person-to-person *persona a persona*
credit card *tarjeta de crédito*
post office *correo*
general delivery *lista de correo*
letter *carta*
stamp *estampilla, timbre*
postcard *tarjeta*
aerogram *aerograma*
airmail *correo aereo*
registered *registrado*
money order *giro*
package; box *paquete; caja*
string; tape *piola; cinta*

AT THE BORDER

border *frontera*
customs *aduana*
immigration *migración*
tourist card *tarjeta de turista*
inspection *inspección; revisión*
passport *pasaporte*
profession *profesión*
marital status *estado civil*

single *soltero*
married; divorced *casado; divorciado*
widowed *viudado*
insurance *seguros*
title *título*
driver's license *licencia de conducir*

AT THE GAS STATION

gas station *gasolinera*
gasoline *gasolina*
unleaded *sin plomo*
full, please *lleno, por favor*
tire *llanta*
tire repair shop *vulcanizadora*
air *aire*
water *agua*
oil (change) *aceite (cambio)*
grease *grasa*
My . . . doesn't work. *Mi . . . no sirve.*
battery *batería*
radiator *radiador*
alternator *alternador*
generator *generador*
tow truck *grúa*
repair shop *taller mecánico*
tune-up *afinación*
auto parts store *repuestos*

VERBS

Verbs are the key to getting along in Spanish. They employ mostly predictable forms and come in three classes, which end in *ar, er,* and *ir,* respectively:
to buy *comprar*
I buy; you (he/she/it) buys *compro; compra*
We buy; you (they) buy *compramos; compran*
to eat *comer*
I eat; you (he/she/it) eats *como; come*
We eat; you (they) eat *comemos; comen*
to climb *subir*
I climb; you (he/she/it) climbs *subo; sube*
We climb; you (they) climb *subimos; suben*

Got the idea? Here are more:
to do or make *hacer*
I do or make; you (he/she/it) does or makes *hago; hace*
We do or make; you (they) do or make *hacemos; hacen*
to go *ir*
I go; you (he/she/it) goes *voy; va*
We go; you (they) go *vamos; van*
to go (walk) *andar*
to love *amar*
to work *trabajar*
to want *desear; querer*
to need *necesitar*
to read *leer*
to write *escribir*
to repair *reparar*
to stop *parar*
to get off (the bus) *bajar*
to arrive *llegar*
to stay (remain) *quedar*
to stay (lodge) *hospedar*
to leave *salir* (regular except for *salgo,* "I leave")
to look at *mirar*
to look for *buscar*
to give *dar* (regular except for *doy,* "I give")
to carry *llevar, cargar*
to have *tener* (irregular but important: *tengo, tiene, tenemos, tienen*)
to come *venir* (similarly irregular: *vengo, viene, venimos, vienen*)
Spanish has two forms of "to be." Use *estar* when speaking of location or a temporary state of being: "I am at home." *"Estoy en casa."* "I'm sick." *"Estoy enfermo."* Use *ser* for a permanent state of being: "I am a doctor." *"Soy doctora."* *Estar* is regular, except for *estoy,* "I am." *Ser* is very irregular:
to be *ser*
I am; you (he/she/it) is *soy; es*
We are; you (they) are *somos; son*

NUMBERS

0 *cero*
1 *uno*
2 *dos*
3 *tres*
4 *cuatro*
5 *cinco*
6 *seis*
7 *siete*
8 *ocho*
9 *nueve*
10 *diez*
11 *once*
12 *doce*
13 *trece*
14 *catorce*
15 *quince*
16 *dieciseis*
17 *diecisiete*
18 *dieciocho*
19 *diecinueve*
20 *veinte*
21 *veinte y uno* or *veintiuno*
30 *treinta*
40 *cuarenta*
50 *cincuenta*
60 *sesenta*
70 *setenta*
80 *ochenta*
90 *noventa*
100 *ciento*
101 *ciento y uno* or *cientiuno*
200 *doscientos*
500 *quinientos*
1,000 *mil*
10,000 *diez mil*
100,000 *cien mil*
1,000,000 *millón*
one half *medio*
one third *un tercio*
one fourth *un cuarto*

TIME

What time is it? *¿Qué hora es?*
It's one o'clock. *Es la una.*
It's three in the afternoon. *Son las tres de la tarde.*
It's 4 A.M. *Son las cuatro de la mañana.*
six-thirty *seis y media*
a quarter till eleven *un cuarto para las once*
a quarter past five *las cinco y cuarto*
an hour *una hora*

DAYS AND MONTHS

Monday *lunes*
Tuesday *martes*
Wednesday *miércoles*
Thursday *jueves*
Friday *viernes*
Saturday *sábado*
Sunday *domingo*
today *hoy*
tomorrow *mañana*
yesterday *ayer*
January *enero*
February *febrero*
March *marzo*
April *abril*
May *mayo*
June *junio*
July *julio*
August *agosto*
September *septiembre*
October *octubre*
November *noviembre*
December *diciembre*
a week *una semana*
a month *un mes*
after *después*
before *antes*

Courtesy of Bruce Whipperman, author of *Moon Pacific Mexico*. Corrected for Ecuadorian usage by Jean Brown.

Suggested Reading

Many of the out-of-print books listed below are available in libraries or from **Powell's Books** (40 NW 10th Ave., Portland, OR 97209, www .powells.com). Titles published in Ecuador can often be found at the Libri Mundi bookstore in Quito.

DESCRIPTION AND TRAVEL

Cárdenas, José-Germán, and Karen Marie Greiner. *Walking the Beaches of Ecuador.* Quito: J.G. Cárdenas and K.M. Greiner, 1988. An account of the authors' journey by foot down the entire coastline of Ecuador.

Clynes, Tom. *Wild Planet! 1,001 Extraordinary Events for the Inspired Traveler.* Visible Ink Press, Detroit MI, 1995. Festivals and celebrations around the world, including many in South America.

Sienko, Walter. *Latin America by Bike.* Seattle: The Mountaineers, 1993. Excellent reference book on cycling in Central and South America.

Urrutia, Virginia. *Two Wheels and a Taxi: A Slightly Daft Adventure in the Andes.* Seattle: The Mountaineers, 1987. The author, a grandmother, rode through Ecuador with only her sense of humor and an Ecuadorian taxi driver as backup.

HISTORY

Casas, Bartolomé de las. *A Short Account of the Destruction of the Indies.* New York: Penguin USA, 1999. Originally written as a plea to Prince Philip of Spain in the 16th century, this is a searing indictment of European cruelty toward the native peoples of the New World.

Hemming, John. *The Conquest of the Incas.* San Diego: Harcourt Brace & Co., 1973. Probably the best account of the Spanish arrival in the New World and its aftermath. A long but surprisingly readable account, exhaustively researched.

Vega, Garcilaso de la. *Royal Commentaries of the Incas & General History of Peru.* Austin: University of Texas Press, 1966. Out of print. First-hand account of the Incas at the time of the Spanish arrival and afterward.

ECUADORIAN CULTURE

Acosta-Solis, Basaglia, et al. *Ecuador: In the Shadow of the Volcanoes.* Quito: Ediciones Libri Mundi, 1991. English version by Pamela Gordon-Warren and Sarah Curl. General reference book on the country.

Anhalzer, Jorge. *Quito.* One of Anhalzer's many gorgeous coffee-table books available in Ecuador, filled with incredible photos. Others include *Amazonia, Llanganati, Galapagos, Ecuador: A Bird's Eye View,* and *Cotopaxi.*

Buchanan, Christy, and Cesar Franco. *The Ecuador Cookbook: Traditional Vegetarian and Seafood Recipes.* Christy Buchanan, 1998. A bilingual cookbook that uses easy-to-find ingredients.

Carvalho-Neto, Paulo. *Antología del Folklore Ecuatoriano.* Quito: Ediciones Abya-Yala, 1994. Anthology of folklore from around the country. In Spanish.

Carvalho-Neto, Paulo. *Cuentos Folkloricos del Ecuador, Sierra y Costa, Vol. I–III.* Quito: Ediciones Abya-Yala. Folklore from the Andes and the coast. In Spanish.

Cuvi, Pablo. *Crafts of Ecuador.* Quito: Dinediciones, 1994. Beautifully photographed book on Ecuadorian crafts.

González, Claudio Malo. *Cuenca Ecuador.* Quito: Ediciones Libri Mundi, 1991. Large-format book on Cuenca's historical treasures.

Paymal, Noemi, and Catalina Sosa. *Amazon Worlds*. Quito: Sinchi Sacha Foundation, 1993. A beautifully photographed coffee-table book on the indigenous cultures of the Ecuadorian Amazon.

ECUADORIAN LITERATURE

Adoum, Jorge Enrique, ed. *Poesia Viva del Ecuador, Siglo XX*. Quito: Grijalbo, 1990. Out of print. Collection of 20th-century Ecuadorian poetry.

Beardsell, Peter R. *Winds of Exile: The Poetry of Jorge Carrera Andrade*. Oxford: Dolphin Book Co., 1977. Out of print.

Cuvi, Pablo, et al. *Ten Stories from Ecuador (Diez cuentistas ecuatorianos)*. Quito: Ediciones Libri Mundi, 1990. A bilingual selection of modern Ecuadorian authors.

Izaca, Jorge Juan. *Huasipungo: the Villagers*. Carbondale, IL: Southern Illinois University Press, 1973. Landmark novel about peasant life in Ecuador that caused a furor when it was originally published in the 1930s. Brutally honest.

Spindler, Frank, trans. *Selections from Juan Montalvo*. Tempe: Center for Latin American Studies, Arizona State University, 1984. Out of print.

GENERAL INTEREST

Bemelmans, Ludwig. *The Donkey Inside*. New York: Paragon House, 1990. Out of print. The French author of the famous *Madeline* series for children traveled in Ecuador in the late '30s and early '40s. Subtle, always perceptive and sympathetic, and at times biting characterizations of Ecuadorians and their attitudes.

Buchet, Martine. *Panama: A Legendary Hat*. New York: Assouline, 2004.

Burroughs, William S. *Queer*. New York: Viking Penguin, 1996. A companion piece to Burroughs's first novel, *Junky* (1953), *Queer* describes a fictional addict's sexual escapades during a "hallucinated month of acute withdrawal" in Guayaquil and Mexico City.

Lourie, Peter. *Sweat of the Sun, Tears of the Moon*. Lincoln: University of Nebraska Press, 1998. First-hand account of an obsession with the treasure in the Llanganatis.

Michaux, Henri. *Ecuador: A Travel Journal*. Evanston, IL: Marlboro Press/Northwestern, 2001. Out of print. A short, quirky account of the Belgian-born author's travels in Ecuador in 1927. An interesting and very philosophical read, even spiritual at times.

Noble, Judith. *Introduction to Quechua: Language of the Andes*. Lincolnwood, IL: Passport Books, 1999. A book and tape package that covers everyday phrases, grammar, and vocabulary.

Poole, Richard. *The Inca Smiled: The Growing Pains of an Aid Worker in Ecuador*. Oxford, UK: Oneworld Publications, 1997. Out of print. The story of a British volunteer in Ecuador in the '60s, with interesting takes on the Andean indigenous personalities and Third World development.

Theroux, Paul. *The Old Patagonian Express: By Train Through the Americas*. Boston: Hougton Mifflin Co., 1997. The author travels from Canada to the tip of Chile by train. One chapter on the Quito–Guayaquil line, even though he didn't ride it.

Thomsen, Moritz. *Living Poor: A Peace Corps Chronicle*. Seattle: University of Washington Press, 1969. Out of print. Describing two years on a farm in Esmeraldas in the 1960s, this is said to be one of the best books on the Peace Corps experience. The narrative continues in *The Farm on the River of Emeralds* (Boston: Houghton Mifflin Co., 1978) and *The Saddest Pleasure: A Journey on Two Rivers* (St. Paul: Graywolf Press, 1990). All are eloquent and wrenching.

THE AMAZON

Emmons, Louise. *Neotropical Rainforest Mammals*. Chicago: University of Chicago Press, 1997. This scientific field guide has become the standard for studying these types of mammals.

Forsyth, Adrian, and Ken Miyata. *Tropical Nature*. New York: Touchstone, 1987. A great introduction for the nonscientist, this book makes tropical ecology fascinating and understandable.

Kane, Joe. *Savages*. New York: Vintage Departures, 1996. First-hand account of the Huaorani's fight against oil exploration, missionaries, and environmentalists.

Kricher, John. *A Neotropical Companion*. Princeton, NJ: Princeton University Press, 1999. Another good introduction to tropical ecology.

Montgomery, Sy. *Journey of the Pink Dolphins: An Amazon Quest*. New York: Simon & Schuster, 2000. An exhaustive, lyrical account of the author's many trips to the Amazon in search of the elusive pink river dolphins. Contains color photos and discussions of the people, flora and fauna, politics, and ecology.

Oxford, Pete, and Renee Bush. *Amazon Images*. Quito: Dinediciones, 1995. Beautiful photos.

Richards, Paul. *The Tropical Rain Forest: An Ecological Study*. Cambridge, UK: Cambridge University Press, 1996. A new revised edition of the 1964 botanical classic, based on more than 60 years of experience in rainforest ecology.

Smith, Randy. *Crisis Under the Canopy*. Quito: Abya Yala, 1993. Nonfiction work on tourism and the Huaorani.

THE GALÁPAGOS

Angermeyer, Johanna. *My Father's Island: A Galápagos Quest*. New York: Viking, 1989. Out of print. Life in the Galápagos through much of the 20th century.

Castro, Isabel. *A Guide to the Birds of the Galápagos Islands*. Princeton, NJ: Princeton University Press, 1996. Presents every species to have been recorded within the archipelago, including accidentals and vagrants. Thirty-two color plates.

Darwin, Charles. *The Origin of Species by Means of Natural Selection*. New York: Signet Classics, 2003. The book that shook the world—and, as a bonus, it's one of the few groundbreaking scientific works that's truly readable.

Darwin, Charles. *The Voyage of the Beagle*. New York: Penguin USA, 1999. A classic of early travel literature written by a wide-eyed, brilliant young man setting out to see the whole world. You can almost witness his theories being born.

Darwin, Charles, and Nora Barlow, ed. *The Autobiography of Charles Darwin, 1802–1882*. New York: W.W. Norton & Co., 1993. A simple and straightforward look into Darwin's mind and the forces that shaped it.

Darwin, Charles, and Mark Ridley, ed. *The Darwin Reader*. New York: W.W. Norton & Co., 1996. Selections from Darwin's works, including *The Voyage of the Beagle* and *The Origin of Species*.

De Roy, Tui. *Spectacular Galápagos: Exploring an Extraordinary World*. Westport, CT: Hugh Lauter Levin Associates, 1999. Text and breathtaking photographs by one of the islands's foremost advocates. De Roy lived in the Galápagos for 35 years and also wrote *Galápagos: Islands Born of Fire* (Warwick Publications, 2000).

Green, Jonathan. *Galápagos: Ocean, Earth, Wind & Fire*. Naturalist guide and photographer Green has assembled some excellent shots of the landscape and wildlife. Available in Quito or from the author (macarena@uio.satnet.net).

Horwell, David, and Pete Oxford. *Galápagos Wildlife*. Bucks, UK: Bradt, 1999.

Humann, Paul, ed., and Ned Deloach, ed. *Reef Fish Identification: Galápagos*. Jacksonville, FL: New World Publications, 1994.

Hurtado, Gustavo Vasconez. *Isle of the Black Cats*. Quito: Ediciones Libri Mundi, 1993. Novelized account of Floreana's soap operas.

Jackson, Michael. *Galápagos: A Natural History*. Calgary: University of Calgary Press, 1994. This definitive guide to the islands is a must-read for every visitor.

Latorre, Octavio. *The Curse of the Giant Tortoise*. Quito, 1990. Covers the strange history of the islands.

McMullen, Conley. *Flowering Plants of the Galápagos*. Ithaca, NY: Cornell University Press, 1999.

Vonnegut, Kurt, Jr. *Galápagos*. New York: Delta, 1999. The emperor of irony's take on what would happen if the only people to survive a worldwide epidemic were the passengers on a Galápagos cruise ship.

Weiner, Jonathan. *The Beak of the Finch: A Story of Evolution in Our Own Time*. New York: Vintage Books, 1995. Describes the work of Rosemary and Peter Grant, who have studied 20 generations of finches on Daphne Major over two decades.

Wittmer, Margaret. *Floreana: A Woman's Pilgrimage to the Galápagos*. Wakefield, RI: Moyer Bell, 1990. First-hand account of early Floreana settlers.

HEALTH

Bezruchka, Stephen, M.D. *The Pocket Doctor*. Seattle: The Mountaineers, 1999. A handy travel health reference.

Forgey, William, M.D. *Travelers' Medical Resource*. Merrillville: ICS Books, 1990. Absolutely comprehensive. Includes a toll-free computer database update service.

Rose, Stuart, M.D. *International Travel Health Guide*. Northampton, MA: Travel Medicine, Inc. Updated yearly.

OUTDOOR RECREATION

Brain, Yossi. *Ecuador: A Climbing Guide*. Seattle: The Mountaineers, 2000. The most up-to-date and detailed guide to climbing Ecuador's major peaks.

Kunstaetter, Robert, and Daisy Kunstaetter. *Trekking in Ecuador*. Seattle: The Mountaineers, 2002. Details on short and long foot journeys throughout the country.

Rachowiecki, Rob, Mark Thurber. *Climbing & Hiking in Ecuador*. Bucks, England: Bradt, 2004. A wide-ranging book that covers mountaineering and hikes of various lengths throughout the country.

BIRDING

Fjeldsa, Jon, and Niels Krabbe. *Birds of the High Andes*. Copenhagen: Apollo Books, 1990. Covers birds the length of the Andes above 2000 meters, beautiful plates. More than 880 pages.

Ridgely, Robert, and Paul Greenfield. *The Birds of Ecuador: A Field Guide*. Ithaca, NY: Comstock Publishing, 2001. The long-awaited guide to Ecuador's wealth of avifauna. More than 800 pages.

Rodner, Clemencia, Miguel Lentino, and Robin Restall. *A Checklist of the Birds of Northern South America*. New Haven: Yale University Press, 2001. Covers Ecuador, Colombia, and Venezuela.

Wheatley, Nigel. *Where to Watch Birds in South America*. Princeton, NJ: Princeton University Press, 2000. Site-specific, includes maps.

Internet Resources

GENERAL ECUADOR WEBSITES

EcuadorExplorer.com
www.ecuadorexplorer.com
Complete online guide.

Ecuador.com
www.ecuador.com
News, features, cultural and business information.

Exploring Ecuador
www.exploringecuador.com
Tourism, business, arts, cultural organizations, and news.

LatinWorld: Ecuador
www.latinworld.com/sur/ecuador/ index.html

Yahoo! Ecuador page
dir.yahoo.com/regional/countries/ ecuador/
Links to just about everything.

Ecuaroads
www.ecuaworld.com/ecuaroads
Road trips through Ecuador.

InQuito
www.inquito.com
Online guide to Quito, in English, German, and French.

VirtualTourist.com
www.virtualtourist.com/vt/8c0/
Ecuador travel page: "Real travelers sharing real info."

THE GALÁPAGOS ISLANDS

International Galápagos Tour Operators Association
www.igtoa.org

The Charles Darwin Foundation and the Charles Darwin Research Station
www.darwinfoundation.org

Galápagos Conservation Trust
www.gct.org

Discover Galapagos
www.discovergalapagos.com
Natural history, conservation issues, and travel information.

Galápagos Coalition
www.law.emory.edu/PI/GALAPAGOS
Scientists and lawyers interested in Galápagos conservation and its relation to human activities.

NEWS AND MEDIA

Hoy **online**
www.hoy.com.ec
Quito-based national daily newspaper, in Spanish.

El Comercio **online**
www.elcomercio.com
Quito-based national daily newspaper, in Spanish.

El Universo **online**
www.eluniverso.com
Guayaquil-based national daily newspaper, in Spanish.

Miami Herald
www.miami.com/mld/miamiherald/ news/world/americas
Coverage of Latin America.

South America Daily
www.southamericadaily.com

BBC News Latin America coverage
news.bbc.co.uk/hi/english/world/ americas

GOVERNMENT

Ecuadorian Embassy in Washington D.C.
www.ecuador.org

U.S. Department of State background notes country index
www.state.gov/www/background_notes/whabgnhp.html
Click on "Ecuador" for the most recent posting.

CIA World Factbook: Ecuador
www.odci.gov/cia/publications/factbook/geos/ec.html

U.S. Department of State's *Ecuador: A Country Study* online
lcweb2.loc.gov/frd/cs/ectoc.html

U.S. Embassy in Ecuador
www.usembassy.org.ec

WEATHER AND THE NATURAL WORLD

Yahoo! Quito weather forecast
weather.yahoo.com/forecast/ECXX0008.html

Instituto Geofisico-Escuela Politecnica Nacional
www.igepn.edu.ec
Local volcano watchers provide daily updates, seismograms within 15 minutes of events, and photos.

Smithsonian Institution Global Volcanism Program
www.volcano.si.edu/gvp
Includes recent worldwide activity.

LANGUAGE

Yahoo! Babel Fish
http://babelfish.yahoo.com

SpanishDICT.com

www.spanishdict.com
Online Spanish dictionary.

Learn Spanish
www.studyspanish.com
Free, award-winning online tutorial.

THE ENVIRONMENT

Planeta.com
www.planeta.com
Eco-travel in Latin America.

Fundación Sinchi Sacha
www.sinchisacha.org
Helps the indigenous population of Ecuador by encouraging self-directed development and fair trade.

Fundación Natura
www.fnatura.org
Ecuador's largest environmental organization.

Jocotoco Foundation
www.fjocotoco.org
Purchases land to preserve avifauna and biodiversity.

OTHER WEBSITES

Cultures of the Andes
www.andes.org
Quechua language links, songs, and pictures.

Instituto Geofisico
www.igepn.edu.ec
Volcano watch, with up-to-date information on what volcanoes are doing in Ecuador.

Saraguro Community Page
www.saraguro.org
Saraguro links, music, culture, history, anthropology, archaeology, tourism, and pictures.

Human Rights Watch
www.hrw.org/americas
Information on human rights issues in Ecuador.

Index

A

Abya Yala: 37
Academia Superior de Arte: 47
accommodations: general discussion 427-428;
    see also specific place
Achupallas: 19, 166
acute mountain sickness (AMS): 432
Agato: 90-91
Agora: 36
agriculture: 391-392
AIDS: 431
air travel: general discussion 413-416, 421;
    see also specific place
Alausí: 19, 166
albatross: 332
Alcedo Volcano: 358
alcoholic beverages: 404
All Fools' Day: 400
All Saints' Day: 400
All Souls' Day: 400
Alusí: 166-167
Amaluza: 422
Ambato: 135-139
Amigos de la Naturaleza: 70
Andean geographical region: 366-367
Apuela: 101-102
archaeological sites: Agua Blanca museum
    234; El Cajas National Park 282-283;
    El Salitre 124; Gualimán 102; Ingapirca 9,
    11, 17, 19, 285-286; Las Tolas de Cochasquí
    92-93; Machalilla National Park 233;
    Pumapungo ruins 273; Rumicucho Ruins
    68-69; Todas Santos 274
Arco de la Reina: 33
art: general discussion 398-401; see also
    specific place
arthropods: 336
art lessons: 47
astronomy: 36
Atacames: 218-219
Atahualpa: 144
ATMs: 437
avalanches: 368
Avenida Amazonas: 11, 37
Avenue of the Volcanoes: 8, 118, 366
Awá-Kwaiker people: 395

B

Bachas Beach: 345
Baeza: 8, 174-175
baggage: 415, 420, 422
Bahía de Caráquez: 223-226
ballet: 41
Banco del Azuay: 275
Baños (central Sierra): 19, 141-151
Baños (southern Sierra): 282
Baños de San Vicente: 242
bars: see nightlife
Bartolomé Island: 355
basilica (Riobamba): 157
Basílica La Dolorosa: 104
bats: 330
Battle of Pichincha: 400
beer: 404
Bellavista (central Sierra): 147
Bellavista (Santa Cruz Island): 345
bicycling: general discussion 412, 418-419;
    Alandaluz 235; Baños 147; Galápagos
    Islands 350; Isinliví 133; Quito 44;
    Vilcabamba 299, 300
Bilsa Biological Station: 212-213
birds/bird-watching: general discussion 408-
    409; Antisana Ecological Reserve 172-173;
    Baeza 175; Cabañas Ecológicas Copalinga
    295; Cerro Blanco Protected Forest 261;
    Cerro Golondrinas 111; Cotopaxi National
    Park 123-126; Cuyabeno Wildlife Refuge 178-
    179; Galápagos Islands 330-336; Intag Cloud
    Forest Reserve 101; La Perla Forest Reserve
    212-213; Limoncocha Biological Reserve
    183-185; Loja 292; Los Cedros Biological
    Reserve 100; Machalilla National Park 233-
    234; Manglares Churute Ecological Reserve
    262; Mindo 70, 71, 72; Parque Condor
    84; Pasochoa Protected Forest 73-74;
    Podocarpus National Park 296; Riobamba
    159; Río Napo 186, 187; Salinas 241; Sangay
    National Park 163; San Rafael Falls 176
Black Sheep Inn: 16, 134
Black Turtle Cove: 345-346
blackwater rivers: 372
Bolívar, Simon: 247, 384-385
Bolívar: 113
Bolívar's Birthday celebration: 254
boobies: 331-332

books/bookstores: Ambato 135; birding 409; literature 399; Otavalo 81-82; Quito 37, 42-43, 409
Borbón: 215
border towns: 422
Bospas Fruit Forest Farm: 110-111
Bucarám Ortiz, Abdalá: 388-389
Buccaneer Cove: 354
budgeting: 438
Bullcay: 284
bullfighting: 47, 412
Bureau of Consular Affairs: 436
business hours: 441
bus travel: general discussion 419-420; see also specific place
butterflies: 71, 186, 195, 197, 345, 376

C

Cabañas Aliñahui and Butterfly Lodge: 197
Cabañas San Isidro: 188-189
cable car: 41
Café Art Gallery: 104
Cagañas Albergue Español: 198
Calderón: 65-66
Calle Numa Pompilio Llona: 250, 251
Camino de la Antena: 175
camping: see specific place
Cañar: 17, 284-285
Cañari people: 284, 394
Canelos Kichwa people: 163
Canoa: 222-223
canoeing: 192
Canonization Anniversary: 210
Canonization Festival (Bahía de Caráquez): 225
Canonization Festival (Bñanos): 146
Capilla de Catuña: 31
Capilla del Hombre: 39
Capilla Santa Ana: 251
Caranquis: 394
Carcel de las Mujeres: 35
Carnival: 400
Carnival (Ambato): 138
Carnival (Guaranda): 154
Carnival (Guayaquil): 254
car travel: general discussion 416-418; see also specific place
Casa de Benalcázar: 34
Casa de la Cultura (Cuenca): 272
Casa de la Cultura (Guayaquil): 252
Casa de la Cultura (Latacunga): 130
Casa de la Cultura (Quito): 11, 36
Casa de los Marqueses: 130
Casa del Suizo: 198

Casa de María Augusta Urrutia: 32-33
Casa de Montalvo: 137
Casa de Sucre: 33
Casa Mojanda: 88
Cascales: 177
casinos: 253
Catamayo: 297
Catedral (Plaza Grande): 29
Catedral Antigua: 272
Catedral Nueva: 17, 272
cathedral (Macas): 202
caves/caverns: Canoa 223; Gruta La Paz 113; Jumandy Caves and Tourist Complex 190; La Cueva de los Tayos 203-204
Cayambe: 93-94
Celebration of Apostle Santiago the Elder: 140
Centro Cívico: 254
Centro Commercial Malecón: 250
Centro Cultural Metropolitano: 30
Centro Cultural Sarao: 254
cerebral edema: 432
Cerro Brujo: 353
Cerro Crocker: 345
Cerro Dragon: 346
Cerro Santa Ana: 250-251
Cerro Sararucu: 95
Chachis: 395
Chagas' disease: 431
Charles Darwin Research Center: 13, 344-345
chicha: 404
children, traveling with: 428
cholera: 430
Chordeleg: 17, 284
Christmas/Christmas Eve: 400
Christmas festival (Cuenca): 275-276
Chugchilán: 134
cinema: Bahía de Caráquez 225; Cuenca 275; Guayaquil 248, 254; Machala 263; Quito 41
City Hall (Quito): 29
Ciudad Blanca cemetery: 253
classical music: 41
climate: 368-369
climbing: see mountaineering
cloud forests: general discussion 369-370; see also ecological reserves and protected areas
coastal birds: 334
coastal forests: 371
coastal geography: 367
Coca: 179-182
cockfights: 412
Cofán people: 396-397
coffee: 404
Cojimíes: 222

Coliseo Rumiñahui: 41
Collanes Plain: 19, 165
Colombia: 116, 117, 230, 422
colonial period: 382-383
Columbus Day/Día de La Raza: 254, 400
comorants: 333
conduct and customs: 423-424
Conejo: 210
consulates: Cuenca 281; Guayaquil 259;
   Quito 59
Convent Museo Santa Catalina: 35
Convento de la Concepción: 157
Convento de las Conceptas: 273
Convento San Alfonso: 157
Convento y Museo de San Agustín: 30
Corona del Diablo: 363
Corpus Christi: 400
Corpus Christi (Cuenca): 275
Corpus Christi (Salasaca): 140
Cotacachi: 97-99
courier flights: 414-415
crafts: Cañar 284; Chordeleg 284; Cotacachi
   97; Cuenca 276; Gualaceo 283-284;
   Guayaquil 254-255; Ibarra 104; Otavalo 78,
   80-82; Peguche 88; Quito 42; San Antonio
   de Ibarra 107; Saraguro 287, 288; Sigsig
   284; see also specific place
credit cards: 437
crime: 434-436
Crucita: 230
cruises: freighters 416; Galápagos Islands 309
Cubilche: 107-108
Cuenca: 9, 11, 19, 269-282
Cuenca's Independence celebration: 275
curanderos (native healers): 91, 108
currency: 436-437
customs and imports: 422

D
dance lessons: 47
Daphne Major: 346
Darwin Arch: 365
Darwin Bay Beach: 365
Darwin, Charles: 314-315, 316
Darwin Island: 15, 365
Darwin Lake: 359
Darwin's finches: 334-335
Data de Posorja: 244
Data de Villamil: 244
Day of the Dead: 400
Day of the Dead (Salasaca): 140
demographics: 393-394
dengue fever: 431

Devil's Nose: 19, 166
Día de la Raza: 400
diarrhea: 430
disabled travelers, tips for: 428
diseases: 430-431
diving: 15-16, 232, 311-312, 340, 350, 412
dolphins: 330
drugs: 435
dry season: 13
Duran: 262

E
earthquakes: 368
Easter: 400
ecological reserves and protected areas:
   general discussion 378; Alandaluz
   Ecological Tourist Center 234-235;
   Antisana Ecological Reserve 18, 172-173;
   Bellavista Cloud Forest Reserve 18, 72-73;
   Cayambe-Coca Ecological Reserve 94-96;
   Cerro Blanco Protected Forest 261; Cerro
   Golondrinas 111; Chimborazo Fauna Reserve
   152-154; Cotacachi-Cayapas Ecological
   Reserve 99-100, 216-217; Cotopaxi National
   Park 8, 18, 123-126; Cuyabeno Wildlife
   Refuge 178-179; El Angel Ecological Reserve
   112-113; El Boliche National Recreation Area
   126; El Cajas National Park 11, 19, 282-283;
   Iliniza Ecological Reserve 121-123; Intag
   Cloud Forest Reserve 101; Jatun Sacha
   Biological Station 195-197; Jumandy Caves
   and Tourist Complex 190; La Perla Forest
   Reserve 212-213; Limoncocha Biological
   Reserve 183-185; Los Cedros Biological
   Reserve 100-101; Machalilla National Park
   8-9, 18, 233-234; Manglares Churute
   Ecological Reserve 9, 18, 262; Maquipucuna
   Biological Reserve 18, 69-70; Mindo-
   Nambillo Protected Forest 70; Pasochoa
   Protected Forest 73-74; Pedagogical
   Ethnobotanical OMAERE Park 199; Playa del
   Oro Reserva de Tigrillos 217; Podocarpus
   National Park 9, 19, 295-297; Pululahua
   Crater and Geobotanical Reserve 13, 68;
   Puyango Petrified Forest 265; Reserva
   Ecologica Mache-Chindul 212; Reserva
   Ecológico Manglares Cayapas-Mataje
   215; Río Palenque Science Center 211-212;
   San Francisco Cloud Forest 296; Sangay
   National Park 162-166, 202; Sumaco-
   Napo Galeras National Park 189; Tambillo
   Protected Forest 287; Tzanka Ecological
   Refuge 295; Yarina Biological Reserve 183

economy: 391–393
ecotourism: 378
Ecuadorian Orchid Society Botanical
Gardens: 253
ecuavolley: 412
edema: 432
education: 397–398
educational opportunities: 425, 426
egrets: 334
El Altar: 19, 164–166
El Angel: 112
El Barranco: 275
El Chato Tortoise Reserve: 345
El Cisne: 297
electricity: 441
El Indio Guarango: 154
Elizabeth Bay: 359
El Loco: 388–389
El Muerto: 352
El Niño: 324–325
El Panecillo: 34–35
El Quinche: 67
embassies: Guayaquil 259; Quito 59
employment: 425
entertainment: general discussion 398–401;
see also specific place
environmental issues: 376–378
Epiphany: 400
equator: 13, 67–69, 82–83
Esmeraldas: 11, 213–214
Española Island: 363–364
Espumilla Beach: 355
Estadio Olímpico: 41
ethnographic museum (Mitad del Mundo): 67
etiquette: 423–424

F
fauna: general discussion 369–371, 374–376;
Galápagos Islands 318–319, 322, 325–338
Feast of San Sebastian: 291
feminism: 424
Feria Agropecuaria: 229
Fernandina Island: 359–360
Festival de la Chicha de Jora: 287
festivals and events: general discussion 399–
401; Quito 12; see also specific event; place
Fiesta de la Lana: 154
Fiesta de la Santissima Virgen de la
Merced: 130
Fiesta de las Frutas y las Flores: 138
Fiesta de los Lagos: 104
Fiesta del Provincialización: 115

Fiesta del Virgen de la Paz: 113
Fiesta del Virgen del Carmen: 104
Fiesta de San Juan (Cotacachi): 97
Fiesta de San Pedro y Pablo: 94
Fiesta Municipal (Tulcán): 115
Fiesta of San Juan (Otavalo): 81
finches: 334–335
fish/fishing: 220, 240, 241, 282–283, 408
flamingos: 334
flightless cormorants: 333
flora: general discussion 369, 370, 372–374;
Galápagos Islands 338–339
Floreana Island: 360–363
flower exports: 122
folk music: 40
food: general discussion 401–404; see also
specific place
Foundation of Cuenca: 275
Foundation of Guayaquil festival: 254
Founding of Riobamba: 157
freighters: 416
French Museum: 68
frigatebirds: 332–333
frostbite: 432
fruit: 403
Fundación Golondrinas: 111
Fundación Quito colonial: 67–68

G
Galápagos Fur Seal: 330
Galápagos Islands: 303–365; accommodations
341–343, 350–351; climate 324–325; diving
311–312; entertainment and events 340,
350; fauna 318–319, 322, 325–338; flora
318–319, 338–339; food 343, 351; history
312–314, 314–315, 316, 317–320; information
and services 343, 351; maps 305, 316, 323;
planning your trip 306–312; shopping 340;
tours 308–311, 350; transportation 307–308,
343–344, 351–352
Galápagos penguin: 332
Galápagos sea lion: 329–330
Gardener Bay: 363–364
gay and lesbian travelers: 428
gender issues: 424
Genovesa: 364–365
geography: 366–367
geology: 368
giant tortoise: 326–327
Girón: 286
government: 390–391
Granary Trail: 175

gratuities: 311, 438
greater flamingos: 334
Gruta La Paz: 113
Guagua Pinchincha: 69
Gualaceo: 17, 283-284
Gualaquiza: 204
Guallupe: 110
Guamote: 166
Guano: 162
Guápulo: 74
Guaranda: 154-155
Guayaquil: 237-238, 244-262; maps 239, 245, 248-249
Guayas: 250
Guayllabamba: 66-67
guides: 406; see also tours
Guitig factory: 121
gulls: 333
gyms: 47

H
Hacienda Cusín: 87
Hacienda Pinsaquí: 11, 91-92
haciendas: 427-428
Hacienda Tinalandia: 18, 211
Hacienda Zuleta: 96
handicapped travelers, tips for: 428
healers: 91, 108
health and safety: 429-436
helados de paila: 106
hepatitis: 10, 430, 431
Heroes del Cenepa: 68
herons: 334
hiking/backpacking: general discussion 406-407; Baeza 175; Baños 146-147; Cerro Golondrinas 111; Chimborazo Fauna Reserve 153-154; Cuenca 277; El Boliche National Recreation Area 126; El Cajas National Park 282-283; Imbabura 108; Intag Cloud Forest Reserve 101; Isinliví 133; Laguna Quilotoa 135; Mindo 71; Mirador La Cruz 225; Otavalo 84; Oyacachi Trail 95-96; Pasochoa Protected Forest 74; Piñan Lakes 108-109; Pululahua Crater 68; Riobamba 159; Sangay National Park 163; Saraguro 288; Vilcabamba 299; Volcán Cotacachi 100; Volcán Reventador 176-177; see also mountaineering
Historical Museum: 251
hitchhiking: 418
HIV: 431
Hobbs Bay: 352

Hola Vida: 199
holidays: 399-401
homestays: 427
horseback riding: general discussion 412; Alandaluz 235; Baños 147; Hacienda Pinsaquí 92; Hacienda Zuleta 96; Puerto López 232; Puluulahua Crater 68; Quito 46-47; Riobamba 159; Sangay National Park 163; Vilcabamba 299
horse-drawn carriage tours: 41
hospitality: 424
Hostería San Jorge: 18, 69
hotels: see specific place
Hotel San Francisco de Quito: 19, 49
hot springs: Aguas Hediondas 116; Apuela 101; Bainearios Aguas Termales 116; Baños (Central Sierra) 8, 19, 146; Baños (Southern Sierra) 11, 282; Chachimbiro 109-110; Los Elenes 162; Papallacta 174; Rodas 11, 282; Zaruma 265
Huaorani people: 396
Huaquillas: 265, 422
hypothermia: 432

I
Ibarra: 11, 102-107
Iglesia de Guápulo: 74
Iglesia de la Merced: 33-34
Iglesia de Nuestra Señora del Agua Santa: 1
Iglesia de San Francisco (Latacunga): 1
Iglesia de San Vicente: 251
Iglesia El Carmen de la Asunció
Iglesia El Pedestal: 290-291
Iglesia El Sagrario: 29
Iglesia La Merced: 104
Iglesia San Agustín: 30
Iglesia San Antonio de P
Iglesia San Francisco (C
Iglesia San Francisco
Iglesia San Sebastia
Iglesia Santo Domi
Iglesia Santo Dom
Iglesia Santo Do
iguanas: 322, 3
Iliniza Norte: 1
Iliniza Sur: 12
Illuchi: 147
Ilumán: 91
IMAX mo
immuni
Incas:
Inca
Jacch
Jambel
James B
milio:
86, 292, 380-381

Independence Celebration (Latacunga): 130
independence from Spain: 383-386
Independence of Guayaquil: 254, 400
Independence of Loja: 291
Independence of Riobamba: 157
indigenous people: general discussion 394-397; Achuar people 204-205; Casa de María Augusta Urrutia 16, 32-33; Centro Cultural Metropolitano 16, 30; Cuyabeno 178; El Cajas National Park 282-283; hide paintings 16, 17; Itchimbia Cultural Center 16, 36-37; itinerary suggestions 16-17; Laguna Quilotoa 16, 134-135; language 104, 204, 397; Latacunga Loop 16, 132-135; markets 8, 283-284, 401; organizations 171, 192; Peguche 16, 88; Puyo 198
industry: 392-393
information and services: general discussion 436-441; see also specific place
Ingañan: 286
Ingapirca: 9, 11, 17, 19, 285-286
insects: general discussion 376; diseases from 430-431; Galápagos Islands 336
International Theater Festival: 229
internet access: 439-440
Isabela Island: 356-359
Isinliví: 133
Isla de la Plata: 9, 233
Isla de los Monos: 185
Isla de Puna: 244
Isla Lobos: 352
tchimbia Park and Cultural Center: 16, 36-37

igua Ecuadorian Folklore Ballet: 41
: 264
y: 354-355
31
ico Reindaldo Espinosa: 291

nedo International Airport: 10
seum: 251
ka l discussion 409-411; see
kaya.
Kichwa
Kicker Rc
La Balbaner
08

La Basílica: 35
Labor Day: 400
La Candelaria and Los Chiguales: 225
La Cima de la Libertad: 34
La Compañía: 32-33
La Concepción: 29-30
La Esperanza: 107-108
La Galapaguera: 352
Lago Agrio: 177-178
Laguna Amarilla: 19, 165
Laguna Colta: 162
Laguna Cuicocha: 99-100
Laguna de San Pablo: 86-87
Laguna Doñoso: 109
Laguna El Junco: 352
Laguna Limpiopungo: 124
Laguna Quilotoa: 8, 134-135
Lagunas de Mojanda: 88
Lagunas de Piñan: 108-109
Laguna Yahuarcocha: 108
lahars: 368
Lake District: 173-174
La Libertad: 242-243
La Lobería: 352
land: 366-369
land iguanas: 328-329
landslides: 368
language: general discussion 397; Achuar 204; English language courses 426; Quechma 104; Spanish courses 60-61, 85, 150-151, 281, 425
La Ronda: 32
La Rotonda: 250
La Selva Jungle Lodge: 186-187
Las Orguideas: 199
Las Peñas: 250-251
Latacunga: 128-132
Latacunga Loop: 132-135
La Tola: 215
La Toma Airport: 297
laundry: 441
lava lizards: 329
lava tunnels: 345
leishmaniasis: 431
lesbian and gay travelers: 428
lighthouse: 251
Límon: 204
Limoncocha: 184
literature: 399
Lligua: 147
Lloa: 69
Llullu Llama Hostal: 16, 133
Loja: 9, 19, 288-297

Los Gemelos: 345
Lowland Quechuas: 395, 397
luggage: 10, 435

M

Macará: 297, 422
Macas: 200-203
Machachi: 121-123
Machala: 262-265
machismo: 424
magazines: 43, 440
mail: 438
malaria: 430-431
Maldonado: 117
Malecón del Salado: 253
Malecón 2000: 248, 250
Mama Negra: 130
mammals: general discussion 370, 371,
   374-375; Galápagos Islands 329-330
Manglaralto: 236
mangroves: 11, 371
Manta: 226-230
Manta Day: 229
maps and tourist information: 441
marimba: 215
marine iguanas: 327-328
marine invertebrates, Galápagos Islands:
   337-338
marinelife, Galápagos Islands: 326
Mariscal Sucre International Airport: 10, 62
markets: general discussion 401; see also
   crafts; specific place
Mascarilla: 111
Media Luna: 345
Méndez: 203
Mindalae Ethnic Museum: 37
Mindo: 70-73
mining: 392
Mirador El Lechero: 84
Mirador Turi: 282
Misahualli: 193-195
Mitad del Mundo: 13, 67-69
mockingbirds: 335
Molinas de Monserrat: 130
Monasterio de la Merced: 34
Monasterio del Carmen: 273
Monasterio El Carmen Alto: 33
Monasterio El Carmen Bajo: 30
money: 436-437; safety tips 434-435
Monjas Grande: 19, 165
Montañita: 235-236
Montecristi: 231

Monumento Olmedo: 250
Monumento Sucre: 250
Monument to the Heroes of Independence: 252
Moorish Clock Tower: 250
Moreno, Gabriel García: 386
Morona: 203
motorcycles: 416-417
mountain biking: see bicycling
mountaineering: general discussion 44-46,
   404-406; Cerro Saraurcu 95; Cubilche
   107-108; El Altar 164-166; Iliniza Norte 123;
   Iliniza Sur 122-123; Otavalo 84; Pichinchas
   volcanoes 69; Quito 44-46; Santa Cruz
   Island 345; Volcán Antisana 173; Volcán
   Carihuairazo 153-154; Volcán Cayambe 95;
   Volcán Chiles 117; Volcán Chimborazo 8, 19,
   152-153, 159; Volcán Corazón 122; Volcán
   Cotopaxi 124-125; Volcán Imbabura 107-108;
   Volcán Rumiñahui 125-126; Volcán Sangay
   164; Volcán Sumaco 189; Volcán Tungurahua
   143-144; Yana Urcu de Piñan 100
mountain sickness: 432
movie theaters: see cinema
Muisne: 221
Municipal Museum: 252
Murcielago: 227
Museo Alberto Mena Caamaño: 30
Museo Amazonico: 37
Museo Antropológico y de Arte
   Contemporaneo: 17, 248
Museo Arqueológico Municipal (El Angel): 112
Museo Arqueológico Municipal (Macas): 202
Museo Colonial y de Arte: 36
Museo de Arte Moderno (Cuenca): 272-273
Museo de Arte Moderno (Quito): 36
Museo de Arte Religioso: 290
Museo de Artes Populares: 274
Museo de Ciencias Naturales: 137-138
Museo de Esqueletología: 274
Museo de Instrumentos Musicales: 36
Museo de la Ciudad: 33
Museo de la Historia de la Medicina: 274
Museo de la Musica: 290
Museo de la Provincia: 138
Museo de las Ciencias Naturales: 39
Museo de las Culturas: 97
Museo de las Culturas Aborigines: 274
Museo de las Fuerzas Armadas: 34
Museo del Banco Central (Cuenca): 273
Museo del Banco Central (Loja): 290
Museo del Banco Central (Manta): 227
Museo del Banco Central (Quito): 36
Museo del Obraje: 81

Museo de los Metales: 274
Museo del Sombrero: 274
Museo de Sitio Inti-Ñan: 68
Museo de Traje Indígena: 36
Museo El Fortin de Santa Ana: 251
Museo Fray Pedro Bedon: 32
Museo Fray Pedro Gocial: 31
Museo Fundación Guayasamín: 39
Museo Jacinto Jijón y Caamaño: 37
Museo "Los Amantes de Sumpa": 242-243
Museo Manuel Agustin Landivar: 274
Museo Nacional de Arte Colonial: 34
Museo Nahim Isaias B.: 250
Museo Naval: 250
Museo Presley Norton: 253
Museo Regional Banco Central del
    Ecuador: 104
Museo Remigio Crespo Toral: 274
Museo Salango: 234
music: general discussion 398-399; see also
    nightlife; specific place

N
Nabón: 288
Nanegal: 70
Nanegalito: 70
Napo Wildlife Center: 185-186
Nariz del Diablo train ride: 166
Natabuelas: 394
National Science Museum: 157
Neotropical Field Biology Institute: 186
newspapers: 43, 440
New Town (Quito): 11, 18, 37, 38, 39
New Year's Eve/New Year's Day: 400
nightlife: Atacames 219; Baños 145-146;
    Cuenca 275; Galápagos Islans 340, 350;
    Guayaquil 253; Loja 291; Macas 202;
    Machala 263; Manta 229; Otavalo 81; Playas
    243; Quito 40-41; Riobamba 159; Salinas
    240-241; Santo Domingo de los Colorados
    210; Tena 190; Tulcán 115; Vilcabamba 299
Nuestra Señoradel Agua Santa: 146

O
Obispo: 19, 165
observatory: 36
officialdom: 435-436
oil industry: 392-393
Old Town (Quito): 11, 27, 28, 29-35
Olmedo: 215
Olon: 236
Orellana, Francisco de: 180-181

Organization for the Defense and Conservation
    of the Ecology of Intag (DECOIN): 101
Oriente: 18, 168-205, 367; maps 170, 184,
    185, 196
Otavaleño people: 89, 394
Otavalillo: 109
Otavalo: 11, 78-86, 89
oxbow lakes: 372

P
packing: 10, 307
Palacio Arzobispal: 29
Palacio de Gobierno (Quito): 29
Palacio de Justicia: 275
Palacio del Gobierno (Guayaquil): 250
Palacio Legisiativo: 36
Palacio Municipal (Guayaquil): 250
Palacio Municipal (Ibarra): 104
panpipes: 88
Papallacta: 13, 173-174
paragliding: 104, 412
paramo, 370-371
parks: see ecological reserves and protected
    areas
Parque Amazonico La Isla: 190
Parque Bolívar: 130
Parque Calderón (Cuenca): 272
Parque Central (Loja): 290
Parque de la Independencia (Loja): 290
Parque de los Iguanas: 252
Parque El Ejido: 36
Parque Histórico Guayaquil: 17, 253
Parque Jipiro: 291
Parque La Alameda: 36
Parque La Carolina: 39
Parque La Filantrópica: 130
Parque La Libertad: 157
Parque Maldonado: 157
Parque Montalvo: 137
Parque 21 de Abril: 157
Parque Universitario La Argelia: 291
Parque Vicente León: 130
Paseo de los Monos: 199
passports: 10, 422
Patate: 140-141
Patio de Comedias: 41
Patriotism Day: 400
Peach Festival: 284
Pedernales: 222
Peguche: 88, 90
Penal García Moreno: 35
peñas: 40

penguins: 332
performing arts: *see* theaters and concerts; *specific place*
Peru: 265, 297, 422; border struggles with 387, 388, 389
pharmacies: 433
Píllaro: 139-140
Piñan Lakes: 100, 108-109
Playa del Oro: 217
Playa El Manglesito: 352
Playa Escondida: 11, 220-221
Playa Ochoa: 352
Playas: 243-244
Plaza Centenario: 252-253
Plaza Colón: 251
Plaza del Quindé: 37
Plaza del Teatro: 11, 30
Plaza Grande: 29-30
Plaza San Francisco: 31
Plaza San Sebastian: 272-273
Plaza Santo Domingo: 32
Plazoleta del Carmen: 273
police: 435-436
politeness: 423-424
politics: 390-391
Pomasqui: 67
Pompeya: 185
Portón de la Ciudad: 290
Portoviejo: 231
postal service: 438
Post Office Bay: 13, 362-363
Prince Philliip's Steps: 365
prison visits: 35
Pro-Bici: 19, 159
Puente San Francisco: 147
Puente San Martín: 147
Puerto Ayora: 15, 339-345
Puerto Baquerizo Moreno: 348, 349, 350-352
Puerto Cayo: 231
Puerto Chino: 352
Puerto Egas: 354
Puerto Grande: 352-353
Puerto López: 18, 231-233
Puerto Santa Ana: 251
Puerto Velasco Ibarra: 362
Puerto Villamil: 357-358
Pujilí: 135
pulmonary edema: 432
punctuality: 423
Punta Brava: 236
Punta Carnero: 242
Punta Cormorant: 362

Punta Espinosa: 13, 360
Punta Montañita: 236
Punta Moreno: 358-359
Punta Pelada: 243
Punta Pitt: 352, 353
Punta Suárez: 13, 364
Puntzan: 147
Puyo: 198-200

QR

Quechua people: 13, 93, 277, 395, 397
Quesera de la Cooperative Salinas: 154
Quevedo: 212
Quinta de Mera: 137
Quinta de Montalvo: 137
Quito: 21-65; accommodations 48-51; entertainment and events 12, 40-41; food 52-56; information and services 56-58, 59, 60-61; maps 24-25, 28, 38; shopping 42-43; sights 27, 29-37, 39; sports and recreation 44-47; transportation 62-65
Rábida Island: 355-356
rabies: 10, 432
radio: 440-441
rafting: general discussion 407-408; Baños 147; Quito 46; Tena 8, 13, 191-192
rail travel: *see* train travel; *specific place*
rainforests: 371-376
rats: 330
rays: 336-337
religion: 397
reptiles: 326-329
reserves: *see* ecological reserves and protected areas
restaurants: 402-403; *see also specific place*
RICANCIE: 192
Río Aguarico: 407
Río Anzu: 408
Riobamba: 19, 155-162
Riobamba agricultural, livestock, and crafts fair: 157
Río Blanco: 20, 46, 407
Río Due: 407
Río Hollin: 408
Río Jondachi: 408
Río Misahualli Bajo: 407-408
Río Napo: 179, 181, 183-188, 407; maps 184-185
Río Oyacachi: 95
Río Palenque: 211-212
Río Pastaza: 19, 147
Río Patate: 147, 408
Río Piatua: 408

Río Quijos: 20, 46, 407
Río Toachi: 46
Río Topo: 147, 408
Río Upano: 408
Ritmo Tropical Dance Academy: 47
rivers: hydrology 372; rafting and kayaking 407-408; see also specific river
roads: 417
Rucu Pichincha: 69
Runa people: 394
Runtún: 146-147

S

Sacha Lodge: 185
safety tips: 311, 429-436
Salango: 234
Salasaca: 140
Salinas (Central Sierra): 154
Salinas (Santa Elena Peninsula): 240-242
Same: 220
San Antonio de Ibarra: 107
San Antonio del Pichincha: 67
San Cristóbal: 15, 348-353
Sangolquí: 73
Sani Lodge: 18, 187
San Juan celebration: 400
San Lorenzo: 11, 215-218
San Martín, José de: 247
San Miguel de Yahuarcocha: 108
San Miguel festivals: 400
San Pablo celebrations: 400
San Pedro: 215
San Pedro and San Pablo: 225
Santa Catalina: 35
Santa Cruz Island: 339-346
Santa Elena Peninsula: 9, 238-244
Santa Fé: 346-347
Santa Isabel: 286
Santa Mariana de Jesús: 23
Santa Rosa: 345
Santiago (Southern Oriente): 203
Santiago Island: 353-355
Santo Domingo de los Colorados: 209-211
Santos Reyes and Santos Inocentes: 216
Santuario de La Virgen del Cisne: 297
San Vinicio festival: 140
Saraguro: 287-288
Saraguro people: 287, 394
scams: 435
seabirds: 330-334
sea lions: 329-330
seals: 330

seasons: 9
sea turtles: 329
senior travelers: 428-429
sexually transmitted diseases: 431
Seymour Norte: 347
sharks: 336-337
sherbet: 106
shopping: see specific item; place
Shuar-Achuar people: 163, 395-396
Sierra geographical region: 366-367
Sierra Negra Volcano: 358
Sigchos: 133-134
Sigsig: 284
Simón Bolívar's Birthday: 400
Siona-Secoya people: 396
SISA: 81
snakes: 432
snorkeling: see diving
soccer: 47, 412
soil: 372
Solar Culture Museum: 68
Sombrero Chino: 356
Son Latino: 47
South Plaza Island: 347
Spanish conquest: 381-382
spectator sports: see specific place; sport
sports and recreation: general discussion 404-412; equipment 43, 405-406; see also specific activity; place
Steve Devine's Butterfly Farm: 345
Súa: 219-220
Sucúa: 203
sugarcane liquor: 404
Sugarloaf Volcano: 355
Sullivan Bay: 353-354
sunburn: 430
surfing: 235, 236, 241, 243, 350, 408
sustainable development: 377-378

T

Tabernacle: 19, 165
Tagus Cove: 359
Tandayapa Lodge: 18, 72
Tarqui: 227
taxes: 415, 438
taxis: 418
taxonomy: 326
Teatro Bolívar: 30
Teatro Malayerba: 41
Teatro Nacional Sucre: 30
Teatro Politecnico: 41
Teatro Prometeo: 36

Teatro Variedades: 30
telecommunications: 438-439
teleférigo: 41
television: 440-441
Temple of the Sun: 286
Templo de la Patria: 34
Templo del Sol: 104
Tena: 8, 13, 190-193
Tena founding celebration: 190
Textile Market (Otavalo): 78, 80
textiles: Agato 90-91; Gualaceo 283-284; Guano 162; Otavalo 78, 80; Peguche 88; Salasaca 140
theaters and concerts: Guayaquil 254; Quito 41
thermal baths: see hot springs
Tigua hide paintings: 17
time: 423, 441
Tío Tigre: 210
tipping: 311, 438
topiary: 112, 130
tortoises: 326-327
Tortuga Bay: 344
tourist seasons: 13
tourist visas: 10, 421-422
tours: general discussion 409-411; Bahía de Caráquez 225; Baños 148; Coca 179-180; Cuenca 277; Cuyabeno Wildlife Refuge 178-179; Galápagos Islands 308-311, 340-341, 357; Guayaquil 255; Latacunga 130; Loja 292; Macas 202; Machalilla National Park 234; Manta 227; Misahualli 193-194; Otavalo 82-84; Puerto López 232; Puyo 199; Quito 41, 44-45; Riobamba 159; Río Napo 187-188; Salinas 241; Santo Domingo de los Colorados 210; Súa 220; Tena 190-192; Vilcabamba 299-300
train rides and attractions: 166
train travel: general discussion 420-421; see also specific place
transportation: see specific place
travelers' checks: 437
travel resources: 441
Tropical Dancing School: 47
Tsachila people: 395
Tufiño: 116-117
Tulcán: 113-116, 422
turtles: 329
typhoid fever: 10, 430
typhus: 431
Tzawar Mishki: 140

UV
Ulba: 147
Universadad Nacional de Loja: 291
Urbina Bay: 359
vaccinations: 10, 429
Vilcabamba: 9, 297, 298, 299-302
Vilcabamba festival: 299
Virgen de La Merced: 225
Virgen del Cisne: 291
Virgen del Loja: 290
Virgen Mirador: 146
visas: 10, 421-422
visual arts: 398
Vivarium: 18, 39
Volcán Antisana: 173
Volcán Carihuairazo: 153-154
Volcán Cayambe: 95
Volcán Chiles: 117
Volcán Chimborazo: 152-153
Volcán Corazón: 122
Volcán Cotacachi: 100
Volcán Cotopaxi: 124-125
Volcán Imbabura: 107-108
volcanoes: 321-322, 368; see also specific place; volcano
Volcán Reventador: 176-177
Volcán Rumiñahui: 125-126
Volcán Sangay: 164
Volcán Tungurahua: 143-144
volleyball: 412
volunteering: 425
volunteer programs: 196-197

W
water, drinking: 430
waterfalls: Cascada Inés María 147; Cascada San Miguel 147; Cascadas de Peguche 88, 90; El Pailón del Diablo 151; Maldonado 117; Podocarpus National Park 296; Puyo 199; San Rafael Falls 176
waved albatross: 332
weather: 368-369
weaving: see textiles
Weilbauer collection: 37
Western Union: 437
wet season: 13
whales: 330
whale-watching: 232
whitewater rivers: 372
Wildsumaco Lodge: 189-190
wine: 404
Wolf Island: 15, 365

women travelers: 428
World Banana Fair: 263
World of Whales Festival: 232

XYZ

Yachana Lodge: 188
Yacuambi: 205
Yaku: 34
Yamor: 81
Yanacocha: 18, 72

yellow fever: 10, 431
Yungilla Valley: 286
Yuturi Lodge: 187
Zamora: 295
Zapara people: 397
Zapotillo: 422
Zaruma: 265
zoos: Quito Zoo 18, 66-67; San Martín Zoo 147; Zoo El Pantanal 262; Zoologico Amarú 274
Zumba: 422
Zumbahua: 135

Map Index

Ambato: 136
Bahía de Caráquez: 224
Baños: 142
Cuenca Center: 270-271
Darwin's Voyage on the *Beagle*: 316
Ecuador & the Galápagos Islands: 2-3
Galápagos Islands, The: 305
Guayaquil: 245
Guayaquil and the Southern Coast: 239
Guayaquil Center: 248-249
Ibarra: 103
Latacunga: 129
Loja: 289
Macas: 201
Manta: 228
North Coast and Lowlands: 208
Ocean Currents Affecting the Galápagos: 323
Orellana's Journey 1542-1543: 181
Oriente, The: 170

Otavalo: 79
Otavalo and Vicinity: 86
Puerto Ayora: 341
Puerto Baquerizo Moreno: 349
Quito: 24-25
Quito, New Town: 38
Quito, Old Town: 28
Quito, Vicinity of: 66
Riobamba: 156
Riobamba, Central: 158
Río Napo, Lower: 184-185
Sierra, Central: 120
Sierra, Northern: 77
Sierra, Southern: 268
South America: 367
Tena: 191
Tena and Upper Río Napo: 196
Tulcán: 114

Acknowledgments

I would like to thank many friends around Ecuador who so freely contributed their time, local knowledge, assistance, and logistical support to this project: Gustavo Aguilera (Cuenca), Fabián Altamirano (Loja), Gabriel Ampuero (Playas), Camilo Andrade (Imbabura), Jim and Linda Belote (Saraguro), Ros Cameron (Galápagos), Beto Chico (Cajas), Franklin Chango (water taxis), Pilar Chiriboga (Riobamba and Chimborazo), Fausto Cortez (absent from Galápagos), Eliza Cutcher (Puyo), Dan Dixon (jungle rivers), Jorge Espinosa (La Mirage), Mary Ellen Fieweger (Intag), Mimi Foyle (PVM), Kevin Goulash and Diane Hillis (Puerto López), Pete Hall (volcanoes), Rosa Jordan (Playa del Oro), Niels Krabbe (birds), Marcos Lema (Peguche), Nicola Mears de Proaño (Bahía), Jorge Montiel (Guayaquil), Alfredo and Victoria Pincay (Salango), Fernando Polanco (Zuleta), Eduardo Rodríguez (Esmeraldas), and Graham Watkins (Darwin Station).

Over the years many others have contributed to my general knowledge of Ecuador and accompanied me on various adventures. Those not already listed above include Ned Addis, Alison Brown, Juan Gabriel Carrasco, Martha Clayton, Juan Diego Domínguez, Ken "Davie" Gadow, Ingemar Höök, Cheri Johnson, Durrell Kapan, Daniel Kouperman, Joan Kroll, Robert and Daisy Kunstaetter, Sue Mann, Eugene Metz, Presley Norton, Richard Parsons, Ali Sharif, Randy Smith, Lee Stice, and Clarice Strang.

Very special thanks to Cati Cajilema and the staff of Safari Tours for covering for me, making it possible for me to escape from the office, and for setting up my travel logistics. Thanks also to the staff of the South American Explorers, for filling in a few gaps, and to Julian Smith, who had the confidence to recommend that I try and fill his shoes for this fourth edition.

Last, but definitely not least, thanks to Alick Paterson (Quito) who in the course of a few months of diligent investigation became an expert on Quito churches, museums, and other places of interest, and who further put his expertise to use by proofreading the text.

www.moon.com

DESTINATIONS | ACTIVITIES | BLOGS | MAPS | BOOKS

MOON.COM is all new, and ready to help plan your next trip! Filled with fresh trip ideas and strategies, author interviews, informative blogs, a detailed map library, and descriptions of all the Moon guidebooks, Moon.com is all you need to get out and explore the world—or even places in your own backyard. As always, when you travel with Moon, expect an experience that is uncommon and truly unique.

MAP SYMBOLS

▦	Expressway	**C**	Highlight	✗	Airfield	⚲	Golf Course
▦	Primary Road	○	City/Town	✗	Airport	**P**	Parking Area
▦	Secondary Road	◉	State Capital	▲	Mountain	🛆	Archaeological Site
▦	Unpaved Road	⊛	National Capital	✛	Unique Natural Feature	♠	Church
------	Trail	★	Point of Interest			🛢	Gas Station
··········	Ferry	•	Accommodation	〰	Waterfall	〰	Glacier
▰▰▰	Railroad	▼	Restaurant/Bar	▲	Park		Mangrove
▰▰▰	Pedestrian Walkway	▪	Other Location	⊓	Trailhead		Reef
▥	Stairs	⋀	Campground	✗	Skiing Area		Swamp

CONVERSION TABLES

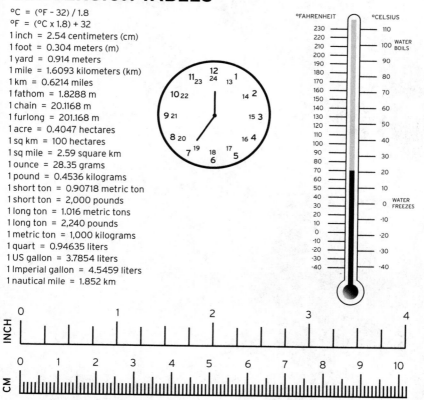

°C = (°F − 32) / 1.8
°F = (°C x 1.8) + 32
1 inch = 2.54 centimeters (cm)
1 foot = 0.304 meters (m)
1 yard = 0.914 meters
1 mile = 1.6093 kilometers (km)
1 km = 0.6214 miles
1 fathom = 1.8288 m
1 chain = 20.1168 m
1 furlong = 201.168 m
1 acre = 0.4047 hectares
1 sq km = 100 hectares
1 sq mile = 2.59 square km
1 ounce = 28.35 grams
1 pound = 0.4536 kilograms
1 short ton = 0.90718 metric ton
1 short ton = 2,000 pounds
1 long ton = 1.016 metric tons
1 long ton = 2,240 pounds
1 metric ton = 1,000 kilograms
1 quart = 0.94635 liters
1 US gallon = 3.7854 liters
1 Imperial gallon = 4.5459 liters
1 nautical mile = 1.852 km

MOON ECUADOR
& THE GALÁPAGOS ISLANDS
Avalon Travel
a member of the Perseus Books Group
1700 Fourth Street
Berkeley, CA 94710, USA
www.moon.com

Editor: Annie M. Blakley
Series Manager: Kathryn Ettinger
Copy Editor: Mia Lipman
Graphics Coordinator: Deb Dutcher
Production Coordinator: Lucie Ericksen
Cover Designer: Nicole Schultz
Map Editor: Kevin Anglin
Director of Cartography: Mike Morgenfeld
Cartographers: Chris Markiewicz, Kat Bennett,
   Jon Niemczyk
Proofreaders: Jamie Andrade, Kia Wang
Indexer: Greg Jewett

ISBN-10: 1-59880-134-1
ISBN-13: 978-1-59880-134-7
ISSN: 1095-886X

Printing History
1st Edition – 1998
4th Edition – March 2009
5 4 3 2 1

Front cover photo: Llamas, Chimborazo, Ecuador,
South America, © Alfredo Maiquez/Lonely Planet.
Title page photo: Puñay mountaintop ruins on the
way to Ingapirca, © M Joan Kroll.
Other front matter photos: © Jean Brown

Printed in the United States by RR Donnelley

KEEPING CURRENT

If you have a favorite gem you'd like to see included in the next edition, or see anything
that needs updating, clarification, or correction, please drop us a line. Send your
comments via email to feedback@moon.com, or use the address above.

ABOUT THE AUTHORS

© ALISON FLYNN

Julian Smith

"A life has to move or it stagnates." –Beryl Markham

Julian Smith has been writing since he learned to read, and traveling since his first family trip to Cape Cod as a toddler. A pre-college summer in Brazil sparked a love affair with (and in) Latin America, fueled by a stint studying the cloudforests of Costa Rica. Days after wrangling a degree in biology from the University of Virginia, he found himself hopelessly entangled in a self-publishing venture that resulted nine months later in the one-pound, eight-ounce *On Your Own in El Salvador*, the first in-depth guide to the country.

Moon Ecuador came two years later, inspired by a trip the length of the country in 1996. Since then, he's made many friends in the country as well as climbed Cotopaxi and dived off the Galápagos Islands, which he counts among the most incredible places he's ever been.

He has contributed to *Outside* magazine, the *Washington Post*, *Los Angeles Times*, *National Geographic Traveler*, *New Mexico Magazine*, *Road Trip USA*, *Online Travel Planning for Dummies*, and other publications. His *Moon Four Corners* won the Society of American Travel Writers' Lowell Thomas Award for best guidebook in 2004. He also managed to earn a master's degree in wildlife ecology along the way, studying grizzly bear tourism on the coast of British Columbia.

As far as normal jobs go, Julian has done pretty well. He's worked as a Canyonlands National Park ranger, guided tourists through the Central American rainforest, and tried (in vain) to protect the vegetable garden of one of the richest men in the world from marauding rodents. Along the way he's found himself freezing atop Kilimanjaro, meditating in a Japanese Zen temple, doused with rum in a Cuban Santería ceremony, and fleeing from Ugandan pygmies, through absolutely no fault of his own.

He currently lives in Santa Fe, NM, where he gets outside as much as humanly possible. For more travel writing, photography, and assorted oddities, stop by his website, www.juliansmith.com.